INTERIOR HOUSE-PAINTING
COLOURS AND TECHNOLOGY
1615–1840

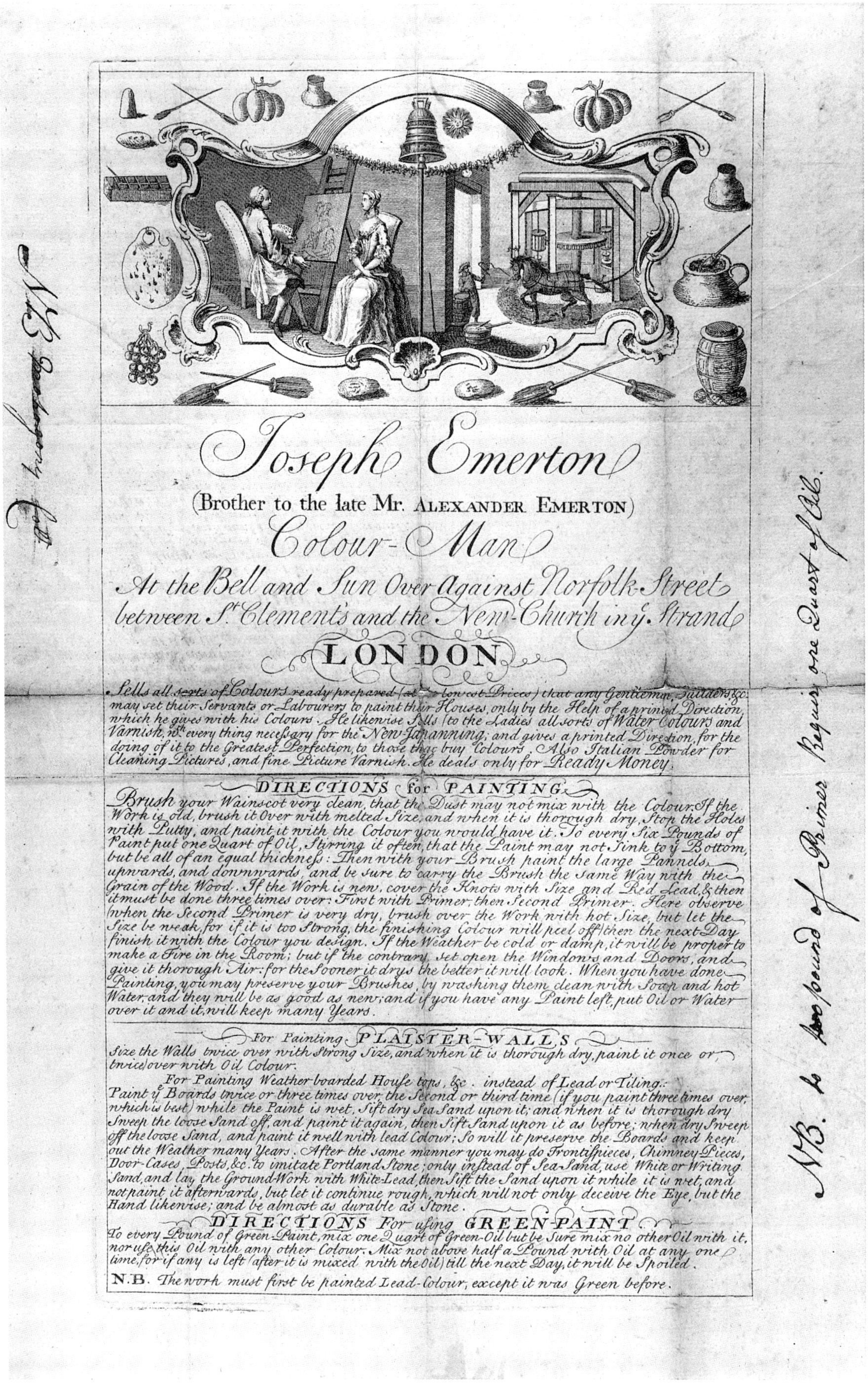

Joseph Emerton

(Brother to the late Mr. ALEXANDER EMERTON)

Colour-Man

At the Bell and Sun Over Against Norfolk-Street between S^t. Clements's and the New-Church in y^e. Strand

LONDON

Sells all sorts of Colours ready prepared (at the lowest Prices) that any Gentleman, Builders &c. may set their Servants or Labourers to paint their Houses, only by the Help of a printed Direction, which he gives with his Colours. He likewise Sells (to the Ladies) all sorts of Water Colours and Varnish, wth every thing necessary for the New-Japanning; and gives a printed Direction, for the doing of it to the Greatest Perfection, to those that buy Colours. Also Italian Powder for Cleaning Pictures, and fine Picture Varnish. He deals only for Ready Money.

DIRECTIONS for PAINTING

Brush your Wainscot very clean, that the Dust may not mix with the Colour. If the Work is old, brush it Over with melted Size, and when it is thorough dry, Stop the Holes with Putty, and paint it with the Colour you would have it. To every Six Pounds of Paint put one Quart of Oil, Stirring it often, that the Paint may not Sink to ye Bottom, but be all of an equal thickness: Then with your Brush paint the large Pannels upwards, and downwards, and be sure to carry the Brush the same Way with the Grain of the Wood. If the Work is new, cover the Knots with Size and Red Lead, & then it must be done three times over: First with Primer, then Second Primer. Here observe (when the Second Primer is very dry, brush over the Work with hot Size, but let the Size be weak, for if it is too Strong, the finishing Colour will peel off) then the next Day finish it with the Colour you design. If the Weather be cold or damp, it will be proper to make a Fire in the Room; but if the contrary, set open the Windows and Doors, and give it thorough Air: for the Sooner it drys the better it will look. When you have done Painting, you may preserve your Brushes, by washing them clean with Soap and hot Water, and they will be as good as new; and if you have any Paint left, put Oil or Water over it and it will keep many Years.

For Painting PLAISTER-WALLS

Size the Walls twice over with Strong Size, and when it is thorough dry, paint it once or, twice) over with Oil Colour.

For Painting Weather boarded House tops, &c. instead of Lead or Tiling.

Paint ye Boards twice or three times over, the Second or third time (if you paint three times over, which is best) while the Paint is wet, Sift dry Sea Sand upon it; and when it is thorough dry Sweep the loose Sand off, and paint it again, then Sift Sand upon it as before; when dry Sweep off the loose Sand, and paint it well with lead Colour; So will it preserve the Boards and keep out the Weather many Years. After the same manner you may do Frontispieces, Chimney-Pieces, Door-Cases, Posts, &c. to imitate Portland Stone; only instead of Sea-Sand, use White or Writing Sand, and lay the Ground-Work with White-Lead, then Sift the Sand upon it while it is wet, and not paint it afterwards, but let it continue rough, which will not only deceive the Eye, but the Hand likewise; and be almost as durable as Stone.

DIRECTIONS For using GREEN-PAINT

To every Pound of Green-Paint, mix one Quart of Green-Oil but be Sure mix no other Oil with it, nor use this Oil with any other Colour. Mix not above half a Pound with Oil at any one time, for if any is left (after it is mixed with the Oil) till the next Day, it will be Spoiled.

N.B. *The work must first be painted Lead-Colour, except it was Green before.*

N.B. Ready Money

N.B. to a ~~two~~ pound of Primer Requires one Quart of Oil.

1. Joseph Emerton's 'DIRECTIONS for PAINTING' (*c.* 1744).

INTERIOR HOUSE-PAINTING COLOURS AND TECHNOLOGY 1615–1840

IAN C. BRISTOW

PUBLISHED FOR
THE PAUL MELLON CENTRE FOR
STUDIES IN BRITISH ART
BY
YALE UNIVERSITY PRESS
NEW HAVEN AND LONDON
1996

Designed by John Trevitt

Set in New Baskerville by Best-set Typesetter Ltd., Hong Kong
Printed in Hong Kong

Library of Congress Cataloging-in-Publication Data

Bristow, Ian C.
Architectural colour in British interiors, 1615–1840 / Ian C. Bristow.
p. cm.
Includes bibliographical references and index.
ISBN 0–300–03866–6 (cloth)
1. Interior decoration—Great Britain—History—17th century.
2. Interior decoration—Great Britain—History—18th century.
3. Interior decoration—Great Britain—History—19th century.
4. Color in interior decoration. I. Title.
NK2043.B75 1996
729′.4′0942—dc20 95–45152 CIP

A catalogue record for this book is available from the British Library

CONTENTS

CONTENTS

SOURCES AND ABBREVIATIONS USED IN NOTES

TABLES

ACKNOWLEDGEMENTS

In the twenty years since I started work on the research which has led to the present book and its companion volume I have received help and advice from a large number of institutions and individuals. Without it, this study would have been greatly impoverished, and I am delighted to acknowledge here all the support and assistance I have received. Inevitably, my thanks are due in the first instance to Dr Derek Linstrum, who conceived the research fellowship at the Institute of Advanced Architectural Studies in York to which it was my good fortune to be appointed in 1975. Sponsorship for this was obtained by the University from Berger Paints, to whom, together with Dr Jeremy Taylor, then Director of Research at the Institute, whose guidance during the three years of my Fellowship was invaluable, I am most grateful.

My research at York immediately attracted a remarkable range of support from outside sources, most notably the Victoria and Albert Museum, the interest of whose Departments of Conservation and Furniture was crucial. When Keeper of the former, Norman Brommelle kindly arranged for me to use the facilities of the Museum's laboratories, thus introducing me to Jo. Darrah to whom my especial thanks are due for help and guidance in the use of microscopy and associated techniques. When Keeper of Furniture and Woodwork, Peter Thornton took a keen interest in the project (continued enthusiastically in his present role as Curator of Sir John Soane's Museum); and I am especially grateful to him and his former colleagues, notably Frances Collard, John Hardy, Simon Jervis, Dr Clive Wainwright, and James Yorke. The National Trust too greatly interested itself in my work, and for much information and assistance I am grateful to Belinda Cousens, Dudley Dodd, St John Gore, Martin Drury, Gervase Jackson-Stops, Julian Gibbs, Anthony Mitchell, Christopher Wall, and Merlin Waterson. Other institutions have been similarly kind, including the Department of the Environment, through the Property Services Agency and the former Directorate of Ancient Monuments and Historic Buildings, the latter's interest being continued by English Heritage. In addition, I must acknowledge the very positive help and support of John Harris and his former colleagues at the R.I.B.A. Drawings Collection, especially Jill Lever, Jane Preger, and Margaret Richardson; and also the considerable aid given by Frank Dimes, Alan Jobbins, and Patricia Statham of the Institute of Geological Sciences, now part of the Natural History Museum.

On the historical side, I have benefitted from invaluable help and a wide range of information provided by John Addy, Dr Geoffrey Beard, David Beevers, Jeannie Chapel, Howard Colvin, Dr Thomas Cocke, John Cornforth, Abbott Lowell Cummings, Monica Dance, Caroline Davidson, Elaine Evans Dee, Sam Dornsife, Paul Drury, Dr Kate Fielden, Peter Foster, John Fowler, David Freeman, Dr Terry Friedman, Mark Girouard, Ian Gow, Leslie Harris, Karen Hearn, Dr Sally Jeffery, Christine Meadows, John Morley, Dr David Parker, Dr Nicholas Penny, Dr Jan Piggott, Fiona Pilkington, Paul Quarrie, Dr Anthony Quiney, Joseph Rishel, the Hon. Jane Roberts, Jessica Rutherford, John Sambrooke, Stephen Sartin, Rosalind Savill, Christina Scull, the Earl of Shelburne, James and Ann Simpson, Basil Skinner, Dr Nicola Smith, the late Francis Steer, Dorothy Stroud, the late Sir John Summerson, the Hon. John Thorneycroft, Dr Simon Thurley, Karin Walton, Giles Waterfield, Juliet West, and Robin Wyatt. This was matched on technical matters by help and encouragement from Marigene Butler, Dr Anthony Crawshaw, Gillian Lewis, Peter and Ann MacTaggart, Dr John Mills, David Paull, Westby Percival-Prescott, Joyce Plesters, Morgan Phillips, Prof. Stephen Rees-Jones, R.A. Snowden, and Raymond White.

British firms too have been generous in providing samples and materials for my work, and in this connection I should particularly like to thank British Oil and Cake Mills Ltd, English China Clays Ltd, H. Haeffner & Co. Ltd, Lamp Metals Ltd, Reckitts (Colours) Ltd, and A.F. Suter & Co. Ltd.

Particular thanks are also due to all those owners of historic buildings who permitted me to visit them and carry away samples of paintwork, or who commissioned me to do this. They include Her Majesty the Queen; Bradford City Council; His Grace the Duke of Buccleuch; the late Dowager Marchioness of Cholmondeley; the Clerical, Medical & General Life Assurance Co. Ltd; the Department of the Environment; the Trustees of the Dickens House Museum; the Eagle Star Group; Ealing Borough Council; English Heritage; the Greater London Council; Gulfpark Property Management Ltd; Leeds City Council; Lloyd's; the Corporation of London; the National Trust; the Office of Public Works, Dublin; the Royal Academy; the Trustees of Sir John Soane's Museum; the Borough of Tamworth; and York City Council. For the generosity and kindness shown by all these and many others I am most grateful.

Finally I must thank the Paul Mellon Centre for British Art for providing funds towards publication, and acknowledge the initiative and help of John Nicoll at Yale University Press in effecting this. To John Trevitt I owe an enormous debt for hard work in editing and design, and thank both him and Sue Jackson for their patience in dealing with my many queries and requests.

IAN C. BRISTOW

PREFACE

This book provides the primary technical background to my study of paint colour in architecture, which is uniformly published under the title *Architectural Colour in British Interiors 1615–1840*. The latter deals with the aesthetic ends to which colour was put: the present volume concentrates on the materials available to the house-painter during the period, the ways in which they were combined to make paint of various types, the manner in which the latter was applied, and the different colours which could be mixed. Both volumes result from the research fellowship which I held at the University of York in 1975–8 and my subsequent DPhil thesis 'Interior House-painting from the Restoration to the Regency' submitted in 1983. While the overall aim of my research has been an understanding of the architectural uses of colour, the technical studies were essential to this end, most particularly in the interpretation of building accounts and in the examination of paint samples from interiors whose original colours had been obliterated by subsequent schemes of redecoration.

The method of approach and sources used are fully described in the preface to the companion volume, which is reproduced here as Appendix F. Needless to say, no single historical publication provided complete information on the subject, and it was necessary to compile material from a fair number of works, each of which needed critical appraisal. Many house-painters' materials were used in common with artists, and recent studies from this viewpoint were also important, notably Rosamond Harley's *Artists' Pigments c. 1600–1835*, first published in 1970. Outside the field of pigments, however, it has been less easy to supplement the strictly architectural literature; and in some cases (notably the natural resins used in varnishes) it has not been possible to obtain a completely coherent picture of sources and types employed.

Nevertheless, the general accuracy of the information initially provided by historical printed works was unequivocally confirmed by studies of painters' bills and accounts, and also by the technical examination of paint samples from various interiors. Material obtained from these two sources has, of course, also been included in the text below, both being of particular importance in establishing the use made of newly developed pigments such as Naples and patent yellows, which do not appear very quickly in printed British material. Further studies will, no doubt, provide additional supplement.

Finally, in presenting this study in published form it is necessary to warn that many of the materials discussed are toxic, some extremely so; and, in an age when health and safety are treated as paramount, a strict injunction is issued that the information here given is for historical interest only, and that personal experiment except in safe laboratory conditions should not be attempted.

PART I

MATERIALS

INTRODUCTION

In general, the materials employed in the painters' trade were destined for one of three main products: water-based paints, or 'distempers'; oil-based paints; and varnishes. The first usually consisted of a white base pigment (generally crushed chalk) mixed with a solution of an organic binder (normally animal-glue size) in water. When the latter evaporated, the binder would consolidate the pigment, providing an opaque finish. Distempers of this type were cheap, but water-soluble; and where a harder-wearing or weather-resistant surface was needed, oil paint would be used. In this case the base pigment (usually white lead) would be dispersed in an oil medium (commonly linseed oil) which, rather than evaporating, would harden by polymerisation to provide a tough protective film, binding the pigment particles to themselves and the ground. The process of polymerisation (known colloquially as 'drying') is often rather slow, but can be accelerated by the action of a range of metallic compounds known as 'driers'. These could either be dispersed in oil, like pigment, and mixed with the paint, or, in cases where the resulting darkening of the oil was unimportant, heated with it prior to its use. To adjust the viscosity of the paint, or to lessen the sheen with which it dried, a 'thinner' (generally oil of turpentine), which would evaporate before polymerisation took place, might be added.

Transparent finishes were provided by a range of varnishes, made by dissolving one or more naturally occuring resins in an organic solvent. Those used in house-painting may be divided into three broad groups, depending on the solvent used. In the first (called 'spirit varnishes'), ethyl alcohol was used to dissolve a resin such as shellac; in the second, a harder resin (often copal) was dissolved in linseed oil; and in the third the solvent was oil of turpentine. Particular resins were appropriate to specific solvents, and the resulting varnishes had different uses. Thus the first group was reserved for interior finishes; but the second could be employed either indoors or out; while the third found employment mainly as an additive to oil paint to increase its lustre when dry.

The basic oil- or water-based paint was (as will be appreciated from the base pigments already mentioned) generally white in colour, but could be tinted to produce a desired hue by the addition of one or more coloured pigments. On occasion these were also added to varnish, but, where transparency in the latter was to be maintained, various dyestuffs or coloured resins soluble in the relevant medium were substituted.

Pigments, the first of the materials to be considered in detail in the following chapters, are needed as a primary constituent of paint to provide obliterating power, to give colour, and, in the case of oil paint, to enhance the protective qualities of the oil by providing greater substance and resistance to weather in the dried paint film. Although a large number of white, black, or coloured substances exist in nature or can be manufactured, very few are suitable for employment in paint, lacking one or other of the practical qualities needed. Of prime importance is the inert nature of the pigment, so that, for paints fulfilling a protective function, substances appreciably soluble in water cannot be used. Nor should a pigment react with its fellows, other constituents of the paint, the atmosphere, or commonly encountered compounds to which it may be exposed. Pigments should also be light-fast, not fading on exposure, especially to sunlight. Even today it is not possible to meet these apparently simple conditions completely: much less was it feasible during the seventeenth and eighteenth centuries, and of the few dozen substances discussed below, several are notably deficient in one or other of these respects. Patent yellow, for example, discoloured on exposure to atmospheric impurities; orpiment was not compatible with many other pigments; and the organic reds and yellows, the latter needed especially to produce bright, clear, and delicate tints, were generally fugitive, some of them extremely so.

When in use as a pigment, each of the substances discussed has different properties. Where its refractive index is comparable with that of an oil medium the pigment becomes more or less transparent, thus having little or no ability to obliterate the surface to which the paint is applied, a quality measured today in terms of *covering power*. These are often known as *glazing pigments* to distinguish them from those which are opaque in oil and called *body pigments*; although it is important to realise that the one category merges imperceptibly into the other and many pigments fall between the two extremes of complete opacity on the one hand and total transparency at the other end of the scale. In effect this means that some white pigments in particular cannot be used in oil, although they are of considerable importance in an aqueous medium. With others the phenomenon may be exploited, especially in such work as graining or marbling in which transparency is required; and for work of this nature, special varieties of some pigments, having greater transparency than those in general use (for example the siennas and umbers among the earths) were particularly selected. Moreover, different pigments, or even different batches of the same pigment, have widely varying powers to tint paints to the desired depth of colour, a quality known as *tinting strength* or *staining power*; while whites on the other hand are spoken of as having *reducing power*. This characteristic had, as today, to be balanced against cost, cheaper varieties of the same pigment often being inferior in this respect, so that larger quantities were required to produce the same degree of colouration.

Price was also often determined by other factors, reflecting the expense and rarity of the substance composing a pigment, the distance from which it had to be brought, the cost of its production, and the degree of preparation required to fit it for use. Some earths in particular needed refinement to free them from large or gritty particles, a process generally effected by agitating the crude earth, once ground to powder, in water, and then allowing it to stand. The coarser matter would settle out first, allowing its desired separation from the more finely-divided particles. During the period under review, this was known as 'washing' or 'levigation'. Quite apart from any question of their tinting strength, cheaper pigments were often dull in tone compared with more expensive alternatives, and even different batches of the same pigment could differ in colour or quality. This was particularly the case where, as with the organic pigments, the raw materials needed for their manufacture were expensive, and successive degrees of extraction could make the most economical use of them. Often, too, certain otherwise unsatisfactory, but cheap substances could be used to make more expensive pigments go further without unduly affecting the properties of the dried paint film. These are known as *extenders*, and were widely used with white lead for undercoats and other less critical applications; but the ill-defined boundary between such legitimate use and adulteration was notorious. Some idea of the wide variations in price between pigments, and hence the enormous constraints cost could impose on the choice of paint colour, may be obtained from the table drawn up from items contained in one of the early nineteenth-century annual stock-taking lists of the London colourman and manufacturer Lewis Berger (table 1). This shows clearly not only the differences which might be expected between different qualities of the same pigment, but also the enormous range between the valuations of certain earth pigments at $\frac{1}{4}$*d.* or less per pound, and those of the vastly more expensive organic pigments, whose price was often such as to preclude their use for the ordinary purposes of house-painting.

Two further general points about the nature of certain pigments have also to be made. The deliberate addition of particular metallic substances to oils in order to increase the speed at which they dry is discussed more fully in Chapter 10 in connection with driers, but it is useful to point out here that certain pigments too have this prop-

Table 1. *Prices per pound at which Lewis Berger valued selected pigments in his stock on 1 January 1806* (Berger MSS., stock 1805–6). Dots show prices of individual items

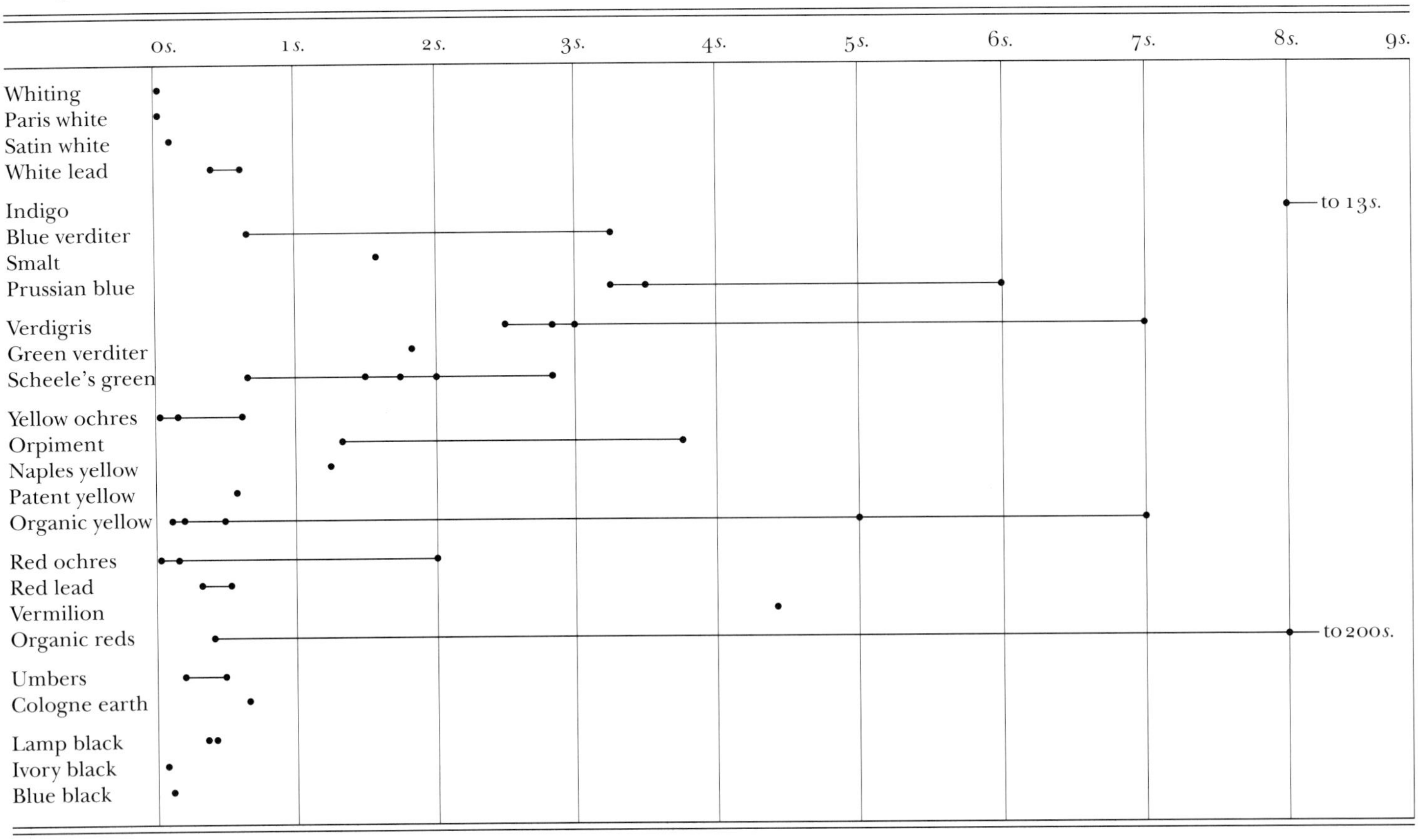

erty. These are said to 'dry well', and include, for example, red lead, verdigris, and umber; while others seem to retard the rate of drying. This, it may be noted, does not appear to have been a major constraint in the choice of paint colour. Also, the toxic nature of certain eighteenth-century pigments may be mentioned, especially that of the arsenical greens and of white lead, both of which were a contemporary cause of concern.

CHAPTER 1

WHITE PIGMENTS, EXTENDERS, AND ADULTERANTS

White pigments were of primary importance to the house-painter since they were normally used to form a base paint which would later be tinted to the colour desired. Their properties were therefore of particular significance, and although during the period considered in this study a fair number of white substances found employment in paints of different types, many were far too expensive for use in house-painting. Three were of major importance in this field: chalk, lime, and white lead. Only the last was suitable for use in oil; and the first two, apart from widespread employment of chalk as an adulterant for white lead, were used only in an aqueous 'distemper' medium.

CHALK, MARL, AND CALCAREOUS CLAY

Chalk, which occurs naturally in the south-east of England and in northern France, consists of practically pure calcium carbonate, although a small proportion of silica, sometimes about 3 per cent, may be present.[1] When crushed it is used as a pigment known generally today as 'whiting'. Some white earths, however, may contain a mixture of chalk with china clay, and, being made up from various proportions of calcium carbonate and aluminium silicate, form marls or calcareous clays intermediate between the two.[2] Following crushing and removal of coarse particles by levigation, the earth is dried by heat, which must be carefully controlled in order to prevent the formation of calcium oxide. This would soon absorb atmospheric moisture to form calcium hydroxide, making the pigment alkaline and thus incompatible with alkali-reactive tinting pigments such as Prussian blue, verdigris, chrome yellow, or emerald green.[3] White earth pigments belonging to the whole of this group are more or less transparent when ground into an oil medium, and for this reason were used chiefly in distemper, or as a cheap extender or adulterant for white lead. They were also used as a base for the preparation of some of the red and yellow organic pigments discussed below.

As the common base for distemper, 'whiting' was naturally included among the six pigments the plasterers of the City of London secured a right to use in this medium by Act of Parliament in 1603.[4] It was also commonly known during the seventeenth and succeeding centuries as *Spanish white*, although some writers, especially those concerned with pigments for artists, seem to have applied the term to satin white (q.v.). When Chorley Church, Lancashire, was restored in 1635–6, however, two pounds of chalk and three pounds of Spanish white were charged for at the identical rate of 2*d.* per pound, indicating that for house-painting purposes they were probably one and the same.[5] Much later, the Swiss author P.F. Tingry (whose *Traité* of 1803 was published in English as *The Painter and Varnisher's Guide* the following year) indicated that Spanish white was properly a pure clay, although he noted that washed chalk was often sold under the name;[6] and in 1821, when William Butcher published *Smith's Art of House-Painting* (a considerably revised edition of John Smith's seventeenth-century work on house-painting, *The Art of Painting* (1676, second edition 1687)), he included in the patchily updated text an additional note that 'what they [colourmen] call SPANISH . . . is merely common whiting'.[7]

The terms 'white', 'whiting', and 'Spanish white' are found ubiquitously in the run of Exchequer and Augmentation Office rolls covering the years 1615 to 1640,[8] and the mid-seventeenth-century architect Sir Roger Pratt enthused over the whiteness and smoothness obtained by the use of Spanish white for the whitening of ceilings.[9] At the end of the century, William Leyburn illustrated its use as an extender in a formula for an oil primer;[10] and likewise, in his *Directions for House and Ship Painting* of 1812, the American author Hezekiah Reynolds used Spanish white as an extender for white lead in undercoats and a grey finish for exterior application.[11]

Another term commonly encountered is *Paris white*, which is mentioned in a number of later eighteenth- and early nineteenth-century documents. This appears to have been regarded as a higher grade of pigment than ordinary whiting, the London pigment manufacturer and wholesaler Lewis Berger, for instance, listing it in his early nineteenth-century annual stock lists at 5*s.* per cwt. against 1*s.* 6*d.* for the latter;[12] but it is not clear to what extent its higher value was due to the nature of the raw earth or to the care taken in its preparation. Certainly at the end of the nineteenth century George H. Hurst indicated that it received more thorough grinding than the ordinary grades of whiting,[13] but it seems likely that by then the name had lost any association with a specific source of raw material, and in this century it has come to be applied simply to the finest grades of pigment.[14] Undoubtedly, however, the term must originally have come from material obtained from the vicinity of Paris, notably from Bougival and Meudon. The former lies about eight statute miles from the centre of Paris in the vicinity of Marly on the west side of the city. In *L'Art du peintre, doreur, vernisseur*, the first edition of which appeared in 1772, Jean Félix Watin described 'le blanc de Bougival, autrement blanc d'Espagne' as 'une terre, ou marne blanche', commenting in some detail on its industrial preparation by washing and levigation.[15] Tingry too described Bougival white as a 'very fine marly earth', indicating that it was a better pigment for house-painting than chalk, which constituted one third of its composition.[16] At Meudon, a village lying about eight miles south-east of Bougival, Watin indicated that ordinary 'blanc de craie' was obtained. Such pigment was, he noted, employed for whitening ceilings, observing that it was harder than Bougival white, which it otherwise resembled.[17] Probably, therefore, it was the Bougival product which has originally known in England as Paris white, and the price difference between it and ordinary chalk obviously reflected a significantly superior product.

In 1819 Peter Nicholson referred to 'French white' as a pigment, although he was probably confusing this term (only otherwise encountered as the colour name listed in Appendix A below) with Paris white.[18] It may nevertheless be useful to review other French sources of white pigments briefly, especially since, despite its everyday nature and ubiquitous working in the south and east of England (areas which Tingry's later editor mentioned),[19] documentary references to specific British sites from which whiting was extracted during the period covered by the present study seem elusive. The late seventeenth-century writer A.C. D'Aviler referred to the use of 'blanc de Rouen' in size-bound distemper, and listed it amongst those pigments in ordinary use for house-painting;[20] and a contemporary reference to 'blanc de Roüen ou blanc de craye' as the pigment ordinarily used in that medium is made by Pierre Bullet.[21] Just over a century later Tingry, who seems to have researched his data on white earths with some care, described Rouen white as a marl consisting of clay and calcium carbonate.[22] Another source of white in France was Troyes, which lies ninety miles east-south-east from Paris in the département of Aube. Tingry described 'white of Troyes' from the vicinity as a 'white chalk',[23] and the English editor of the revised version of his book (published in 1830) indicated its nature similarly as 'whiting'.[24] Besides these sources, Watin indicated that pigment was also obtained from Burgundy, the province lying to the south of Champagne (in which Troyes is situated);[25] and in addition Tingry referred to chalk from Briançon, which lies near the Italian border about forty-five miles east-south-east of Grenoble in the south.[26] He also mentioned 'White of Moudon or Morat' from the town known today as Murten, which lies in his native Switzerland in the Pays-de-Vaud, about twenty miles west of Berne. This was, he said, a pure clay, and thus in his opinion 'a real Spanish white'.[27] Tingry also noted sources of pipe-clay in the Auvergne and Normandy,[28] but his enthusiasm for clay whites was not matched by later English writers, and both Hurst and Heaton noted that china clay, which occurs extensively in Cornwall, was little used as a pigment.[29]

The form in which white earth pigments were sold was discussed by Watin and Tingry. The former noted that the best qualities of Bougival white were sold 'en petits bâtons', but the coarser settlings were allowed to form lumps of a pound to twenty ounces in weight.[30] Tingry, on the other hand, simply mentioned that Bougival white was sold in the form of oblong cakes, while Troyes white was marketed either in large square cakes weighing 10 or 12 pounds, in rolls and cylinders of 16 to 20 ounces, or cut into long square sticks to resemble tobacco-pipe clay.[31] In this connection, it is interesting to note that Berger's early nineteenth-century stocks of the latter comprised '255 Doz. Pipe Clay in $\frac{1}{2}$ Balls'.[32]

In his *Handmaid to the Arts* of 1758 Robert Dossie gave descriptions of the preparation of a number of white pigments used by artists. These included 'Troy white or Spanish white' which were in effect satin white (q.v.) together with two fine qualities of calcium carbonate: 'Pearl white' was, he indicated, made by powdering pearl or oystershell, and was used in miniature painting;[33] and 'egg-shell white', for watercolour, was made from crushed and levigated egg-shells.[34] Both pigments were listed by Thomas Martin in his *Circle of the Mechanical Arts* of 1813 and Peter Nicholson in his *New Practical Builder* of 1823–5;[35] but the origin of both lists was Dossie's *Handmaid*, which was copied quite uncritically, and the two latter references should, therefore, be treated as quite unreliable in connection with house-painting. Indeed, a third early nineteenth-century author, Nathaniel Whittock, explicitly observed in his *Decorative Painters' and Glaziers' Guide* of 1827 that pearl, oyster-shell, and egg-shell whites were used only by portrait and historical painters.[36] Occasionally, however, oyster shells were burnt to produce lime (q.v.) and could perhaps have been used for house-painting in this way.

A bill among the papers at Boughton House, Northamptonshire, includes an item of 1*s.* paid for 12 lb. of 'Spanish whiting' supplied on 11 October 1705 (a price equivalent to 9*s.* 4*d.* per cwt.);[37] while in 1803 the architect John Soane paid 3*d.* per dozen for a total of 24 dozen cakes of 'fine Whiting'. Another item was for '18^{lb} fine Whiting', which cost 6*d.* (the equivalent of 3*s.* 1*d.* per cwt.);[38] and, assuming the price per pound was the same, each cake would thus have weighed $\frac{3}{4}$ lb. Lewis Berger's stock of whiting rose from 40 cwt. on 1 January 1802 to 95 cwt. in 1806, and by 1 January 1810 stood at $121\frac{1}{2}$ cwt., the valuations being made at the rate of 1*s.* 6*d.* per cwt. on the first two occasions and 1*s.* 9*d.* on the last. His stock of Paris white in 1802 and 1806 was, by comparison, $90\frac{1}{4}$ cwt. and just over $184\frac{3}{4}$ cwt. respectively, in both cases valued at 5*s.* per cwt.;[39] while elsewhere records recently published relating to the decoration of two houses in Doncaster between 1798 and 1802 show that various amounts of Paris white were charged for retail at a rate of 1*s.* per stone, the equivalent of 8*s.* per cwt.[40]

GYPSUM

Gypsum, or calcium sulphate, which can be used as a pigment in a similar way to chalk, occurs freely in Europe and the New World. John Hill, the mid-eighteenth-century translator of the work on geology by the classical writer Theophrastus, noted the occurrence of gypsum as '*Parget*, or Plaister-stone' in Derbyshire and Yorkshire, and at Montmartre on the north side of Paris, adding that it was burnt to form plaster of Paris.[41] Hurst indicated that a temperature of 300°F. is needed to effect this, and named Chellaston and the neighbouring village of Aston upon Trent as the two principal sources in Derbyshire;[42] while in the early nineteenth century there were gypsum pits at Elvaston, a third village in the vicinity.[43] Hurst also indicated that large quantities of gypsum were obtained from Newark-on-Trent, Nottinghamshire; Fauld, Staffordshire; and Netherfield in Sussex, adding that the pigment, prepared from it by grinding, was completely neutral in its properties and could be mixed with all the others then in use without affecting them in any way.[44] The use of gypsum was mentioned by Tingry who, perhaps reflecting a southern European outlook rather than British practice, said that it was extremely valuable for whitewashing and painting in distemper, and could produce a more delicate white than chalk;[45] but English writers hardly refer to gypsum, and it was probably on the strength of Tingry's remarks that Whittock included it among the 'preparations of clay or chalk' which were used in distemper.[46] It is therefore difficult to assess to what extent it was used in distemper in Britain, although its free occurrence in this country should have allowed it to be easily available. Possibly too it could have found employment as an extender for white lead, although its slight solubility in water would have made it a poor choice for exterior work.

LIME

Chalk and limestones may be burnt to produce quicklime (calcium oxide), and this, when slaked with water, becomes slaked lime (calcium hydroxide). On exposure to the air, which contains carbon dioxide, the latter gradually reverts to calcium carbonate, this chemical process forming the basis of the setting mechanism of lime mortar. Several varieties of lime were commercially available in the eighteenth century, since certain limestones contain a proportion of clay, producing when burnt a natural cement which would set under water and whose quick set was valuable in masonry. To achieve complete slaking and a smooth consistency for plastering, on the other hand, lime had to be matured wet after slaking; and for this purpose it was therefore necessary to use lime burnt from chalk which was pure and would not set during the process. In 1703 Richard Neve mentioned the employment in London of such chalk lime from Kent and Sussex;[47] but stone lime was brought from further afield, notably from the River Tamar between Devon and Cornwall *via* the port of Plymouth, and Lewis Berger was using 'Plymouth Stone Lime' during the early nineteenth century in connection with the manufacture of blue verditer (q.v.).[48] Possibly this was similar to the 'rock lime' which the London colourman T.H. Vanherman recommended for making satin white (q.v.) in his *Painter's Cabinet, and Colourman's Repository* of 1828. This, he observed, was available at Nine Elms Wharf, Lambeth, London;[49] and it may therefore also be identical with the 'Vauxhall stone lime' mentioned by Phillips in connection with limewash.[50] In addition, Neve observed that 'the Shells of Fish, as of Cockles, Oysters, &c. are good to burn for Lime',[51] and although no reference to the use of such lime for house-painting in London has been encountered, oyster shells were being burnt for lime at Taunton, Massachusetts, in the early nineteenth century;[52] while a notice appeared in the *New York Gazette* on 3 April 1780 advertising 'oyster-shell white for white washing',[53] and it seems most likely that this referred to lime made in this way rather than to crushed shells.

As a material ubiquitously available on the building site, lime was used extensively for the simple whitening of surfaces, and a number of references to 'lime whitening' will be found in Chapter 17. Tingry's editor, indeed, seems to have preferred lime to chalk for this purpose, describing it as excellent for whitewashing ceilings. That from the burning of hard stone had, he said, a better colour than chalk lime, and produced a brighter white than chalk; but, he added, since lime was scarce in London, the latter was here more generally employed.[54] By this he seems to have meant that it was stone lime which was at a premium, since in his builders' price-book the surveyor John Phillips gave the rate for 'New work, whiten only' as 2*d.* per square yard, when 'Lime whiting once over' was only $1\frac{1}{2}$*d.*; but for the same 'with the Vauxhall stone lime' the price was $3\frac{1}{2}$*d.*[55] Lime was essential also in formulae for casein-bound paints, where its alkaline nature and subsequent carbonation to a neutral compound were exploited. These too are discussed in Chapter 17, together with the use of lime in solution as lime-water for the preliminary sealing of plasterwork.

SATIN WHITE

In the late nineteenth century Hurst described satin white as essentially a mixture of calcium sulphate and aluminium hydroxide prepared by the mixture of slaked lime in water with a solution of aluminium sulphate;[56] but during the period covered by the present study it seems clear that alum (potassium aluminium sulphate) was used rather than the latter. This would have produced a similar pigment, but the product would require careful washing to free it from the highly alkaline potassium hydroxide arising as a by-product. Comparable pigments were being prepared for watercolourists by the opening years of the seventeenth century, and at least one formula, that published by Henry Peacham in 1606, calls for the lime to be burnt from chalk with which a third part of alum had already been allowed to react in aqueous solution.[57] Confusingly, he referred to the resulting pigment as 'Spanish white'; and in his 'Catalogue of Simple and Mixt Colours', published in the *Philosophical Transactions* of the Royal Society in 1686, Richard Waller also indicated that his sample of 'Spanish white' was made in this way.[58] As already mentioned, Dossie too provided a related method for the production of 'Troy or Spanish white' by the mixture of chalk and a solution of alum,[59] which was picked up by Martin and Nicholson (their 'Troy White')[60] and by Whittock (his 'Spanish white').[61] While it is possible, therefore, that for fine-art purposes these terms may have been applied to satin white, it seems unlikely that for house-painting they were applied to anything other than chalk (q.v.).

Although no English reference to the use of satin white in the ordinary decoration of buildings during the seventeenth or eighteenth centuries has been encountered, the late seventeenth-century French writer D'Aviler observed: 'Le Blanc qu'on nomme des Carmes se fait sur des murs bien secs avec de la chaux de Senlis éteinte, où l'en mêle de l'alun: on prend le dessus qui est le plus pur dont on met 5. ou 6. couches'.[62]

The slightly earlier author André Félibien had also described the preparation of *blanc des Carmes* from Senlis lime in 1676, remarking specifically that when used on stone or plaster it did not go yellow.[63] Undoubtedly, however, its cost (discussed below) would have militated against its common use; and it is clear that later its major role lay in the specialised business of wallpaper printing. It was also, as Heaton indicates, particularly useful as a base for lake pigments, and manufactured for that purpose:[64] several formulae for satin yellow (q.v.) prepared in this way are to be found among those used by Lewis Berger and his sons in the early nineteenth century. Vanherman was probably exceptional, therefore, in using it as a constituent of his 'Impenetrable or Anti-corrosive' and 'Aromatic' paints (the latter for interior, the former for exterior use), and, indeed, described it as 'the satin white of the paper stainers'. To prepare it, he directed, 8 lb. of rock lime were slaked with a volume of water sufficient to make 6 gallons of strained liquid. A similar weight of alum was dissolved in a further 6 gallons of water, added to the first, and the whole stirred for half an hour. After three hours had elapsed, it was stirred again and allowed to stand overnight, when it would be ready for use.[65] His formula was repeated by Tingry's editor, who draw attention to the alkaline nature of the product.[66]

Several sets of detailed instructions for the preparation of satin white are contained in the records of Lewis Berger's company, the earliest being dated 1815, although he had used it in the production of satin yellow in 1809. In this and succeeding formulae prior to 1837 a small quantity of orchill (q.v. Chapter 2) was also added, presumably with the intention of giving the pigment a bluish-white colour; and the formulae are also interesting in showing the care taken to wash away the alkaline by-product.[67] In 1815 the pigment cost 8*s.* per cwt. to produce, and in 1831 6*s.*, suggesting it retailed at about 12*s.* or 15*s.*; and on 1 January 1806 and 1810 Berger valued his stock at a rate of 14*s.* per cwt. It seems likely, therefore, that the figure of 84*s.* in his 1802 stock-list was an error, although he then had only just over $3\frac{1}{2}$ cwt. in stock against nearly $35\frac{3}{4}$ cwt. in 1806 and nearly 23 cwt. in 1810.[68]

LEAD WHITE

None of the white pigments so far described is of use in oil since, their refractive indices being comparable with that of such a medium, they become transparent and lack body. White lead (basic lead carbonate) is, however, an almost ideal pigment in oil, being opaque, compatible with most other pigments, and drying well. Its formation of an organic compound, or 'lead soap', with drying oils, enhancing their protective qualities is well known; and in 1676 John Smith described it as the only white used in oil, a statement which, subject to minor exceptions and admixture of the pigment with extenders and adulterants, remained true throughout the period under consideration.[69] It does, however, tend to blacken slightly in sulphurous atmospheres, and is toxic, presenting when used carelessly a health hazard to painters in daily contact with it; while used in exterior work, it tends to produce a paint film subject to surface powdering, or 'chalking'. Although principally suited to use in oil, white lead can be used in an aqueous medium; but it has little advantage for this purpose, and is very expensive compared with chalk. Nevertheless, it does seem to have been used in this way on occasion, and instances are described in Chapter 17.

Manufacture of white lead was known in classical antiquity, and described by Vitruvius.[70] In 1678, Sir Philiberto Vernatti published an account of its manufacture in the *Philosophical Transactions of the Royal Society*:

> First Pigs of clean and soft Lead are cast into thin Plates a yard long, six inches broad, and to the thickness of the back of a Knife. These are rolled, with some Art, round; but so as the Surfaces no where meet to touch: for where they do no *Ceruss* grows.
>
> Thus roll'd, they are put each in a Pot just capable to hold one, upheld by a little Bar from the bottom, that it come not to touch the Vinegar, which is put into each Pot, to effect the conversion.
>
> Next a square Bed is made up of new Horse-dung, so big as to hold 20 Pots abreast, and so make up the number of 400 in one Bed.
>
> Then each Pot is covered with a Plate of Lead; and lastly all with Boards, as close as conveniently can be. This repeated four times, makes one heap, so called, containing 1600 Pots.
>
> After three Weeks the Pots are taken up, the Plates unrolled, laid upon a Board, and beaten with Battledores till all the Flakes come off. Which, if good, prove thick, hard and weighty: if otherwise, fuffy & light; or sometimes black and burn'd, if the Dung prove not well order'd: and sometimes there will be none.
>
> From the Beating-Table the Flakes are carried to the Mill; and with Water ground between Millstones, until they be brought to almost an impalpable fineness. After which it is moulded into smaller parcels, and exposed to the Sun to dry till it be hard and so fit for use.[71]

This method, known as the 'stack' or 'Dutch' process,[72] remained very similar in England until comparatively recently, except that spent tanner's-bark later became substituted for the horse-dung, a patent being awarded to Richard Fishwick for this improvement in 1787;[73] but it should be noted that many published descriptions were inaccurate, including those of the normally reliable authors Hill, Dossie, and Tingry. They all indicated that the lead was brought into direct contact with the acetic acid; but the product of the ensuing reaction would then have been lead acetate rather than lead carbonate.[74]

Tingry's editor expressed a preference for '*London* white lead',[75] and at least since the seventeenth century the pigment had indeed been manufactured in and around the capital. In 1679, for example, there was a manufactory in Hatton Garden,[76] and in 1747 Robert Campbell mentioned its production at Whitechapel and in other London suburbs:[77] later trade cards survive in the Castle Museum, York, in connection with works at Tooley Street, London, and also at Derby.[78] During the seventeenth century, Venice seems to have been a celebrated source, and was referred to by John Smith, who observed significantly that the greatest quantities had formerly been made there.[79] This seems to be confirmed by Watin, who, writing almost a century later, remarked that (apart from a particularly finely prepared variety of the pigment) the best came from Venice, but added that otherwise the English and Dutch had taken over this branch of commerce.[80] During the early nineteenth century, a clear preference was expressed for use in the best work of white lead several years old. Nicholson observed in his *New Practical Builder* that the pigment improved with keeping, and should be two or three years old for the best white,[81] and in *The Mechanic's Companion* (1825) called for 'good old white lead' to be used in finishing coats.[82]

White lead was also known as *ceruse*, the name used by Vernatti, although this seems to have changed its connotation in succeeding years. In the first edition of his book, John Smith indicated that it was a more refined variety of the common white lead which was held in particularly high regard by artists, and in the second edition that ceruse was 'the most pure and clean part'.[83] Dossie and Nicholson, however, appear to have treated the terms as synonymous;[84] and Tingry's later editor simply observed that ceruse was the name formerly applied to white lead.[85] Moreover, definite deterioration in the quality of the pigment to which the term was applied by the mid-eighteenth century in France is revealed by the Comte de Caylus, who noted in 1755 that *céruse* contained 'une petite quantité de terres crétassées, dont les Fabriquans la sophistiquent';[86] and Watin too distinguished between *céruse*, and *blanc de plomb* 'que d'autres appellent céruse pure'. The first was, he indicated, white lead mixed with chalk or marl, either in equal parts, or in a ratio of six parts of white lead to ten of marl, adding that *céruse*, 'se distingue du blanc de plomb par sa couleur, qui est moins blanche, & par son poids, qui, à volume égal, est moins lourd'. *Céruse de Rome* was, however, beautiful, heavy, and expensive.[87] Butcher's description also indicates that the name had come to be applied to an adulterated pigment since, editing John Smith's seventeenth-century account of ceruse, he described it firstly as 'a very beautiful white, but much dearer than white-lead', before adding his own observation that it was 'not of so good a body'.[88]

Undoubtedly therefore, as Nicholson and Watin explicitly observed, white lead was frequently adulterated.[89] Dossie mentioned the use of chalk or powdered talc (q.v.) for the purpose;[90] and Butcher indicated that 'some colourmen, for the sake of gain, are apt to adulterate it with what they call SPANISH, which is merely common whiting'. This treatment, he explained 'renders the colour harsh in using, and greatly reduces the beauty of the white';[91] while Vanherman, who referred to the employment of 'Paris white, and other cheap articles' for adulteration, also warned against the practice. He mentioned in particular the discolouration to which such pigment was subject, and suggested a test by which sophistication could be detected.[92] Nevertheless, whiting was often legitimately used as an extender, especially in undercoats in the way suggested by Reynolds.[93] Later, in place of chalk, barytes (q.v.) was extensively employed; and in the 1820s, J.C. Leuchs (whose *Anleitung zur Bereitung aller Farben und Flüssigkeiten* of 1825 was translated into French in 1829 as *Traité complet des . . . matières tinctoriales et des couleurs*) noted that white lead adulterated with one part of barytes was known as *Venice white*; if two parts of barytes were present, the pigment was called *Hamburg white*; and if three parts were used it was called *Dutch white*.[94] This list was repeated by Andrew Ure in 1839 in *A Dictionary of Arts, Manufactures, and Mines*.[95]

In contrast to 'ceruse', *flake white* seems always to have been a term reserved for a high grade of white lead. Thus, in their *Treatise of Japanning and Varnishing* of 1688, John Stalker & George Parker quoted its price ground in walnut oil as twice that of ordinary white lead in the same medium;[96] but although John Smith was uncertain both of its origin and of the reason it was 'by some accounted the best white of all others', mentioning that it was said to be found 'only under the Lead of some very old Buildings',[97] Watin was quite unequivocal in his description of *blanc de plomb en écailles* as simply the product of the stack process.[98] Dossie, however, had described 'White flake' as being of Italian origin, and made by the corrosion of lead by means of the 'pressings of the grape', adding that it surpassed all ceruse or white lead made in England, which was much cheaper.[99] As usual his description was echoed by Martin and Nicholson, while Whittock simply remarked that flake white was manufactured in a similar way to white lead, but using other acids.[100] Flake white appears among other pigments which Lewis Berger was offering for sale in several of his letters dated between 1780 and 1788, its quoted prices being about double those of ordinary white lead; although the gap had closed slightly by the first decade of the nineteenth century in the valuations (q.v. below) made as part of his annual stocktakings. Nevertheless, it seems to have retained its superior status for many years to come, since Butcher observed that it was a very pure white 'used for particular purposes, being much higher in price'; while Tingry's editor remarked that it appeared to be white lead purified by washing and levigation, and formed into drops.[101] These (fig. 2) were made by passing the levigated slurry through a funnel and laying the shell-like drops on a piece of chalk to dry.

Nottingham white also was considered a superior quality of white lead, and was especially recommended by early nineteenth-century writers for use in finishing coats, particularly those which were 'flatted', a technique used to produce a dead matt finish, which is described in Chapter 15. The earliest reference to white lead under this name so far encountered appears to be an entry in accounts for painting at Egremont House, London, dated 11 April 1764 for 'Nottingham mixt & a Gally pot & tools';[102] and it is significant that quantities of Nottingham white in bills for the supply of painting materials at Osterley between 1779 and 1781 are often associated with items for oil of turpentine.[103] The pigment is mentioned in the Berger archive in a letter of 1786, while another of 1788 quotes a

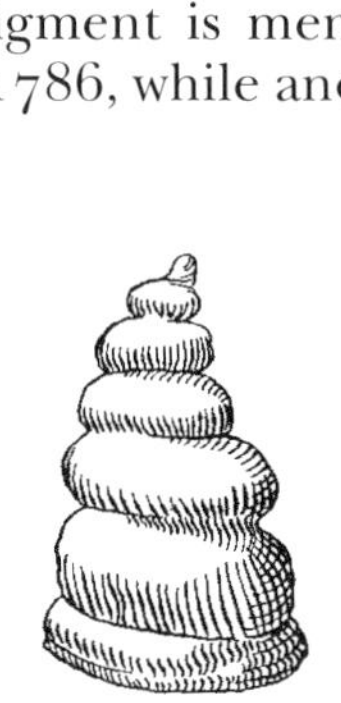

2. A 'drop' of pigment.

price for its supply at about fifty per cent above that of ordinary white lead. It appears too in the early nineteenth-century stock-lists at a similar differential, as may be seen from the analysis of prices (table III, p. 12). The author of the *Practical Treatise on Painting in Oil-Colours* (1795) distinguished Nottingham white from ordinary white lead by saying that alegar was used in its manufacture in place of ordinary vinegar. This, he thought, contained less 'vinous acid' than the latter, which, he believed, possessed the 'virtue and spirit of the hop';[104] but in 1835 the colourman George Field simply observed that it was prepared from flake white.[105] John Pincot recommended use of Nottingham white 'for finishing the inside of best rooms' in his *Treatise on the Practical Part of Coach & House Painting* of about 1811;[106] and items 'flated dead white with the best Nottingham lead' appear in the 1810 and 1813 editions of *Taylor's Builders Price-Book.*[107] Phillips provided similar entries in the 1812 and 1821 editions of *Crosby's Builders' New Price Book*;[108] Martin referred to Nottingham white lead as the most esteemed for flatting;[109] Nicholson repeated this, and adverted to the use of 'fine old Nottingham lead';[110] while Butcher too specified its employment in this connection.[111]

During the second half of the eighteenth century, attempts were made to develop methods other than the stack process for the production of white lead. In 1749 Sir James Creed patented a forerunner of the modern chamber process in which the lead is corroded in a specially built chamber into which currents of carbon dioxide, acetic acid vapour, air, and steam are passed;[112] while Watin referred to 'la céruse de Crems' from the small town of that name in Austria, which was, he said, an expensive pigment.[113] Field mentioned that 'Crems or Cremnitz' white was a lead carbonate imported from Vienna in 'cakes of a cubical form';[114] but Cremnitz (now Kremnica) is, of course, a town in modern Czechoslovakia, and for some reason the two (both formerly in Austria-Hungary) seem to have become confused. At the end of the century, Hurst described the method adopted for the manufacture of 'Kremnitz white' in Germany by the exposure of trays containing a mixture of litharge (lead oxide) and either acetic acid or lead acetate to carbon dioxide, a process parallel to that of Creed;[115] but it is not clear that this method was in use at Crems during the eighteenth century, especially since in the 1820s Leuchs noted that pigment had not been made there for fifty years,[116] and Tingry had provided analyses showing that 'Cremnitz white' could contain a mixture of substances. Some specimens contained bismuth oxide (bismuth white, q.v.), others white lead, and some were mixed with a great deal of chalk; while he himself suggested its preparation from tin nitrate, zinc oxide (zinc white, q.v.), and white chalk, but such a pigment was, he added, too expensive for house-painting.[117] It is therefore difficult to assess the use or nature of pigments sold under this name, but it is clear there was a continuing search for alternatives to white lead produced by the stack process.

In 1797 the Earl of Dundonald secured a patent for making white lead by treating litharge with salt and water, washing the resulting lead oxychloride, and boiling it with potassium carbonate to form white lead, which was washed and dried for use.[118] Another method, first patented in England by Edward Noble in 1808, seems to have been of French origin, and consisted in the precipitation of white lead by passing carbon dioxide through a solution of a basic lead salt.[119] Noble used lead acetate for this, and Tingry's later editor mentioned a patent granted in 1821 to John Sadler for a similar process.[120] Vanherman also referred to two comparable methods of preparing white lead, one closely related to the above, the other transforming lead oxychloride in water by the action of carbon dioxide;[121] while in 1837 Button & Dyar secured a patent for the same process (later described by Ure and Hurst) using a solution of basic lead nitrate.[122] There is little information to suggest how important these processes were in terms of house-painting, but it seems unlikely that they were of great significance, since Ure quite specifically referred to the stack process as that used in this country.[123] Other contemporary developments seem also to have been less than totally successful,[124] and as late as 1940, Noël Heaton remarked that although countless processes designed to supersede the stack process had been patented and put into operation, for the most part they had failed to become established, on account of either their expense or the inferiority of their product.[125] Over the last few decades, however, the stack process has been superseded, at least in England, by other methods of manufacture; and modern white lead differs from the earlier product in some respects, principally in its smaller particle size, which affects its handling characteristics.

Looking at prices for white lead, 3 pounds were charged for in connection with the restoration of Chorley church, Lancashire, in 1635–6 at a cost of 6*d.* per pound.[126] Later, in 1703, Neve remarked that white lead for painting was commonly sold in London at 2½*d.* or 3*d.* per pound dry, or at 5*d.* per pound ready ground in oil.[127] The latter is identical with the rate charged in a bill among papers at Boughton House, Northamptonshire, for a barrel containing nearly 3 cwt. of 'fine white lead Gro[und]' supplied in 1705.[128] During the late seventeenth century, the pigment was also available ground in walnut oil, and Stalker & Parker indicated: 'Flake white, finely ground in Nut-oyl, is sold at 2*s.* the pound. White lead, ground in the same oyl, 1*s.* per pound.'[129] The price of 5*d.* per pound for the ordinary product ground in linseed oil seems to have fallen to 4*d.* by 1734, the date at which Willam Salmon published the retail price list of the Strand colourman Alexander Emerton in his *Palladio Londinensis.* 'Best White Lead ground in Oil' was 4*d.* per pound, but could also be purchased by the hundredweight, in which case it was priced at 36*s.*[130] Salmon's different categories of white lead paste seem to have formed the basis of those in the price-book first published by John Phillips in the early years of the nineteenth century. This contained a summary of prices charged between 1760 and 1790 in addition to those current from 1790 to 1803; and it is instructive to set these out in tabulated form, with the addition of those in the revised 1812 and 1821 editions, in order to show the movements in the value of money occasioned by the war with France, since these also affected the other painting materials described below (table II, p. 12).

These prices appear to accord well with examples noted in painting accounts. For example, 40lb. of 'prepar'd White Lead' was supplied to William Blaithwaite, Esq., at

Dyrham Park, Gloucestershire (now Avon), on 7 May 1781 at a rate of $4\frac{1}{2}$*d.* per pound, which is equivalent to 42*s.* per cwt.;[131] a total of 393 lb. of white lead was supplied at Tredegar House, Newport, Monmouthshire (now Gwent), at various dates in 1792 and 1793 at a rate of 6*d.* per pound, which is equivalent to 56*s.* per cwt.;[132] while John Soane settled an account for the supply of painting materials in 1803, which contained items for 2 cwt. 1 qr. of 'Genuine Gro[d] White Lead' at 56*s.* per cwt. provided on 5 March, and two further items for very similar quantities of 'White Lead' supplied on 9 May and 11 July of that year at a rate of 60*s.* per cwt.[133] Nevertheless, the rates given by Phillips (especially in his second list)[134] may be less reliable than they seem, since, although at the bottom end of the price scale they compare well with those in the records of Lewis Berger, at the upper end they considerably exceed those at which he valued his stock. Berger's rates are shown in tabulated form, together with the quantities which were of course also recorded in the manuscripts (table III). By 1828 it seems likely that prices had fallen back further, since Vanherman gave the cost of dry white lead as 34*s.* per cwt.[135]

Table II. *Prices of white lead per cwt. given by William Salmon and John Phillips 1734–1821*

	Salmon (1734)[1]	Phillips (1804)[2] 1760–90	Phillips (1804)[2] 1790–1803	Phillips (1812)[3]	Phillips (1821)[4]
Best white lead ground in oil	36*s.*	38*s.*	60*s.*	76*s.* 9*d.*	76*s.*
Second primer ground in oil	36*s.*	36*s.* 6*d.*	58*s.*	69*s.* 6*d.*	66*s.*
First primer	36*s.*	30*s.*	38*s.*	45*s.*	42*s.*

References
1. p. 57. 2. p. 130. 3. pp. 210–11. 4. pp. 168–9.

ZINC WHITE

Although zinc white (zinc oxide) had been known for many years, it was not until the closing decades of the eighteenth century that serious attempts were made to use it as a non-toxic substitute for white lead. In a paper dated 1782, Guyton de Morveau considered all the then known white pigments and suggested zinc white was the best alternative to white lead. It was, he noted, being sold at 6fr. per pound.[136] In 1794 and 1796 John Atkinson, a colourmaker from the Liverpool area, took out patents for its preparation, calling it *mineral white*;[137] and Vanherman provided a description of its manufacture by the melting of zinc in a large deep crucible inclined at an angle of forty-five degrees. The secret of success was the nice control of the process to produce a reasonable yield of oxide (which was raked off from the surface of the molten metal) without discolouration.[138]

Although the author of the *Practical Treatise* said it was possible that zinc white might be procured in sufficient quantities to supply the place of ceruse, even for house-painting,[139] no evidence has been found to suggest that it came into general use for this purpose until the mid-nineteenth century. In the fourth edition of his book, Watin referred to Guyton de Morveau's paper, but observed that zinc white was too expensive to be employed in decorating, and he had never known it used.[140] Moreover,

Table III. *Prices of white lead from figures contained in Berger archive 1788–1810*

	Letter book[1] 20 June 1788	Stock 1801–2[2] 1 January 1802	Stock 1805–6[3] 1 January 1806	Stock 1809–10[4] 1 January 1810
Ground in oil				
Nottingham lead	–	70*s.* ($4\frac{1}{2}$ cwt.)	–	60s. (5 cwt.)
'Genuine' white lead	40*s.*[5]	46*s.*[6] ($43\frac{1}{4}$ cwt.)	58*s.* (68 cwt.)	52*s.* (16 cwt.)
'Second' white lead	36*s.*	42*s.* ($13\frac{3}{4}$ cwt.)	55*s.* ($24\frac{3}{4}$ cwt.)	49*s.* ($12\frac{3}{4}$ cwt.)
'Common' white lead	–	38*s.* ($3\frac{1}{2}$ cwt.)	52*s.* & 50*s.*[7] ($9\frac{1}{4}$ cwt.)	46*s.* ($\frac{3}{4}$ cwt.)
Dry pigment				
Flake white	75*s.*[8]	70*s.* (1 cwt.)	82*s.* (2 cwt.)	76*s.* (3 cwt.)
Nottingham white	56*s.*	50*s.* ($4\frac{1}{2}$ cwt.)	–	–
White lead	36*s.*	42*s.* (32 cwt.)	57*s.* & 54*s.* ($29\frac{1}{4}$ cwt.)	46*s.* & 45*s.* (53 cwt.)

Notes and references
1. p. 289.
2. pp. 48, 54, 55, 56, 58.
3. pp. 10, 11, 25, 30, 31.
4. pp. 8, 13, 14, 20.
5. 'Fine' white lead.
6. 'Gro[d] Lead'.
7. 'Gro[d] White Lead'.
8. Elsewhere, letters dated 14 June and 20 August 1780 contain prices for flake white of 65*s.* and 75*s.* (Letter book, pp. 29, 30).
N.B. Weights in stock given to nearest $\frac{1}{4}$ cwt.

no mention of the pigment is to be found in the early nineteenth-century Berger papers,[141] and Vanherman's reference to it is also indicative that zinc white was not in use in England even by the late 1820s. He said it was more expensive than white lead, but, he felt, might compete with it if the duty then charged on it was removed, adding that the principal objection to its use was that it was 'hungry', and required a great deal of oil to make it sufficiently fluid to work well. Nevertheless, he suggested, this could be overcome by thinning it, once ground into oil, with copal, mastic, or turpentine varnish and oil of turpentine; and expressed the hope that a proper zinc paint manufactory might be started.[142]

That the pigment did come into use during the following thirty years is evident from T.L. Donaldson's *Handbook of Specifications* of about 1859, in which he quoted a French specification calling for the employment of zinc to the exclusion of white lead, and in another specified it for use in white-painted rooms with gas lights.[143] Presumably white lead tended to blacken very quickly in such interiors, and the introduction of gas for illumination may thus have given some impetus to the development of zinc oxide in England. Nevertheless, it would seem that even by that date it was still treated as a special pigment, and not expected to be in normal use.

BARYTES AND BARIUM CARBONATE

Barium sulphate occurs naturally as *barytes* or 'heavy spar', and is found in the counties of Derbyshire, Cornwall, Devonshire, Cumberland (now part of Cumbria), and Shropshire, the Malehurst mines in the latter county being particularly mentioned by Heaton.[144] Its occurrence is often closely associated with that of lead ore, and it was known to the miners of this mineral as *cawk*.[145] Barytes seems to have come into use as an artists' water-colour towards the end of the eighteenth century, and was called *permanent white* or *constant white*;[146] while Vanherman described it as 'the only constant white in water colours'.[147] In oil it is transparent, but it became used as an extender or adulterant for white lead and other pigments. Lewis Berger's sons were experimenting with barytes, which appears subsequently as an extender in a number of pigments for which formulations are given among the firm's papers, from at least 1816, and a method for the artificial preparation of barium sulphate from barium carbonate is noted in 1824;[148] while Tingry's later editor referred to William Duesbury's patent of 1825 for the purification of native barium sulphate.[149]

Although today barytes is distinguished from *witherite*, the naturally occurring form of barium carbonate, it appears the former name could be applied to both during the early nineteenth century. Barium carbonate can be employed in much the same way as barytes, although it is softer, less dense, and has a higher oil absorption, and has been used to a small extent in this century for water paints.[150] Vanherman observed that there were two kinds of 'the Barytes, or ponderous spar – the sulphate and carbonate', indicating that the latter only was to be used, since, he believed, 'the sulphuric acid of the first acts on gums and mucilage, and changes the whiteness'. In fact, the sulphate is almost completely inert as a pigment; while, since the carbonate is decomposed by acids, as Vanherman himself warned, the latter compound is highly toxic. Nevertheless, he described a method for its manufacture by grinding and washing, and mentioned its use as a 'water-white for ceilings', recalling that he had purchased 20 tons in 1814 from a lead mine near Minsterley, about twelve miles west of Shrewsbury, at £10 per ton, although he felt the current price might be much lower.[151] This rate works out at approximately double that of Paris white (q.v.) and it therefore seems unlikely that, unless it had become very much cheaper, barium carbonate would have been widely used in distemper. Tingry's editor, who quoted extensively from Vanherman's book, also mentioned barium carbonate, or 'Cocks comb spar', referring to that from Murton in Cumberland besides the former's Shropshire source.[152]

TALC

The use of 'talc' as an adulterant for white lead was mentioned by Dossie.[153] Although today the term is applied to a form of hydrated magnesium silicate, it is possible Dossie may have had a form of gypsum (calcium sulphate) in mind, since Félibien had indicated that this was its composition.[154]

CROTIA

Vanherman used sifted road-dust as a pigment in the fish-oil-based paints of which he published details in 1805,[155] and later in his 'Impenetrable or Anti-Corrosive Paint' for exterior use. The sweepings of a road made with flints, clinkers, granite, or any stony substance were collected and passed through a 'forty-five hole wire sieve' for use. He gave the name *crotia* to the product, which cost 1*s.* 6*d.* per cwt.[156] 'Road Sand', together with fish-oil, another substance with which Vanherman was concerned, were mentioned in derogatory terms by Pincot, who seems to have been a business rival of the former;[157] and both substances were discussed by Martin and the author of *The Painter's and Varnisher's Pocket Manual* (1825); while Tingry's later editor also referred to Vanherman's road-dust.[158]

BONE WHITE

Calcined hartshorn or 'bone white' was recommended by Dossie as a watercolour pigment, and was included in the lists published by Martin and Nicholson, who plagiarised Dossie's work quite uncritically.[159] Clearly, it was a pigment never intended for house-painting, and indeed Whittock indicated that it was used only by historical and portrait painters.[160]

BISMUTH WHITE

Although Martin and Nicholson included bismuth white in their pigment lists,[161] it seems most unlikely to have been used for house-painting; and, as Tingry's editor (who described bismuth oxide or *magistery of bismuth* from Cornwall as *pearl white*) pointed out, was used chiefly as a cosmetic.[162]

CHAPTER 2

BLUE PIGMENTS

During the seventeenth century, the only blue pigment which was more or less satisfactory for house-painting purposes in an oil medium was indigo, although the colour it would produce was dull in tone. For a brighter hue, either azurite or its manufactured equivalent, blue verditer, had to be pressed into service. These were not particularly well suited to the medium, however, although excellent for use in distemper; while smalt possessed considerable limitations on the way in which it could be used, and ultramarine, although almost perfect technically, was far too expensive. This problem was fortunately solved by the discovery of Prussian blue during the first decade of the eighteenth century, and, apart from a slight tendency to become greenish in colour, the preparation of blues in oil presented little difficulty from then on; while, at the very end of the period under consideration, Prussian blue was supplemented by artificial ultramarine.

INDIGO

Indigo is a naturally occurring dye prepared from leaves of plants belonging to the genus *Indigofera*. Seventeenth-century sources of that used in England included India, and (*via* Spain) Guatemala on the central American mainland; although, by the early nineteenth century indigo from the East Indies (trade with which was dominated by the Dutch) seems also to have been common. As will be seen from the analysis of prices below, there are many references to 'East India Indigo' in the Berger archive; and Tingry listed indigo from the East Indies together with dye from the West Indies, although, he observed, that from Guatemala was the best and most esteemed.[1] His later editor too mentioned 'Flora or Guatemala' dye together with 'Carolina' indigo, and gave an analysis of a specimen of 'Caraca *Flora*' (presumably from Caracas, now in Venezuela, South America). This, he indicated however, contained only 54½ per cent of indigo, against 75 per cent in some specimens from the East Indies and 79½ per cent in samples from Calcutta.[2] Quality was, therefore, highly variable and, quite apart from the care taken in extraction of the dye (which was effected by soaking the leaves in water, beating them to a pulp, and allowing the indigo to settle out), could depend on which from a series of harvests the dye came.[3] John Smith gave a brief description of dye extraction,[4] and Tingry observed that it was imported in flat, square pieces which were not very hard, floated on water, and were inflammable. According to him, that called 'cupreous indigo', which left a green, bronze-like colour when rubbed on the fingernail, was the best.[5] It was necessary to reduce the cakes of dye to powder form for use as a pigment, and the author of *The Painter's, Gilder's, and Varnisher's Manual* [*c.* 1830] illustrated two mills for the purpose.[6]

Unlike many other natural dye-stuffs, indigo prepared in this way can be used directly as a pigment, and it was mentioned by D'Aviler as one of those used for painting grotesques on a prepared white field.[7] It is serviceable in both oil and distemper, and John Smith indicated that the longer it was ground in oil the more beautiful its colour became.[8] Although a vegetable dye which, the late nineteenth-century colour chemist A.H. Church indicated, loses from one third to one half of its intensity when exposed to sun-light for five years,[9] it seems to have been considered sufficiently light-fast, at least during the seventeenth century, to have been used to mix a bluish grey for exterior use. John Smith mentioned that it was much used with white for the 'last colours of Windows, Doors, Pales, Posts, Rails, Pallisadoes, &c.'; but, he added, since it was rather expensive 'Blew Balls' were substituted for it by vulgar painters. These, which he dismissed as 'not so good a colour neither for beauty nor lasting',[10] have been identified by Dr Harley with *florey*, prepared from the froth on top of dyeing vats, which could contain either indigo or woad. The latter, a cheaper dye extracted from the plant *Isatis tinctoria*, was grown and prepared in England, but was virtually obsolete as an artists' material by the beginning of the seventeenth century.[11] Nevertheless, its production in the 1690s in Gloucestershire was described by Celia Fiennes, who noted that the lettuce-like tufts the plant produced were cut off close to the ground, leaving the root to produce more leaves. These were ground to a paste in a horse-mill, the product being made up into balls, which were air-dried under cover. The smell, she noted was 'so strong and offencive you can scarce beare it at the Mill', adding 'I could not forse my horse neare it'.[12]

Use of florey before the Civil War is illustrated by its inclusion in lists of painting materials for work at Whitehall and Greenwich palaces in 1630–1 and 1639–40 respectively;[13] but indigo was clearly preferable, and in 1670 John Evelyn advocated its use in blue oil paint.[14] A little later, John Smith indicated that the colour produced by mixture of indigo with white lead was known as *lead colour*.[15] Although Watin too suggested that the pigment was used with white in oil, and employed it for example in *gris argentin*,[16] its use in this medium would no doubt have declined rapidly following the introduction of Prussian blue during the first quarter of the eighteenth century. Certainly in 1755, probably thinking in terms of fine art, Caylus observed that this had led to its complete abandonment by painters;[17] and, while Butcher, Nicholson, and the author of the *Painter's . . . Pocket Manual* all gave recipes for *lead colour* in which indigo was used, these probably represent an uncritically accepted survival from Smith's seventeenth-century text.[18] Indeed, although Butcher also included Smith's description of the pigment in his general discussion of those in use, in common with other contemporary authors who referred to *lead colour*, he proposed elsewhere in his text its mixture by the combination of white with lamp black, tending to confirm that indigo had passed out of normal use in oil.[19]

In distemper, on the other hand, the pigment seems to have had continued employment throughout the period under consideration, no doubt owing to the instability of Prussian blue with alkalis such as that found in fresh lime plaster. Bullet, for example, used it with Rouen white to make *gris perle*;[20] Watin employed it in mixtures for *gris argentin* and *olive* distemper;[21] a small quantity was included together with other distemper pigments and materials in an account of 1802 for painting a house in Doncaster;[22] and Nicholson recommended its use for 'inferior greys' in distemper.[23] By this date, however, it is likely that it was often 'extended' with the rather cheaper Prussian blue; and a formula for 'Indigo wash' contained in the Berger archive gives details of a preparation containing indigo, Prussian blue, and barytes, the resulting combination costing 25*s.* per cwt. to produce.[24]

The indigo purchased in connection with the Doncaster house mentioned immediately above was priced at a rate equivalent to 8*s.* per lb., but, as might be surmised from the wide range of qualities mentioned above, considerable variations are met with in the price of the dye, quite apart from the marked difference between the 'Spanish' varieties from Central America and those from the East Indies. On 1 January 1806, for example, Lewis Berger had a small stock of 3 lb. of the former valued at 13*s.* per lb., and $4\frac{3}{4}$ lb. of the East Indian variety at 8*s.* per lb.; the price difference no doubt reflecting Tingry's already-mentioned assertion that Guatemala indigo was more esteemed. By 1810, Berger's stock had risen to a total of $112\frac{1}{2}$ lb. 'Spanish Indigo' at 7*s.* 10*d.* per lb., while overall he had 1147 lb. 'East India Indigo' at prices ranging from 3*s.* 2*d.* to 4*s.* 8*d.* per lb.[25] As in the case of white lead, however, the prices given by Phillips were rather higher, and he suggested that Spanish indigo would cost 14*s.* or 19*s.* per pound, against 'Indigo blue, common sort' at 9*s.* 6*d.* In addition he quoted a price for 'Rock Indigo will stand well' at 18*s.* or 24*s.* 4*d.* (the latter term, Dr Harley has indicated, being a corruption of 'rich indigo').[26]

ORCHILL AND LITMUS

Orchill, which was used by Lewis Berger's company in a formula for satin white (q.v.), is a dye of fugitive character yielded by various lichens of the *Roccella* genus, notably *R. fuciformus*, native in the British Isles to Wales, Scotland, and the north of England. Its extraction by grinding the lichen with urine and quicklime (the resulting chemical reaction producing ammonia) was known from the beginning of the period here considered,[27] and was described by Tingry, who referred to preparation of the dye in his day on a large scale in London, Paris, and Lyons from material imported from the Canary and Cape Verde Islands.[28] In addition, Ure noted a variety from the Auvergne.[29] The dye is red in acid conditions and blue in alkali, and Tingry's editor observed that when, a few days after treatment began, the dye was purplish red in colour it was known as 'archil'; but that when it eventually turned blue it was then called 'litmus'.[30] In the context of the tendency of satin white to alkalinity, it would therefore have been employed by the Berger firm as a blue to heighten its apparent cleanliness of colour; and in 1802 Lewis Berger had stocks of just over $11\frac{3}{4}$ cwt. valued at 38*s.* per cwt.[31] Otherwise, no other mention of the dye for purposes of interior decoration has been encountered, although it is interesting to note that in 1898 S.O. Addy referred to the then surviving and supposedly old-established practice of employing orchill in exterior colour-washes in the north of England.[32]

SMALT

The crushed blue glass known as smalt was used widely in painting from at least the mid-sixteenth century. Its manufacture is reputed to have been started at Neudek (now Nejdek in north-west Czechoslovakia) about 1540, but Dr Harley suggests that since blue glass was known well before this, the pigment could have been available earlier.[33] It was made from *zaffre*, which was described by Tingry's later editor as crude cobalt ore roasted with about twice its weight of powdered flints, although Ure, in his slightly later description, substituted two or three parts of sand for the latter.[34] Sixteenth- and seventeenth-century methods of smalt manufacture are discussed by Dr Harley, and later processes by Hurst;[35] but although accounts of the production of the blue glass itself vary in detail, the general principle was to roast silica, in the form of either flints or sand, with potash and zaffre in more or less equal parts. The blue glass was then crushed for use, but suffered from two major disadvantages. In the first place, if finely ground to reduce its grittiness the colour paled: in the second, its refractive index being akin to that of an oil medium, the pigment was without body. Thus John Smith and Watin both described it as 'blackening' in oil, while its staining power was not high enough to permit the addition of a body white to overcome this while still producing a blue of any depth.[36] For this reason two grades of fineness were evolved, each used in a different way.

To achieve the deepest colour the coarser variety, known as 'strewing smalt' (referred to by Watin as *azur à poudrer*) was employed. John Smith's book contains a whole chapter on the method of its use, from which the following extract is taken:

> Smalt being a Colour that gives its greatest Lustre by the way of strowing only, I shall lay down the true method of performing this work: First temper up White-Lead pretty stiff with good clear drying Oyl; let it be as stiff as it well can be to spend well from the Pencil, with this

white Colour cover over the Superficies of the work you intend to strow with Smalt; and if it be the Margent of a Dial whose Figures are already Gilt with Gold, let every part between the Figures, and where there is no Gold laid on, be done over, and be very exact in the work, for the Smalt takes no where but on this new and moist ground; then take Smalt, and the Work to be done over with it lying flat, strowing it thick on the thing to be coloured, and with the feather edge of a Goose-Quill stroke over it, that it may lie even and alike thick on all Places; and then with a Bunch of Linnen Cloath, that is soft and plyable, dab it down close, that it may take well upon the ground to be thoroughly dry, then wipe off the loose Colour with a Feather, and blow the remainder of it off with a pair of Bellows, so is your Work finished.

In all other Cases, where the Work to be strowed over with Smalt does not lye flat, you must take Smalt up upon a flat bunch of Linnen Cloath, and so dab it upon the ground you are to lay it upon.[37]

Applied in this way, he enthused, 'there is not a more glorious Colour in the World'.[38]

The second, fine variety he called 'Oyl Smalt', and Watin *émail*; but Dossie and James Smith, whose *Panorama of Science and Art* was published in 1815, called this *bice*, a usage not to be confused with the seventeenth-century application of the name to azurite discussed in the section dealing with that pigment below.[39] This variety was intended for grinding up in oil and mixture with white lead; but even so John Smith criticised its lack of body and said that it worked with great difficulty,[40] while, as mentioned above, its colour would have been extremely pale.

Stalker & Parker gave the price of 'the best fine smalt' as 4*s.* or 5*s.* per pound in 1688,[41] while in 1676 the husband of the portrait painter, Mary Beale, recorded the acquisition of four pounds of the 'best and finest ground smalt that ever came into England' valued at 8*s.* per pound.[42] Unfortunately, no information on contemporary prices of the coarser, strewing smalt is to hand; but by the late eighteenth century this seems generally to have been rather cheaper. In 1788, for example, Lewis Berger was offering 'Strewing Smalts' at 1*s.* 6*d.* per pound, and 'Smalts' at 1*s.*, 1*s.* 2*d.*, or 1*s.* 4*d.*; while between 1802 and 1810 he valued his stocks of strewing smalt at rates between 1*s.* 6*d.* and 1*s.* 9½*d.*, and a more expensive quality 'Smalts HFE' at 2*s.* 9*d.*[43]

Before the Civil War, strewn smalt appears to have been extensively used. Paint samples have shown that this technique was employed for the earliest scheme, almost certainly of the 1630s, on the enriched ceiling beams and entablature of the Queen's Cabinet at the Queen's House, Greenwich. These had first been painted dull yellow and the mouldings and enrichments oil-gilded, following which the interstices and other areas between the gold were picked in with white, on the surface of which lies a thick layer of smalt.[44] This process, it will be noted, follows the sequence described by John Smith; and it is of interest that two documentary references to other royal works reflect the same order: in 1636–7 an account mentions 'painting guilding and laying with smalte in oyle' a picture frame at Oatlands, Surrey;[45] while another for 'divers times pryming payntinge & guildinge wth fyne gold and strewinge wth fayre blew' occurs in an account for an armorial at Whitehall Palace in 1629–30.[46] Strewn smalt has also been found on the ground of a pulvinated frieze of a mid-seventeenth-century doorcase now at Tamworth Castle, Staffordshire;[47] and it is of interest that, probably in the 1660s, the Devon plasterer John Abbott noted apropos strewn smalt, 'you see soe excellent a blew in Roode lofts done many years agone, & yet sheweth very faire'.[48]

In 1670, Evelyn noted that smalt had to be strewn,[49] and strewing smalt clearly remained in use during the second half of the seventeenth century; but it may, perhaps, have been employed more sparingly for interior architectural purposes. John Smith, who described it as 'the most glorious colour of all, if it lie at a distance', added 'near the Eye, the beauty is not so great', and the illustrations he chose for its use were on clock dial-boards or inn signs, both of which could have been laid flat for ease of application.[50] An instance of such employment occurs in 1700, when John Martin repainted the 1637 dial-board of Watford Church, Hertfordshire, strewing the ground between the figures with smalt, which, he noted, was carefully dried beforehand.[51] It also had a particular use on exterior ironwork, and has been found strewn on a layer of white on the seventeenth-century iron gates at the Royal Hospital, Kilmainham, Dublin;[52] while those at Ham House were painted 'Smalt blew' in 1673–4.[53] Probably, therefore, it is to strewn smalt that Robert Streeter's 1694 account refers, when he repainted the ironwork of the Tulip Stairs at the Queen's House, Greenwich, 'w:^th^ fine Smalte'.[54]

Following the introduction of Prussian blue in the early eighteenth century, it seems likely that this laborious technique for the use of smalt would have been abandoned, and although Lewis Berger held significant stocks of strewing smalt during the 1800s,[55] it must be borne in mind that the pigment was used for many purposes quite unconnected with house-painting, such as ceramic glazes, paper-making, and laundry blue; and again, no reliance can be placed on its appearance in the colour lists of Martin and Nicholson, since the former seems to have plagiarised Dossie, who was not exclusively concerned with house-painting, and the latter transcribed Martin more or less word for word.[56] While it is true that Nicholson added the information that smalt had to be strewn, it should not be forgotten that by the time he was writing William Butcher had published his revised edition of John Smith's book, in which the description of strewing smalt is a survival from the seventeenth-century text.[57] There appears, therefore, little direct evidence that the pigment remained in use by the 1800s.

In the case of oil smalt, D'Aviler listed *émail* together with indigo and azurite as being used for painting ornaments on a white ground.[58] In such instances he may have had it in mind that it was to be used as a glaze without admixture with white, but Bullet suggested the employment of *émail* with white in *gris perle* oil paint.[59] Examination of paint samples from the doorcase at Tamworth already mentioned showed a layer of white lead in oil, attributable to the seventeenth century, which contains a little smalt;[60] and others from the ceiling of the Hall at the Queen's House, Greenwich, indicate that the 'Collour' picked in by Robert Streeter between the 1630s gilding in 1694 consisted of white lead with a small admixture of this pigment, no doubt giving it a greyish tone.[61] In addition, samples taken from the wainscot of the Marble Hall at Petworth House, Sussex, contained a layer of grey attributable to the early eighteenth century, produced by the use of smalt.[62] Some fifty years later, however, Dossie stated that while formerly employed in oil, the finer smalt was by then largely disused;[63] and Watin writing slightly later said of both fine and coarse varieties that they were only employed externally, since the blue yellowed in an oil medium if used indoors.[64]

Tingry alone suggested that smalt was used in some kinds of distemper.[65] Otherwise, no reference has been encountered to its employment in this way, and it cannot be doubted that indigo or blue verditer were more useful in this medium.

Altogether, smalt seems to have been a pigment employed fairly extensively for house-painting purposes in the seventeenth century, either strewn to produce an intense blue or mixed with white lead in oil for bluish greys; but to have been superseded rapidly by Prussian blue in the 1700s.

AZURITE

From well before the period under consideration, a pigment known as *blue bice*, made by crushing and levigating the mineral azurite (a naturally occurring form of basic copper carbonate), was in use. The main source of supply seems to have been Germany, although it is possible that some may have been of Central American origin, and Hill observed that the mineral occurs in the British Isles.[66] By the early years of the seventeenth century, an artificial variety of blue copper carbonate known as blue verditer was also being prepared, and Rosamond Harley indicates that the natural pigment fell into disuse by artists towards 1700, although its employment was revived during the nineteenth century. During the eighteenth century the term *blue bice* became applied to verditer and other pigments, but Dr Harley is firmly of the opinion that during the seventeenth century it was applied exclusively to pigment prepared from azurite.[67]

A sample of paint from the sixteenth-century ceiling of Wolsey's Closet at Hampton Court, Middlesex, has revealed that azurite was used for its blue ground;[68] and in the Exchequer rolls of the 1620s are several references to *blue bice* or *fair bice* being used on architectural elements. At Whitehall Palace, it was used in redecorating the ceiling of the Tudor chapel in 1621–2, 'layinge all the blewe in the ffrett with faire bice', a treatment no doubt echoing that of the ceiling in Wolsey's Closet.[69] A similar effect may have been employed in 1622–3 in the short-lived apse in Inigo Jones's Banqueting House, which was 'pickt in with faire bice';[70] but other references are to its employment on smaller elements. Blue bice was used in 1620–1, for example, on the frieze in a chamber at Whitehall;[71] while the shafts of the upper order of columns of the chimneypiece in the Queen's New Cabinet Room at Somerset House were painted with 'rich blewe Byce' in 1629–30.[72]

The medium employed in any of these instances is not mentioned, and it is unclear whether the pigment was commonly used in water or oil for architectural purposes. There are, however, several seventeenth-century references to bice being strewn, probably (accepting Dr Harley's view that it is not this material) in a similar way to smalt. In 1670, for instance, Evelyn wrote 'of *Smalt* and *Byce*, which is onely done by *Strewing*',[73] and a significant number of entries referring to the strewing of bice in the painting of clock-dials appear in the pre-Civil-War Exchequer rolls. In 1615–16, for example, the great dial at Westminster Palace was 'strawed wth faire bice'; and at Greenwich payment was made 'for pryming paynting guylding and strewing wth fyne Byce three lardge dyalls'.[74] Similar items in connection with the painting of dials appear at Somerset House in 1618–19; at Hampton Court, Oatlands, and Nonsuch in 1619–20; at Whitehall in 1622–3; and at Hampton Court in 1631–2.[75] It is also of interest in this connection that parts of the taffrails of the King's barge were 'newe gilt and strawed wth fare Bise' in 1630.[76] Writing in the second half of the seventeenth century, it is true, John Smith referred to the use of blue bice in oil, observing that it had the best body of all the bright blues, although it was the palest in colour and was inclined to be sandy. For this reason, he indicated, it required good grinding on a very hard stone.[77] It seems likely, however, that by the time he was writing, azurite was obsolecent; and, as Dr Harley explains, it would lose its colour if finely ground, for this reason simply being mixed with oil or water for use.[78]

Stalker & Parker gave the price of 'Blew Bise' (which they noted was only useful for mixing greens, a remark again seeming to suggest it had fallen from favour by the late 1680s) as 4*d.* or 6*d.* per ounce,[79] showing that it was extremely costly compared with white lead (q.v.). In France, D'Aviler listed 'cendre bleüe' as one of the blue pigments used for painting grotesques and ornaments on a white ground;[80] but the French applied this term equally to natural and artificial varieties of copper carbonate, and although Watin described the origin of *cendre bleue* as a blue stone found in the copper mines of Poland and the Auvergne, it seems possible that by his time much of that used in France was the artificial pigment of British manufacture and his definition was accordingly archaic.[81] The most likely explanation for this is, as Dr Harley has pointed out, that the method of manufacture for blue verditer was regarded as an English speciality and was not understood in France during the eighteenth century.[82] Indeed, the formula that Watin gave for it was that for the obsolete blue frit described by Vitruvius, which, although relying on the presence of copper for its colour, was a completely different substance.[83] Nevertheless, Leuchs appears to describe production of pigment from azurite in the Tyrol as late as the 1820s.[84]

Altogether, it seems possible to conclude that, although an expensive pigment, azurite had been used on a fairly large scale in opulent interiors of the sixteenth century, and that this continued into the first half of the seventeenth. Its later employment is more difficult to assess on the basis of the evidence to hand, but it seems likely that on account of the introduction of blue verditer, its use in house-painting in Britain declined in parallel with its employment in fine art, and that, having had more limited application after 1660, by about 1700 it was of negligible importance.

MANUFACTURED COPPER BLUES

Although other varieties of artificial copper blue are described in earlier literature,[85] the only type which appears from documentary sources to have been employed for house-painting in England during the first two centuries of the period under review was that produced as a by-product of silver refining, known as *blue verditer*. Chemically, this was a basic copper carbonate, and may thus be described as an artificial variety of azurite. In the early nineteenth century, however, a series of related, but different, copper blues came to be developed, to which the same name was sometimes applied.

In the early seventeenth century, blue verditer seems to have been of fairly recent introduction,[86] but a quantity was supplied in connection with work at Whitehall Palace in 1624–5.[87] Its use appears to have been well established by the second half of the century, although it is not an entirely satisfactory pigment for general use in oil, since its refractive index is similar to that of the medium, and it thus becomes transparent. Also, poorer qualities have a tendency to discolour. John Smith accordingly characterised it as less satisfactory than 'blue bice' (azurite), having no body, a sandy texture, poor colour, and a tendency to turn green;[88] but it is nevertheless clear that it was used to a fair extent in oil, and certainly became of great importance in an aqueous medium, to which it is better suited.

The process of manufacture carried out by the silver refiners was described by Christopher Merret in 1678. Crude silver, which contained copper, was dissolved in nitric acid, when any gold impurity, being insoluble in the acid, settled out, leaving a solution which was a mixture of silver and copper nitrates. After this liquid had been decanted from the gold, copper plates were suspended in it, and the silver in turn allowed to precipitate leaving a solution of copper nitrate. This was then poured onto chalk (calcium carbonate), 100lb. of which were employed at a time, the mixture being stirred for some hours daily. When the blue colour of the solution paled, the liquor was poured off and replaced by a further quantity, the process being repeated until all the chalk had been converted to verditer, which was then dried ready for sale.[89]

The hue of copper carbonate can vary from quite a good blue, only slightly more greenish than azurite, to a green having a distinctly bluish cast. Green verditer is discussed in Chapter 3 and may be made by the same process as the blue, although much more exacting conditions are required to produce the latter; and during the seventeenth century the verditer makers seemed to be at a loss to understand why a green product often resulted. For this, it was said, 'they can assign no reason, nor can they hit on a certain rule to make constantly their Verditer of a fair Blew, to their great disprofit, the Blew being of manifold greater value than the Green'.[90] How far this apparent vagueness was a blind to protect what was a valuable trade secret it is difficult to say, but it has recently been shown that the technique for producing the blue lay in accurate control of the concentration of the copper nitrate solution, its temperature, and in frequent stirring. It seems likely that on account of the second of these the pigment could be made only during the colder months of the year, and another subtlety lay in increasing the size of the pigment particles and hence the depth of colour by including pigment already made in a new batch of chalk and copper nitrate.[91] As late as 1834, 'Refiners Verditer' was being made in a similar way by Lewis Berger's sons, although they employed 'Pinnings Dutch lead' (which may have been barium carbonate)[92] in place of chalk, and also added 'Bleach' at the end, once the verditer had been made and washed.[93]

By this date, cheaper methods of making blue and green copper pigments had been developed, and it seems probable that the term *refiners verditer* (employed by Lewis Berger from at least 1802, and in the 1820s by Vanherman)[94] was used not merely to distinguish the product of the older process, but specifically the blue variety. Thus, reference is made in an early nineteenth-century patent to 'refiners blue verditer',[95] and Nicholson called for the use of 'refiners verditer' to mix a grey in distemper.[96] Its continued manufacture despite its higher price indicates that it enjoyed advantages, and was almost certainly of a better colour and possessed greater stability than the newly developed pigments.

In place of the slow 'refiner's' process, copper carbonate may be produced by precipitation from a solution of a copper salt such as copper sulphate by the addition of potassium carbonate, the main constituent of pearl or Russia ash (potash subjected to red heat in order to increase the percentage of carbonate).[97] Pigments made using the latter substances, however, would invariably have contained a proportion of copper hydroxide (from the potassium hydroxide in the potash) and seem to have suffered from two defects, a comparatively pale colour and a tendency to turn green. Such methods were known by the mid-eighteenth century, and a variety of treatments to deepen the colour and achieve better stability by alterations to a greater or lesser degree in the copper compounds produced were developed. Dossie, for example, suggested the preparation of a 'dark' variety of 'verditer', which he listed among the blue pigments, by the addition of starch to a solution of copper nitrate prior to precipitation by means of pearl ash;[98] but the product of direct precipitation is often green in colour (invariably so where the solutions are hot when mixed) and by the late eighteenth century methods had been evolved in France for further treatment of the precipitate in order to enhance its blueness. In 1792, Bertrand Pelletier published a paper entitled 'Examens chimiques des cendres bleues' in which he explained that the pigment, which he had been told was a product of silver refining, was supplied to France by the English, although an inferior variety was made at Paris by precipitation from copper sulphate solution with potash and treatment of the precipitate with lime and ammonium chloride to make it blue. He put forward an improvement on this, precipitating copper hydroxide directly from a solution of copper nitrate using lime, filtering off the green precipitate, and grinding it with quicklime to make it blue.[99] Further improvements were suggested by the French industrial chemist J.A.C. Chaptal during the opening decade of the nineteenth century, in particular the substitution of lime-water for the ground lime;[100] and, possibly as a result of the work of the two

French chemists, related formulae appear in the early nineteenth-century documents of Lewis Berger's company. From at least 1817, a pigment called 'azure blue' was manufactured by precipitating copper carbonate from a solution of copper sulphate, this time in the presence of a small proportion of cream of tartar (potassium hydrogen tartrate), followed by a final treatment with lime-water;[101] and in another series of formulae for 'Blue Verditer', which commence the previous year, copper hydroxide was precipitated from copper sulphate by the addition of lime. Common salt (sodium chloride) was also present, and some later formulae contained tartaric acid to produce a deeper tint.[102]

Similar methods were published by Tingry, Colin Mackenzie, Leuchs, and Ure, the latter in particular citing a method used in France for the production of *cendres bleues en pâte* in which calcium chloride was used instead of common salt and the product further treated with lime paste, pearl ash, ammonium chloride, and copper sulphate. When dried the pigment was known as *cendres bleues en pierre*.[103] Many such products seem likely to have been a complex of copper compounds, and appear analogous to certain greens discussed in connection with green verditer and copper chloride Brunswick green in Chapter 3. By the end of the nineteenth century, they were grouped under the umbrella of *Bremen blue*, and were described by Hurst as having a pale greenish blue colour; but although at one time made on a large scale, he indicated that by the time he was writing they had been replaced by artificial ultramarine and cobalt blue.[104]

These developments in the production of copper pigments had an almost immediate effect on prices at the beginning of the nineteenth century. In the letter-books of Lewis Berger, quotations of 2*s.* to 2*s.* 6*d.* per lb. are given between 1778 and 1788 for the supply of 'common' and 'fine' blue verditer, with a price of 4*s.* 6*d.* for 'finest blue verditer' in 1788 (against those for green verditer at 1*s.* 3*d.* or 2*s.*). These are more or less comparable with the prices for 'refiners verditer' given in his annual stock-lists during the first decade of the nineteenth century: on 1 January 1802, for example, Berger had a stock of $\frac{3}{4}$ cwt. 'Finest' refiners verditer valued at 4*s.* per lb., together with just over 1 cwt. 'Refiners Verditer (Secc^{d})' at 2*s.* 9*d.*, while in 1806 and 1810 his stock of refiners verditer stood respectively at nearly 4$\frac{1}{4}$ cwt. at 3*s.* 3*d.* per lb., and nearly 4$\frac{3}{4}$ cwt. at 3*s.*[105] Against these, the prices given for simple 'Blue Verditer' in his stock lists at the same period are extremely low, and since these are broadly comparable with those given in connection with his production formulae for precipitated blues,[106] it is probably safe to assume they represent pigment made by precipitation. By way of example, on 1 January 1802 Berger's stock of 'Blue verditer' was nearly 20$\frac{1}{2}$ cwt. valued at 9*d.* per lb.: in 1806 this had risen to just over 61$\frac{1}{4}$ cwt. at 8*d.*; while in 1810 he had a total of just over 21$\frac{1}{2}$ cwt. valued at 8$\frac{1}{2}$*d.* per lb.[107]

Although best used in distemper, blue verditer has been identified as the pigment employed for the 'fair blew in Oylle' applied to the entablature, doorcases, and other elements in the Dining Chamber (now the Round Gallery) at Ham House, Surrey, in 1638;[108] and it was used on its own in a linseed oil medium for picking out the enrichments above a white ground in the Saloon at the Casino, Marino, Dublin, in the late 1760s.[109] In both cases the particle size was large, and the colour was found to be in an excellent state of preservation. It will be recalled that John Smith, writing during the second half of the seventeenth century, had included the pigment among those used in oil, noting that, while it had disadvantages in several respects, it was useful for mixing greens;[110] and it is not uncommonly observed either on its own or in combination with yellow in late eighteenth-century paint layers.[111] In the 1820s, Vanherman (who indicated it was best ground with the oil as and where required since it was apt to 'fatten' on keeping once ground) included a small quantity of refiners verditer in one of his greens for commercial production and use in oil;[112] a similar use in connection with Scheele's green is illustrated in a patent of slightly earlier date;[113] and Butcher suggested its use as an alternative to Prussian blue in mixing French grey.[114] Such evidence runs counter to Watin's assertion that blue verditer, though much used in distemper, was of no use in oil,[115] a view in which he was followed by Tingry, who stated categorically that it was not used in oil since it went dark (an observation arising from the similarity of its refractive index to that of oil, which, as already mentioned, had been noted by John Smith over a century before).[116] Probably, however, Watin and Tingry represent a Continental view, especially bearing in mind the English origin of high-quality pigment; and in Britain it was clearly used in this way, even after the introduction of Prussian blue. Even so, it does not seems to have been regarded as a totally satisfactory pigment in oil, Whittock, for example noting that to become opaque it had to be mixed with white lead;[117] and the author of the *Painter's . . . Pocket Manual* (who commented, like Watin, that the pigment was only proper for distemper) indicated that it could not be used in oil except with a considerable admixture of white.[118] Thus, while Laxton included 'blue verditter' among his list of oil-paint colours in *The Improved Builder's Price Book*,[119] it is possible he was using the pigment name to describe a paint colour made from other ingredients, probably to match that of the dry pigment, a practice apparent from a reference by Phillips in his list of painters' colours to blue verditer 'by mixture'.[120]

As a distemper pigment, on the other hand, there is no doubt that blue verditers were extensively employed, and in an aqueous medium were capable of developing the intense colour displayed by many wallpapers of the period, unaffected by the yellowing effect of oil. The author of the *Practical Treatise*, indeed, observed that refiners verditer, which he described as blue, was consumed principally by the 'paper stainers'.[121] Pincot, for example, retailed a 'blue verditter' water colour, which he recommended for ceilings;[122] while Nicholson suggested the preparation of 'fine' greys in distemper by means of white with refiners verditer.[123] Moreover, although green verditer seems a natural choice where a finish of that colour was required, Watin, in describing mixtures for green distemper to be varnished, suggested the use of *cendres bleues* with *céruse* and *stil de grain* (an organic yellow pigment discussed in Chapter 5), indicating that Prussian blue produced a duller, less intense colour. He also used *cendres bleues* in mixing *vert d'eau* in distemper.[124]

PRUSSIAN BLUE

Prussian blue, known chemically as potassium ferric ferrocyanide, was discovered during the first decade of the eighteenth century by Ghislain Diesbach, a Berlin colour maker, and was first advertised in 1710 for use as an artists' pigment at a price said to have been scarcely one-tenth that of ultramarine.[125] In 1724 an account of its manufacture was published by Dr Woodward in the *Philosophical Transactions*;[126] and by the mid-1730s the pigment was evidently sufficiently cheap to be in commercial use for house-painting since 'Fine Sky Blue mixed with Prussian Blue' was advertised in Alexander Emerton's range of ready-ground paint colours at 8*d.* or 12*d.* per lb. (against 'Best White Lead' at 4*d.*). His price list was published in the first edition of William Salmon's *Palladio Londinensis* (1734), and this also contained a table of rates for painters' work, including '*Prussian* blue' at 10*d.* per square yard.[127] Together (since the pigment is not mentioned in the 1723, nor indeed the 1738 or 1753 editions of John Smith's *Art of Painting*), these seem to provide the first printed references to the use of Prussian blue for ordinary house-painting; although in 1722 reference was made to its possible employment by William Kent in colouring the grounds of the *trompe l'oeil* coffers on the ceiling of the Cupola Room at Kensington Palace, London.[128]

Woodward's account of the method used for the manufacture of Prussian blue, originally written in Latin, was published in English by Dossie.[129] In essence, a solution of potassium ferrocyanide was prepared by the calcination of bullock's blood with potash and extracting the soluble part of the product with boiling water. A solution of alum and ferrous sulphate was then added, and the greenish precipitate treated with hydrochloric acid to turn it blue. At the end of the nineteenth century Hurst indicated that in his day the use of alum was widespread, and made the pigment easier to grind, although its colour would be lighter; and observed also that the precipitate will turn blue without the addition of hydrochloric acid if simply exposed to the air, although this produced a pigment of inferior colour.[130] With regard to the locations at which it was manufactured, Campbell mentioned that the pigment was prepared chiefly in Southwark, and Watin that it was made in Berlin and London.[131] Its quality was variable, Dossie commenting that there were many different degrees of brightness and strength, while the colour could vary from a true blue to a purplish or light tint. He added also that in use the colour was inclined to yellow, 'as may be seen in all blue wainscots, or other work done by house-painters; which in a short space of time turn to an olive or greenish grey colour'.[132] Cheap qualities of Prussian blue for use in distemper were kept in a damp or wet state and sold in this form, being known accordingly as *wet blue* or *damp blue*. John Phillips, for example, referred to 'Damp blue in water', while Whittock remarked of Prussian blue that for use in distemper it was usually kept ready ground by colourmen under the name of damp blue.[133] Vanherman also mentioned the use of wet *Antwerp blue* in mixing green,[134] this being a variety of Prussian blue which was being stocked by Lewis Berger in the early nineteenth century and manufactured by his sons in the 1820s.

A considerable amount of information of Prussian blue is contained in the surviving documents of Berger's company which is thought to have commenced its manufacture in London in 1766. From the large number of formulae relating to the pigment, the earliest to survive being dated 1816, the basic method of manufacture seems to have changed little from that of Diesbach a century before, although the ferrocyanide was produced from animal hooves rather than blood, and hydrochloric acid does not seem to have been used at the end of the process. The improvements reputed to have been made by Berger were probably, therefore, either by way of an increase in the quality of the raw materials, or in the systematisation of manufacture to produce consistent results. Certainly on the evidence of the surviving records considerable trouble and effort continued to be put into the latter after his death in 1814, and the formulae books, and experimental notebooks, are an impressive record of this.[135] Of particular interest is the sample book, which contains smears of pigment dated between 1789 and 1802. A page from this is illustrated (fig. 3, p. 99) and shows clearly the differences of colour between the grades and the prices applicable to each, which in this instance range between 1*s.* 4*d.* per lb. and 32*s.* per cwt. for the cheaper grades. Earlier, the letter book shows that in 1779 Berger had been offering 'Dry Prusian Blue' at rates from 2*s.* to 12*s.* per pound, and the same rates appear in other letters of the period.[136] In 1802, 1806, and 1810 he valued his stocks, which were never less than a total of 13 cwt. at prices from 1*s.* 8*d.* to 7*s.* 6*d.* per pound; and in 1802 and 1810 had smaller stocks ($\frac{1}{2}$ lb. and 37$\frac{1}{2}$ lb. respectively) of Antwerp blue at 13*s.* or 8*s.* per lb. At the same time, he also had small stocks (18 to 60 lb.) of Prussian blue in ground form valued at rates between 3*s.* and 4*s.* per pound.[137] (The reason these were small was probably that the pigment did not keep well in this form, and on this account it had been included by Vanherman among those pigments 'best ground in oil, when wanted, as they are apt to become fat or liverry'.)[138] Turning to the very cheap variety, wet blue, in 1779–88 Berger had been offering this for sale at prices between 31*s.* 6*d.* and 80*s.* per cwt., but in 1802, 1806, and 1810 valued his stocks (which fluctuated widely from 1$\frac{1}{4}$ to 22$\frac{1}{2}$ cwt.) from 36*s.* to 45*s.* per cwt.[139]

Apart from the price of 56*s.* per cwt. charged for Prussian blue by Lamb & Jones, Oil and Colourmen of Little Pultney Street, London, in 1776, and the same figure for damp blue given by Vanherman, these are generally considerably lower than other prices encountered.[140] At Tredegar House, Newport, Monmouthshire (now Gwent), in 1793, for example, 1*s.* 4*d.* was paid for the supply of '1 ounce prussion blue to ye plaisterer';[141] a figure of 9*d.* per oz. is mentioned in documents recently published relating to the transactions of a York builder in 1800;[142] and Soane was charged at a rate equivalent to 1*s.* per oz. for a total of 1 lb. 10 oz. of the pigment in 1803 (the same rate in this instance applying to both dry and ground varieties).[143] As usual, the prices given by Phillips are also well above those at which Berger valued his stock. He quoted 17*s.* per lb. for Antwerp blue in 1812 and 1821, and gave rates of 130*s.* 8*d.* and 112*s.* per cwt. for 'Damp blue in water' in these years respectively.[144]

While the precise date of its introduction for house-painting between 1710 and 1734 is uncertain, there is no doubt that once its use become economical Prussian blue was used extensively for the decoration of buildings in both oil and distemper, although its use with lime was precluded since the pigment is adversely affected by alkalis. It could also (as in the Drawing Room at Bolling Hall, Bradford, in the 1770s)[145] discolour in distemper applied to lime plaster. Its everyday employment continued throughout the eighteenth and early nineteenth centuries, and in 1828 Vanherman described the pigment as 'the most general and useful blue we have, either for inside or out-door painting. Its combination with some of the reds, and most of the yellows, produces purples and greens, of numberless tints and gradations'.[146] In addition, Whittock mentioned its transparent nature, and explained that for this reason it was frequently used as a glazing pigment without white lead in such operations as marbling, for which this is a considerable advantage.[147]

NATURAL ULTRAMARINE

The blue pigment known as ultramarine was manufactured from the semi-precious mineralised limestone *lapis lazuli* which occurs in several parts of the world, notably Afghanistan and Siberia, the Kokcha valley in Badakshan, Afghanistan, being the source most commonly exploited until modern times. The stone contains hauyne, lazurite, and sodalite, the two latter forming the strongest blue components, which were separated from the unwanted portions of the crushed material by mixing it with a paste of wax, resin, and oil, and kneading the resulting mass in hot water. This allowed the desired pigment particles to escape, while the useless matter was retained by the waxy dough. The best pigment was the first to emerge, the poorest and greyest obtained in the final stages being known as *ultramarine ashes*.[148] Natural ultramarine has always been extremely costly, and Stalker & Parker, for example, gave prices ranging from twenty shillings to seven guineas per ounce, as against 4*d*. or 6*d*. for 'Blew Bise' (azurite).[149] These relate well to those recorded by Mary Beale's husband, who noted £2 10*s*. per ounce in 1672 and £4 10*s*. in 1674;[150] and John Smith remarked that it was 'so vastly dear, that 'tis not to be used except in pieces of great price',[151] so that the absence of the pigment from the group suggested by D'Aviler for painting blue ornament and grotesque on a white ground is not surprising.[152] Nevertheless, reporting on William Kent's work at Kensington Palace in May 1722, two members of the committee appointed to inspect the ceiling of the Cupola Room, Jan Van der Vaart and Jacob Rambour, were unable to judge whether he had used true ultramarine, while Alexander Nisbett though his pigment 'Nothing but Prussian Blew, in which perhaps there may be some Ultramarine mixt'.[153] Although there may have been a considerable element of political sour grapes in these remarks, if it is assumed that they apply to the ground within the coffers of the ceiling it could be concluded that in royal works, at least, natural ultramarine may have been expected to be used on strictly limited architectural elements despite its expense. Watin, however, stated quite definitely that the pigment was not used in house-painting, and Tingry too observed that it was particularly reserved for pictures on account of its price.[154] Hence, although ultramarine is included in the pigment lists of Martin and Nicholson, both writers copied uncritically from Dossie, whose list was of more general application to the arts rather than confined to the limited subject of house-painting;[155] while Whittock observed that its high price precluded its use in any quantity, although for finer work it was sometimes essential.[156] Even in 1812 and 1821 Phillips quoted £3 15*s*. 6*d*. per lb. for 'Ultramarine blue';[157] and it seems clear that the pigment can never have been used for the ordinary purposes of room decoration, although it is possible that it may have been used very occasionally for particular motifs, as for example in heraldic work or touches of colour in arabesque.

FRENCH ULTRAMARINE

During the first quarter of the nineteenth century, prizes were offered by the Society of Arts and the *Société d'Encouragement pour l'Industrie Nationale* for the successful manufacture of an artificial variety of ultramarine. That of the latter body was awarded in 1828 to a French chemist, Jean Baptiste Guimet, who established a factory at Fleurieu-sur-Saône in 1831.[158] Although it is apparent that it came into use very quickly for fine-art purposes on the Continent and was of outstanding importance for house-painting from the middle of the nineteenth century, artificial ultramarine seems insufficiently established as a pigment by the terminal date of the present study to have been of very much significance. Examples of its use in high-class decorative work in the 1840s, are cited in Chapter 21.

COBALT BLUE

Cobalt blue seems to have been discovered in 1802. It was, apparently, an article of commerce in France within five years, and was listed for fine-art purposes in England by 1816.[159] Mention of the pigment in connection with house painting, however, seems elusive, apart from the description of its manufacture by roasting cobalt phosphate with alumina included in the 1830 edition of Tingry's book;[160] while in 1831 Lewis Berger's firm appears to have made experimental batches of the pigment, but no production formula or costing appears.[161] Modern cobalt blue is described by Heaton as 'a combination or solid solution of cobalt oxide and aluminium oxide', but it seems likely the earlier pigments produced by Thenard in France and Leithner in Germany may have differed from their present day equivalent, the former containing cobalt phosphate and the latter cobalt arsenate.[162] The modern pigment, having a refractive index similar to linseed oil, is transparent when ground in that medium. In the absence of any information on early nineteenth-century prices, it is impossible to suggest the usefulness of the pigment in house-painting at that date, but its omission from Vanherman's book is probably more significant than its mention in the 1830 edition of Tingry, whose later editor made no suggestions for its employment.

CHAPTER 3

GREEN PIGMENTS

Although ten green pigments are reviewed in this chapter, only two, verdigris in oil and green verditer in distemper, were of primary importance for house-painting during the majority of the period under consideration. Nevertheless, although verditer was excellent in distemper, it was of low staining power in oil, and verdigris was often subject to discolouration in that medium. By the end of the seventeenth century, and probably earlier, verditer appears to have superseded its forerunner, crushed natural malachite; while neither terre verte nor sap green seem to have been important in the present connection. From the second half of the eighteenth century, there appears to have been much experiment dedicated to production of a green pigment to supersede verdigris in oil, the earliest moderately successful development probably being copper chloride Brunswick green. From about 1780, Scheele's green was available, although the full extent of the use made of it is difficult to judge; but emerald green was clearly of importance following its introduction in the second decade of the nineteenth century. Only towards the end of the period was chrome yellow Brunswick green developed, a pigment which answered for the first time most of the technical requirements for a bright stable green in oil.

Naturally, in an age of experiment and development, with processes often carefully shrouded from public knowledge for fear of competition, at least some contemporary literature bearing on the nature of new pigments is obscure. In addition, there seem to have been a number of processes in use which would have resulted in the production of complexes or mixtures of different compounds; and the names given to new products often became confused. In particular, terms such as 'English verdigris', 'Bremen green', 'mineral green', and 'patent green' were applied to more than one pigment, and, as illustrated below, it cannot always be certain to which variety they relate.

VERDIGRIS

Verdigris, a basic copper carbonate, was made during the seventeenth century at Montpellier and elsewhere in France. Most English supplies seem to have come from that source, John Smith mentioning Montpellier verdigris as being the best; and a detailed description of the manufacturing process, which was organised on cottage-industry lines, was published by John Ray, a fellow of the Royal Society, in 1673.[1] In essence, copper plates were corroded by the action of acetic acid vapour above wine vinegar, the corrosion product, or verdigris, being scraped off, formed into cakes, and sold for use. The ordinary pigment prepared in this way could be refined by recrystallisation after solution in acetic acid which had been purified and concentrated by distillation. It was then known as *distilled verdigris.* Tingry observed that this process was carried out by the Dutch using pigment imported from France, describing the production of pyramids of crystals about a foot high with a two-inch-square base, each weighing between three and four pounds. The product was, he believed, better for grinding in oil when aged, or powdered and either heated or exposed to the sun to dehydrate it.[2]

Distilled verdigris was an expensive pigment. John Smith remarked that while excellent for fine work it was too dear for use in 'vulgar painting', and Tingry observed that on account of its high price, which prevented its general use, it was reserved for painting 'of the noblest kind' and for delicate purposes in varnish.[3] Stalker & Parker listed it at 1*s.* per ounce, against the 3*s.* per pound for *'Vert-de-Greece'* suggested by Evelyn in 1670, presumably for the ordinary variety.[4] By the late eighteenth century, Lewis Berger was offering distilled verdigris to merchants at 5*s.* or 5*s.* 6*d.* per pound, although 'French verdigrease' was about half this price, rates quoted lying between 2*s.* 4*d.* and 3*s.* per pound. In the early nineteenth century, prices increased considerably, his stock of distilled verdigris being valued at 8*s.* 6*d.* per pound in 1802; at 7*s.* in 1806; and at 10*s.* 6*d.* in 1810. 'Dry Verdigrease', on the other hand, was valued at 2*s.* 6*d.* in 1802 and 1806; and 4*s.* 8*d.* in 1810. In all three years, the quantities of distilled verdigris held were always significantly smaller than those of ordinary pigment, being $4\frac{3}{4}$ lb. against $\frac{3}{4}$ cwt. in 1802; nearly 2 cwt. against $10\frac{1}{2}$ cwt. in 1806; and just over $\frac{1}{2}$ cwt. against $5\frac{1}{2}$ cwt. in 1810. In addition, Berger had small stocks of 'Ground Verdigrease' totalling just over $\frac{3}{4}$ cwt. in 1802, but only 13 lb. in 1806, and just over $\frac{1}{4}$ cwt. in 1810, valued at 2*s.* 6*d.*, 3*s.*, and 5*s.* per pound respectively, suggesting that on occasion the pigment could also be purchased ready-ground into oil.[5]

Besides France, Dossie mentioned Italy as a supplier of verdigris, and observed too that a manufactory had recently been started in England.[6] The term *English verdigris* should, however, be treated with caution, since other pigments discussed below were known under the name during the early nineteenth century.[7] Nevertheless two of the recipes for 'English verdigris' given by Tingry's later editor do relate to copper acetate pigments, although the first contained also alum and zinc sulphate. These formulae, together with that of Vanherman for 'another Bremen green' depended on a reaction between copper sulphate and lead acetate to produce copper acetate in pure form. In general, therefore, such pigments would have been equivalent to distilled verdigris made by recrystallisation, and Vanherman described that produced by his formula as 'one of the best, for intensity and durability of colour, and for solidity of body'.[8] It should be noted, however, that the term *Bremen green* was also applied to certain copper chloride pigments (q.v.) discussed below.

John Smith said of verdigris that it was used on most occasions where a green was required, and described how the addition of a little organic yellow corrected a tendency to blue, making a delicate grass green. Watin too used an organic yellow (with distilled verdigris) in three mixtures, but other formulae given by these authors illustrate employment of the pigment without such addition.[9] For house-painting purposes verdigris appears to have been of service in two basic ways, either in combination with white lead in oil as an opaque paint, or on its own in oil as a glaze. Suggestions for greens in which it was mixed with white lead were made by Smith, Bullet, Watin, and Reynolds, proportions varying from 1 part of ground verdigris in 10 of ground white lead, to equal parts of each.[10] Watin's proposal for the use of 1 part of verdigris with 2 or 3 of white lead in mixing a green for garden trellises was endorsed by Tingry, who also noted that the latter proportion would reproduce in oil the colour of green verditer in distemper, a point duly repeated in the *Painter's . . . Pocket Manual.*[11] This straightforward way of using verdigris was detailed by Butcher in his revised edition of John Smith. He directed that equal quantities of white lead and the best French verdigris were to be mixed, and applied over a ground colour of 'a good pleasant blue' made from Prussian blue and white, adding: 'When the verdegris is laid over the blue ground, it will not at first appear green, but will change, in a few days, to a beautiful colour.'[12] The change of colour on exposure had earlier been noted by Tingry, who advocated the use of a white ground in place of the yellow he noted was customary among painters (a practice also mentioned by Evelyn in 1706, probably quoting a French source).[13]

In contrast to its employment in opaque finishes, use of verdigris as a glaze was suggested by John Smith and Bullet, the first noting that this would produce *willow green*, and the second using it with an equal part of *vert de montagne* (see discussion of malachite below) in *vert de treillages.*[14] A similar suggestion was made by D'Aviler, who noted verdigris was a cheap substitute for the latter pigment, but had a greater tendency to blacken.[15] Instability of verdigris, caused by its reaction with atmospheric carbon dioxide and sulphur dioxide, was clearly a problem, Dossie observing that the colour 'soon flies when used in oil', and both Watin and Tingry's later editor remarking on its yellowing.[16] For this reason, it was often used in a varnish medium, which conferred superior stability, a technique particularly found in coach-painting. Thus, Watin illustrated employment of distilled verdigris (here mixed with white lead) in varnish in two formulae for this application; and it is of interest that Pincot was proud to record with some emphasis he had lately seen a coach-body still in a satisfactory state which he had painted a glazed verdigris green eighteen years previously.[17] It appears, however, that the method was also used for house-painting in seventeenth-century England, since in 1670 John Evelyn recommended that verdigris ground in linseed oil should be diluted with '*Joyners Vernish*, . . . till it run somewhat thin' and be applied over a white ground, although it is not clear whether he had an interior or exerior use in mind.[18] It is probably significant, though, that a wainscot of seventeenth-century style painted in a green which could have been achieved in this way is shown by William Hogarth in his picture *The Election Entertainment.*[19]

The best way of using verdigris in varnish is, however, not simply to grind the pigment into oil and add it to the latter, but to dissolve it in the medium using heat, to produce a copper resinate. Examples probably representing this practice have been found on panelling dating from the 1730s to 1760s in New England;[20] but comparable eighteenth-century British instances have so far proved elusive, although as discussed in Chapter 19 such glazes were used above metal leaf, and it seems likely that copper resinates were being mixed with white lead to produce high-quality opaque greens. Evidence for this comes from the Strand colourman Alexander Emerton, whose instruction sheet for use of his products contained a special set of 'DIRECTIONS for using the GREEN PAINT':

> To every Pound of Green Paint, put one Quart of Green Oyl, and be sure mix no other Oyl with it, nor use this Oyl with any other Colour. Mix not above half a Pound with Oyl at one Time, for if any is left (after it is mix'd with Oyl) till the next Day it will be spoil'd.[21]

The injunctions that the oil should not be mixed with any other colour, and that it should be combined with the paint as required, strongly suggest the presence of dissolved verdigris or other copper pigment (although it is just possible that the 'Green Oyl' could have been freshly expressed hempseed oil, since this is a bright yellow-green in colour);[22] and it is of significance that Salmon gave the covering power of Emerton's 'Fine deep Green' as 20 square yards per lb. against only 8 for his other colours.[23] Moreover, copper resinates mixed with white lead certainly seem to have been in use to produce a green 'japan' finish on chairs and other furnishings during the second half of the eighteenth century, and were probably of especial importance for this purpose.[24]

That verdigris was still in use for house-painting in the early nineteenth century seems evident, since Phillips mentioned paintwork finished with 'verdigrease green', and an item for 'Four times in oil flated green with verdigrease green' appears in early nineteenth-century editions of the *Builders Price-Book.*[25] Its use by Reynolds has already been mentioned, and Whittock too noted it was the most common green pigment used in ordinary work, although his description may have been inspired by Butcher's recent re-publication of John Smith's seventeenth-century text.[26] In the 1820s, it is true, Leuchs noted its use had diminished; but Hurst seems to imply its continuing employment into the 1890s, although, he noted, use of distilled verdigris had ceased.[27] Regarding its employment in distemper, only Tingry's later editor suggested this; but his comment seems unreliable since the pigment reacts chemically with both chalk and lime to form calcium acetate, and Watin remarked quite explicitly that it was not used in this way.[28]

TERRE VERTE

As its name implies, terre verte is a pigment of natural origin. It consists chiefly of the mineral *glauconite*, and occurs in several parts of the world. In modern times, high-grade pigment has been obtained from Cyprus, but the noted historic source was Verona. Green earth 'ex Agro Veronesi' was listed by Michele Mercato in his catalogue of the Vatican mineral collection, which he formed in 1574; and in 1820, Giovanni de Brignoli de Brunnhoff described the mines on Monte Baldo, from which it was obtained.[29] In the mid-eighteenth century, Hill said that the pigment was generally imported from Italy, although, he observed, it was 'to be met with entirely as good here at home'.[30] Hurst particularly mentioned the Mendip Hills, Somerset, as a source of terre verte, but noted also its occurrence in France, Italy, and Cyprus; while Church referred particularly to that found at Bentonico near Verona.[31] The green colouration is due to the presence of silicate of iron, and since the refractive index of the pigment is similar to that of oil, it lacks body and becomes translucent in that medium.

Small quantities of 'Teravert' totalling 14lb. are included in an account dating from 1705 preserved at Boughton House, in which they are billed at 7*s.* and 8*s.* per lb.[32] It cannot be certain, however, that these were for house-painting; and although the pigment was listed by Martin and Nicholson, its inclusion in their colour-lists must as usual be treated with reserve since they clearly originate from Dossie, whose interests were not confined to such coarse applications.[33] The only more positive evidence suggesting use of terre verte as a house-painting pigment comes from the two Continental authors Watin and Tingry, although neither suggested its employment in any of the colour mixtures they proposed. Tingry described it as good in both oil and distemper, while Watin mentioned two varieties, *terre verte commune* and *terre verte de Vérone*.[34] In this connection it is interesting that Rondelet listed *terre verte commune* at 1fr. 60 per lb. and *belle qualité* at 3fr.[35] Curiously, Watin stated that the pigment was never used in distemper, a pronouncement apparently contradicted by the author of the *Painter's . . . Pocket Manual*, who indicated that 'Italian green' was used only in this medium,[36] although his description may be traced to Tingry, and he was probably confused about the nature of the green earths he was discussing. Use of terre verte in English house-painting is, therefore, an open question; but lack of stocks in 1802 and 1806, and the limited quantity of a mere 47lb. held by Lewis Berger on 1 January 1810, albeit at the fairly modest valuation of £5 per cwt. (equivalent to about 10½*d.* per lb.),[37] besides omission of the pigment from any of the more authoritative English books such as those of John Smith and Vanherman, suggest that if employed at all this was not general practice.

SAP GREEN

At least from the early seventeenth century, sap green was prepared by evaporating the juice expressed from ripe buckthorn berries, or those from other species of the genus *Rhamnus*. Typical descriptions of the process were given by Dossie (who, in fact, specified the use of unripe berries) and Watin, the former stating that the concentrated mass thus obtained was used only in an aqueous medium.[38] However, although Watin described 'verd de vessie' as used in water, he observed that it was normally employed in fan-painting, adding, 'il ne vaut rien à l'huile, & ne sert ni aux bâtimens ni aux équipages'.[39] Tingry repeated unequivocally that it was used only by fan-painters and for colouring maps.[40] Nor did Watin employ it in any of his suggested mixtures for green distempers;[41] and the inclusion of sap green for house-painting in their lists by Martin and Nicholson cannot be regarded as significant in view of their obvious derivation from Dossie, whose book was concerned with the arts in general.[42] Moreover, although Lewis Berger had significant stocks of sap green, totalling nearly 2¼cwt. on 1 January 1802, 2¾cwt. in 1806, and nearly 3 cwt. in 1810, it was not a cheap pigment, being valued at 4*s.* 6*d.* per lb. in the first two instances, and 4*s.* 7*d.* in the latter (with a small quantity of a cheaper variety at 2*s.* 6*d.* in 1806).[43] Rondelet listed it at 5fr. 50 per lb.[44] It seems certain, therefore, than the pigment was not employed for house-painting; and John Phillips, indeed, specifically listed it as 'Fine sap green for water-colours', quoting prices of 2*s.* 5*d.* and 10*s.* 6*d.* per pound.[45]

MALACHITE

During the seventeenth and eighteenth centuries a pigment was made by crushing malachite, a naturally occurring form of basic copper carbonate. John Smith, referring to it in the terminology of his day as *green bice*, described it in 1687 as sandy and not much used.[46] It was not mentioned in the first edition of his book, and no further English references to its use for house-painting have been encountered, although *vert de montagne*, as the pigment was known in France, was listed by D'Aviler, Bullet, Watin, and Rondelet (who priced it at 3fr. 50 per pound against 6fr. for artificial copper carbonate *cendres vertes*); while Tingry suggested the use of *mountain green* for 'sea green' paint.[47] The main source of this material, which may also have contained chrysocolla (copper silicate), appears to have been the Carpathian mountains in eastern Czechoslovakia, Leuchs listing Neusohl (now Banská Bystrika), Schmoelniz (now Smolnik), and Herrengrund (or Urvölgy, which is about 4 miles NNW of Neusohl). The first of these was mentioned as a source of chrysocolla by the mid-sixteenth-century writer Agricola, and both Watin and Tingry refer to Hungary (then including modern Czechoslovakia) as the source of mountain green.[48] In addition, the latter referred to Saxony, while Leuchs described its continuing manufacture at Schwaz in the Austrian Tyrol by crushing and milling. Interestingly, he records that 1250 quintals (approximately 60 tons) were produced in 1819, average production between 1809 and 1811 having been 464 quintals (roughly 20 tons).[49] These quantities do not appear, however, to imply use on a very large scale, and it seems likely that since (as already mentioned in connection with blue varieties of copper carbonate pigments) the artificial forms were an English speciality, these references may represent anachronistic practice. In Britain at least, the latter would have provided a cheaper alternative to natural pigment from an early date, and malachite is notably absent from Dossie's book. It was also omitted completely from the list of pigments in Butcher's revised edition of John Smith's work. For this reason it seems unlikely that it ever enjoyed much use for house-painting in Britain, even during the first half of the seventeenth century.

GREEN VERDITER

As already noted, the silver-refiners' process described in connection with the manufacture of blue verditer more often produced, at least during the seventeenth century, a pigment of greenish colour. In parallel with the blue form, green verditer was described by John Smith as sharing the undesirable qualities of its natural counterpart (malachite), being sandy, and lacking body in oil. On this account it was not, he indicated, greatly used.[50] Hence, although 'Best green verditer' appears among other green oil-paint colours in the *Builder's Price-Book* published by I. & J. Taylor, it seems likely that a similar hue was generally produced in this medium by the employment of verdigris with white lead in the way suggested by Tingry.[51] This recommendation was repeated by the author of the *Painter's . . . Pocket Manual*, who (again taking his cue from the latter, but without ruling out its use in oil) unequivocally indicated that green verditer was better adapted as a pigment to employment in distemper.[52] In this medium, it undoubtedly found extensive use, and 'green verditter', for example, appears in the range of proprietary 'water colours' for use in interiors retailed by Pincot during the early years of the nineteenth century.[53]

By this date, it is clear that, in common with blue verditer, the pigment was also being manufactured on an industrial scale by precipitation from a solution of copper sulphate by the addition of potassium carbonate. In 1812 Jacob Zink took out a patent for the manufacture of *British verdigris* by this means, and Tingry's later editor provided a similar formula for the manufacture of *English verdigris* (names which must be approached with caution since they were not invariably applied to copper carbonate pigments).[54] Papers preserved in the archive of Lewis Berger's firm show that a similar method was used to prepare a pigment called *French green*; and although the first formula for production of the latter does not appear until 1816,[55] the name is present in the firm's stock-list for 1 January 1802.[56] Also, a note in the 'Lake & Carmine Book' dated 1808 details the preparation of 'Second French Green' (a name later applied by the company to a variety of Scheele's green, q.v.), a derivative pigment containing, in addition to French green, Dutch lead and princess blue.[57] In 1831 French green was made according to the following directions:

> Dissolve 3 Tubs (abt 0 cwt. 2 [qrs.] 17 [lb.] each) Roman Vitriol in Copper – which will make 6 strikings. Dissolve abt 4½ Pails (abt 0 [qrs]. 26 lb ea[ch]) Pearl Ash in Copper
>
> Let down Vitriol & strike with Ash for 3 successive times then turn precipitate over into large Tub & fill up with water
>
> 36 Strikings make 1 days work
>
> The precipitate from 36 Strikings to be wash'd 4 times & fill out thro' a 68 Sieve laid on Chalks & taken off in a damp state.[58]

Experiment suggests that to make such green pigments the solutions were mixed hot.

In 1831, the production cost of French green made according to this formula was 9½*d.* per lb., suggesting it was sold at about 1*s.* 6*d.* or 1*s.* 9*d.*, prices comparable with those at which Lewis Berger had valued his stocks during the first decade of the nineteenth century. In 1802 and 1806, these amounted to approximately 13 cwt., but by 1810 stood at nearly 22 cwt.[59] Bearing in mind the inflation caused by the wars with France, it seems that the artificial pigment prepared by precipitation was cheaper than the green verditer (prepared, presumably, by the older method) for which Berger was quoting prices of 1*s.* 3*d.* per lb. in 1778 and 1779, and 2*s.* in 1788.[60] Certainly, the absence of 'green verditer' from his early nineteenth-century stock-lists and formula books suggests that, since the green produced by precipitation was stable in colour, the earlier method of manufacture had been superseded except for the production of blue verditer (q.v.).

In 1819, Nicholson indicated that French green was used in the preparation of pea-green distemper,[61] and it is possible that it may have formed the basis of Pincot's proprietary 'French green' watercolour for rooms.[62] Interestingly, too, there is evidence to suggest that by the 1760s cruder versions of precipitated copper carbonate pigments were being prepared on a domestic basis for colourwashing rooms.[63]

Finally, it may be noted that precipitated green copper carbonate pigments seem also to have been used in oil, since Vanherman described the preparation of a 'fine green' by precipitation in the presence of borax and grinding the pigment into oil;[64] while its use with Scheele's green, refiners verditer, and white lead to make a bright pea-green oil paint for house-painting is suggested in a patent of 1812.[65]

COPPER CHLORIDE BRUNSWICK GREEN AND RELATED PIGMENTS

During the second half of the eighteenth century and early part of the nineteenth there was a continuing search for alternatives to green verditer and verdigris. In this, cost and the need of a better pigment for use in oil were probably major factors. By the 1820s, Leuchs noted that many copper compounds has been tried, citing among others its hydroxide, oxalate, malate, borate, phosphate, selenate, arsenate, arsenite, antimonate, antimonite, and silicate.[66] One of the earliest marketed commercially appears to have been *Brunswick green*, launched by the brothers Gravenhorst of that city in 1764, which Leuchs believed, consisted of copper carbonate and lime or chalk, and often (significantly) contained ammonia. It was thought best of as an oil pigment, and, although more opaque than verdigris, it needed the addition of at least an equal quantity of white lead. It retained its colour, which became stronger in the course of a few days' exposure, better in the open air than indoors.[67] Ure appears to have copied this reference, noting that Brunswick green was 'a mixture of carbonate of copper with chalk or lime, and sometimes a little magnesia or ammonia'.[68]

In 1771, Leuchs continued, the Gravenhorst brothers launched 'distilled Brunswick green'. This, he considered, was composed of copper tartrate; but, although intended to replace verdigris, was no longer greatly used.[69] It was probably to this that the author of the *Practical Treatise on Painting in Oil-Colours*, (1795) referred, conjecturing that 'Brunswick green' was a 'precipitate of copper which has been dissolved in tartar and water by coction [boiling], and which, by evaporation of the lixivium, is deposited in the form of a cupreous tartar', describing it as 'a very valuable and newly discovered colour'.[70]

That any of the compositions suggested by Leuchs are completely accurate seems doubtful, and it is significant that in the early nineteenth century Chaptal noted: 'What is called in the arts, *Brunswick Green*, is made by moistening copper filings with a solution of sal ammoniac [ammonium chloride] in close vessels'. The product of the reaction was washed and dried, and the pigment used in oil and for printing wallpaper.[71] A few years later, James Smith also described 'Brunswick green' as produced from copper and ammonium chloride, adding that it was commonly called *mineral green*,[72] a nomenclature noted too by Leuchs, who observed that although the name was usually given to Scheele's green (q.v.), it was also often applied to material prepared similarly to Brunswick green.[73] Hurst notes the reaction took about two months, and that the product was basic copper chloride, otherwise known as copper oxychloride.[74]

Tingry's later editor described a similar way of making a pigment he called *English verdigris*,[75] and among the records of the Berger firm is a note dated 1824 giving a comparable method for the manufacture of 'Strick's Verdigrease Green';[76] but this does not seem to have been a commercial product, and such names were also applied to other copper pigments, including both true verdigris and green verditer (qq.v.). Vanherman too gave comparable details for the preparation of a copper chloride pigment, calling the product (like his copper acetate pigment discussed in connection with verdigris above) *Bremen green*, and recommending the addition of lead acetate and Venice turpentine to increase its lustre, thus implying its use in oil.[77] It appears, however, that true Bremen green, which was probably related chemically, was a pigment of blue or bluish green colour; and the complex manufacturing process used in various German cities, including Bremen was described by Ure.[78]

Another name given to copper chloride green was *Frise green*, a term used by Chaptal and properly translated into English as 'Friesland' green.[79] Leuchs indeed notes that it was first made in that region and exported in great quantities to America, but by the time he was writing it was made in several places in Germany and Holland. The process involved dissolving 5 parts of potash and 2 of sal ammoniac in water, filtering the liquid, pouring it into a solution of copper sulphate, and washing and drying the precipitate. The product, which contained copper carbonate, was, he said, a pale lively green which could be used in oil.[80]

In the 1820s, Leuchs provided an extensive summary of names and processes for making a variety of copper chloride greens, some of which would have resulted in complexes containing varying proportions of carbonate, hydroxide, tartrate, or other ions. Other metallic compounds, including some of calcium and zinc might also be present,[81] and there was inevitably confusion, especially over terminology, in much nineteenth-century literature. During the 1820s and 30s, for instance, the Berger firm was making a pigment they called *patent green*, although the name had earlier been applied to other varieties.[82] The product seems likely to have been a complex of copper tartrate and chloride, and there may also have been a residue of the French green (a copper carbonate pigment discussed above in connection with green verditer) which was used as a base. The full process in 1821 was as follows:

> Take 1cwt French Green (in a state fit for Sale)
> " 6lb Lime, slaked one day before used, then levigate in Water using such a quantity that the whole may not exceed 3 Gall^s when levigated
> " $1\frac{1}{4}$lb Salt Tartar is next to be added to the 3 Gall^s levigated Lime & when properly mixed the same is to be put thro a wicker Sieve to the French green, when the ingredients are well mixed by beating, the solution of
> " 3lb 6 oz. Ammoniac in ab^t 3 or $3\frac{1}{2}$ Gall^s. Water is to be gradually added & when the whole is perfectly smooth, pass it thro a wicker Sieve & let it stand in that state for 3 whole days 2 *days* are not sufficient.[83]

The 1831 transcription of this formula has an added note that the cakes of pigment should be made very thin and had to be dried in a moderate heat. The pigment cost 1*s.* 1*d.* per pound to produce, suggesting it was sold by Berger at about 2*s.* or 2*s.* 6*d.* per pound.[84]

To assess the use made of copper chloride greens is not easy. Nevertheless, 'the insoluble muriatic combination of copper' certainly seems to have impressed Sir Humphry Davy, who observed that it would probably be found to be more permanent than the greens found in classical antiquity;[85] and it has recently been identified in an early nineteenth-century, intense, verditer-like green distemper on the plaster walls in the main stair hall at the Gardner-Pingree House of 1805 in Salem, Massachusetts.[86] From the evidence reviewed above, however, it seems that pigments of this type were probably intended primarily for use in oil, and enjoyed a certain popularity until superseded by emerald green and chrome yellow Brunswick green; but by the end of the nineteenth century Hurst observed that copper chloride greens were quite obsolete.[87]

SCHEELE'S GREEN

In 1778, C.W. Scheele, a Swedish chemist, published details of the green pigment which bears his name, and which by his own account he had discovered three years previously.[88] It is known chemically as copper arsenite, and is extremely toxic. Hurst described it as unsatisfactory, with low covering power, fading on exposure to light and air.[89] Descriptions of its manufacture by precipitation from hot solutions of potassium arsenite (formed by reaction between arsenious oxide and potassium carbonate) and copper sulphate were published by Leuchs, Tingry's later editor, and Ure (who gave *Mittis green* as an alternative name);[90] while in 1812 William Parker had taken out a patent for a similar method of making the pigment, which he referred to as *mineral green*.[91] Although generally applied to Scheele's green, this term does, however, have to be approached with a little caution, since it was also applied to other pigments.[92] Parker's patent is of interest as providing the only really firm published suggestion for the use of Scheele's green in house-painting, since in it he described a 'bright mineral pea green' oil paint made by admixture of one pound of his mineral green with a pound of copper carbonate made from copper sulphate and pearl ash, a pound and a half of refiners blue verditer, and three pounds of white lead, using lead acetate as a drier. He also described a method by which this mixture could be used for flatting walls.

Although Dr Harley has linked the *patent green* described by Butcher as 'so called from a patent being lately obtained for the making of it' with Parker's patent, there is nothing in the patent specification itself to justify the attribution.[93] Butcher's description of the pigment as 'a beautiful green, and of a good body: . . . used in most cases where verdigris would be too expensive, and . . . sold at most of the colour-shops' could equally be applied to other pigments, particularly, perhaps, Zink's 'British verdigris' (also patented in 1812) which has been discussed above in connection with green verditer (q.v.). This was a copper carbonate pigment and, as is known from other sources, was the basis of at least two hybrids known as patent green.[94] It is worth noting also that, later in his book,[95] Butcher referred to 'Fowler's patent green', a pigment or colour also mentioned by Phillips;[96] but no patent is listed in classes 50 or 54 of the *Patents for Inventions Abridgements of Specifications A.D. 1618–1866* (1871) under that name. References to 'patent green', including that in the list of prices fixed by the Painter-Stainers Company of London in 1803, and those made by Laxton and the authors of the *Painter's . . . Pocket Manual* and *Skyring's Builder's Prices* cannot, therefore, be accepted as unequivocally indicating the use of Scheele's green.[97]

In considering the use of the pigment in house-painting, it is accordingly necessary to look at less direct evidence. A formula dated 1811 amongst the records of Lewis Berger's company shows that he was then producing a variety of Scheele's green under the name *Olympian green*, but whether this was the same pigment as the Olympian green for which he was quoting prices of 1*s.* 3*d.* per lb. in 1778, and 2*s.* in 1779 and 1780 is, perhaps, open to doubt, since 1778 is the generally accepted year in which Scheele published details of his discovery. It is nevertheless clear that from 1811 Berger was invariably applying the name to pigments of copper arsenite type,[98] and it seems likely, therefore, that Nicholson was recommending Scheele's green when he suggested the use of 'Olympian green' in 1819 for the preparation of pea-green distemper.[99] It may also be significant that in the same year, Stitt gave prices for 'Olympian green' in distemper,[100] but the coincidence of name is not, of course, conclusive.

Further evidence from the Berger archive is circumstantial, but it seems significant that the firm manufactured a large number of different varieties of the pigment. The earliest surviving formula is that dated 1810 for 'Petre's green', and formulae appear in 1811 for 'Fine Green' and 'Olympian green'; while in 1812 details are given for the preparation of 'Fine 2nd Mineral Green' (fig. 4).[101] Between 1815 and 1818, no fewer than nine varieties were

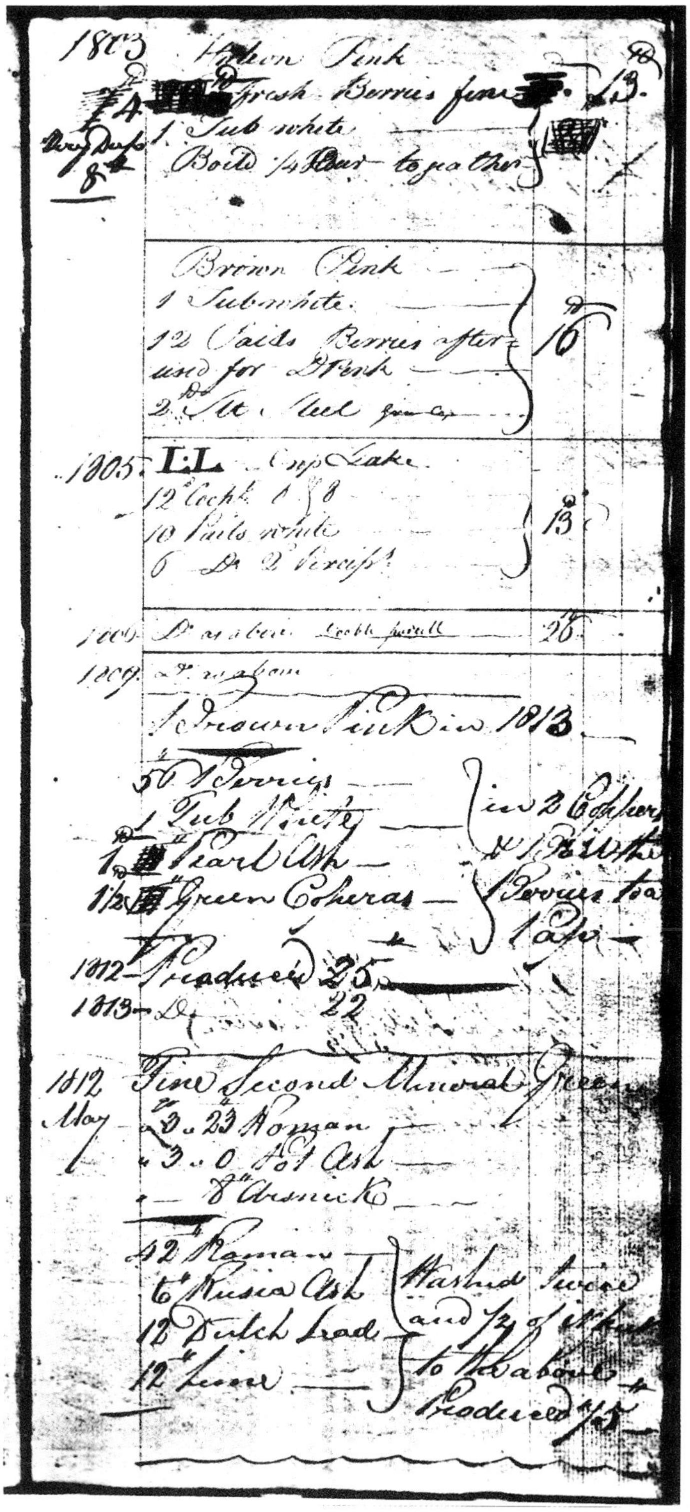

4. Page from the 'Lake & Carmine Book' of Lewis Berger showing formulae for various pigments made in the early nineteenth century.

listed, and in 1831, seven. The range of formulations in use during the former period is shown in table IV. Throughout all of these the basic method of precipitation remained standard, and in 1831, for example, the formula for *second French green* (not to be confused with the firm's French green discussed in connection with green verditer above – q.v.) was as follows:

1 cwt.	2 [qrs].	14 [lb.]	Roman Vitriol
——.	2.	16	Russia Ash
——.	1.	14	Flace Lime
——.	——.	7	Arsenic

The Ash & Arsenic to be melted together in Iron Pan in small quantity Water – The Lime to be slackd [a footnote adds in $7\frac{1}{2}$ gallons of boiling water] & levigated & then wash'd in upon the Ash & Arsenic, fill up Pan with water making the Temperature abt 80°F –

The Roman to be dissolved & added to abt 2 Inches Water in the Frame then strike the Ash Arsenic & Lime upon it fill up with water & afterwards wash twice more.[102]

The use of lime and other additional substances in the Berger formulae was no doubt intended to vary the colour and working properties of the pigment, possibilities mentioned by Mérimée, who gave Scheele's original formula and commented on ways in which it could be varied.[103]

The wide range of proprietary names applied by the Berger firm to Scheele's green may be seen from the table; and in general these, including *African green*, *Olympian green*, and the various varieties of *mineral green*, also appear in the 1831 formula book, but with amended quantities in their formulations, and with other modifications.[104] Production costs per pound for the 1831 range were as follows:

Deep mineral green, 1*s.* $2\frac{1}{2}$*d.*
Second deep mineral green, 1*s.* $1\frac{1}{4}$*d.*
Second mineral green, $10\frac{1}{2}$*d.*
Second French green, 5*d.*
African green, $3\frac{3}{4}$*d.*
Olympian green, $3\frac{1}{2}$*d.*
Common green, 3*d.*

Such an extensive range suggests a fairly large demand for pigments of this type, and their prices would certainly have favoured their use for house-painting. Moreover, although employment of Scheele's green in the printing of wall-paper (an industry for which Lewis Berger had supplied pigment) must not be forgotten, the stocks held by him between 1802 and 1810 were extremely large, and certainly greater than would have been justified by a purely fine-art market. Thus, on 1 January 1802, for example, these stood at a total of over $4\frac{1}{2}$ tons including qualities ranging in valuation between 2*s.* 9*d.* and 8*d.* per lb.; in 1806 he had only slightly less in stock at prices between 2*s.* 10*d.* and 8*d.*; while in 1810 his total stock was again in the region of $4\frac{1}{2}$ tons, this time valued at rates between 2*s.* 10*d.* and $6\frac{1}{2}$*d.* per lb. Although small by comparison, in the latter two years he held stocks of the pigment ground into oil totalling nearly 1 cwt. and $\frac{1}{2}$ cwt. respectively, in both cases valued at 1*s.* 6*d.* per lb., showing that the pigment was available in a state immediately suitable for oil-painting.[105]

Nevertheless, it is difficult to draw any firm conclusions on the basis of such evidence, either as to the extent to which Scheele's green was used for house-painting, or as to the date of its introduction for the purpose. The pigment is notably without mention by Vanherman, but this is perhaps consistent with his expressed aversion to those of a poisonous nature; and in the final analysis it is possible only to observe that it was capable of employment in both oil and distemper, and that its price would not have precluded this. By the late nineteenth century, however, Hurst remarked that Scheele's green had gone out of use.[106]

EMERALD GREEN

Leuchs states that emerald green, to which he referred as *Schweinfurt* green, was discovered by F.V. Rusz and G. Vilhelm Sattler at Schweinfurt in 1814 and put on the market in 1816.[107] In 1822, the chemists Liebig and Braconnot published papers on its preparation, and a formula was given by Tingry's editor in 1830.[108] Emerald

Table IV. *Tabulated formulae for pigments based on Scheele's green contained in the 'Lake & Carmine Book' in the Berger archive*[1] (Quantities given as equivalents in pounds.)

	Roman vitriol	Russia ash	Potash	'Arsenic'[2]	Lime	'Dutch lead'[3]	Common salt	Cream of tartar
Fine green (1815)[4]	182	72		$4\frac{1}{2}$	42	7		
Yellow green (1816)[5]	182	72		26	42[8]		10	
African green (1818)[6]	182	72		26	44[9]	50	10	
Olympian green (1818)	182	72		$4\frac{1}{2}$[7]	44[9]	50	10	
Second French green (1816)	[Not legible]							
Deep mineral green (1815)	112		84	7	9			4
Second deep min. green (1816)	112		84	7	8	4		$1\frac{1}{2}$
Second mineral green (1816)	112		84	7	18	15[10]		
Common mineral green (1816)	112		84	5	18	28[10]		

Notes and references
1. pp. 346, 348, 350, 352, 354, 360, 362, 364, 366.
2. Presumably white arsenic, arsenious oxide.
3. Nature unknown, see note 94 to chapter 1.
4. 'Struck cool'.
5. 'For yellowing the sec[d] French & Olympian Greens'.
6. 'Struck at 130°[F]'.
7. Uncertain, original obliterated.
8. Chalk lime specified with 44 lb. Plymouth stone lime as an alternative.
9. Plymouth stone lime.
10. Whiting later substituted.

green consists chemically of copper aceto-arsenite, and has an extremely distinctive colour, Hurst, who noted it was generally known in America as *Paris green*, described its high opacity, good covering power, and ability to work well in oil and water, but drew attention to its incompatibility with pigments containing sulphur, such as French ultramarine, which cause it to discolour, and its tendency to become brown in damp conditions.[109] It is also affected by alkalis, and like Scheele's green it is extremely poisonous. Use of the pigment for house-painting by the end of the period under consideration appears likely, since Schweinfurt green was added to the list of pigments included in the *Painter's . . . Manual* [*c.* 1830];[110] while the Berger company had noted Braconnot's process in 1829 and seems to have commenced production of the pigment by 1830.[111] The formula used in 1831 was given as follows:

> Take 100 lb Roman Vitriol & dissolve the same in ab.t 40 Gall.s boiling Water [.] Take 152 lb Sugar Lead & dissolve in ab.t 44 Gall.s *Cold* Water, add this solution of Acetate Lead to the solution of Sulphate Copper – When the Sulphate Lead has subsided draw off the Acetate Copper & add to the precipitated Sulphate Lead a further quantity of ab.t 20 Gall.s cold Water The Acetate Copper from this to be added to the former making Sp[ecific] Gr[avity] abt 1033
>
> Boil 30 Gall.s Water & at the boiling point put in 29 lb Sub Carbonate Soda [15 lb. of pearl ash was later substituted], let this completely dissolve & keep the liquor on the strong boil when 66 lb Powder White Arsenic is to be added & when this is completely dissolved add the same to the Acetate Copper: Stir well for ½ *hour* when struck.

The cost of production was 1*s.* 9*d.* per pound.[112] It is clear that by the middle of the nineteenth century the pigment was in service for high-class decorative painting,[113] and it may often be seen in layers of house-paint dating from its second half.[114] It was used also in wallpaper printing, an application mentioned specifically by both Church and Hurst, although the latter indicated its employment had been on the decrease during the closing decades of this period.[115]

CHROME YELLOW BRUNSWICK GREEN

Called by Vanherman *Brunswick green*, the term by which it is now generally recognised, it is important to distinguish this preparation from the earlier copper chloride pigment discussed above which went by the same name. In essence this later pigment is an intimate mixture of chrome yellow and Prussian blue, but its inclusion here as a pigment in its own right is occasioned by the practice described by Vanherman of adding the blue during manufacture, immediately after precipitation of the yellow and before filtration.[116] Heaton describes pigment made by dry mixture of the ingredients as being duller in colour and having a tendency to separate out on standing when made up into paint, the blue coming out on top, and in twentieth-century terminology defines a pure mixture of Prussian blue and chrome yellow as 'chrome green', 'Brunswick green' being reduced with barytes.[117]

Vanherman described Brunswick green (which, he indicated, was reduced with white lead or whiting) as 'the best standing bright green we have', adding, 'it is a recent discovery, is much in requisition, and gains ground in reputation.'[118] The Berger firm had been making the pigment under the names *Prussian green* and *chrome green* (which are liable to confusion with the green version of Prussian blue discussed under that name below, and the artists' pigment oxide of chromium) from at least 1824; but from 1831 the name Brunswick green was used exclusively and its production cost in the latter year was around 3*d.* per pound.[119] On account of this and its immensely superior stability to other green pigments and mixtures then available in oil, it obviously became rapidly adopted for house-painting in this medium, although it is unsuitable for use in distemper on account of the interaction between chrome yellow and alkalis.[120] Evidence for its use before 1828, when Vanherman's observations show it was becoming well established as a pigment, is, however, elusive; but since its availability was dependent on that of chrome yellow (q.v.) it is likely that employment of the two developed in parallel.

PRUSSIAN GREEN

Although the term *Prussian green* was often applied during the 1820s to the pigment described above under the hearing 'Chrome yellow Brunswick green' the name was earlier used for a green pigment prepared by omitting the hydrochloric acid from the manufacture of Prussian blue. In the absence of other references to Prussian green in connection with house-painting, its inclusion by Martin and Nicholson in their lists of pigments should probably be disregarded in view of their obvious derivation from Dossie, who described the pigment in a much wider context, adding, moreover, that its employment was then neglected.[121]

CHAPTER 4

INORGANIC YELLOW PIGMENTS

Of all groups of pigments available for house-painting prior to the mid-eighteenth century, the yellows undoubtedly presented the painter with his greatest problems. Although yellow ochre is one of the most stable pigments known, even today, and works with equal facility in both oil and distemper, the brightness of its colour is limited; while the two brighter inorganic pigments available during the seventeenth century, orpiment and lead-tin yellow, were both considerably more expensive. Employment of the latter was probably limited by this factor to fine-art purposes, while orpiment was worked only with difficulty and was, moreover, an extremely unpleasant substance to handle; so that, although both were reasonably stable, these constraints seem more or less to have precluded their use in everyday house-painting. In contrast, the organic yellow pigments, which were reasonably cheap and of bright colour, were extremely fugitive; and although they worked well in both oil and water, they were transparent and of low staining power in the former medium, so that their full potential for depth of colour could be exploited only in distemper or when used as a glaze in oil. They were thus unsuited to application over large plain areas as oil colours, and hence, for house-painting purposes, were pre-eminently distemper pigments.

It may not have been until the middle of the eighteenth century that a practicable substitute, Naples yellow, was introduced to the house-painting palette. It was, however, expensive and of only moderate staining power, and appears to have had a reputation for grittiness in use. About 1770 another alternative, patent yellow, was discovered; but although bright in tone and cheaper in price it was subject to discolouration in both oil and distemper. Thus it was only at the very end of the period under consideration, when it became possible to manufacture chrome yellow at a moderately economical price, that the earlier problem of a suitable bright yellow pigment, needed especially for the mixing of greens in oil, was overcome in an adequate way.

NATIVE OCHRES AND RAW SIENNA

Yellow ochre occurs extensively in many parts of the world as a natural coloured earth. It forms one of a group of pigments, the ochres, siennas, and umbers, which being naturally formed substances vary slightly in composition, so that it is often difficult to place any one specimen in a particular category. In general, however, ochres contain no manganese, the colouration being entirely due to the presence of various hydrated ferric oxides in the earth or clay; siennas contain a much greater proportion of colouring matter together with a small proportion of manganese oxide, rendering the pigment more transparent in oil; while umbers contain still more manganese oxide and are brown in colour. In all cases the hue of the pigment may be changed by roasting to produce red ochre, burnt sienna, or burnt umber.

References to English ochre occur in the Exchequer rolls for 1619–20 and the early 1630s;[1] and small quantities were supplied for use at Osterley Park in 1779 and 1780.[2] Yellow ochres have been obtained from many places in Britain: Heaton lists ochre from Oxfordshire which he describes as 'soft and transparent, with a peculiar brownish-yellow tone'; ochre from the Golden Valley near Bristol, 'browner in tone than the French ochres, and more opaque than the Italian'; Derbyshire ochres from the Matlock district, 'dark and reddish in tone'; and a bright ochre found in the Vale of Avoca, Co. Wicklow, 'of fine texture and deep golden colour, slightly transparent'.[3] Samples of the last of these, in addition to specimens from the Bristol area and the vicinity of Tavistock, Devon, are to be found in the collections at the Institute of Geological Sciences, South Kensington, together with material deposited from mine-water in old Cornish workings which has also, apparently, been exploited as a pigment.[4] Hurst mentioned ochre from Cornwall, and indicated the existence of deposits in Scotland, Cumberland (now part of Cumbria), Merioneth, Caernarvon, and Anglesey (the last three now welded together as Gwynedd), describing the Welsh varieties as rather duller than Oxfordshire ochres.[5] Yellow ochre occurs too in the Forest of Dean, Gloucestershire, pigment from this source being mentioned by the seventeenth-century contributors to the *Philosophical Transactions*, Henry Powle and Richard Waller.[6]

Although, since Reynolds specified its use,[7] it is clear that English ochre was being exported to America during the early nineteenth century, the extent to which British sources were individually exploited during the period under consideration is in most cases obscure. In 1786, however, Lewis Berger was in correspondence with John Pyne Esq. at East Down, Devon, asking to be sent samples of the ochre he could supply, suggesting that Devon pigment may have been on the market during the late eighteenth century;[8] while reference to 'common Brown or Bristol Oker' was made by Pincot in the early nineteenth, and 'Bristol Yellow Ochre' was mentioned by Vanherman.[9] Bristol ochre was listed also by Tingry's editor,[10] and it is clear that ochres from the vicinity of the city (perhaps from the Golden Valley near Wick, or from some parts of the Mendips, where Hill had mentioned seeing ochre),[11] were in fairly common use, especially since Berger had a stock of nearly 131 cwt. of 'Bristol Oker' on 1 January 1810.[12] Undoubtedly, however, it was the Oxfordshire pigment which was the most famous, probably on account of the superb quality of that obtained from Shotover Hill, which lies four or five miles east of the university city. John Smith observed that 'Plain-Oaker' was,

> a certain concret, or stony substance, found among stiff Clays in divers parts of this Kingdom; but those parts that contain most of it, is the *Shotover-Hills* near *Oxford*, from whence most of the Yellow-Oaker, that is sold in *England*, is dug out; 'tis a Colour, that with pains, will grind very fine, it bears an excellent body, and resists the weather well.[13]

A detailed account of the extraction of ochre at Shotover in the second half of the seventeenth century was published by Robert Plot in his *Natural History of Oxford-Shire* (1677). The diggings were, he indicated, on the east side of the hill to the right (i.e. presumably south) of the road from Oxford to Wheatley, the vein, which was between two and seven inches in thickness, lying at a depth of between seven and thirty feet. The ochre was of two kinds, the *stone ochre*, which was ready for use as soon as dry, and the *clay ochre*, which, he continued,

> because of the natural inequality in its goodness, they wash and steep two or three days in water, and then beat it with clubs on a plank into thin *broad cakes*, of an equal mixture both of good and bad: they then cut it into squares like Tiles, and put it on hurdles laid on trestles to dry, which when thoroughly done 'tis fit for the *Merchant*.

He also mentioned that a bed of slightly more reddish colour underlaid the yellow, and that elsewhere in the vicinity, at Garsington and Pyrton, there were deposits of less good quality; while ochre obtained from between Ducklington and Witney, which lie just over ten miles west of Oxford, was employed for inferior purposes.[14]

The term *stone ochre* continued in use well into the nineteenth century, when it seems to have been applied to ordinary grades of Oxfordshire pigment, rather than the very finest, which was, as indicated below, considerably more expensive. These were, however, of high grade compared with other English ochres, and were used for purposes of house-painting where a good quality of pigment was required. Large amounts of stone ochre were supplied in connection with work at Osterley in 1779–81, often associated in the accounts with Prussian blue, and thus probably for mixing greens;[15] a small quantity was bought by John Soane in 1803;[16] while Pincot suggested its purchase for house-painting ready ground in oil, and mentioned its use also in coach-painting.[17] Butcher included it in oil mixtures for fawn, green, and Portland-stone colour, and also indicated its employment in tinting grounds for the imitation of oak.[18] References occur, moreover, in the archive of Lewis Berger's company to 'Secc.[d] Oxford Stone Oker', and in *Crosby's Builders' New Price Book* to 'Oxford stone ochre'.[19] Besides *stone ochre*, about 1800 James Crease indicated that Oxford ochre was alternatively called *light ochre*,[20] a term employed by Nicholson, who used 'light ocher' in the preparation of olive colour, elsewhere suggesting the use of Oxford ochre to make olive green oil paint.[21]

English ochres varied widely in price. In 1802, for example, Lewis Berger had modest stocks of 'Lump English Oker' valued at 6*s*. 6*d*. per cwt. and the same in powder form at 7*s*. In 1806 the price of the latter had risen to 8*s*., and in 1810 his total stock of lump and powder English ochre was just over 108 cwt. at prices comparable with those already mentioned.[22] In this latter year, he had in addition nearly 131 cwt. of 'Bristol Oker' valued at 7*s*. per cwt., which compares well with the price of 6*s*. quoted by Vanherman some years later.[23] In contrast Berger valued his stock of 'Fine Oxford Oker' at 84*s*. per cwt. in 1802, 'Oxford Oker' appearing at the same rate in 1806 and at 90*s*. in 1810, his stock in that year being less than a mere $2\frac{3}{4}$ cwt. Although 'Secc.[d] Oxford Stone Oker' was markedly cheaper in 1802, being valued at 28*s*. per cwt., by 1806 its price had risen to 50*s*., and by 1810, when his total stock was nearly $27\frac{1}{2}$ cwt., the rate stood at 57*s*.[24]

In view of the considerable range of pigments furnished by British sources it is, perhaps, at first surprising to notice the large quantities of yellow ochre imported from Europe. In the first edition of his book, John Smith divided yellow ochres into two classes, English and foreign: the first (called in the second and later editions *plain ochre*) was, he said, light in colour; and the second (subsequently called *Spruce ochre*) darker in shade.[25] Rosamond Harley indicates that 'spruce' is an old form of the word Prussia, or Prussian, an observation corroborated by references such as that of Tingry's editor to 'Dutch or spruce ochre' since a great deal of pigment seems to have been shipped from Dutch ports.[26] Although John Houghton, who included Plot's account of the Shotover workings in his series of pamphlets *A Collection for Improvement of Husbandry and Trade*, issued between 1692 and 1703, stated that only one barrel of ochre was imported from Holland in 1697,[27] Dr Harley, by research among eighteenth-century customs ledgers, has been able to show that increasing quantities later became shipped into England.[28] As might be expected, therefore, spruce ochre appears in the letter books of Lewis Berger, who was quoting prices of 16*s*. per cwt. for the supply of fine spruce ochre in 1788, common spruce ochre being offered at rates from 9*s*. to 12*s*. Although in 1802 he valued his stock of just over $9\frac{1}{2}$ cwt. 'Dutch Lump Oker' at 15*s*. per cwt. and $5\frac{1}{2}$ cwt. 'Dutch Spruce oker' at 17*s*., these prices rose rapidly during the first decade of the century. In 1806, when his combined stock stood at nearly 61 cwt., the rates had become 18*s*. and 21*s*.; and in 1810 30*s*. and 32*s*. (the latter price here being for 'Gen[uin][e] Dutch Spruce Oker', with an additional price of 28*s*. being given for 'Spruce Oker Mix'd'), while his combined stock of all Duch ochres had fallen to just over $43\frac{1}{2}$ cwt.[29] It seems clear, therefore, that these imported ochres represented a middle quality occupying the gap between the comparatively expensive but high-quality Oxfordshire ochres, and the common pigment obtained from elsewhere in the British Isles.

A similar relationship in price between the cheapest ochres and that known in France as *ocre de ru*, which was described by Caylus as being of deeper colour,[30] is apparent in the price list published by Rondelet, who gave a rate of 45c. per pound for the latter against only 17c. for *ocre jaune commun*.[31] With regard to specific French sources of pigment, Watin and Tingry mentioned *jaune de Berry*, which Rosamond Harley indicates had been obtained at Vierzon from Roman times until the nineteenth century; and Tingry referred also to yellow ochre from the Auvergne.[32] Although 6lb. of 'fine french Oaker' are mentioned in an account dated 1704 among the papers at Boughton House, French varieties of yellow or red pigment do not seem to be mentioned by English writers on house-painting during the period under consideration;[33] but, passing over their omission by John Smith, it has to be borne in mind that little treating the subject of house-painting in any completeness was published in England during the eighteenth century, and that it was not until after the disruption of trade by the Napoleonic wars that any comprehensive works appeared. Nevertheless, it is clear that French pigment of either yellow or red colouration was being imported during the eighteenth century, since Lewis Berger was giving quotations for 'French Oker in Lumps' at prices from 18*s.* to 20*s.* per cwt., and the same 'in Powder' at 12*s.* to 18*s.* in 1780.[34] There is, however, no mention of French ochre in his early nineteenth-century stock-lists.

Yellow ochre also occurs notably in Italy, Cyprus, and India, pigment from the last of these sources being mentioned by Whittock in connection with the imitation of Siena marble in distemper.[35] With the particular exception of *terra di Siena*, however, neither of the other two is mentioned by English writers on house-painting, although both were probably being exploited during the eighteenth century, Caylus, for example, noting that ochres from Italy were more golden than those sold by the Paris merchants.[36] Certainly too, umber (q.v., Chapter 8) was being imported from Cyprus, but this, of course, need not necessarily imply importation of ochre from the same source. With regard to Italian ochres, Lewis Berger had small stocks of 'Roman Oker' amounting to 2 cwt. in 1802 and just over 1 cwt. in 1806, in both cases valued at 7*s.* per cwt.; while in 1810 he again had 1 cwt., this time valued at 8*d.*[37] These prices were, of course, very close to that of the cheapest English pigment, and, while English writers on fine art from the seventeenth century onward make mention of Roman ochre, which was regarded as having a reddish cast,[38] it seems unlikely to have been imported extensively on that account for house-painting.

The yellow earth from the vicinity of Siena, which came to be known as *raw sienna*, on the other hand, was undoubtedly used to a certain extent in graining, and possibly too for other decorative work. *Terra di Siena* was described by Dossie and by Watin, and its transparency in oil compared with ordinary yellow ochre was clearly its most valuable property.[39] Whittock particularly included it in his list of transparent pigments used without white lead as glazes and, together with Butcher, Vanherman, and Nicholson, mentioned its use in graining, where this property was sought.[40] However, although he suggested in addition that it had considerable value as a distemper pigment,[41] and Lewis Berger had small stocks of 'Yellow Sienna' in the first decade of the nineteenth century at prices comparable with those of the Dutch ochres, the pigment was generally much more expensive than these; and it seems most probable that Whittock was referring to graining or marbling executed in a distemper medium rather than the employment of raw sienna as a tinting pigment for ordinary purposes. In this connection, it is probably significant that the quantity of 1 ounce supplied at Osterley in 1780 is followed by an item including a graining brush.[42] In 1788 Lewis Berger was quoting 6*s.* per lb. for 'Terra de Sienna', but by 1802 he valued his stock of over 18 cwt. at the rather lower figure of 84*s.* per cwt.; and the price seems to have fallen slightly further in subsequent years, so that his stock of nearly 80 cwt. in 1806 was priced at 80*s.* per cwt., and his 1810 stock of just over $21\frac{1}{2}$ cwt. at only 70*s.* In 1802 he had in addition just over $2\frac{1}{2}$ cwt. of 'Small Terre de Sienna', valued at 40*s.* per cwt., together with 2 cwt. 'Yellow Sienna' at only 17*s.*, a similar quantity of the latter appearing at the same rate in 1806.[43] By comparison, 'Distemper Oker' was a much cheaper pigment than even the last of these, being valued by Berger at 7*s.* per cwt. in 1802, and 5*s.* 9*d.* in 1806 and 1810. Although his stock was fairly small in 1802 at just over $12\frac{1}{2}$ cwt., by 1806 it had risen appreciably to over 177 cwt., and in 1810 stood at $181\frac{1}{2}$ cwt. with, in addition, a further quantity of nearly 22 cwt. valued at the rather higher price of 10*s.*[44] It seems most unlikely, therefore, that even the cheap varieties of raw sienna would have been destined for use in common distemper work.

The general position regarding the use made of different varieties of yellow ochre, a pigment of almost universal application in both oil and size media, thus seems clear. Local sources of varying quality would undoubtedly have been exploited from very early times and employed for vernacular purposes; and, on account of its everyday utility, yellow ochre was naturally one of the six pigments the London plasterers were allowed to use under the 1603 Act of Parliament.[45] During the eighteenth century cheap varieties of the pigment, often brownish or dull in colour, were used extensively in distemper and for inferior painting in oil, particularly perhaps for exterior work. For better quality interior painting, ochres obtained from Holland or France were employed when available, together with the second grades of Oxford ochre. Thus, Vanherman summed up the useful character of spruce ochre as:

> a pleasant, warm, and friendly pigment in forming greens, buffs, and stone colours; . . . [which], combined with reds or browns, produces countless tints of pleasant drabs, sage, olive, tea greens, &c.[46]

For graining or marbling, however, the finest Oxford ochre and Italian raw sienna, with their increased transparency, were needed, but obtained at considerably greater expense.

As indicated by Pincot and Tingry's editor, besides being sold in lump or powder form, yellow ochres were available ready ground in oil.[47] As early as 1619–20, 'Englishe Oker grounde' appears in connection with work at Greenwich Palace,[48] and Stalker & Parker mentioned its sale in this form.[49] Lewis Berger was offering 'Spruce Oker in Oil' for sale in 1788 at 36*s.* per cwt., and had modest stocks of 'Gro.[d] Spruce Oker' during the first decade of the nineteenth century, generally valued at twice or one and a half times the price of that supplied in the lump. These amounted to 3 cwt. in 1802, nearly $4\frac{1}{4}$cwt. in 1806, and nearly $1\frac{1}{4}$cwt. in 1810, priced at rates of 34*s.*, 38*s.*, and 40*s.* per cwt. respectively.[50] It must be observed, however, that in general retail prices for yellow ochres seem to have been considerably higher than those used by Berger for the valuation of his stock; although these, being employed for business purposes, must undoubtedly be regarded as reliable, and, as indicated above, correlate well in the case of the Bristol ochre with the price given by Vanherman, himself in the retail trade. Thus at Doncaster in 1825, even for colour-washing the Workhouse, yellow ochre was bought at a cost of 3*d.* per pound, the equivalent of 28*s.* per cwt,[51] a figure considerably in excess of those between 5*s.* and 10*s.* for distemper ochre appearing in the Berger archive; and spruce ochre was supplied both to Soane in 1803 (some in ground form) and at Tredegar House, Newport, Monmouthshire (now Gwent), in 1792–3 at a rate of 6*d.* per lb., equivalent to 56*s.* per cwt.,[52] against the figures of 9*s.* to 17*s.* which appear in the Berger archive between 1788 and 1802. Moreover, the general retail price of yellow ochre for house-painting about 1800 seems to have been 4*d.* per lb. (i.e. 37*s.* 4*d.* per cwt.), this being the rate charged for the supply of pigment in connection with sundry works at Doncaster between 1798 and 1803 and for pigment sold to Soane in 1803.[53] Interestingly, the same rate is found in an account dated 1705 at Boughton House, Northamptonshire, for a quantity of 'English Oaker' totalling just over $\frac{3}{4}$cwt.; $\frac{1}{4}$cwt. 'Reff[d] English Oaker' being billed at 5*d.*; and 6 lb. 'fine french Oaker' being costed at 8*d.*[54] Although the reasons for the discrepancies in price are obscure, it is significant that the differentials, even if slightly telescoped, are maintained throughout; and the same is true of those given by Phillips in 1812:

English ochre	$8\frac{1}{2}$*d.* per lb.
Spruce ochre	10*d.*
Lump ochre	1*s.* $2\frac{1}{2}$*d.*
Oxford stone ochre	1*s.* $2\frac{1}{2}$*d.*
Raw terra Sienna	3*s.*

These are, as usual, well above those encountered elsewhere and similar to those he gave in 1821.[55]

MANUFACTURED IRON OXIDE – MARS YELLOW

The recipe for *York brown* dated 1824 which appears in the second of the Berger company's experimental notebooks, and was later transcribed in slightly amended form into the 1831 formula book, is the only reference so far encountered to an artificial yellow iron oxide pigment in a possible house-painting context; although such pigments had been known since the seventeenth century and seem to have come into use for fine-art purposes during the late eighteenth.[56] The formulae among the Berger papers rely on the double decomposition of lime and ferrous sulphate to produce iron oxide and calcium sulphate; but at least by the late nineteenth century precipitates based on aluminium hydroxide, formed in a way comparable with that used in the preparation of lake pigments, seem also to have been available, and there is no reason why these too should not have been in use at a much earlier date.[57] Although in 1810 Lewis Berger's stock of just over 3 cwt. of York brown had been valued at 80*s.* per cwt., in 1831 the production cost of pigment made by the following method was noted as 9*s.* 10*d.* per cwt.:

> 0 cwt. 1[qr]. 21 [lbs.] Flace lime [the 1824 formula employed 'Common Lime'] Slack'd with cold Water, to which add ab.[t] 17 Pails more cold water & pass same thro' a 68 *Wire* Sieve into Iron Pan –
>
> Dissolve 1 cwt. 2. 0. Sulphate Iron in ab.[t] 20 Pails boiling Water & when settled add it in that state to the Lime
>
> Let the whole stand together for ab.[t] 2 Days [stirring] when draw off as much of the water as is necessary for filling [filtering] out thro' a Hair Sieve, when stiff enough lay upon racks in thick Cakes & carry into Stove – when dry expose it for some time [five or six weeks are mentioned in the 1824 recipe] to the action of the air.[58]

No information is presently available, however, to indicate the extent to which such pigment may have been used or what advantages if any it may have possessed, since, unlike natural ochre, artificial pigment prepared by the above method would have contained a large percentage of calcium sulphate.[59]

ORPIMENT, KING'S YELLOW, AND REALGAR

Two sulphides of arsenic occur in nature, orpiment (arsenic trisulphide) which is yellow, and realgar (arsenic disulphide) which is of a deep red colour and known alternatively as red orpiment. They are found in a number of places, including Somerset; but British sources are not of commercial significance, and Hill writing in the mid-eighteenth century mentioned Germany as a source of material used in England. He described orpiment as 'a very beautiful Substance, composed of large Flakes . . . of a glorious Yellow, very weighty', suggesting that yellow orpiment could be burnt to produce red orpiment with the emission of a nauseous smell. He also observed that there were,

> two other less beautiful Kinds; the one composed of an impurer Substance, resembling common Sulphur . . . the other more impure than the last, and tinged of a paler or deeper Green in many Places.

Later he remarked of these poorer qualities, 'the yellow looking more like dirty Fragments of common Brimstone, and the red like dusty pieces of bad Bole [red ochre]', that they were,

> purchased by our Painters for Cheapness; and they say, with proper Management, make as good Colours as the finer Pieces; though, in their Barrels, they look more like Ashes than the beautiful Substances they really are.[60]

This last observation no doubt referred to the process of refining by sublimation mentioned by his near contemporary, Dossie, who remarked that the pigment was rarely used in its natural state, and was known after purification as king's yellow. However, Dossie also described the artificial manufacture of king's yellow by roasting twenty parts of arsenious oxide with one of flowers of sulphur. The product could, he indicated, by made more orange by increasing the proportion of sulphur, and following sublimation was levigated to fit it for use.[61] Watin too mentioned artificial orpiment, observing that this was the more commonly encountered and should be as red as possible, although the natural variety, which should be of a golden yellow, was, he said, held in higher estimation. They produced, he noted, a marigold colour.[62] This, Tingry observed, could also be achieved by slight calcination of the yellow pigment,[63] an idea repeated by the author of the *Painter's . . . Pocket Manual*.[64]

Although king's yellow is a bright pigment with a good body in oil, it has a number of disadvantages in practical use. In the first place it discolours when mixed with pigments containing lead or copper, in particular white lead and verdigris, owing to the formation of the blackish sulphides of these metals; while Butcher also observed that it would blacken if touched with an iron knife.[65] Secondly, when used in oil the pigment has a tendency to clump together over a period of years, producing a speckled effect unsatisfactory in appearance; and thirdly, compounds of arsenic are notoriously toxic. Hence Dossie described the pigment as poisonous and unpleasant, and rejected by many,[66] and John Smith too cautioned that orpiment was,

> a good Colour for some uses, but very troublesome to grind, being a Mineral stony substance of a poysonous nature; therefore take care that the fumes of it don't offend the brain in the time of grinding.[67]

Even when applied to the wall as a paint it provided problems, and Vanherman warned he thought it,

> necessary to caution the use of it, unless any one has a wish to be driven out of house and home with his family; in that case, he has only to order one small apartment to be painted with King's yellow, and he will be gratified; for the smell cannot be confined, but sends its vile effluvia into every corner of the house, and, instead of growing weaker, it gains strength every day, and the only remedy . . . is to bestow on it two coats of patent yellow, and then two coats of light carriage varnish. This pigment . . . should be excluded, not only on account of the above annoying quality, but also its antipathysing with most other colours.[68]

These references and others to king's yellow in books on house-painting do not suggest its use was favoured, although it was apparently employed for fine-art purposes and in heraldic painting.[69] Instead one gains the impression that discussion was more for the sake of completeness and to warn against such arsenical compounds than for any practical use to which they might be put. Thus, Watin listed *l'orpin ou realgal* among colours which were dangerous and which he advised should be used as little as possible, and although he mentioned they could be employed in combination to mix *jaune citron ou aurore* in oil, he suggested the substitution of pink or Naples yellow.[70] Probably taking his cue from the latter, Tingry later indicated that the former was an obsolete method for the preparation of lemon yellow.[71] He nevertheless used realgar in a mixture for golden yellow,[72] and, based on this, the author of the *Painter's . . . Pocket Manual* also used them in gold colour and lemon yellow.[73] Significantly, John Smith did not mention either in the pigment list he gave in the first edition of his book; and their unpopularity at the beginning of the nineteenth century is underlined by the low stocks held by Lewis Berger. In 1802, 1806, and 1810 his stocks of yellow orpiment stood only at 2 lb., 5 lb., and 26 lb. respectively, his holding of king's yellow at the same dates being 87 lb., 36 lb., and 195 lb.; while of 'Orange Orpiment' he had similarly low amounts of 1 lb., 7 lb., and 69 lb.[74] Hence, although red and yellow orpiment were not excessively expensive as pigments (Lewis Berger quoting prices for supply of the latter at between 1*s.* and 1*s.* 6*d*, per lb. in 1780 and valuing his stocks of yellow and orange orpiment at prices between 1*s.* $1\frac{1}{2}$*d.* and 1*s.* 8*d.* per lb. during the first decade of the nineteenth century), it seems clear that the practical limitations on their uses militated against their general employment for house-painting. King's yellow, whose use was similarly limited, was rather more expensive, Berger valuing his stocks between 1802 and 1810 at prices between 3*s.* 6*d.* and 6*s.* per lb.;[75] but it was put forward by Whittock for mixing cinnamon and a light delicate green in distemper, and also for the rather specialised purpose of a glaze in the imitation of *verde antico* marble in distemper.[76] His suggestion that it formed a most beautiful green with blue may, however, be traced to Dossie, and is therefore unreliable as evidence for its use in house-painting.[77] Whittock's comments suggest, nevertheless, that it was used in distemper (perhaps smelling less unpleasant than in oil), and realgar certainly seems to have enjoyed a very specialised use (described in Chapter 20) in the production of clouded ceilings during the first decades of the nineteenth century.

LEAD-TIN YELLOW

From at least the fourteenth century, lead-tin yellow (lead stannate) was prepared for use as a pale yellow pigment. It does not appear to have possessed a distinctive name, but was commonly referred to as *giallolino* or *massicot*, terms also applied to canary litharge (lead monoxide, discussed in Chapter 10), which it resembled, and possibly too to Naples yellow (q.v. below). This obscurity of terminology was discussed by Mrs Merrifield in 1849, and has recently been re-examined by Dr Harley.[78] Although references to *massicot* are found in house-painting literature throughout the period being considered, it is accordingly difficult to know to which pigment they referred; but it seems likely that lead-tin yellow was too expensive for common use in this way, and was virtually obsolete by the mid-eighteenth century.

In 1686 Waller referred to 'masticot' as an 'improper calx of tin';[79] and lead-tin yellow has been identified in European paintings ranging from the early fourteenth to the mid-eighteenth centuries.[80] It seems likely its colour could vary, since John Smith referred to 'White Masticote' and 'Yellow Masticoate';[81] and in 1688 Stalker & Parker gave the cost of 'Yellow and pale Masticoate' as 2*d.* per oz.,[82] a price equivalent to 2*s.* 8*d.* per lb., which may be compared with that of 6*s.* 8*d.* for 'Masticotte' contained in a manuscript of *c.* 1600 attributed to Edmonde Barton.[83] Since litharge would undoubtedly have been much cheaper than this, it seems probable that these references are to lead-tin yellow, and hence that the latter is unlikely to have been used for general purposes in house-painting, although it might have found employment in high-class decorative work. In this connection, it appears significant that John Smith, who described 'Masticote' as 'a good light-yellow for most uses' which ground very fine and had a good body in oil, noting too that it was especially useful for making greens of several types, did not include it in any of his suggested mixtures for house-painting, and illustrated its use only in colouring maps.[84]

In the mid-eighteenth century, Dossie observed that 'Masticot' stood well in oil or water, but noted that it was not greatly used; and it is significant that he described it as made by the gentle calcination of white lead, a process which would produce lead oxide rather than lead stannate.[85] Watin too, who included it in his category of 'dangerous colours' to be used as little as possible, also indicated the manufacture of *massicot* in this way, describing three forms, which he said were obtained by different degrees of heat. These were *blanc, jaune.* and *doré*, which no doubt represent the three forms in which litharge is commercially available today.[86] Tingry repeated this, but identified massicot specifically with canary litharge, adding significantly that it had been employed before being superseded by Naples and patent yellows.[87] Later writers repeated similar information,[88] and it is clear that knowledge of the preparation of lead-tin yellow had become obscure, if not totally forgotten.

References to massicot in nineteenth-century British house-painting literature are scant; and although a mixture of 'masticot' with an organic yellow pigment appears in the list published by Phillips in his builders' price book, this contains a number of pigments more or less reserved for use by artists.[89] Only Nicholson and the author of the *Painter's . . . Pocket Manual* referred to massicot in an unambiguously house-painting context, the former suggesting its use in mixing straw-coloured distemper, and the latter in making gold colour;[90] but neither seems to carry much weight, although it is just possible that lead-tin yellow was still on the market. In 1802, for example, Lewis Berger had a small stock of just over $1\frac{1}{2}$cwt. of 'Masticott' which was valued at 9*d.* per pound against rates equivalent to approximately $3\frac{1}{2}$*d.* or 6*d.* for litharge, suggesting it was different from the latter; but he had no stock in 1806 or 1810.[91] Rosamond Harley notes that the London artists' colourman, Ackermann, was supplying 'massicot' in cake form for watercolours at the beginning of the nineteenth century,[92] and a sample appears in the notebooks of George Field, dated 1809.[93] The nature of these is, however, unclear; and it is notable that in 1835 Field described massicot simply as an 'oxide of lead'.[94] The latter, however, blackens quickly in oil, and can never have been very suitable for house-painting; and nineteenth-century references to massicot in the present context are probably archaic. It is nevertheless noteworthy that throughout the period the term *litharge* was more or less exclusively applied to lead oxide used as a drier, the word *massicot* being reserved for a yellow staining pigment.

NAPLES YELLOW

The yellow compound, lead antimonate, was prepared artificially in the ancient world, and used extensively in ceramics in Egypt and Mesopotamia. By the early sixteenth century it was being used in Italy for the decoration of *maiolica*, formulae for its preparation in this context being recorded by Cipriano Piccolpasso in the second half of the 1550s;[95] and, while possibly in use for fresco during the latter part of the sixteenth century, it has been positively identified in easel paintings from the early 1630s onwards.[96] In the seventeenth century there was a widespread belief that the substance known as Naples yellow was of natural origin; but although lead antimonate occurs naturally as the mineral bindheimite, doubt has been cast as to whether this was used as a pigment.[97] In 1676, for instance Félibien noted that '*Jaune* de Naples' was a type of dirt or slag ('crasse') found in the vicinity of sulphur mines;[98] and in 1755 Caylus reported that painters who had travelled in Italy were convinced Naples yellow was a mineral taken from the heart of the earth near Naples. Nevertheless, he continued, a colour which resembled it perfectly could be made from antimony and red lead.[99]

In 1766 Auguste Fougeroux de Bondaroy read a paper to the Académie Royale des Sciences, in which he dismissed the natural origin of the pigment and put forward a method for its manufacture. Research in Italy had informed him that the secret of the process was in the possession of an aged Neapolitan, who would not communicate it for fear of losing his life. He was told, however, that the pigment was made by exposing metallic ingredients to a lively heat for twenty-four hours in a potters' furnace. His first experiments showed that a yellow approximating to that of Naples yellow could be made from red lead and 'antimoine diaphorétique' (antimony oxide),[100] but his final formula called for 12 oz. 'céruse' (lead carbonate), 3 oz. 'antimoine diaphorétique', 1 oz. 'alun' (aluminium potassium sulphate), and 1 oz. 'sel ammoniac' (ammonium chloride) placed in a covered, unglazed flat dish, and exposed to a moderate fire for seven to eight hours.[101]

A modified version of this formula was published by Tingry,[102] but was later subjected to critical comment by Mérimée, who indicated that the nature of certain ingredients had suffered from mistranslation between the Italian source and the French of Fougeroux de Bondaroy, so that it did not produce a successful pigment. Instead, he published a formula given to him by J.B. Guimet (whose success in producing artificial ultramarine was mentioned in Chapter 2), in which 2 parts of red lead and 1 part of potassium antimonate were mixed and ground together before being dried, powdered, and exposed to a 'moderate red heat' for four or five hours.[103] These and other formulae of the eighteenth and nineteenth centuries have recently been tabulated and published elsewhere.[104]

Dossie (to whom the nature of the pigment was unknown, although he suspected it was manufactured), indicated that it was generally used only in oil, and on account of its brightness, which was inferior only to that of king's yellow, was 'much received into practice'. It had, however, a gritty texture which could not be satisfactorily removed by levigation in water, and would discolour in contact with iron in the presence of moisture.[105] At the end of the nineteenth century, Church too noted it was troublesome to grind on account of its gritty nature, and was liable to discolouration in water,[106] although Hurst indicated it was equally useful in both water and oil.[107]

Naples yellow was put forward by Watin, who knew Fougeroux de Bondaroy's work, as a substitute for orpiment in the preparation of *jaune citron ou aurore.* He also employed it in *couleur d'or* and *chamois*, stipulating its plentiful addition in the latter.[108] His suggestion that it might be used for lemon and golden yellows was repeated by Tingry (who mentioned also its employment for yellows generally, and illustrated its use in distemper, oil, and varnish);[109] and similar ideas duly appeared in the *Painter's . . . Pocket Manual.*[110] Evidence for practical employment of the pigment in the 1770s may be found in accounts for the purchase of painting materials relating to Osterley Park: four ounces of 'Naples yellow Ground' were supplied in 1774 at a cost equivalent to 4*s.* per lb.; and the following year half a pound, presumably of dry pigment, was supplied at a rate of 2*s.* 6*d.* per lb. Further quantities totalling $4\frac{3}{4}$ lb. were purchased in 1779 and 1780 at the same rate, including 1 lb. 'Naples Yell.w in Turpeñ.'[111] In addition, the pigment has been identified together with Prussian blue in an oil green of 1780 in the meeting room of the Royal Society at Somerset House.[112] Less definite, but probably significant, evidence for its employment is furnished by the use of paint of 'naples Yellow' colour in the early 1770s in the Dining Room of a house at Norwood, Middlesex, associated with the Osterley Park estate;[113] while in 1774 payment was made for painting the 'plain parts' of the ceiling and walls of the newly refurbished chapel at Queens' College, Cambridge, 'a Naples yellow'.[114] A decade later the Long Bow Room at Gordon Castle, Morayshire, (demolished 1961) was painted 'Naples Green',[115] here probably reflecting use of the pigment with blue in mixing greens, although in none of the latter instances can it be absolutely certain that the name necessarily implied employment of the pigment itself.

Interestingly, the stocks Lewis Berger possessed in the first decade of the 1800s were subject to considerable fluctuation. In 1802 and 1810, for example, he listed Naples yellow at 2*s.* 9*d.* and 3*s.* per lb. respectively, and 'Levigated Naples Yellow' at 1*s.* and a price equivalent to 1*s.* 3*d.* per lb. His combined stock in 1802 stood at a mere $10\frac{1}{2}$ lb., but in 1806 he had nearly $9\frac{1}{2}$ cwt, at a price equivalent to 1*s.* 3*d.* per lb.: by 1810 this had fallen again to just over 3 cwt.[116] Retail prices given by Phillips in 1812 and 1821 at 3*s.* 7*d.* and 3*s.* 6*d.* respectively, were, as usual, higher.[117] Although the pigment was thus clearly still available in the early nineteenth century, it remained quite costly, and it may be significant that little evidence for its use is found in later literature. Martin and Nicholson, of course, included Naples yellow in their colour lists transcribed more or less directly from Dossie, but mentioned its practical use only in connection with graining;[118] and it is notable that Butcher, although he included it in a group of pigments discoloured by contact with a steel knife, did not list it in his main series of house-painting pigments, nor indicate its use for any purpose in his text.[119] Morever, mention of the pigment is omitted entirely from Whittock's authoritative work on graining, and also from Vanherman's eminently well-informed book.[120] It thus seems likely that employment of Naples yellow for house-painting was quickly rivalled in the 1780s by that of patent yellow, a pigment which at least had the advantage of price on its side, if not durability when used in oil or distemper; while in the 1820s, both were largely superseded by chrome yellow.

PATENT YELLOW

Patent yellow, basic lead oxychloride, had been discovered by C.W. Scheele approximately ten years before James Turner took out a patent for its manufacture in England in 1781.[121] This indicated that to a given quantity of litharge or red lead, a solution of half as much by weight of sea salt (sodium chloride) was added, the mixture ground, and allowed to stand for twenty-four hours. The resulting white substance was washed to free it from the caustic soda which formed the other product of the reaction, and heated until the colour desired was produced. This would, the patentee observed, 'be of different tints, according to the continuance of the calcination, or the degree of heat employed'.[122] Possibly to protect his process from piracy, it is notable that Turner did not indicate the material had to be melted, a procedure mentioned by Chaptal in 1807.[123] Later, Mérimée gave further details of this, observing that once the white material had been dried and powdered, it was,

> exposed in the receiver of a reverberatory furnace, until it assumes the yellow colour required; this powder is then to be thrown into a crucible which has been brought up to a red heat, and is then returned into the furnace, where it is only allowed to remain until the composition has melted; thus fused, it is thrown on a plate of iron; and when cool, it forms a crystalline mass striated transversely.[124]

This seems to tally with Field's description of a sample in 1809 as being in 'hard, ponderous, lumps, of a lamelated, sparkling fracture – a fine bright yellow – opake', his painted-out rectangle of it being close to Munsell reference 7.5 Y 9/8.[125] In England, the pigment became known as *Turner's yellow*; but Tingry recorded that although at one time it had been imported into France from Britain in cakes which were half an inch thick, Chaptal had set up a manufactury in his home town, and the pigment had thus become known in France as *Montpellier yellow.*[126] In this connection, it may be noted that Chaptal's process, which was primarily motivated by extraction of the alkaline product, was published in 1794 and differed from Turner's patent in the proportions of raw materials used, the account noting that four volumes of litharge and one of common salt were mixed together in four volumes of water.[127]

In his patent specification, Turner advertised his pigment as being for use in water as well as oil; but, although Tingry (who re-published Chaptal's formula) indicated it was used for the same purposes as Naples yellow,[128] it appears to have had a reputation for being subject to discolouration, so that, Field observed, on this account it was little used 'except for the common purposes of house-painting'.[129] Despite this seemingly unsatisfactory tendency, Butcher described patent yellow as 'a beautiful colour, of great utility', adding too that it was 'much used by coach painters'. For house-painting he suggested its employment in preparing fine yellow paint, and also to make greens in combination with French verdigris and Prussian blue;[130] while Nicholson too suggested its use for yellow and for mixing with Prussian blue to make a good green.[131] The application of patent yellow in coach-painting was mentioned by Pincot, who used it combined with about four per cent of stone ochre;[132] while Vanherman noted that coachmakers had been the chief consumers of patent yellow.[133] No doubt the varnish medium they employed helped to confer superior stability to the pigment.

The earliest reference so far encountered to practical employment of patent yellow in a house-painting context is in an account dated 1787 for painting 55 square yards at Osterley Park 'once in oil & twice patent yellow' at a rate of 1*s.* per yard, together with a run of skirting 'the plinth patent yellow'.[134] The pigment has been identified alongside Prussian blue in green paint used in the Outer Library at Attingham Hall, Shropshire, in the mid-1780s;[135] and confirmation of its employment elsewhere to mix greens in this way is provided by a letter of 1809 noting the despatch of a consignment of paint (presumably green) together with 'a small quantity of Prussian blue – with which you make it Darker – and some pattent yellow with which you can make it Brighter'.[136] It is thus curious that Vanherman suggested it was unsuitable for mixing greens since it was, he said, 'unfriendly with the blues'.[137] Patent yellow was used at the Royal Pavilion, Brighton, in 1802;[138] a quantity was supplied to John Soane in 1807;[139] and technical investigation of the two first-floor drawing rooms at the Soane Museum has indicated that about 1812 these were painted yellow using patent yellow, a scheme repeated following enclosure of the loggia in 1833, the finish in both cases being varnished.[140] This would have acted to protect the pigment against discolouration, and it is of interest in this connection that in a passage suggesting the use of patent yellow in place of orpiment, Vanherman recommended the subsequent application of two coats of 'light carriage varnish'.[141] Further confirmation for its employment in house-painting comes from the price-books of Laxton and Skyring, in both of which 'patent yellow' is mentioned as a paint colour.[142]

By the time Vanherman was writing he indicated that patent yellow had been superseded by chrome yellow. He nevertheless recommended it as a good ground colour for the latter, a suggestion which must have made sense when the prices of around 70*s.* per cwt, for patent yellow in the 1806 and 1810 stock-lists of Lewis Berger are compared with the likely price of chrome yellow (q.v.) in 1831 of about 225*s.* per cwt.[143] Tingry's later editor concurred that the pigment had been superseded by chrome yellow, but added that it was often used as an adulterant for it;[144] and in this connection it is worth drawing attention to the practice of Berger's firm during the second decade of the nineteenth century of using patent yellow as a base for a pigment they called 'Dutch mineral', discussed in connection with yellow lakes below. By the end of the nineteenth century it seems clear that the pigment was almost completely obsolete, and Hurst recorded that use of patent yellow had been more or less abandoned.[145]

CHROME YELLOW, ORANGE, AND RED

Lead chromate, or chrome yellow, must be regarded as the pigment for which the eighteenth century had been waiting. It presented an ability to provide a stable bright yellow in oil without the problems (other than its toxicity) presented by the other pigments reviewed above, and was especially useful in its capacity for combination with Prussian blue to produce the range of greens discussed under the heading 'Chrome Yellow Brunswick Green' in Chapter 3. The precise date at which chrome yellow was introduced is uncertain; but the French chemist L.N. Vauquelin, who published his first paper on Siberian chrome ore in 1797 and isolated the element chromium the following year,[146] noted in 1809 that its beauty, good working quality, and permanence were already well known to painters. By then, he recorded, supplies of ore had been discovered at Var in France,[147] and from 1808 material was being obtained from the Pennsylvania-Maryland region of the United States.[148] In Britain, deposits were discovered in the Shetland Islands in 1817.[149]

Chrome yellow was mentioned as a pigment by Sir Humphry Davy in 1815, who observed that it was 'a much more beautiful yellow than any possessed by the ancients', and that there was reason to suppose that it was 'quite unalterable';[150] while Field tested samples at about the same time.[151] This and other evidence suggests that it was well established as an artists' pigment by the end of the second decade of the nineteenth century;[152] and it is notable that a list of 'expensive colours' used in the lavish decoration of the Music Room at the Brighton Pavilion in 1818 includes 'Crome, Yellow' alongside carmine, lake, and vermilion; while the following year, the walls of the Yellow Drawing Room were painted 'light Chrome yellow'.[153] Even in 1831 it was still fairly expensive, the cost prices of the range manufactured by the company founded by Lewis Berger lying between 11½*d*, and 1*s.* 1½*d.* per lb., which suggests a retail price in the region of 225*s.* per cwt. By 1837, however, a cheaper variety called *canary yellow*, which was extended with barytes, was manufactured at a cost of 15*s.* per cwt.; and another, known as *imperial yellow*, this time extended with gypsum, followed in 1840 at 13*s.* per cwt.

The pigment is produced by ionic exchange on addition of a solution of potassium bichromate to one of lead acetate. The first experimental notes on the manufacture of chrome yellow to survive amongst the Berger material are dated 1824, but reference is also made to a batch prepared in 1823. The cost price in 1824 was 2*s.* 5*d.* per lb.; and successive entries, including the production formula of 1826, show improvements and modifications to the process, bringing the price down to those of the 1830s quoted above, together with an increase in the range of colours produced. By 1831 pale, mid, deep, and orange varieties were produced; extra pale, red, and extra red followed within two or three years; while in 1841 and 1844 the names *Chinese red* and *Persian red* were applied to pigments of this type.[154] The range of colours possible results from variations in the proportion of basic lead chromate associated with the normal yellow chromate. As the amount of basic chromate increases, the pigment becomes a deeper orange, while the red pigment is the most basic of all, containing up to two molecules of basic chromate to one of the yellow. The orange chromes may be used in distemper, but the yellow varieties are unstable in this medium, being attacked by alkalis and converted to the orange variety.[155]

The first printed reference to chrome yellow encountered in connection with house-painting is by Vanherman, who described its preparation and praised the pigment as surpassing all others for brilliancy, beauty, and intensity of colour. He also mentioned that orange and lemon varieties were manufactured, and that the pigment had superseded patent yellow, suggesting its use in paint of stone colour and for mixing various greens.[156] Tingry's editor of 1830 quoted Vanherman's formula, saying that for a time the pigment had been scarce and expensive; but by the time he was writing it was being produced commercially, although it was often adulterated with white lead or patent yellow. In particular, he observed that a superior type was being made at Chelsea by Dr Bollmann,[157] whose contribution to the manufacture of the pigment has been discussed by Dr Harley.[158] Chrome yellow also received mention in the more or less contemporary *Painter's . . . Manual*,[159] and was included by Nicholson in the revised edition of the *Builder's and Workman's New Director*, in which he described it as an excellent yellow lately much used.[160] The pigment was not mentioned by Butcher or Whittock, but it seems likely that, having been used for the exceptionally lavish and high-class decorative work at Brighton, it became more widely available during the 1820s at a price appropriate for house-painting, and that by the end of the decade it enjoyed extensive use in oil. Use of the darker red varieties is, however, unlikely to have become common until rather later.

ROTTEN STONE

Rotten stone, not normally regarded as a pigment, is mentioned in Chapter 18 below in connection with its main purpose, the polishing of varnishes. Nathaniel Whittock, however, called for its use in staining yellow grounds for the imitation of oak and satin wood, and in the megilp which formed the basis of the glaze for the former, since, he believed, yellow ochre was too deep in colour and would impart an undesirable greenish tone to the work;[161] but the use of rotten stone in this way was probably exceptional.

CHAPTER 5

ORGANIC YELLOW PIGMENTS AND DYESTUFFS

Organic yellow pigments, whose properties and relationship to the inorganic yellow compounds used for house-painting were briefly described in the introduction to Chapter 4, were prepared in the form of lakes from a variety of naturally occurring yellow dyes. In connection with eighteenth-century terminology, however, as Dr Harley has pointed out, it is important to note that, whereas the word *lake* is now of general application, it was formerly applied only to reds, the equivalent term for yellows being *pink*.[1] In general two white bases were in use as vehicles for the dye, chalk and aluminium hydroxide; although in certain circumstances white lead, satin white, and even patent yellow were employed. In most cases the dyes would be mordanted on the base by the use of alum (exceptionally, ferrous sulphate, often known as *copperas*, was used for brown pink); but in the case of aluminium hydroxide it is also possible to form the white *in situ* by adding an alkali to dye previously dissolved in water together with a quantity of alum. The latter base was used for the more expensive qualities of pigment; and these were considerably higher in price than those in general use for house-painting, as may be seen from table v, which shows the cost prices per cwt. of the range of pigments being made by Lewis Berger's company in 1831.

YELLOW DYESTUFFS

Although the berries of various species of *Rhamnus* were apparently the most widely used source of dye until the extensive import of quercitron bark at the end of the eighteenth century, to at least some extent these and other dyestuffs seem to have been used interchangeably, so that the pigments produced would have varied slightly in colour and in other properties, particularly their light-fastness. Nevertheless, all should be regarded as fugitive compared with the inorganic pigments described above. In addition some dyes were used for purposes other than the preparation of pigments, such as the production of coloured lacquers and for staining timber, and notes on these varieties and their uses for such purposes are included for convenience.

Annatto

The seeds of *Bixa orellana*, a South American plant, contain the dye *bixin* which is of an orange colour and soluble in water and alcohol. This was used by Dossie in an orange lake of his own invention.[2]

John Smith described how 'ornato' might be used to provide an oil of golden colour, although this hint was omitted from the 1723 and subsequent editions of his book;[3] while Stalker & Parker (who referred to 'Ornator') and the early nineteenth-century authors Tingry and Vanherman described the use of annatto in coloured lacquers.[4]

Barberry

A substantive yellow dye, *berberine*, may be extracted from roots of the species *Berberis*, a shrub which grows in England. Only one author, Tingry, seems to have made reference to it in the context of house-painting pigments, giving it as a constituent in a recipe for a brownish variety

Table v. *Cost prices of yellow lake pigments manufactured by Lewis Berger's sons in 1831*

Italian pink (aluminium hydroxide base)	3*s.* 6*d.* per lb.	(equivalent to 392*s.* o*d.* per cwt.)
Fine yellow lake (aluminium hydroxide base)	1*s.* 10*d.* per lb.	(equivalent to 205*s.* 4*d.* per cwt.)
Brown pink (aluminium hydroxide base)	1*s.* 10*d.* per lb.	(equivalent to 205*s.* 4*d.* per cwt.)
New yellow (base of 'Dutch lead')	4*d.* per lb.	(equivalent to 37*s.* 4*d.* per cwt.)
Satin yellow (satin white base)	3¼*d.* per lb.	(equivalent to 30*s.* 4*d.* per cwt.)
Dutch pink No. 1 (chalk base)		22*s.* 6*d.* per cwt.
Dutch pink No. 2 (base of chalk and 'Dutch lead')		18*s.* o*d.* per cwt.
English pink (chalk base)		10*s.* 8*d.* per cwt.

(Berger MSS., 1831 formula book, pp. 63, 65, 67, 69, 71, 139, 141, 143.)

of Dutch pink in which he suggested the use of a mixture of dyes extracted from one part of barberry with two of yellow berries.[5] Being a substantive dye, however, barberry would not combine with alum to form a proper lake and would have remained in the form of dyestuff particles.

Fustic

Dyes extracted from two distinct species share the name fustic, that from the West Indian and South American tree *Chlorophora tinctoria* (formerly known as *Morus tinctoria*), which grows also in India, being distinguished as *old fustic*; while that from another West Indian tree, flourishing too in southern Europe and the Levant, *Rhus cotinus*, is referred to as *young fustic*. The former species contains the dyes *morin* and *maclurin* (also known as *moric* and *morintannic acids*), and the latter *fustin* (otherwise called *fisetin*). James Smith referred simply to the use of 'fustic' in the manufacture of brown pink;[6] but formulae specifically employing old fustic for the preparation of Dutch pink and English pink appear in 1813 and 1815 in the Berger archive (although its use here was soon superseded by that of other dyes). In the Berger papers, reference is often made to the dyestuff as 'Wood' or 'Old Wood', a reference to 'Old Wood (Fustic)' in 1813 making the identification clear; while, to corroborate this, a slightly later formula in which old fustic is listed amongst the ingredients calls in the description of the method to be adopted for the 'Wood' to be boiled.[7] The alternative name 'yellow Brazil wood' has been used in the present century.[8]

Quercitron bark

Quercitrin and *quercetin* are present in varying degrees in the bark of oak trees. They are contained to an exceptional extent in the American species *Quercus velutina* (known formerly as *Q. tinctoria*), first imported by Edward Bancroft, who was responsible for the name quercitron, during the last quarter of the eighteenth century, and occur also in *Q. citrinia*, *Q. digitata*, *Q. nigra*, and *Q. trifida*. Bancroft's activities have been discussed by Dr Harley, but his letters patent allowing him sole rights for extraction of the dye expired in 1798,[9] and it is not surprising, especially bearing in mind its economy in use, to find Lewis Berger and his successors using oak bark in many formulae for yellow lakes from 1807 onwards. There seem, however, to have been a wide range of qualities, and in 1823, for example, careful distinction was made between 'Common Querc^{n} Bark', which cost 5*s*. per cwt., and 'Fine Bark' at 18*s*.[10] Elsewhere, reference was made simply to 'Quercitron Bark', 'Bark', 'Fine Bark', 'Fine Querc^{n} Bark', 'Common Bark', or 'Oak Bark'; but on one occasion the use of fine bark for a bright yellow lake was noted, with a direction that common bark should be used for a darker colour.[11] Since no alteration in the quantities was specified (while in the first example mentioned it was still necessary to use 2 cwt. of the fine bark in place of $2\frac{1}{2}$ cwt. common bark) it seems likely that it was the quality of the dye which could be extracted rather than the quantity which determined the grade.

Saffron

The stigmas of the autumn crocus, *Crocus sativus*, contain the substantive dyes *crocin* and *crocetin*. Use of saffron in the production of coloured lacquer is mentioned by Stalker & Parker, here as a substitute for turmeric;[12] but the dye was often confused with the latter (*safran des Indes*) or with the red dye from safflower (*safran bâtard*). Extraction of the colouring matter with water, followed by digestion in alcohol was described by Ure.[13]

Turmeric

The substantive dye *curcumin*, soluble in water and alcohol, is obtained from the root of the far eastern plant *Curcuma tinctoria*. It was mentioned in connection with pigment production by Dossie, who suggested the employment of one part to four parts of French berries in the preparation of Dutch pink;[14] but as a substantive dye it would not have combined with alum to form a lake in the usual way. Stalker & Parker, and also Vanherman, referred to its use in coloured lacquers;[15] while Watin described the use of *terra merita* in staining parquet, giving the alternative names *Curcuma longa* and *saffran des Indes*.[16] *Terra merita* was one of the two yellow dyestuffs listed by Rondelet, who indicated its cost as 2fr.25 per pound.[17]

Weld

The yellow dye *luteolin* may be extracted from the leaves and stems of the European plant *Reseda luteola*. It seems to have been regarded as the least fugitive of the yellow dyes available,[18] and Tingry (whose text was incorrectly translated into English, 'woad' being substituted for 'weld') mentioned it was used for the best pigments.[19] It was employed extensively by Lewis Berger's firm during the first three decades of the nineteenth century in the production of yellow lakes, and it certainly appears to have been reserved for use in special varieties such as Dutch mineral and satin yellow, and for the expensive qualities intended for fine-art purposes. It is difficult to obtain a clear idea of the size of Berger's stocks, since these were reckoned by the 'load' and 'bundle'; but these increased steeply during the first decade of the nineteenth century: starting at only £8 worth in 1802, in 1806 he valued these at over £100, and in 1810 the figure stood at £216.[20]

Yellow berries

A yellow dye known as *rhamnetin* may be extracted from the unripe berries of many species of *Rhamnus*, the English variety of which, known commonly as buckthorn, is *R. frangula*. It is clear, however, that berries from foreign sources enjoyed considerable use, and were imported particularly from France and the eastern Mediterranean. Dossie, for example, referred to French berries as being used in the preparation of Dutch pink and light pink, and James Smith in the production of brown pink.[21] In France the berries of *R. alaternus* and *R. infectorius* were known as *graine d'Avignon*. Watin described them as from 'un arbrisseau nommé petit *noir-prun*' and added, 'il faut la choisir sèche, assez grosse, & bien nourrie', although Tingry indicated that the term was applied to the berries when they were green;[22] while Rondelet listed *graine d'Avignon* at 2fr.50 per pound.[23] In contrast to the absence of French ochres from his early nineteenth-century stock-lists, Lewis Berger had stocks of French berries increasing from just over $\frac{1}{4}$ cwt. in 1802 to 4 cwt. in 1806 and over 11 cwt. in 1810 valued at diminishing rates of 70*s*., 30*s*., and 28*s*. per cwt. respectively;[24] while in 1817 the firm used French berries in a formula for brown pink.[25] Although the majority of the formulae refer simply to 'Berries', and occasionally to 'fine Berries' or 'fresh Berries', other specific varieties called for included 'Turkey Berries' and 'Persian Berries'. The former, possibly *R. sacatalis* from Smyrna (now İzmir) or Aleppo, were used in 1789 and 1816 in the manufacture of Dutch pink and in formulae of about 1815 for brown pink;[26] and were valued at £6 6*s*. per cwt. in 1810 when Berger's stock stood at nearly 26$\frac{1}{2}$ cwt.[27] Turkey berries also seem to have been used in 1834 in the manufacture of 'Dark Com.ⁿ Italian Pink',[28] but had apparently been superseded by French berries in the preparation of brown pink, presumably since, as a note referring to the formula of 1817 already mentioned indicates, they were too yellow in colour. Persian berries may also be identified with *R. sacatalis*, but in addition with *R. amygdalinus* and *R. oleiodes*, and were employed by the firm in 1820 and 1831 in the making of Italian pink; while in the latter year they were used also for a variety of Dutch pink.[29] The extent to which imported as against native berries were used in commercial pigment manufacture during the period considered in this book is not, however, clear; but the valuation of the 25$\frac{1}{4}$ cwt. of 'Berries' Berger had in stock in 1802 at 100*s*. per cwt. and the total of just over 15$\frac{1}{2}$ cwt. 'Fine' and 'Com.ⁿ' berries he possessed in 1806, both at £7, do not suggest that even if the unqualified term represented non-imported dyestuff it had any advantage in price.[30]

ORGANIC YELLOW PIGMENTS

Having briefly considered the yellow dyestuffs employed for pigment manufacture, attention may be turned to the pigments themselves, commencing with the cheaper varieties, often known as yellow pink, Dutch pink, and English pink. As already mentioned, these were commonly prepared by mordanting the dye on chalk, although other bases were in use; while aluminium hydroxide was reserved for more expensive pigments such as Italian pink.

Yellow pink and Dutch pink

The names *yellow pink* and *Dutch pink* are linked by Stalker & Parker, who indicated that 'Yellow or Dutch Pink' might be purchased ready ground into oil at 3*d*. per ounce.[31] Such pigments were evidently in sufficiently common use in the 1670s to warrant the inclusion of 'Pink-Yellow' among those listed by John Smith in the first edition of his book. It was, he indicated, 'a good light Yellow, a little inclining to a green', and he commented also that it was 'a Colour that grinds very easie, and bears a good body', illustrating its use in mixing grass-green oil paint.[32]

The mid-eighteenth-century writer Robert Dossie gave a formula for the preparation of Dutch pink from French berries and turmeric root on a chalk base, indicating that white lead was sometimes used instead;[33] and Watin gave a similar chalk-based formula for the manufacture of *stil de grain* by adsorption of the dye extracted from *graine d'Avignon*. It could, he remarked, be ground in both distemper and oil, instancing its use in both media in mixing *vert de composition*.[34] Tingry, in the translation of whose work the term Dutch pink is consistently used as the equivalent of Watin's *stil de grain*, gave a series of similar recipes for its preparation. In the first of these, weld was used as the dye, while the last was particularly designed for white lead in oil and employed a base of two parts of white lead to one of chalk. He too commented that the pigment was much used in house-painting in both oil and distemper, and repeated Watin's formula for mixing 'compound green' for the decoration of rooms in oil.[35]

The formulae employed by Lewis Berger, who was making Dutch pink from Turkey berries by 1789, were broadly comparable, although the range of dyestuffs utilised by his sons was more extensive than the species of *Rhamnus* so far mentioned, and included old fustic and quercitron bark.[36] For a similar pigment, which they called *new yellow*, weld (the dye from which, as already mentioned, enjoyed a reputation for greater lightfastness than those from other sources) was employed.[37] Both Dutch pink and new yellow were formed on a base of 'Dutch lead' which seems, however, unlikely to have contained any white lead;[38] and it seems uncertain, therefore, that formulae based on white lead, such as those suggested by Dossie and Tingry, were in commercial production. In addition, in 1815 the firm was making a yellow lake from weld on a base of patent yellow, calling the pigment *Dutch mineral*;[39] but this seems to have been discontinued by 1831, as had other varieties of Dutch pink made between 1818 and 1826 incorporating a proportion of orange lead.[40] Manufacture of new yellow, on the other hand, continued beyond that date, and its superior nature was reflected in the cost of production, which in 1831 was equivalent to 37*s*. 4*d*. per cwt. against those of the two more ordinary grades of Dutch pink at 22*s*. 6*d*. and 18*s*.[41]

The prices at which Lewis Berger's stocks of Dutch mineral, new yellow, and Dutch pink were valued during the first decade of the nineteenth century are generally remarkably consistent, the first at 84*s*. or 90*s*. per cwt., the second at the equivalent of 56*s*. or 65*s*. 4*d*. per cwt., and the last at 26*s*. or 27*s*. (In addition, however, he had in 1802 a small stock of 'Fine Dutch Pink' valued at 45*s*. per cwt., together with a rather larger quantity of 'Secᵈ' new yellow valued at a rate equivalent to 28*s*.) In 1802 his stocks of ordinary Dutch pink stood at nearly 22 cwt., rising to nearly 57 cwt. in 1806, and in 1810 were almost 29 cwt.[42] Over the same period his stocks of new yellow rose from about 4$\frac{1}{2}$ cwt. in 1802 to nearly 7 cwt. in 1806, and to just over 14$\frac{1}{2}$ cwt. in 1810;[43] while those of Dutch mineral in the same years stood respectively at just over 5 cwt., nearly 11 cwt., and nearly 22 cwt.[44] Curiously, the price at which he was offering Dutch pink for sale in 1779 and 1780 was considerably higher than those so far mentioned, this being consistently 84*s*. per cwt., although it had fallen to 75*s*. in 1788.[45] Perhaps the most likely explanation for this dramatic reduction in price by the 1800s is that by then, as already indicated, Berger had commenced manufacture of the pigment himself and was no longer merely supplying that produced by others.

Retail prices of Dutch pink at the beginning of the nineteenth century seem to have been about 8*d*. per pound, the rate at which a quantity of 9 lb. was purchased for painting at a house in Doncaster in 1802;[46] although Phillips quoted a price of 1*s*. 6*d*. per lb., which is, as usual, higher than those found elsewhere.[47] Other ingredients in the Doncaster account include glue and items whose general nature suggests that the Dutch pink was to be employed in distemper rather than oil, and it seems clear that the former was the medium in which the pigment enjoyed most common use. Dossie, indeed, observed that the pigment did not work well in oil, also drawing attention to its fugitive nature, and indicated that its principal use was for 'common purposes' in water.[48] Thus, in the early nineteenth century, Nicholson illustrated its employment in the preparation of straw-coloured distemper;[49] Pincot retailed a proprietary watercolour for the decoration of rooms under the name Dutch pink;[50] and Whittock noted that Dutch pink was used only in distemper.[51] Nevertheless, in his revised edition of John Smith's book, Butcher suggested the use of Dutch pink to make a fine yellow oil paint (albeit with the suggestion that patent yellow was preferable);[52] and, bearing in mind its use in oil greens by Smith and Watin, it seems clear the pigment enjoyed at least some use in oil also, although experiment suggests that its staining power in this medium was limited.

English pink and light pink

Besides Dutch pink, Stalker & Parker also mentioned *English pink*, which, Dossie remarked, was a lighter and coarser variety of the same pigment containing a greater proportion of chalk.[53] Although Dossie distinguished two varieties of *light pink*, one of which was made as a true aluminium hydroxide lake, the other was, he indicated, like Dutch pink but with much less colour;[54] and, writing some years later, the author of the *Practical Treatise* used the two names as synonyms, observing that English pink was sometimes termed light pink.[55] Martin and Nicholson also treated the two as one and the same, applying to both Dossie's description of English pink as a pigment inferior to Dutch pink;[56] while Tingry's editor too remarked on the comparatively poor quality of English pink.[57]

Confirmation of this already clear evidence for its relation to Dutch pink is provided by the formulae and prices in the records of Lewis Berger's company. The formulations contained in the surviving documents show that English pink was invariably made on a base of whiting, dyes mentioned including old fustic and quercitron bark; although, since the first formulae do not appear before about 1815 (the date at which these dyestuffs superseded the use of yellow berries in the manufacture of Dutch pink), there is no reason why the latter should not have been employed for several years before.[58] By way of comparison with the cost prices of Dutch pink (which, as already mentioned, were the equivalent of 22*s*. 6*d*. and 18*s*.) in 1831 English pink was costed out at 10*s*. 8*d*. per cwt.;[59] and its sale price in earlier years consistently bore more or less the same relationship to that of Dutch pink. Thus, during the late eighteenth century Berger was offering the pigment at prices ranging from 35*s*. to 42*s*. per cwt.,[60] and in the early nineteenth century valued his stock at prices between 14*s*. and 20*s*. per cwt. In 1802 he possessed a quantity in excess of 35 cwt., and in 1806 nearly $23\frac{1}{2}$ cwt.; but although by 1810 this had fallen further to a figure just less than 7 cwt. the quantities nevertheless suggest strongly that the pigment was one in common use.[61] As with Dutch pink, Pincot retailed a watercolour taking its name from English pink, and this too reflected the price difference between the qualities, being sold at half that of the former.[62] Although Butcher mentioned the use of both English and Dutch pink in oil,[63] the limits on employment of the latter in this medium have been mentioned above, and it seems most likely, especially in view of its inferior staining power, that use of English pink would almost invariably have been confined to distemper.

Satin yellow

By the end of the first decade of the nineteenth century Lewis Berger was producing a lake pigment which he called *satin yellow*. This was made on a base of satin white, and it seems most likely that it too was a special formulation for use in wallpaper manufacture. The earliest formula in the Berger archive (for 'Yellow Sattin') is dated 1809 and employed weld with either quercitron bark or yellow berries, while a later formula of 1815 made use of weld with old fustic. In 1831, however, weld alone was used, the cost price of the pigment being $3\frac{1}{4}$*d*. per pound (equivalent to 30*s*. 4*d*. per cwt.).[64]

Italian pink and other more expensive yellow lakes

True yellow lakes, that is those made by the direct precipitation of aluminium hydroxide from solutions of alum and an alkali in the presence of the dissolved dying agent, were known during the second half of the seventeenth century and described by Antonio Neri.[65] Although Lewis Berger was manufacturing yellow drop lakes from 1793, the method of preparation at that date is slightly obscure; but by 1803 it is apparent this was to employ weld as the source of dye, a base of previously prepared aluminium hydroxide (which he called lake white),[66] and an alum mordant with a small addition of sugar of lead. At this date he used *Rhamnus* berries in the preparation of Italian pink (fig. 4, p. 27); but by about 1815 all the ingredients were similar to those for the earlier of his yellow lakes, although formulae of that date for 'common' yellow lake pigments employed quercitron bark. The system of precipitating the white separately from the mordanting of the dye continued beyond 1831 in the case of the Italian pink, but was replaced by its preparation *in situ* for the yellow lakes from 1824. From 1820 Persian berries were used for Italian pink, while in 1831 bark was used to provide the dye for other yellow lakes, providing an illustration of the interchangeability of the dyestuffs which were in use.[67]

Pigments on an aluminium hydroxide base were extremely transparent and also expensive, the price of the yellow lake offered by Berger in 1780, for example, being 12*s.* per pound, that is sixteen times the price of Dutch pink in the same lists, and over thirty times that of English pink.[68] By the opening of the nineteenth century, prices of such yellow lakes had fallen in parallel with those of Dutch and English pink, although the proportional differences were maintained. Thus in 1802, 1806, and 1810 Berger valued his stocks of yellow lake and Italian pink at rates from 5*s.* to 7*s.* per pound, and their comparative rarity is reflected in the smallness of his combined stocks of both pigments which stood at 68 lb., 11½ lb., and just over 64½ lb. in the same years respectively.[69] Their higher price is seen too in the production formulae of 1831 in which 'Fine Yellow Lake' is shown as costing 1*s.* 10*d.* per lb. to produce, and Italian pink 3*s.* 6*d.*[70] In view of their consistently high price and the apparent absence of references to true yellow lakes in connection with house-painting by writers on the subject, it seems clear that these are unlikely to have been used ordinarily for such purposes, although yellow lake is mentioned in connection with a sample of rosewood graining executed at the Royal Pavilion, Brighton, in 1802, and it thus seems probable that they found occasional employment in high quality decorative work of this nature.[71]

Brown pink

A variety of yellow lake of brown colour was in use by artists of the second half of the seventeenth century. Stalker & Parker referred to it as 'Brown or glasing-Pink', remarking that it was very dear and that 'the bigness of a Nutmeg grinded will stand you in 6d.'; and Dossie observed that it was generally very fugitive and on that account much discused, although, he believed, it had been of better quality in the past.[72] Formulae in the Berger papers (fig. 4, p. 27) reveal that it was made during the early nineteenth century in the same way as his yellow lakes of contemporary date, in that the dye, here obtained from *Rhamnus* berries, was adsorbed onto a base of aluminium hydroxide, this time in the presence of pearl ash. The mordant, however, was ferrous sulphate rather than alum, and this was undoubtedly the constituent responsible for the brown colouration. In 1819 the firm's practice was to use berries which had first been employed to make Dutch pink, but from that date quercitron bark was substituted and the aluminium hydroxide was formed *in situ.* The same method continued in use until after 1831, when the cost of production was 1*s.* 10*d.* per pound, the same as that of fine yellow lake.[73] During the first decade of the century, Berger valued his stocks at prices in some cases equivalent to those of yellow lake, and on other occasions roughly double these. In 1802, for example, he had an extremely small stock of only 4¾ lb. valued at 10*s.* per lb., and by 1806 still had only 42 lb., this time priced at 5*s.* per lb. In 1810 he had just over 7 lb. at the same price together with 6¼ lb. at 13*s.*[74] This last was singled out as 'Brandrams', and (like Newman, to whom Berger was supplying both brown pink and a yellow lake, which he called 'Spanish yellow', similar to Italian pink),[75] Brandram was an artists' colourman. Like yellow lake, therefore, especially bearing in mind both its cost and the small stocks held by Berger, it is unlikely that brown pink would have found any use for the general purposes of house-painting; although the pigment is included in the rather dubious lists of Martin and Nicholson (copied from Dossie's book),[76] and is listed also by Rondelet and Phillips, the latter quoting rates of 14*s.* to 19*s.* 2*d.* per lb. for its purchase in 1812 and much the same in 1821.[77] However, Soane purchased 2 oz. for 6*d.* in 1803 along with other house-painting pigments,[78] and it seems just possible, therefore, that the pigment may have enjoyed limited use in such decorative work as graining for which its transparency would have commended it, although it was not mentioned by Whittock in his list of pigments for decorative painting.[79]

Orange lake

Both Martin and Nicholson included orange lake in their lists of pigments copied wholesale from Dossie, who put the pigment, made from annatto, forward as one of his own invention.[80] Although Lewis Berger also appears to have made a batch of orange lake in 1796, the details of its formulation are not clear, and it does not seem to have become one which he made regularly.[81] In 1802 he had a tiny stock of 6¼ lb. valued at 8*s.* per lb.,[82] and it is clear that, even if available for artists' use, such a pigment is extremely unlikely to have been used for house-painting.

CHAPTER 6

INORGANIC RED PIGMENTS

In many ways the seventeenth and eighteenth centuries were extremely fortunate in the group of three red mineral pigments which they inherited from the middle ages, especially when these are compared with the yellows considered above. Red ochres corresponded closely with yellow ochres as cheap and extremely stable (though dull) pigments, working well in oil or water; and again a range of qualities and degrees of transparency were available which could be applied to more or less specialised purposes. In contrast with the unsatisfactory nature of all the bright inorganic yellows, the bright reds, vermilion and red lead, gave reasonably satisfactory service; and although much more expensive than the cheaper varieties of red ochre (vermilion particularly so) it was often only necessary to employ the organic reds to modify their tone rather than as alternatives in their own right. Although of slightly orange colour, on account of its comparatively economical price red lead tended to be used in distemper, while vermilion was reserved for oil.

RED AND BROWN OCHRES, NATURAL AND ARTIFICIAL

Red ochres occur naturally in the form of *haematite*, or may be obtained by roasting yellow ochres. They may also be manufactured artificially. Their colour, which can vary widely from dark purple to red, orange, or brown, is owed in all cases to the presence of ferric oxide in its anhydrous form, and this may compose anything from below ten to over ninety per cent of the pigment. Red ochres from all three sources were used ubiquitously in house-painting; and terminology is confused, since the names of distinctive naturally-obtained pigments such as 'Venetian red' came quite early on to be applied to others, and in the case of 'Indian red' were even used for varieties of markedly different colour. It is, therefore, often difficult to be certain as to whether a natural or an artificial pigment is implied in any particular instance.

Natural red oxides

Red ochres occur extensively in the British Isles, many from the iron mines in the Forest of Dean, Gloucestershire, having been particularly noted for the high quantity and purity of the ferric oxide they contained. The late seventeenth-century writer Henry Powle, for example, mentioned the ochre of the Forest;[1] and, writing in the mid-eighteenth century, Hill mentioned that he had visited the pits and talked to the workmen, who informed him that the ochre they dug up was sent to London to be sold as '*Indian* red'. 'On comparing it with some of the true *Persian* Kind, which I had from the *East-Indies*,' Hill recorded, 'I find it of a paler Colour, but of a much finer Texture'.[2] Specimens at the Institute of Geological Sciences, London, show that a range of colours from dark purple to orange in hue have been obtained from the Forest, and include a sample of bright scarlet 'vermilion' ochre from the Highmeadow Mine near Coleford. Noël Heaton particularly mentions the *Crawshay red* from this area, indicating that it contained up to 98 per cent of ferric oxide and a remarkable freedom from grit combined with a fine colour.[3] The I.G.S. samples from the St Annal's Mine show that this was a bright orange red similar to that of the Highmeadow specimen.[4] On the other hand, since the term 'Spanish brown' (which as will be shown below was generally applied to inferior pigments) is known to have been used in connection with ochre from the Forest of Dean during the early seventeenth century, it seems likely that much of the pigment obtained from this area in earlier times may have been of less high quality.

Hill had also visited pits in Derbyshire and Staffordshire which were 'peculiarly worked for this Substance', but although the ochre was good, it was, he said, much inferior in all respects to that from the Forest of Dean.[5] Witney, Oxfordshire, too seems to have been a source of lower-grade pigment, which was referred to by Waller as *reddle*;[6] and Tingry's later editor mentioned the Mendips as presenting a plentiful supply of red ochre.[7] This also would probably have been less brilliant than that from the Forest of Dean, since Heaton observed of the red ochres from Bristol and the West of England that they are generally of low grade and often brownish in tone, an observation true at least for the specimens at the I.G.S. from Wick, Gloucestershire (now Avon), and Winford, Somerset.[8] Heaton also mentions Cumberland oxide, but describes it as unsuitable for paint manufacture, having a tendency to separate on standing;[9] while Hurst provided an analysis of a sample from Ulverston, Lancashire (now in Cumbria);[10] and there are in addition samples at the I.G.S. from Westmorland (also now part of Cumbria), Rutland (now part of Leicestershire), and Co. Antrim.[11]

True *Indian red* came from the island of Hormus in the Persian Gulf, and was described by Dossie as having a hue inclining to purple, a quality certainly possessed by the specimen from the Gulf at the I.G.S.[12] However, as already mentioned, Hill described the substitution of ochre from the Forest of Dean, a practice still current at the end of the nineteenth century;[13] and Dossie observed that the true pigment was rarely to be found since it had been supplanted by an artificial oxide. Although in *The New Practical Builder* Nicholson merely repeated Dossie's comment that the natural pigment was scarce, a decade later in the new edition of *The Builder's and Workman's New Director*, which he published in 1834, he omitted the statement, indicating instead that Indian red was an extremely useful pigment imported from the East Indies.[14] It is possible, therefore, that supplies were again becoming available at an economical price; but Nicholson cannot really be regarded as a reliable authority, for this; and, although Lewis Berger had a stock of 3 lb. 'Indian Red' in 1806 (none in 1802 or 1810), this appears to have been valued at the equivalent of over £50 per cwt., making it seem likely that he was applying the term to another substance, perhaps Indian lac dye.[15]

Another natural red ochre well known, at least by name, during the eighteenth century was *Venetian red*, which Mrs Merrifield indicated in 1849 came from the vicinity of Verona.[16] Heaton describes pigment from this source as having a pale and rather orange shade;[17] while Dossie defined the pigment in the first instance as a native red ochre inclining to scarlet rather than crimson, and hence similar to artificial Indian red but 'fouler'. On the other hand, he suggested, a substitute was easily prepared by mixture of an ordinary red ochre with one of artificial preparation;[18] and such mixtures were probably commonly sold, since John Martin, for example, noted at the beginning of the eighteenth century that he had used a mixture of light red and brown red in painting the ground of the clock dial-board at Watford Church, Hertfordshire, which, he added 'M.[r] Jo: Glover of Watford calls Venetian-Red'.[19]

A third foreign source making its contribution to English terminology was Spain, where the Malaga district provides an excellent source of fine grades of pigment.[20] However, although in the first edition of his book John Smith described *Spanish brown* as being of Spanish origin,[21] the term had been applied to English pigment for at least half a century. Letters patent granted in 1626 referred to the 'Ocker digged in the fforeste of Deane called Spanishe Browne';[22] and it is interesting that Smith omitted the suggestion from the second and subsequent editions of his text. It seems fairly clear, in fact, that the term (found as early as 1619–20 in the Exchequer rolls)[23] was generally applied to British pigment of natural origin; and (although John Atkinson, whose artificial pigments are discussed below, named one of them 'Spanish brown' in his patent of 1794)[24] Dossie, Whittock, and Tingry's later editor consistently referred to Spanish brown as a naturally occurring pigment, the first describing it as a native red earth similar to 'Venetian red' but fouler, obtained from several parts of England, and the last mentioning that it was plentiful in the West of England.[25] It may be concluded, therefore, that, while the term *English brown* is also occasionally encountered, *Spanish brown* was the name generally in use for low-grade, usually natural, red ochres, often from British sources. Their poorer quality is reflected in the prices discussed below at which they were sold, together with those of 6*s*. and 6*s*. 6*d*. per cwt. at which in 1806 Berger valued his stocks of lump and powdered 'Eng.[h] Brown Oker' respectively (which totalled nearly 107 cwt.).[26] In connection with such pigments of poor colour it may also be noted that Dossie treated the term *brown red* as synonymous with Spanish brown, although Stalker & Parker had applied the name to a pigment made by calcining *brown ochre*, which Dossie indicated was a pigment of a warm brown or foul orange colour.[27]

Completing this survey of native ochres significant during the period under consideration, Watin and Tingry naturally referred to the French sources in Berry and the Auvergne;[28] but it is not clear that red pigments from these areas were necessarily imported into England. Farther afield, it is possible that Turkey or Cyprus supplied a limited amount of pigment, since Berger had a smallish stock of nearly $1\frac{1}{4}$ cwt. 'Turkey Red' in 1802;[29] and although by the end of the nineteenth century Hurst mentioned the name only in connection with a variety of artificial red oxide, Church, writing a few years before, had remarked on Cappodocia as one of the sources of native red ochre in classical times.[30] This part of the world also gave its name to the soft red ochre much used in gilding and known as *Armenian bole*; but the mid-eighteenth-century translator of Theophrastus' work on geology, John Hill, indicated that at that date common reddle was often sold under the name.[31] Hill also mentioned a red ochre which had been obtained from New Jersey in North America and used both in painting and medicine. Known as 'Blood-stone' it was obtained, he said, from a depth of fifteen to twenty feet, but by the time he was writing was 'disused, and not known in the Shops'.[32] Subsequently, Tingry's later editor referred to ochre from the Magdalen Islands in the Gulf of St Lawrence, adding that pigment from this source had been sold in auction at 3*d*. per pound, a price putting it slightly above those of the better grades used in ordinary house-painting.[33]

Red ochres from the calcination of yellow ochre

Waller included *burnt ochre* in his table of pigments, describing its production from yellow ochre by roasting it over an open fire;[34] and Hill mentioned that this practice of burning yellow ochre to produce red pigment was in his time much employed among the people who dealt in colours.[35] Reynolds too seems to have regarded it as an everyday practice, and Dossie indicated that *red ochre* was commonly Oxford ochre calcined, a statement repeated by Martin, Nicholson, and Whittock;[36] while Watin also described the *ocre rouge* commonly sold as being made red by calcination.[37] Stalker & Parker and Dossie also mentioned *light red*; which the latter defined as a light red ochre of a scarlet cast manufactured by the calcination of yellow ochre to the desired degree, giving *light ochre* as a synonym. As already noted, however, he regarded *brown red* as being the same as the naturally occurring pigment 'Spanish brown', although Stalker & Parker had described it as burnt from brown ochre.[38] It is not possible, of course, to make the generalisation that the terms *light red* and *red ochre* stood exclusively for pigments prepared by roasting yellow ochres, but it seems, nevertheless, that this was often the case during the seventeenth and eighteenth centuries. Hence it is difficult to assess the degree to which such pigments were used in preference to those of virgin natural origin; but it is clear that some varieties at least could be far more costly than the latter, and the two certainly identifiable pigments of this nature which Berger had in stock during the early years of the nineteenth century were both extremely expensive. Furthermore, of these, 'Burnt Stone Oker' appears only in his 1802 list,[39] when he had a mere two pounds in stock valued at a rate equivalent to 168*s.* per cwt. (over fifty times the price of his Spanish brown), the same as the valuation given for his stocks of 'Burnt Terre de Sienna'.

During the period under review, *burnt sienna* was clearly regarded as a very special pigment produced by roasting the yellow earth occurring naturally at Siena in Italy. It was mentioned by Dossie, and listed by Rondelet at a price of 7fr. per pound, that is thirty-five times the price of the cheapest red oxide.[40] Lewis Berger's stock in 1802 was a mere 3 lb., although by 1806 this had increased to just over 2 cwt. at a price equivalent to 224*s.* per cwt.; but both stock and price had fallen back in 1810 to 16 lb. and the equivalent of 112*s.* respectively.[41] Despite its expense, it had a particular use in house-painting, since on account of its transparency in oil it was valuable in the preparation of graining glazes. Butcher, Whittock, Vanherman, and Nicholson all mentioned its use in this way, and it seems most likely that it was for such an application that in 1803 Soane purchased a total of five ounces, some ready ground in oil at rates equivalent to 672*s.* and 896*s.* per cwt.[42] No such special character, however, would have been possessed by ordinary grades of ochre prepared by calcination, and the extent of their use accordingly remains obscure.

Artificially manufactured red ochres

The preparation of red ferric oxide by roasting ferrous sulphate was known at least by the end of the sixteenth century, when 'burnt Vitrioll' was mentioned in Haydocke's translation of Lomazzo.[43] This reaction was widely used by the eighteenth century for the industrial preparation of sulphuric acid, which distilled over from the heated iron compound, the iron oxide being left as a residue in the retort. Dossie described the method as that used for the manufacture of *scarlet ochre*, giving a related procedure for preparing 'common Indian red'. This latter pigment had, he said, by its cheapness prevented the import of the true Indian red for a long time: 'So that the true teint of the original kind, being in some measure forgotten, this has been gradually made to vary from it, till it is in fact a quite different colour.' Accordingly, he described it as verging on a scarlet hue, while the true Indian red tended to be purplish in colour.[44] The author of the *Practical Treatise* also indicated that the common 'Indian red' was the washed and dried residue left after the manufacture of sulphuric acid by the distillation of ferrous sulphate, but mentioned that the colour could be varied from red to purplish.[45] By far the fullest description of the process was given by the French author Watin. *Rouge brun* or *brun rouge d'Angleterre* was, he said, made at Deptford, near Greenwich, seven miles from London,

> en calcinent les feux de la couperose dans un fourneau de réverbere, & les remuant continuellement jusqu'à rougeur parfaite: on les lave pour enlever l'acrimonie vitriolique; quand elles sont seches, on les met dans un cofre où sont enfermées deux boules de fer. Le coffre est suspendu; en l'agitant, le coffre fait rouler les boules, que réduisent, en deux heurs, trois cent livres de couleur rouge en poudre impalpable.[46]

The location of the factory at Deptford is no doubt related to the manufacture of copperas which had been carried on there at least since the second half of the seventeenth century, and was described by David Colwall in the *Philosophical Transactions* in 1678.[47] Possible evidence for production of pigment too at this time is provided by the Italian painter Andrea Pozzo, who observed in the description of materials used for fresco painting appended to the second part of his *Perspectiva* published at Rome in 1700 that 'Rossetto d'Inghilterra' could be used instead of burnt vitriol, since it was itself 'of the nature of vitriol'.[48] Details of the process for pigment manufacture were repeated by Tingry and Ure, the latter indicating that the *English red* thus prepared was much in demand in France.[49] Rondelet gave the price of *rouge brun d'Angleterre* as 30c. per pound against 20c. for ordinary *ocre rouge*; while *rouge de Prusse*, which was described by Watin (who was uncertain as to whether it was made by the calcination of copperas or yellow ochre) as a brighter and more lively pigment, was 45c.[50] Tingry, however, indicated unequivocally that it belonged to the former class, prepared from ferrous sulphate.[51]

By the end of the eighteenth century, artificially prepared pigments of this nature were known under many other names. John Atkinson's patent of 1794 describes the manufacture of 'Venetian red' and 'colcothar vitriol' by calcination of ferric residues, the former having been subjected to eight hours in a reverberatory furnace, and the latter sixteen. Atkinson's 'Spanish brown' was a similar pigment made by calcining the same residues with a native yellow ochre.[52] The 'Venetian red' (and presumably the other two) were produced in cake form, and it is possible, therefore, that Lewis Berger's stocks of 'Cake Venetian' during the early nineteenth century represented such an artificial pigment rather than a native ochre, since pigments including English brown and Spanish brown appear in his stock-lists in 'lump' rather than 'cake' form.[53] The 'purple oxide of iron' which, Tingry's later editor remarked, was commonly called *purple brown* was also prepared artificially by Atkinson, who produced more than one shade of this name. To produce 'Chocolate purple brown' his patent specification called for 'the slime of sulphurous copper ore' (which no doubt contained a significant percentage of iron sulphide) to be calcined for eight hours in a reverberatory furnace; while 'Blue purple or dark purple brown' required a preliminary roasting in the same way for six hours, following which it was ground and again calcined for sixteen hours.[54] There is no reason, however, why such darker shades of iron oxide should not have been produced in previous years by roasting ordinary red or yellow native ochres; and, as in the case of 'Spanish brown' and 'Venetian' red, Atkinson again seems to have taken over the name of a pigment already in use. Lewis Berger, for example, was offering purple brown for sale in 1788; and the real significance of methods of manufacture such as those of Atkinson may lie in the cheapening of better grades of pigment. Thus, although Berger was quoting 36*s.* and 42*s.* for the supply of purple brown in 1788, by the early nineteenth century he was valuing his stocks at only 12*s.* or 12*s.* 6*d.* per cwt. These, moreover, rose from a mere 7 cwt. in 1802 to just over $33\frac{1}{2}$ cwt. in 1806, and by 1810 stood at just over 224 cwt. indicating that there was considerable demand for such dark oxides once available at an economical price.[55]

The applications of red ochres in house-painting

Red ochres are one of the most reliable pigments known, and work well in both oil and water. They were, moreover, generally extremely cheap compared with many others in use during the eighteenth century, and naturally took their place among the group of six basic pigments that the London plasterers were permitted to use under the 1603 Act of Parliament.[56] They were sold either dry or ground into oil, Lewis Berger, as will be seen from the analysis of prices below, having stocks of both Spanish brown and Venetian red in paste or powder form; but although terminology is confusing, so that it is difficult to be certain whether these pigments were of natural origin or artificial manufacture, it is possible to draw a number of conclusions as to the place each occupied in house-painting.

As indicated above, *Spanish brown* is universally mentioned as the cheapest variety of the pigment, and was probably most often of native type. John Smith remarked on its universal application in priming timber on account of its cheapness and ability to dry reasonably quickly while allowing the oil to penetrate into the fibres, adding that it received the colours to be superimposed well, and described it as a dull, dark red of a horse-flesh colour.[57] The same application was described in more detail by Leyburn, and Dossie too mentioned Spanish brown as being much used for grounds and coarse work by house-painters.[58] At the beginning of the nineteenth century, in his *Hints for the Preservation of Wood-Work exposed to the Weather* (1808), James Crease remarked that although Spanish brown provided the cheapest finish, 'it is not deemed a pleasant colour', recommending that the pigment should not be used on its own and suggesting instead the use of chocolate-brown paint in which it was, of course, often a constituent.[59] Vanherman gave formulae employing Spanish brown for the preparation of both red and chocolate-colour paints for external use, indicating that its price was 8*s.* or 16*s.* per cwt.,[60] which may be compared with the figures of between 5*s.* and 5*s.* 9*d.* at which Lewis Berger valued his stocks of lump and powder pigment during the first decade of the nineteenth century. These totalled nearly 43 cwt. in 1802, just over 197 cwt. in 1806, and just over $73\frac{1}{4}$ cwt. in 1810,[61] together with just over 2 cwt., 1 cwt., and just over $3\frac{1}{2}$ cwt. in paste form in these three years respectively (valued at between 18*s.* and 20*s.* per cwt.).[62] Both the size of his stock and its availability in paste form show that the pigment was one in common use.

Although Reynolds suggested its employment in a red paint for use externally,[63] *Venetian red* seems ordinarily to have been preferred for interior work. Vanherman suggested its use in the production of a 'dark blotting-paper colour' for a picture gallery, mixed with white and a little lamp black, and recommended its employment as a ground for crimson. It was, he observed, 'a sure standing colour, and very useful, as, with white and black, vermillion and ochre, it produces an infinity of tints, particularly of the drab kind, which are always admired, for their solid appearance and quiet tone.'[64] Dossie mentioned Venetian red in connection with graining, and Whittock also suggested its extensive use for this and for marbling.[65] Again Berger possessed large stocks in both cake and powder form totalling just over 139 cwt. in 1802, over 170 cwt. in 1806, and nearly $76\frac{1}{2}$ cwt. in 1810, the prices at which these were valued ranging from 13*s.* 6*d.* to 15*s.* 9*d.* per cwt.;[66] while in addition in 1802 he had nearly 4 cwt., and in 1810 $3\frac{1}{2}$ cwt. in ground form valued at 36*s.* per cwt.[67] It seems, therefore, as one would expect, to have been rather more expensive than Spanish brown; but qualities of both probably varied between quite wide limits, and Phillips listed it in 1812 at only $8\frac{1}{2}$*d.* per lb. against the latter at 8*d.*, while in 1802 Soane had been charged at a uniform rate equivalent to 56*s.* per cwt. for both 'Span.[h] Brown' and 'Gro[d] Venetian Red'.[68] The same rate had been charged for the supply of 'fenesion red' at Tredegar House in 1793.[69]

Indian red ochre, on the other hand, does not seem to appear in Berger's stock-lists for 1802, 1806, or 1810, so that its relative cost is difficult to assess; but as already mentioned Dossie referred to the use of an artificial variety in connection with house-painting, and Nicholson suggested the use of 'India red' in the preparation of red, chocolate, pearl, and flesh-coloured paint.[70] It is probable, however, that the ordinary varieties sold under the name would have been placed among the better qualities of pigment used for house-painting; and Reynolds suggested its use in graining (for painting the veins in the imitation of red cedar), while Whittock made very extensive use of 'Indian red' in both graining and marbling.[71] The prices given by Phillips in 1812 and 1821 suggest respectively that common varieties of Indian red sold retail at 1*s.* 10*d.* or 1*s.* per lb. (one-and-a-half or two-and-a-half times those he gave for 'Venetian red'), while the 'best sort' cost 8*s.* 5*d.*;[72] but his lists are often unreliable, and the true position thus remains obscure.

Against this, both Berger (as already mentioned) and Phillips, who priced it at 3*s.* 8*d.* per lb.,[73] indicated clearly that *burnt sienna* was a much more costly pigment than the ordinary grades of red ochre. Thus, although Nicholson suggested its use in mixing 'Fine yellow fawn colour' in oil, and for fawn distemper,[74] its expense would surely have precluded its ordinary use in this way; and it would undoubtedly have been reserved for the finer decorative operations such as graining and marbling.

RED AND ORANGE LEAD

Red lead was used as a pigment in antiquity and throughout the middle ages. Although regarded until comparatively recently as a mixture of the monoxide and dioxide of lead, it is now considered to be a compound of formula Pb_3O_4.[75] Vitruvius described its manufacture by roasting white lead,[76] but by the second half of the seventeenth century ordinary red lead was generally prepared by roasting litharge. John Smith provided a précis of the description published by John Ray, a contemporary Fellow of the Royal Society, who gave details first of the preliminary conversion of metallic lead to litharge. This was ground through coarse and fine stones in a mill, washed, and placed in a reverberatory furnace for two or three days during which it was kept continually stirred with an iron rake until it had attained the correct colour, described by Smith as a 'fine pale Red'.[77] Writing in the middle of the eighteenth century, Campbell noted that red lead was made at Whitechapel, among other places, and Richard Watson recorded in his *Chemical Essays* that it was produced also in Derbyshire and at Holywell in Flintshire (now part of Clwyd).[78]

As a pigment of moderate price, red lead seems to have enjoyed a wide variety of applications throughout the period under consideration, and was employed both in oil and in distemper, although, as Cennini had warned, it could not be used in true fresco since it rapidly discoloured.[79] It was one of the six basic pigments that the London plasterers were permitted to use 'mingled with size' under the 1603 Act of Parliament, and its employment in an aqueous medium was mentioned by both Dossie and Watin;[80] while even in the late 1820s Whittock remarked that it was sometimes used in this way.[81] In oil, however, there seems always to have been a marked reluctance to use red lead as a tinting pigment in finishes, possibly on account of the reputation Dossie and Whittock seem to suggest it had for blackening in this medium.[82] Indeed, the former remarked quite explicitly that on account of its tendency to blacken in oil the pigment was not much used except for very gross purposes; and although experiment with a modern sample has suggested that in oil red lead was in fact one of the more stable pigments among those in use for house-painting during the eighteenth century, it is possible that the earlier product was less satisfactory in this respect. Another reason for its apparent unpopularity may be contained in John Smith's observation that the pigment was difficult to grind, since it tended to be hard and sandy, a second drawback absent in the modern substance;[83] while Vanherman drew attention to its tendency to separate out from an oil medium, observing that it 'adheres so strong to the bottom of the paint-pot, that it proves a troublesome task to liberate it and bring it into a working condition again'.[84]

In other respects, however, red lead had many valuable attributes, John Smith remarking on its opacity in oil and its quick-drying properties.[85] On account of the latter it was undoubtedly one of the most important driers in use, both in the treatment of oils and as a direct additive in primings, undercoats, and dark colours, and also in formulae for knotting, all of which are discussed in Chapters 10, 15, and 16. Moreover, at least by the end of the period being considered, its protective qualities in the prevention of rust seem to have been appreciated, since Nicholson recommended its use with only a small admixture of white lead for the first coat on external ironwork, and in the mid-nineteenth century Alfred Bartholomew specified three coats of 'red lead paint' for the same purpose.[86] On account of its opacity red lead was a natural choice in providing a suitable undercoat or 'ground' for vermilion, a much more expensive pigment, although Dossie warned against this practice.[87] Nevertheless, it seems to have been common, and was mentioned by Tingry in particular connection with buffets; but red lead was, perhaps, used most extensively in coach-painting for both the body and the wheels in the ways described by Pincot and Vanherman respectively.[88] Red lead was also a favourite adulterant for vermilion, a practice discussed in connection with that pigment below; but perhaps found its greatest employment in house-painting in grounds for graining. Reynolds, for example, recommended the use of red lead in the undercoats for 'red cedar color',[89] while Vanherman observed that red lead was seldom used in house-painting except as a ground for the imitation of mahogany.[90]

Nevertheless, it seems clear that red lead was used occasionally as a straightforward tinting pigment in finishes; although, until the growth in the early nineteenth century of a fashion for walls decorated in Pompeian red, the limited extent to which bright red or orange paint was employed in interiors must be borne in mind. Thus Watin observed of red that it was not commonly used in interior decoration, and of red lead in particular (which he included in a list of dangerous pigments to be used as little as possible) remarked picturesquely that it gave 'les couleurs d'enfer dans les décorations'.[91] Tingry, on the other hand, noted employment of the pigment in coach- and house-painting to compose beautiful reds, and it was listed in a house-painting context alongside vermilion and other reds by Reynolds and Nicholson, the former mentioning it specifically in connection with interior decoration while suggesting also its combination with Spanish brown to produce a red paint for exterior applications.[92] Besides this, he advocated its use with yellow ochre to mix orange paint for exteriors;[93] while John Smith had recommended a similar combination to make brick colour. Nicholson too suggested its use with yellow to produce an orange, although neither English author indicated whether he had an interior or exterior context in mind.[94] Otherwise, the only further suggestion encountered for employment of red lead in tinting an interior finish is that provided by Tingry, who recommended a small addition of the pigment in the preparation of buff (for which Watin had used vermilion, and in mixing which William Butcher employed either vermilion or orange lead).[95]

Orange lead, which was used also by Butcher in preparing the ground for the imitation of mahogany,[96] seems to have been a slightly different form of red lead, although contemporary details are obscure. Clearly, however, it was a more expensive product, since Rondelet gave the price of *mine orange* as 1fr.25 per pound against 80c. for *faux minium ou mine rouge*;[97] and a similar relationship is found in the prices at which Berger valued his stocks. Thus, in 1802 red lead was priced at 26*s*. per cwt. against 48*s*. for orange lead, while in 1806 and 1810 the proportional differences were maintained between 38*s*. and 60*s*. and between 36*s*. and 58*s*. respectively. It is also interesting to note that in the same years Berger had always considerably less red lead than orange lead in stock, the figures for 1802, for example, being just over $7\frac{3}{4}$ cwt. and nearly 60 cwt. respectively; while in 1806 he had 6 cwt. of red lead against nearly 17 cwt. of orange lead, and in 1810 merely about $4\frac{1}{4}$ cwt. of the first against nearly 63 cwt. of the latter. (In addition in 1802 he had a small stock of 11 lb. 'Washd Orange Lead' valued at a rate equivalent to 84*s.* per cwt.)[98] At the end of the nineteenth century, Hurst described orange lead as made by roasting white lead rather than litharge, an interesting return to the method of manufacture practised in classical times. The product was, he indicated, rather paler in colour than ordinary red lead and also lighter in weight, but otherwise identical in its properties and used for very similar purposes.[99]

Altogether, therefore, it seems clear that the principal use for red or orange lead in house-painting was as a drier or in undercoats. Although it had certain uses in oil, mostly in mixing oranges, for red finishes and other tinting applications in this medium it was regarded as considerably inferior to vermilion, an attitude perhaps best expressed by Vanherman who indicated that it was employed on waggon or cart wheels, while vermilion was used on those of coaches.[100] This relationship is reflected too in the expense of the latter pigment against red lead, which seems to have retailed at prices varying from 4*d.* per pound in the 1630s, to 5*d.* at the beginning of the eighteenth century, and $4\frac{1}{2}$*d.* at the beginning of the nineteenth, although the more expensive variety, orange lead, was then available.[101] Probably, however, it was more extensively used in distemper, particularly perhaps as a substitute for vermilion in the preparation of pinks by admixture with the cheaper varieties of red lake, a possibility discussed at greater length in Chapter 21.

VERMILION

Vermilion (mercuric sulphide) occurs naturally as the mineral *cinnabar.* Ure described the chief European beds as being at Almaden, near Cordova in Spain, and at Idria in upper Carinthia (now Idrija in western Slovenia, Yugoslavia, 23 miles west of Ljubljana).[102] However, although natural pigment has been used since classical times, and Leuchs suggests the continuing production of small quantities in the 1820s,[103] it was being prepared artificially well before the period here being considered. Mediaeval methods of manufacture are touched on by Dr Harley; and it is notable that, while Watin mentioned the natural *cinnabre* and Rondelet listed it at a price of 10fr. 20 per pound against 6fr. for *vermillon,* no English author has so far been noted who referred specifically to the natural pigment in connection with house-painting.[104] Indeed, Hill observed: 'The purer native Cinnabar has been used to be much esteemed . . . but our factitious kind equalling it in Beauty, and being much cheaper, has banished it from among the Painters.'[105]

Many authors, including both John Smith and Dossie, described the manufacture of vermilion by the 'dry' method in which mercury is added to molten sulphur to produce on cooling a mass of black mercuric sulphide known as 'Ethiops'.[106] This was then crushed and sublimed to produce the red form of the sulphide, or vermilion, which can vary from orange to bluish red in tone depending on its physical structure, notably the size and shape of the particles.[107]

Manufacture of the pigment needs great care if a good colour is to be obtained, and the principal sources of vermilion in eighteenth-century England were Holland and China. Pigment was being made in Amsterdam in the seventeenth century,[108] and a full description of Brand's works outside the Utrecht gate of that city was published in 1790. This shows that the sublimed pigment was ground in water between horizontal stones and sieved before sale.[109] The method used for manufacture of vermilion in China, on the other hand, appears to have been shrouded in mystery until as late as 1883, but was then shown to be similar to that used in Holland, the difference in quality being owed to the greater care taken by the Chinese.[110] By research into eighteenth-century customs ledgers, Dr Harley has been able to show that Dutch vermilion was imported regularly and in increasing amounts in the eighteenth century, these reaching a peak in 1760, after which greater quantities were purchased from China (whence supplies had occasionally been obtained earlier) and Germany.[111] Nevertheless, in the early nineteenth century the Swiss author Tingry still noted that the pigment was chiefly produced in Holland;[112] but Nicholson observed that the best was imported from China, and that Dutch vermilion was an imitation.[113] Samples of both Chinese and Dutch pigment are contained in the notebooks of the London colourman George Field dating from the early nineteenth century, the former having a purplish cast, and the latter a brighter tone.[114] Lewis Berger had employed Chinese vermilion in the 1780s as a base for cochineal lakes,[115] and Vanherman too expressed a preference for pigment 'if genuine' from this source.[116]

Adulteration of the pigment with red lead seems to have been common, warnings of this being given by Dossie, Butcher, Whittock, and Vanherman;[117] and it was probably this practice which led to Watin's condemnation of 'vermillon d'Angleterre'.[118] Whether pigment was being manufactured in Britain at this time, or simply re-exported, is unclear, and it seems significant that no English manufacturies were listed by Leuchs in the 1820s;[119] but by 1825 the Berger company was experimenting with preparation of the pigment by the dry process, when notes were made on milling requirements for dark and pale varieties,[120] and production had clearly commenced by 1831 when the pigment cost 2*s.* $3\frac{1}{2}$*d.* per pound to prepare.[121]

The latter figure relates well to information concerning cost of the pigment from other sources. This suggests that the retail price (in common with others, about twice that the Berger manuscripts note for manufacture) remained fairly stable from the late seventeenth well into the nineteenth century. Stalker & Parker, for example, listed vermilion at the equivalent of 5*s.* 4*d.* per pound,[122] and Berger was offering the pigment for sale during the 1780s at prices between 5*s.* and 5*s.* 6*d.*[123] His stocks during the first decade of the nineteenth century were fairly modest, amounting to 27 lb. in 1802, and by 1810 stood at only 157 lb.; while in 1806 he had 17 lb. of 'Deep Vermillion' in stock. These were valued at rates ranging from 4*s.* 5*d.* to 5*s.* 4*d.* per pound.[124] However, although Berger held stocks of Chinese vermilion, it is difficult to evaluate the cost and extent of these, since they were recorded by the 'packet';[125] but the prices given in *Crosby's Builders' New*

Price Book (while as usual rather higher than those encountered elsewhere) suggest that the oriental 'Chinese' product at 12*s.* per lb. may have been sold retail at about one third to one half above that charged for the European or 'English' at 8*s.* 5*d.*[126] This seems to be confirmed by the prices of 7*s.* 6*d.* per pound for 'Chinease Vermillion' quoted in a costed lake formula of 1787 contained in the Berger archive.[127]

Although the method was known in the late seventeenth century,[128] it was not until the end of the eighteenth that Konstantin Kirchoff published his influential report on the alternative 'wet' process for the manufacture of vermilion, which was eventually to supersede the 'dry' process so far described. In its early form, this still entailed producing the black sulphide or 'Ethiops' by grinding mercury with flowers of sulphur; but, instead of subliming it, a warm aqueous solution of caustic potash (potassium hydroxide) was added, and grinding continued. Gradually, the colour became brown, and then rapidly red. The vermilion produced was washed several times in a dilute solution of more caustic potash, and finally with water.[129] It appears, however, that this was not very successful commercially, and it was superseded by a further method in which the pigment was produced directly from metallic mercury by reaction with potassium pentasulphide. Hurst reported one such method, the Firmenich process, which had been published in 1862;[130] and Zerr & Rübenkamp described the Döbereiner process as having quickly superseded the method of Kirchoff.[131] It was, perhaps, to such a development that Ure's editor referred in 1860, commenting that Kirchoff's process was so greatly improved as to furnish a vermilion whose brilliancy equalled that of the Chinese.[132] In terms of British manufacturing practice, it is of interest that a transcription of Kirchoff's process taken from published sources appears in one of the Berger experimental notebooks in 1830,[133] although Armitage indicates the firm did not abandon the dry process until after some time after 1853, when free trade laws led to German competition.[134]

During the period under consideration, vermilion seems generally to have been purchased in powder form, since it was priced in this category by Stalker & Parker, and Tingry's later editor recommended it as best to grind it in oil oneself, possibly because, as Vanherman pointed out, it is apt to 'fatten' or settle on standing.[135] No doubt also it was easier to detect sophistication in the dry pigment. Although it can be used in water,[136] it seems likely that in distemper its place was generally taken by the much cheaper red lead. In oil, however, vermilion clearly enjoyed extensive employment, although Nicholson described it as too expensive for common use,[137] and Pincot remarked that 'Vermillion' was an extravagant colour costing an extra 8*d.* per square yard above that of ordinary paint.[138]

In the seventeenth century, John Smith, probably thinking in terms of clock dial-boards rather than panelling or other domestic joinery, ranged vermilion alongside smalt and lake as providing 'the most glorious Ground of all others for Gold';[139] while, in the early nineteenth, Tingry illustrated its employment (in varnish) for the painting of buffets.[140] Reynolds and Nicholson too included it among pigments which could be used for making red paint, and Pincot referred to its use in carriage painting.[141] Although in the eighteenth century it seems likely that use of such bright reds was generally confined by prevailing tastes to comparatively limited areas, by the opening decades of the nineteenth vermilion clearly found at least occasional employment on large expanses of wall. It was used, for example, in combination with an extender and a small quantity of black to produce a deep red on the walls in John Soane's Study at 13 Lincoln's Inn Fields, London;[142] and it seems likely that the 'scarlet' walls in the Dining Room at Eaton Hall, Cheshire, may have been produced by a comparable formulation.[143] In this connection it is notable that Vanherman, who observed that vermilion was a most useful and extremely beautiful colour, but powerful and to be used with caution, noted that it 'adds brilliancy to all other reds', and suggested its employment with lake to make a bright scarlet, or with rose pink to make a crimson colour which he recommended for libraries.[144]

More generally, throughout the period being considered, vermilion was used in mixing pinks and other tints. For the former, it was often used with an organic red, the combination of a delicately transparent but fugitive lake with the more stable, opaque vermilion having obvious advantages both aesthetic and technical; and in this connection it is of significance to recall that vermilion was employed by Berger as a base for red lakes. Such a mixture was recommended, for example, by John Smith, who advocated the use of vermilion with lake and white lead to mix a flesh colour;[145] while Watin suggested its combination with carmine and white lead to make *couleur de rose*,[146] and a comparable formulation was proposed by Nicholson for apricot and peach colours.[147] As suggested by Vanherman, vermilion could also be used with yellows to tint white to buff or orange:[148] Watin, for example, recommended its employment with Naples yellow in *chamois*;[149] and Butcher noted its combination with stone ochre in fawn.[150] Combinations with blue were, moreover, suggested by the author of the *Painter's . . . Pocket Manual*, who mixed violet in this way,[151] and by Butcher, who, among other alternatives, noted the use of vermilion with Prussian blue to mix French grey.[152]

Vermilion was used also in graining and marbling. Both Reynolds and Whittock recommended its employment in preparing grounds for the imitation of various timbers, the latter making extensive use of it both for this and to a more limited extent in marbling, and employing it both for grounds and for the superimposed glazes.[153] Altogether, it is clear that vermilion occupied an important position in better-quality interior work in oil, although it was probably rarely used in distemper.

CHAPTER 7

ORGANIC RED PIGMENTS AND DYESTUFFS

In many ways the position occupied by the organic reds corresponds with that of the organic yellows discussed in Chapter 5. Thus the cheap qualities enjoyed widespread use in distemper, although they were liable to similarly rapid fading on exposure to light; while the transparency of the more expensive grades, which were rather more lightfast, made them useful for graining. There was, however, one important factor which led, despite their expense, to a further role for the higher-grade lakes, since, while red lead and vermilion provided good bright stable colours (in a way not paralleled during most of the period under consideration by the inorganic yellows) they were of a rather orange hue for many applications. The red lakes were accordingly used to modify this by lending them a more purple cast, and are often to be found in formulae for the mixing of high-quality pinks in oil. They were also sufficiently stable to be used in deeper reds and lilacs, and were a common constituent of colours such as French grey, where only small quantities were needed. The methods used for the preparation of organic red pigments were generally comparable with those described in the case of the yellows, and similar white bases were employed, although vermilion was sometimes also pressed into service. However, whereas the yellow dyes seem to have been regarded as interchangeable, different red pigments were in general related much more specifically to particular dyestuffs, possibly on account of the wider variations in cost between them which were reflected in the end product. As with the yellow lakes, the dyes themselves are first briefly discussed; and again, for convenience, an example used to stain parquet is included.

RED DYESTUFFS

The dyes used for lake-making fall into three main classes: those produced by several species of scale insect, including, most importantly, carmine from cochineal; those extracted from various dyewoods, notably brasil wood; and finally that present in the root of the madder plant.

Carmine and related insect dyes

Red dyes of related type are produced by the females of three varieties of scale insect: kermes, *Kermes vermilio* Planch., native to southern Europe; the lac insect, *Laccifer lacca* Kerr (formerly known as *Coccus laccae*), native to India and neighbouring countries; and the American cochineal beetle, *Dactylopius coccus* Costa (formerly known as *Coccus cacti* L.).[1] Although the dye, principally *kermesic acid*, extracted from kermes, which lives on the kermes or scarlet oak, *Quercus coccifera* L., was widely used during the middle ages, it is the weakest of the three, and seems to have become more or less obsolete by the beginning of the seventeenth century.[2] Lac dye from India was, however, still in use at this date, but was rapidly superseded by that from cochineal. The red dye, principally *laccaic acid*, is present in the ovarian fluid of the female insects, who become trapped in the sticky exudation of lac resin with which they surround themselves on the twigs of the host tree (which may be one of a number of species). Cultivation today concentrates on the resin, used to manufacture shellac, and the dye is run to waste after it has been washed out of the lac, which is broken from the branches and granulated for the purpose. Formerly, however, the dye was precipitated from the washing water with lime to form a coarse powder which contained about ten per cent of the colouring matter,[3] a process possibly carried out in England on occasion, since Dr Harley observes that considerable quantities of unrefined 'stick lac' were imported during the eighteenth century.[4] In the case of cochineal the dye, *carminic acid*, is extracted directly from the bodies of the killed and dried insects which live on cactus plants; and cochineal, which was being imported by Spain during the sixteenth century,[5] was priced at 35*s*. per pound in an early seventeenth-century English manuscript.[6] This is remarkably similar to the rates of between 27*s*. and 35*s*. at which Lewis Berger valued his stocks during the first decade of the nineteenth century, which amounted to 225 lb. in 1802, nearly 505 lb. in 1806, and 421 lb. in 1810.[7]

Brasil and logwood

Markedly fugitive dyes, purplish red in alkaline conditions, are contained in trees of the genus *Caesalpinia* native to South America and the West Indies, and may be extracted by boiling the timbers in water. That from the latter source is known generally as *sapan wood* and is inferior to that from the former which has been known by a large number of names, but most generally as *brasil wood* (a name derived from the Latin *rosa*, rather than from the country, Brazil).[8] Even by the mid-nineteenth century the different species to which the names were applied had not been completely rationalised, and in earlier years the timbers were often known by their place of origin, or by the names of places from which apparently similar material had been obtained. In the first half of the seventeenth century Sir Theodore Turquet de Mayerne, a Genevan physician resident in London, noted the use of Pernambuco brasil in the preparation of 'Rosette';[9] and during the early nineteenth century, as will be shown, the Berger firm was using 'Nicaragua wood', which was also referred to as 'Cutt wood', for making rose pink (q.v.). Timber under the former name, used notably in the making of violin and cello bows, is generally identified today with *C. echinata*, although Ure suggested *C. brasiletto*, which, he indicated, was little inferior to the first species of brasil he mentioned, *C. crista*, and had been especially abundant in the West Indies. However, on account of its slightly cheaper price than the latter, demand for it had been, he said, so great that nearly all the trees in the British possessions were cut down and the timber was consequently scarce on the English market. He was, on the other hand, uncertain even over the genus to which 'Nicaragua wood' belonged, suggesting that it might be a species of *Haematoxylon*, and commented that, going also under the names 'Peach wood' or 'Santa Martha wood' it yielded an inferior quantity, though better colour, of dye.[10]

Trees of the genus *Haematoxylon*, for example *H. brasiletto*, may yield a dye of similar colour to that of the brasil woods already described; but that obtained from other species of this genus, such as the South American *H. campecheanum*, otherwise known as *logwood* or *Campeachy wood*, and obtained, Ure remarked, from the bay of the latter name, is bluish purple in colour in alkaline conditions and similarly fugitive. (Both red and purple extracts are indicator dyes, and turn yellow in acids.) This species, Ure recorded, had been grown in Jamaica since 1715;[11] but although its importation into England, which had been prohibited in 1581,[12] was again permitted on repeal of the statute by a second Act of Parliament in 1662,[13] no references to its use in connection with the preparation of a pigment for house-painting have been encountered. Its employment was, therefore, probably restricted to fabric dyeing and similar purposes. Nevertheless, Berger had a stock of 50 tons of 'Logwood' in 1806, valued at £17 per ton;[14] and at the end of the nineteenth century, Hurst published a number of formulae for violet lakes calling for its use.[15]

Returning to the species yielding red dyes, Berger also held stocks of both 'Cut Wood' and 'Braziletto Wood'. Each almost certainly falls within this category, the former on account of the applications to which it is assigned in his pigment formulae (one of which for rose pink refers to it as 'Cut Nic Wood') and the latter on account of its name. Interestingly, the Nicaragua 'Cut' wood commanded a marginally higher price, since his stocks of 2 cwt. in 1806 were valued at the equivalent of £31 per ton, while he had 3 tons of the 'Braziletto' valued at £28 per ton. The prices of these timbers, however, seem to have been subject to considerable fluctuations, since by 1810 he was valuing his tock of 13 cwt. of the former at the equivalent of only £15 10*s*. per ton, and 8¼ tons of the latter at £12 10*s*.[16] Since the two rates moved together, maintaining the same proportional relationship, it seems more likely that the fluctuations in price were connected with market conditions than with variations in the quality of the timber; and it is possible, therefore, that these reflect the difference noted some years later by Ure (to which reference has already been made) between material from the mainland and that from the British possessions in the West Indies. Whatever the truth of this, though, the price seems to have stabilised at the lower figures, and 14*s*. per cwt. for 'Nicaragua wood' is recorded in a costed formula of 1831, again for rose pink.[17]

Madder

The roots of *Rubia tinctorum* and related species yield *purpurin* and *alizarin*, and the plants were cultivated extensively in Europe and the Levant for use in the dyeing industry. The major source of madder during the whole of the period under consideration seems to have been Holland. Depending on the care taken in the process and in the selection of the madder, the colour of the dye extracted may vary from purple to brown, the better qualities coming from the central fibres of the root only. This was known as *crop madder*; and cold water was used for extraction in order to avoid contamination of the more brilliant fractions by browner elements which are progressively more soluble as the temperature is increased. The dyes from madder are much faster to light than any of those so far described, being much prized on that account; and the development of the madder industry has been fully discussed by Dr Harley.[18] In 1806 Berger had a stock of nearly 192 cwt. of madder valued at 65*s*. per cwt.; and in 1840 the firm was using 'best crop Madder' at 1*s*. per lb. for lake-making.[19]

Orchill and Litmus

The indicator dye from this source, red in acid and blue in alkali, has been dealt with above in the section on blue pigments.

Safflower

The petals of *Carthamus tinctoria* yield two dyes, one yellow and the other red. Ure indicated that the latter only was of use, and was extracted by the application of sodium carbonate once the yellow dye had been washed out of the petals by simple solution in water.[20] Tingry's later editor observed that the dye from *Carthamus* was used in the cosmetic called 'Spanish vermilion';[21] and Watin mentioned that it was used for staining parquet. He referred to it as *safran bâtard*, observing that druggists called it *safranum*; and on this account especial care is necessary to avoid confusion with both true saffron and with turmeric (*safran des Indes*) which have been discussed above. The best dye, Watin believed, came from the Levant, although it was, he said, grown also in Alsace and Provence.[22]

ORGANIC RED PIGMENTS

Indian lake

Turning now to the pigments prepared from the dyestuffs listed above, the only specific reference to Indian lake is that by John Smith in the 1687 edition of his book. Although the text relating to this remained otherwise almost exactly the same, it was amended from the third edition of 1701 onwards to refer simply to 'Lake', an indication, no doubt, that lac dye had been generally superseded by cochineal.[23] He described the pigment as,

> the best of all dark Reds, being a most pure Crimson; 'tis a Colour that will grind very fine, and lies with a good Body, but there must be good store of pains taken with it in the grinding, for if it be not well and throughly ground, its Colour will want much of its glory; and besides this, 'twill work with some difficulty, so that 'twill be apt to cling up together, after 'tis laid on, just as you see warm Water do upon a greazy Trencher, when washed in it; . . . of this colour there be divers sorts at the Colour-Shops, very different in their Colours, some being of a more dead and pale Colour; . . . the best sorts come from *Venice* and *Florence*.[24]

Carmine and carminated lakes

Lake pigments made from cochineal were apparently known in England at least by the early seventeenth century under the name 'Lake of spayne'.[25] The dye precipitated from the imported insects, known as *carmine*, was an extremely expensive commodity. It was prepared by boiling the pulverised beetles in water and treating the decoction, which was filtered off, with various precipitating agents or mordants such as alum (potassium aluminium sulphate), cream of tartar (potassium hydrogen tartrate), borax (sodium borate), or tin salts (either stannous chloride or stannous nitrate). The resulting liquid was allowed to stand, often for a period of some days, in order to allow the carmine to settle out. The use of different salts in this way, either singly or in combination, allows the colour of the pigment to be varied; while Dossie referred to carmine as cochineal dye 'brighted with aqua fortis' (nitric acid).[26] The formulae of Lewis Berger, which commence in 1787, show him using various combinations of the substances listed above; and reveal also that from the start in many instances he was forming the dye in the presence of vermilion,[27] a practice to which reference was made by nineteenth-century writers.[28] Varieties containing this were produced more cheaply, the pure grades of carmine in the firm's 1831 range, for example, costing 6*s.* 5*d.* and 5*s.* 1*d.* per ounce to manufacture, against 2*s.* 8*d.* and 1*s.* 3*d.* for those containing vermilion.[29] Between 1778 and 1780 Berger was offering different qualities of carmine for sale at prices from 10*s.* to 24*s.* per ounce; and during the early nineteenth century, when he valued his stocks in 1802, 1806, and 1810, for example, at prices ranging from 14*s.* 3*d.* to 2*s.* per ounce, these were proportionately small, in none of these years rising above a total of 18 pounds.[30] One would not, perhaps, expect to find such an expensive pigment used in house-painting; but nevertheless, Watin remarked: 'Nous l'employens quelquefois dans les décorations, pour, dans les couleurs vigoureuses, soutenir la laque'.[31] Clearly, however, this must be regarded as unrepresentative of ordinary practice.

For more general use, cochineal was used to prepare aluminium hydroxide lakes, which were often known as *carminated lakes*. The late seventeenth-century writer, Richard Waller (who mentioned also the obsolete dye from kermes and the obsolescent dye from lac), described the preparation of red lakes in this way;[32] and Watin distinguished between *laques fines* made using the same method, and *laques ordinaires* which were made with chalk, usually using the inferior dyewoods.[33] In the former category he included both *laque de Venise* and *laque de Florence*, to which, it will be remembered, John Smith had also drawn attention as of the best quality. Dossie too referred to both aluminium hydroxide and chalk-based pigments as lakes;[34] and, since the unqualified term was clearly, therefore, not exclusive to the former, it must be approached with a degree of caution in the interpretation of recipes for the mixing of paint colours. Various grades of lake were made, some from the coloured liquor left over from the production of carmine, and others from 're-cycled' dye extracted from red rags; and Dossie, for example, said of lake that in former times it had no doubt been made from lac, but by his time was seldom prepared from anything other than cochineal, brasil wood, or scarlet rags.[35] To extract the dye from the latter, it was only necessary to boil them in a solution of an alkali such as potassium carbonate, a procedure described by Tingry.[36]

Although it is possible to prepare an aluminium hydroxide lake by the simple addition of a solution of potassium carbonate to that of the alum and dye, Ure observed that this produced a poor colour in the case of cochineal, and for this reason freshly precipitated aluminium hydroxide was added to the dye bath, a method used, he indicated, in other instances where the affinity of the dye for this base was strong.[37] It is of particular note, therefore, that this was the procedure followed by the Berger firm, who prepared such a 'Lake White' from alum and pearl ash.[38] Interestingly, too, Ure observed that the colour of lakes made from cochineal on a bright day was better than that of those made in dull conditions, perhaps explaining the excuse offered by Lewis Berger in a letter of 10 March 1785 that lake production had been held up by severe weather.[39]

The development of Berger's lake production followed closely that already described in the case of carmine, and the firm made a range of drop and other lakes, many of which contained vermilion.[40] In 1831 the range contained ten varieties of drop lake, production costs lying between 26*s.* and 12*s.* 10*d.* per lb. for varieties (which are identified by letters such as 'L', 'LL', or 'SB') free from vermilion, and between 15*s.* 7*d.* and 4*s.* 6*d.* for those in which it was used (numbered 2 to 8). Wet lakes (presumably kept in a damp state like the varieties of Prussian blue intended for use in distemper), some of which again contained vermilion, were cheaper to produce at between 2*s.* 2*d.* and 9*d.* per lb.; while rose lake, which although a true aluminium hydroxide lake also contained barytes, cost 2*s.* per lb. to manufacture. In addition the firm was producing a range of three purple lakes at costs running between 6*s.* 8*d.* and 8*s.* 8*d.* per lb.[41]

Although considerably cheaper than carmine, it may be seen, therefore, that even the more modestly priced grades of wet lake were still moderately expensive pigments for house-painting purposes. Between 1779 and 1780 Berger was offering drop lakes at prices from £5 to

20*s.* per lb. and wet lakes from 6*s.* to 2*s.* As with carmine, his early nineteenth-century stocks reflected their high prices, and, valued in 1802, 1806, and 1810 at rates from 73*s.* 6*d.* to 10*s.* per lb., these did not rise in any of these years above 218 lb. in total.[42] Hence, although Butcher and Nicholson indicated that lakes were used in mixing red paint,[43] and Laxton included 'lake colours' in the most expensive group for which he gave prices,[44] Vanherman observed that lake was expensive and not much used in house-painting except for apartments of the first order. Nevertheless, he indicated, it harmonised with Prussian blue to provide a variety of beautiful purples and with chrome yellow to provide brilliant oranges of various gradations, the former use being mentioned also by Nicholson.[45] Undoubtedly, however, its primary employment in house-painting would have been in the production of pinks and such tints as lavender or French grey, where only small quantities were required to produce the desired blush; and cochineal has recently been identified as the colourant in the lake used in mixing a pink in one of the panels of the ceiling of the Drawing Room from Lansdowne House, designed by Robert Adam in 1766.[46] Tingry, Nicholson, Butcher, and Vanherman all mentioned the use of lake in this or similar ways.[47] Being transparent in oil, it was also used to a considerable extent as a glazing pigment in graining and marbling; and Vanherman suggested its employment in connection with the finishing touches in the imitation of mahogany,[48] while Whittock too relied on red lake, drop lake, and crimson lake in both grounds and glazes.[49]

Rose pink and cheaper varieties of lake

The cheaper varieties of organic red pigment, generally known as *rose pink*, were made by the same process as the cheap organic yellows, by adsorption of the dye onto chalk. In general the dye used was that from timbers such as brasil rather than cochineal, and although Whittock did suggest the use of the latter as an alternative, the more authoritative authors, Dossie and Tingry referred only to the use of dyewoods (which could, as they also mentioned, be used to make true aluminium hydroxide lakes).[50] Formulae for rose pink appear in the Berger papers from 1805, made from 'Cutt Wood', 'Cut Nic Wood', or 'Nicaragua wood', the liquor extracted from which was in all cases mordanted onto chalk by the agency of alum; and in 1831 the pigment cost 24*s.* per cwt. to manufacture.[51] From 1779 to 1788 Berger had been offering rose pink for sale at prices between 63*s.* and 84*s.* per cwt., but in 1802, 1806, and 1810 he valued his stocks at prices of 42*s.*, 50*s.*, and 34*s.* per cwt. respectively.[52] The contrast between these prices and those quoted above for carmine and carminated lakes needs no emphasis; and, although in the latter two years his stocks had fallen to around 7 cwt., in 1802 he had over $35\frac{1}{2}$ cwt., indicating clearly that the cheaper product was one in fairly common use.

Apropos the term 'roset', Dr Harley has pointed out that it shares with brasil the common Latin root *rosa*,[53] and it is significant that 'Russet' (references to which occur throughout the pre-Civil-War Exchequer rolls)[54] was one of the six basic tinting materials the London plasterers were allowed to use in distemper under the 1603 Act.[55] In 1618–19, 'Brasill Cullor distempered' was used on the bearers of a close chair at Royston, Hertfordshire;[56] but the cheaper lakes based on brasil wood were not mentioned by John Smith, indicating that they were not generally used in the more expensive oil medium. This was undoubtedly owing in a large measure to the extremely poor reputation enjoyed by pigment prepared from brasil wood; and Dossie, for example, warned that it could never be expected to stand when used in either oil or water, and was seldom employed for any purpose than the coarse work of house-painting or in wallpaper.[57] Tingry's later editor also warned that it was fugitive, adding that for this reason it was stored by colourmen in damp, dark cellars;[58] but Vanherman, who noted that rose pink was a substitute for lake, while cautioning that it was to be depended upon even less than the latter, added more hopefully that he had been informed that the pigment prepared by some suppliers stood the test of time better. He was, he said, carrying out tests to check this, but the results, if ever published, are not known. Experiment has shown his caution was fully justified, but he nevertheless used rose pink in mixing lavender, crimson, and French grey for interior use.[59] Whittock, however, used rose pink to a certain extent in graining glazes, but took pains to point out that this was possible only since the end product was varnished and would thus be protected from the action of the atmosphere;[60] Nicholson too recommended its use in a glaze for the imitation of mahogany.[61] Reynolds's suggestion that rose pink could be used in red or purple paint seems, therefore, a dubious one, assuming that (as with his other formulae) he had oil in mind;[62] but Field remarked that rose pink was used in wallpaper manufacture 'and in the commonest distemper painting', and in these ways it would undoubtedly have enjoyed everyday use.[63]

Madder lakes

Although Tingry and his later editor gave a number of recipes for the preparation of madder lakes, and Vanherman too included a madder formula among those towards the end of his book, no direct reference to the use of such pigments in house-painting seems to be made.[64] The reason for this was clearly expressed by the author of the *Painter's . . . Manual* published about 1830, who observed: 'Madder being itself abundant and cheap, the costliness of madder lakes has been hitherto entirely owing to the extremely tedious and complicated methods pursued in the manufacturing of them.' In this it seems clear that he was referring to the care necessary to extract dye of sufficiently good colour from the crushed roots, but although he drew attention to recent improvements in technique, he still described madder lakes as being nearly the same in price as cochineal lakes.[65] It is most unlikely, therefore, that house-painters would have been able to take advantage of the relative permanence of madder compared with cochineal during the majority of the period under consideration, and even in 1832, when the first production formula appears in the Berger archives (the firm had been experimenting with it since at least 1816), its cost price was 11*d.* per ounce, making it doubtful that it was ever used for this purpose.[66]

CHAPTER 8

BROWN PIGMENTS

Apart from brown pink, which has been discussed above in connection with the organic yellows, and the bitumenous pigment Vandyke brown, whose uses were limited to quite specialised purposes, the only brown of importance in house-painting was the earth pigment known as umber.

UMBER, RAW AND BURNT

The naturally occurring pigment known as umber is closely related to the yellow and red ochres discussed in Chapters 4 and 6, but differs from them in containing a certain proportion of manganese dioxide. It is fairly transparent and quick-drying in oil, both in its raw state and when burnt to darken and redden the colour. Sir Roger Pratt observed that in its crude form umber was of a 'muskish' colour, but that when burnt it was almost of a liver colour.[1] Its use as a drier is discussed further in Chapter 10. The most famous source of umber is Cyprus, pigment from this area being known as *Turkey umber*, and specimens may be seen at the I.G.S.[2] It was, therefore, probably to Cyprus that John Smith referred when he described umber as being 'dug out of a certain Island in the Mediteranian Sea'.[3] His contemporary, Plot, described a number of varieties found in Oxfordshire;[4] and deposits also occur elsewhere in the British Isles, notably in Devon, the Mendip Hills, Derbyshire, and Ireland. Vanherman mentioned the use of raw Devon umber,[5] sources in this county including Ashburton (specimens from which are to be found at the I.G.S.)[6] and Milton Abbot. Both were referred to by the late nineteenth-century author George Hurst, who also mentioned umber from Veryan near Truro in Cornwall and pigment from Wales. Derbyshire umber was, he observed, rather violet-brown in hue;[7] and this source, together with Flintshire (now part of Clwyd) and the Mendips, was referred to by Nicholson, who mentioned also pigment from Co. Wexford.[8] The variety from Ireland which was to become more famous, however, was the *Cappagh brown* from Co. Cork, a sample of which is contained in Field's notebook; but the mine, which Church recorded was first opened in 1814, has now been exhausted.[9] In general, the English varieties were considered inferior to those from Cyprus, a matter expressed explicitly by Tingry's later editor, and reflected in the price differences mentioned below.[10]

General use of umber to produce dark brown colours does not seem to have been advocated in the published literature on house-painting of the period here considered, and it is likely that a mixture of red ochre and black, which would in any case have been much more opaque in oil, would have provided a cheaper way of mixing such dark tones. Nevertheless, in 1638 the Little Hall and Passage at Ham House, Surrey, were given two undercoats of 'Umber in Oylle';[11] and several rooms at Dyrham Park, Gloucestershire (now Avòn), were painted 'umber colour' in 1694.[12] In general, however, it seems likely that umber was mainly used in the tinting of warm off-white colours, and, in the early nineteenth century, for the dulling of greens. John Smith, for example, mentioned the use of burnt umber with white to mix the colour of new oak wainscot;[13] Watin mentioned its combination with white and other ochres in timber colours such as *bois de chêne* and *bois de noyer*, advice repeated by Tingry;[14] Reynolds referred to its combination with other pigments in light stone colour;[15] Nicholson used burnt umber in fine yellow fawn colour;[16] Butcher employed burnt umber in Portland stone colour;[17] and Vanherman included raw umber in several greens for both interior and exterior application, remarking also that with white it produced a number of 'pleasant quaker tints', and of burnt umber that, used in this way, it would mix warm drabs.[18] Although in some cases it is not clear whether burnt or raw umber is intended, most writers mentioned the practice of burning the pigment, and it seems certain from the above that it was frequently employed in both states.

Umber was used also in decorative work where its transparency in oil was a valuable asset, and found particular employment in graining. John Smith, Reynolds, Whittock, and Vanherman all mentioned it in the latter connection;[19] while Smith indicated in addition that it was the natural choice for shadowing gold,[20] an application of the pigment well illustrated in John Martin's account of the method used in repainting the clock dial-board at Watford Church, Hertfordshire, in 1700.[21] The pigment works well in oil or distemper, and it seems surprising that it does not appear among those the plasterers were allowed to use in the latter medium under the 1603 Act of Parliament.[22] Whittock, indeed, commented that it was useful in distemper,[23] and its employment for common purposes in this medium appears most likely.

It was, therefore, in almost all respects a widely-used pigment. Lewis Berger had fairly substantial stocks during the first decade of the nineteenth century, especially of *Turkey umber*. In 1802 these stood at just over $28\frac{1}{2}$ cwt., and although they had fallen by 1806 to only just over $5\frac{1}{2}$ cwt., by 1810 they stood at nearly 230 cwt. Against these, his stocks of *English umber* never rose in any of these years above 16¼ cwt. The prices of these pigments were liable to quite wide variations, but a clear relationship between the price of the two varieties may be discerned. During the 1780s, for example, Berger was offering Turkey umber for sale at 36*s.* per cwt. and English umber at 24*s.*; while in 1802 he valued his stocks of the former at 35*s.*, a price still close to that a decade or so earlier. By 1806, however, this had risen to 60*s.* per cwt., with English pigment at 24*s.*, but in 1810 the prices had fallen dramatically to 20*s.* and 12*s.* respectively.[24] It is therefore interesting to note that in 1828 Vanherman gave the price of raw Devon umber as the equivalent of 28*s.* per cwt.[25] In addition, Berger held much smaller stocks of burnt umber, which, while again fluctuating, always maintained a markedly greater superiority over the price of the ordinary pigment. These amounted to ½ cwt. in 1802 valued at 70*s.* per cwt., 34½ lb. in 1806 valued at a rate equivalent to 112*s.* per cwt., and 52 lb. in 1810 valued at 35*s.* per cwt.[26] Retail prices as usual seem to have been rather higher than those at which Berger valued his stocks of umber: 6 lb. were supplied at Boughton House, Northampton, in 1704 at a cost of 6*d.* per lb.; the same price was charged in 1793 for 2 lb. Turkey umber at Tredegar House, Newport, Monmouthshire (now Gwent); and Soane was charged 8*d.* for 1 lb. in 1803.[27] In addition he purchased 3 oz. of burnt umber at a rate equivalent to 2*s.* 8*d.* per lb. These prices establish a fairly clear hierarchy of grades, even if it is difficult to suggest a reason for their wide fluctuations from year to year; and it may be suggested, therefore, that unless specifically qualified as Turkey or burnt umber, it was generally the raw pigment of lower grade which was intended.

VANDYKE BROWN (CASSEL EARTH, COLOGNE EARTH)

Natural varieties of soft impure brown coal or lignite containing a certain proportion of ferric matter may be ground and prepared for use as pigment. Material from Cologne, often called *Collen's* or *Cullen's earth*, was known in England during the first half of the seventeenth century; and pigment from Cassel, often referred to from the end of the eighteenth century onwards as *Vandyke brown*, also came to be imported.[28] Lewis Berger held very small stocks of both during the early nineteenth century, having 4 lb. of the latter in 1802 valued at 1*s.* per lb. and 4¾ lb. of Cologne earth in 1806 valued at 8*d.* per lb.; while in 1810 he had 8 lb. each of Vandyke brown and Cologne earth valued at 2*s.* 6*d.* and 2*s.* per lb. respectively.[29] Apart from the slight difference in price, the practical difference between the two is not clear; but both varieties fall into the more expensive range of pigments where house-painting is concerned, and (although Whittock proposed the use of Vandyke brown in warm brown and cinnamon colour distempers)[30] use of pigments of this type seems generally to have been limited to certain specialised purposes in decorative work. John Martin, for example, described the employment of burnt umber with a little 'Cullens-earth' in shadowing certain details of the clock dial-board at Watford Church, Hertfordshire, in 1700;[31] and both Whittock and Nicholson mentioned the use of Vandyke brown in graining, the former making extensive use of it in this connection.[32] Such applications would have exploited the transparency of the pigments, and would have justified expenditure on their additional cost over the price of other browns such as umber; so that (despite the listing of Cologne earth by both Martin and Nicholson, who copied uncritically from Dossie) it seems unlikely that pigments of this type would have found much use for common purposes.[33]

BISTRE

As with Vandyke brown, inclusion of this pigment in the lists of Martin and Nicholson can be traced to Dossie, who described it as an artists' watercolour.[34] It was made, he indicated, by boiling the soot of beech wood in water, decanting the resulting liquid from the solid matter while still hot, and evaporating it to dryness. Phillips listed the pigment at prices of 7*s.* 3*d.* and 18*s.* per lb.,[35] which, even allowing for the discrepancies often encountered in the case of other pigments between the rates he mentioned and those found elsewhere, show that it was a great deal more expensive than others generally used in house-painting. It is, therefore, quite unlikely to have been used for this purpose.

ASPHALTUM

Another brown pigment used by artists, asphaltum, was listed by Martin and Nicholson, copying uncritically from Dossie.[36] References by other authors on house-painting are, however, only to its employment in japan gold sizes and varnishes, and the substance is accordingly described below in the section on materials used for this purpose.

CHAPTER 9

BLACK PIGMENTS

The black pigments in use for house-painting during the period under consideration mostly owed their colour to the presence of carbon, some being practically pure forms of the element, although naturally-occurring manganese dioxide may have been used to a limited extent. Mineral sources, however, do not seem to have been important in the context of interior work, for which, especially for dark solid shades in oil, lamp black appears to have been employed; while animal or wood charcoal blacks were used for the more delicate tints. The latter pigment had a notably bluish cast which made it especially suitable where it was desired to avoid any tendency to yellowing.

LAMP BLACK

Lamp black, as its name implies, is the soot made by burning hydrocarbons such as oil or rosin in a confined space. John Smith described it as 'Soot raised from the roseny and fat parts of Fir-Trees', adding that it came generally from 'the Northern Countrey's, as *Sweden* and *Norway*';[1] while Stalker & Parker and Dossie described its manufacture from oil, the latter saying that the soot was collected and sold without further preparation.[2] Smith and Tingry's later editor explained that the raw pigment did not dry well, and that it had to be burnt to improve its performance in this respect;[3] while Vanherman recommended particularly in this connection that it should be raised to 'a strong red heat' in an iron box or crucible.[4] By removing its natural oiliness in this way the pigment would also presumably be worked more easily in water, and suffer less from any tendency to brownish discolouration.

John Smith, who also described a finer variety which he called *candle black*, said that lamp black was more generally used than any other black on account of its 'plenty and cheapness', and that it was suitable for most uses.[5] Watin indicated, however, that it did not work well in distemper (a medium with which Smith was not concerned);[6] and, for use in his 'aromatic' emulsion paint, Vanherman suggested the alternative use of blue black as equally good and less troublesome.[7] D'Aviler and Bullet also included *noir de fumée* in their lists of basic pigments,[8] and Pincot too employed it as one of the staples of the house-painter's trade, which, Tingry remarked, provided its principal application.[9] As might be expected, therefore, Lewis Berger held fairly substantial stocks of lamp black during the first decade of the nineteenth century, amounting to nearly 20 cwt. in 1802, 43¼ cwt. in 1806 and nearly 63½ cwt. in 1810, valued at rates varying from the equivalents of 32*s.* 8*d.* to 51*s.* 4*d.* per cwt.[10] Although a small amount was supplied for painting a house in Doncaster in 1802 at a rate equivalent to 37*s.* 4*d.* per cwt.,[11] other retail prices encountered are rather higher: Soane, for example, was charged at the equivalent or 112*s.* per cwt. in 1803;[12] and two quantities of 1 lb. each were supplied at Tredegar House, Newport, Monmouthshire (now Gwent), in 1792 and 1793 at rates equivalent to 168*s.* and 186*s.* per cwt. respectively.[13] These are, unusually, more or less in line with those of 1*s.* 7½ *d.* or 1*s.* 6*d.* per lb. published by John Phillips during the second decade of the nineteenth century.[14]

Lamp black was recommended by Watin and Tingry for use in making black paint for ironwork;[15] and, on account of its opacity compared with the relative transparency of ivory black, it seems natural that it should have been used in this way. Reynolds too specified its employment for mixing black paint for exterior use, and suggested its use to dull green and stone colour in oil.[16] He also used it with Spanish brown to mix claret colour and chocolate colour,[17] the latter a combination suggested too by Butcher and Tingry's later editor, and one which had, no doubt, always been widely exploited.[18] On the other hand, although John Smith and Nicholson recommended employment of lamp black with white to mix ash colour, Bullet its use in the same way for *couleur de fer*, and Reynolds for an exterior slate colour, Watin classified such mixtures as producing simply *gris ordinaire*.[19] Thus, despite its high staining power (which would in any case have been offset by the lower cost of other black pigments), its employment for more subtle tinting purposes in better class interiors may well have been less universal, since finer, more delicate greys could be produced by means of ivory and charcoal blacks, or by other means. It was, however, used quite extensively in grey undercoats, which are discussed in Chapter 15. Also, although Whittock employed lamp black for veining in the imitation of *verde antico* and veined white marble in distemper,[20] on account of its slight greasiness it was probably less used in an aqueous medium. Nevertheless, D'Aviler noted its use in mixing grey distemper,[21] and in the Doncaster account mentioned above the pigment appears alongside others, which suggests that its employment in this medium was intended, so that it may have been used in this way on occasion.

IVORY BLACK AND BONE BLACK

Ivory black is prepared by the calcination of ivory or bone (when it may be known as bone black) in a closed vessel from which air has been excluded. In contrast to other black pigments discussed, it usually contains only about ten or twenty per cent of carbon, the remainder being composed of calcium phosphate: hence it is more transparent than the others, tending also to have a brownish cast. Tingry gave *Cologne* or *Cassel black* as alternative names for pigment genuinely prepared from ivory,[22] which seems to have been the material from which most seventeenth-century varieties were made. John Smith remarked that ivory black was expensive and not used in common work, an observation repeated in the early nineteenth century by Whittock (probably quoting Butcher's edition of John Smith);[23] but in the mid-eighteenth century Dossie stated it was prepared for common use in large quantities from bones and was sold at a low price. It was also, he observed, frequently sophisticated with charcoal dust, which gave it a bluish cast.[24] In addition, Watin mentioned *noir de composition*, prepared by calcination of the animal residue left after the manufacture of yellow prussiate of potash (potassium ferrocyanide) as part of the process for making Prussian blue, a product also mentioned by Hurst.[25]

Common use of the pigment at this date is consistent with prices noted for it. In the late 1770s and 1780s, Lewis Berger was offering ivory black for sale at prices ranging from 16*s.* to 20*s.* per cwt., and by the first decade of the nineteenth century was valuing his stocks at even lower prices lying between 9*s.* and 15*s.* 3*d.* per cwt.[26] By then, therefore, the price of lamp black was several times that of commercial 'ivory' black, probably more generally prepared, as Dossie suggested, from bone. The price of the genuine article, by comparison, may be seen from a costed formula of 1826 for 'Drop Ivory Black' in the Berger archive in which ivory, itself costing 10*s.* per cwt. to purchase, was burnt to produce the pigment at a cost of 17*s.* per cwt. To this 'Deep [Wet Prussian] Blue' was added, making a final cost price of 23*s.* per cwt., suggesting it would have retailed at around 50*s.* per cwt.[27] In 1810, Berger had, indeed, a stock of just over 3½ cwt. 'Lump Ivory Black' valued at this figure, and it seems likely, therefore, that this was of a similar nature.[28] His stocks of the cheaper varieties were, however, considerably more substantial, and exceeded too those he held of lamp black (q.v.), amounting to just over 33 cwt. in 1802, nearly 69½ cwt. in 1806, and over 140 cwt. in 1810.[29] Altogether, it seems clear that the cheap varieties were used quite extensively for house-painting, in which their main application was for tinting greys, lamp black, as mentioned above, being generally recommended for more solid shades including blacks and browns. Its particular advantage over lamp black lay in its being more easily miscible with water, and thus more suitable for use in distemper. Thus D'Aviler used ivory black in mixing grey distemper, and Nicholson too recommended its use for 'inferior greys' in this medium;[30] while Watin employed it in the production of greys and for greying whites in general.[31]

CHARCOAL (BLUE BLACK)

Besides blacks prepared from animal substances, crushed wood charcoal too was used as a pigment. Particularly fine qualities were prepared for artists from peach stones and other special vegetable matter, and Church indicated that such pigments should be washed to remove soluble alkalis prior to use.[32] In the first edition of his book John Smith described willow charcoal as a good black for ordinary purposes, mentioning that, although coarse, it had good drying properties; but in the second edition he remarked that 'being not so easy to be gotten as the Lam[p]-black' it was seldom used.[33] On the other hand, *noir de charbon* was listed by D'Aviler for use in greys and with yellow ochre in *couleur d'olive*,[34] and was described by Watin, who commented that it gave a beautiful grey in distemper. He illustrated its use in this medium to eliminate any tendency to yellow in whites, and used it with blue in both oil and distemper to mix *gris argentin* and *gris de perle*.[35]

Dossie defined *blue black* as a wood charcoal pigment, adding that the best was said to be that made from vine stalks and tendrils;[36] and Watin, who also referred to the use of *noir de pêches* as a watercolour, described *noir de vigne* as the most beautiful of the blacks.[37] Tingry too was conversant with both these sources of pigment, remarking particularly that charcoal produced from vine twigs would produce with white lead a silver white otherwise unobtainable;[38] and Vanherman mentioned that vine wood burnt to charcoal would confer on white a rich and beautiful satin tint, while cautioning that it had to be used sparingly.[39] Besides these varieties of charcoal, Watin also described *noir d'Allemagne*, which, he indicated, was a powder made at Frankfurt, Mainz, and Strasbourg from roasted wine lees;[40] and Tingry described a similar pigment which was identified by his later editor as *Frankfurt black*.[41] In 1802 Lewis Berger had a stock of just over ¼ cwt. of 'For.^{n} Francfort Black' valued at £7 per cwt., and in addition a further 4½ cwt. 'Francfort Black' valued at the much lower rate of 50*s.* per cwt. The same price was applied to his stock of 2¾ cwt. in 1806, while just over 1½ cwt. were valued at 60*s.* per cwt. in 1810.[42] From formulae of 1829 and 1831, it seems almost certain that these lower-priced grades were, in fact, a commercially produced substitute based on charcoal with the addition of Prussian blue and ivory and lamp blacks, which was designed to imitate the bluish cast of the much more expensive genuine product. In 1831 it was made from:

210 lb. charcoal
84 lb. 'Burnt Ivory'
15 lb. fine lamp black
10 lb. deep wet blue
10 lb. common lamp black
7 lb. soda (sodium carbonate).[43]

It may well, therefore, have been such a preparation that Vanherman had in mind when suggesting that Frankfurt black could be used to colour varnish.[44]

Even so, the imitation Frankfurt black, being comparable in price with lamp black, was considerably more expensive than the ordinary charcoal 'blue black', of which, as might be expected, Berger had fairly extensive stocks. These were valued at prices more or less comparable with his cheaper 'ivory' blacks, and stood at 40½ cwt. in 1802, 12 cwt. in 1806, and just over 11 cwt. in 1810, the first two being priced at a rate of 12*s.* per cwt. and the last at 15*s.*[45] The same relationship with the price of ivory black may be seen in the rates at which he was offering blue black for sale during the late 1770s and 1780s, which varied between 16*s.* and 24*s.* per cwt.;[46] while in the late seventeenth century Stalker & Parker had quoted a common price for the pigments ground into oil.[47] In 1802, besides the varieties already mentioned, Berger had also a small stock of 1 cwt. blue black ground in oil which was valued at 38*s.* per cwt.;[48] and it is thus clear that the pigment was used in both oil and water, although for house-painting it was, no doubt, more often prepared from more common varieties of charcoal, such as the beechwood mentioned by Tingry,[49] than the special materials mentioned above.

In general, the uses for blue black described by early nineteenth-century authors are similar to those suggested by D'Aviler and Watin, which have already been mentioned. Vanherman, for example, used blue black in a mixture for green paint;[50] while Nicholson described the pigment as useful in mixing inferior greys in distemper, and indicated that it could be added to white oil finishing coats, no doubt on the basis that it would reduce any tendency to yellowing.[51] It is tempting to suggest that the two ounces supplied to the plasterer at Tredegar House in 1793 were destined for the same purpose in distemper;[52] and, apart from the fact that, as Vanherman remarked, it was less trouble to use than lamp black (which, although more expensive, has a higher staining power), it seems likely that its bluish cast was one of the main criteria for its choice in preference to either this pigment or ivory black.[53] Charcoal has, moreover, been identified in the blue oil paint of an early colour scheme in the Library at Kenwood House, Middlesex, used again, no doubt, with the intention of dulling the blue without any tendency to yellowing and consequent production of a greenish tinge;[54] and, probably with the same desirable property in mind, Nicholson suggested the use of blue black for veining in the imitation of veined white marble, here mixed with a little Prussian blue.[55] No mention seems to be made, however, of its use in mixing deep blacks, and it is most likely that this role was better performed by lamp black.

COAL AND OTHER MINERAL BLACKS

In the first edition of his book, John Smith included 'Sea-Coal' among the black pigments, indicating that it dried well;[56] but he omitted any mention of it from the second, which suggests, perhaps, that it had become virtually obsolete.

In the 1820s, Vanherman employed 'mineral black' as a tinting pigment in his 'Impenetrable or Anti-Corrosive Paint' for exterior application, giving its cost as 14*s.* per cwt., but did not provide any information as to its nature.[57] In 1835, however, Field described *mineral black* as 'a native impure oxide of carbon, of a soft texture, found in Devonshire';[58] and both references may, perhaps, be identified with the pigment obtained since the late eighteenth century from Bideford in that county, especially since one of Field's early nineteenth-century notebooks contains a sample of 'mineral black' noted as coming from the Union Mine at Bideford.[59] More recently, *Bideford black* has been described by John Remington as being 'of the nature of a pasty clay, occurring in rocks of the carboniferous age, the local name being "Culm measures"'. To prepare the pigment for marketing it was dried to remove the natural 12–15 per cent moisture content, the product containing approximately $\frac{1}{3}$ carbon, $\frac{1}{3}$ silica, $\frac{1}{3}$ alumina, and small amounts of ferric oxide and other compounds.[60]

Heaton indicates that other varieties of *mineral black* may be known as *black chalk*, noting the existence of extensive deposits in Spain and Italy, which require only grinding and levigating for use as a pigment.[61] In his *Natural History of Staffordshire*, published in 1686, Plot referred to a black chalk which he had been told was found in the strata in Langley Close, near Stainsop;[62] and 'Italian black chalk' was priced by Phillips as 2*s.* 2*d.* per lb. in 1812 (a price amended to 2*s.* in 1821).[63]

MANGANESE DIOXIDE (BLACK WADD)

Tingry's later editor referred to the employment of black manganese oxide as a pigment, noting that the ore was known as *black wad* or *wadd* in Derbyshire, but occurred also in Devon and Somerset.[64] Wadd was described by Ure as a mixture of manganese with an equal weight of iron oxide,[65] and Heaton observed that pigment prepared from the crude ore had a greenish cast.[66] Vanherman and Tingry's later editor suggested its recent use for the protection of exterior ironwork, 'tar oil' being employed as the medium since the pigment was apt to cause the spontaneous ignition of linseed oil.[67] Its colour was, Vanherman added, dull and unpleasant; and the pigment seems most unlikely to have been used for interior work.

CHAPTER 10

DRIERS, DRYING OILS, AND THEIR PREPARATION FOR USE

Certain oils, chiefly of vegetable origin, have the property of hardening by polymerisation or 'drying' when exposed to the atmosphere. Others, for example olive oil, do not dry but remain fluid; and an intermediate group, which contains rape-seed oil (used for lamps during the eighteenth century), dries poorly. Of the so-called *drying oils* only three – linseed oil, walnut oil, and poppy oil – seem to have been in normal use for house-painting, the first being by far the most commonly employed.

The mechanism by which oils polymerise is complex, but in essence the drying power of an oil depends on the proportion of unsaturated fatty acid present. The molecules of unsaturated organic compounds, such as the *linolic* and *linolenic* acids in linseed and other drying oils, have the ability to link up and regroup to form chains, or polymers, in this case *linoxyn*; and this mechanism, involving the absorption of oxygen from the atmosphere, produces the tough flexible film associated with paints.

DRIERS

The speed of drying can be enhanced by various means, in particular by the addition of certain metal salts known as *siccatives* or *driers*, the most important substances used during the period here considered being red lead and litharge (both oxides of lead), sugar of lead (lead acetate), white copperas (zinc sulphate), and umber. Their accelerating effect is not proportional to the quantity in which they are used, and beyond about two per cent they are injurious to the paint since they speed up further changes in the dried film, and thus shorten its life.[1] Driers may be used in two ways, either previously dissolved in the oil, or in paste form as a direct addition to the paint. Formulae for the first of these applications are discussed below in connection with the drying oils themselves, but first the substances used for both methods will be described and their general characteristics discussed. The choice between drying method and between different driers for immediate addition to paint will be summarised in Chapter 15.

Red lead

Red lead has been discussed above in Chapter 6. It was also used extensively as a drier throughout the period under consideration, especially in priming coats and in making boiled oils. Although at 28*s*. or 38*s*. per cwt. it appears from Lewis Berger's early nineteenth-century stock lists to have been marginally cheaper than litharge (q.v.), its colour prevented its direct use as a drier in all finishes but the very darkest (Evelyn, for example, suggested it could be used in blue made using indigo),[2] and the boiled oil produced using it tended to be deep in colour from the length of time it had to be heated to achieve adequate solution.

Litharge

Litharge has been mentioned in Chapter 4 in discussion of the pigment lead-tin yellow, and attention there drawn to the apparently invariable use of the name for lead monoxide when used as a drier during the period being considered. The substance was made as a by-product of silver refining, the process being described by the seventeenth-century author John Ray: pigs of impure silver obtained after smelting the ore, which contained a great deal of lead, were re-melted in a reverberatory furnace; when at the right temperature, air was blown in and the lead monoxide which formed on the surface was blown off, the silver gradually solidifying at the bottom.[3]

Several authors on house-painting refer to different varieties of litharge known as *litharge of lead, litharge of silver*, and *litharge of gold*, these terms having been used in classical times by Pliny in connection with his description of various naturally occurring substances found in silver mines.[4] Tingry in particular discussed litharge at some length, and described how on first heating a *grey oxide* is formed.[5] This, a mixture of lead monoxide and metallic lead, was called *ashes of lead* by Martin, but it is still known commercially as grey oxide.[6] Tingry continued by describing how, on further heating in a reverberatory furnace during the process of silver refining or 'cupelling', litharge was formed on the surface. The colour, he observed, varied, two varieties being produced. The red, called *litharge of gold*, had, he suggested, suffered least from the fire, while that called *litharge of silver* was more vitrified and of a greenish-yellow colour. In addition, Watin noted that the first was cooled in a mass, the second spread out.[7] The distinction owes its explanation to the fact that lead monoxide exists in two different crystalline forms, tetragonal and orthorhombic. The latter, corresponding with litharge of silver, is canary yellow in colour and for that reason often known as *canary litharge*. If pure it is stable only above 489°C, but it can also exist at normal temperatures when small impurities are present.[8] The tetragonal form on the other hand is stable below this temperature, but always exists at atmospheric temperatures in association with orthorhombic litharge; and the mixture, orange-red in colour, corresponds with litharge of gold.

John Smith used 'Litharge of Lead' in the preparation of boiled oil, but the suggestion made by Nicholson that 'ashes of lead' or 'litharge of lead' could be used simply mixed with linseed oil as a drier seems unreliable since it would discolour the paint.[9] Tingry, indeed, stated that this variety of litharge was not used in painting,[10] and it is most likely therefore that it was the pure monoxides which found employment. Thus, Stalker & Parker and Tingry recommended litharge of gold, the latter indicating that it was preferable to litharge of silver.[11] His later editor remarked, however, that although the distinction between the two varities had formerly been recognised, by his time it was unknown.[12] Other English authors do not seem to express any preference, generally using the term litharge without qualification, and Lewis Berger simply listed 'Litharge' in his early nineteenth-century stock lists, mentioning 'Prepar'd', 'Fine', and 'Com^{n}' varieties. Between 1802 and 1810 he valued his stocks of these at rates between 27*s.* and 54*s.* per cwt., these being in each year marginally above the prices for red lead, his total stocks rising from just over 12 cwt. in 1802 to just over 20½ cwt. in 1806, and nearly 96 cwt. in 1810.[13] Retail prices encountered seem consistent with Berger's rates, 2 lb., for example, being supplied at Dyrham Park in 1779 at 5*d.* per lb., and Soane being charged at 5*d.* and 6*d.* per lb. for small quantities at Pitzhanger Manor, Middlesex, in 1803.[14]

Litharge was used, as will become apparent, to a large extent in the production of boiled oils throughout the period under consideration, and it is mentioned by most writers on the subject. The earliest reference to its use as an added drier which has been noted, however, is that by Watin.[15] Nevertheless, the examples mentioned above, together with the 3 lb. of litharge purchased in 1780 in connection with work at Osterley (2 of which were ground in oil), the 1 lb. of 'Litharge dry' purchased for 3*d.* the following year, and the 'Pot of . . . Litharge ground' supplied at Dyrham also in 1781 probably illustrate its use in this way at that date;[16] and there is no reason to suppose that this was not common well before then. As with red lead, its colour tended to rule out its universal use in finishing coats, especially those of light or delicate tint, and hence Tingry's later editor recommended it for drying purposes specifically in dark colours.[17]

Sugar of lead

Lead acetate, or sugar of lead, a white crystalline substance, is especially suitable for use as an additive drier, although it may also be used in the preparation of boiled oils. Earlier writers do not seem to mention it, but Dossie described its preparation by the solution of lead in vinegar, and its use in finer work.[18] In a letter of 1788 Lewis Berger quoted for its supply at 168*s.* per cwt., while in 1802, 1806, and 1810 he valued his stocks, which never amounted to more than 10 cwt. in any of these years, at rates equivalent to 219*s.* 4*d.*, 168*s.*, and 140*s.* per cwt. respectively, the average being roughly the equivalent of 1*s.* 6*d.* per lb.[19] In 1779, 1 oz. was purchased at Osterley for 12*d.*, although 3*d.* was paid for a similar quantity the following year; and in 1803 Soane was charged at a rate of 3*s.* per lb. for a total of 6 pounds, the same rate as that given by Phillips in 1812 and 1821.[20] Lead acetate can therefore be seen clearly as a considerably more expensive substance than almost all others used as driers, in particular red lead, litharge, or white copperas. Pincot and Nicholson both referred to it under the alchemical name *saccharum saturnae*, describing it respectively as used for flatting coats and for fine whites;[21] and it seems clear that its principal employment was an added drier in high quality work at least from the mid-eighteenth century.

White copperas

Dossie described *white vitriol* (zinc sulphate) as a mineral obtained from Hungary (then including modern Czechoslovakia);[22] and Tingry's later editor gave an account of the process used for its preparation in Germany by roasting blende, a zinc ore (zinc sulphide), exposing the residue to the air, and extracting the sulphate by solution in water. He added that he believed it was also being prepared from zinc ore in the Mendip Hills, and advised that the pure form of the salt made by dissolving zinc in sulphuric acid was unnecessary for painting.[23] Lewis Berger was offering white copperas for sale in 1788 at 75*s.* per cwt. and valued his stocks, which rose from just over 6 cwt. in 1802 to nearly 22¾ cwt. in 1806 and just over 75 cwt. in 1810, at rates between 44*s.* and 85*s.* per cwt., prices more or less comparable with the cheaper varieties of litharge.[24]

Dossie, Tingry, and Whittock gave formulae for boiled oils (reviewed below) in which white vitriol features among other ingredients, but it is fairly clear that its main application was as an added drier. It was certainly being used in this way during the late seventeenth century, but the term 'copperas' was often used without qualification and it is not always possible to be sure that zinc sulphate was implied, since in the late nineteenth century Hurst indicated that green copperas (ferrous sulphate, also known as green vitriol) rendered anhydrous was frequently used as a drier.[25] Blue copperas (copper sulphate, also known as blue or Roman vitriol), however, would not have been used for this purpose; and, since Watin observed that only white copperas was commonly used as a drier,[26] it seems most likely that the unqualified term was applied to zinc sulphate. John Smith, for example, observed:

> Some Painters to make their Colours dry, take Copperas, and having beaten it to pouder, burn it in a Fire-shovel; . . . that is, they set it on the fire, . . . till all the moysture be exhaled, and the matter remain a dry white Calx; some of this pouder of burnt Copperas, being added to the Colours in grinding, shall make the Colour dry very well.[27]

The white colour of the anhydrate shows clearly that it was the zinc salt to which Smith referred, and the practice of dehydration was also advocated by Watin.[28] Butcher seems

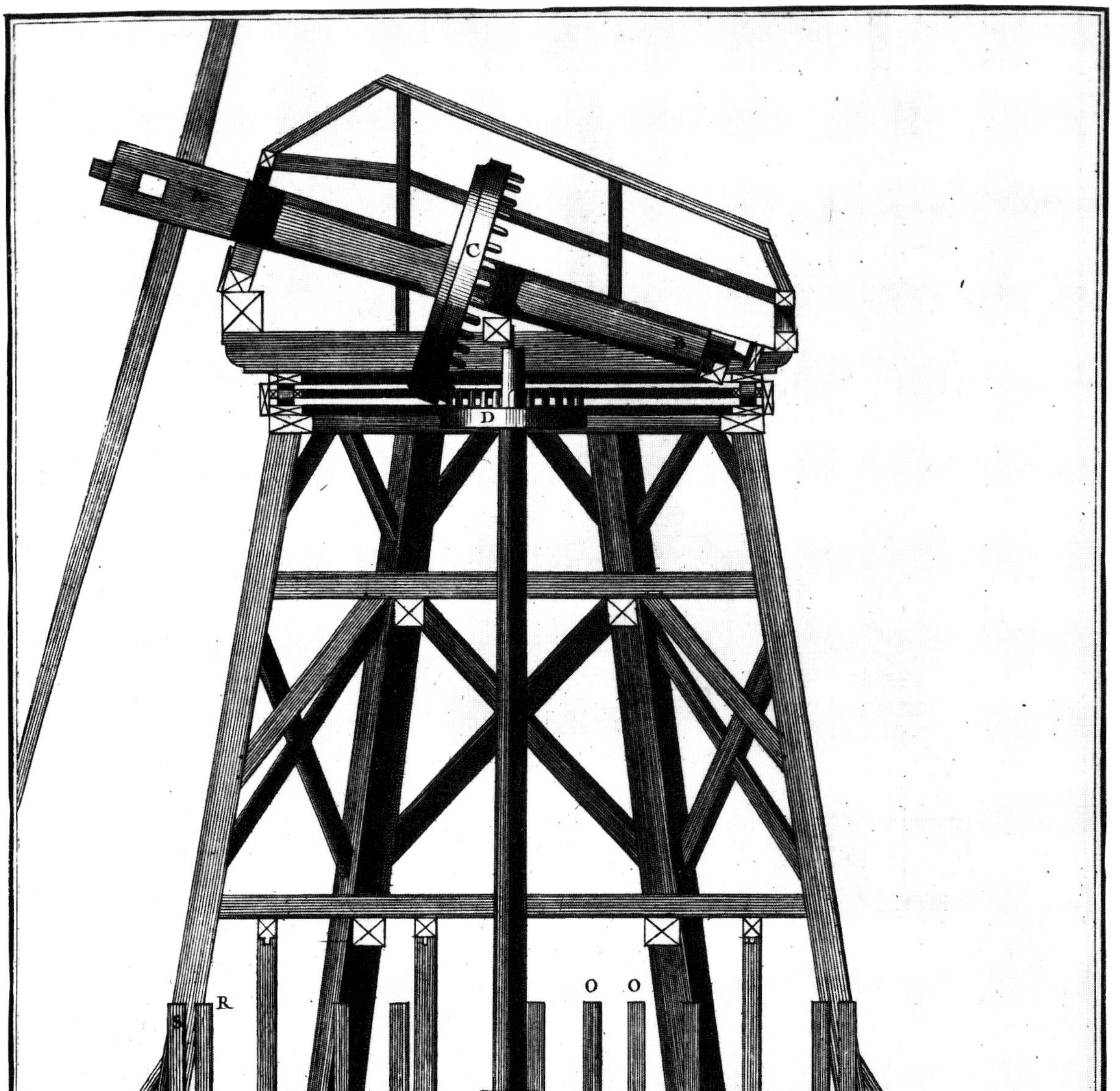

OEconomie Rustique,
Moulin a exprimer l'Huile des Graines.

5. Mid-eighteenth-century oil mill.

to have used white copperas extensively, recommending its employment in black, and that of 'copperas' in white, grey, stone colour, green, and other colours;[29] but although Dossie implied that white vitriol was used in fine work, other authors regarded it as less satisfactory; and Tingry's later editor, for example, remarked that it was 'not calculated for white and other delicate colours, it being apt to deteriorate the colour'.[30] Nevertheless, it emerges as a very generally used substance: far greater quantities than of litharge or lead acetate were purchased, seemingly ground in oil, in connection with work at Osterley between 1774 and 1781;[31] and it was the only drier which Lewis Berger stocked in paste form during the early nineteenth century, although his stocks were small. These amounted to 14lb. in 1802, but stood at nearly $1\frac{3}{4}$ cwt. in 1810, and were valued at 9*d.* or 10*d.* per lb.[32] It was also, as Vanherman and Tingry's later editor observed, especially suitable for use with zinc white, for which other driers were less satisfactory.[33]

Umber

The brown pigment umber, described in Chapter 8, contains manganese dioxide which acts as an efficient drier. Its dark colour more or less precluded its use other than in the preparation of boiled oils; and formulae which include it for this purpose, always in association with other driers, were given by Dossie, Watin, Martin, and Nicholson. These are described below.

Green copperas

Although the late nineteenth-century author George Hurst indicated that green copperas (ferrous sulphate) rendered anhydrous was frequently used as a drier,[34] no explicit reference to its employment in house-painting before this date has been encountered. While Lewis Berger had extensive stocks of green copperas during the first decade of the nineteenth century, amounting in each of the years 1802, 1806, and 1810 to several tons valued at rates between 7*s.* and 11*s.* 6*d.* per cwt., it must be remembered that the substance was used by him for other purposes, most notably the manufacture of Prussian blue.[35] There is no reason to suppose, therefore, that it was generally used as a drier during the period being considered; and unqualified references to 'copperas' probably imply the use of white copperas (q.v.).

Iron oxide

Dossie mentioned the use of *colcothar* in the preparation of boiled oils, and had earlier defined the substance as a residue left in the necks of the retorts used for the distillation of sulphuric acid from ferrous sulphate.[36] This was no doubt an impure form of ferric oxide, and may in Dossie's mind have possessed analogous properties to the red ochres which had always been used extensively in primings on account, it was thought, of their gentle drying properties compared with those of other substances, allowing the oil to penetrate more deeply into the pores of the ground before polymerising. However, he did not mention it again in any of the detailed formulae which followed; and although it was mentioned later by Whittock in his list of driers,[37] this was undoubtedly copied from Dossie, and the substance can probably be disregarded.

Verdigris

The pigment verdigris, discussed in Chapter 3, also possesses excellent drying properties. It was recommended by Evelyn as a drier for blues made using indigo, and in later editions of John Smith's book as a drier for lamp black.[38] No doubt in dark blue or black paint its strong colour would have been unimportant.

White lead

The pigment white lead, discussed in Chapter 1, was also used to a limited extent for its drying qualities, quite apart from its utility as a base pigment for oil paint. As described below, Watin and Whittock, for example, mentioned its employment in the preparation of sun-bleached oils, and Martin included it with other ingredients in a formula for the production of boiled oil. Watin and Tingry also used roasted white lead, presumably thus containing a proportion of lead monoxide, in similar formulae;[39] but in general it does not seem to have been a very important substance for such purposes.

Talc

Talc, whose nature has been discussed briefly in Chapter 1 in connection with its possible use as an adulterant, was used in combination with other substances by Watin in formulae for sun-bleached and boiled oils.[40] Its drying properties in this connection are, however, unlikely to have been significant, and it was probably intended as a vehicle to aid precipitation of the mucilage.

DRYING OILS

As the most commonly used drying oil, linseed oil is described first; and, since many methods for the treatment of drying oils are common to all those considered below, the principles which lie behind them are discussed in detail in connection with it. Variations in the case of other oils, however, are separately discussed under the appropriate headings.

Linseed oil

Linseed oil is expressed by pressure from the seed of the flax plant, *Linum usitatissimum*, and was known in Roman times. In sixteenth- and seventeenth-century England, the industry was confined to the counties of the East Coast, but it spread during the eighteenth to other parts of the country, and seed was increasingly imported.[41]

In 1765, Diderot & D'Alembert described in their *Encyclopédie* a windmill used for all types of oil production, and provided an illustration of it (fig. 5). Power from the sails was transferred to a horizontal shaft (H) fitted with wooden cams which lifted stampers. The seed from which oil was to be extracted was first pulverised in the mortars (f) and put in horsehair bags. These were placed in the press-box between two iron plates (1 and 5) and the remainder of the cavity packed with blocks of wood, including two wedges, the second of which was reversed. One of the stampers was then brought into operation to knock in the first wedge, thus exerting pressure on the seed, oil from which flowed out through an aperture into pots placed underneath. When oil had ceased to run, a second stamper was used to knock in the reversed wedge, additional wooden blocks were placed in the cavity, and pressure again exerted on the seed to produce a further quantity of oil. The process was repeated until no further expression of oil was possible. The product of this first pressing was 'virgin' oil, drawn cold. The residue which remained was afterwards heated with a little water in hemispherical kettles enclosed in masonry furnaces, the mixture being kept moving by means of the anchor-shaped stirrers illustrated (fig. 6), and the whole re-pressed between heated iron plates to yield a second quantity of oil.

Some substances, Diderot & D'Alembert noted, had first to be bruised in the edge-runner mill of which they also provided an engraving (fig. 7).[42] That a similar process was in use in the late seventeenth century in Lincolnshire is clear, since in 1696 Christopher Merret noted that rape

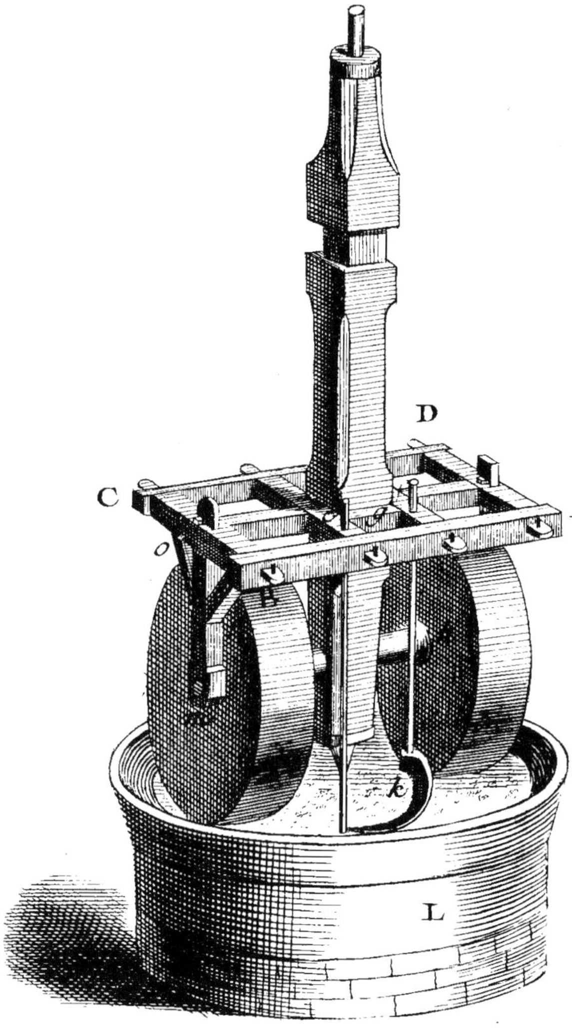

7. Edge-runner mill used to bruise the seed prior to pressing.

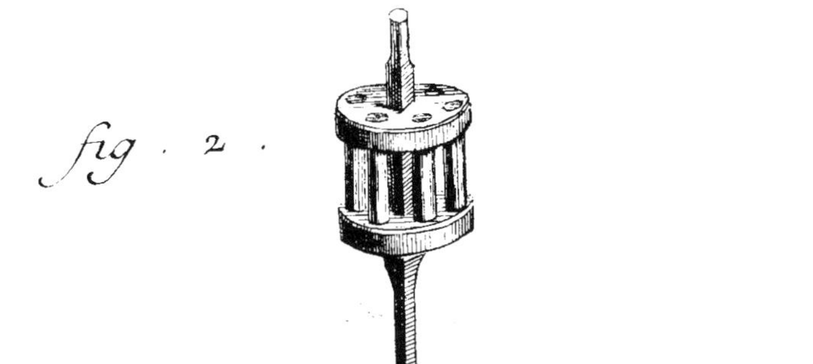

6. Kettles in which the seed was heated prior to a second pressing.

seed was grown between Spalding and Crowland 'whereof they make Oyl, by breaking it between two great black Marble Stones of near a Tun Weight, one standing Perpendicularly on the other'. These were, he said of German origin, remarking too that some of the mills 'go with Sails', indicating they were wind-powered.[43] In 1651, John French had described the process of making 'Oyles by expression', including linseed oil, directing that the material had to be bruised and strongly pressed, and noting that it 'must stand in the press some houres, because the Oyle drops by little, and little'. He referred also to the use of heat, but warned that although the quantity of oil obtained would be greater, it would not keep so well.[44]

In the eighteenth century Dossie referred to the use of water-mills for the manufacture of linseed oil,[45] and the efficiency of water- and wind-mills was investigated by John Smeaton, who published the results of his work in 1760.[46] In the mid-nineteenth century, Ure illustrated a 'Dutch mill' press box of the type described by Diderot & D'Alembert (fig. 8), but indicated that mills of this description, formerly driven by water or horse power, were obsolete. His commentary adds, though, useful detail to that given in the *Encyclopédie*, and he noted that a dozen blows of the stamper, which weighed between 500 and 600

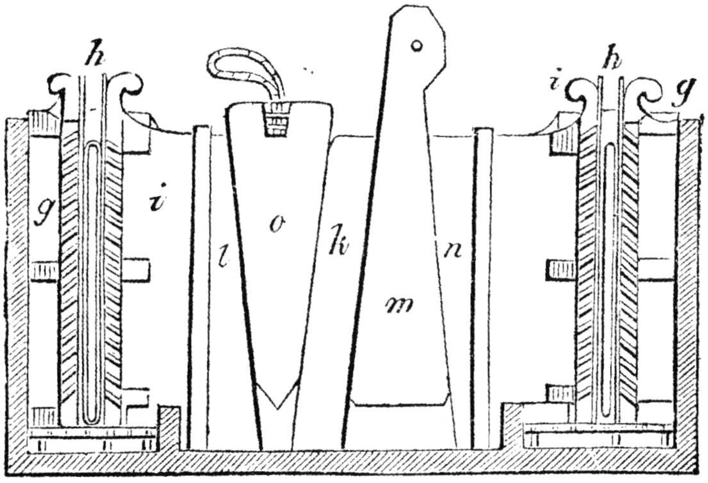

8. Detail of 'Dutch mill' press box.

pounds and fell through a height of 16 to 21 inches, were needed to drive in the wedge (o), after which the press was allowed to stand for a few minutes to permit the oil to flow out from the horsehair bags in which it was confined. By the time he was writing, however, use of steam-powered hydraulic presses (which he also described) seems to have been well established; and he mentioned the import of seed from Archangel, Odessa, and eastern India.[47]

According to Church, the use of heat enabled an average oil-yield of 27 per cent of the weight of seed against 20 per cent if pressed cold;[48] but oil drawn in this way is darker in colour than cold-drawn oil, more viscous, and of poorer quality. The practice was mentioned by the twelfth-century writer Theophilus in his treatise *De Diversis Artibus*;[49] and, as implied by the references quoted above, seems likely to have been ordinary commercial procedure throughout the period under consideration. This was certainly the case in the early nineteenth century, and the continental authors Chaptal and Tingry both referred to it, the latter, indeed, particularly describing linseed oil as requiring the greatest degree of heat in its extraction, and for that reason always being coloured and thick. On this account, it was, he noted, used for coarse work; and by 1830, his later editor observed that oil extracted without heat was reserved for medical purposes.[50]

Raw oil obtained either with or without heat is dull or cloudy in appearance, and is not used today without further refinement. It is also desirable to increase the speed at which it will dry, and techniques were devised at an early date to effect both these improvements, and also to bleach the colour. Dossie described the processes in use for such 'fattening', listing long keeping, the addition of certain pigments, and exposure to the sun and air as the main methods employed.[51] The latter was particularly used to prepare the thick 'fat oil' which formed the basis of gold-sizes, and is discussed in more detail in connection with gilding in Chapter 19, but the bleaching action of sunlight was sometimes used also to reduce the yellow colour of oils used for other purposes. The *Dutch process* as practised at the beginning of the nineteenth century was described by Chaptal and Martin, both of whom indicated that one-third part of fine white sand, one-third part of water, and one-third part of linseed oil were placed in a well-glazed earthenware pot, which was covered by a sheet of glass and exposed to the sun. The whole was stirred daily, and exposure continued until the oil was white. It was then allowed to stand for two days to settle, and the refined oil decanted.[52] At the end of the nineteenth century, Church mentioned the same practice, indicating that a temperature of 80° or even 100°F should be maintained.[53]

Dossie described such methods as making the refined oil reluctant to dry,[54] and in recommending a similar process, John Smith had included the use of a drier:

> Put the afore-mentioned quantity of Linseed-Oyl [1 quart] to the like quantity of Litharge [2 ounces]; put the mixture into a Glass, and set it in the hot Sun, for a Month, in the Summer time, stirring the Litharge and the Oyl well together, twice a Week, during the whole time, and you shall not fail in that time to obtain ⟨not only⟩ an Oyl very white and clear (for the Sun takes away all Colour, either from Linseed or Wallnut-Oyl) but also, it will become in that time very fat and thick, and attain to a very drying quality.[55]

Similar processes were described by Watin, Martin, Whittock, and Vanherman,[56] the first and third of these using white lead as the drier, and the others litharge; but it is difficult to judge the extent to which such methods were in commercial use. At the end of the eighteenth century, however, an advertisement was placed in a Hull newspaper by an oil-mill superintendent 'possessed of the Dutch Process of Refining Rape and Linseed Oil', suggesting such knowledge was desirable;[57] and in 1825 Nicholson suggested the use of bleached linseed oil in white finishing coats.[58] This seems, however, to have been exceptional, and Dossie remarked of linseed oil that it was generally used without any preparation other than mixing it with the appropriate drier. It was, he noted however, improved by long keeping;[59] and Vanherman believed that if kept for two years it would lose its colour.[60] Martin and Nicholson also mentioned filtration, followed by standing two or three years to precipitate and clarify, the latter describing the Dutch process as giving 'the effect of age'.[61] In general, therefore, the majority of linseed oil used for house-painting was probably unbleached, and untreated by the Dutch process.

Much of the linseed oil used commercially today has been refined by treatment with sulphuric acid. This process, *acid refining*, was described in some detail by Vanherman and Tingry's later editor in connection with linseed oil for house-painting, the latter describing Matthias Wilks's patent specification of 1822 while remarking that it had been practised in his presence in about 1800.[62] Chaptal, however, had mentioned the process only in connection with lamp-oil,[63] and an English patent had been taken out by Daniel Bridges for a similar purpose as early as 1748, in which it was described as a 'New method to refine, purify, and meliorate . . . rape [seed] oyl'.[64] Thus, since Dossie did not mention this method at all in connection with linseed oil, and Tingry's editor did not refer to it in such a way as to suggest it was in common commercial use, it seems questionable that the process was important during much of the period presently being considered.

The quickest way to produce a fast-drying oil is to heat raw oil with one of the metal salts discussed above which act as driers. The product is generally known as *boiled oil*, but has also been called *drying oil* or *fat oil*. However, although effective and efficient, the method has a serious disadvantage for interior paintwork in that the oil produced is dark in colour, and yellows whites and other delicate tints. Its use was generally advocated, therefore, in connection only with dark colours for exterior use, suggestions to this effect being made by Pincot (with particular reference to the colder months of the year), and Butcher (for black), while Crease remarked that it was most properly used for external purposes.[65]

In the first edition of his book, John Smith described red lead as the only pigment used in the production of drying and fat oils;[66] but in his 1687 recipe used litharge for the purpose, only adding red lead as an alternative in later editions, in which he directed:

> To a Quart of Linseed Oyl, add two Ounces of the Litharge of Lead, which may be had at every *Druggist's* Shop, (some use Red Lead) powder it finely before you put it to the Oyl; when you have mix'd it, set it on the Fire in an Earthen Pan, and boyl it for near an Hour, more or less, 'till the Oyl be grown fat, or almost of the thickness of Treacle that comes from Sugar; then set it on Fire with a lighted Paper, and stir it well while burning, then put out the Flame, after it hath burnt a Minute or two, and let the Matter stand till it be throughly cold, and the Litharge well settled to the Bottom; then pour off the clear Oyl, and keep it for Use in a Bladder close tyed up, or for Want of that, in a Glass Bottle.[67]

The practice of setting fire to the oil on completion of the boiling seems both dangerous and unusual, and does not appear in any other formulae noted. Stalker & Parker too suggested the alternative use of red lead or litharge (of gold), the latter in a formula for a better grade of boiled oil;[68] while in the early nineteenth century Reynolds advocated the use of red lead.[69]

Boiled oil was, however, commonly purchased during the eighteenth century ready-prepared, and Dossie gave a typical commercial formula in which 1½ lb. of red lead were boiled with a gallon of linseed oil. A more complex recipe 'for coarser work' employed 1 lb. of litharge of gold or silver, ½ lb. of white vitriol, ½ lb. of sugar of lead, and ¼ lb. of umber boiled with one gallon of linseed oil;[70] and similar formulae requiring mixtures of the several driers already mentioned in this connection were given by Tingry, Nicholson, and Whittock.[71] Tingry also recommended the addition of garlic or a small onion, but this seems to have been without much appeal to the English palate. Instructions as to the length of time for which the oil should be boiled range from 15 minutes to 3 hours, but Dossie generally advised boiling only so long as the discolouration of the oil would permit, while Tingry recommended boiling until a skin formed;[72] and Nicholson observed: 'The method of ascertaining whether the mixture is sufficiently heated is to put a quill in it, which will in that case be immediately consumed.'[73] A further feature of Dossie's recipes is the addition of gum arabic and sandarac resin, an additional aspect of oil preparation discussed below in Chapter 15 in connection with gloss paint finishes. Nicholson, probably transcribing Martin,[74] included 'plaster' in a formula for boiled oil which seems to be based on that containing talc suggested by Watin.[75] In it he called for 1 lb. of linseed oil to be boiled with ½ oz. each of litharge, white lead, umber and plaster, and directed that the scum which formed was to be skimmed off from time to time, the process being stopped when the oil began to rarefy and become red. The scum was, he indicated, called *smudge* and was used for external applications,[76] a suggestion he later repeated, recommending that both the scum and dregs (known today as *foots*) provided a good drier for dark colours, and mentioning that this was often used in exterior work.[77]

Linseed oil was undoubtedly the most widely used medium for oil painting throughout the period being discussed despite its yellowish colour, and was supplied in connection with work at Whitehall Palace in 1632–3.[78] In general its price seems to have risen steadily, and reached its maximum during the opening years of the nineteenth century. Stalker & Parker indicated that it cost 8*d.* per quart in 1688,[79] but by 1734 in his *Palladio Londinensis* Salmon suggested a figure of 10*d.*, amended in another work by him, the *London and Country Builder's Vade Mecum* (1745) to a rate of between 10*d.* and 1*s.*[80] A price equivalent to 1*s.* 4*d.*, which seems to be on the high side, appears in the accounts for painting at Egremont House, London, in 1761 and 1763; but in 1781 linseed oil was supplied to Tredegar House, Monmouthshire (now Gwent), at a rate of 1*s.* 2*d.* per quart,[81] and in 1803 Soane was charged at between 1*s.* 2*d.* and 1*s.* 6*d.*[82] The London surveyor John Phillips recorded the progress of its price as follows: between 1760 and 1790 it was sold at 1*s.* per quart; between 1790 and 1803 at 1*s.* 6*d.*; and in 1812 he quoted 2*s.* 9*d.*, while by 1821 the price had fallen back slightly to 2*s.* 6*d.*[83] As usual with the rates he quoted, however, these seem to be slightly exaggerated, and although Pincot referred to its price as having reached 2*s.* at one stage,[84] in 1806 Lewis Berger still valued his stocks, which amounted to nearly 1300 gallons, at a rate equivalent to 10½*d.* or 11*d.*[85] In 1825 the London colourman John Lingard was selling it at a price equivalent to 11*d.* per quart.[86]

Naturally, boiled oil was slightly more expensive, Salmon quoting 1*s.* per quart for 'Best drying Oil' in 1734, and that supplied at Egremont House in 1763 costing 1*s.* 6*d.* or 1*s.* 8*d.*[87] The latter was also the price charged for 'prep^{d} oil' at Tredegar House in 1793.[88] In 1802 Berger valued his stocks of 20 gallons at a rate equivalent to 1*s.* 1¾*d.*, although this fell to 1*s.* in 1806 when his stock was 58 gallons, but rose steeply to 1*s.* 9½*d.* in 1810 when he had 120 gallons.[89] Phillips again recorded his maximum price in 1812, quoting 4*s.* 6*d.* for 'Best drying oil',[90] but in 1810 and 1813 Taylor suggested only 2*s.* 6*d.*;[91] while in 1825 Lingard gave a much lower figure, the equivalent of 1*s.* 0¾*d.*[92]

In the earlier editions of his book, John Smith suggested that annatto could be steeped in oil to enhance its properties as a medium for vermilion, red lead, orpiment, or massicot; but this advice was omitted from 1723.[93] In the 1740s, Alexander Emerton provided a special 'Green-Oil' for use with his green paint. It may have contained dissolved verdigris and has accordingly been discussed in Chapter 3 in connection with that pigment; while Vanherman's linseed-oil emulsion, or 'Incorporated Oil', is described below in Chapter 17.

Walnut oil

Walnut oil, expressed from the nut kernels of the tree, *Juglans regia*, has drying properties similar to those of linseed oil, but possesses the great advantage of being paler in colour. It was prepared for a variety of purposes, and Evelyn mentioned its employment not only for house-painting, but also for polishing walking sticks, and as a frying-oil. He described a bushel of nuts as yielding 15 lb. of peeled and clear kernels, from which $7\frac{1}{2}$ lb. of oil could be obtained, observing, 'the sooner 'tis drawn, is the more in *quantity*, though the dryer the *Nut*, the *better* in *quality*'. The lees were, he remarked, used to fatten hogs.[94] Ageing of the nuts was also mentioned by Hurst, who indicated that they were collected and placed in heaps for about three months until they had begun to decompose before being pressed.[95] Dossie described the oil as being pressed from the kernels (which he emphasised should have been peeled) by means of a screw press, and noted that it was used without any preparation other than keeping.[96] In the early nineteenth century, however, Tingry observed that the common kind which was applied to painting was extracted with the assistance of a small degree of heat. He also provided a number of recipes for boiled walnut oils, including a method which was, he said, used by English artists: in this, 2 lb. of nut oil were boiled with 3 lb. of water and 2 oz. of white vitriol until only a little water remained. The oil was then separated from the water by means of a funnel, and allowed to stand for use. Another formula he gave, simply called for 1 lb. of oil to be boiled with 3 oz. of litharge.[97]

After describing the methods for boiling and sun-bleaching linseed oil which have been quoted above, John Smith observed:

> By the same methods may Nut-Oyl be made to dry as well as that of Linseed, it being preferred before that of Linseed, for all White Painting that is not exposed to the open Air, for 'tis observed, that in all close places, Linseed Oyl is apt to make White-Lead turn Yellow.[98]

That walnut oil was indeed in fairly common use for house-painting in the mid-seventeenth century is evident from Sir Balthazar Gerbier's defence of the wages paid to carpenters. They were, he remarked in his *Counsel and Advise to all Builders* (1663), 'as deserving to be well payd as the Painters, who do but spend the sweat of Wall-nuts (to wit oyle) the Carpenters that of their browes'.[99] His contemporary Pratt also adverted to walnut oil, specifically mentioning its use in avoiding the yellowing of paint;[100] and references to its employment in house-painting may be found in late seventeenth- and early eighteenth-century painting accounts, such as those for Kensington Palace of the 1690s and Montagu House, London, of the 1700s, both of which contain items for white paint in nut oil.[101] It was, however, dearer in price than linseed oil, and although Rondelet listed *huile de noix* at the same price as *huile grasse* (boiled oil),[102] it seems always to have been a much more expensive commodity in England. Stalker & Parker listed it at 1*s.* 4*d.* or 1*s.* 6*d.* per quart, twice the price of linseed oil;[103] and Lewis Berger's small stock in 1806 of merely six gallons was valued at the equivalent of 1*s.* 9*d.* per quart, while in 1810 he listed only one gallon, this time at the equivalent of 3*s.* 6*d.*[104] For this reason walnut oil was always regarded very much as a luxury. The author of the *Builders Price-Book* and Butcher mentioned it in connection with superior flatted white finishes,[105] and Nicholson remarked that walnut oil was sometimes used in this way, but, on account of its high price, not often.[106] In 1830 Tingry's editor stated that it was not greatly used in England, although Whittock on the other hand had described the oil as much used in ornamental painting.[107] It may be concluded, therefore, that while walnut oil was fairly widely used to obtain a good white on large areas of house-paint during the earlier part of the period under consideration, this practice had declined during the eighteenth century (probably following the introduction of 'flatting' discussed in Chapter 15). It probably continued in use, however, for the very best ornamental or decorative work.

Poppy oil

The drying properties of the whitest of the vegetable oils considered here, poppy oil (sometimes known as *oil of pinks*), were discussed during the first half of the seventeenth century,[108] and were clearly known earlier. It has recently been identified in a painting of 1485–90,[109] and was described by Dossie as pressed from ripe poppy seed and as having similar properties to nut oil, but drying better.[110] The more modern authorities Church and Heaton, however, contradict this, describing it as drying rather slowly.[111] Ure, Church, and Hurst mention the species *Papaver somniferum* as providing the seed, while Watin indicated that the seeds of the *pavot noir* were employed;[112] but Tingry referred to those of the white poppy.[113]

Use of poppy oil by house-painters is mentioned in William Cogan's patent of 1742,[114] and in 1745 it was advertised for sale by the Ripon varnish maker, Williamson.[115] Its employment for grinding pigments in connection with house-painting was mentioned by Charles Seguin in his additions to the 1788 edition of Bullet's *Architecture pratique*;[116] and in the early nineteenth century, Tingry provided a special recipe to improve its drying qualities which called for 2 lb. of poppy oil to be boiled with 3 lb. of pure water and 1 oz. of white vitriol until one-half or two-thirds of the water had evaporated. He mentioned its particular employment in white paint and illustrated its use, notably in delicate greys.[117] The only price list noted to include poppy oil is that of the Continental author Rondelet, who gave its price as 1fr.20 per pound against good quality linseed oil at 1fr.00.[118] In England on the other hand it was described by Nicholson as being 'rather expensive',[119] and Whittock remarked that nut oil would answer for decorative painting.[120] Since no other mention of poppy oil in connection with house-painting has been encountered in English works, however, there seems little doubt that the oil was of limited importance in this context.

Hempseed oil

Vanherman mentioned hempseed oil in the context of other drying oils, but did not suggest that it was in use for house-painting.[121] Hurst indicated that it was expressed from the seed of the plant *Cannabis sativa*, being greenish in colour when fresh, but that it was rarely used on account of its price although often present as an impurity in linseed oil, since the Russian growers often mixed it with the linseed.[122] No evidence for its deliberate use during the period being considered has been encountered, although, as mentioned in Chapter 3 in connection with the pigment verdigris, it is just possible that the special 'Green-Oil' applied by Alexander Emerton during the 1740s may have been hempseed oil rather than a copper resinate in linseed oil.

Beech-nut oil

Vanherman also mentioned beech-nut oil in the context of drying oils;[123] but it seems most probable that this reflects his quest for new materials, and it is unlikely that it would have enjoyed any use for house-painting. Indeed, Ure included it in his category of non-drying oils. It was, he indicated, expressed from the nuts of the beech tree, *Fagus sylvatica*, and used for cooking purposes in France and as a lamp oil.[124]

Fish-oils

In 1805, Vanherman received a reward from the Society of Arts for his method for making fish-oil drying. The first step was to put 12 lb. of litharge and 12 lb. of powdered white copperas into 32 gallons of 'good common vinegar' in a 40-gallon cask. This was to be shaken and rolled twice a day for a week, the vinegar, he noted, being used to dissolve the litharge, the copperas accelerating this and increasing the drying quality. The product was to be shaken and mixed with a ton of whale, cod, or seal oil, although he preferred the 'Southern whale oil' on account of its good colour and minimal smell. It was then allowed to stand until the next day, when the clear upper seven-eighths was to be poured off. To this, 12 gallons of linseed oil and 2 gallons spirit of turpentine were to be added, shaken together, and allowed to stand two or three days, when it would be fit to grind with white lead and fine colours. The residue of the fish-oil could, he claimed, be clarified using half its quantity of lime-water to make an excellent oil (which he called 'incorporated oil') for coarse exterior paints, a suggestion perhaps looking forward to the emulsions he later advocated, which are discussed in Chapter 17.[125]

The sifted road-dust or 'crotia' which Vanherman used in his formulae for various colours has already been reviewed in Chapter 1, and both this and his fish-oil attracted caustic comment from Pincot, who adverted to 'Various Quackerys . . . of cheap colours, . . . Fish Oil and Road Sand, . . . of so rough a nature as to encourage wet and Vermin'.[126] Nevertheless, Thomas Martin commented that Vanherman's product appeared to be good for exterior use, but dried slowly;[127] and later in the nineteenth century 'menhaden oil' from the species *Alosa menhaden* seems to have enjoyed a certain degree of use, especially in America, being described by Hurst as drying fairly well.[128] By 1828, however, Vanherman appears to have relinquished the idea of using fish-oil in paint. He did not mention it in connection with his 'Impenetrable or Anti-corrosive Paint' for exterior application, and he confined his comments on such oils to their refinement for burning.[129] It is thus unlikely that fish-oil was of importance in connection with the present study.

COAL-TAR

In his 1805 paper on fish-oil, Vanherman noted that a subdued green paint made using the residue resulting from its preparation would cost less than half the price of coal-tar paint of similar colour.[130] With the development of gas-lighting in the closing years of the eighteenth century and early part of the nineteenth, increasing supplies of coal-tar, the oily part of the liquid condensate resulting from the destructive distillation of coal, became available. This contains a rich mix of hydrocarbons, and its attempted employment as a paint medium was seemingly one of the earliest uses to which it was applied, probably in succession to the wood-tars discussed in Chapter 11. The extent to which it was at first refined before use is unclear, but the commercial availability of such paints in 1816 is demonstrated by a brochure of that date issued by the Patent Colour-Company, who were then marketing chocolate, brown, black, and invisible green 'MINERAL OR REFINED COAL-TAR PAINTS' for 'Common Outside Work';[131] and in another brochure described them as 'composed of the English Ochres, in combination with a MINERAL OIL, extracted by a peculiar process from *Lithanthrax* or *Pit-Coal*'.[132] It is improbable that these products enjoyed any employment for interior purposes, although as technology developed during the nineteenth century more refined coal-tar products, in particular naphtha, were developed and came to be used in varnish-making.[133]

CHAPTER 11

TURPENTINES AND THEIR DERIVATIVES

The crude oleo-resins or *turpentines* which exude from various species belonging to the Pinaceae family of coniferous trees were used in the manufacture of varnish, but may also be separated by distillation into the liquid hydrocarbon known as *oil of turpentine* and a solid residue called *rosin*. The former was the most commonly used thinner in oil paint and one of a variety of solvents used in varnish-making, while the latter was used in both varnishes and oil paints. Wood-pitch and tar, used as a medium for some cheap exterior paints, were also manufactured from the same family of trees.

In the late seventeenth century Houghton described 'Terpentine' as a clear, oily liquor, transparent and clammy, with a yellowish-white colour, and quoted Thomas Bent's contemporary description of its collection and subsequent processing as practised near Marseilles, on the Mediterranean coast of France:

> In the spring, when the *sap* runs most, they pare off the bark of the *pine*, to make the *sap* run down to the hole, which they cut at the bottom to receive it; . . . then they take up the juice in spoons from the bottom, and when they have a good quantity, they strain it . . . What runs through easily, is the common *turpentine*; what remains, they distil in an alembick with a sufficient quantity of water [elsewhere he mentioned four volumes]; and what comes over, is oil of *turpentine*, and the *calx* remaining is common *rosin*. Then they cut the stock of the tree into large chips, and pile them hollow in a cave, covering it on the top with tyles, but so as to let some air come in to feed the fire; then burning them, there runs a thick juice to the bottom, . . . and that . . . is *tar*. Then boiling it gently to consume more of the moisture, they set it to cool, which when cold, is *pitch*.[1]

Hurst described a similar system of tapping as being practised in America during the late nineteenth century, but observed that this was leading to concern about the destruction of the forests, and that the French industry was conducted on a rather more scientific principle. In France, he said:

> The trees are cut in February or March, and the sap is caused to flow into an earthenware vessel placed at the foot of the tree. The trees are tapped for five years in succession, when they are not touched again for a few years, and then tapping commences again; when the tree has got somewhat exhausted, the final tapping takes place, and a large yield of resin obtained, but the tree is killed. It is felled, and another planted in its place.[2]

Developments in distillation methods are obscure, but Heaton believed that the system of steam distillation, which was described by Hurst, was introduced during the first half of the nineteenth century.[3]

CRUDE TURPENTINES

A variety of oleo-resins obtained virtually exclusively from several different species of Pinaceae in ways comparable with that just described was directly exploited in painting and varnish manufacture during the period being considered. The principal varieties were *common turpentine*, from various species of European and American pine; *Venice turpentine*, from the European larch; and *Strasbourg turpentine*, from the silver fir. In addition, resin from the Norway spruce was sold as *Burgundy pitch*, and mention is made by some authors of *Chios turpentine*, from the turpentine tree of Greece, Turkey, and the Near East, which belongs to the family of Anacardiaceae. As may be seen from the tabulated list of resins (table VI, p. 76), each varies in its composition; and contemporary discussion of them centred around their particular properties in varnish-making, rather than in connection with their distillation to make rosin and oil of turpentine. By the late nineteenth century, however, the majority had become obsolete for the former purpose, and were dismissed summarily by Hurst.[4]

The common variety of crude turpentine is obtained from several species of *Pinus*. In addition to the Mediterranean, Houghton mentioned that crude turpentines were obtained from New England.[5] This source had been known from at least the 1630s, since in 1634 William Wood commented on 'Rozin and Turpentine' from the New England 'Firre and Pine';[6] and American produce was probably important in Britain. The French author Watin, however, mentioned material only from the Pyrenees and Bordeaux,[7] which Tingry identified as coming from the wild pine of the south of France.[8] This species (cited by Heaton as *Pinus maritima*)[9] is given by Howes as *Pinus pinaster*, the maritime or cluster pine; and he indicates that it was the most widely exploited in France for the distillation of oil of turpentine, calling the oleo-resin *Bordeaux turpentine* or *galipot*.[10] In connection with this nomenclature, it may be noted, Watin and Tingry reserved the term *térébenthine* for the liquid as it first ran from the incision in the tree; *galipot*, on the other hand, was material which had begun to harden or become more viscous; and *barras* was similar but contaminated by bark or wind-blown matter.[11] Although Tingry ruled out the use of common turpentine in varnish-making,[12] Watin had described it as more often used than either Venice or Chios turpentines;[13] and possible uses are found in earlier English literature. John Smith, for example, recommended the addition of some 'good clear Turpentine' to oil paint to improve its gloss and permanence;[14] and Dossie mentioned that crude turpentine was used as an adulterant for oil of turpentine.[15] Other references to its employment are discussed in connection with varnishes in Chapter 18 below.

As indicated by Evelyn in 1670, *Venice turpentine* is the product of the larch, *Larix decidua* Mill.[16] Like some other early English writers whose works have been noted in connection with the present study, Houghton distinguished it alone from common turpentine, commenting that it came from France and Germany, and was often known as 'Ausburg turpentine'.[17] Watin described *la térébenthine de Venise* as the best for use in varnish, mentioning also its medicinal application, but indicated that it was expensive, and that inferior varieties were often substituted.[18] It seems to have been obtained from many regions of the Alps, since Heaton cited its principal origin as the Tyrol,[19] and Tingry noted its supply from Grisons, Savoy, and Grenoble. In addition, he mentioned the extraction of Venice turpentine from the larches of the Apennines,[20] perhaps explaining Watin's references to *térébenthine de Pise* in two varnish formulae.[21]

Strasbourg turpentine is obtained from the fir *Abies alba* Mill.[22] Tingry mentioned its source as the silver fir, and commented that it took its name from the city where it was most traded. He also called it *turpentine of Alsace*, noting that it was obtained as well from north Germany and Switzerland.[23] Watin, indeed, appears to have called it *térébenthine de Swisse*.[24] In the present century, Heaton stated that it was collected chiefly from the white fir of the Vosges (citing the species as *Abies pectinata*);[25] and Mills & White note that the drying properties which it exhibits are probably conferred on it by the presence of neutral abienol in its composition.[26]

Besides the Mediterranean and New England, Houghton mentioned that crude turpentines were obtained from Norway;[27] and it thus seems likely that material from the Norway spruce, *Picea abies* (L.) Karsten,[28] was being imported into Britain by the latter part of the seventeenth century. In the early nineteenth, Tingry stated that *Burgundy pitch* or *white pitch* was the turpentine of the 'spruce fir, *picea* or *epicea*', describing it as 'a white resinous and pretty thick substance' which exuded from the bark and was collected in the summer, melted, and strained. He noted, however, that a mixture of *galipot* and *barras* was often sold under the same name, although this soon became friable and possessed neither the unctuosity, viscidity, tenacity, nor smell of the true material.[29] In the mid-nineteenth century, Ure defined 'frankincense' as the product of '*Abies excelsa*, the Norway spruce fir',[30] and referred to *Burgundy pitch* as 'frankincense (*Abietis resina*)' which had been refined by melting in water and straining through a course cloth. He also commented, however that the material which was usually sold under this name was 'common resin incorporated with water and coloured with palm oil', noting that in some cases American turpentine was employed.[31] It thus seems clear that the term *Burgundy pitch* must be approached with some caution especially since Watin had applied the designation *poix de Bourgogne* to a wood tar (q.v. below).

Chios turpentine is obtained from *Pistacia atlantica* Desf., a species, not of the Pinaceae, but of the Anacardiaceae family, sometimes considered to be a variety of *P. terebinthus* L. It grows in parts of mainland Greece, Turkey and the Near East, besides the island of Chios.[32] Watin coupled *la térébenthine de Chio* with Venice turpentine as the best for varnish making, but it was, he observed, expensive and used for medicinal purposes;[33] and Tingry too described it as the most esteemed, but rarest.[34] It seems doubtful, therefore, if it would have had much employment in connection with house-painting.

Information on prices for crude turpentines is scant. Stalker & Parker described the clearest, finest, and whitest Venice turpentine as sold at 18*d.* or 20*d.* per pound,[35] while Lewis Berger had stocks of 'Turpentine' amounting to 25 cwt. in 1806 and nearly 14 cwt. in 1810.[36] These were valued at rates of 72*s.* and £10 10*s.* per cwt. respectively the equivalents of about $7\frac{3}{4}$*d.* and 1*s.* $10\frac{1}{2}$*d.* per pound, but further information has so far proved elusive.

OIL OF TURPENTINE

Oil of turpentine is now imported from several countries but although different varieties have varying chemical characteristics, unlike the crude oleo-resins discussed above all behave in much the same way as far as their practical application in house-painting is concerned.[37] On the Continent, most is distilled from the turpentine yielded by *Pinus pinaster* (known also as *P. maritima*); but the only early author to identify the source used, Tingry mentioned that produced from the turpentine of the silver fir, generally known as Strasbourg turpentine.[38] At the end of the nineteenth century, Hurst said that very little French oil of turpentine was exported to England;[39] but minimal information is available from earlier publications on house-painting to indicate the source most commonly used during the period considered in this study. However, as already noted, Houghton adverted to the importation of crude turpentines from the Mediterranean, Scandinavia and New England; while Martin mentioned that which emanated from the Canadian fir.[40] Both references suggest the existence of an established trade with these areas, and the exploitation from an early date of non-European species.

Although properly called oil of turpentine, and referred to by Watin as *l'essence*, *l'huile*, or *l'esprit de térébenthine*,[41] by the 1770s it had become known in England as *turps*,[42] and was also known loosely simply as 'turpentine', a fact which can give rise to confusion. Its use as a thinner for oil paint was practised throughout the period here discussed, and it also formed the solvent for an important group of varnishes discussed below. Although in common with other painting materials its price seems to have remained more or less constant from the latter part of the seventeenth century until towards the end of the eighteenth, it appears to have suffered slightly more from inflation after this period than many others, possibly since trade with France and America, both important suppliers of the commodity, was disrupted; and Englefield refers to the quest for a substitute in 1779 on account of its high price.[43] At the end of the seventeenth century, Stalker & Parker quoted 8*d.* per pound, a price roughly equivalent to 1*s.* 3*d.* per quart;[44] while Salmon indicated its cost as 1*s.* per quart in 1734, the same price as that charged in supplying oil of turpentine at Dyrham Park in 1781.[45] Both are close to the figure of 1*s.* 1½*d.* per quart suggested about 1811 by Pincot as its 'normal' cost 'except under the unpleasant circumstances we now labour in respect to our relations with Holland, America, &c.'. It was not long, he indicated, since its price had been the equivalent of 10*s.* per quart;[46] but this may have been something of an exaggeration, since the increases tabulated by John Phillips do not approach anything like this figure. Starting from 1*s.* between 1760 and 1790, its price had, he indicated, risen to 2*s.* per quart between 1790 and 1803, while in 1812 it stood at 3*s.*, falling back to 2*s.* 9*d.* in 1821.[47] That supplied at Tredegar House in 1793, costing 1*s.* 8*d.* per quart, partly bears this out, although Berger still valued his stock of 40 gallons in 1806 at the equivalent of 1*s.* 1½*d.*, and the same figure appears in the volumes of the *Builders Price-book* for 1810 and 1813.[48] By 1825, however, Lingard indicated the price of the commodity as 1*s.* 9*d.* per quart, showing that to whatever heights it may have risen the price had by then fallen back still further.[49]

ROSIN

The residue remaining in the retort after distillation of oil of turpentine was run off and solidified to form *rosin.* Although quite commonly referred to in earlier literature as 'common resin', or simply 'resin' it is more properly known as rosin in order to distinguish it from other substances forming the large group of natural resins described in Chapter 13. Watin called the material which remained with the water in the retort and solidified *la térébinthine cuite*, noting that after recovery and remelting it became *la colophone* or *l'arançon.*[50] To these names, Tingry added *brai sec* and *poix grecque*;[51] while Nicholson referred to 'the boiled turpentine of commerce'.[52]

Like Watin, Houghton, it will be remembered, described the production of rosin (to which he also referred as *colophony*) by distillation of the crude oleo-resin with four volumes of water, and in the mid-seventeenth century, French had added four volumes of water in the distillation of Venice turpentine;[53] but it is clear that addition of the latter was by no means an invariable practice. Dossie, for example, described white rosin as having been distilled with water, but a brown variety as the result of distillation in its absence;[54] and Stalker & Parker had described the boiling of Venice turpentine with and without water to produce white and amber-coloured products.[55] Tingry too mentioned the difference in technique as producing yellow and black varieties,[56] but later in the nineteenth century, possibly after the introduction of steam distillation, Ure (who reserved the term *colophony* for black rosin) indicated that the difference between the colours was a function of the length of time for which they had been heated.[57] Still later, Hurst observed that the colour differences were dependent on the quality of the original resin and the season in which it had been collected, while Heaton referred to the practice of bleaching the rosin in sunlight to obtain the very palest grades;[58] but there is no evidence to confirm that these subtleties were practised commercially at an earlier date.

The main constituent of rosin is abietic acid ($C_{20}H_{30}O_2$) which exists in a number of isomeric forms. The commodity is insoluble in water, but dissolves in most organic solvents. It is brittle, but softens at about 80°C, giving it poor properties for use in paint or varnish.[59] Nevertheless, it seems to have been widely employed in linseed oil and turpentine varnishes during the eighteenth century (formulae for which are discussed in Chapter 18); and it was also used to add lustre to oil paint, suggestions to that effect being described in Chapter 15. Stalker & Parker described the best 'Rosine' as clear, transparent, and clarified, and sold at 3*d.* per pound, while 'White Rosine' cost 4*d.* to 6*d.*[60] At Tredegar House in 1793 a small quantity of black rosin was supplied at 6*d.* per pound, while Lewis Berger had a stock of nearly 68 cwt. of black rosin in 1806 valued at 12*s.* per cwt., roughly the equivalent of 1½*d.* per pound.[61]

WOOD-TAR AND PITCH

Watin provides a little amplification of Thomas Bent's late seventeenth-century description of wood-tar manufacture quoted at the beginning of this chapter. When logs from the trees which yield turpentine were placed on the fire, he observed that a slightly viscous whitish matter first exuded from their ends, which was called *poix résine blanche.* This was followed by a black oil, and finally a black pitch, which he called *poix de Bourgogne*,[62] although the term 'Burgundy pitch' was generally applied to a crude turpentine (q.v. above).

The earliest description of pitch-making so far located is that provided by John Winthrop the younger, Governor of Connecticut, quoted by John Evelyn in 1664. It was made, he recorded, from the American pitch pine, which grew on barren plains and hills. These often blew down, and when the ground was burnt annually by the Indians the bodies of the trees were consumed, leaving behind knots of timber from the point at which the boughs joined the trunk. The latter were collected and fired in a furnace made with a sloping clay floor which had an outlet for the tar. The knots were piled on this in a similar manner to that employed in charcoal-burning, and covered with clay. During firing, the air supply was carefully regulated, and the tar ran out at the bottom. The same process could, he noted, be performed with the whole tree, but there was a plentiful supply of the knots, which saved labour. From the tar, pitch could be made 'by boiling it to a sufficient *height*'.[63]

In the early nineteenth century Tingry provided engravings of two commercial methods used in Russia;[64] and a few years later Edward Clarke reported on the manufacture of tar in Sweden, noting on a journey from Umeå to Safvar that barrels of this were seen in every creek, ready

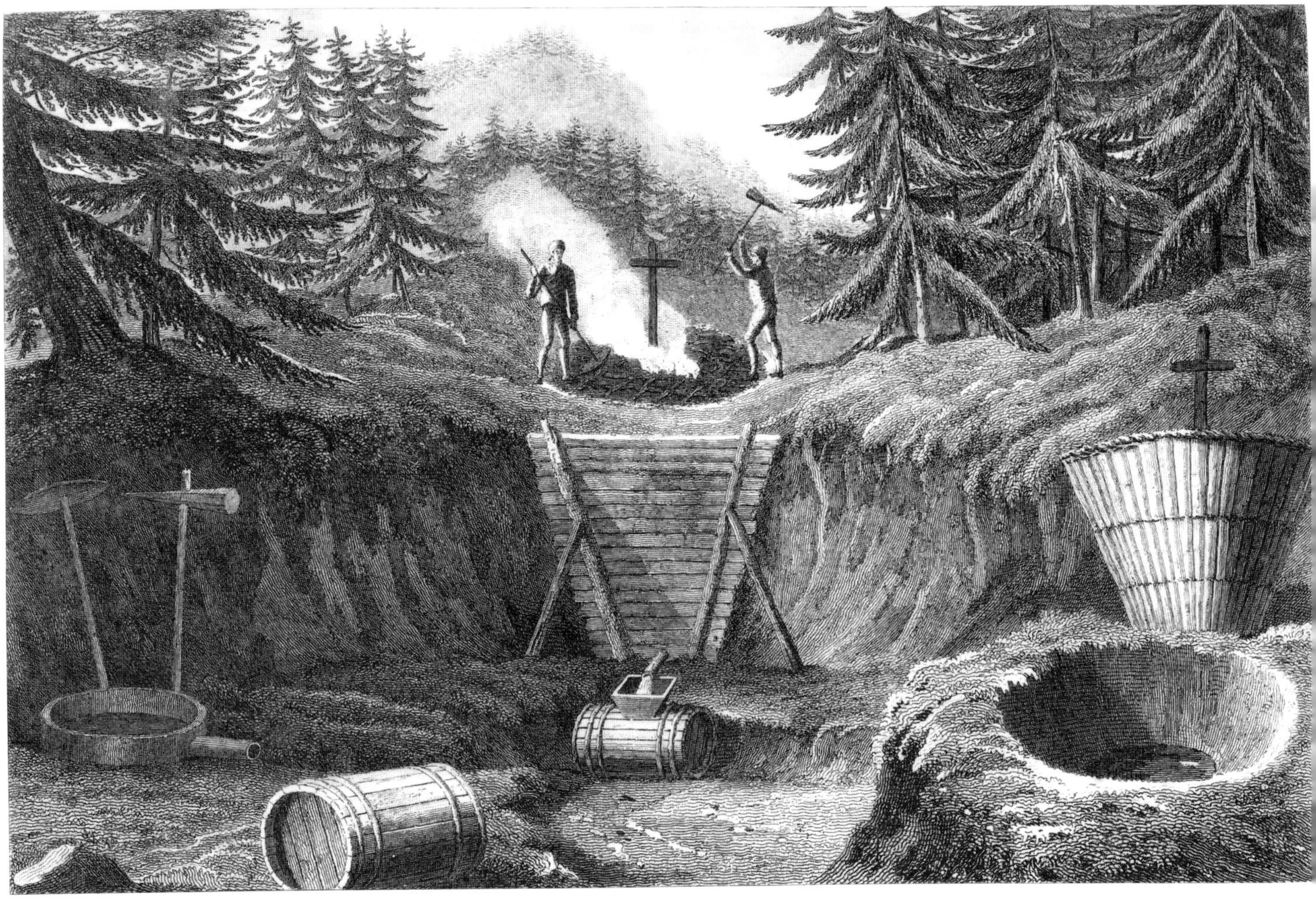

9. Wood-tar manufacture in Sweden in the early nineteenth century.

for export all over Europe, its quality being much superior to Russian or American tar.[65] From the most southern parts of Westro-Bothnia to the northern extremity of the Gulf, the inhabitants were engaged in its manufacture, and on a journey from Piteå he halted to inspect a tar-works. He described the process, which he illustrated (fig. 9), as follows:

> A conical cavity is . . . made in the ground (generally in the side of a bank or sloping hill); and the roots of the fir together with logs or billets of the same, being neatly trimmed into a stack of the same conical shape, are let into this cavity. The whole is then covered with turf, to prevent the volatile parts from being dissipated, which, by means of a heavy wooden mallet, and a wooden stamper, worked separately by two men, is beaten down, and rendered as firm as possible above the wood. The stack of billets is then kindled; and a slow combustion of the fir takes place, without flame, as in making charcoal. During this combustion, the *tar* exudes; and a cast-iron pan being at the bottom of the funnel, with a spout, which projects through the side of the bank, barrels are placed beneath this spout, to collect the fluid as it comes away. As fast as the barrels are filled, they are bunged, and ready for immediate exportation.[66]

Ure, who quoted this description, noted that the varieties of tar which were imported into Britain comprised Stockholm, Archangel, and American produce.[67]

Pitch and tar were used as vehicles for cheap exterior paints (suggestions to this effect being made, for example, by Dossie and Crease)[68] but were not employed for the finer requirements of interior decoration, although Pratt commented that to prevent warping, cracking, and rotting of wainscots, especially those set against external or stone walls 'it's thought very good to pitch them on the back'.[69] In 1781, various quantities of tar were purchased for an unknown use at Osterley Park at a rate of 1*s.* 4*d.* per gallon, a barrel costing 32*s.*;[70] and the previous year 10lb. of pitch cost 1*s.* 10*d.*[71] In 1803 Soane purchased a small quantity of pitch for an unknown purpose at a rate of 3*d.* per pound.[72]

CHAPTER 12

SOLVENTS AND THINNERS OTHER THAN TURPENTINE

Besides oil of turpentine, a number of other organic solvents were used in paint or in varnish manufacture. Apart from ethyl alcohol, the most important for the latter purpose, all were of vegetable origin.

ETHYL ALCOHOL

Ethyl alcohol is obtained by the fermentation of sugars in solution to provide a weak aqueous mixture, the alcohol generally amounting to a maximum of 12 to 13 per cent. To obtain a higher concentration it is necessary to distill the product, the resulting fluid having been known throughout the period considered in this book as *spirit of wine*. By a single distillation only moderate concentration of the spirit is possible, but by careful repetition of the process it is possible to obtain concentrations of around 95 per cent of alcohol. This further refinement was known as rectification, the product being referred to as *rectified spirit of wine*. The procedure was known in the middle ages and was described in detail by John French, who illustrated a linked series of stills for the purpose in 1651 (fig. 10), commenting: 'By Furnaces and Vessels made after this insuing figure there may be made four rectifications of any Spirit at once.'[1]

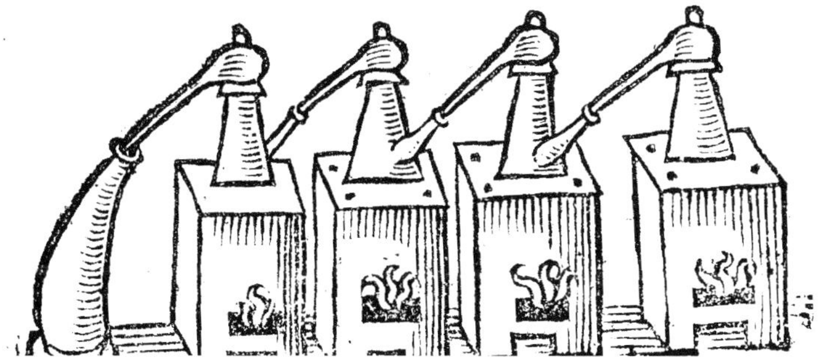

10. A system of linked stills proposed in the mid-seventeenth century for the rectification of ethyl alcohol.

To free the alcohol completely from water it is necessary to absorb the latter chemically. The thirteenth-century writer Ramón Lull appears to have produced absolute alcohol by a triple distillation of spirit with which quicklime (calcium oxide) had been mixed,[2] and the same method was practised in the mid-seventeenth century, when French directed:

> Take of the best rectified spirit of Wine, with which imbibe the strongest unslaked lime, until they be made into a past; then put them into a Glass-gourd and distill off the spirit in ashes: This Spirit pour on more fresh Lime, and doe as before, doe this three or four times, and thou shalt have a very subtile Spirit able to dissolve most things.[3]

Ure noted that it was necessary to leave the alcohol in contact with the quicklime for twenty-four hours before re-distillation, and both he and Church noted a range of alternative substances which could be used.[4] Of these, it appears that dried salt of tartar (anhydrous sodium tartrate) was of early introduction, its simple mixture with 'Brandy, (as they call weak spirit of Wine of the first distillation,)' being described by Robert Boyle in 1671.[5] By the eighteenth century it was being used in distillation, but Watin noted that such 'esprit-de-vin tartarisé' could prove troublesome in use.[6]

Pure, or *absolute*, alcohol has a specific gravity considerably less than that of water, and this provides a ready means of determining the relative percentages in a given sample, providing the temperature of the mixture is known. The proportion of alcohol can then be expressed by either weight or volume. In 1816, Tingry's English editor gave the specific gravity of rectified spirit of wine at 55° to 60°F. as 0.830, implying an alcohol content of roughly 91 per cent by volume;[7] and Ure gave figures fixed by the London, Edinburgh, and Dublin Colleges of Physicians of 0.838 or 0.840, the equivalents of approximately 88 or 88.5 per cent by volume.[8] Hurst too gave 0.838, indicating that this was equivalent to 86 per cent of alcohol.[9] On the evidence available, however, it seems that such high concentrations may not always have been in common use for varnish-making, at least during the earlier part of the period being considered. Thus in 1688 Stalker & Parker provided the following advice on purchase of the commodity:

> To make Varnish you must have Spirit of Wine, which must be strong, or it will spoyl the Varnish, and not dissolve your Gums, and consequently hinder your design; for the stronger your spirits are, the better will the Varnish be; the Spirits only being to dissolve the Gums, in order to make them spread, or lie even upon the work. After it hath performed that work, the sooner they evaporate the better, and the higher the Spirits are

> drawn, the less flegm or watery parts are in them; and the less of watery parts are in the Varnish, the sooner it dries, and is fit for polishing, is more permanent, and will come to the greater and better gloss. But this is of little use now Varnish is so much used; for the Distillers have learned by practice and custom to make Spirits that just dissolve the gums, only it requires the longer drying: Yet these Spirits that are commonly used will sometimes be too weak, either by neglect or dishonesty of the Distiller, who hath not sufficiently deflegm'd or drawn all the watery from the spiritous parts. Therefore the best way to prove your Spirits, is to take some in a spoon, and put a little Gun-powder in it, and then set the Spirit on fire with a little paper or candle, as you do Brandy, and if it burn so long till it fire the Gunpowder before it go out, it is fit for use, and will dissolve your gums.[10]

The test they suggested is, of course, the old method for determination of *proof spirit*, defined by 58 Geo. III, c. 28 as weighing twelve-thirteenths of an equal volume of distilled water at 51°F. Ure gave this as the equivalent of a mixture having a specific gravity of 0.919 at 60°F., or roughly 57 per cent by volume, although at the end of the century Hurst gave 0.926 indicating that this corresponded with 49 per cent of alcohol.[11] Interestingly, Watin too described the gunpowder test, noting it was just about adequate, although, he advised, one could be surer of one's spirit by comparing its weight with that of a known sample.[12] The time-honoured method was, however, rejected by Tingry, who advocated the use of the hydrometer, a device with which Boyle had been experimenting over a century earlier.[13]

Use of mere proof spirit during at least some of the period examined thus seems possible, and it is worth noting that this concentration is similar to that achieved by primary commercial methods during the first half of the nineteenth century. Ure, for example, described the Dorn still in which two distillations took place, providing a product of 60 per cent; and an improvement, the Coffey still, patented in 1830.[14] *Proof spirit* and *rectified spirit* were, he indicated, the two commonly sold concentrations.[15] The stress laid by Stalker & Parker on the desirability of using the strongest possible spirit is, however, significant; and it is of moment too that Watin stipulated it was necessary that the spirit should be well rectified and as concentrated as possible.[16] These references suggest, perhaps, that during the earlier years covered by this study proof spirit was regarded as the absolute minimum which could be used; but by the late 1820s, when nomenclature seems clearer and standards had been set for the concentrations sold, it is notable that Vanherman mentioned the employment of 'Rectified Spirits of Wine' as a thinner for his 'Aromatic Paint'.[17] By 1860, the recently introduced duty-free methylated spirit appears to have become widely employed, Ure mentioning its extensive use in varnishes and lacquers, and giving its constitution (since modified) as spirit of wine having a specific gravity of not less than 0.830 with an addition of 10 per cent of wood spirit (methyl alcohol) to prevent its consumption.[18]

OIL OF CARAWAY

'Oil of carraway' was suggested by Cadet-de-Vaux as an alternative to linseed oil in his recipe for milk painting, especially in the preparation of a fine white (a suggestion copied by Butcher), and by Vanherman as a constituent of the thinner for his 'Aromatic Paint'.[19] Ure indicated that it was extracted from the seeds of the plant *Carum carui*, but it seems unlikely to have been used to any great extent.[20]

OIL OF LAVENDER OR SPIKE

Tingry described the manufacture of essential oil of lavender by the distillation of the flowers or tops with water, indicating that essential oil of spike was the same, but produced from a different variety of the plant.[21] Ure gave the species as *Lavendula vera* and *L. spicata* respectively, mentioning that the latter was used by porcelain painters and by artists in making varnish.[22] Church too referred to both varieties, stating that they were used for painting without any treatment other than re-distillation, which, he cautioned, should be carried out after contact with quicklime for twenty-four hours and not following treatment with caustic potash. Oil of spike was, he indicated, a powerful solvent for many resins.[23]

Between 1630 and 1635, seventy yards of painting were executed in connection with the new chapel at Somerset House 'in white lead and spicke';[24] and an agreement of 1665 with Robert Streeter (the Sergeant Painter) for the painting of Clarendon House, Piccadilly, stipulated the inclusion of spike oil in the second undercoat.[25] In addition, the seventeenth-century French author Félibien mentioned its use as a thinner for oil paint.[26] Writing in the early nineteenth century, however, the author of the *Painter's . . . Pocket Manual* indicated that it was hardly ever free from impurity and its use was generally renounced;[27] while Whittock remarked that although oil of spike or lavender had formerly been employed by house-painters instead of oil of turpentine the latter was by his time preferred and the former was only used for enamelling.[28] It seems doubtful, however, that *Lavendula* oils would have been used for house-painting, other than in exceptional cases, at any date.

OIL OF RHODIUM

It was laid down that oil of rhodium (which, Ure indicated, was extracted from the wood of *Convolvulus scoparius*)[29] was to be used in the finishing coat for the painting of Clarendon House, Piccadilly, in 1665.[30] This seems, however, to have been an exceptional specification.

CHAPTER 13

RESINS AND OTHER SUBSTANCES USED IN VARNISH

Besides many of the materials already described, a wide range of natural resins and other substances was used in the manufacture of varnish during the period under review. These are now discussed under three main headings: the resins (variously soluble in linseed oil, oil of turpentine, or alcohol) forming its basic constituent; camphor, used on occasion to improve flexibility; and colouring agents, some of which were resins, and others dyes capable of solution in organic solvents.

BASIC VARNISH RESINS

The subject of natural varnish resins is extremely complex, and even today some of the species from which the substances have been obtained have not been completely identified (notably those yielding the copals, damars, and elemis), although others are better defined. Nor have all the organic constituents been determined. Early writers were often obscure in their nomenclature, and, writing at the beginning of the present century, A.H. Sabin remarked that one of the most serious difficulties in approaching the subject was posed by the fact that in different countries different names were given to the same resin, and the same name to different resins.[1] Moreover, many of the materials formerly exploited are now virtually obsolete commercially, and interest in the subject is more or less confined to botanists or those concerned with craft techniques used in a wide range of historical artifacts, ranging from ethnographic objects to fine art. On this account, the amount of directly relevant recent research is limited; but, following the development of more subtle analytical methods, in particular gas chromatography, allowing more detailed identification of organic constituents, increasing attention is being given to the subject of historic varnishes. Such modern analytical techniques provide considerable potential, although many of the substances originally present in varnish formulae undergo changes with time, volatiles evaporate, complex polymers are formed, and progress is hampered by the lack of a complete *corpus* of knowledge of the species of plant exploited in the first instance. Besides this, many harder resins were melted before incorporation with the solvents, a process described by Theophilus (probably about 1100),[2] which will also have altered their original character.

In the discussion of individual resins which follows, it has not been thought necessary for present purposes to include descriptions of the organic compounds forming their constitution, even where these have been adequately identified, but a summary based on the important résumé published by John Mills & Raymond White is provided (table VI, p. 76). The general basis for their classification is division of resins into two distinct classes, those containing diterpenoids, which come from certain species of the order Coniferales and the Leguminosae family of the Rosales, and those containing triterpenoids from several families of broad-leaved trees. For more detailed information on individual constituents, however, attention is directed to their paper.[3]

With the exception of lac, which is produced by insect activity, resins are the product of trees and occur in the form of sticky exudations on the trunk or branches. Before describing these in more detail, a number of definitions have to be made. In the first place, although the term *gum* has often been applied to resins, a clear distinction is now made between the two groups: *resins* are insoluble in water and dissolve only in organic solvents; whereas *gums* are more or less soluble in water, or may swell to form a jelly-like mass when placed in it, but are insoluble in organic solvents. *Oleo-resins* are a mixture of a resin with an essential oil, the crude turpentines discussed in Chapter 11 being one example. In their fresh state resins from vegetable sources are known as *recent resins*, but many may be found in a fossilised or semi-fossilised state, and have been imported as *fossil resins*. The latter group has been widely used for the manufacture of oil varnishes, while the recent resins are generally softer and used in spirit varnish. Fossil resins do not dissolve easily in linseed oil, and in order to achieve solution must first be *run*, that is, heated to melting point, altering the structure of the complex substances of which they are composed. The technique was used by Watin,[4] and at the beginning of the nineteenth century. Tingry described a special furnace for the purpose (fig. 11).[5]

Amber

The fossil resin amber, known mineralogically as *succinite*, occurs in the greensand beds of the Cretaceous period in a belt extending from England to the Baltic coast and beyond. English sources, principally comprising pieces washed up on the shores of East Anglia, seem to have been of strictly limited importance, and those of the Baltic, where large deposits have been mined or quarried as well

Table VI. *Notable components of resins yielded by different species as given by Mills & White, 'Natural Resins' (1977)*

Class	Order	Family	Genus	Species	Product	Components	
DITERPENOIDS							
Gymnospermae	Coniferales	Pinaceae	*Pinus*	various	Common turpentine	abietadiene and lesser amounts of pimaradiene acids	–
			Do.	extinct	Amber		abietane, pimarane, and labdane compounds
		Do.	*Picea*	*abies*	Burgundy pitch		–
		Do.	*Abies*	*alba*	Strasbourg turpentine		neutral abienol (or its oxidation products)
		Do.	*Larix*	*decidua*	Venice turpentine		manool, larixol, and larixyl acetate
	Do.	Cupressaceae	*Tetraclinis*	*articulata*	Sandarac resin	phenols, communic acid (or its polymers), and pimaradiene acids (especially sandaracopimaric acid)	
	Do.	Araucariaceae	*Agathis*	*dammara*	Manila copal	sandaracopimaric, agathic, & polymerised communic acids	–
			Do.	*australis*	Kauri resin		abietic acid & co-polymerised communic acid & communol
Angiospermae (sub-class Dicotyledoneae)	Rosales	Leguminosae (sub-family Caesalpinioideae)	*Hymenea*	various	Brazil and East African copals	labdanes of the enantiomeric series and derived compounds, polymers probably from ozic acid or a related compound	
TRITERPENOIDS							
Angiospermae (sub-class Dicotyledoneae)	Guttiferales	Dipterocarpaceae (sub-family Dipterocarpoideae)	*Hopea*	various	Damar	dammarane compounds, and sometimes oleanane and ursane compounds	
Do.	Sapindales	Anacardiaceae	*Pistacia*	*lentiscus*	Mastic resin	keto-acids of euphane skeleton, oleanonic acid, and compounds of the euphane and oleanane series	
Do.	Rutales	Burseraceae	*Canarium*	*luzonicum*	Manila elemi	α- and β- amyrin	'elemi acids' (euphanes)
		Do.	*Bursera*	various	S. American elemis		–
		Do.	*Protium*	various			
OTHER							
Angiospermae (sub-class Dicotyledoneae)	Ebenales	Styracaceae	*Styrax*	various	Benzoin	coniferyl benzoate	

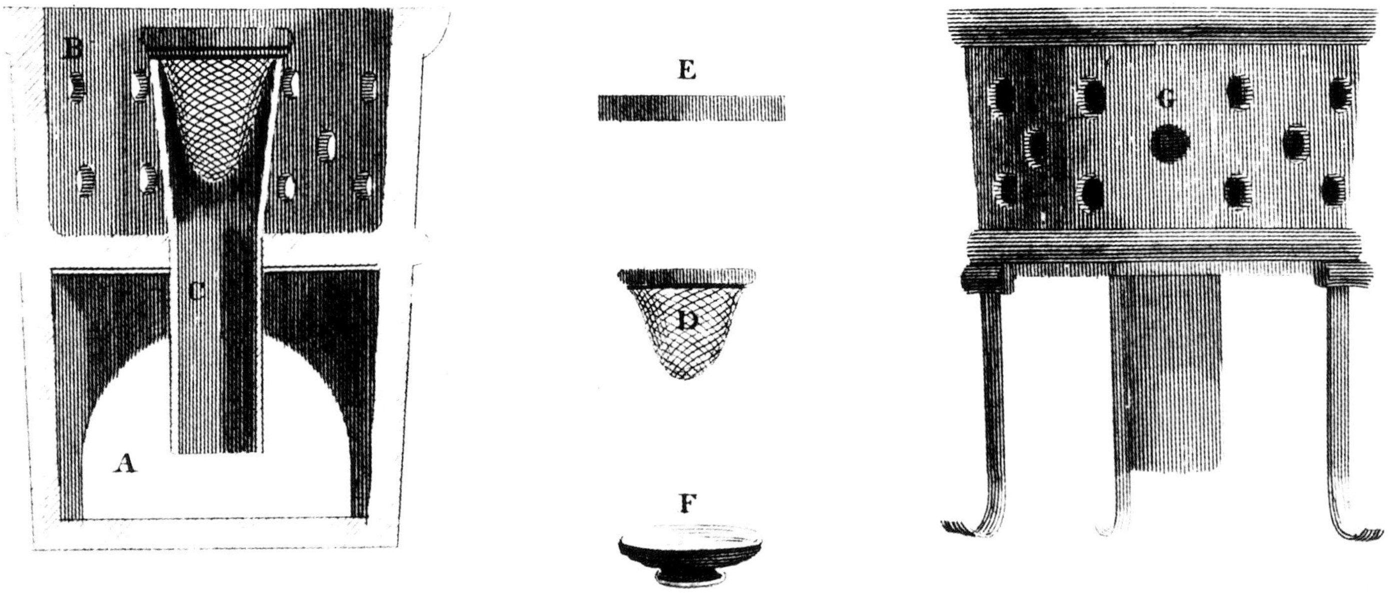

11. Early nineteenth-century furnace for melting copal and amber.

as collected from the coast or dragged from the sea, were the most extensively exploited.[6] Recently, by analysis of its organic chemical constituents, it has been possible to confirm the long-standing theory of its natural origin as the oleo-resin of one or more extinct species of *Pinus*.[7] Amber was the hardest of the varnish resins, and had to be run to become sufficiently soluble in linseed oil or oil of turpentine, although it is more or less insoluble in alcohol, and varies in colour from off-white to brown or red. Its use for fine-art purposes was recommended in the second half of the seventeenth century, when it was included in at least one formula for a picture varnish;[8] but it had been known since classical times, when it was called *electron* on account of its electrostatic properties. Watin, who described amber (*karabé*) as commonly found in the sea at Danzig (now Gdansk), stated that together with copal it was the principal constituent of oil varnishes, but also drew attention to an apparently similar substance obtained at the beginning of the eighteenth century from Marseilles, and warned particularly that the Dutch passed off an American material called 'gomme de look' in its place.[9] The so-called Travancore ambers occur in the East Indies, and several similar substances are found in other parts of the world.[10]

The extent to which varnishes containing amber were in use for house-painting purposes is not clear, although Vanherman indicated that these were prepared in a similar way to copal varnishes;[11] but the author of the *Painter's . . . Pocket Manual* (1825) remarked that, while amber varnish had been in very general use, 'of late, copal, on account of its being less coloured, has obtained a preference', and Vanherman too had drawn attention to the 'high coloured' nature of the former.[12] Ure recorded the importation of rough amber in 1855 and 1856 as 7 cwt. and 1 cwt. respectively, suggesting that by that date it was hardly ever employed;[13] and Hurst, while mentioning that it yielded the finest and most durable varnish, giving a firm and elastic coat which resisted the action of the atmosphere exceedingly well, observed that on account of its dark colour and expense it was rarely used.[14]

Animi

See under *Copal* below.

Benzoin

Hurst gave the origin of benzoin (which was often known during the seventeenth century as *benjamin*) as the species *Styrax benzoin* growing in Sumatra, Java, Borneo, Siam, Laos, and other parts of the Malay Archipelago, although other species of the same genus may also have been exploited. He indicated that Sumatra and Siam (Thailand) were the principal commercial sources, and described the cultivation of trees from seed in the former country. These were tapped by means of incisions made in the bark when seven years old, and yielded resin over a period of nine years, although in the interior regions resin was collected from wild trees. The Siamese and Sumatran products, he indicated, differed slightly in their appearance: that from Siam was imported in the form of milk-white tears, or an agglomerate of these in a yellowish matrix, while the Sumatran product was rather greyer in colour, having white tears in a darker translucent matrix.[15] The resin is soluble in alcohol and has a distinctive fragrant odour which seems to have provided the main reason for its use in varnishes. Watin, for example, drew attention to this characteristic,[16] and Ure remarked that it was principally used in perfumery and in the composition of certain varnishes for snuff-boxes and walking-sticks to provide an agreeable smell when these were warmed by the hand.[17] Hurst too indicated that it was used principally on this account.[18]

The descriptions of both Watin and Tingry tally well with Hurst's account of the two varieties of benzoin, Watin in particular drawing attention to the two forms in which it was found, *en larmes* and *en masse*, adding that the former was preferable, but more expensive and not in common use.[19] Stalker & Parker also provided advice on selection of the resin, recommending that in choosing 'Benjamin, or Benzoine' the best was that of a bright reddish colour 'very like to clarified Rosine, but never so fine, freest from dross or filth'. Its price, they indicated, ranged from 4*d.* to 6*d.* or 8*d.* per ounce, depending on its quality.[20]

Copaiva balsam

Vanherman included 'Capavi' in a list of soft resins.[21] This no doubt refers to copaiva balsam, which Heaton defined as the oleo-resin obtained from various species of *Copaifera* in South America, and was used as a plasticiser.[22] Ure called it *capivi*, citing the principal species from which it was obtained as *C. officinalis*, growing in Brazil and Cayenne (French Guiana), although he listed others. It was, he said, soluble in absolute alcohol, but only partially so in spirit of wine, and it was used as a constituent in many lacquers and varnishes.[23] 'Copaiba' balsam was mentioned by the mid-seventeenth-century medical writer Guliemus Piso, who indicated that the trees easily yielded copious quantities and described the manner in which they were tapped.[24]

Copal, animi, and kauri resins

The term 'copal' has come to be used for a large group of resins, most generally those characterised by their hardness and relatively high melting point. They are the product of trees of the Leguminosae and Araucariaceae families and can be found both as recent resins and in a fossilised or semi-fossilised state. The latter 'hard' and 'half-hard' copals have to run to make them soluble in drying oils, but the 'soft' copals are used in spirit varnishes. Most of those freely exported in the past are, however, no longer exploited, and the principal though still limited imports today are generally of soft copal from the East Indies.[25]

Modern writers define five basic groups of copal resins, those from East Africa, West Africa, and South America produced by various Leguminosae species belonging to the sub-family of Caesalpinioideae, and those from eastern Asia and New Zealand from species of the family Araucariaceae. In the mid-eighteenth century, Dossie mentioned that supplies of 'animi' and 'copal' were brought from the East and West Indies and Africa,[26] other available evidence tending to suggest that America was the main source exploited until the second half of the eighteenth century or beginning of the nineteenth; while material from New Zealand was not commercially available until later.

Although the term copal appears to have been used by some authorities to denote a hard resin suitable for use in oil varnishes, and Watin, for example, described it and amber as the principal constituent of these,[27] Tingry included a recent resin under the same collective noun which was at least partly soluble in alcohol and oil of turpentine;[28] and, as already mentioned, modern 'copal' resin is of the spirit-soluble type. Stalker & Parker too suggested that 'copal' should be dissolved in alcohol, and by way of general advice directed that the best 'Gum Capall' was:

> the whitest, freest from dross, and thick dark stuff that is incorporated with the Gum. It is of it self a thick whitish heavy Gum, and rarely without that dark and drossy mixture; but that which is clearest and freest from the said stuff is the best.

The price was, they added, 1*s*., 1*s*. 4*d*., or 1*s*. 6*d*. per pound according to the quality.[29]

1. East African copal

It has been suggested that the trade in East African copal began as early as the tenth century when the Arabs exchanged it for cotton cloth, although it may not have been significantly developed until the second half of the eighteenth. The export of copal and ivory were made a monopoly of the Sultan of Zanzibar in 1839, and American merchants were actively involved from 1859.[30] Howes gives the species from which the celebrated fossilised or semi-fossilised resin originated as *Trachylobium verrucosum*,[31] but more recently this has been reconsidered, and the tree responsible is now thought to belong to the genus *Hymenea*, and is hence known as *H. verrucosum*.[32] In the nineteenth century, the noted source of high-quality fossil resin was the island of Zanzibar, and Hurst described the method of collection there and on the neighbouring mainland, where the ground was prodded during the rainy season by collectors using iron rods in order to locate the pieces of buried resin, which occurred generally at a depth between eighteen inches and three feet. The pieces were cleaned to reveal their pale yellow or amber-coloured interior, which was second only to amber in hardness. He described the resin as soluble in linseed oil and in oil of turpentine after running, but not in alcohol.[33] Heaton adds that it was scarce, expensive, and used only in the highest quality varnishes. It was, he notes, formerly obtained primarily from Zanzibar; but he mentions that digging there had declined and the trade transferred to Tanganyika (now Tanzania), resin from this source being exported from Lindi. He refers also to a similar resin called Mozambique or Inhambane copal, and mentions importation during the first half of the present century of fossil copal from Madagascar,[34] a source discussed in the first half of the nineteenth by the French writer N.J.B.G. Guibourt.[35]

On the evidence to hand, it is impossible to judge the extent to which East African resins were used for varnish-making during the eighteenth century and before. Although the mid-sixteenth-century physician Georgius Agricola was certain that amber-like fossil resins were obtained from Africa, he noted the silence of earlier writers on their precise origin;[36] and it is unclear whether, in mentioning islands around Africa as a source of what appear to have been recent resins, the contemporary medical writer Amatus Lusitanus was necessarily referring to Zanzibar or Madagascar.[37] Nor does terminology help. Dossie certainly mentioned Africa as a source of 'animi';[38] but although Hurst reserved the term *animi* for East African or Zanzibar copal (a nomenclature followed also by Heaton)[39] it is obvious that earlier writers did not restrict it in this way, and commonly applied it to soft resins from various countries, which often contained entrapped insects. Thus, although Tingry described an 'animi' from Ethiopia, he also applied the name to a resin from Brazil discussed below, noting that the latter was more common in commerce;[40] and Ure too mentioned 'animé' of South American origin.[41] It is also evident that the use made of 'Gum animæ' by Stalker & Parker in a formula for an oil gold-size without running rules out its identification with Zanzibar fossil copal;[42] while both Tingry and Whittock used 'animi' in spirit varnishes, clearly eliminating any possibility that the term was earlier reserved for hard East African resin.[43]

2. West African copals

A large number of both fossil and recent resins has been obtained from West Africa, particularly during the last hundred years, although the species yielding these have still not been completely identified. Hurst described the fossil resins as resembling those from East Africa, and second only to them, although not quite so hard. They were known generally by the names of the countries from which they were shipped, and he listed Sierra Leone copal; Angola copal; and varieties from Gaboon (now Gabon) and Loango (now in the country known as the Congo). Each had slightly different properties, but no living tree was known yielding such resins, although, he observed, it was possible that one or more species might be found once the inland areas became better known. Both he and Church described Sierra Leone copal, in particular the variety known as pebble copal, as the best, and soluble in linseed oil only after running; but the latter indicated that it was partially soluble in oil of turpentine and that the species from which it was obtained had been identified as *Copaifera guibourtiana*.[44] Later, Heaton observed that the supply of fossil resin from Sierra Leone was practically exhausted, and that it was the recent resin from this species which was imported;[45] while, more recently, Howes notes that resin from the Congo, which Hurst had described as available only in small quantities, had been the most important in the period between the two World Wars.[46] No specific reference to West African copals has been encountered in the earlier literature on house-painting which has formed the basis of the present study, although Dossie referred to Africa as a source without qualification,[47] and recent resins were certainly being obtained from the area in the mid-sixteenth century, when Amatus Lusitanus noted that the Portuguese brought them from Guinea (then probably referring to the whole stretch of coast from the country currently known by that name right down to the Congo or Angola). In particular, he mentioned Mina (now Elmina in Ghana) as a source of supply.[48]

3. South American, Caribbean, and Mexican resins

As in Africa, resins are produced in South America by trees belonging to the genus *Hymenaea* of the sub-family Caesalpinioideae of the Leguminosae, and have been procured in either a fossilised or a recent state, in the latter case often being in the form of a soft 'elemi'. The species most generally mentioned is *H. courbaril*, and the two sources particularly noted in late nineteenth- and twentieth-century literature are Brazil and British Guiana (now Guyana), the latter having provided the fossil Demerara copal which Hurst described as an excellent oil varnish resin, not soluble in alcohol. It was collected, he noted, in much the same manner as 'animi and copal' (by this he meant African fossil resins); and, once freed from the outer crust, was quite clear and transparent, commonly occurring in large masses of 10 or 12 lbs. weight.[49] Earlier, however, it seems that recent resins were of major importance, and material of this character was also obtained from Mexico and the islands of the West Indies.

Resins from the South American mainland appear often to have been known in the nineteenth century as *animi*, Hurst, indeed, adverting to the alternative name 'Demerara animi' for fossil Demerara material. Ure noted that 'animé' exuded from the courbaril of Cayenne (French Guiana) and elsewhere in South America, and was a pale brown-yellow in colour.[50] He further commented that the trees appeared to belong to the genus *Hymenaea*, and the resin often contained insects belonging to living species, thus meriting the term 'animé'. After running, it was extensively used by varnish-makers.[51] Of 'Gum Anima', which was, he said, produced by the courbaril, Tingry noted it came particularly from Brazil (this being more commonly found in commerce than the variety from Ethiopia), noting that the best pieces were fairly large and appeared marbled with white, opaque, and yellow transparent veins. He commented too on its sweet and agreeable smell.[52]

This latter characteristic was particularly attributed to American animi by the sixteenth-century Spanish physician Nicholas Monardes, who differentiated the latter from copal (which, he said, had less aroma), noting: 'THEY doe bryng from the newe Spaine twoo kindes of Rosine, that be both a like, much one to the other, the one is called Copall, and the other Anime.' Animi, he said, was the resin of a large tree. It was white in colour, and similar in appearance to incense, although the particles were somewhat larger and 'beyng broken, it hath a yeallowe colour, as Rosine hath'. Copal (which, he reported, was used by the Indians as incense) was, on the other hand, very white and came in large pieces.[53]

It seems clear that, following their discovery, American resins were rapidly promoted in Europe for medical purposes; and it appears of particular semantic significance for study of the developing resin trade that the mid-seventeenth-century writer Guliemus Piso noted 'copal' was the word the American Indians applied to all aromatic resins and gums.[54] Whether it was thus to American material that Stalker & Parker referred as 'Capall' is unclear;[55] but this seems quite likely, and in the mid-eighteenth century Dossie was certainly familar with use in varnish of resins from the area, although he did not differentiate between animi and copal.[56] Watin and the author of the *Practical Treatise*, however, specifically referred to copal from New Spain (Mexico in its former, larger borders). This, Watin differentiated from resin from Cayenne (French Guiana) and the Antilles (West Indies);[57] and Tingry and Ure too seem to distinguish it from that of the South American mainland, discussing resin from Mexico under the heading *copal* rather than *animi*.

Of copal, Tingry noted that it distilled naturally from a large tree abundant in New Spain, and was procured in the form of a hard solid which was transparent with a shining surface of faint lemon colour sometimes inclining to orange. It was, he added, partially soluble in pure alcohol, or, after treatment, in oil of turpentine.[58] Ure, who also noted that it exuded spontaneously, indicated that it was imported in the form of small flat fragments, which were hard, rough, usually yellow, and without taste or smell. He cited the producing species as *Rhus copallinum* indicating that it came from the Antilles, Mexico, and North America.[59] The 1810 edition of the *Encyclopaedia Britannica* also names New Spain as the source and cites the same species as producing copal.[60] Mexican copal was mentioned by Church, but not by Hurst or Heaton, suggesting that it had ceased to be of commercial importance by the end of the nineteenth century.[61]

4. Asiatic copals

Howes lists various sources of copal resin in the East Indies, indicating that although these were originally exploited in fossil form, recent resins are widely obtained; and most copal available today is of this latter type.[62] Heaton described the East Indian resins as forming a group ranging in hardness from varieties about as hard as Congo copal to those almost as soft and soluble as damar, discussed below. They were, he observed, often referred to in general as Manila copals, although similar material was obtained from other islands.[63] Hurst noted that Manila copal was partly soluble in oil of turpentine, but completely soluble in alcohol and employed in spirit varnishes.[64] The trees yielding the resin belong to the genus *Agathis*, modern writers mentioning *A. alba* or *A. dammara*;[65] although during the nineteenth century Ure regarded one source as *Elaeocarpus copalifer* and noted that the resin was soft and transparent and dissolved completely in oil of turpentine.[66] Earlier authors who mentioned the East Indies as a source of copal include Dossie and Tingry, the latter remarking, however, that it was rarer than copal from the West Indies.[67]

5. Kauri resin

Another species of *Agathis*, the Kauri pine, *A. australis*, growing in New Zealand produces a resin which has been obtained in both fossil and recent states, although in this case the fossil variety is thought to be of comparatively recent age, perhaps only hundreds of years old.[68] It was considered by Hurst as far from equalling the African copals, and he noted that in the form in which it was obtained it was partially soluble in oil of turpentine and alcohol, and completely so after running, although its properties in this respect could vary.[69] In the mid-nineteenth century, Ure described the resin as a 'new and peculiar substance' imported under the name *cowdie resin*;[70] and it seems unlikely to have been of any importance during the period under consideration.

Damar

Resin is yielded by trees belonging to the sub-family Dipterocarpoideae of the Dipterocarpaceae family found over a wide area of the Far East, including the Seychelles, Philippines, New Guinea, Malaysia, and Indonesia, the total number of species numbering over five hundred. The harder of these have been exploited as damar resin, and modern examples are thought to emanate from a species of *Hopea* so far unidentified;[71] although late nineteenth-century writers such as Church and Hurst mentioned *H. odorata* and *H. micrantha* as providing 'rock damar'; and also species of the genus *Dammara* (*D. orientalis*, producing 'Singapore' or 'white damar'), *Vateria* (*V. indica*, and *V. acuminata*, the former providing 'piney resin', also known as 'white damar', and the latter a similar product from Ceylon (now Sri Lanka)), and *Shorea* (*S. robusta*, from which 'sal damar' was obtained). The resins occur generally in the form of hard white nodules or in stalactitic form, and are insoluble in alcohol but soluble in oil of turpentine: this had been regarded as distinguishing them from the 'copals', although Hurst indicated that they were sometimes classed within this general group.[72] Although Howes relates that the word damar first came into English usage when the earliest British traders visited Malaya, no explicit reference to damar has been encountered in any of the early nineteenth-century literature or earlier works on the subject of house-painting which has formed the basis of the present study. He remarks, moreover, that to natives of the producing areas 'copal' and 'damar' were the same, pointing out that the latter was the native term, the word copal being of Mexican origin.[73] It is possible, therefore, that damars of varying type were in use for turpentine varnishes during the period presently being considered.

Elemi oleo-resin

Soft oleo-resins may be obtained from a number of species belonging to the family of Burseraceae which are distributed from the East Indies to Mauritius, West Africa, South America, and the West Indies. The Manila elemi imported today is the product of *Canarium luzonicum* but, although Mills & White note that the Philippines have been known as a source since about 1700, the only references encountered in eighteenth- and early nineteenth-century literature on house-painting are to African or South American supplies.[74] Of these, Tingry regarded that from Ethiopia as the genuine kind, indicating that it contained reddish veins and was superior to material from America on account of the toughness and odiferous qualities which it imparted to varnishes.[75]

The products of the West Indian, and South and Central American genera *Protium* and *Bursera*, which Mills & White note have sometimes gone under the name 'elemi', were, they mention, imported to Europe from the sixteenth century onwards.[76] In the mid-seventeenth century, Piso noted that 'Elemni' came from an olive-like tree,[77] and in the mid-eighteenth Watin described *elemi* as a yellowish or slightly greenish-white substance obtained from the wild olive of Mexico, which was imported in pieces weighing two or three pounds wrapped in leaves of the Indian cane. He advised that those pieces should be chosen, which, being dry on the outside, were like molasses within, and noted the use of *elemi* to give flexibility and body to spirit varnishes and enable them to take a polish, adding, however, that turpentines were often substituted.[78] The author of the 1810 edition of the *Encyclopaedia Britannica* and Ure gave the species yielding the substance as *Amyris elemifera*, the former mentioning the West Indies and the latter South America, in particular Brazil.[79]

In the 1860 edition of Ure's *Dictionary* the editor noted that the description in the former edition was incorrect, and that most elemi was imported via Holland from the Dutch settlements.[80] Since the East Indies were also mentioned as a source in the 1810 *Encyclopaedia Britannica*,[81] it therefore seems likely that during the first half of the nineteenth century this area took over as the main source of supply, especially because, although Hurst mentioned resin from both Mexico and Brazil, he indicated that Mexican material was not very common and confined his main account to Manila elemi which, he said, was white or greyish in colour with a granular appearance, noting its solubility in alcohol.[82] It appears probable, therefore, that the majority of seventeenth- and eighteenth-century material was from South America; and Stalker & Parker, who described the best 'Gum Elemni' as the hardest, whitest, and clearest, most free from dross or dirt, and imported wrapped in the bark or husk of a tree, indicated that it cost 4*d.* or 5*d.* per ounce.[83]

Kauri resin

See under *Copal* above.

Lac

The sticky exudation formed by the Indian lac insect, *Laccifer lacca*, on the branches and twigs of the host trees has already been mentioned in connection with the red dye also present which was used to prepare a lake pigment. The crude lac, known as *stick lac*, is removed from the twigs, beaten, sifted and washed to remove the dye. In this form it is known as *seed lac*, which, as its name implies, is in the form of granules having a dark reddish-brown colour. The seed lac may then be melted, strained, and either drawn out or cast into transparent sheets which are broken into smaller pieces and marketed as *shellac*. Tingry, for example, described the method of casting the lac on a marble table,[84] while Ure noted use of the smooth stems of the banyan tree for the same purpose.[85] Modern specimens of seed lac resemble earlier descriptions closely, but much of the shellac imported today has received further treatment to bleach its natural colour. The resin, the only one exploited in connection with house-painting to be of animal origin, is soluble in alcohol to give a brownish solution, making what is often called French polish.

Stalker & Parker described the best 'Gum Lac, *called* Seed-Lac' as large-grained, bright, and clear, free from dust, sticks, and dross, pricing it from 1*s.* 2*d.* to 1*s.* 6*d.* per pound; and the best 'Shell-Lacc' as the most transparent and thin, which when melted down drew out the longest and finest thread, and costing 1*s*. 6*d*. to 2*s*. per pound.[86] Interestingly, Dossie argued that seed lac and shellac were quite different substances,[87] but Watin described accurately the relation between the three forms in which it was imported.[88]

Mastic

Mastic resin was known to the ancients and used in varnish throughout the middle ages. It is obtained from incisions in the bark of the small Mediterranean tree, *Pistacia lentiscus*.[89] The main source of supply is Chios, which was mentioned by the late seventeenth-century author Houghton,[90] although Church noted other sources of similar material in India.[91] The resin is soluble in alcohol and turpentine, and Heaton described its uses as comparable with damar, adding that since it was considerably more expensive than the latter it was mainly used for high-quality picture varnishes.[92] It was in this connection also that Vanherman referred to its employment.[93] Stalker & Parker mentioned mastic,[94] and Watin described the resin as being procured in the form of seeds or tears nearly as big as barley, and inclining to lemon in colour.[95] This is matched by modern samples. It could, he observed, be distinguished from the similar-looking resin sandarac in that the latter does not soften when placed on the tongue, while mastic becomes sticky; and it was, he indicated, the principal constituent of turpentine varnishes. In 1810 Lewis Berger had a small stock of 1 lb. of mastic valued at 5*s*.[96]

Rosin

Rosin has been discussed in Chapter 11.

Sandarac

Sandarac resin, also known as *gum juniper*, exudes naturally from trees native to the mountains of North Africa, although production is increased by making incisions in the bark. The species is now known as *Tetraclinis articulata*; but Heaton and the late nineteenth-century writers Church and Hurst cited this as *Callitris quadrivalvis*, while Ure regarded it as *Thuya articulata*.[97] The resin, which was known to the ancients and in the middle ages, is completely soluble in alcohol and partially soluble in oil of turpentine. Watin described sandarac as the principal ingredient of spirit varnishes, and obtained in clear tears which were shiny and transparent, whitish in colour but inclining to lemon, a description matched by modern samples.[98] Stalker & Parker, who indicated that the best 'Gum Sandrick' was the largest and whitest with the least tendency to yellow, gave prices of 1*s*. or 1*s*. 2*d*. per pound;[99] while in 1806 and 1810 Lewis Berger had stocks of 28 lb. and 2 lb. respectively, valued at 4*s*. and 1*s*. 8*d*. per lb.[100]

Turpentines

Crude turpentines have been discussed in Chapter 11.

NON-RESIN PLASTICISERS

Camphor

Only one non-resin plasticiser, camphor, has been noted in the literature examined. This aromatic ketone occurs naturally in the wood of the camphor tree native to Japan and Borneo. Tingry described the source as a kind of laurel found in thc East Indies and Japan;[101] and Ure, who indicated that camphor was found in a great number of plants, noted that the only species from which it was extracted for manufacturing purposes were *Laurus camphora* and *L. sumatrensis*. He described its preparation by distillation of the wood with water, adding that it could also be prepared chemically.[102] The hard translucent solid obtained was described by Watin;[103] and Tingry, who suggested its employment in formulae for both spirit and turpentine varnishes, indicated that its main use was in facilitating the solution of certain resins while adding toughness to the product and preventing cracking. A quantity of $\frac{5}{8}$ ounce per pound of spirit of wine should not, he added, be exceeded.[104] Vanherman employed camphor in a white copal varnish.[105]

COLOURING AGENTS

Although several yellow colouring agents used in both varnish and pigment manufacture have already been described in Chapter 5 certain substances, generally soluble only in organic liquids, remain to be discussed.

Alkanet

Tingry's later editor mentioned the use of the red dye extracted from alkanet root in coloured lacquers, or 'changing varnishes'.[106] Ure gave the species as *Anchusa tinctoria*, a variety of borage grown at Montpellier and in the Levant, indicating that the roots imparted a fine red colour to alcohol and oils, but only a dirty red to water. It seems unlikely to have been in extensive use for lacquers, however, since he only mentioned its employment in ointments and pomades, although he described also a method for its use in staining marble a flesh colour.[107]

Annatto

Annatto has been described in Chapter 5.

Asphaltum

A number of naturally occurring bitumens containing varying proportions of asphalt have been used in the manufacture of black and brown varnishes and were employed for fine-art purposes as glazes, especially during the eighteenth century.[108] They consist essentially of hydrocarbons of high molecular weight associated with complex organic derivitives often containing sulphur and nitrogen, mixed with mineral matter. That from Val de Travers in Switzerland, for example, contains only about ten per cent of asphalt, while that from the great asphalt lake in Trinidad is mixed with about thirty to forty per cent of a fine clay in suspension.[109] Although Dr Harley indicates that American sources have been known since the seventeenth century,[110] and by the late nineteenth Church and Hurst were familiar with material from Switzerland, Albania, Trinidad, Barbados, and Peru,[111] references in the earlier literature connected with house-painting examined are only to material from the Near East. Dossie remarked that *asphaltum* was obtained from Asia,[112] while Watin described *l'asphalte ou bitume de Judée*.[113] This was also known as *Jew's pitch*, and came, Tingry indicated, from 'Lake Asphaltis' (the Dead Sea). It was, he observed, an almost black, brittle solid having a brilliant surface as if polished.[114] It is soluble in oil of turpentine.

Stalker & Parker employed 'Gum Efpaltum' in oil-based gold size,[115] and Dossie also mentioned the use of asphaltum for this purpose;[116] while the author of the *Painter's . . . Pocket Manual* reserved it for bronzing or very pale gilding.[117] Vanherman suggested its employment in making a black turpentine varnish,[118] and Watin used it for the same purpose in oil.[119]

Dragons blood

Three varieties of dragons blood have been recognised: that from *Dracaena cinnabari* growing on Socotra, which, Howes observes, was described by Dioscorides and Pliny; that from *D. draco* of the Canary Islands, which was in use by the fifteenth century; and that from certain *Daemonorhops* species of palm growing in the East Indies and Malaya.[120] (The species from the latter area was called by Hurst *Calamus draco*.)[121] The substance is soluble in alcohol, but not to any extent in oil of turpentine, and was used to impart a red colour to lacquers, instances being given in Chapter 18. Stalker & Parker described the best as that which was the brightest red and most free from dross. It was, they indicated, bought in drops made up in a kind of leaf or husk, and cost 8*d.* or 1*s.* per ounce.[122] This description matches that given by Hurst of the Socotran product, which was obtained by tapping the tree, but it differed in appearance from the Far Eastern variety, which he also described. This, which formed on the fruit of the tree as it approached maturity, was collected by shaking the fruit into baskets, and sifting the resin to separate it from the stems and particles of woody fibre. It was then heated and cast into rolls by wrapping it in a palm leaf. It was, he observed, the type most generally imported by the late nineteenth century, very little then being obtained from the Canaries.[123] It is, however, difficult to suggest that this was necessarily the case during the eighteenth century, since descriptions are not specific. Watin, for example, stated only that the best was that imported in the mass as when taken from the trees;[124] while Tingry mentioned the Canaries, Jamaica, and the East Indies as sources of resin, which he described as dry, friable, and inflammable, of a dark red or brown colour, and readily soluble in water, adding that two varieties were sold, the first in globules, the second of softer consistence.[125]

Gamboge

The yellow gum-resin gamboge, obtained from South-east Asian trees belonging to several species of *Garcinia*, has been imported since the early seventeenth century.[126] It contains both a gum soluble in water and a resin soluble in alcohol, and is produced from incisions made in the bark of the tree. The gum-resin is melted and poured into hollow pieces of bamboo to form rolls, and is sold in this form.[127] Tingry noted its production from trees growing in 'Gamboge' (Cambodia), Siam (now Thailand), and China, describing it as a dry, solid, compact, hard, opaque, inflammable substance, and gave it the alternative name *gum guttae*;[128] while Watin referred to it as *la resine gutte*.[129] Stalker & Parker, Watin, and Vanherman illustrated its use in making coloured lacquers, the first quoting a price of 6*d.* per ounce for the best quality;[130] but otherwise it was used only as an artist's watercolour, and was mentioned by Dossie only in this connection.[131] In 1802 Lewis Berger had a stock of 18 lb. 'Powder Gambouge' valued at 2*s.* per pound, his stock rising to over 150 lb. in 1806, when he priced it at roughly 5*s.* 4*d.* per pound; but by 1810 he had only about half this quantity in stock, half of which was valued at a rate of 4*s.*, the 'Fine Gambouge' forming the balance being costed at 6*s.* 6*d.*[132] These prices are not far removed from those given by John Phillips, who indicated the cost of the substance as 8*s.* 8*d.* and 8*s.* in 1812 and 1821 respectively.[133]

Red sandal wood

Tingry's later editor described the use of the red dye which may be extracted from red sandal wood (otherwise known as red saunders wood) in lacquers. He gave the species from which it was obtained as *Pterocarpus santalinus* growing in India and Ceylon, indicating that the bright red timber darkened on exposure to air, yielding a dye soluble only in alcohol.[134] Ure noted that the timber (discussed in Appendix B in connection with its imitation in paint) which was imported from Calcutta in logs, was much used for dyeing and occasionally for turning, but evidence for its common use in lacquers is elusive.[135]

Saffron

The yellow dye obtained from saffron has already been described in Chapter 5.

Turmeric

This too has been described in Chapter 5.

CHAPTER 14

SIZES, CASEIN, AND WATER-SOLUBLE GUMS

The distinction made today between gums, which are water-soluble, and resins, which are not, has already been mentioned in Chapter 13. In general, although used for various fine-art purposes, gums found little or no application in house-painting, animal glue sizes of varying quality being used in their place. Nevertheless, they are briefly described below, since a limited number of references to their employment may be found.

GUMS

Gum arabic

Gum arabic occurs as an exudation on various species of *Acacia* growing in Senegal, the Sudan, and northern Sahara, and appears to have been an article of commerce since classical times.[1] Of the several varieties available, that known as *gum Senegal* was regarded at least during the late nineteenth century as the best for use in the preparation of artists' watercolours.[2] Gum arabic is generally encountered in the form of roundish globules, ranging from almost colourless to brownish in tint, which may be transparent or nearly opaque;[3] and, being almost completely soluble in water, is thus a true gum.

Stalker & Parker described the best as clear, transparent, and white in colour, observing that it would cost 1*s.* per pound;[4] and Tingry noted its yellowish-white colour, its brilliance, and brittle nature.[5] In 1802 Lewis Berger had $6\frac{1}{2}$ lb. of 'Pick'd Gum Arabic' in stock, valued at 2*s.* 6*d.* per pound, while in 1806 he had $12\frac{3}{4}$ lb. of gum arabic valued at a rate of 1*s.* 6*d.* By 1810, however, he had a total stock of just over $3\frac{3}{4}$ cwt. of fine and second qualities, valued at rates roughly equivalent to 1*s.* $11\frac{1}{2}$*d.* and 1*s.* $6\frac{1}{4}$*d.* respectively; and listed in addition nearly 4 cwt. gum Senegal, valuing it at a rate equivalent to $11\frac{1}{4}$ *d.* per pound.[6] Gum arabic was used, rather surprisingly, by Dossie as a constituent of a drying oil for coarse work;[7] but this seems exceptional, and no other references to its possible use in house-painting have been noted.

Gum tragacanth

Another true gum, gum tragacanth, exudes from several species of *Astralagus* growing in the mountainous regions of Asia Minor, Syria, Iraq, and Iran, and is obtained in the form of horny strips or long roundish pieces.[8] Tingry described it accurately, observing that it is more or less white and inodorous, and swells to a mucilage in water.[9] Its main use appears to have been in the printing of fabric.[10] Although D'Aviler suggested the use of *gomme adracanthe* in alcoholic solution for application to joinery, it seems likely since gum tragacanth is insoluble in this medium that his intention was rather to recommend the use of dragons blood (*sang-dragon*) as a spirit stain.[11]

SIZES

Size is an impure form of gelatin, containing also a similar substance known as chondrin.[12] It is extracted by boiling skin, horn, or other animal matter in water; and the solid prepared by evaporating the product to dryness was sold as carpenters' glue, a full description of the entire process as practised during the mid-nineteenth century being given by Ure (fig. 12).[13] Throughout the period considered, different qualities of size were in use, which, for present purposes, will be divided into three categories: common size; sizes made from better qualities of leather; and isinglass.

Common size

Dossie described common size as made by boiling leather in water.[14] On the Continent, size made by this method seems to have been known as *la colle de Flandres*, and Watin, who noted that it was made from scraps of sheep or other animal skins, described it as the type most commonly used in decoration.[15] Tingry observed that common Flanders glue dissolved in water was very often used in place of size of higher quality, noting that this was made by boiling skins for three or four hours in eight parts of water, making a strong jelly. A further two parts of water could be added to make a size of moderate consistence.[16]

In England, Emerton gave directions for the preparation of 'Size the Plaisterers use in White-washing', indicating that 'A Pound of Glue boyl'd, will make two Gallons of Size';[17] although Reynolds used the same quality of glue in a single gallon of water.[18] In the seventeenth century, size appears commonly to have been prepared on site directly from leather offcuts, and in the Exchequer roll for 1627–8 'Leather shriddes to make Size' are itemised in connection with work at Newmarket, together with 'wood to boile Size'.[19] Similar items, often simply for shreds, occur elsewhere in the series of rolls;[20] and in an

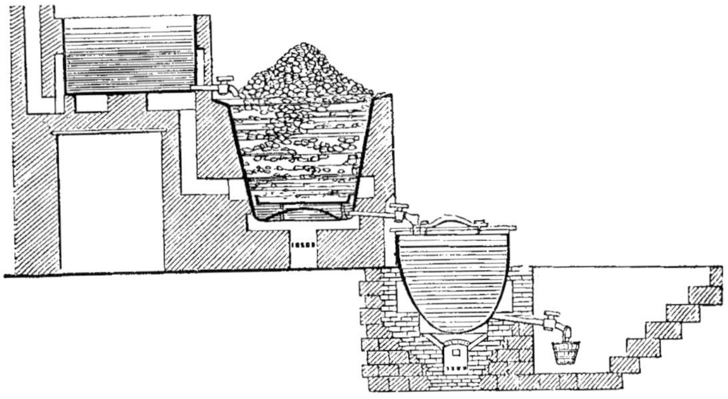

12. Extraction of glue from animal matter in the mid-nineteenth century. The boiler was fed by warm water from the tank at the top, and the liquid product run into the vessel at the bottom to settle before being drawn off for evaporation.

account relating to the restoration of Chorley church, Lancashire, in 1635–6, there are two items for 'Patches' (one of which amusingly also includes payment to the 'boy that brought them').[21] Even at the end of the eighteenth century the practice continued, as shown by an item for 'spetches' in an account for painting the Mansion House in Doncaster.[22] A domestic recipe preserved at Claydon, Buckinghamshire, notes in connection with the preparation of distemper that one should boil 1 lb. of leather parings with 6 quarts of water until this was reduced to 4 quarts. The size was then to be strained off, and a further quantity prepared by adding $\frac{1}{2}$ lb. of fresh parings to the old ones and boiling with a fresh 6 quarts of water as before.[23]

It is also apparent that common size was often purchased in liquid form, two strengths being commonly available. Salmon, for example, referred to *single size* at 1*d.* per quart, and *double size* at 2*d.*;[24] although the *Builders Price-Book* merely listed 'Size' at a rate of 4*d.* per gallon, a price equivalent to that of Salmon's single size.[25] This probably equates, therefore, with Emerton's formula, which is in any case the proportion generally used today, but the precise relationship of this with double size is not made explicit by any of the eighteenth-century sources noted. In *Rivington's Series of Notes on Building Construction*, published in the late nineteenth century, however, it was indicated that double size 'is boiled for a greater time so as to be stronger'.[26] A clue to its specific use in house-painting is given by Phillips, who referred to 'Double size, used for painting new work first'; and he also gave details of the movement of prices during the late eighteenth and early nineteenth centuries. From 1760 to 1790 he gave the same rates as those already mentioned for single and double size (giving also rates per firkin of 1*s.* 6*s.* and 5*s.* respectively), while between 1790 and 1803 he quoted 2*s.* 6*d.* and 6*s.* 6*d.*[27] The latter price receives corroboration from the rates equivalent to 6*s.* 6*d.* and 7*s.* at which Soane was charged for double size in 1803.[28] Later prices recorded by Phillips were 3*s.* 8*d.* and 7*s.* 8*d.* in 1812, falling back slightly to 3*s.* 6*d.* and 7*s.* 6*d.* in 1821.[29]

Sizes made from better qualities of leather

For fine purposes, Dossie recommended that size should be prepared from glovers' leather,[30] and it is of note that an entry in the Exchequer roll for 1637–8 refers specifically to the supply of 'glovers shreds and glovs to make size'.[31] Watin indicated that *la colle de gants* was made from clippings of white sheepskin boiled in water for three or four hours, and advocated its use for colours which were not to be varnished.[32]

An even better quality of size, *la colle de parchemin*, was, Watin indicated, prepared from parchment which had not been written on. One pound of clippings were to be boiled in six pints of water for four hours, until the liquor was reduced by half. The solution was then strained and allowed to cool to a strong jelly. A further pint of water could be added to make a less strong size, or four pints to make a weak size. This *parchment size* was used when one wished to varnish or gild above it. *La colle de brochette*, on the other hand, was an inferior variety made from common parchment. It was less expensive and only used for gross work.[33] Tingry too described the preparation of size from parchment, noting that waste pieces were soaked in warm water for twelve to fifteen hours, and then boiled for five or six hours and strained. It could, he said, be used in all cases where great cleanliness was required, and could be substituted for fish glue (isinglass).[34] Watin had advocated the use of parchment size in his special white distempers *cipolin* and *blanc de roi* (discussed in Chapter 17);[35] and it was probably Tingry's endorsement of its appropriateness in these that led Nicholson to specify the use of parchment size for distemper.[36]

Isinglass

The finest size, said by Church to consist of nearly pure gelatine, was made from the air bladder and other selected parts of the sturgeon inhabiting the Black Sea and coasts of Denmark,[37] although Dossie simply described it as made from the cartilages of some large fish.[38] It was known to Eraclius in the tenth century.[39] Stalker & Parker noted that the best was that 'which is the clearest and whitest, freest from yellowness', adding that it was 'if good, worth 3 or 4*d.* the ounce' although it was more cheaply available, they suggested, by the pound.[40] Dossie described the preparation of isinglass size by boiling $\frac{1}{2}$ oz. of beaten isinglass in $1\frac{1}{2}$ pints of water until it had dissolved. The solution was to be strained while hot, and in that state formed a strong size. For a weak size an equal part of water was to be added.[41] Tingry, who described the product as *fish glue*, or *ichthyocolla*, directed on the other hand, that the 'membranous matter that furnishes it' should be boiled in water until a cooled sample set to a trembling jelly.[42]

Although Nicholson remarked that isinglass was too expensive for use in distemper,[43] Dossie mentioned its employment in the finer parts of good quality work;[44] and William Chambers recommended that the cove in the Saloon of the Casino at Marino House near Dublin should be 'done with Izing glass & flake white' in order that it should be of a more brilliant white than the entablature and other white elements.[45] It seems likely, therefore, that isinglass may have been used on occasion in very high quality interiors.

CASEIN

The complex acid substance casein is present to the extent of about half an ounce per pint of milk. It is soluble only in alkaline conditions, and this property may be utilised in the preparation of a washable paint by mixing skimmed milk or prepared casein with lime and water. On exposure to atmospheric carbon dioxide the alkaline lime is gradually converted to neutral calcium carbonate, thus setting the casein free in its original form as an insoluble binder. This property has been known since early times, and instances of its exploitation during the period being considered are described in Chapter 17.

PART II

PAINT MANUFACTURE AND APPLICATION

INTRODUCTION

Having surveyed the materials which were economically available to the house-painter during the period extending from the early seventeenth century to the first decades of the nineteenth, attention may be turned to the way in which they were made up into paints and varnishes, and how these products were applied as decorative finishes. The two most common painting mediums in use over the whole of this time were oil and water, the choice between them in any instance depending on several factors, including their relative cost, the durability required in the situation to which they were to be applied, and (since some pigments worked better in one or other medium) the finish colour required. As a general rule, ceilings and plaster walls in everyday interiors were decorated using water-based paints, notably size-bound distempers, while joinery would be painted in oil. In finer rooms, oil might be used also on plaster walls and ceilings, and could be made having varying degrees of sheen, more glossy formulae, for example, finding favour on joinery during the seventeenth century and earlier part of the eighteenth, and a fashion for matt paintwork prevailing from the 1740s.

Besides oil and water, varnish was used to a limited extent as a paint medium, especially on the Continent and for provision of a durable finish on furniture. Its main use, however, was as a glossy protective finish for timber or painted imitations of decorative woods and marbles, and several types adapted to different purposes were in use. Thus, copal oil-varnishes were particularly tough and suited to exterior applications, while spirit-based types were often preferred for more delicate interior work.

Another important decorative technique was that of gilding, practised widely throughout the period being considered. Two basic methods were in use, water gilding and oil gilding. Although the former could take a far higher burnish, it was much more expensive than the latter, and was accordingly generally confined to furniture and picture frames, while architectural gilding would be executed more cheaply on an oil size.

The imitation of decorative timbers and marbles formed a specialised branch of the house-painter's task. It was practised most popularly during the first century and latter decades of the period under consideration, and could involve the use of both oil and water-based paints, varnish, and gilding. Besides graining and marbling, the house-painter was also expected to be able to imitate freestone, bronze, and other decorative materials, and, especially in the latter part of the period being considered, to produce on ceilings the effect of a clouded sky. Besides the general discussion in Chapter 20 of the tools and techniques used, appendices providing glossaries of the different varieties of timber and marble imitated are provided at the end of this volume.

The final topic considered is the way different colours were mixed. Colour-mixing in the period being considered was greatly constrained by the limitations of the individual pigments available, and new developments in pigment production clearly led to changes in practice. Perhaps the most illuminating aspects of the subject are the way different colour names were often associated with particular pigments or pigment combinations, and the manner in which the relative costs of the different tinting materials affected the prices for different colours. These matters are considered in Chapter 21, and a glossary of colour names and tinting methods associated with them heads the series of appendices. For the architectural uses made of the colours and the other materials and techniques described, the reader is, however, referred to the companion volume.

CHAPTER 15

MANUFACTURE AND FORMULATION OF OIL PAINT

The use of oil paint in house-painting was well established by the beginning of the period under review, and instances of its employment may be found promiscuously throughout the Exchequer rolls of the first half of the seventeenth century.[1] The 1638 accounts for the redecoration of Ham House, Surrey, show its extensive application on panelling and cornices;[2] and its widespread employment in the painting of interiors has continued to the present day. In general, the basic concept of oil painting was very similar to that still prevailing, priming being succeeded by one or more undercoats and a finishing coat, although the latter was generally of very different appearance from the high-gloss finishes common at present. In this chapter, the formulae in use and methods by which oil paint was prepared are described; and in the next, attention will be turned to its application, together with consideration of costs and pricing of work.

PREPARATION AND STORAGE OF THE PASTE

The first stage in the preparation of oil paint was to incorporate the pigments required separately with the oil, making a stiff paste similar in character to the form in which artists' oil colours are still supplied today. Apart from the burning of lamp black to reduce its greasiness mentioned in the description of it in Chapter 9, no preliminary treatment of pigments by the painter was generally considered necessary for house-painting; and although John Smith devoted a chapter to the removal of coarse particles by washing or levigation, he concluded by remarking, 'unless you intend to bestow some cost on a piece, you need not be at the trouble to wash [i.e. levigate] your Colours, but use them for coarse ordinary work, as you buy them at the Shops.'[3]

Some pigments such as indigo or Prussian blue were, of course, naturally very much finer than others; but as a comment on standards acceptable in the early nineteenth century, it may be noted that John and Samuel Berger were screening their finest carmine and drop lake No. 2 through a '100 sieve', while for other pigments, including rose pink, French green, azure blue, and York brown, a '68 sieve' was used.[4] Vanherman, moreover, employed a '45 hole wire sieve' in the manufacture of his 'Impenetrable or Anti-corrosive Paint' (an emulsion intended for external use) and a '60 hole wire sieve' for his interior 'Aromatic Paint', which suggests that this was regarded as a reasonable standard for inside work.[5] All these are, of course, much coarser than the screens used for many modern pigments.

The main function of paint grinding is to ensure thorough 'wetting' of the pigment by breaking down clumps of particles to achieve their even dispersion in the oil medium. This was commonly effected by means of a *slab* and *muller*, a third tool known as a *voider* being used to remove the ground paste from the slab. The process is shown on several trade cards, including that of the Bethnal Green oil and colourman, J. Sholl junior (fig. 13). In 1687, John Smith (later additions to whose text are given in angle brackets) described the tools and procedure fully:

> the Stone must be a hard . . . ⟨Rance,⟩ Marble, ⟨or some other⟩ of a close grain [in the early nineteenth century, slate was said to be unsuitable][6], . . . about a foot and half square, and so thick, that its weight may be sufficient to keep it fast and steady, and not apt to be moved when Colours are grinding on it.
>
> The Muller is a pebble Stone, of the form of an Egg, the bigger end of which is to be broken off, and with sharp Sand or Emery, it must be ground smooth and flat ⟨on some other hard flat Stone; and the Edges of it must be well rounded off, that the Colours may the better slide under it when it is moved round⟩: this Stone ought to be about two Inches Diameter, or ⟨three⟩ at most, on the flat end, and about five Inches high, that so you may command it the more easily in the time of grinding.
>
> To these belong a Voider, being no other than a Lanthorn Horn, about three Inches one way, and four the other; this Voider is to clear off the Colours from the Stone when ground, and also to keep them together in the time of grinding when it spreads too much.[7]
>
> When you come to grind Colours, let your Grinding-stone be placed about the heighth of your middle; let it stand firm and fast, so that it joggle not up and down; then take a small quantity of the Colour you intend to grind (two spoonfuls is enough) for the less you grind at a time, the easier and finer will your Colour be ground: lay this two Spoonfuls of Colour on the middest of your stone, and put a little of your Linseed Oyl to it, (but be sure you put not too much at first) then with your Mulier mix it together a little, and turn your Mulier three or four ⟨five or six⟩ times about, and if you find there be not Oyl enough, put a little more to it, ⟨and grind it⟩ till it come to the consistence of an Oyntment

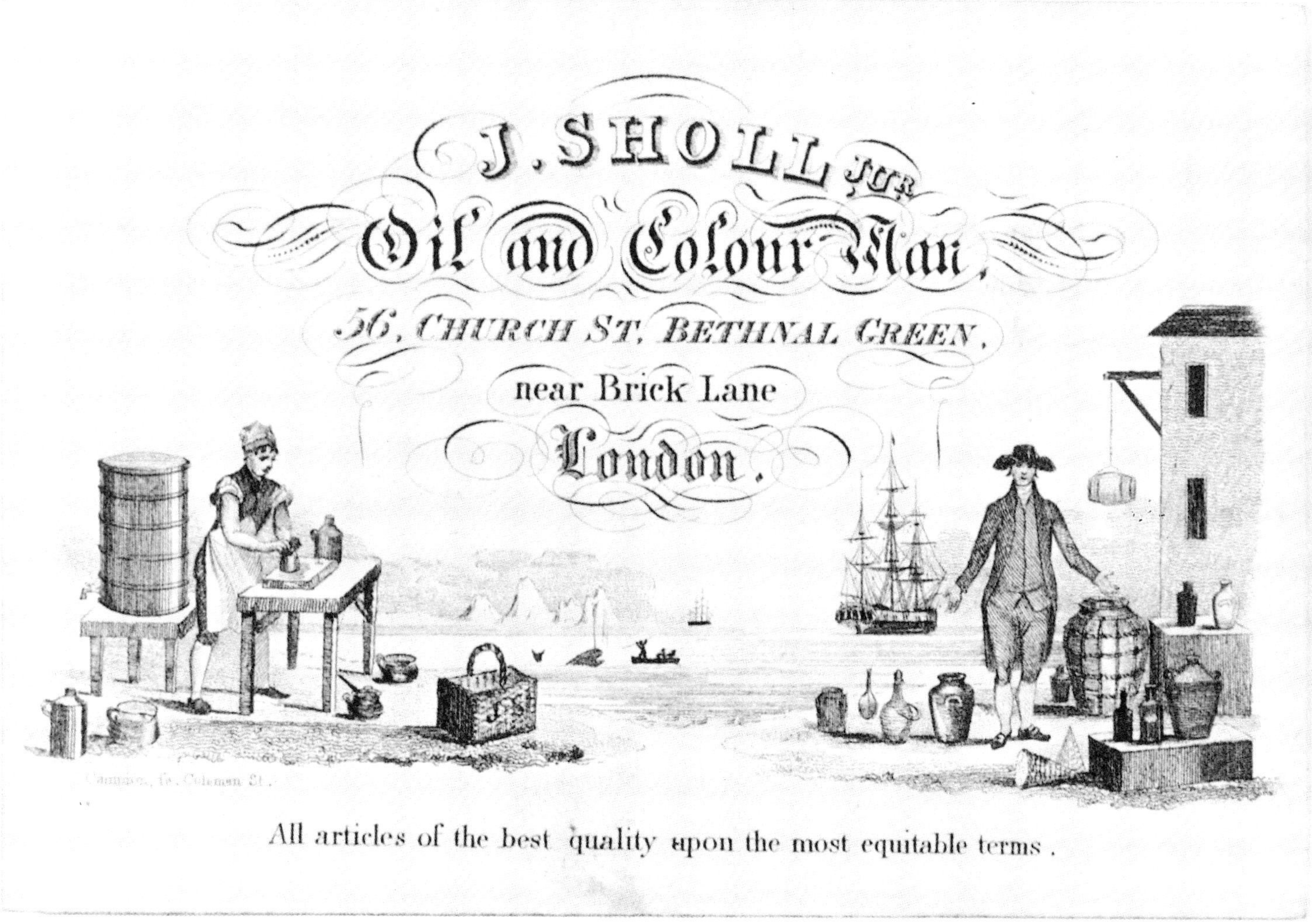

13. Grinding pigment into oil using a slab and muller (trade card of J. Sholl, Jnr., Bethnal Green, London).

⟨; or appears free from any sort of lumps, and smooth as the most curious sort of Butter⟩; for then ⟨when stifish,⟩ it grinds much better and sooner than when it's so thin as to run about the Stone: You must oftentimes, in the grinding, bring your Colour together with a Piece of a Lanthorn Horn, and with the same keep it together in the middle of your Stone; when you find you find you have ground it fine enough, by the continual Motion of your Mulier about the Stone, holding it down as hard as your strength will permit (which you must also move with such a sleight, as to gather the Colour under it) and that no knots nor grittiness remains, but be as fine even as the Oyl it self, then with your Horn cleanse it off the Stone into a Galley-Pot, Pan, or what ever else you design to put it into, and then lay more Colour on your Stone, and proceed to grinding as before.[8]

Tingry added a further hint, noting 'the absorption of the oily fluid, which becomes greater as the division of the parts is completed [i.e. dispersion proceeds] requires the addition of more colour to bring the mixture to a proper consistence'.[9] This procedure may be seen clearly on the trade card of the Gloucester painter and gilder, William Hardwick, a detail from which is reproduced (fig. 14). The process was undoubtedly responsible for a great deal of the lead poisoning with which the painting trade was beset, on account of the inhalation of dry white-lead powder by those engaged in grinding it into oil, a fact recognised at least by 1796 when details of a French arrangement to protect the operative by means of a hood and heat-convected air extraction system were published by the Society of Arts.[10]

The hand process was clearly laborious when large quantities of paint were required, and in 1718 Marshall Smith took out a patent for a 'Machine or Engine for the Grinding of Colours, to be vsed in all kinds of Paintings . . . vsually Ground with a Muller on a Flatt Stone, by Mocion in the Mechanicks, exactly Imitating those of the Handes'; but no details of his invention are given in the specification, and it is by no means certain that it was successful.[11] Within a few years, however, improved processes were in commercial use. Thus, seemingly in 1741, Elizabeth Emerton advertised that she was continuing the business of her late husband Alexander Emerton (to whom reference has already been made in Chapter 2 in connection with Prussian blue) claiming that as her colours were,

ground in Horse-Mills, of which there is not the like in England, they are prepared in much greater Perfection, and sold considerably Cheaper than by any of the Trade, that have not such Conveniencies, but grind

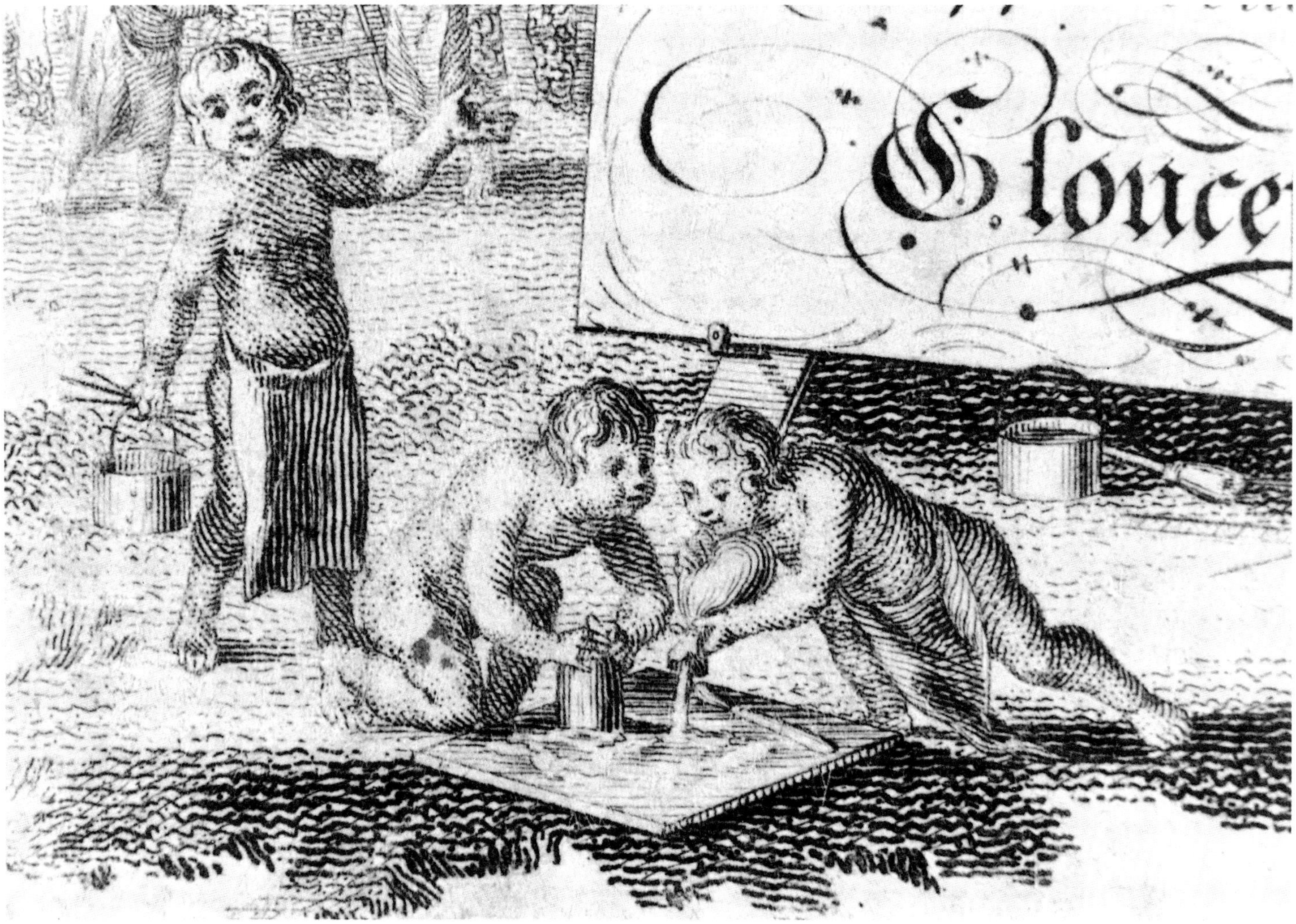

14. Addition of further pigment during the grinding process (trade card of William Hardwick, Upper College Lane, Gloucester, detail).

their Colours in Hand-Mills, or upon a Stone, with great Expence and Labour.

One Pound of Colour ground in a Horse-Mill, will paint twelve Yards of Work, whereas Colour ground any other Way, will not do half that Quantity.[12]

The mill is illustrated on the trade card and 'DIRECTIONS for PAINTING' issued by her successor, Alexander Emerton's brother Joseph, the British Museum copy of which (fig. 1) is dated to 1744 by a bill made out on its reverse; while another illustration of it heads a late eighteenth-century card issued by the same firm when it had become Emerton and Manby (fig. 15). Although it has been suggested that this was a machine used for crushing dry pigment,[13] it seems clear from Elizabeth Emerton's advertisement that the mill was used in the production of paste; and, indeed, Dossie writing only a few years later observed: 'For coarser work, the colours demanded in great quantity are ground by hand or horsemills with the oil; and the others on a stone with a muller.'[14]

Emerton's mills probably worked like those for grinding flour, using a pair of horizontally mounted grindstones, the conical element seen at the bottom of each revolving shaft being a funnel down which oil and pigment were fed. A developed form of such a machine was illustrated and described by Ure in 1839 (fig. 16), its frame being of timber or cast iron. The millstones (C & F) were of cast iron, channelled as shown, the lower of the two being surrounded by an iron hoop (D) which served to retain the ground pigment. This could flow out only through the sluice-hole (E), dropping into the tub (X) beneath. Pigment to be ground was placed in the hopper (R), and fed via the bucket (S), which was continually agitated, into the hole in the centre of the upper millstone.[15] A drawing of a similar mill (of perhaps slightly earlier form) was included in his scrap-book of material relating to floor-cloth manufacture by Robert Barnes in 1857 (fig. 17), the hopper being particularly evident.

Use of steam power to drive a battery of paint mills during the early nineteenth century is shown by Edward Holl's design of 1817 for a paint and sheet-lead mill built at Chatham Dockyard, Kent, for the Royal Navy. His drawing (fig. 18) shows the beam engine which provided the motive power, transmitted to the individual mills via a horizontal shaft. The building still stands, and retains traces of the shafting and marks of the engine.[16]

Other developments may also be noted, although probably unimportant within the bounds of the present study. In 1804, for example, the Society of Arts illustrated in their *Transactions* a hand-operated rotary paint mill;[17] and

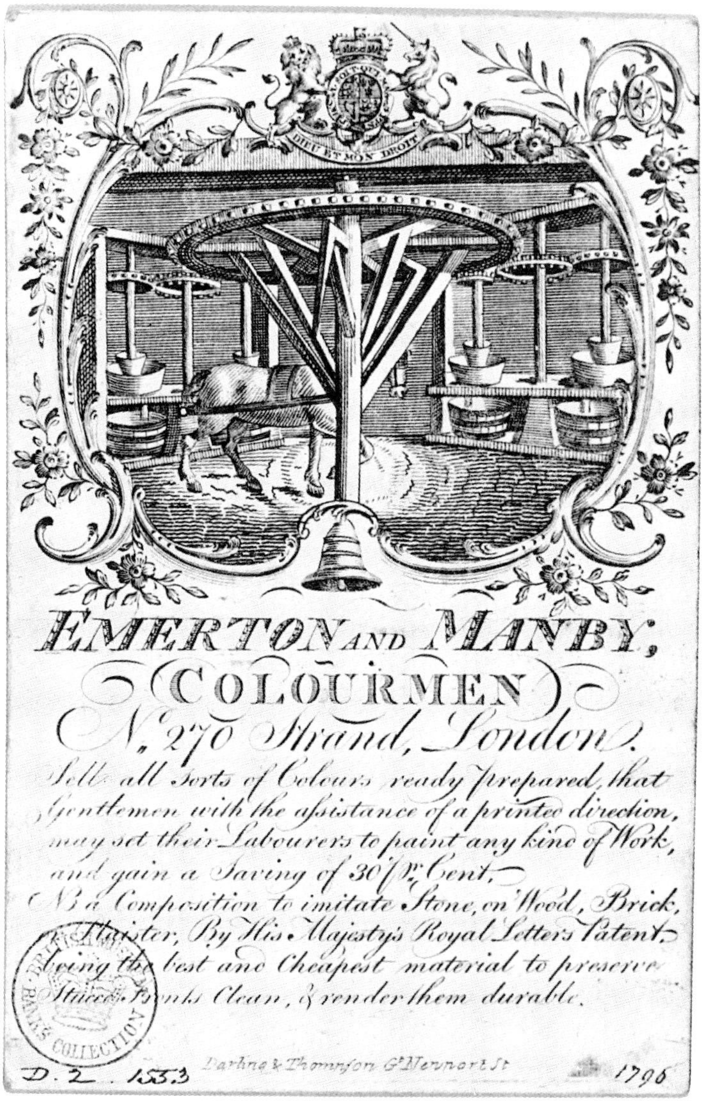

15. Emerton's horse-mill for grinding pigment into oil.

in 1860 Ure's editor included a comment that steel rollers were used in the preparation of printing-inks.[18] The development of roller-mills for the preparation of house-paint seems not to have taken place, however, until the second half of the nineteenth century, when Clark's roller-mill was introduced following the form patented by J.K. Geyelin in 1852; but by the end of the century, Hurst noted, they were extensively used.[19] Pollard's patent grinding mill of 1824, which employed a flat slab and batteries of mullers which could be operated by 'any suitable power', on the other hand, seems not to have been of importance in the present connection.[20]

Throughout the period being examined, commonly used pigments could be bought at colour shops, either in powder or in paste form. In 1619–20, for instance, 'Englishe oker grounde' was supplied in connection with work at Greenwich Palace;[21] and John Smith suggested:

> Those that list not to be at the trouble of grinding Colours themselves, may have of any sort, . . . ready ground, at the Colour-Shops, at reasonable rates ⟨either in smaller or larger Quantities as they have Occasion, from an Ounce to any weight they desire⟩.[22]

Alexander Emerton's colour list, published by Salmon in 1734, shows that he was supplying ready-mixed tints by the pound weight:[23] that these were in paste form and had to be diluted with oil for use is made explicit in his 'Directions for Painting'.[24] Stalker & Parker, however, indicated that distilled verdigris, brown pink, and lakes were preferably purchased in powder; while vermilion, carmine, smalt, blue bice, massicot, and red orpiment were generally sold in that way.[25] Pincot recommended that red lead and lamp black should be purchased dry,[26] and Tingry's later editor suggested that the finer pigments were better ground in oil by oneself, instancing vermilion and verdigris.[27] Of these, it will be remembered that some, such as vermilion, were liable to adulteration which could be

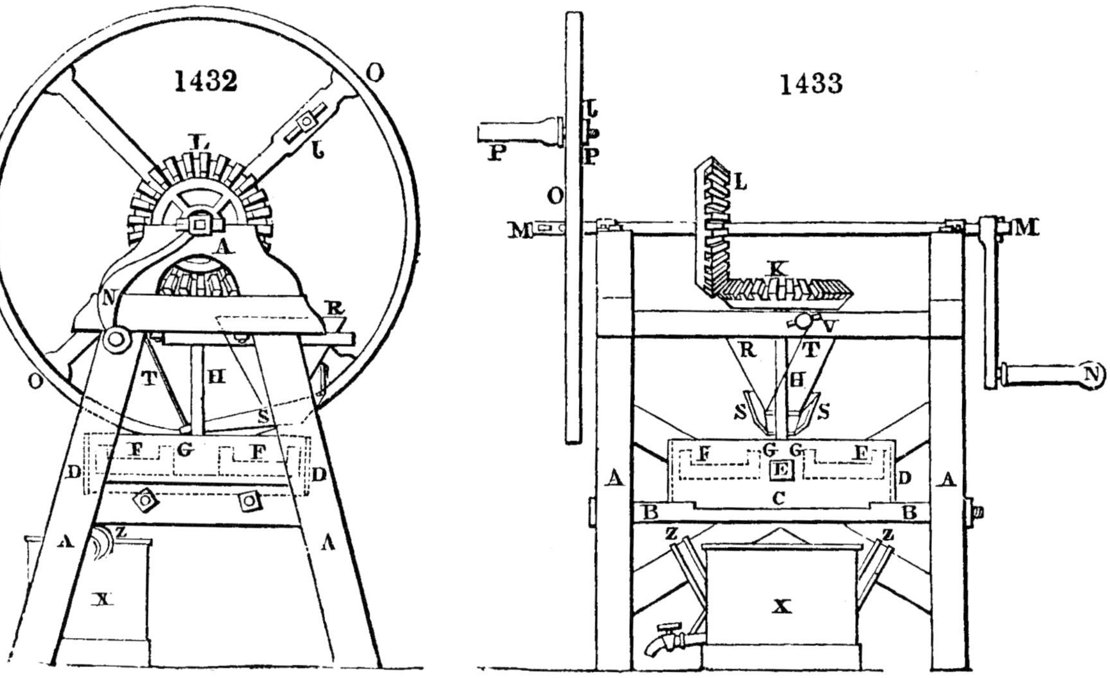

16. Nineteenth-century paint mill.

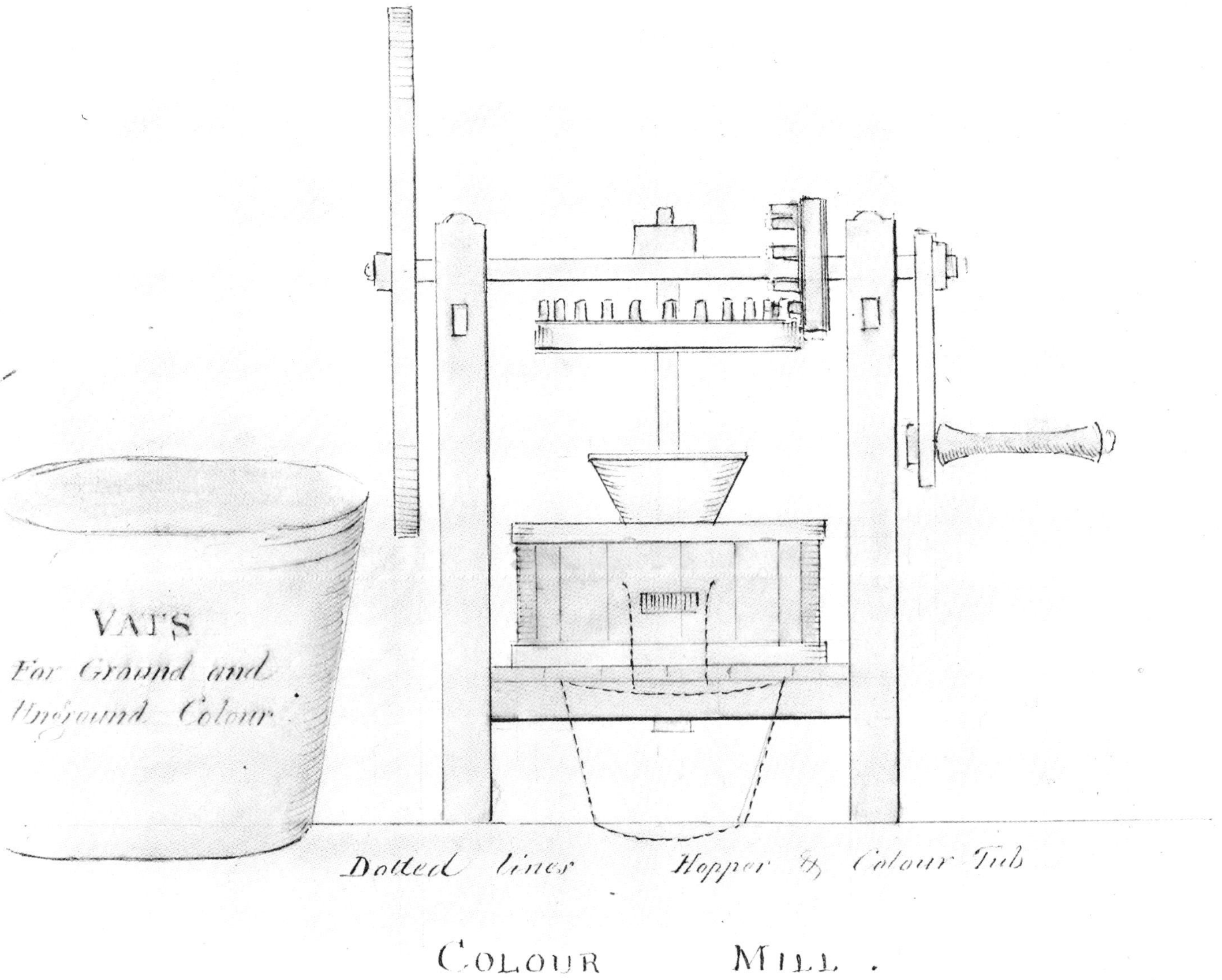

17. Another nineteenth-century paint mill.

better detected in the dry state; and others did not keep well once ground, having a tendency to settle out of suspension. Each circumstance would provide a sound reason why procurement in paste form was to be avoided. Otherwise, ground pigments could be kept for many years, a convenient practice pointed out by John Smith to prevent a man 'Daubing of himself too often by grinding of Colours'. To effect their storage he recommended they,

> be put up and tyed close in Ox Bladders, or in the Bladders of Hogs or Sheep, according as your quantities are; this will preserve them from drying or spoiling a long time together.
>
> I remember I had a parcel of Colours given me in the year 1661. by a Neighbouring Yeoman, that were as he said, left at his House by a Trooper, that quartered there in the time of the Wars, about the year 1644. This Man was by profession a Picture-Drawer, and his Colours were all tyed up in Bladders, according to the Method before prescribed, and when I had opened them, I found them in a very good condition, and to my thinking as fit for use, when mixt with a little fresh Oyl, as if they had been but very lately ground, though they had remained in this condition about seventeen years.[28]

This practice was also advocated by Dossie,[29] and bladders of colour still survive in the effects removed from the studio of J.M.W. Turner which are now at the Tate Gallery: examples are illustrated in the trade card of William Jordan, thought to date from 1792 (fig. 19). Larger quantities of paste were preserved under water, Emerton, for example, recommending in his 'DIRECTIONS', 'if you have any Paint left, put Oyl or Water over it, and it will keep several Years.'[30] Tingry's later editor also referred to this method, describing how to remove the head from the wooden casks in which London white lead was supplied, and the preservation of any unused paste by covering it with an inch of water.[31] An illustration of such a cask is, perhaps, provided by the trade card of the London colourman James Stone (fig. 20), whose premises in

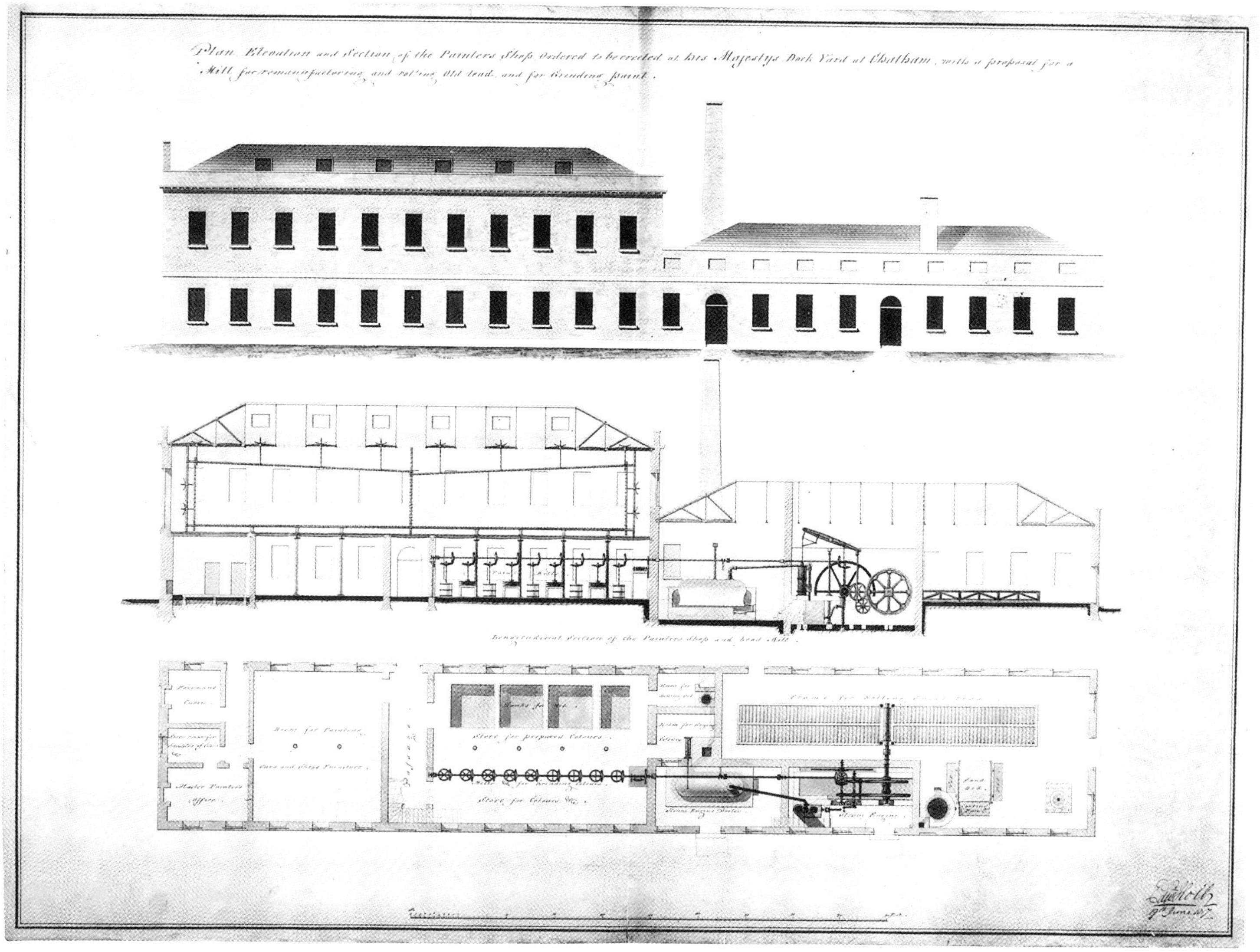

18. Mill-building designed for Chatham Dockyard in 1817.

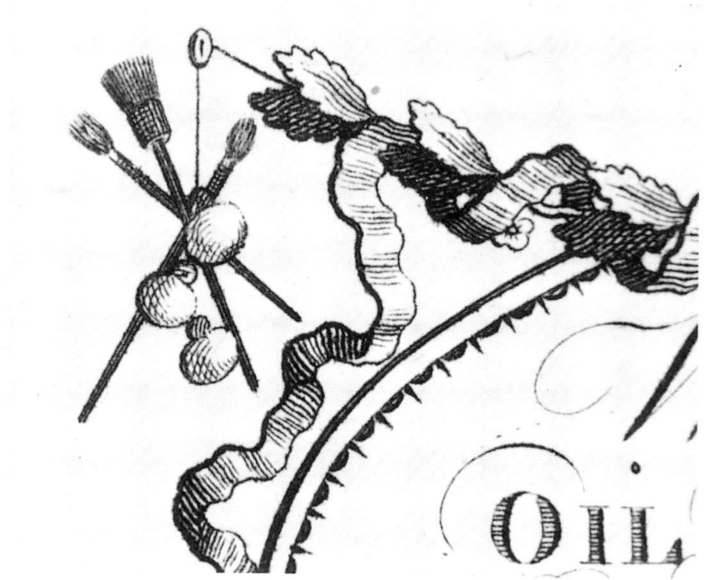

19. Brushes and the bladders used to store small quantities of pigment ground in oil (trade card of William Jordan, Fetter Lane, Holborn, London, detail).

Bishopsgate could be recognised by the sign of 'the Olive Tree & Colour Barrel'.

When desired, the paste, usually white lead (possibly containing extenders), which formed the basis of the paint, was tinted with other pigments in paste form, on occasion, seemingly, before dilution to a suitable consistency for application. Both John Smith and Pincot, for example, suggested this order of procedure;[32] but, no doubt, the colour would also be tinted or adjusted subsequently in many instances.

DILUTION OF THE PASTE

For use, John Smith recommended the addition of oil to the ground paste until the colours 'be so thin as not to let the ground on which they are laid be seen through them', but at the same time cautioned against applying the paint in too thick a state. On the other hand, he warned, painters commonly over-thinned paint to save the cost of paste.[33] Watin, however, provided a different criterion, advising that no colour diluted with oil or a mixture of oil and oil of turpentine should ever form a thread at the end

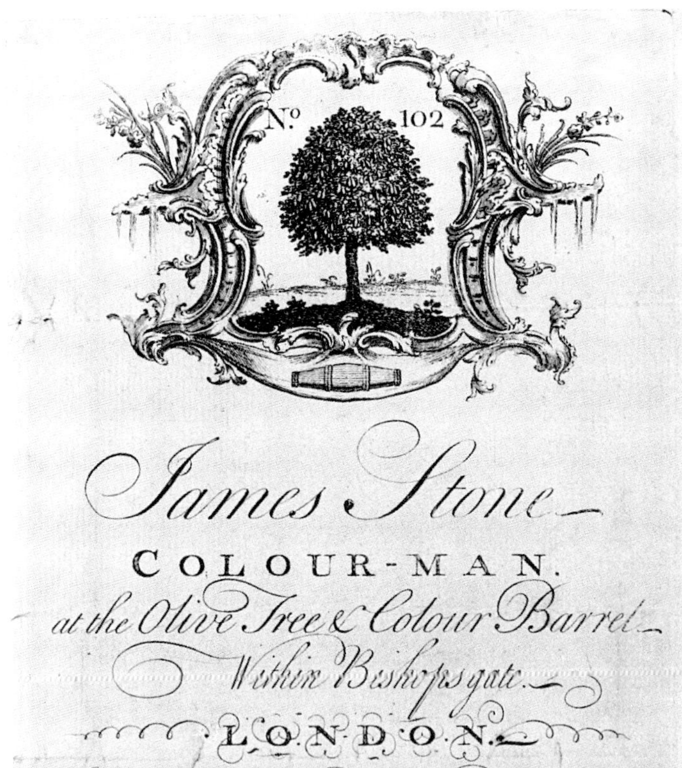

20. Trade card of James Stone, Bishopsgate, London, showing a colour barrel.

of the brush, a suggestion copied by Tingry.[34] Both pieces of advice are of practical use in illustrating the consistency desirable in paint prepared for application, and possibly of more immediate help than the few precise details of quantities which are available.

In considering these, it must be borne in mind that paste prepared by different painters or suppliers might have varied somewhat in its consistency; and also, as D'Aviler instanced with yellow ochre, some pigments required more oil to make them workable than others.[35] In fact only Watin seems to have given a complete specification for dilution, although this was in connection with a priming mix rather than an undercoat or finish: 14 ounces of ceruse required, he said, 2 ounces of oil for grinding, and 4 for dilution.[36] For thinning his proprietary tints, ground presumably in a horse-mill, Alexander Emerton specified a quantity equivalent to $\frac{1}{3}$ of a pint of oil per pound of paste;[37] and Parker in his patent of 1812, $\frac{1}{7}$ of a pint per pound of his green colour, a figure matching Watin's formula closely.[38] In contrast, Tingry's later editor gave a figure which seems very high, stating that in general the equivalent of $\frac{3}{5}$ to $\frac{4}{5}$ pint were generally added to each pound of ground white lead.[39] These figures may be compared with the figure close to $\frac{1}{7}$ of a pint per pound for finishes in the model *Specification for Repainting Work* issued by the Lead Industries Development Council in 1939, bearing in mind that for these a mixture containing a small proportion of oil of turpentine, which would improve the workability of the paint, was used.[40]

The addition of oil of turpentine to the drying oil in this way was practised from an early date. In 1676, John Smith referred to it as being added by some to paint in the process of dilution to assist in drying, but added that for exterior use it would not then resist the weather so well, a point echoed in the early nineteenth century by Crease.[41] In 1706 Evelyn too advocated the addition of 'some *Oyl of Terpentine*', noting specifically that he was speaking of '*work* within-doors';[42] and in describing the dilution of white-lead paste, D'Aviler suggested pure oil or a mixture of oil with an equal part of oil of turpentine as alternatives.[43] By the mid-eighteenth century Dossie referred to the practice as if it was a matter of course, saying that after grinding the colours were put in pots, 'and there mixed with oil of turpentine and drying oil, according to the particular purposes to which they are employed';[44] and it appears certain from the later literature discussed below that by then and in succeeding years, when flat finishes were fashionable, the addition of oil of turpentine was the norm. However, since the degree of gloss with which the paint film dries falls off with increasing proportions of oil of turpentine (a fact specifically noted by Tingry's later editor),[45] it seems probable that thinning with mixtures containing it would not invariably have been practised in interior work during the seventeenth and early eighteenth centuries, when glossiness seems often to have been considered a desirable attribute; and it may be significant that Emerton, who (as will be described below) was certainly attempting to maximise the glossiness of his paint on wainscot, did not mention its use in his 'DIRECTIONS', which were clearly envisaged as applying to interiors.[46]

The addition of oil of turpentine has obvious advantages in making oil paint less viscous and more easily applied. Moreover, during the late seventeenth century John Smith, as mentioned in the last paragraph, had suggested its addition made for quicker drying. This view was shared by Dossie,[47] although the early nineteenth-century writer Crease dismissed the idea as erroneous.[48] Clearly, though, the oil of turpentine would evaporate fairly rapidly, increasing the apparent speed of drying in the early stages and leaving a paint film less thickly bound with oil.

Reduction in the proportion of oil also had the benefit of ameliorating the tendency of paint films to yellow with age, and it was for this reason that in 1706 Evelyn advocated the use of oil of turpentine with walnut oil in interior finishing coats, observing that this 'preserves it from *ternishing*, and losing *colour*'.[49] Probably for the same reason, in the early nineteenth century Butcher indicated that a mixture of oil of turpentine with linseed oil was used where nut oil, preferable for a pure white, was too expensive.[50] Hence, although as late as 1812 the American author Hezekiah Reynolds was still recommending the addition of a mere one part of oil of turpentine to forty parts of linseed oil for interior work, European practice for many years seems to have been to use it in much greater proportions.[51] Watin, for example, stated: 'Les couleurs broyées à l'huile, s'employient quelquefois à l'huile pure, plus souvent à l'huile coupée d'essence, & très-souvent avec l'essence de térébenthine pure.'[52] The last formulation referred to the special finish known as *flatting* (to be discussed in a moment), but for the lower coats Watin generally specified one part of oil of turpentine to three of oil.[53] The proportions usually recommended by later English authors in which the two should be combined for ordinary finishes are either one part oil of turpentine to two parts of oil, or in equal quantities, although in one particular case Nicholson suggested a formula containing two-thirds oil of turpentine.[54]

Although no reasons for the choice of proportion of turpentine to oil seem to be put forward in any given instance, and at first glance they seem to have been employed interchangeably in both undercoats and finishes, it is nevertheless possible to detect a noticeable pattern in their use, since general practice seems to have been to dilute successive coats with oil and oil of turpentine mixed in uniform proportions, or to increase the quantity of the latter layer by layer. Thus, for new inside work Butcher primed using $\frac{1}{3}$ oil of turpentine, undercoated with the same, and finished using $\frac{1}{2}$ oil of turpentine;[55] Pincot, again for new interior work primed in size (see below), used pure oil for thinning the undercoat, and used $\frac{1}{3}$ oil of turpentine for the finish;[56] while Nicholson primed using pure oil, added a very little oil of turpentine to the undercoat, and employed $\frac{1}{2}$ oil of turpentine in his ordinary finish, succeeding this where desired with the finish already mentioned containing $\frac{2}{3}$ oil of turpentine.[57] The only exceptions so far encountered to this seemingly general rule are provided by a pure oil of turpentine primer proposed by Tingry, which will receive further consideration below, and the use made by Pincot in a repainting specification of pure oil of turpentine to thin his undercoat.[58]

SELECTION AND USE OF DRIERS

Techniques for increasing the speed with which oil paint dried have been discussed in Chapter 10. John Smith and Watin made it clear that only some pigments needed the addition of a drier, the latter particularly noting *stil de grain* and the blacks.[59] Nevertheless, the employment of driers or use of boiled oil seems to have been common. Dossie, for example, described the addition of lead acetate or zinc sulphate as generally practised, although he thought it to be of dubious efficacy;[60] and Tingry's later editor cited yellow ochre as requiring more drier than chocolate, olive, yellow, blue, or brown colours, suggesting that its addition to all these was the norm.[61] Earlier, John Smith had recommended the use of one part of boiled oil with three parts of raw oil, even for pigments such as umber, verdigris, and red lead where it was not strictly necessary, in order to increase their lustre when dry.[62]

Reasons for the choice between boiled oil and solid driers in any particular instance are not explicitly stated in the published literature examined in connection with the present study, although Watin suggested the use of litharge for dark colours, zinc sulphate for light colours, and boiled oil for yellows and greens.[63] John Smith, on the other hand, treated the use of boiled oil as the most obvious choice, describing zinc sulphate in terms suggesting its more occasional use, but it seems quite likely he may have been referring here primarily to practice for exterior work.[64] Crease indeed described boiled oil as the most proper for outside purposes, although this statement does not of course necessarily rule out its use internally in addition;[65] but otherwise Nicholson is the only author to mention boiled oil in a formula, this time specifically for external application.[66] From this rather negative evidence, especially taking into account the fact that, except for greens and fairly dark browns, boiled oil would soon discolour interior paint (a matter of particular significance during the second half of the eighteenth century when extreme delicacy of tint was sought), it seems plausible to suggest that boiled oil was not generally used for interiors during this period. The slightly greater lustre it would impart, however, could well have encouraged its employment on wainscot and joinery of dark colour at an earlier date, and this may have persisted on such elements as brown-painted doors and skirtings.

Apparently confirming the avoidance of boiled oil for interior work during the latter part of the eighteenth century, the use of driers in solid (no doubt, paste)[67] form is exclusively and consistently mentioned by later English writers. It is moreover, possible to see fairly clearly the way in which a choice was made between these. Red lead was used in priming coats and sometimes to a small extent in undercoats, as may be seen, for example, in formulae given by Pincot, Butcher, and Nicholson; although in addition Butcher used it in black paint, and it seems likely therefore that it may also have been employed in the darker browns.[68] For finishes, zinc sulphate seems to have been the most generally employed drier, being mentioned by writers from John Smith onward, although Watin and subsequent authors reserved it for lighter tints, using the more or less comparably priced litharge for the darker shades.[69] Mixtures too enjoyed application, and among other authors Nicholson seems to have favoured these, recommending in one case two parts of zinc sulphate with one of litharge, a suggestion he later amended to equal parts of each. For fine whites, on the other hand, he advocated the use of lead acetate, which, as already suggested in Chapter 10, seems to have been reserved for high-class purposes since it was considerably more expensive than either litharge or zinc sulphate.[70] Whichever drier was employed, however, Watin stipulated that it should be added immediately prior to use of the paint.[71]

With regard to the quantities in which these substances were employed, earlier writers do not mention amounts; but half an ounce per pound of paste was generally recommended by authors from Watin onwards, and Tingry's later editor indicated that the amount used should not normally exceed this figure, which is almost precisely comparable with those given in the Lead Industries Development Council model *Specification*.[72] On the other hand, less was often used. Nicholson recommended use of a walnut-sized amount of sugar of lead (which is in any case more energetic than the other commonly employed substances) for twenty pounds of paint (roughly equivalent to $\frac{1}{10}$ ounce per pound);[73] and general practice seems to have been to reduce the amount of drier in successive coats. Thus, for example, Butcher recommended the addition of 1 ounce of zinc sulphate, 1 ounce of litharge, and 1 ounce of red lead to each 6 pounds of white lead paste for priming; 1 ounce of zinc sulphate, ½ ounce of litharge, and ¼ ounce of red lead to the same quantity of paste for the second coat; and zinc sulphate alone to the third.[74] Indeed, only in this formula and in one of Pincot's[75] is drier in the last coat specified; and, bearing in mind Watin's precept that drier should be used sparingly in whites,[76] it seems quite likely that it was sometimes omitted altogether from finishes, which could often be allowed longer to dry.

OIL PRIMERS

The first coat of paint on a virgin surface, known throughout the period under consideration and today as *priming*, was of a rather special nature, and generally thinned with a rather greater quantity of oil than subsequent coats. This was, no doubt, in recognition of the fact that, as Wilsford remarked, 'the priming spends most colour (if the wood be dry) but is usually the worst'.[77] John Smith too remarked, 'if the Colour to be mixt be your priming Colour, (that is the first Colour you lay on) it ought to be made very thin, that it may have Oyl enough to pierce into the Wood, which is much for its preservation';[78] and William Leybourn observed that the first coat would spend as much oil as the two succeeding coats.[79] Although it will be remembered that Watin suggested a fairly normal rate of dilution, common practice seems to have been to increase the proportion of oil, and the early nineteenth-century author James Crease observed that the priming should be made 'tolerably thin' with oil;[80] while a marginal note on the British Museum copy of Joseph Emerton's 'DIRECTIONS for PAINTING' (fig. 1) seems to suggest that a pint of oil should be added to each pound of paste.

Pincot and Nicholson suggested the use of pure oil for the dilution of priming coats; although Watin proposed a mixture containing one-quarter part of oil of turpentine, and Butcher one-third.[81] Exceptionally, Tingry advocated the use of pure oil of turpentine for internal work in diluting the paste for the 'first stratum', since, he believed, in the first place it would carry off the odour of the oil; in the second it would tend to make the later colours more brilliant; and in the third it possessed hardening properties. It was beneficial also, he suggested, when added to the first coat on ironwork, since it aided adhesion of the paint to the bare metal;[82] but this may not reflect general practice.

On plaster one or more coats of pure oil might be applied as a primer, Smith recommending this for plaster clock-dials, and Nicholson a coat of drying oil on stucco.[83] In the former case at least, the context is external; and only the Continental authors Félibien and Watin referred specifically to the practice internally.[84] No operation of this nature seems to be itemised in any of the English trade price-books, although as may be seen from the summary of prices given in table VII (p. 108) painting on stucco was priced separately at a higher rate than on timber in some of these, and it is not entirely clear that this procedure was usual for day-to-day work.

Priming formulae given by authors writing up to the mid-eighteenth century differ from those later recommended, and were generally based on red ochre. John Smith, for example, recommended the use of Spanish brown on its own,[85] and Dossie observed that this pigment was much used by house-painters for grounds and primings in coarse work.[86] Leyburn on the other hand suggested its mixture with whiting, advising that:

> Painting of Outside-works; as Doors, Shop-Windows, Window-Cases, Pediments, Architraves, Friezes and Cornices, and all other Timber-works which are exposed to the Weather, ought at first setting up to be primed with Spanish Brown, Spanish White, and Red Lead (about a 5th part) to make the other two Colours to dry, well grown'd with Lintseed Oyl, will make excellent Primer.[87]

In addition, Dossie proposed a mixture containing ochre and white lead.[88] Combinations such as these are commonly encountered in seventeenth- and early eighteenth-century work, and examples have been found on the wainscots in the North Drawing Room at Ham (1637–8),[89] the Marble Hall at Petworth, Sussex, (1692),[90] and in the Saloon at Beningbrough Hall, Yorkshire, (*c.* 1715).[91] The photomicrograph of paint layers in a sample from the Banqueting House at Studley Royal, Yorkshire (1728–38) shows the typical appearance of a red oxide priming (fig. 21). Besides priming, such formulae were used also for painting the backs of wainscots to prevent damp affecting the glue used in their assembly; and Neve, for example, suggested that the most effectual way to prevent failure of the joints from this cause was 'by priming over the Backsides of the Joynts well with *White-lead, Spanish-brown*, and *Linseed-oyl*'.[92] Watin too recommended two or three coats of coarse red in linseed oil for this purpose,[93] and an item appears in the Kensington Palace accounts of 1691 for 'Colo^r on ye back of ye Wainscott', charged at 3*d.* per yard.[94]

Watin's ordinary priming formula which contained white lead, plus presumably small quantities of paste drier,[95] has already been mentioned in connection with the dilution of the basic paste, and stands in considerable contrast with these earlier types. Later oil formulae are similar, invariably being based on white lead and resembling the pink lead primer of recent times. Thus, although in the early nineteenth century Pincot advertised that he made a 'light chocolate colour' for priming externally, he had at first recommended two coats of 'flesh colour' for new exterior work. This was made from 14 pounds of white lead and 1 pound of red lead in linseed oil, and Nicholson too gave a similar mixture.[96] The general absence of dark red primings from samples of late eighteenth- and early nineteenth-century work confirms that these had been more or less superseded, at least for interior purposes; and a typical example of the new type is shown on the second photomicrograph illustrated (fig. 22). There seems no doubt that it was the increasing use of white on joinery during the eighteenth century which led to adoption of the pink formulation; and it is of interest that, rather than the usual dark red of the earlier period, pale brownish primers, perhaps representing an intermediate type, have been found on the panelling in the Saloon at the Royal Academy, originally painted white in the 1720s,[97] and on the entablature and joinery in the

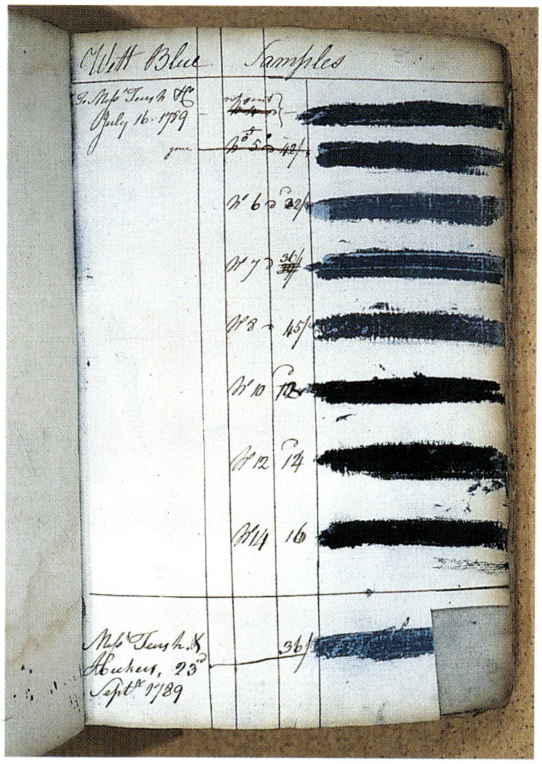

3. Samples of Prussian blue supplied by Lewis Berger in 1789.

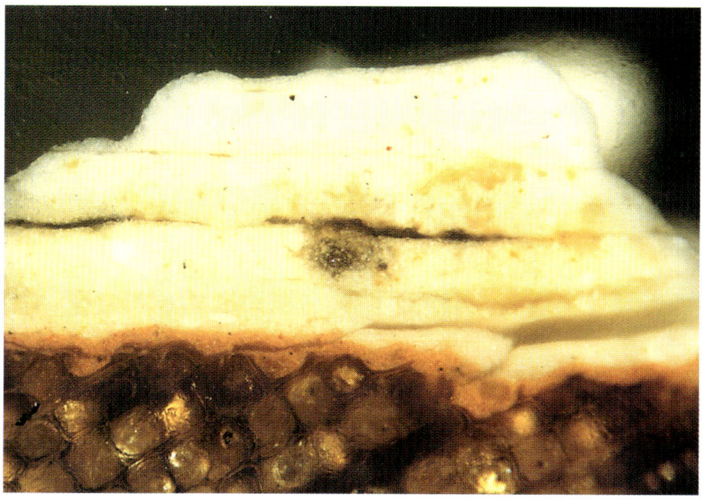

21. Cross-section from joinery in the Banqueting House, Studley Royal (*c.* 1730–40), showing typical red-oxide oil priming of the period, followed by various coats of white lead.

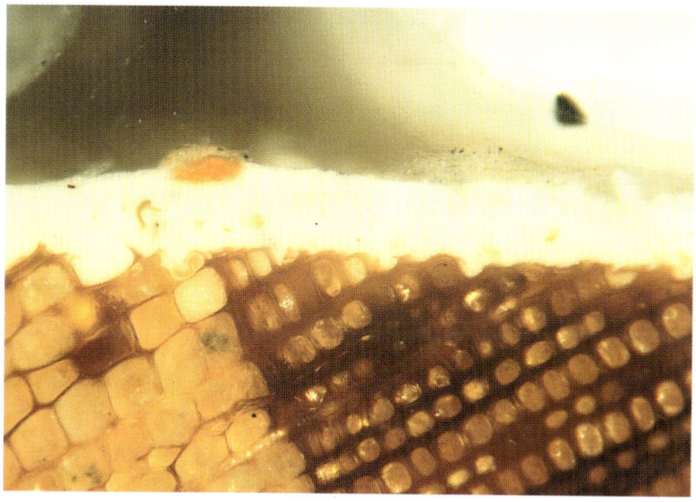

22. Cross-section from the Corridor, Frogmore (*c.* 1795), showing typical pink primer of the type which became popular from the mid-eighteenth century.

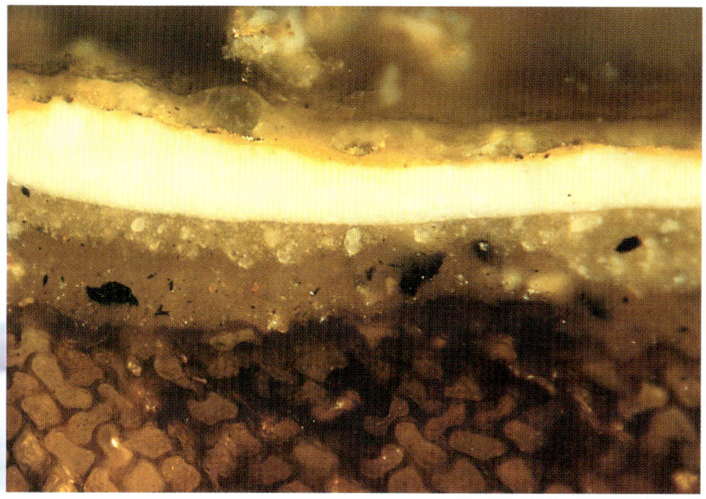

23. Cross-section from joinery of the 1630s in the Hall at the Queen's House, Greenwich, showing the rather transparent nature of seventeenth-century undercoats.

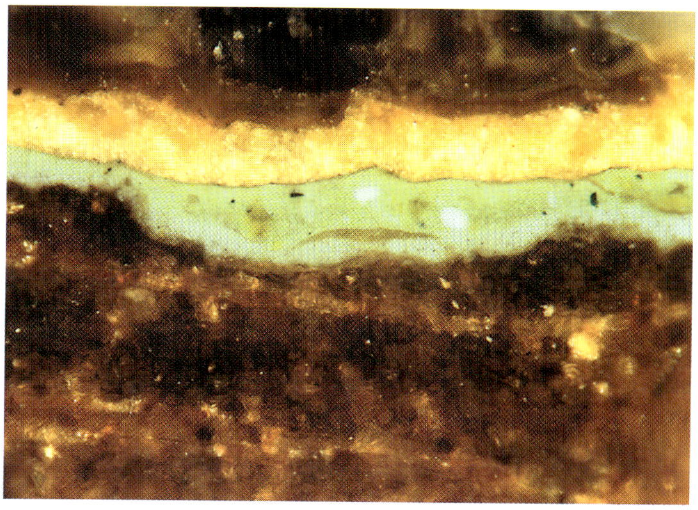

24. Cross-section from early nineteenth-century panelling in the Drawing Room, Tamworth Castle, showing a grey undercoat beneath a green finish.

Egyptian Hall at the Mansion House, London, painted a very pale off-white in the 1750s.[98] Indeed, as early as 1706, Evelyn, who in 1670 had only mentioned the normal primer of 'Oaker and *Spanish-white*', advocated the use of white lead as a primer below two subsequent coats of white, commenting: 'The ordinary priming with *Red*, being a *Cheat* among *Painters*: seeing *White* upon *White* must render the Colour still *whiter* and fairer.'[99]

By the 1830s, virtually pure red-lead primers were in use on exterior ironwork. Nicholson, for example, recommended the employment of red lead with a small admixture of white lead for the purpose,[100] and Bartholomew referred to the application of 'red lead paint' for the first three coats.[101] It seems possible that John Smith's reference to the painting of window bars with red lead may indicate the use of similar formulations in the seventeenth century.[102]

SIZE-BOUND PRIMERS AND UNDERCOATS

For internal work, an oil primer was not always used. Emerton, for example, observed: 'Outside Work must be primed with Oyl Primer; but Inside Work may be primed with Size';[103] and Pincot too suggested: 'In new houses the inside work may be Primed with strong double Size, just stained with a little Spanish Brown, merely to see where the brush has been.'[104] In 1662, payment was made for work at the Queen's House, Greenwich, 'Layed in Sise & coured [covered] over with oyle';[105] and prices for 'Inside painting, twice in oil and primed in size' appear in various editions of the *Builders Price-Book* published by I. & J. Taylor, the first of which appeared in 1776.[106] Moreover, in the later version of Emerton's 'DIRECTIONS' it is suggested that plaster walls should receive two coats of strong size before painting (fig. 1).

The practice of using size for priming was condemned by Dossie, who warned:

> Even in the case of house or coach painting, the clear-coating with size and whiting ought to be omitted; and, in its place, a coat of drying oil with some white lead and ochre . . . should be used as the first priming. . . . This method would both preserve the work much better, and prevent the blistering and peeling, and in some degree, the sinking in of the colours that attend the common method.[107]

Pincot himself acknowledged that surveyors would object to the use of size in the way he had suggested, although, he protested, he had never found one who could give him a sufficient reason for this;[108] and its use continued to be advocated. Reynolds, for example, directed that following other preparation work one should 'dissolve one pound of Glue in one gallon of boiling water; add two pounds of Spanish White; and when cold, and well mixed; lay it on carefully; and even with the grain of the wood, with a clean brush.'[109]

It will be observed that both Dossie and Reynolds mentioned the addition of whiting to the size, making a form of distemper. Such preparations were also used, especially in the redecoration of interiors, as a cheap undercoat which was known as *clearcole*, a corruption of the French term 'claire colle' (rendered 'Cold-clear' by Stalker & Parker, who used it correctly for size alone).[110] Prices for 'clearcole and finish' appear in Salmon's *London and Country Builder's Vade Mecum* (1745) and the *Builders Price-Book* at rates of 4*d.* and 3*d.* per yard respectively, against 5*d.* for two coats of oil;[111] and Martin described it as the cheapest method.[112] Although whiting seems to have been the pigment most commonly employed, Nicholson, who referred to the preparation of clearcole from whiting and size, also specified the use of white lead.[113] Pincot too provided a recipe for a white-lead-based clearcole, to make which 1 pound of white lead ground in water was to be added to 1 quart of size 'which when chilled is rather thicker than cream';[114] and items such as 'Clear cold whitelead & 2ce in Oil' appear in accounts for the decoration of Norfolk House, London, in 1753 and 1755.[115] In addition, these accounts contain items showing that lead-based clearcole was used between undercoats and finishes, for example '4 times in Oil Dead white & between the Second & third colour a Clear cole with Whitelead';[116] while Pincot advocated the application of 'a coat of single Size with a little White Lead ground in water, just white enough to see where the brush goes', between the undercoat and finish in new houses.[117]

Although this technique resembles that deliberately used by Emerton to increase the lustre of the finishing coat (see discussion of gloss finishes below), it seems more likely that at Norfolk House at least, where the finish was to be flat, it was intended to prevent the uneven 'sinking in' of the paint, a problem which, as Sir Roger Pratt noted, had often to be overcome.[118] Like Dossie, however, Vanherman strongly deprecated the use of clearcole as an undercoat in redecoration, remarking that it was 'often detrimental; for if the sun or damp interfere, the first will surely blister, and the second detach the paint from the wood'.[119] Nicholson warned specifically that it was of no use externally, but although he believed it was not greatly used at the time he was writing, it seems clear that its employment in interiors had been widespread, especially for cheap work.[120] Pincot, for example, mentioned it particularly in connection with rooms for servants;[121] and in accounts for painting work at Osterley between 1772 and 1774 an item is to be found for 'Clearcoal and finish in maids room' at a rate of 3*d.* per yard.[122] The same price was charged for clearcole and finish in certain rooms at Somerset House in 1787.[123]

OIL UNDERCOATS

During the seventeenth century, oil undercoats were often based on whiting rather than white lead, producing a much less opaque paint film. Thus Evelyn suggested in 1670:

> Your first *Priming* shall be of Oaker and *Spanish-white*, very thinly ground: The *second* with the same, a little *Whiter*; but it matters not much. The *third* and last, with *White-lead* alone; some mingle a little *Spanish-white* with it, but it is better omitted.[124]

Similarly, in 1700 Leyburn suggested following his dark red priming (based on red ochre, whiting, and red lead) first 'with the same Colour (but much more whiter) for second primer; and lastly with fair white'.[125] This explains the rather transparent undercoats commonly seen on cross-sections of seventeenth-century work, examples including those beneath the original white finish in the Hall at the Queen's House at Greenwich (fig. 23) and on the wainscoting in the North Drawing Room at Ham, both dating from the 1630s.[126] By 1706, however, Evelyn was advocating pure white lead in primer, undercoat, and finish, suggesting that although this would involve 'a small charge' it would be 'more fair and durable';[127] and at the beginning of the eighteenth century it seems clear that undercoats of seventeenth-century type were being superseded.

Little information is given by John Smith on the colouring of undercoats, although the way Leyburn softened the transition from red primer to white finish will have been observed. Where, on the other hand, as was common, interior panelling was painted grey or brown, it seems that the undercoat and finish might be the same colour. At Beningbrough Hall, Yorkshire, for instance, the stiles of the wainscot in the Saloon were undercoated and finished in pale grey above a dark red primer about 1715;[128] while samples taken from the wainscot in the Servants' Hall at Boughton House, Northamptonshire, which is known from surviving accounts to been painted with two coats of oil paint about 1700, suggest that in this instance the undercoat and finish were both of the same brown.[129] In the Balcony Room at Dyrham Park, Gloucestershire (now Avon), on the other hand, two coats of white form the ground for the marbling and imitation porphyry executed in 1694 which lie beneath the present grained finish.[130]

The marbling at Dyrham was executed by a Huguenot painter, and it is possible the white undercoat represents French practice. Certainly in the second half of the eighteenth century Watin advocated the use of white as a ground for two coats of a verdigris green for external use;[131] and elsewhere stated as a precept that everything should be laid on a ground of white.[132] By this date, of course, taste in England had changed, and the vogue was for rooms with white mouldings and ornaments set off against coloured fields. Here, everyday practice was now first to paint the whole room white, and then to colour the grounds. This was called 'picking in'. Many colours would not cover in one coat, however, experiment suggesting that yellow ochres, Naples yellow, patent yellow, verdigris, and Scheele's green were particularly liable to produce a streaky finish. The difficulty was therefore most acute when using yellow or green, although other colours, including dark browns, could be made easily to cover a white ground in one coat without difficulty.

Rather than apply two coats of an expensive colour such a blue or green, practice was naturally to use cheaper undercoats wherever possible. For this purpose, greys made by tinting white with black were the obvious choice; and Emerton, for example, stipulated a lead-colour undercoat for his green paint.[133] Examples of this practice have been found in the course of examination of paint samples from rooms of the second half of the eighteenth century, including the grey undercoat used (probably in the early 1780s) beneath the delicate blue finish in the Morning Room at Heveningham Hall, Suffolk,[134] although the blue in the staircase was applied directly above white.[135] The use of grey undercoats persisted into the nineteenth century, and Pincot, Bentley, and Vanherman all recommended lead colour as a ground for a large number of greens.[136] An example of this, probably dating from 1807–11, has been found on cross-sections from the Drawing Room at Tamworth Castle, Staffordshire (fig. 24);[137] and grey was used also about 1830 as a ground for blue in the redecoration of one of the service apartments at Somerset House, London.[138] For fine greens, Vanherman recommended the use of French grey, often a rather expensive colour (see Appendix A), but here, perhaps, no more than white tinted with black;[139] and lead colour was advocated by Pincot as a base for chocolate.[140] Examples of this practice have been found on nineteenth-century exterior ironwork.[141]

Other colours than grey were used for grounds. Pincot, for example, suggested the use of a light blue as a ground for verdigris greens,[142] and Butcher specified Prussian blue and white as an alternative to grey for a similar purpose;[143] but for two coats of verdigris green externally, Tingry (endorsing Watin's advocacy of white) observed that the general practice of painters was to use a yellow undercoat.[144] This would, no doubt, have been cheaper than blue; and for fine green externally, Crease suggested the use of two coats of the dark 'invisible green' (q.v. in Appendix A below) as undercoats beneath two of the finer finish.[145] Reynolds used a mixture of Spanish brown and red lead as a ground for a red exterior finish made using Venetian red,[146] and in connection with the finer qualities of red paint Dossie referred to the common use (which he deprecated) of red lead as a ground for vermilion.[147] The same practice was followed by Pincot in coach-painting;[148] while Vanherman recommended a ground of rose pink and Indian red for crimson.[149] In addition to these examples, it is worth noting that Pincot used a ground of white lead beneath patent yellow on coach bodies, and Tingry recommended the use of yellow ochre in grounds for patent and Naples yellows.[150] Later, of course, patent yellow itself came to be used as a ground for chrome yellow, a practice mentioned by Vanherman.[151]

Regarding the depth of tint used in undercoats, Nicholson observed: 'If the stucco be intended to be finished of any given tint, a grey, light green, apricot, &c. it will be proper, about the third coat of painting, to prepare the ground for such a tint, by a slight advance towards it';[152] and Reynolds suggested the use of white 'slightly tinged with yellow' in this way as an undercoat for straw colour.[153] This practice may be compared with D'Aviler's suggestion that an undercoat containing *céruse* and *vert de montagne* should be used beneath a finish on garden furniture made from the latter alone;[154] but this formula would have been archaic by the early nineteenth century. In contrast to Nicholson, Vanherman recommended that the shade of the ground colour should be a little darker than the finishing tint, in order to prevent the work looking 'sheery' and badly covered.[155] No doubt practice would have varied between different painters, but, as will be shown in the next chapter, great emphasis was laid in the early nineteenth century on achieving a solid even finish, and the depth of the undercoat was important to this.

GLOSS FINISHES

During the second half of the seventeenth century it is clear that a good gloss finish was considered desirable. The advocacy by Stalker & Parker of varnish-paints on wainscot will be dealt with in Chapter 18, but even in the context of more day-to-day practice John Smith observed:

> Take notice also, That all simple Colours used in House Painting, appear much more beautiful and lustrous, when they appear as if glazed over with a Varnish, to which both the drying Oyl before-mentioned contributes very much, and also the Oyl of Turpentine that the Painters use to make their Colours dry soon.[156]

Elsewhere, with even greater enthusiasm, he remarked that the use of boiled linseed oil would add such a beauty and lustre to the colours that they would 'dry with a gloss, as if they had been varnished over', adding: 'Some Colours indeed don't need to have their drying hastned by a fat Oyl . . . but yet fat Oyl [i.e. boiled linseed oil] added to these also, [doth] add a great beauty and lustre to the Colour.'[157] Moreover, the Hull painter John Fletcher advertised that his colours dried 'quick & hard with a fine Gloss';[158] and in his 'DIRECTIONS' of the 1730s Alexander Emerton advocated a coat of hot weak size on top of the oil undercoat, indicating specifically that its purpose was to make the paint look glossy.[159] In these contexts, however, the term must be seen as a relative one within the confines of early paint technology, and clearly cannot be related directly to modern standards.

Besides the simple techniques already mentioned, it is notable that Dossie remarked on the frequent adulteration of oil of turpentine with rosin.[160] John Smith, moreover, deliberately suggested the advantages of oleo-resins in the production of a glossy finish, observing:

> experience teaches, that some good clear Turpentine, dissolved in the aforesaid Oyl of Turpentine, before it be mixt with the Oyl-Colours, shall make those Colours shine ⟨much⟩ when dry, and preserve their beauty beyond all other things, drying with an extream glasey surface, and much more smooth than Oyl alone, and shall also better resist the injuries of air and weather ⟨, provided too much be not put in⟩.[161]

Tingry too recommended the use of a resinous preparation for interior house-painting, noting that it 'exhibits all the qualities of a varnish'. His formula called for 3 pounds of rosin to be dissolved in 10 pounds of oil by the application of gentle heat, after which 6 ounces of turpentine were to be added. This prepared drying oil was to be allowed to stand, but was to be used fresh, being diluted with oil of turpentine in the normal way;[162] and Reynolds specified the addition of a teaspoonful of rosin to each pound of white lead in the preparation of ice-colour paint for interior use.[163] In comparison with this, Dossie had provided a series of formulae for resinous drying oils, observing too that the normal boiled-oil manufactured for sale could be much improved by the addition of sandarac resin. For common purposes 2 pounds of sandarac and 1 pound of gum arabic were to be added to every gallon of linseed oil while it was being 'boiled'; and in thinning it for use it was, he indicated, necessary to use a rather larger proportion of oil of turpentine than normal.[164]

Such formulae approach very closely the preparation of varnish, and Félibien, probably in more of a history-painting context, had suggested the addition of varnish to paint in order to avoid the necessity of having to varnish the painting later.[165] Probably, though, the practice was common, since in a domestic receipt of 1756 to 1770 for the finishing coat for painting rooms the addition of turpentine varnish to white lead is noted with the comment 'and you may depend on't you'll have a clear gloss';[166] and Reynolds similarly advocated the addition of 1 gill of copal varnish as an alternative to the use of oil of turpentine in each gallon of oil for interior painting.[167] Tingry's later editor too suggested a similar practice, indicating that an oil-of-turpentine-based varnish (Tingry's No. 13 of which details are given in Chapter 18) could be added to finishing coats to give a greater gloss, but advised that it was better to varnish the work as a separate operation once dry.[168] This last procedure had been discussed by Watin,[169] and will receive further consideration below in connection with the application of varnish.

FLAT OR 'DEAD' FINISHES

By the early 1740s, at least, a fashion for completely matt oil paint in interiors had arisen. This was achieved by a process known as *flatting*, in which the white-lead paste was diluted with a large proportion of oil of turpentine, generally without the addition of any oil, the resultant finish being called *dead white*. An estimate of 1743 for the interior of 44 Berkeley Square, London, includes an item for 'clean white done in turpentine', and a large number of items for dead white in other London interiors appear in the accounts for Henry Pelham's house (the part remaining now lying behind 22 Arlington Street) of 1745–50, and Norfolk House of 1753–6.[170] By the second part of the century it had become the standard finish in high-quality work, even on joinery, being ubiquitous in accounts of the period. With only a single exception, Watin specified dilution in pure oil of turpentine for all his normal interior oil finishes;[171] and prices for 'Fine flat white' appear in editions of Taylor's *Builders Price-Book* from the date of its first issue in 1776.[172]

Flatting was generally executed as an additional coat laid on top of the ordinary oil finish, although Watin used two coats on wainscot, and Nicholson observed that large surfaces would need two coats, noting that this was an almost general rule on stucco.[173] Expensive ingredients such as Nottingham white lead were often used, and it also required some skill in application: Butcher warned that it should be made up and used 'off hand; for if it stands to set, it will leave a mark' on account of the volatile nature of the oil of turpentine.[174] Vanherman too indicated that speed in application was essential, requiring two men on large wall surfaces;[175] and, as acknowledged by Tingry's later editor, flatting was thus highly priced and regarded as a superior process.[176] Skyring, for example, stipulated an additional 6*d.* per yard above the cost of ordinary white paint,[177] and the implications of this together with other comparative prices will be seen from the list set out in table VII (p. 108).

Butcher described the preparation of a flatting coat by mixing the best Nottingham white lead (paste) with pure oil of turpentine, although he suggested that a small quantity of nut oil could also be added, directing that it was to be laid on 'above third colour, or second colour, as you think proper' (that is on an undercoat and ordinary finish, or on a single undercoat – see discussion of these terms in the next chapter).[178] Both Pincot and Nicholson also recommended the use of Nottingham white lead, the former specifying sugar of lead as a drier.[179] Although Butcher mentioned the use of nut oil, and the fourth and eleventh editions of the *Builder's Price-Book* contain an item for work 'flated with nut-oil', Nicholson remarked that, while sometimes employed, this was not often the case since it was rather expensive, adding that the same was true of paste ground in poppy oil.[180] Use of these oils, even in a limited way, does of course serve to point what was undoubtedly one of the basic reasons for the favour accorded to dead white, quite apart from its flat finish. The low linseed oil content would have minimised the yellowing effect of the medium, and hence, for example, Nicholson observed that it was 'to be preferred for all superior work, not only for appearance, but preserving the colours and purity of tint'.[181]

Finally, it should be noted that although often referred to as *dead white*, the process was used also for finishes of various colours, no doubt for the same reasons which led to the adoption of flatted whites in the first place. French grey, blue, and greens, including 'verdigrease green', are priced flatted in later editions of the *Builder's Price-Book*;[182] while 'Dead French Gray' had been supplied at Dyrham Park in 1781,[183] and flatted French grey and green had been used at Somerset House, London, in 1790.[184] To these colours Nicholson provided the addition of fawn.[185]

CHAPTER 16

THE APPLICATION OF OIL PAINT

KNOTTING

John Smith did not mention the process of knotting, or prevention of the resin present in the knots of the timber from bleeding through the paint film and producing an unsightly stain on the finished work. The reason for this omission is not clear, since the problem would no doubt have been appreciated at the time, but is most likely to have been since his description of the painting process was conceived more in terms of exterior work.[1] Alexander Emerton, however, directed that the knots in wainscot should be covered with 'Oyl Primer',[2] and a similar method was recommended by Watin and Tingry, although they indicated that extra litharge should be ground into the priming, the latter author directing that it should then be applied locally to the knots.[3] Red lead too was a favoured drier for the purpose, mixtures of red and white lead in linseed oil being given by Nicholson;[4] while Butcher specified that to kill knots red lead and litharge should be applied with a small quantity of oil and a greater proportion of oil of turpentine.[5]

In contrast with the oil-based formulae, aqueous preparations containing a drier bound with size were in use. In Joseph Emerton's edition of the 'DIRECTIONS', for example, a mixture of size and red lead appeared in place of the 'Oyl Primer' in Alexander Emerton's text, a possible indication, perhaps, that this had not always proved effective (fig. 1). An early nineteenth-century paint manufacturer, Thomas Bentley, too gave a similar formula, recommending that knots in new timber should be killed by the application of three parts of white lead and one of red lead in weak glue or strong size;[6] and Tingry's later editor suggested employment of a strong solution of glue with red lead.[7] Even Vanherman, who was extremely critical of size priming and clearcole, specified the use of red lead finely ground in water and diluted with double size for knotting, directing that two coats of this preparation were to be applied hot;[8] and it is clear that such formulae represent common practice.

Other treatments were, nevertheless, advocated. Nicholson suggested a preliminary application of freshly slaked lime, which was allowed to remain on the knots for twenty-four hours before being scraped off; and also gave a pair of two-coat knotting formulae combining coats of size and oil. The first of these called for a primary layer of red lead in strong size, followed by a 'second knotting' of white and red lead in oil; while the second, presumably intended for better-quality work where light colours were being used, required the application of ceruse in parchment size followed by white lead in oil with the addition of one-fourth part of red lead.[9] In a later work, however, he suggested the use of such an oil knotting on top of two coats of size as a third line of defence only where there was doubt as to the efficacy of the first two.[10]

In general it seems reasonable to suggest that simple knotting with red lead in size remained general practice throughout the period considered in this study, although oil-based formulae were also in use. Two coats (on occasion one of oil succeeding a layer of knotting in size) might also be employed, as is evident from the Norfolk House accounts in which items for 'twice knoted' appear.[11] Besides these, for work of exceptionally high quality, silver leaf might be used to seal the knots, applied on a coat of gold-size. Although Nicholson is the only writer to mention this practice, suggesting its use in one instance in principal rooms, and in another reserving it for application above the undercoat if the knots persisted in bleeding through,[12] an example of its employment has been found in the Saloon at Uppark, Sussex;[13] and knotting with silver leaf appears also in one of the clauses of Bartholomew's *Specifications*.[14]

STOPPING

Even the most carefully executed joinery will contain joints which require filling before the application of paint, and external cracks and shakes which appear in timber which has been exposed to the weather also need stopping up to prevent the entry of rainwater. In 1668 Leybourn mentioned the practice of 'stoping',[15] and John Smith directed:

> let the first business therefore be, to stop up these places smooth and even, with a ⟨substance by the Painters called⟩ Putty made of Whiting and Linseed Oyl, well beaten together on the grinding-stone, with a Wooden Mallet, to the consistence of a very stiff Dow [Dough].[16]

Pincot, no doubt speaking from experience, described putty as made by mixing whiting and linseed oil, 'as the women make a pudding, but so stiff as not to hang about your fingers, which is very unpleasant';[17] and Vanherman provided a more detailed description of its manufacture. Whiting was first dried in an oven, rolled, and sifted through a 45-hole wire sieve. It was then formed into a stiff paste with raw linseed oil on a painters' stone and left until the next day, when pieces weighing three or four pounds each were beaten again. The finished product was stored in glazed pans covered with a wet cloth, but in the event of its becoming hard it could be warmed over a fire or by immersion in boiling water, and again beaten to regain its former consistency.[18]

In contrast to the above, Evelyn stated that putty was made from '*White* and *Red-lead*, and some *Spannish-white* (not much)', and Tingry mentioned the use of 'white lead cement', presumably made in a similar way to the hard stopping of more recent times, using a proportion of white-lead paste with ordinary putty.[19] Such formulations seem, therefore, to have been in at least occasional use. Otherwise, the only alternative noted is the 'badigeon' mentioned by Nicholson. This was, he indicated, a mixture of plaster and freestone, or of sawdust with glue which was used for stopping;[20] but the first of these alternatives seems to stem from Watin's *badigeon* which, he noted, was used for the walls of churches and the outsides of old houses to lighten them and afford them the colour of new stone,[21] and references to *putty* appear generally to indicate the ordinary mixture of whiting and size. Prices seem to have ranged between $3\frac{1}{2}$*d.* and 4*d.* per pound up to about 1790, and to have risen to 6*d.* thereafter. Salmon, for example, quoted 4*d.* in 1734, while Leadbeater indicated prices of between $3\frac{1}{2}$*d.* and 4*d.*;[22] but 6*d.* per pound was paid at Tredegar House, Newport, in 1792, and the compiler of the *Builders Price-Book* quoted the same figure in 1810 and 1813.[23] All these prices are consistent with those given by Phillips in *Crosby's Builder's New Price-book*.[24]

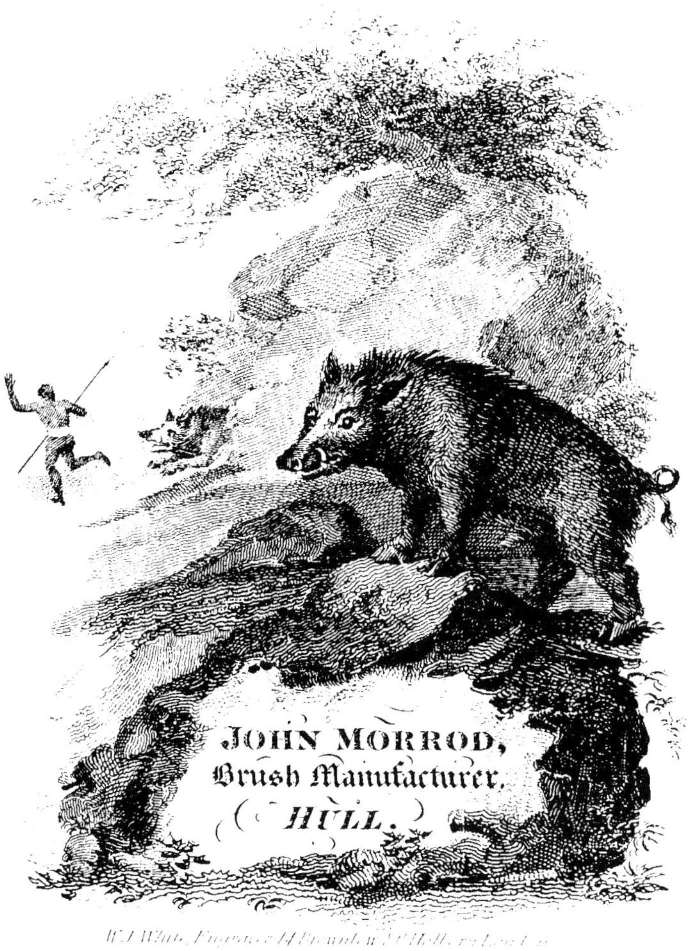

25. Trade card of John Morrod, brush-manufacturer, Hull.

BRUSHES AND OTHER UTENSILS

Paint brushes were divided by John Smith into three categories. Those usually used for house-painting were, he observed, made of hogs hair, were round in shape, and varied in diameter from 2 inches to $\frac{1}{4}$ inch. Flat hog's-hair brushes, on the other hand, were used for drawing lines and in graining and marbling; while 'pencils' were made of a finer and smaller hair, either bound into quills of various sizes, set in tin ferrules, or, for larger sizes, bound into wooden stocks like the ordinary brushes. He emphasised the need for careful selection of pencils and brushes, observing in the case of the latter that the bristles should be fast-bound in the stocks, and that the hairs should be strong and lie close together. Should they become loose, he suggested in later editions that wooden wedges be driven between the threads binding them.[25] Watin too discussed brushes, demanding that the bristles be straight and that they should present a neatly trimmed flat end. He divided them into two categories, those made with the hair of the wild boar alone, and those in which this was mixed with pig's hair.[26] In 1615–16 a quantity of brush hair was supplied at 20*d.* per lb. in connection with work at Greenwich Palace; and the trade card of John Morrod, a Hull brush manufacturer (fig. 25) illustrates the raw material.[27]

Although several names for house-painters' brushes of this ordinary type are encountered in early nineteenth-century English literature, it seems likely that they cover only two basic varieties, directly related to Watin's division. Tingry's later editor, for example, described only two categories, the 'common brushes' which, he indicated, contained coarse hairs only, and 'ground tools' consisting of white and fine hair. The former were, he noted, used in the application of undercoats, brushes of the latter type being used for the finish.[28] For their part, Pincot and Vanherman differentiated only 'dusters' and ground tools, the latter observing that when worn down 'long Hair Dusters' made the best brushes for painting.[29] Tingry's later editor also remarked that the common brushes became finer from use.[30] Furthermore, although Lewis Berger stocked 'Brushes', 'Dusters', and 'Ground Brushes', the first two were priced at identical rates and the last category alone at a higher price, so that, for example, in 1806 a dozen 'No. 3' brushes or dusters were valued at 8*s.* 6*d.*, against 10*s.* 6*d.* for the same quantity of ground brushes.[31] It seems most likely, therefore, that the ordinary grade of brush was commonly broken in for use by dusting down the work over a period, and was accordingly known as a 'duster'. An illustration of a 'dusting brush' taken from a later nineteenth-century book is reproduced (fig. 26); although it seems likely that by this date improved methods of manufacture, such as that described by Ure,[32] had been introduced. Another name encountered, which seems also to have been used interchangeably for the cheaper quality, was 'pound brush'. Two were supplied at Tredegar House, Newport,

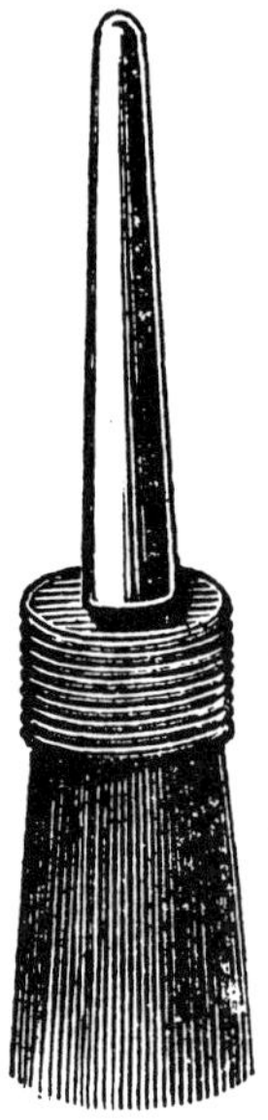
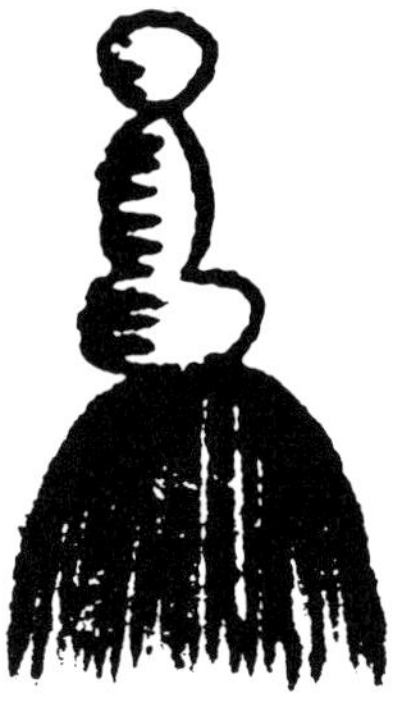
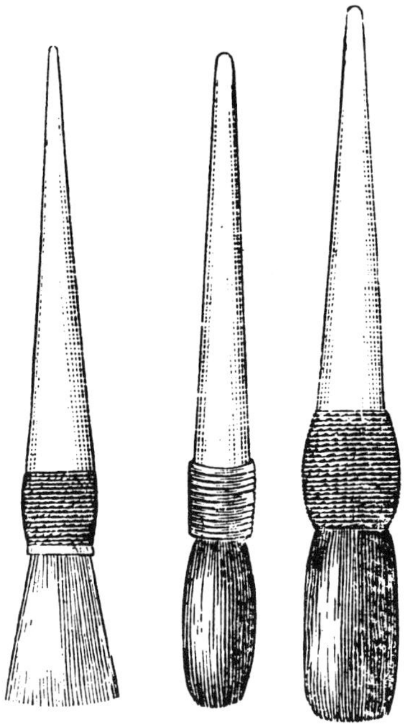

26. Nineteenth-century 'dusting brush'.
27. Seventeenth-century illustration of a 'Painters Laying Brush'.
28. Nineteenth-century sash tools.

in 1793,[33] and Martin described pound brushes as made from hog's hair, remarking that they were first used as dusters.[34] Nicholson repeated this, explaining that pound brushes were thus employed 'till the soft part is worn away', the previous wear, he indicated, adapting it better 'for spreading the colours for which it is afterwards used'.[35] In connection with this term, it is of interest that the Italian renaissance painter Cennino Cennini noted that a pound of hair was used in making a hog's-hair brush.[36]

Of the three brushes illustrated by Moxon in 1703 (fig. 32, p. 115), that in the middle is notably close in form to the mid-nineteenth-century duster just mentioned, and although he included this in a plate of plasterers' tools, it probably represents the type used equally by painters. Similar round brushes with flat ends may be certainly be seen, for example, on the trade cards of Hardwick and Jordan (figs. 14, 19), although those shown by Joseph Emerton in the mid-1740s (fig. 1) have shorter stocks and appear to be of a more pointed shape. Unless purely for artists' use, these may, however, represent the softer quality used for finishing or 'laying off' the work. The hog's-hair brush illustrated in the 1680s by Holme (fig. 27) may also have been used for this purpose, since he described is as a 'Painters Laying Brush', and his illustration, though crude, perhaps suggests hair of a more flexible nature than that shown by Moxon.

Before using a new brush, Watin suggested that it should be soaked in water for half an hour to remove the sawdust used to secure the bristles, and to swell the binding string and the wood;[37] but no author seems to suggest the painter himself binding the hairs in the way which persisted well into the present century,[38] although with 'long hair' dusters in particular this might have been expected. For cleaning brushes after use, John Smith recommended washing first in clean linseed oil, followed by warm soap suds, and Emerton the use of soap and hot water.[39] Pincot too recommended the use of soap.[40]

Besides the large round brushes so far discussed, it will be remembered that John Smith had mentioned the use of flat hog's-hair brushes for special purposes, in particular for graining and marbling. By the early nineteenth century, brushes of this form were also known as 'varnishing brushes', and their use in both fields is discussed in Chapters 18 and 20 below. For painting sashes, small brushes known as 'sash tools' were used. These were probably round in shape, corresponding to the small hog's-hair brushes mentioned by John Smith, although little information about them is given by authors writing during the period being considered. Pincot, for example, referred merely to 'small' brushes 'for sashes',[41] while four were supplied at Tredegar House in 1793,[42] and Lewis Berger stocked a range of sash tools of different sizes.[43] A late-nineteenth-century illustration (fig. 28) shows a number of forms; but even at this date all still appear to be round in shape, like the small brushes shown on Jordan's trade card (fig. 19). Pencils, to which John Smith also referred, were used extensively for imitations, in signwriting, and for other decorative work. Stalker & Parker described them as made from camel's hair; and Nicholson, writing much later, referred to 'camel hair pencils', of which Lewis Berger had stocks in 1802 and 1810.[44] Watin, on the other hand, stated that pencils were made from badger's hair, or from that of the Siberian squirrel;[45] but the author of the *Painter's . . . Pocket Manual* observed that brushes made from badger's hair were seldom used, generally being found only abroad.[46] The different sizes made were, as already mentioned, related to the quills from different birds into which the hairs might be bound: Watin gave the extremes as swan and lark, the former being mentioned among others by John Smith;[47] while the complete series given by Stalker & Parker ranged through goose, little goose, and duck, to swallow quills.[48] Of these, during the early nineteenth century Lewis Berger stocked only 'Swan Quill Pencils'; but besides a few 'Quill Tools' had in addition some 'Com^{n} Pencills', 'best Pencils', and 'Fitch Pencils'.[49] Fitched pencils had been mentioned by John Smith, and were also listed by Vanherman (who included too 'a few French Tools', although it is unclear what these were).[50]

Other painting tools and implements seem to have received scant attention by writers, but in 1806 Berger had a small stock of palette knives;[51] and Vanherman referred to 'Pallet Knives, large and small', a 'Putty or Stopping Knife', 'Single or Hand Pots', and 'double Paint Pots'.[52] Pots, probably of earthenware and metal type, may be seen on a number of trade cards (figs. 1, 13, 14).

PREPARATION AND PAINTING PROCEDURE

The first maxim to be observed in house-painting was, Pincot remarked, to '*rub it bare and lay it fair*'. The inexperienced, on the other hand, he suggested, would more generally work on the principle '*lay it on thick and some will stick*'.[53] By far the most comprehensive account of the way in which a room should be painted was given by Vanherman, whose 'Aromatic paint' (an early form of emulsion), to which it more strictly applied, is described in

Chapter 17. The work was, he said, to be knotted and dusted and the floor covered,[54] after which the priming was laid on with a ground brush. New sashes, however, were, he indicated, always primed before installation, and did not require a second priming. In this connection it is worth noting that during the mid-seventeenth century Pratt had observed that iron and timberwork were to be painted as soon as wrought; while in the agreement of 1665 relating to the painting of Clarendon House, London, it was laid down: 'The Joyners at no hand to stay for priming, and the Works to be finished when once set up with all expedition'.[55] After priming, Vanherman continued, a day was allowed for the paint to harden before it was lightly rubbed down with a pumice stone.[56] The work was then dusted again, and stopped with putty, after which the 'second colour' was applied. After a further day had elapsed, the work was rubbed down a second time, on this occasion with glasspaper, again dusted, and the 'third colour' applied. Another day's rest was allowed, and the wood rubbed down using glasspaper, again dusted, and the 'fourth colour or finish' executed.[57]

Of the other authors noted in the course of research, only Nicholson mentioned rubbing down between coats in this way,[58] and it seems likely that, as today, this was frequently skimped, especially since Vanherman felt it necessary to remark that many painters thought it lost time to rub down so often. There was, on the other hand, he stressed, 'no comparison between work executed in this way and the slovenly mode practised in general'.[59] With regard to the length of time allowed between coats, the clear day specified by Vanherman no doubt related to the speed at which his 'Aromatic Paint' would dry (modern paints are adjusted to dry much more quickly). With ordinary oil paint, on the other hand, it seems likely that longer was often required, and Nicholson, otherwise the only author noted to comment on this, observed that if time would permit, two or three days between each coat would not be too long.[60] Experiment with formulations of contemporary type has tended to confirm this. Stopping was carried out by Nicholson after application of the 'second colour' rather than after priming as suggested by Vanherman, and by John Smith (for exterior work) before priming.[61] It seems most likely that general practice for interior painting would have conformed to that of Vanherman and the present day in stopping after application of the primer.

Turning to repainting work, no references to the use of paint strippers have been encountered, and the first mention of burning-off located is in one of Bartholomew's mid-nineteenth-century specification clauses, in which the contractor was enjoined to prepare all the interior and exterior joinery, and 'to burn off therefrom all . . . blistered and other defective parts of the painting'.[62] Significantly, this possibility was not mentioned by Vanherman, who again provided the most punctilious account of the preparation necessary. Previously painted surfaces were, he directed, to be washed down with soap and water and pumiced, the latter a procedure specified also by Pincot and Nicholson. Chips and blisters were then to be brought forward with three or four coats of paint applied locally, and when these were dry, the work was stopped and rubbed down ready to receive the 'second colour' or undercoat. From then on painting continued as in new work.[63] For the cheap method of redecoration, clearcole and finish, Nicholson suggested merely dusting and stopping before application of the clearcole;[64] while Emerton dusted and sized the old paintwork on wainscot before stopping and application of the finish.[65]

Cleanliness and the avoidance of dust are obviously of prime importance in achieving a good finish in any kind of paintwork, and Pincot, who stressed too its role in the avoidance of lead poisoning, remarked:

> In *Inside Painting* a great help to your work would be to let the woman wash, and clean it well; you will here have the advantage of the Painter, circumstances not affording him that opportunity though always done in Ireland by women employed by Painters for that purpose, who clean before and after workmen: I have often had a well painted room spoiled by women carelessly splashing it over in cleaning the floor, which ought to be done previous to your laying on the last coat of paint.[66]

Undoubtedly, the last word in preparation lies in a mid-nineteenth-century French specification quoted by Donaldson:

> L'entrepreneur de Peinture sera avec le plus grand soin tous les *traveaux préparatoires* en usage, tels que les époussetages, égrenages, gratages, lavages, rebouchages, lessivages, poinçages, et tous autres nécessaires pour obtenir la perfection désirable.[67]

During the course of painting, informed opinion suggested that ventilation combined with a degree of warmth was necessary, the two no doubt combining to prevent dampness or humidity affecting the paint. In pricing work, Laxton noted that a small fire should be allowed in each room;[68] and Emerton recommended: 'If the Weather is cold or damp, it will be proper to make a Fire in the Room; but if the contrary, set open all the Windows to give it Air. For the sooner it dries, the better it looks.'[69] This advice seems not always to have been followed, since Bentley directed that when applying his 'New Metallic, or Aromatic Oil Paint', in contrast with 'the usual mode of Painting, it is absolutely necessary that the windows should be kept open, to have all the air possible during the operation'.[70] Vanherman too implied that this was not general practice, and writing in turn of his own product, advised:

> Unlike the usual method adopted by painters, of keeping close shut up during the operation, it is necessary that all doors and windows should be open when the Aromatic Paint is used, as it is an erroneous idea, that affording air at this time injures the whiteness of paint; it is quite the reverse – air and light bleach all colours.[71]

He also provided a detailed account of the order in which the various elements of the room were generally tackled, observing:

> Most painters begin with the backs of the shutters, and linings, and then the sashes . . . and the sofit, and shutter fronts; after these, the cornice and frieze; next commence the wall or wainscot, beginning at the top, and so proceed downwards to the dado, which you leave until all the four flanks, or sides, are gone over. You are now to cover the doors, and then the dado and skirting, and,

Table VII. *Prices for painters' work in pence per yard super for ordinary white or common colours*
N.B. Figures in square brackets are for exterior work, those in round brackets for painting on stucco.

	1659[1]	1665[2]	1690–4[3]	1696[4]	*c.*1700[5]	1734[6]	1745[7]	1745–8[8]	1776[9]	1783[10]	1787[11]	1789–91[12]	1790–1803[13]	1803[14]	1810[15]	1816[16]	1818[17]	1831[18]
New work																		
One coat of oil ('once in oil')	[3]	–	3[19]	–	4	–	–	3	2	–	2(2½)	3½	3½(3½)	3	5(5)	5	5	4
Two coats of oil ('twice in oil')	[6]	–	–	–	6	–	–	4½	4	4½	4(5)	4½	5½(6)	6	8(8)	7	8½	6
Three coats of oil ('three times in oil')	[9]	10[12]	10	8	9	6[6–8]	6	6(7)	6(6–8)	6½	6(7½)	6	7½(8)	8½	11(11)	10	11½	9
Four coats of oil ('four times in oil')	–	–	–	–	12	–	8	8(9)	8–10[20]	8½	8(10)[20]	8	9½(10½)[21]	10½	14(14)	11	14	12
Two coats of oil on a size primer ('twice in oil primed in size')	–	–	–	–	–	–	–	–	5	–	5	–	6½	–	9	–	–	–
Old Work																		
Two coats of oil ('second colour and finish')	–	–	–	–	–	–	5	–	–	–	5	–	7	–	–	–	–	–
One coat of oil on a distemper undercoat ('clearcole and finish')	–	–	–	–	–	–	4	–	3	3½	3	–	4½	5	6	6	–	5½
Flatting																		
Single coat of flatting ('dead white once in oil')	–	–	–	–	–	–	–	–	–	–	4	–	6	–	–	–	7	6
1 coat of oil plus one coat of flatting ('twice in oil dead white', or 'once in oil and flatted')	–	–	–	–	–	–	–	–	–	–	7	–	9	–	12	–	12	10
2 coats of oil plus one coat of flatting ('three times in oil dead white', or 'twice in oil and flatted')	–	–	–	–	–	–	–	7(8)	9	10	10	–	11	13	15	12	15½	15
3 coats of oil plus one coat of flatting ('four times in oil dead white', or 'three times in oil and flatted')	–	–	–	–	–	–	–	9(10)	12	12	12–14	13	16	15	18	15	18½	18
4 coats of oil plus one coat of flatting ('four times in oil and flatted')	–	–	–	–	–	–	–	–	–	14	–	–	–	17	21	–	–	–

Notes and references

1. Wilsford (1659), p. 26.
2. Gunther (1928), p. 147 (contract for Clarendon House, Piccadilly, London).
3. P.R.O. MSS., WORK.19/48/1, ff. 50(iv), 64(iii), 93(iii) – accounts for Kensington Palace.
4. R.I.B.A. MSS., WRE/2/19, 20 (tenders for Greenwich Hospital).
5. Boughton MS., vol. i, pp. 159–69 (accounts for Boughton, Ditton, and Montagu House).
6. Salmon (1734), p. 56.
7. Salmon (1745), p. 47.
8. R.I.B.A. MSS., PEL/1, pp. 82–6 (accounts for 22 Arlington Street).
9. *Builders Price-Book* (1776), pp. 90–1.
10. Englefield (1936), pp. 180–1 (prices fixed by the Painter-Stainers Company).
11. *Builders Price-Book* (1787), pp. 135, 138.
12. Woburn MS.
13. Phillips (1804), pp. 126–7.
14. Englefield (1936), pp. 185–6.
15. *Builders Price-Book* (1810), pp. 81, 83–4.
16. Englefield (1936), pp. 190–1.
17. Laxton (1818), p. 96.
18. Skyring (1831), p. 88.
19. Painting on the back of wainscot.
20. On stucco from a ladder, 12*d.*
21. On stucco from a ladder, 14*d.*

> lastly, the chimneypiece, if it is wood. When two men are employed in the same room, the work is executed with more facility, especially if the flanks are of great dimensions; in that case, one takes the top and the other the bottom, so that both meet in the middle; this is particularly essential, when an apartment, hall, or staircase, is to be flatted.[72]

Should the colour scheme comprise both dark and light colours, Pincot suggested execution of the dark colours last, since the dark paint covered the light better at junctions than vice versa, thus producing a neater job.[73]

Considerable concern was expressed over the quality of the final finish in oil paint, which, Tingry observed, had a character of solidity which caused it often to be preferred to varnish or distemper.[74] It will be remembered that Vanherman recommended the use of a dark undercoat for the particular purpose of preventing the work looking badly covered, and it will be recalled too that at a much earlier date John Smith had stipulated thinning the paint only to the extent that the ground (which was of course often primed in a dark red colour) should not grin through. It was suggested above that this problem of opacity in the finish was greater with some colours than others, and there seems little doubt it was for this reason that Reynolds specifically directed a half-worn brush should be used in laying a blue finish made with Prussian blue.[75] Indeed, most significantly, the author of the *Painter's . . . Pocket Manual* indicated that the test of the complete workman was that he left no brushmarks behind him;[76] but to achieve this, quite apart from a properly tinted undercoat and correctly chosen brush, the way in which the latter was handled was critical, and Pincot therefore gave detailed instructions over this aspect of painting practice:

> Now, in laying on the colour always take a full brush laying a little here and there at distances within your reach, rubbing it out till the whole is spread fair and even, a yard square at a time is sufficient; and, when equally spread, cross it first one way and then another, lying it off lightly with the grain of the wood.[77]

Vanherman too stressed the need in laying colour on panels, stiles, or indeed any flat work, to 'cross the brush, both backwards and forwards, and in all directions, to equalise the paint', and then to 'lay it off, by beginning at the top and drawing your brush firmly down, and then from the bottom upwards, to meet and make the joining good', adding with final emphasis: 'Be careful not to leave any hair marks on the work'.[78] Even at a much earlier date, Emerton, who it will be recalled also stipulated the need for a grey undercoat for his green paint, took care to direct that the panels of wainscot should be painted the way of the grain;[79] and the hallmark of good work was summed up by Martin, who observed that although cheap painters cared little about it: 'Good painting is known by the *fullness* and *solidity* of its appearance without any marks of the brush'.[80]

OIL PAINT SYSTEMS FOR INTERIORS

The minimum recommended by authors from the late seventeenth century for new interior work was, put into modern terms, priming, an undercoat, and a finishing coat. Where an oil primer was used this was known as *three times in oil*, but where the work was primed in size as *twice in oil and primed in size*. On stucco, however, Nicholson regarded four coats of oil paint as the minimum sufficient, that is *four times in oil*.[81] These terms may be seen in table VII, which shows prices for ordinary colours taken from various accounts and trade manuals of the period; and it will be seen that painting on stucco (the term being applied to internal plaster as well as exterior rendering) was more expensive than painting on timber. More coats than the minimum mentioned above might of course be used. Nicholson, for example, suggested an oil primer followed by four or five coats of oil paint; an estimate dated 1771 signed by James Adam for painting the major interiors at the Shire Hall, Hertford, contains items for five coats of oil on the stucco; and at Somerset House up to five coats were applied.[82] The maximum noted to date were the six coats of white in nut oil used on ceilings at Montagu House, London, in 1705;[83] but this seems exceptional, and for ordinary work three coats remained the norm. A contract dated 1770 for the erection of a bakehouse and dwelling in Middlesex, for example, specified that all the interior and exterior joinery was to be painted three times in oil;[84] and, although in the first edition of his book John Smith noted that two or three primings followed by four or five coats of finish might be used externally, for wainscoting he particularly remarked that two coats of finish only were required.[85] In 1667 Stephen Primatt priced only for three coats of oil on 'Bannisters for Stair-cases',[86] and the tenders of *c.* 1696 for interior painting at Greenwich Hospital were all for three coats.[87] Emerton too envisaged the application of a primer and two coats of finish on wainscot.[88] Two coats alone are also occasionally met with, as in the Servants' Hall at Boughton House painted about 1700;[89] and in other instances the work might be primed in size, followed by two coats of oil, this being recommended, for example, by Joseph Emerton in the painting of stucco (fig. 1).

In repainting old work, the cheap method known as *clearcole and finish*, using a distemper undercoat, was described in the previous chapter, and found a place in many eighteenth- and early nineteenth-century price books. Its oil equivalent of undercoat and finish was known as *second colour and finish*, and by way of explanation Pincot defined *second colour* as 'a term used by Painters, which is the second coat layed on new work, and the first on work which has been painted before, the old work being considered equal to a primed state'.[90] Nicholson too indicated that the term was used in this way.[91]

The nomenclature applied to flatting was, however, slightly less clear cut. The earlier system seems to have been to regard the flatting as forming the last oil coat, and thus in the late 1740s at Henry Pelham's House in Arlington Street, London, three times *dead white* was priced at 7*d.* per yard against 6*d.* for three times in oil and 8*d.* for four times in oil.[92] The same system was followed in eighteenth-century editions of the *Builder's Price-Book*, so that in 1787, for example, 'Dead white to old work once in oil' was priced at 4*d.* per yard against 5*d.* for 'Second colour and finish', showing clearly that only one coat was intended. In the first edition of 1776 'Dead white to old work three times in oil' at 9*d.* (as against 10*d.* in 1787) must therefore have been intended to represent two coats of normal oil followed by the flatting coat, and 'Fine flat white four times in oil' at 1*s.* three coats plus the flatting.[93] William & James Pain also gave prices on the same system during the closing years of the century in their *British Palladio*.[94]

A variant term was used, however, by the Painter-Stainers Company, who regulated the prices of painting in London, when in 1783 they fixed a rate of 1*s.* 2*d.* per yard for 'four times in oil and once flatted white'.[95] In this instance it seems probable that a total of five coats was intended, since the *Builder's Price-Book* of 1787 quoted 1*s.* to 1*s.* 2*d.* for dead white to old work 'four times in oil',[96] and at Woburn Abbey between 1789 and 1791 1*s.* 1*d.* was charged for 'three Oyl & flatted'.[97] In the 1810 edition of the *Builder's Price-book*, after the severe rise in prices occasioned by the wars with France, 'Once in oil, and flated dead white' was priced at 1*s.* per yard against 5*d.* for once in oil, the difference of 7*d.* between these no doubt representing the cost of a flatting coat.[98] The conclusion that the new mode of expression implied the application of two coats of paint is confirmed by the fact that this latter figure was given by Laxton in 1818 for 'Flatting, dead colour once', while he too priced one coat of oil at 5*d.*[99] Martin moreover defined 'Three times in oil and flat' as three coats of oil plus a flatting coat, but confused the issue by defining 'Thrice in oil and flat' as two coats of oil plus a flatting coat.[100] It seems fairly clear, however, that *thrice* is a misprint for *twice*; especially since Nicholson, who based his text of 1823–5 directly on Martin's article, amended it to 'THRICE IN OIL', explaining that this meant two coats of oil plus one of flatting.[101]

MEASUREMENT OF WORK FOR PRICING

Painter's work could be measured for pricing in a number of ways: by the superficial area, by the piece, by the foot run on items such as mouldings, or by the time and materials expended. The first of these provided, of course, the method applied to most straightforward paintwork, but the second too was in use by the beginning of the period under review, and was employed in connection with such elements as window lights and iron casements, sash frames (the fixed part of the window joinery) and sash squares (the opening parts), iron bars, catches, and chimneypieces. Wainscot on the other hand was naturally priced by the superficial yard, although Isaac Ware noted in 1756 that it was measured in feet and the figure reduced to yards. To square up a room, he directed, the perimeter of the wall was taken and multiplied by the height. For the latter dimension, measurement was made as if all the mouldings were flattened out, being 'girt by a line bending it into every moulding' so that although the horizontal component of the calculation was the same as that used by the joiner, the vertical element was increased.[102] Earlier writers too referred to the same method, Wilsford observing that 'Painters do measure with a string all moulded works', and Leybourn also mentioning this procedure;[103] while the latter's near contemporary, Venterus Mandey, noted that one should begin with a piece of string from the top of the cornice.[104] Window shutters had of course to be painted both sides, and Neve noted: 'They always reckon double Work for Painting of Window-shutters, if both sides are Painted alike';[105] while Ware tabulated 'the back and edges to the shutters' and also the 'Back edge to the architrave' in his addition.[106] The area occupied by the chimneypiece would be deducted if it was not to be painted in with the wainscot, Ware making this allowance too in his example. Another detail of the measuring method was noted by Neve, who observed that although, 'they reckon Sash-frames by themselves, (at so much *per* Piece, and likewise Mantle-pieces) when there is no Painting about them; . . . if they stand in the Wainscot, they measure them as plain Work, deducting nothing for the Vacancy.'[107]

Staircase bannisters were also often measured by the square yard. Leybourn remarked that although they could be girt they would sometimes be priced as if flat, adding 'I have seen the experiment tryed, and the difference would not countervalue the trouble of Girting'.[108] His observation was repeated by Neve, who enlarged on the method thus: 'Both sides of the Ballisters are measured as if it were flat Measure, including the Vacuity betwixt the Ballisters; which being cast up in Feet and Parts, it's reduced into Yards as other Plain Painting is.' It stood to reason, he argued, that this should produce the same result as the other method 'because it's the Custom to set them but their Square or Diameter asunder, and then the Flanks make good the Vacuities'.[109]

During the eighteenth century, with more widespread elaboration in interior painting and increasing use of stucco, the system evolved further. In 1663 Gerbier, for example, had priced only carved and gilded frames and mouldings by the foot run, and in 1734 Salmon only exterior cornices in this way;[110] but by 1787 the *Builder's Price-Book* noted that carved mouldings, modillions, cornices, fascias, and skirtings were all measured by the foot run, and the first edition of 1776 had priced cloak pins, stall plates, bell wires, and Ionic entablatures in this way.[111] Furthermore, although Salmon had observed that all carving in rooms was so varied that it would have to be valued by the time and material expended, by 1787, perhaps as a result of a greater consistency of architectural style, the *Builder's Price Book* indicated that although many such items had still to be valued in this way, 'Chimney pieces, ornamental ceilings, and other enriched work picked in, and small detached pieces done with variegated, or fancy colours' were priced by the square foot.[112] This method, found used in many accounts of the neo-classical period including, for example, those for Somerset House,[113] reflects the revolution in the use of paint colour in interiors which took place during the mid-eighteenth century, and is described in the companion volume.

CHAPTER 17

WATER-BASED PAINTS

Although in certain instances, some of which are mentioned below, water-based paints were applied to timber, such finishes were more generally reserved for the decoration of plasterwork. Campbell, for example, referred to 'plaistering and white-washing the Ceiling, and such Part of the Walls as require it, or are not to be wainscoted';[1] while Dossie remarked that distemper was used for ceilings and 'common hangings', meaning by the latter those of paper rather than fabric.[2] Thus, in a contract dated 1770 for the erection of a house and baker's shop in Middlesex, the joinery was to receive three coats of oil paint, while the plasterwork of the walls and ceilings was to be finished in a water-based coating.[3] Such preparations in their simple form were naturally rather cheaper than those in which oil was used as the medium; and, the author of the *Painter's . . . Pocket Manual* declared, although much used in the interior of houses, distemper was inferior to oil paint.[4] When applied to new walls before they had properly dried out, on the other hand, oil could give trouble, a disadvantage stressed by J.C. Loudon in connection with exterior work in 1833;[5] and it seems likely therefore that, as remained common practice until quite recently, the plasterwork in newly finished interiors would often be decorated first in a porous water-based paint, pending final decoration in oil a year or two later. This was certainly the case at Henry Pelham's house in Arlington Street, London, the accounts for which show that the whole of the staircase had been painted in this way by January 1746 and was not decorated in oil until about two years later.[6]

At Arlington Street, as elsewhere, it was the plasterer who was responsible for the application of water-based finishes, work in oil being executed by the painters and charged accordingly in a separately measured account. The same split in responsibility is implicit in the wording of the specification forming part of the contract dated 1770 mentioned above; and Campbell, moreover, remarked particularly: 'The Plaisterer is always Whitewasher'.[7] This division of work seems to have prevailed since at least 1603 when, as a result of energetic lobbying on the part of the Painter-Stainer's Company, an Act of Parliament was passed preventing 'any of the Company of Plaisterers' from applying oil paint.[8] The statute gave the Painter-Stainers sole right to the use of oil 'within the City of *London* and the Suburbs and Liberties of the same', and the plasterers were limited to the use and application of whiting and a restricted range of five tinting pigments 'mingled with Size only'. Although, in opposing a later Bill of 1664, the Plasterers Company argued that country bricklayers and glaziers commonly laid oil paint on timber and iron,[9] (a submission which suggests that London practice may not always have been followed in the provinces), the principle does nevertheless seem to have been general and to have been maintained well into the nineteenth century. It is reflected, for example, in eighteenth-century price-books, and even as late as 1831 still formed the framework adopted in the 21st edition of *Skyring's Builder's Prices*;[10] while the Act itself was not repealed until 1856.[11]

Of the white base pigments described in Chapter 1, only four (chalk, white lead, lime, and satin white) seem certainly to have been used for house-painting in an aqueous medium. To these may perhaps be added barium carbonate, which Vanherman suggested could be used as 'a water-white for ceilings',[12] and possibly also gypsum. In the case of binders, too, although an appreciable number of alternatives was available,[13] relatively few seem to have been employed; and, for interior work in particular, sizes of varying quality seem to have been used in the vast majority of instances. Indeed, size alone received mention in builders' price-books of the period, and, despite the fact that formulae in which skimmed milk was exploited were also published, references to actual use of these in domestic interiors have proved elusive, so that the true extent to which such casein-bound paints were employed remains obscure. By the early nineteenth century, on the other hand, it seems most likely that oil-bound distempers, using an oil and water emulsion as the vehicle, were being developed and marketed commercially, at least for exterior use. Discussion of these, together with formulae for casein-bound paints, will therefore follow description of the more commonly used size-bound formulations and their method of application.

UNBOUND FINISHES

From the earliest part of the period considered, three basic terms were in use to describe water-based paints: *whitening* (and its close relatives, *white, whited,* and *whiting*), together with *whitewash,* and *distemper.*[14] Of these, it seems that as a general rule the first was often used to indicate a finish to which no binder had been added, the two latter apparently being employed to distinguish paints containing size. The evidence for this is not, however, explicit, and emerges only from usage of the terms. Thus, for example,

Emerton referred to 'Size the Plaisterers use in White-washing';[15] Pincot's formula for 'whitewash' given below contained size, while Neve and Salmon listed 'White-washing with Size' and 'White-washing, with Whiting and Size' respectively, both pricing the item at 2*d.* per yard.[16] The French term *détrempe* was used by D'Aviler and Watin for size-bound paints,[17] and its English equivalent 'distemper' by Dossie, Tingry's translator, and Nicholson in connection with formulae in every case containing size.[18] Prices encountered for painting in 'distemper' are, moreover, comparable with those already mentioned for 'whitewash'. For example, at Somerset House in 1780 3*d.* per yard was charged for two coats, and 4½*d.* for three;[19] and 3*d.* again for two coats at Woburn Abbey, Bedfordshire, ten years later.[20]

Against this reasonably firm evidence for the nature of distemper and whitewash, a clear definition of 'whitening' seems lacking. Comparing prices for this against those for distemper and whitewash, however, it is apparent that in many instances it was a much cheaper process; and since almost the only economy possible would have been omission of the binder, it seems likely that the term often implied a finish applied simply in the form of a suspension of pigment in water. A friable coating of this nature would undoubtedly have been adequate on ceilings or on the upper parts of walls where abrasion from traffic would not be expected, and might also have had certain advantages in freedom from the tendency to yellowing that the presence of poorer qualities of size would impart. Hence, although Gerbier gave a rate of 3*d.* per yard for 'White-washing and stopping', 'Whiting and Stopping of fret Seelings' was 2*d.*, 'Whiting and stoping of old plain wall and seelings' was 1*d.*, and 'Whiting of new walles' was a mere 3$\frac{1}{4}$*d.* per square (100 square feet).[21] In 1694 at Dyrham Park, a house having a large number of enriched ceilings, 2*d.* per square yard was charged for 'Whitening';[22] while in an account of 1780 for work on a house associated with the Osterley estate, 'wash Stop and White to new work' was charged at 1*d.* per square yard, and the same 'to Old Work' at 1½*d.* The latter rate is also found in other bills in the same series covering the years 1779 to 1791, including work at Osterley itself, with an additional item in 1785 for 'Wash Stop & White to Ornament Ceiling' at 4*d.*[23] The rate of 1*d.* per yard for whitening new work is the same as that given by Salmon in 1745 for 'Whitening of new Work', and in the *Builders Price-Book* for 'White only to new work'.[24] By the 1810 edition of this book this had risen to 1½*d.*, while 'Washing, scraping, and whitening to old work' was 2½*d.*, but 'Wash stop and white, in distemper' was 4*d.*[25] Laxton too gave a table in which 'Wash, stop, and white to new work' was 1½*d.*, the same 'to old work' was 3½*d.*, but 'distemper' cost 6*d.*;[26] and Skyring noted 'Whitening to new work' at 2*d.*, specifying the addition of 4*d.* if 'in distemper'.[27] These prices all therefore tend to confirm the suggestion that as a general rule *whitewash* and *distemper* contained size, although *whitening* might not.

An example where the term 'whiting' was associated with size is provided, however, by an account for 1623–4 for 'whiting the ceilings and walls of divers rooms' at Eltham Lodge, Kent, 'in size';[28] while in the early nineteenth century Laxton gave a price for 'white in distemper'.[29] Also, nearly five thousand square yards of 'plain whitening' were executed at the Queen's House, Greenwich, in 1662 at a rate of 2*d.* per yard, matching that quoted by Neve and Salmon for 'whitewashing' with size. The same operation on four fret ceilings (probably the new ceilings in the two bridge rooms and bedchambers created in the south-east and south-west rooms adjoining) was priced at 4*d.*[30]

Examples of 'whiting' are found commonly throughout the Exchequer rolls of the period 1614–40;[31] and, in the finishing of ceilings, Sir Roger Pratt indicated that they should be 'first well sized, and afterwards whited with the best Spanish white', also noting: 'After they are done it is best letting them stand one winter without giving them the last finishing, and the next spring to mend their cracks, and then give them their last whiting.' He recorded too that 'Whiting' was employed in the Hall and Little Parlour, the Clockhouse, garretts, and offices at his own house, Ryston Hall, Norfolk;[32] while plasterers' tenders and agreements for the Mansion House, London, show that they were 'to white' their work in the basement and principal floor in 1748–55.[33] In 1781, the walls of the kitchen in the basement of the east wing of the Strand block of Somerset House were described as 'whited';[34] and the ceilings of the Duchess's Bedroom and the Barrack Room at Gordon Castle, Morayshire, were finished with 'Whitening' in 1782.[35]

Besides the chalk mentioned by Pratt, it is clear that lime too was often used for the purpose, and seems to have provided a finish more or less comparable in price with everyday 'whitening', although this could vary. The brickwork of certain inferior rooms in Sir John Moore's School at Appleby, Leicestershire, was finished with 'limewash' in 1696;[36] but the earliest reference to lime noted in a builders' price-book is that by Salmon who, in 1745, indicated that in London 'Lime White, and Whitening of old Work' cost 2½*d.* per yard.[37] An item for 'Lime-White Twice done' at 1½*d.* and another for 'Lime-white – two coats' at 2*d.* appear in the run of plasterers accounts for work at Osterley in 1784 and 1789 respectively, together with other references to lime-whitening at the same rates;[38] and in 1790, 2*d.* per yard was charged at Woburn Abbey, Bedfordshire, for 'Lime whiting to walls'.[39] Late eighteenth-century editions of the *Builders Price-Book* suggest a rate of 1*d.* for 'Lime-whiteing' (perhaps for one coat, the rate matching that for 'White only to new work'), a figure which rose to 1½*d.* between 1810 and 1813.[40] Phillips, however, suggested that this increase had taken place between 1790 and 1803, giving the same figure as the current price in the 1812 and 1821 editions of *Crosby's Builders' New Price Book.* In these 'New work, whiten only' had increased to 2*d.*, making lime the cheaper alternative, while two coats of 'Lime-whiting' cost 2½*d.* and two coats using 'the Vauxhall stone lime' 3½*d.*[41] Laxton gave 2½*d.* for 'Wash, stop, and lime white' in 1818;[42] and in 1831 Skyring priced 'Lime white' at 1½*d.* against 2*d.* for 'Whitening', two coats costing 2½*d.*[43]

In France, satin white also seems to have been used without a binder during the seventeenth century, since although Watin described the use of size in preparing *blanc des Carmes* for interior walls (his formula is discussed below) D'Aviler did not include this ingredient, directing:

> Le Blanc qu'on nomme des Carmes se fait sur des murs bien secs avec de la chaux de Senlis éteinte, où l'en mêle de l'alun: on prend le dessus qui est le plus pur dont on met 5. ou 6. couches, & quand il est sec on y passe la main avec un gant blanc pour le rendre plus luisant.[44]

Félibien too had described the preparation and application of *le Blanc des Carmes*, observing that it was to be strained and used like milk. Five or six coats were employed, each rubbed down with a brush when dry, and the finish had, he remarked, the especial property of not yellowing when used on stone or plaster.[45]

It is probable that on occasion such unbound finishes were tinted in the same way as distemper, although no evidence for this has been located. In 1833, however, J. Bennett gave a method for the preparation of a 'cheap colouring for the walls of rooms in dwelling-houses' which effectively consisted of a mixture of green verditer with orpiment. Two or three coats were to be applied, and no mention of any binder such as size is made.[46]

SIZE-BOUND FORMULAE

Procedures for the preparation of size-bound distemper and whitewash were described by Watin, Tingry, Pincot, and Vanherman. In principle these were all very similar, calling for whiting to be soaked in water for several hours in order to break down the cakes or rolls in which it was supplied, after which hot size was added at roughly the rate of 1 pint of single size to 2 pounds of whiting. The English authors then recommended allowing the distemper to cool to a jelly for use, but the Continental writers specified its application warm, except for the final coat. If colour was to be added it was first ground into water, but although Vanherman recommended it should be added before the size, Pincot reversed this order. Details of the individual formulae are as follows.

Watin noted that in general to make a pound of distemper which would cover a square *toise* (36 square feet) it was necessary to take 3 *quarterons* of pigment ground in water and add to this four or six ounces of size. On the other hand, to make sufficient *grosse détrempe en blanc* to cover the same area, he later suggested taking nearly two pounds of *blanc de Bougival*, which (having been soaked in water for two hours) was to be diluted with nearly a pint of size.[47]

Tingry, in contrast, indicated that common distemper was made from 'Spanish white of Troyes' broken and soaked in water. To this, half a volume of strong glue was to be added hot. The finished distemper should, he noted, run or drop from the brush in a thread when the latter was taken from the pot, since if it did not run in this way it was too thick and would produce a scaly finish when dry.[48] In his additions to the 1788 edition of Bullet's *Architecture pratique*, Charles Seguin too had commented that distemper would flake if too much size was used.[49]

Pincot gave a particularly good description of the preparation of a *whitewash* for ceilings. To make this, he directed, it was necessary to

> dissolve your whiting in as much water as will render it to the consistence of mortar, thin the same in single size to the consistence of Paint . . . and when well mixed up leave it 6 or 8 hours, or a night to cool, in which state it will be like a jelly, and work without splashing.

For thinning his proprietary 'water colours', however, he observed that the proper consistence for their use was one rather thicker than cream, and that in no case should the size be added hot as it would destroy some of the colours.[50]

Vanherman too gave an excellent account of the method to be followed in making a finish which he called *Royal white*; but despite the similarity of name this bore little relation to Watin's *blanc de Roi* (discussed below) and resembled much more closely the formulae so far noted. It was, he said, to be especially recommended for lodging houses, shops, banks, coffee houses, and offices since it was so quick in use that one day would suffice to do an apartment. To prepare this finish, he directed that 12 pounds of the best whiting should be just covered with cold water and soaked for 5 or 6 hours. The mixture was then stirred and 2 quarts of double size added, after which it was allowed to stand overnight to become a jelly in which state it was to be applied. One pound of the recipe would, he indicated, cover six yards of work once.[51]

Although D'Aviler said that *blanc de Rouen* was used to make distemper, he added that to make the finish more beautiful, white lead or ceruse could be substituted in the second coat.[52] It will be noted also that Watin used proportions of ceruse and white lead in the finishing coats for the special and complex *blanc de Roi* and *chipolin* discussed below, while Tingry remarked on the browning of chalk beneath varnish, preferring 'metallic colours' such as white lead.[53] In England, an account for work executed at Osterley in 1788 includes an item for 'Wash stop & white' on 'enrichd Cornices', which was 'done in white lead' at a rate of 2*d.* per foot run, against 1½*d.* for ordinary whiting.[54] A bill of 1779 includes for 'whiteing with white Lead done in distemper' six plaster busts in the Venetian Parlour in the Mansion House, London; and at the same building the following year an item appears for 'whiteing' a bust of Mark Antony 'with white Lead in Distemper'.[55] A decade earlier, a similar finish was clearly envisaged by William Chambers for the decoration of the Saloon at the Casino at Marino, near Dublin, since in 1769 he wrote to his client, the Earl of Charlemont, recommending 'the cove parts of the Ceiling be done with Izing glass & flake-white to be of a more brilliant white than the Entablature &c &c'.[56] In the early nineteenth century the use of ceruse was given as an alternative to 'French white' by Nicholson, this time in a recipe for straw-colour distemper;[57] and an item in *Skyring's Builder's Prices* also concerned the use of white lead in distemper.[58]

Besides chalk and white lead, it seems possible that lime too was used with size as a binder. Tingry's later editor, for example, remarked that lime was excellent for whitewashing ceilings, although, he added, it (by which he seems to have meant stone, as distinct from chalk, lime) was scarce in London, where for that reason whiting was more commonly employed in spite of its rather duller colour.[59] Despite his use of the term *whitewash* it is quite likely, however, that he had ordinary lime-whitening in mind. Watin, on the other hand, gave a formula for *murailles au blanc des Carmes* which differed from those of Félibien and D'Aviler already discussed in that it quite explicitly contained size. He directed that purified slaked lime to which a little turpentine had been added should be diluted with *colle de gants*, a little alum being mixed with this.[60] It was, he noted, a method which could be used for decorating internal walls, but only those of new plaster or in instances where the plaster was in an almost new state. As with the seventeenth-century formulae, five or six coats were to be applied, the last being rubbed down hard with a hog's-hair brush.[61]

In the seventeenth century, distemper seems quite commonly to have been used on wainscoting and other timber elements. In 1625–6, for example, the wainscoting in one of the bedchambers at Dover Castle was painted timber colour in this medium;[62] and in 1674 items appear in accounts for Whitehall Palace 'ffor paynting white in distemper 3 times in a place the playne waynescott Cornish doores & windowes in y[e] Duke of Yorks bedchamber withdr[g] & presence', and 'ffor washing and painting stone colour in distemper twice in a place the wainscott and windowes in the Queenes withdrawing roome', a similar entry occurring for the Queen's Privy Chamber.[63] Before the Civil War, doors too were painted in this medium, including in 1619–20 the insides of four external doors at Theobalds Park distempered a green;[64] divers doors and a chamber in the Lord Steward's Lodging at Whitehall, similarly coloured in 1622–3;[65] twenty-two doors at Eltham Lodge in 1623–4;[66] and a door in Lady Mary's Gallery at Whitehall painted sad colour three times in distemper in 1633–4.[67] Doorcases too are mentioned, such as that giving into the Presence Chamber at Theobalds, which was distempered in 1619–20;[68] and a door and doorcase at Greenwich painted 'timber colour with size' in 1629–30.[69] Lastly may be noted the deal partition and window shutters in a lodging at Whitehall painted wainscot colour in distemper in 1625–6.[70] Examples of varnished distemper, of both seventeenth- and eighteenth-century date, are discussed below.

The range of colours used in the examples cited above is dicussed further in Chapter 21. In the eighteenth century, of course, many others were used, and distemper was commonly employed for the coloured ceiling grounds fashionable from about 1750, a typical instance being the pink and green used in 1765 in the panel grounds of the ceiling and walls of the Great Drawing Room at Bowood, Wiltshire (now at Lloyd's in London).[71] In addition to such use of distemper, Watin suggested the employment of *stil de grain* and certain organic dyes with *colle de Flandre* to stain parquet, and used earth pigments in alternating coats of distemper and oil to stain floor tiles, which were finally polished in wax.[72] These suggestions were repeated by Tingry,[73] and similar methods were probably in use in England. Thus, the accounts for Henry Pelham's house in Arlington Street contain an item for Bremen paving being painted with Indian red,[74] and comparable house-keeping processes are noted in Appendix D.

Before leaving the subject of distemper formulations, it remains to note the use made of the finer qualities of size. It has already been mentioned that Watin employed *colle de gants* in his formula for *murailles au blanc des Carmes*. He used it also in another formula for the decoration of internal walls, but for the finishing coats of his more elaborate systems *blanc de Roi* and *chipolin* he employed *colle de parchemin*.[75] Nicholson too suggested the use of parchment size in distemper, observing that isinglass was too expensive.[76] This latter, the highest quality of size available, however, had been recommended by Dossie for use in the finer parts of distemper work,[77] and as already noted Chambers had suggested its use in the cove of the Saloon of the Casino at Marino near Dublin to produce a particularly brilliant white for a client who seems to have been concerned to obtain the very best. It is quite possible, therefore, that such an expensive grade might have been used in distempers to be applied to limited areas, even if on very rare occasions; although there can be no doubt that in the vast majority of instances ordinary size would have been employed.

PREPARATION OF THE WORK

Turning to the application of water-based finishes, before painting timber with distemper, Watin recommended that any knots should be rubbed with garlic; but how common this procedure would have been is not clear.[78] Undoubtedly, however, some care was necessary to ensure that surfaces were free from grease, a point stressed by Watin and by Tingry who recommended the preliminary application of a coat of cold size.[79] Pratt, too, it will be recalled, had suggested a similar impregnation prior to the whitening of plaster ceilings.[80] Whether this would also have been normal in the case of rooms hung with paper on stretched canvas to be decorated a plain colour is not clear, but although the practice was not suggested in the published transcription of a letter of 1767 from Rowland Belasis to Lord Fauconberg,[81] it was mentioned that three coats of distemper in all were applied to the paper, so that the first may well have sealed its surface. It is possible too that the paper used may have been well sized in manufacture. Nor is it entirely clear whether plastered walls were commonly lined with paper in the modern way, that is directly on the surface of the plaster, in order to achieve a good finish as a matter of course; but attention may be drawn to the wording of a letter in which a York upholsterer expressed himself 'sure it is much for the advantage of the wall to have a paper upon it to do it in oil or size',[82] a recommendation which does perhaps seem to suggest this, but at the same time to contain a hint that the procedure was not regarded as *de rigueur*. Indeed, Pincot remarked that his 'water colours' were preferable to 'paper' as vermin were not harboured in the 'chasims' behind it, as if to suggest that even during the early nineteenth century stretched paper hangings were a direct alternative to applying paint to the surface of plaster;[83] and the aversion to the use of paper or Irish linen as a ground for *chiaroscuro* friezes pasted up after painting which was expressed by Nicholson suggests too that the practice of lining plaster directly with paper was not always viewed with favour.[84] Nevertheless, Pincot added that his water colours could be applied on top of old paper if it was in reasonable condition, and this practice at least may therefore be assumed.[85]

In the case of redecoration (which, presumably on account of the special preparation needed, was, as will be remembered from the discussion of prices above, considerably more expensive than new work) Pincot advised:

A ceiling if not much clogged with old stuff you may make look very well, by first washing it well with clean water and a brush, after which a coat of what is called single size which sticks fast all the dirt left after washing...

...old stained and patched ceilings are difficult to make a good hand of even by the best regular Plasterers; these, if you attempt them, will want scraping, a trowel would be awkward to you, therefore I recommend an old table knife, drove in a piece of wood longways, and that cut in the form of a battledore, this will serve you to scrape, and stop cracks with, and make good decayed places, which should be done with plaister of Paris.[86]

In a similar way, the author of the *Painter's... Pocket Manual* recommended that on smooth walls a coat of warm glue should be applied, but that if the walls were rough it would be necessary to scrape them clean, in this case specifying a preliminary application of glue and Spanish white;[87] while Vanherman washed, scraped, and stopped with plaster of Paris, following this by a coat of double size before redecoration.[88] A further hint was provided by Nicholson, who suggested that, before distempering, old stained plaster could be 'fixed with a coat of white lead ground in oil and used with oil of turpentine'.[89]

In contrast with these early nineteenth-century English suggestions, the late seventeenth-century French writer D'Aviler simply observed that it was necessary to apply a coat of limewater to old walls before distempering them.[90] Watin too applied limewater, this time after scraping, but specified the use of two or three coats followed by rubbing with a ball of horsehair.[91] It is not clear whether this represents a split between English and French practice, or whether this was an earlier technique which had become obsolete by the early nineteenth century.

BRUSHES AND APPLICATION OF THE FINISH

In the *Academy of Armory* published in Chester in 1688, Randle Holme remarked of the Plasterer:

These kind of Artificers have generally two sorts of Brushes, the one set crooked or bending on the end of a Staff, which is put into it, according to that length the Work Man is to reach....

The other is an Hand-Brush, having an Handle about half a yard, or longer (for shorter they are not to use) by which they lay Whiting and Russet within their own compass or reaching.

His illustration of the first apparently shows too an alternative form of head having a larger diameter (fig. 29); while in connection with his depiction of the second (fig. 30) he commented further that the 'Plaisterers Hand-Brush' was made from hogs bristles and stated that 'according to the Statute' its handle was to be one yard long. Although he again indicated that with this brush the plasterers might 'Whitten, Russet, or Black any Posts, or parts of an House within or without, in water Colours only' (adding rather sternly that they were 'not to meddle in Oyl'), he clearly regarded the first type he had described as more typical of the trade. In repeating the illustration of the 'Plasterers whiting Brush, such as he useth with a long staff' (fig. 31), he remarked that he considered this was the variety which should be placed in their coat of Arms, rather than 'that with an handle, it being rather an House Painters Brush'.[92]

The three plasterers' brushes illustrated by Joseph Moxon in the third edition of his *Mechanick Exercises* (1703), which, he remarked, were used by them to 'white and size their Plastering',[93] are very different from those shown by Holme. The 'Round Brish' and the pencil in the centre and on the right of his engraving (fig. 32) seem much closer in form to the brushes used for oil paint which have already been described; while the 'Stock Brish' (a term also used by Vanherman a century and a quarter later)[94] shown on the left appears to be composed of three closely adjacent tufts of hair, each of circular form. This, of course, resembles in many respects the modern pattern and a mid-nineteenth-century depiction of a 'distempering brush' (fig. 33), and suggests, perhaps, that Holme's

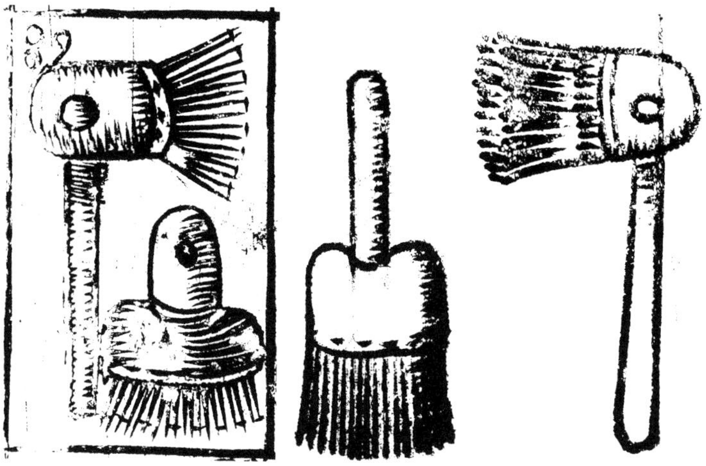

29–31. Seventeenth-century illustrations of plasterers' brushes.

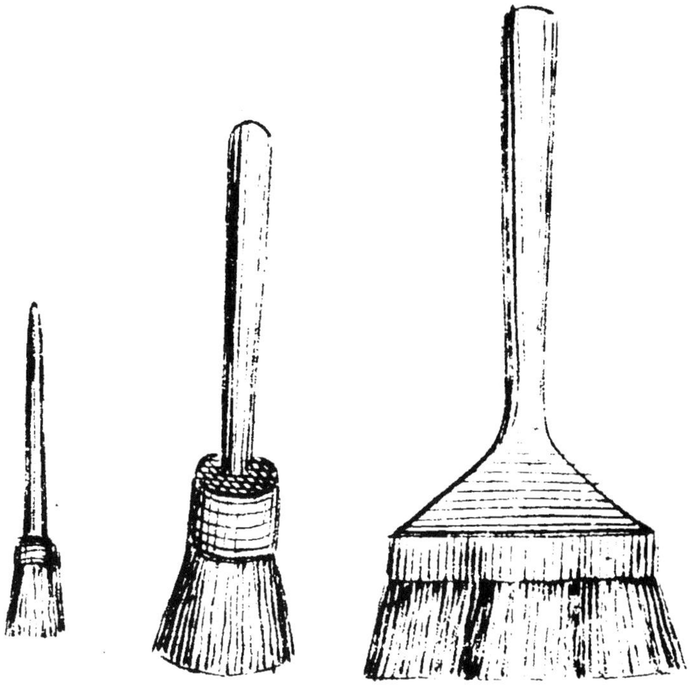

32. Early eighteenth-century illustration of plasterers' brushes.

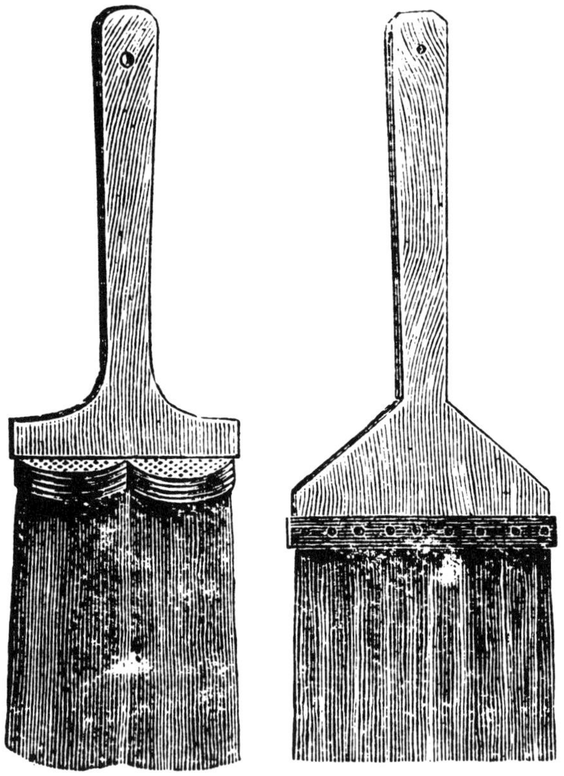

33. Nineteenth-century 'distempering brush'.
34. Nineteenth-century 'white wash brush'.

brushes were archaic. The same mid-nineteenth-century source also illustrated a 'white wash brush' of flat form, which is reproduced here for purposes of comparison (fig. 34).

In applying distemper, Pincot directed: 'do your ceiling over as quick as possible, observing to lay it all one way, and that from the light to the dark part of the room, always beginning on the window side'. His 'water colours' too were to be laid on, 'as quick as you can . . . laying them as even as you possibly can, and observing to leave them lay'd off one way, as the marks of the brush will not then be so much observed'.[95] These instructions are significant and may be compared with those noted in Chapter 16 for the use of oil paints in which other authors stressed the need to provide a solid-looking surface, free from brushmarks.

Two coats of distemper were recommended by D'Aviler, Bullet, and Nicholson;[96] and Pincot recommended the application of his proprietary water colours over a preliminary coat of whitewash.[97] Watin, however, suggested that several coats of common distemper might be applied;[98] and a letter from Rowland Belasis to Lord Fauconberg providing an instance in which three were used has already been noted above.[99] At Bowood, Wiltshire, three coats seems to have been the norm applied by Spinnage in 1765, although two minor rooms received only two.[100] Although the five or six coats recommended for *blanc des Carmes* have already been mentioned (and the much greater number of coats for the other special finishes described by Watin, *blanc de Roi* and *chipolin*, are described below), general practice seems likely to have been restricted to a maximum of three coats only. In preparing successive coats, Tingry drew attention to the care needed to ensure that all were of equal strength in order to avoid trouble from flaking;[101] while the fact that English authors generally recommended application of distemper cold, in contrast to the suggestions of the Continental writers Watin and Tingry, has already been mentioned. Both latter authors, however, directed that the final coat was to be laid on cold; and Tingry seems to have been the source used by the author of the *Painter's . . . Pocket Manual* in making the same recommendation.[102]

MORE COMPLEX FORMULAE AND VARNISHED DISTEMPER

In contrast to the comparatively simple varieties of distemper so far described, Watin included a finish which he called *blanc de Roi*. This was, he indicated, greatly employed in the King's apartments, but was not suitable for rooms used a great deal. It was particularly appropriate in his opinion where gilding was to follow, and indeed the build-up of coats is reminiscent of the gesso ground for water gilding. The operations involved were: (1) *Encoller*, in which a coat of clear size made with the addition of garlic was first applied, followed by a coat of whiting and size; (2) *apprêter de blanc*, in which several more coats of whiting and size were applied; (3) *addoucir et poncer*, or rubbing down; and (4) *reparer*, in which the arrises and angles were sharpened. Two coats consisting of equal parts of ceruse and white lead together with a little indigo in parchment size provided the finish.[103] No other reference to such an elaborate system has been encountered; and it is not, therefore, entirely clear as to whether anything nearly so complicated was ever used in England. Samples taken from the State Bedroom in the Casino at Marino near Dublin, however, suggest that something of the sort may have been carried out about 1770, although it has not been possible to prove this;[104] and at the Mansion House, London, an account referring to work executed in November 1779 included for 'cleaning and whitewashing the mouldings & ornaments of the Cieling and cove' in the Venetian Parlour 'with Kings white'. This is associated with the busts decorated 'with white Lead done in distemper' already mentioned, and the 'Kings white' may accordingly have been similar, especially in view of the rate of 6*d*. per yard at which it was charged.[105] References to the use of 'Kings white' on other ceilings in the building in 1783 also occur in a later bill;[106] but, as already noted, when in 1828 Vanherman gave a formula for 'Royal white', he made it with ordinary whiting.[107]

Another complex formula given by Watin was for a distemper system to be varnished called *le chipolin*. He described it as 'le chef-d'œvre de la peinture d'impression', adding that nothing was so magnificent for a room or apartment than fine timberwork painted in this manner. It would, he said, offer to the ostentatious great richness and the most sumptuous embellishment, while exhibiting the freshness of porcelain, a quality which, he stressed, the finish would keep. The operations were precisely the same as for *blanc de Roi*, up to and including (4) *reparer*, after which three remained: (5) *peindre*, in which two coats of the desired tint were applied in a distemper consisting of equal parts of ceruse and *blanc de Bougival*; (6) *encoller*, using two coats of weak size; and (7) *vernir*, when two coats of spirit varnish were applied.[108]

Although no eighteenth-century British examples have yet been identified, varnished distemper had undoubtedly been employed in England in the seventeenth century. In 1627–8 the linenfold panelling in the tiltyard Gallery at Whitehall was painted lute colour in distemper and varnished;[109] and in 1629–30 the frieze and cornice in the Lord Chamberlain's Cabinet were given several coats of lute colour in distemper finished in the same way.[110] At Oatlands, Surrey, the Queen's Long Gallery was painted green in distemper and varnished in 1636–7, this needing repair for some reason in 1638–9.[111] After the Civil War, Gerbier priced 'Painting of the fairest green, that can be in distemper, and varnisht' at 1*s.* per yard;[112] and it is of interest that in 1828 Vanherman suggested the application of a coat of light carriage varnish above two coats of his 'Royal white' distemper, the varnish being preceded by a coat of size.[113] Tingry, however, indicated that it was preferable to varnish on a coat of white lead in oil of turpentine,[114] and the finishing of oil paint in this way will be discussed further in the next chapter.

CASEIN-BOUND PAINTS

The use of milk or whey as a medium for decorative painting in true fresco (in which the colours are laid on fresh wet lime plaster) was mentioned by Neve,[115] and the properties of casein had undoubtedly been known and exploited in this and similar ways for many years. Watin too described the use of colours *au lait,* but remarked that the method had fallen into disuse on account of the smell.[116] At the end of the eighteenth century, however, an attempt was made by Antoine Cadet-de-Vaux to revive its employment, and an article by him was published in English translation by the Society of Arts in 1801.[117] The influence of this in early nineteenth-century English and American publications has been traced;[118] and it formed the basis of the formulae which appear in Butcher's revised issue of *Smith's Art of House-Painting* and in the *Painter's . . . Pocket Manual.*[119] Such a paint would, Butcher noted, obviate the 'very offensive and injurious smell of common paint to sickly persons' and if made using the quantities given would provide the first coat for 27 yards of work. These were nearly 2 quarts of skimmed milk, about 6½ ounces of freshly slaked lime, 4 ounces of linseed oil, and 3 pounds of whiting. To prepare the paint, the lime was first to be air slaked and sufficient of the milk was to be added to make a mixture resembling thin cream. The linseed oil was then gradually stirred in, followed by the remainder of the milk and whiting, the latter being 'gently crumbled on the surface of the fluid'. For fine whites oil of caraways could be substituted for the linseed oil, and the paint could be coloured by the addition of charcoal or yellow ochre: for exterior work 2 ounces each of linseed oil and white Burgundy pitch were to be incorporated by means of gentle heat and added to the milk and lime mixture, in which an extra 2 ounces of lime were also needed.

In introducing this formula, Butcher presented it as a recipe 'which, we have been assured, will answer for inside work, as paneling, &c. nearly as well as oil-paint'. Despite the attraction of its price, which he estimated at 1½*d.* per yard, compared with those of both oil and distemper, it appears therefore that he had no personal experience of the material in use; and in the absence of any known examples of its employment it is difficult to suggest to what extent milk painting in this way would have been practised.

EMULSIONS AND RELATED DEVELOPMENTS

One feature of Cadet-de-Vaux's milk-painting formula, the combination of oil and water, may, however, have been important, since by the late 1820s it is clear that oil/water emulsions were being developed; and in his book Vanherman described several which he was preparing. The first he called his 'Impenetrable or Anti-corrosive Paint', which seems to have been intended for exterior use. Its manufacture required the preparation of an emulsion or 'Incorporated oil' by churning 3 gallons of freshly prepared wet satin white with 12 gallons of linseed oil and 1 gallon of boiled linseed oil for fifteen minutes. Each gallon of this was used with 7 pounds of a specially formulated combination of pigments in which substantial proportions of his economical invention, crotia (sifted road dust) were included.[120]

The corresponding product for interior use was the 'Aromatic paint', designed, Vanherman indicated, in order to make use of the property possessed by satin white in 'neutrilising' the smell prevalent with ordinary paints. To prepare it, 1 hundredweight of ground white lead was mixed with 1 quart of raw linseed oil and 1 gallon of oil of turpentine to produce a thick cream. To this 10 pounds of the satin white (presumably still wet) were added one quart at a time, and the mixture rubbed through a 60-hole wire sieve. For use, ½ pint of turpentine varnish, made by warming 1 pound of crude Venice turpentine with ½ gallon of oil of turpentine, was to be added. This paint would, Vanherman indicated, dry flat; but for a glossy finish 1 gill of drying oil was added to 'a pot' of colour, and the paint could be thinned with a mixture of 1 gallon of oil of turpentine, ½ pint rectified spirit of wine, and ½ gill oil of caraways which had been shaken together for ten or twelve minutes.[121]

The 'Impenetrable' and 'Aromatic' paints seem to have been the two basic products of Vanherman's maturity, but in addition he described his 'Carniola or Venetian Paint'. It was, he said, his own invention, and, although it seems doubtful that the oil and water would not separate, it could, he suggested, be used either by artists or for house-painting. Its preparation was simple: ½ pint of distilled water was added by degrees to a specially prepared drying linseed oil shaking the mixture until the two were incorporated. The medium was used with pigments which had been ground in turpentine with the addition of a little mastic varnish, and this could also be used to thin the paint when required.[122]

It is of course impossible to say to what extent any of the above emulsions were actually used. Vanherman presented his book as an attempt to reform the paint trade, and implied, as might be expected, satisfaction with his products on the part of his customers. He mentioned, for example, that on account of the disruption caused by the offensive smell of ordinary paint: 'A nobleman, one of my customers, would not suffer a brush of paint in his mansion for five-and-twenty years previous to his having my

Aromatic Paint'; and also that in 1804 the then Duke of Richmond had ordered a new conservatory to receive three coats of 'Impenetrable Paint', but that it should be finished in ordinary white lead and linseed oil. After nine months, he claimed, the latter had disappeared, leaving his own paint 'as hard as stone and as perfect as when first laid on'. He also mentioned the opposition he had experienced from other sections of the trade, and it seems likely that his products were very well known.[123] Altogether, the first decades of the nineteenth century clearly formed an era of continuing experiment, particularly perhaps in the field of external paint; but for interior work it may be doubted whether by the closing years of this study these developments were of importance.

CHAPTER 18

VARNISHES, VARNISH-PAINTS, AND LACQUERS

Varnish was a material having considerable significance for interior decoration during the whole of the period under review. It was used on architectural elements in each of the three distinct ways to which it lent itself: either as a simple transparent glossy finish for timber, oil paint, or distemper; as a medium for opaque paints; or as a coloured transparent lacquer. It was also of importance for japanned or painted furniture, although on fine-cabinet timbers oil or wax were generally used until the popularity of French polish grew in the early nineteenth century. Watin, for example, observed that *bois d'ébénistrie* was generally waxed,[1] and a typical formula for the purpose, calling for 2 ounces of wax to be dissolved in 4 ounces of oil of turpentine, was given by the author of the *Painter's . . . Pocket Manual*.[2]

The practice of varnishing interior architectural joinery of fine colour and quality was mentioned by the French writers D'Aviler and Blondel,[3] and Watin gave a special formula for panelling and oak.[4] Varnish seems to have been used in this way in England before the Civil War, one room at Wimbledon House, the Lord's Closet, being recorded as wainscoted with varnished oak in 1649;[5] while in the mid-eighteenth century the Ripon varnish-maker, Williamson, included 'Pale Wainscot Var[nis]h' in his list.[6] It was also used extensively thoughout the period on imitations, instances including the late seventeenth-century graining and marbling at Kensington Palace,[7] the doors at Somerset House grained in imitation of mahogany in 1780,[8] and on imitative finishes at the Royal Pavilion, Brighton, in the early nineteenth century.[9] References to the varnishing of distemper during the seventeenth and nineteenth centuries have been mentioned in Chapter 17; and it seems too that varnish was also used on occasion on oil paint, since John Smith suggested the renovation of painted joinery and wainscot by washing, and when dry the application of a coat of 'common Varnish' to return the surface to a condition 'as near fresh as when first laid on'.[10] The principal later exponents of varnishing oil paint were, however, the Continental writers Watin and Tingry, the former excepting carved work, which, he noted, was generally stained rather than painted before varnishing in order to preserve the precision of the carving; while both discussed also the use of varnish as a medium for opaque paints in great detail.[11] Although it is not clear that such techniques enjoyed contemporary popularity in England, a century earlier Stalker & Parker had enthusiastically preached the advantages of *japan*, an opaque varnish-paint prepared to imitate that found on Far Eastern furniture, in the decoration of buildings;[12] and, as will be shown, it seems likely that under French influence there was a revival of interest in finishes of this nature during the early nineteenth century. In common with later authors, Stalker & Parker also discussed the addition of alcohol-soluble transparent dyes to spirit varnishes in order to make transparent lacquers of varying colour, generally intended for application to metalwork and gilding.[13]

Compared with oil paint and water-based finishes the subject of varnishes is extremely complex, and a daunting number of formulations arrived at largely by trial and error has been advocated by different writers. In this connection, it has to be borne in mind that house-painting was only one among a number of fields in which varnishes were used; and coach-painting, fine art, and furniture all had considerable importance in the development of techniques. In the present chapter, relevant formulae are first described and the methods by which varnish was applied discussed, taking in the first instance its use as a transparent finish. The use of opaque varnish-paints is next considered, and finally the preparation of transparent coloured lacquers.

In general, three common solvents were in use for varnish-making, and in his authoritative and painstakingly compiled work Watin used these as the basis for varnish classification, linking each to specific resins whose solubilities caused them to be most appropriately employed. In particular he defined first *le vernis clair*, in which alcohol was the solvent and sandarac the principal resin exploited, varnishes of this type, he noted, being used for interior work. His second category, *le vernis gras*, was made using a drying oil as the solvent and either amber or copal; while *le vernis a l'essence de térébenthine* featured mastic as the most widely used resin.[14] Although he described this last variety as an inferior type, it seems to have formed the basis of many recipes for varnish-paint; and, while other resins were used to a considerable extent by other makers, the solvents he listed provide a sound way in which to approach the formulae which they gave.

SPIRIT-VARNISH FORMULAE

The most basic *spirit*, or alcohol-based, varnish is made by dissolving shellac in the solvent, and a simple preparation of this nature was described by Stalker & Parker, who indicated that it was 'commonly used by those that imploy themselves in varnishing ordinary woods, as Olive, Walnut, and the like': 1$\frac{1}{2}$ pounds of 'the best Shell-Lacc' were added to a gallon of 'the best Spirit' and the two allowed to stand for twenty-four hours before being strained. It was, they noted, 'a fit varnish for ordinary work that requires not a polish' and was frequently used by 'common Varnish-dawbers'. It could be improved for use on furniture by the addition of 2 ounces or more of Venice turpentine to each pint, while a further increase in the latter would fit it for use on coaches, signs, or houses when it would 'gloss with very little heat, and, if occasion be, without'.[15] Their formula modified in this way may be compared with Watin's *vernis à l'or* (discussed in more detail below in connection with lacquers) in which stick lac and rosin were combined, and with Vanherman's 'lac varnish' in which 5 parts of lac and 1 part of turpentine were dissolved in 5 times their weight of warm alcohol;[16] while Whittock indicated how a simple spirit varnish could be made by dissolving 5 ounces of shellac in 1 quart of spirit of wine, showing that this most basic form remained in use during the early nineteenth century.[17]

A second type of spirit varnish was proposed by the Continental writers Watin and Tingry, the latter drawing much of his material from Watin's book, but commenting on it and developing the formulae. Their proposals were based on sandarac resin, which had also been used by Stalker & Parker in a varnish they described as 'inferior';[18] but although the latter did not indicate that it could be used in the decoration of rooms, mentioning only its application to prints, Watin and Tingry specifically envisaged its employment for this purpose. Watin's formulae are tabulated for ease of comparison in table VIII. To make the basic white varnish for rooms (A)[19] the sandarac was first dissolved in the spirit of wine, after which the Venice turpentine was added. The only difference between this formula and that designed for application over less clean colours (B)[20] was the use of a poorer quality of turpentine, which had presumably a yellowish cast. Interestingly, on the other hand, he considered Venice turpentine necessary in the varnish for oak panelling and ironwork (C),[21] which represents the basic formula with the addition of shellac and rosin, the former of which would undoubtedly have contributed a darkening of the colour. Tingry reproduced this last formula (his No. 6), but reduced the quantities of sandarac and shellac to 6 and 4 ounces respectively, commenting that he felt Watin's amounts excessive. He also employed 32 ounces of spirit of wine rather than 1 pint, and included 4 ounces of ground white glass, both the latter being features common to other of his formulae. He described this varnish as suitable for wainscoting, balustrades, and rails indoors, and used it as a finish over a darker grey oil paint.[22]

Watin's formula for woodcarvings and the joinery of fanlights (D)[23] was again based on the first white varnish formula, but one-third of the Venice turpentine was replaced by a like quantity of mastic; while that for chimneypieces (E),[24] which could be polished, contained in addition a small proportion of elemi. Tingry reproduced the first of these (his No. 3), but again modified it, using 32 ounces of spirit of wine and adding 4 ounces of ground glass. He described the varnish as used for furniture, chairs, mouldings, and the like, illustrating its use over fine white, light grey, and pearl grey oil paint; but commented also that in his opinion the formula contained too much turpentine and its drying was for that reason delayed.[25] Later Vanherman gave a formula for 'the French polish', dissolving 6 ounces of shellac, 6 ounces of seed lac, 3 ounces of 'juniper' (sandarac), and 2 ounces of mastic in $\frac{1}{2}$ gallon of alcohol;[26] while Whittock combined mastic and shellac alone, specifying the solution of 12 ounces of the former and 1 ounce of the latter in 1 gallon of spirit of wine, and suggesting the use of this varnish as a finish on dark imitations.[27]

A third group of formulae is made up from those containing spirit-soluble copals. Small quantities of 'Gum-Capal' and 'Gum Animae' were used in this way by Stalker & Parker in a formula in which sandarac predominated;[28] and in the early nineteenth century Tingry suggested the combination of 1 ounce of animi (which, it will be remembered from Chapter 13, did not then imply one of the hard copal resins), 6 ounces of sandarac, 4 ounces of elemi, $\frac{1}{2}$ ounce of camphor, 4 ounces of powdered glass, and 32 ounces of spirit of wine (his formula No. 4). The product was intended for use on cut paper, dressing boxes, and the like, but elsewhere he mentioned its use over light grey oil paint.[29] Whittock too combined animi with sandarac in a hard white varnish for furniture made by dissolving 4 pounds of the former and 3 pounds of the latter by standing them in 1 gallon of spirit of wine for two

Table VIII. *Watin's formulae for spirit varnishes*[1]

	Alcohol (pints)	Sandarac (ounces)	Mastic (ounces)	Venice turpentine (ounces)	Elemi (ounces)	Shellac (ounces)	Rosin (ounces)
(A) White varnish for apartments	1	8		6			
(B) Semi-white for less clean colours	1	8		6[2]			
(C) For oak panelling and ironwork	1	8		6		2	4
(D) For carvings, fanlights, and fine work	1	8	2	4			
(E) White for chimneypieces and polishing	1	8	2	4	1		
(F) For use with vermilion	1	6		6[2]		3	4
(G) For dilution of colours	1	2	2	1 quarteron			

Notes and references

1. Watin (1785), pp. 239–42.
2. Pisa or Swiss turpentine (i.e., probably, Venice or Strasbourg turpentine).

days. He also used copal with shellac in another varnish for use on imitations which contained 6 ounces of the former and 2 ounces of the latter in 1 gallon of spirit of wine, a formula close to that which had been suggested by the author of the *Painter's . . . Pocket Manual* in which the proportion of copal was slightly less at the equivalent of 4 ounces for the quantities of shellac and alcohol given by Whittock.[30] No direct evidence for the situations in which any of the above formulae might be preferred for interior use has, however, been encountered.

OIL VARNISHES

Although a form of oil 'varnish' may be prepared by heating linseed oil for a long period to thicken it, and D'Aviler suggested that a varnish for damp situations or for exterior use could be made using a drying oil and litharge,[31] such specially treated oils seem to have been used more generally for varnish-painting or as a gold-size; and for clear varnishes resins such as rosin, copal, amber, and occasionally sandarac were dissolved in the oil. Suggestions made by various authors writing throughout the period under consideration for the addition of crude turpentine or rosin to oil paint in order to increase its lustre have been noted in Chapter 15, and, like John Smith,[32] Whittock recommended use of the latter to make a linseed-oil varnish for exterior application. In this, 1 pound of rosin was added to 4 pounds of linseed oil which had been boiled for one hour, the 'fat' from the surface having been removed with bread; and 4 ounces of oil of turpentine were added for use.[33]

More generally, however, better resins were employed. Watin described copal and amber as the two principal substances used in oil varnishes, observing that they were never used together, amber being reserved for a varnish to be applied over dark colours or gold. Although, he indicated, both could be dissolved directly in hot oil, it was, he believed, better to melt them first as they were then less liable to burn.[34] Varnishes incorporating amber in oil had been in use in fine art since at least the fifteenth century;[35] and in 1672 William Salmon described the preparation of a varnish by dissolving melted amber in hot linseed oil.[36] The date at which the hard copal resins were first introduced for house-painting is obscure, but Watin included melted copal in one of three formulae. *Vernis blanc au copal* was made by adding 4, 6, or 8 ounces of hot linseed oil to each pound of melted copal resin, and 1 pound of oil of turpentine was later added. *Vernis au karabé ou à l'ambre* was the same, the copal being replaced by amber. *Vernis gras à l'or* on the other hand contained lac in addition, 2 ounces being melted separately from 8 ounces of amber before being mixed. About 1 pound of oil of turpentine and $\frac{1}{2}$ pound of linseed oil were then added.[37] Vanherman too gave formulae for copal and amber varnishes, warning that:

> Varnish makers in general discolour their copal and amber varnishes by dissolving these resins in the oil, with a heat little short of boiling; whereas, if they were first melted in essential oil . . . a tepid heat would be sufficient to unite and perfect a colourless copal varnish.

For *white copal varnish* he recommended that 4 ounces of copal resin should be bruised and melted for twelve hours in a moderate oven. It was then to be powdered and $\frac{1}{2}$ ounce of camphor gradually added, after which 3 ounces of white drying oil was to be mixed in by degrees. *Amber varnish* was made in the same way, but was, he noted, 'high coloured'.[38]

Uniquely among the authors noted, Whittock suggested the use of sandarac resin in an oil varnish: 2 pounds of sandarac, 4 pounds of drying linseed oil, and $\frac{1}{4}$ pound oil of turpentine were simply boiled together,[39] although sandarac is generally regarded as easily soluble in oil only after running.[40] Oil varnishes were, Watin indicated, used for external purposes, spirit varnishes being used for interior work; although he added that for public buildings or in the choir of a cathedral *vernis blanc au copal* was to be preferred.[41]

TURPENTINE VARNISHES

Turpentine varnishes using mastic as the resin were in established use for the protection of oil paintings by at least the mid-seventeenth century; and in 1672 Salmon, for example, published a formula for the purpose.[42] Their primary use in house-painting, however, seems to have been as a medium for opaque varnish-paint rather than as a transparent finish, probably because, as Watin pointed out, they were lacking in lustre and could not be polished.[43] He regarded them as inferior to spirit and oil varnishes, but both he and Tingry made extensive use of them with opaque pigments, their formulae accordingly being discussed below. One of those used in this way by Tingry was primarily a picture varnish, and the mastic varnish formula given by the author of the *Painter's . . . Pocket Manual* was specifically for this purpose, so that it seems unlikely that such preparations enjoyed extensive use for ordinary house-painting.[44]

It is possible, however, that cruder turpentine varnishes using rosin in solution were used to some extent in this way, since the same author gave a formula in which 5 pounds of clear rosin were to be dissolved in 1 gallon of oil of turpentine,[45] and Whittock directed that 4 pounds of rosin should be dissolved in 1 gallon of oil of turpentine to make a varnish suitable for outdoor use and for varnishing common work in distemper.[46] These may be compared with Watin's *vernis d'Hollande* discussed below, which he used to make a green paint for coaches.[47] In addition, Whittock observed that oil of turpentine could be substituted for the spirit of wine used as the solvent in his general-purpose spirit varnish based on copal resin in order to make a varnish suitable for exterior work, but how sound this suggestion was is not clear.[48] In general, therefore, it seems unlikely that turpentine varnishes were of much importance for the straightforward finishing of interior work.

VARNISH AS A TRANSPARENT FINISH

Little special preparation seems to have been considered necessary prior to the application of varnish on the surface of new joinery or oil paint, but in re-varnishing coachwork Pincot rubbed down the old surface with powdered pumice in water, and Vanherman stressed the need for work receiving French polish to be free from oil or grease.[49] On distemper, Watin stipulated a preliminary coat of parchment size; and for the special distemper system finished with spirit varnish, *le chipolin*, which was described in Chapter 17, it will be remembered that varnishing was preceded by two coats of weak size. On oil paint, on the other hand, he specifically mentioned that no special preparation was needed; but both he and Tingry emphasised that when it was intended that oil paint should be varnished, the last coat should have been diluted in oil of turpentine. Watin himself used pure oil of turpentine, but Tingry seems to have favoured the inclusion of a small proportion of oil, advising in connection with darker tints that where it was intended to cover them with varnish (as, he observed, was general practice on wainscoting), they must be mixed up with oil of turpentine to which a little oil had been added. This, he indicated, would make them better disposed to receive the varnish.[50]

An exceptionally complex oil-paint system designed to receive varnish was described by Watin. He called it *la peinture à l'huile vernie-polie* and, being 'la chef d' œuvre de la Peinture à l'Huile', it was reserved for choice works such as a superb *salon* or an elegant carriage. After a preliminary coat of ceruse and a little litharge finely ground in linseed oil and diluted with a mixture of the same oil with oil of turpentine, 8 coats of *la teinte-dure* were applied. These consisted of ceruse finely ground in drying oil and diluted with pure oil of turpentine. After rubbing down and polishing, 3 or 4 coats of the desired colour similarly prepared were superimposed; and the whole was finished with 2 or 3 coats of spirit varnish, finally re-polished.[51]

In applying varnish, Tingry observed, the brush should be drawn rapidly over the surface, forwards and backwards, in large strokes; but, he warned, if drawn several times over the same place, the varnish would roll under it, and for that reason the strokes should not be allowed to cross one another. For the application of glossy varnish in this way, large flat brushes were, he indicated, employed; and he later observed that brushes of this form were known as *varnishing brushes*.[52] Watin too described the brushes used, noting that they were made from badger's hair, and that those in the form of a crow's foot were known as *blaireaux à vernir*.[53] The only writer noted to mention the use of a 'rubber' made by wrapping an absorbent material in a piece of cloth was Vanherman, who did so in connection with the application of French polish to furniture.[54] It is quite possible, however, that the method could also have been used in polishing hardwood doors.

Although Vanherman remarked that all spirit varnishes were to be laid on warm,[55] Watin, perhaps reflecting the difference in latitude between France and England, specified their application cold. Nevertheless, he indicated, for the varnish to dry it was necessary for the room to be warm, oil varnishes requiring a slightly higher temperature.[56] Laxton too remarked that varnished works required a fire 'to set the varnish, and prevent it from curdling'.[57] For interior work, Watin, as will be clear from the references above, generally stipulated two or three coats of spirit varnish on both oil and distemper; while in connection with graining and marbling Bartholomew provided the following model specification:

> To varnish with the very best copal the whole of the imitations of wood & marble, the columns . . . having eight (or less as the case may be according to the goodness of the work) coats . . . each . . . polished thoroughly to a perfect gloss, and the other imitations having two coats of varnish.[58]

Rubbing down between coats in this way, using pumice powder, was recommended by Pincot in connection with coach-work, allowing two days for the varnish to dry between each;[59] and the operation of polishing was described in some detail by Watin. For this, three substances were required, powdered pumice, tripoli, and starch. The second of these was described by Heaton as 'originally a variety of diatomaceous earth obtained from North Africa, but the name has been very loosely applied to materials ranging from an impure crystalline quartz to a pure white amorphous silica.'[60] Watin noted that the material was obtained from Brittany, the Auvergne, and Italy, the first being the best, and that from the Auvergne second in quality. It was, Ure remarked, often confused with the English *rotten stone* found in Derbyshire and South Wales which was also used for polishing;[61] and during the early years of the nineteenth century Lewis Berger had small stocks of both, amounting in 1810 to $1\frac{1}{2}$cwt. 'Lump Rotten Stone' valued at 14*s*. per cwt. and 14 lb. 'Tripple' valued at 24*s*. per cwt.[62] Stalker & Parker recorded that 'Tripoly' could be obtained from the ironmongers, and described how to reduce it to powder by scraping the lump with glass or a knife, warning: 'Circumspectly examin your Tripolee and clout, least some mischievous, unwelcom gravel, grittiness, or grating part, unawares steal in, and rase or scratch your work; it will prove no easie matter to hide the flaw and damage.'[63]

The polishing operation for oil varnish as described by Watin consisted of four stages: (1) rubbing with powdered pumice in water; (2) rubbing with powdered tripoli and olive oil; (3) polishing with a soft linen cloth; and (4) finishing off with starch or *blanc de Bougival* and the palm of the hand. For spirit varnish the operations were the same, except that tripoli was used in place of powdered pumice in the first stage.[64]

In 1803 Soane was charged 12*s*. for a quart of 'fine Copall Varnish' and a few years later Pincot recorded that a pint of varnish for coach-painting would cost 4*s*. 6*d*.;[65] while Laxton and Skyring gave the following lists of prices for varnish work:[66]

	Laxton (1818)	Skyring (1831)
Once in best copal	1*s*. per yard	9*d*. per yard
Twice	1*s*. 9*d*.	1*s*. 3*d*.
Three times	2*s*. 6*d*.	1*s*. 9*d*.
Spirit varnish per coat	6*d*.	6*d*.
Hand polishing to either	6*d*.	4*d*.

Earlier, in 1787, 6*d*. per yard was charged at Somerset House for cleaning and varnishing doors;[67] and at Boughton House in 1706 varnishing was charged at 9*d*. per yard.[68] In neither case is the type of varnish or number of coats mentioned, the same being true of late seventeenth-century items in the accounts for Whitehall, Kensington, and Hampton Court Palaces, in each of which varnishing was listed at rates equivalent to 1*s.* 2*d.* per yard,[69] so that the true position over seventeenth- and eighteenth-century prices is unclear.

VARNISH-PAINTING AND JAPAN

So far, varnish has been considered as a transparent finish applied to the surface of timber or paint. It could, however, be pigmented; and, having mentioned the practice of varnishing distemper, Tingry described the use of pigment in a varnish medium, indicating that this method of applying the colour possessed considerable advantages over the first, which, although cheaper, was liable to flake should the timber be damp.[70] Also, as noted in Part I, certain pigments such as verdigris and the lakes are much more stable when used in this way, and Watin remarked that the only way orpiment could be used without inconvenience was in a varnish medium.[71] Quite apart from the enhanced gloss which could also be obtained, it was clearly recognised, therefore, that the method presented certain technical advantages, and from an early date was applied to the decoration of buildings. During the seventeenth century, Stalker & Parker eulogised the use of japan, a varnish-paint, in the following terms:

> Japanning has taught us a method . . . for the splendor and preservation of our Furniture and Houses. These Buildings, like our Bodies, continually tending to ruin and dissolution, are still in want of fresh supplies and reparations: On the one hand they are assaulted with unexpected mischances, on the other with the injuries of time and weather; but the Art of Japanning has made them almost impregnable against both: no damp air, no mouldring worm, or corroding time, can possibly deface it.[72]

All three common varnish mediums were in use at different times, and formulae based on each are first discussed in turn, after which the build-up of coats will be described; and finally a brief assessment made of the importance of varnish-paint at various dates.

Looking first at spirit-varnish based formulae, of the five colours of japan for which Stalker & Parker gave directions for application to furniture or coach bodies, two only, black and red, made use of pigment in the varnish medium, which was made from 1½ pounds of seed lac dissolved in 1 gallon of alcohol. The pigments used were lamp black or vermilion according to the colour desired, white lead being added to the latter to lighten the colour if necessary.[73] Watin too used these two staining pigments in a spirit varnish ((F) in the formulae given above – table VIII, p. 120), illustrating employment of the black on ironwork and finishing it with two coats of clear spirit varnish.[74] This formula was similar to that of his basic white spirit varnish (A) already described, although the amount of sandarac was slightly reduced, and a poorer quality of turpentine was used together with shellac and rosin, presumably in order to lend depth to the colour. For the dilution of colours in general, however, his formula (G)[75] employed the more expensive resin mastic, in this case with a considerably reduced amount of sandarac and with a *quarteron* of Venice turpentine, probably to provide greater workability in the presence of pigment.

Turning to oil-varnish based formulations, in contrast with Tingry, who used turpentine varnishes exclusively with pigment, Watin also used oil-varnish based formulae in three particular instances. The first was for the undercoats in his elaborate system *blanc verni-poli à l'huile* to be discussed below, and the second for his *couleurs d'acier pour les ferrures.* In both, the white copal oil varnish described above was used, the pigments (ceruse, Prussian blue, lake, or distilled verdigris) being ground in oil of turpentine and added to the varnish (with which, in the case of the latter formulation, one-third part of oil of turpentine had already been mixed).[76] He also described the preparation of a black varnish containing Jew's pitch by melting rosin and amber separately, and dissolving the constituents in a drying oil. This was used with the addition of lamp black on a prepared black ground.[77] Vanherman gave a comparable formula, combining asphaltum, oil of turpentine, and a preparation of his 'baked oil'; and suggested also the use of Frankfurt black or vermilion with the same medium, which was prepared by simmering ½ gallon of linseed oil with ½ pound of litharge for fourteen or fifteen hours until a cooled sample could be pulled out into a thread a yard long.[78]

The third and final group is of turpentine-based varnishes for use with pigments, and here Watin provided two formulae. The first of these, used for the dilution of pigments ground in oil, was based on mastic; while *le vernis d'Hollande*, intended for coach-painting using a verdigris and white lead mixture, made use of rosin instead. For the former, 4 ounces of mastic were dissolved in 1 pint oil of turpentine, ½ pound of crude turpentine being added;[79] and Tingry gave a similar formula (his No. 12), the constituents of which were:

12	ounces mastic
1½	ounces turpentine
½	ounce camphor
5	ounces powdered white glass
32	ounces oil of turpentine.[80]

However, although Tingry illustrated its uses for dilution of pearl grey and (for fine work) yellow varnish-paint,[81] he had presented it primarily as a varnish for valuable paintings; and he generally used a varnish of Watin's second type based on rosin for the dilution of pigments ground in oil or in one of a number of varnishes. Watin's formula for *le vernis d'Hollande* contained ½ pound Pisan turpentime (probably Venice turpentine, see Chapter 11) and a quantity of *galipot* in 1 pint oil of turpentine;[82] while the constituents of Tingry's varnish for the dilution of colours (his No. 14) were:

12	ounces *galipot* or white incense (in 1816 edition 'frankincense')
5	ounces powdered white glass
2	ounces Venice turpentine
32	ounces oil of turpentine.[83]

For grinding the pigments prior to dilution, however, he proposed another formula (his No. 13) in which rosin and mastic were combined, indicating that it was similar to the varnish 'of Holland'. The ingredients were:

4 ounces new *galipot* or white incense ('frankincense')
2 ounces mastic
6 ounces Venice turpentine
4 ounces powdered glass
32 ounces oil of turpentine.

The solids were powdered and warmed together in the oil of turpentine for three hours, after which 2 ounces of prepared nut or linseed oil were added for use.[84] However, although in giving this formula he indicated that pigments should be ground with it prior to dilution with his No. 14, in practice he recommended a much greater variety of combinations (table IX).

Having reviewed the formulation of varnish-paints, attention may be turned to the method of their application. *La peinture à l'huile vernie-polie* in which oil paint was finished with a spirit varnish, and the second paint system *blanc verni-poli à l'huile* with which Watin followed this in his section on oil painting, have already been mentioned. The latter, he intimated, imitated and possessed the freshness of marble, a copal-oil varnish being used as the medium. After a preliminary coat of ceruse (with a little copperas as drier) ground in nut oil and thinned with oil of turpentine (unless on stone, when nut oil was used for dilution), seven or eight coats of ceruse finely ground in oil of turpentine and diluted with the white copal oil varnish described above were applied. Each was rubbed down and polished in turn, and he noted that they would dry sufficiently quickly to allow the completion of three coats a day. Over these, two or three coats of white lead ground in nut oil and thinned with pure oil of turpentine were superimposed, followed by seven or eight coats of his white spirit varnish, which were finally polished.[85]

Later in his book, Watin turned to the use of varnish-paint on the panelling of apartments, observing that several houses in Paris had been decorated by this means, and also that all colours could be used in this way. The system was complex, the following operations being required:

(1) 1 or 2 coats of *blanc de Bougival*, as for operation (5) in the special distemper finish *le chipolin* described in Chapter 17 above;
(2) a coat of *blanc d'apprêt* consisting of ceruse and white lead in parchment size;
(3) stopping;
(4) mixing of the colour required;
(5) a coat containing 2 ounces of colour in each *poisson* of varnish;
(6) a coat containing 1 ounce of colour in the same;
(7) a coat containing ½ ounce of colour in the same;
(8) a further coat as (7) to ensure perfection.

Each coat was rubbed down prior to application of the next.[86]

In this complex system, the gradual reduction in the amount of pigment in succeeding coats will be noted. This practice was also followed by Tingry in his directions for painting *buffets* red, stipulating particularly that in general the final coat in varnish-painting should be almost colourless.[87] The extent to which such complicated finishes would have been used on architectural elements seems unclear, however; and it is possible that both these and the seventeenth-century methods of japanning described by Stalker & Parker would have been considerably simplified when applied over large areas of wainscot, even in the most intimate 'japan closets' of the affluent, such as that provided at Dyrham Park in 1694. Nevertheless, Tingry seems to have envisaged the use of varnish-painting even on plaster, since he indicated that for this a preliminary coat of warm size was essential. On wainscot, on the other hand, he proscribed the latter practice, although he said it was the usual custom, recommending instead use of a primer of white lead and one-sixteenth part of litharge which would, he observed, add a splendour and mellow tone to the varnish.[88] This is, of course, consistent with his general aversion to the use of varnish on a distemper ground. Information on the colouring of undercoats is scant; but practice may have been similar to that prevailing with oil paint, and it will be noted that Watin laid his three coats of tinted varnish-paint on a prepared white ground. For his black oil-varnish, on the other hand, he used an undercoat of lamp black with a little umber ground in drying oil and diluted in pure oil of turpentine.[89] Finally, Tingry observed that the odour of turpentine varnishes could be killed by the use of an additional coat of spirit varnish on top;[90] and, as implied by the consistent use of such varnishes in the examples from Watin's book mentioned above, this seems to have been standard recommended practice in interiors.

In assessing the overall importance of pigmented varnish-painting during the period being considered, contemporary technical literature provides few pointers giving an insight into the architectural situations in which it was actually used. It is unclear, too, whether the references to 'painting in lute colour with varnish' wainscoting in two long galleries at Whitehall Palace in 1631–2 imply the employment of varnish-paint, or the overpainting of paintwork with varnish.[91] It is of note, however, that the Japan Closet at Dyrham, now destroyed, was executed at a cost of 5*s.* per square yard;[92] but although in this case it cannot be known whether the room was finished in a plain

Table IX. *Varnish mediums recommended by Tingry for different colours*[1]

Colour name	Ground with	Mixed with
Pearl grey	No. 12 with a little poppy oil	No. 12
Flaxen grey	No. 13 with a little poppy oil	No. 14
Walnut tree wood	drying nut oil	No. 14
Naples yellow, patent yellow, and yellow ochre	½ part drying nut oil and ½ part oil of turpentine	No. 12 or No. 14
Jonquil	No. 13	No. 14
Buff	½ part common poppy oil and ½ part No. 13	No. 14
Blue verditer	No. 13 and a little drying oil	No. 14
Compound green	¾ part oil and ¼ part oil of turpentine	No. 14
Red for buffets	boiled oil and oil of turpentine	No. 14

[1] Tingry (1804), pp. 392–408; (1816), pp. 273–89.

colour of japan or whether it received its name from being embellished with oriental motifs, a few years later Neve indicated that 'plain Japan, either black or white' would cost 3*s.* 6*d.* or 4*s.* per yard.[93] In this connection, however, it is of note that in 1708 only 1*s.* per yard was paid for japanning a mirror-frame black at the Queen's House, Greenwich.[94]

By the mid-eighteenth century, at a date when, as already seen, a fashion for completely matt architectural paintwork prevailed in England, Dossie mentioned the application of japan principally to grounds of copper, iron, or wood.[95] He noted, however, a decline in its use on furniture, observing that it was not 'practised so frequently on chairs, tables, and other furniture of houses, except tea waiters, as formerly', but added that it had been introduced 'for ornamenting coaches, snuff-boxes, and skreens, in which there is a rivalship betwixt ourselves and the French'.[96] Significantly, he had earlier remarked that the art of painting in varnish had been greatly improved by the manufacturers at Birmingham,[97] and it is of note that use of a varnish medium by Chippendale on furniture seems implied in references to chairs 'Japan'd Green & white' supplied by him in 1772 to David Garrick for his house in the Adelphi, London.[98] Nevertheless, although it is clear that several of Watin's formulae were designed specifically for painting the ironwork of balustrades and other small iron elements (while the American author, Reynolds, suggested a modest gill of copal varnish could be added to each gallon of oil for interior work),[99] at the time of writing, nothing has been encountered in any eighteenth-century building account to confirm employment of a varnish medium in England in this way. It may be, therefore, that during the eighteenth century in this country the use of varnish paint became virtually confined to moveable objects including furniture and coachwork.[100]

During the early nineteenth century, however, under the influence of Watin and, perhaps to a greater extent, Tingry (whose book, it will be recalled, was published in English in 1804), it seems possible that such techniques may once again have been applied to interior architectural elements. Evidence for this is provided by the range of 'Antique Ornamental Paints' being produced in 1816 by the London Patent Colour-Works, which may well have been related to a range of 'Couleurs Lucidoniques' made in France about 1800. The latter were described by Rondelet as a new method of painting introduced by Madame Cosseron of the rue Dauphine using colours prepared in spirit of wine. Rondelet listed an impressive range of over forty tints, adding that the paint was ready prepared in liquid form to be thinned with the same solvent if necessary. It was, he stated, odourless and dried with a good gloss, obviating the need for a subsequent coat of varnish, and, having been tried and tested since 1803, was claimed to be suitable for both interior and exterior use.[101]

In Britain, the proprietors of the London Patent Colour-Works advertised the 'Antique Ornamental Paints' as being manufactured without either linseed oil or oil of turpentine, claiming that the vehicle was intended as an imitation of the 'celebrated *Encaustum* of the Ancients',[102] which had been described by the Roman authors Pliny and Vitruvius and involved the use of molten wax. Although a great deal of energy had been expended during the latter half of the eighteenth century in both France and England in attempting to ascertain the medium used for painting during classical times (fig. 35),[103] it seems doubtful that the 'Antique Ornamental Paints' in their final form would have represented great authenticity, and they seem rather to have been a variety of varnish-paint, being claimed to dry within one hour and being 'partly composed of materials possessing a strongly evaporative principle'. The *Memoir on the Antique Paints* published by the same company seems to confirm this:

> Impelled by these considerations, the Inventor of the Paints now offered to the Public, after a series of experiments infinitely laborious and expensive, and pursued with the most unremitting industry, has at length succeeded in producing a combination which he considers to bear an affinity to, and answer the *general* purposes of, the celebrated *Encaustum* of the Ancients. This discovery is likely to be productive of material advantage to the Public, by enabling them to obtain at a comparatively trivial expense, Green and other Fine Colours, appli-

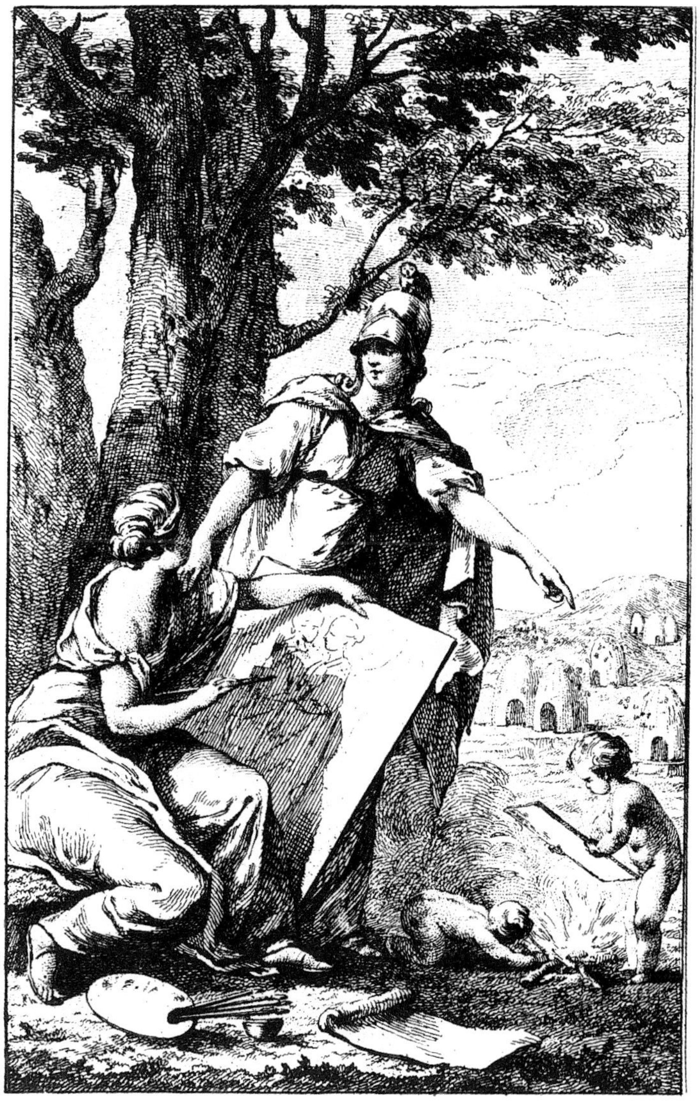

35. Frontispiece from the *Mémoire sur la peinture a l'encaustique* by the Comte de Caylus (1755) depicting the ancient method of painting pictures in wax.

cable to every useful and ornamental purpose, whether interior or exterior, infinitely surpassing in richness and brilliancy of appearance, and fully equalling in durability *any* that can possibly be prepared in the usual method with Linseed-oil, although such of equal quality cannot be manufactured at less than double the expense.

These colours were originally intended to be used with the application of heat; the novelty however of the process of ignition, so materially deviating from the accustomed mode of applying paints, was found to be decidedly incompatible with the long-established prejudices, and occasioned such an infinity of objections, that the Patentee was constrained to entirely relinquish the idea, and, by a variation in the process, afford to the respective Colours a sufficiently increased degree of fluidity to enable purchasers to apply them in the usual method. They consequently will now require no particular management further than that usually adopted with every species of Varnish-Paint.[104]

It thus seems clear that during the early nineteenth century attempts were being made to re-introduce varnish-paints for architectural work in England; but again, the actual extent to which these were successful remains to be seen.

COLOURED TRANSPARENT LACQUERS, OR 'CHANGING VARNISHES'

To complete this summary of the way in which varnishes were prepared and applied, attention must finally be turned to lacquers. Those for interior use seem almost invariably to have been based on spirit varnishes made using lac, a resin which in its unrefined form would confer an orange-red tone, and which for this reason was undoubtedly felt appropriate in adding depth to the colour of fine cabinet timbers.[105] The colour could be further deepened, however, by the addition of certain spirit-soluble dyes and resins; and D'Aviler, for example, seems to have recommended the use of such a lacquer on wainscot, observing that when it was of good quality one merely gave it several coats of varnish made using 'gomme adraganthe' (by which he presumably meant dragons blood rather than gum tragacanth) and spirit of wine.[106] To most other writers, however, the main application of lacquer was on metal, and Dossie in particular defined 'laquering' as 'the laying either coloured or transparent varnishes on metals, in order to produce the appearance of a different colour on the metal, or to preserve it from rust and the injuries of the weather', mentioning its use on brass or copper locks and on nail heads.[107]

Formulae given by different authors are, naturally enough, concerned with coloured lacquers. Stalker & Parker, for example, gave the following directions for making 'common Lacker':

Take one quart of Spirit, put it into a Pottle-bottle [2 quarts],[108] of Shell-Lacc eight ounces, beaten small enough to enter the bottle; shake 'em well together; having stood till quite dissolved, strain it, and reduce to powder a small quantity of Sanguis Draconis, which with a little Turmerick tied up in a rag put into it, grant it a days continuance in that posture, at your leisure hours shaking it. You may alter the colour, heighten or abate it, by adding or diminishing the quantity of the two latter ingredients.

Alternatively, they indicated, dragons blood and saffron could be used for colouring, or annatto and gamboge, adjusting the proportions of each to achieve a redder or more yellow colour as desired. For use in the open air, two pennyworth of Venice turpentine could be added to each quart of liquor; and although in this case, they warned, 'it may look dull and misty immediately after every lackering, that fright, that seeming discouragement, will quickly vanish; that thin cloudy vapour, will be dissipated by its sudden, and piercing lustre'.[109]

In general, Stalker & Parker advocated the use of lacquer in order to make silver leaf look like gold (a practice to which Félibien, John Smith, and Dossie also referred). They were writing with furniture uppermost in their minds, and were thus able to recommend warming the piece to be lacquered, in which case, they noted, a second coat could be applied after fifteen minutes, adding:

If two or three varnishings will not produce a colour deep enough, oblige it with a fourth; but remember, if you should carelessly do it too deep, all assistance will be insignificant, and no remedy whatsoever will avail you.

They concluded by describing how the effect of the lacquer could be heightened by darkening the hollows and the ground of any carving.[110]

Besides Stalker & Parker, a few years earlier Félibien too had noted the use of dragons blood and gamboge in lacquers for silver leaf, and John Smith recommended the use of 'Gum-Lake' (presumably unrefined seed lac) in spirit of wine for the same purpose.[111] Similarly, Watin provided a formula for *vernis à l'or* which contained 4 ounces each of stick lac, gamboge, dragons blood, and rosin, plus 1 ounce of saffron, each of which had been dissolved in 1 pint of spirit of wine and allowed to stand in the sun for fifteen days.[112] Vanherman too described how a lacquer might be made from any spirit varnish by the addition of dragons blood, turmeric, gamboge, or annatto, although he felt that the colour imparted by shellac was 'the most proper';[113] and Tingry's later editor mentioned in addition red sandalwood (which he identified as that from *Pterocarpus santalinus*) and alkanet root to colour lacquers which he referred to as 'changing varnishes'.[114]

The application of lacquers to gilding and silver leaf is discussed in the next chapter.

CHAPTER 19

GILDING AND SILVERING

Gilding has found an important place in the decorative repertoire of many cultures, and its capacity to lend grandeur and sparkle to architecture was naturally exploited during the period being considered. Two main methods were used in interior work, oil-gilding and water-gilding. The latter was the more expensive of the two, and was generally reserved for furniture and other moveable objects where its ability to take a fine burnish could be appreciated to the full; while architectural ornament was generally oil-gilt. Here too, however, a certain amount of finesse was possible and (quite apart from the matter of gilding style which is dealt with in the companion volume to this study) variations could be introduced by such devices as modifying the colour of the leaf. Besides gold and silver, a number of alloys could be used, and it was also possible when occasion demanded to embellish the work further by means of transparent glazes.

MATERIALS AND TOOLS

During the seventeenth century, gold leaf was sold in much the same form as that in which it is available today. Sir Roger Pratt noted that it was obtainable from a gold-beater in Black-horse Alley near Fleet Bridge by the name of Hilliard in books of 25 leaves at a cost of 2*s*. per book (fig. 36). Each leaf was, he said, about 3 inches square, and four books were called a *hundred*. Elsewhere, on the other hand, he noted that the books contained 24 leaves; and John Smith, who gave precisely the same figures for the size of leaf and price of the book, also suggested the contents as only 24 leaves.[1] With regard to eighteenth-century leaf, in 1750 the gold-beater Thomas Evans was paid £115 10*s*. for '38,500 of leaf gold at £3 per mille', a figure which works out on the above basis at roughly 1*s*. 6*d*. per book;[2] although whether this reflected a reduc-

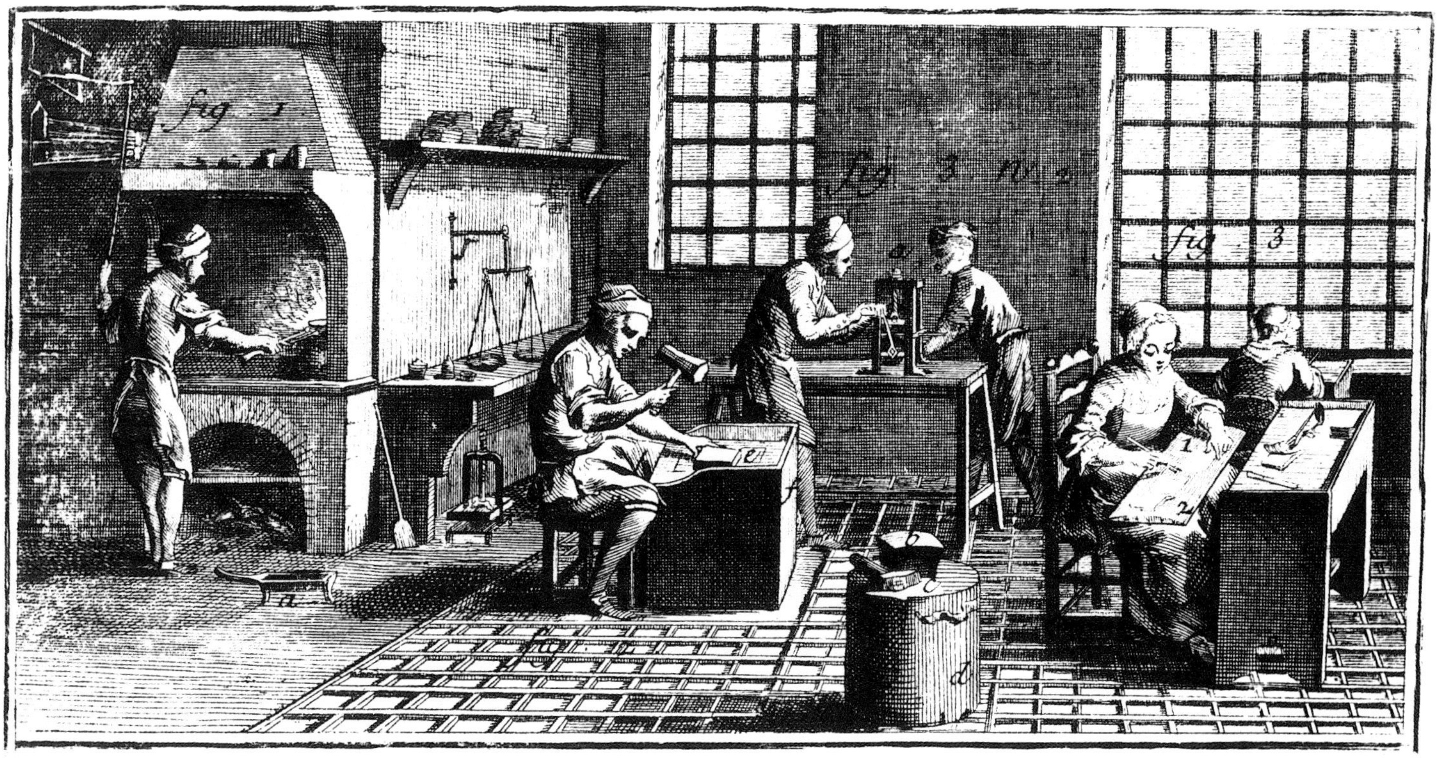

36. Eighteenth-century gold-beater's workshop: (1) furnace for melting the gold; (2) gold being beaten into leaf; (3) leaf being cut to size and put into books; (3.2) gold ingot being milled into sheet.

tion in the price of leaf by that date, or a lower rate charged for a large quantity, is not clear. It seems too that different sizes of leaf were sometimes available, since during the early nineteenth century Lewis Berger had stocks of 'Small Gold Leaf' valued at 6*s.* per hundred, and the French writer Félibien had commented to this effect, observing also that a thicker grade was used on metals than on timber.[3] The latter material, known today as *double gold*, seems to have been used in exterior work during the eighteenth century, since references to 'Double Leaf Gold' in this context appear in the early eighteenth-century accounts for St Paul's Cathedral, London, and 'double Gold' in those of 1772–4 for work at Osterley.[4] It may also have been used on furniture, however, since the pier mirror from the Tapestry Room at Croome Court, Worcestershire, was 'Gilt in the very best Double Burnish'd Gold',[5] although it may be that this implied rather the application of two layers of leaf.

Silver leaf was also manufactured, Berger again having stocks of a 'Small' variety at the equivalent of roughly 1*s.* 8½*d.* per hundred;[6] while Pratt had given its cost as 3*d.* per book, and mentioned also 'party gold' which had one side gold and the other silver. This two-ply economy product cost 6*d.* per book, and was clearly regarded as a poor substitute for proper gold leaf, being, he suggested, used for pageants.[7] This notwithstanding, even more debased products became available, and, writing in the mid-eighteenth century, Robert Dossie mentioned another cheap substitute for gold leaf, remarking:

> There is, besides the true leaf gold, another kind in use, called Dutch gold, which is copper gilt, and beaten into leaves like the genuine. It is much cheaper, and has, when good, greatly the effect of the true at the time of its being laid on the ground; but with any access of moisture, it loses its colour and turns green in spots.

Nevertheless, he indicated, it was adequate for use in theatres, where it would be seen only in artificial light.[8] To date, no further information has come to hand about the use of such substitutes, but it seems likely that in good domestic work genuine gold leaf would generally have been employed.

By alloying the gold with carefully adjusted proportions of other metals, it is possible to vary the colour of genuine leaf. In 1825, for example, the author of the *Painter's . . . Pocket Manual* commented that the principal colours available were red, green, and yellow.[9] Such varied colours were in use in the seventeenth century, and in 1678 the French gilder René Cousin was paid for gilding at Windsor Castle: 'the Ornaments of the Dyall over the Greate Gate that ffronts to the greate Courte being done of a Right Gold Collour, of a green Gold Collour, and of a Brasse [i.e. probably bronze] Collour'.[10] A similar juxtaposition was used by William Kent, who employed leaf of both green and ordinary colour in the ceiling of the Cabinet at Houghton, Norfolk, in the 1730s; the building accounts show that William Chambers contrasted ordinary and green gold in the ceilings of the Library and Council Room of the Royal Academy at Somerset House in 1780; and green gold was used on four bells and their chains in the Gallery at the Royal Pavilion, Brighton, in 1816.[11] (These examples are further discussed in the companion volume.) Employment of such varieties of leaf was not, however, without its dangers, and Dossie sounded a note of caution, indicating that if the gold was alloyed with silver it could become too pale and greenish, while if too much copper was used it would in time 'turn to a yet much stronger green'.[12] His remarks were undoubtedly justified, and the (presumed) green gold in the Boudoir at Attingham Park, Shropshire, has now discoloured in many places.

In order to cut the leaves of gold to size, they were laid out on a *gold-cushion* (fig. 37) made of suede leather nailed over stuffing to a wooden base. John Smith observed that the cushion was 'generally made of a smooth grained Bazil Skin, the flesh-side outward . . . well stufft out with Cotton or Wooll, very hard, plain, and flattish'. Stalker & Parker, however, recommended merely the use of tow as a filler. The size of the cushion could be varied, Smith indicating the use of a wooden base six inches square, although Stalker & Parker specified a 'board 10 inches one way, and 14 the other', dimensions commensurate with those suggested by Dossie. Perhaps, however, Smith had in mind

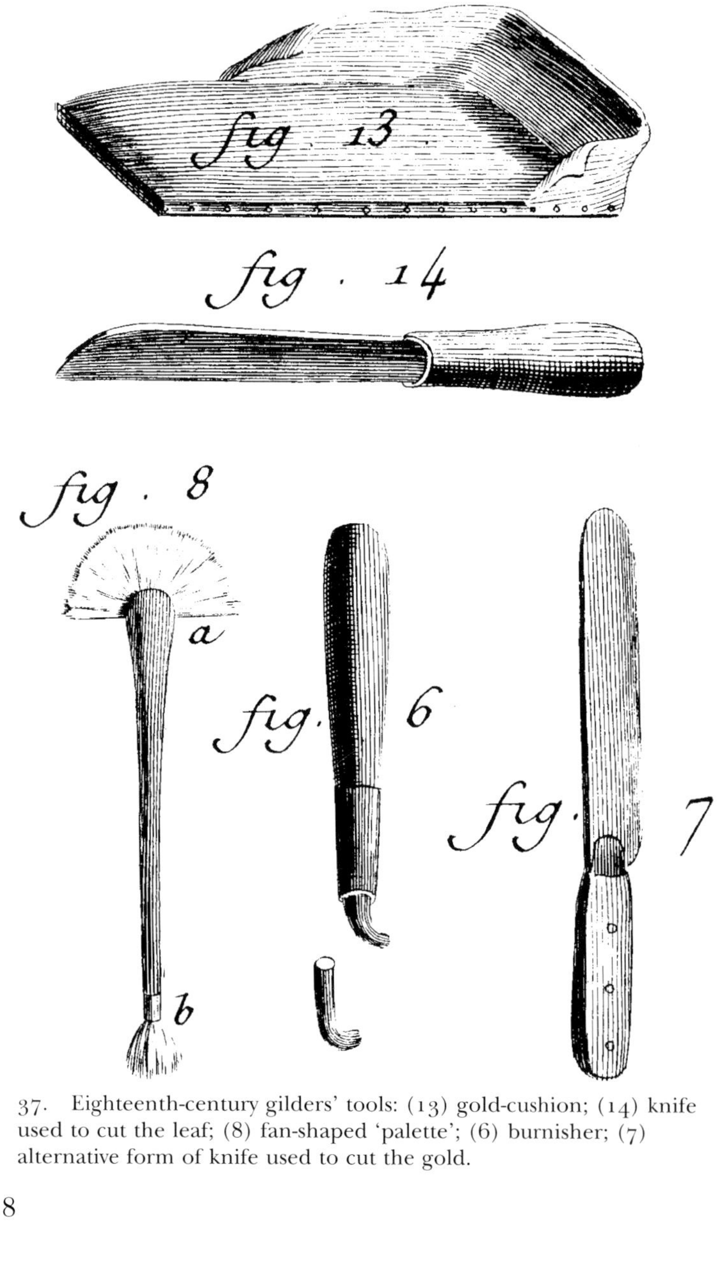

37. Eighteenth-century gilders' tools: (13) gold-cushion; (14) knife used to cut the leaf; (8) fan-shaped 'palette'; (6) burnisher; (7) alternative form of knife used to cut the gold.

that only one leaf was to be dealt with at a time, but Stalker & Parker related that experienced tradesmen would frequently shake a whole book of gold onto their cushion at a time, individual leaves then being singled out as required with the gold-knife to be described in a moment. For this, much more space would obviously be needed; and an added refinement to the cushion might be provided by the gilders, who, they observed,

> commonly border their Cushion at one end, and four or five inches down each side, with a strip of parchment two inches high, intending by this fence and bulwark to preserve their Gold from the assaults of Wind and Air, which if moved never so gently, carries away this light body, which willingly complies with its uncertain motions.[13]

The gold was cut to the size required using a 'thin, broad, sharp, and smooth-edged knife' (fig. 37).[14] According to John Smith this could be either a 'Case-Knife, or else a slip of the hollow Spanish-Cane, cut up to a smooth and sharp edge with a good Pen-knife'. A knife made from cane in this way was, he indicated, preferable to a steel implement, since the gold would not stick to it, whereas to prevent this when using a steel knife it was necessary to wipe it continually on a clean dry cloth.[15]

Once cut, there were several ways in which the gold could be transferred from the cushion to the area to be gilt, which, in architectural work, would generally have been prepared to receive it with an oil gold-size. Smith described one version of the tool, or 'Pallat', used to effect the transfer, indicating that it was made from a flat piece of wood about three inches by an inch, on which was glued a piece of fine woollen cloth. To use it, one breathed lightly on the wool in order to moisten it and placed it gently over the piece of gold which had been cut to size on the cushion. This would then adhere to the wool, and could thus be conveyed to the prepared work. The tool, which was, of course, only suitable for 'flat and plain work', could, he added, be made large enough to carry a complete leaf of gold if desired.[16] Interestingly, Stalker & Parker did not refer to this very basic implement, and indicated instead that the 'Pallet' used by artists for 'taking up and laying on whole leaves at a time' was made from the end of a squirrel's tail, fanned out, and fastened to the broad end of a flat handle split to receive it.[17] Dossie too described a similar item (fig. 37).[18]

If, on the other hand, it was carved work which was to be gilt, Smith indicated an alternative method was used to transfer the leaf. In this case, he said, the 'Painters do usually take up their gold, either from the Book or Cushion, with a bunch of Cotton Yarn, a little moistned with their breath'. By this means the gold could be pressed into the hollows of the work, while, he added, a 'bunch of good fine Wooll' would do as well.[19] For the same purpose, Dossie too recommended the use of cotton wool formed into a ball, but added the refinement of tying it up in a piece of fine linen rag in order to prevent the fibres adhering to the gold-size.[20] Where, on the other hand, the gold was to be 'laid on within the hollows of carved work' (that is, presumably, where the carving was undercut), John Smith later indicated it was necessary to use a fine camel-hair brush to effect the transfer.[21]

OIL-GILDING

The method of gilding used on architectural ornament was generally that known as oil-gilding, in which the area to receive the gold leaf was prepared with an oil-based gold-size. In cases where the work had not received previous decoration in oil paint, Dossie recommended the preliminary application of a special primer made from drying oil and a little yellow ochre. A small proportion of vermilion might, he said, also be added.[22] Stalker & Parker, on the other hand, recommended the use of white lead, ochres, or umber, besides an alternative composition made from the residues of old paint, the washings of brushes, and so on. These were to be strained carefully into a pot, and lightened if necessary with a little white lead.[23] Félibien and Watin also mentioned a similar practice.[24] D'Aviler too suggested the use of a priming where the beads and fillets of wainscot previously painted white were to be gilt. It was made from yellow ochre or rouge brun, but he gave no formula for his gold-size which, he presumably felt, would lack body if applied directly over white.[25] Priming over existing oil paint in this way seems otherwise unnecessary.

Late seventeenth- and eighteenth-century formulae for gold-size are fairly consistent, and invariably contain yellow ochre. It appears, however, that the early nineteenth century saw changes in this. To prepare gold-size, John Smith simply ground yellow ochre in 'fat Oyl'. The ochre was to be of an especially fine quality prepared either by first grinding it with water, which, he said, was the common way, or by levigation to separate the coarse particles. In either case it was, of course, dried before use. The yellow ochre was ground into the oil in the same way as ordinary oil colours, although more labour was necessary, since, apart from the obviously greater viscosity of the oil used, it was, he said, to be ground 'very fine, even as Oyl itself'. The finer it was, the greater would be the lustre of the finished gilding. Regarding the consistency desirable for the size, he indicated it was not to be 'so weak as to run when you have laid it on; nor so stiff, that it may not work well, but of such a competent body, that after it is laid on, it may settle itself smooth and glassy'.

It was for this reason that a 'fat Oyl' was necessary rather than ordinary linseed oil; but, although elsewhere in his book Smith described two methods (noted in Chapter 10 above) for the preparation of 'fat Oyls', he does not seem to have made it clear whether it was simply boiled oil or sun-thickened oil he had in mind.[26] Almost certainly, however, it was the latter, since Stalker & Parker specifically described the preparation of sun-thickened 'Fat Oyl' in connection with their formula for gold-size, which reflects generally that of Smith. Exposure was, however, continued for five or six months, and no drier was added, the process being effected in lead pans rather than in a glass vessel. The product, they suggested, would become,

> as thick as Turpentine, the longer it stands the more fat it will be, and by consequence the Gold will require [sic – acquire?] a better gloss; if it arrive to the consistence of butter, that it may be almost cut with a knife, reserve it carefully, and as the best for use that can possibly be made.[27]

Dossie too described the manufacture of sun-thickened oil in the context of gilding, suggesting that an inch depth of oil placed in shallow pans should be floated on five inches of water and exposed to the sun for six weeks until it approached the consistency of treacle. The oil and water were then to be separated and the oil warmed to allow any impurities to settle before being decanted for use. Oil thickened in this way would, he intimated, be whiter than that prepared without water.[28]

In use, Dossie suggested that the sun-thickened oil could be diluted with ordinary drying oil if too thick to be worked, and could be ground either on its own with the yellow ochre or after being combined with up to an equal part of 'japanner's gold size'. In the latter case it would dry more quickly, but the gilding would be less glossy. In his section on 'japanner's gilding' (for which gold powder rather than leaf was used) Dossie gave two formulae for this variety of size. The first, although complicated, was, he indicated, the generally approved type, but the second, of simple character, was in his opinion just as good. To make the first, 1 ounce of powdered 'gum animi', 1 ounce of asphaltum, $1\frac{1}{2}$ ounces of red lead, $1\frac{1}{2}$ ounces of litharge of gold, $1\frac{1}{2}$ ounces of umber, and 1 pound of linseed oil were boiled together until, when cooled, the product had a thick consistency resembling tar.[29] His second formula consisted simply of 4 ounces of animi boiled with a pound of linseed oil in a similar way. For fine work he recommended the use of two or three coats of gold-size.[30]

Compared with those described so far, the formula given as a 'mordant' by the author of the *Painter's . . . Pocket Manual* possesses a completely different character, being based on oil of turpentine; and, although stained with gamboge, contained no body colour such as the yellow ochre of the eighteenth-century formulae. It consisted of 1 ounce mastic, 1 ounce sandarac, 1 ounce gamboge, $\frac{1}{4}$ ounce turpentine, and 6 ounces oil of turpentine; while, he added: 'For bronzing or very pale gilding, a mixture of asphaltum and drying oil, diluted with oil of turpentine is much recommended.'[31] The extent to which such transparent sizes came in architectural work to supersede those of earlier type is not evident, but extant examples of gold-size containing a dense yellow body reflecting eighteenth-century practice have been noted in the course of technical investigations in the Balcony Room at Dyrham Park, Avon (1694); in the Cabinet at Houghton, Norfolk (*c.* 1730–40); in the Drawing Room at Osterley Park, Middlesex (1772–4); in the Back Drawing Room at 15, St James's Square, London, where the gilding was added at some date following Samuel Wyatt's alterations in 1794; and elsewhere.[32]

Once applied, the size was allowed to dry to a condition in which the gold would adhere without sinking in when applied by the methods described. It was important that this be carefully judged, and Stalker & Parker related two tests which could be used to determine whether the size was in the right condition, suggesting first that one should breathe on it. If the size misted over it was ready for the gold.[33] Their second test was described also by John Smith, who indicated that the correct moment could be determined by touching the size with the tip of the finger, 'for if your Finger stick a little to it, and yet the Colour come not off, then it is dry enough'. He cautioned particularly against laying on the gold if the size was either too wet or too dry.[34]

Once the gold had been applied, Stalker & Parker recommended that a day should be allowed to elapse, and the work beaten over gently with a large fine hog's-hair brush so that the gold might 'be pressed close, and compelled to retire into all the uneven, hollow parts of the Carving'. Afterwards, all the excess gold was to be brushed onto a sheet of paper for re-sale.[35] Later, Dossie recommended the use of a very soft hog's-hair brush for the same purpose.[36]

WATER GILDING

Water-gilding, or *burnished gilding* as it was often called, provided a much higher quality finish than oil gilding. It was, however, more time-consuming to perform, and could not be used externally since the weather would quickly destroy it. The method was fully described by Félibien, Stalker & Parker, Dossie, and Watin, and although there are differences of detail, in essence all their accounts are consistent. The piece to be water-gilt was first sized with one of the better qualities available, such as parchment size; and a ground of *gesso,* generally made with chalk and size, built up by means of a number of coats.[37] When dry, the carving was recut, the work polished and one or more coats of yellow ochre (often known today as 'clay') in size could then be applied and polished prior to laying the final *assiette.* This was generally made from a particularly fine variety of red ochre known universally today as Armenian bole, variations of this name being met with in seventeenth- and eighteenth-century literature. The pigment was mixed with size, often with the addition of black lead (graphite) and a small quantity of some sort of greasy or waxy substance such as tallow, olive oil, or even butter. It was applied warm, allowed to dry, dampened, and, when in exactly the right condition to receive it, the gold was laid on, a matter which required much skill and judgement. After being allowed to dry to a certain, and again nicely judged, extent, the gilding was burnished using a dog's tooth or a piece of agate (fig. 37). Stalker & Parker indicated a strong preference for the latter, which, they said, was 'of late . . . more highly esteemed'.[38]

Using this technique, widely differing degrees of finish could be achieved. Stalker & Parker indicated that in gilding a frame, the ground of the carving and other parts could be left unburnished, 'which being rough in respect of the other, sets off and beautifies the burnishing'.[39] The practice was mentioned by Félibien too, who indicated three degrees of finish: that where the gold was burnished; that where the gold was not burnished; and a third where the ground on which the gold was laid had alone been burnished.[40] A particularly clear example of the juxtaposition of matt and burnished gilding may be seen on at least one of the design drawings by the London cabinet-maker John Linnell, who was active during the second half of the eighteenth century; another is provided by a design by Thomas Chippendale for a mirror at Nostell Priory, Yorkshire; and a third is found on a detail by Robert Adam for an overdoor picture frame at Derby House, Grosvenor Square, London.[41]

The normal place for water-gilding in the English interior seems undoubtedly to have been on furniture, although this might, of course, include the frames of mirrors and pier glasses; and in later years also the gilt mouldings of the wall panels. Dossie, for example, remarked that burnished gilding was, 'seldom practised but upon wood, and at present mostly in the case of carved work, or when carved work is mixed with plain';[42] and, for example, a quantity of 'Reeds and Ribbon to form Pilasters & frames round Glasses' together with the necessary 'Carv'd flowers on Block's Burnish'd Gold' to form the junction between the mouldings were supplied to Thomas Anson for the Front Drawing Room on the first floor of 15 St James's Square, London, in 1794.[43] Nevertheless, Félibien had mentioned the water-gilding of stucco; D'Aviler noted the use of matt or burnished gold as a ground for coloured ornament; and Watin described fully the method for gilding a room in burnished gold.[44] Such references suggest that in France, at least on occasion, water-gilding may have been employed on architectural work, but few items have yet been encountered which might help to indicate whether this too was English practice. Interestingly, the earliest is at Carlton House, a building considerably influenced by French taste. In 1819 W.H. Pyne described John Nash's Golden Drawing Room as 'gilt in burnished and matted gold'; and the accompanying plate seems to have set out deliberately to emphasise the brilliance of the highlights typical of the technique, apparently confirming that it was indeed water-gilding which had been employed.[45] On the other hand, John Rutter's reference in 1823 to the mouldings of the vault in the Oratory at Fonthill developing 'a net-work of burnished gold over our heads' could merely represent poetic licence.[46] Both buildings, however, were obviously of an exceptional opulence, and the water-gilding of architectural ornament would clearly have reflected this.

SILVERING, LACQUERING AND OTHER SPECIAL EFFECTS, AND PRICES

Where silver leaf was to be used, the 'gold-size' was made white in colour. Dossie referred to the use of flake white for the purpose,[47] and John Smith, who in 1687 recommended the addition of 'a very little Yellow-Oaker', later amended his directions to read: 'Silver-Size is made by grinding White Lead with fat drying Oyl, some adding a very little Verdigrease to make it bind.'[48] In water-gilding, Stalker & Parker substituted ground tobacco-pipe-clay for the red bole, indicating in one formula the addition of a little graphite, and in another the optional addition of lamp black if it was desired to produce a size of a light ash colour.[49] Variations might also be made in the colour of the ground where green or red gold were used. Again in connection with water-gilding, Watin indicated that on those parts where *or vert* was to be laid, the size should be made of ceruse, Prussian blue, and *stil de grain* mixed to the colour of *vert d'eau*; while for *or citron*, a combination of ceruse and *stil de grain* alone was to be employed.[50]

Although Dossie observed that, on account of its tendency to tarnish rapidly, silvering was seldom used,[51] examples of its employment in an architectural context may be found. Burnished silver was used by Chippendale, for instance, on carved timber borders surrounding the silk wall-hangings in the Yellow Damask Sitting Room at Harewood house, Yorkshire, in 1775;[52] and silver was used on the fillets and mouldings of the cornice in the Saloon at the Royal Pavilion, Brighton, in 1804.[53] In both instances the accounts show that it was varnished, no doubt to protect it from the atmosphere, a practice noted as necessary by Dossie, who discussed suitable formulae designed to minimise any tendency to yellow.[54]

Elsewhere, Dossie referred to the practice of lacquering silvered picture frames to give the effect of gilding, but noted that the technique was 'now greatly disused'.[55] Earlier, of course, it had been widespread, and was described by Stalker & Parker;[56] while John Smith observed:

> the Common Painters do now more generally in guilding use more Silver than Gold, in most Works that are not much exposed to the air, to which they afterwards give the Colour of Gold, by means of the Lacker-Vernish, . . . made of Gum-Lake, dissolved in Spirit of Wine, and laid over it.[57]

Other formulae for lacquer and the method of its aplication to silver leaf have been described in Chapter 18, and an example of the architectural use of the technique is provided by an account for silvering and lacquering the Tudor ceiling of the Guard Chamber at Whitehall Palace in 1687.[58]

Reference must be made also to the use of green glazes over gold and silver. These often took the form of a copper resinate (see Chapter 3), a technique described by Pierre le Brun in 1635, but of earlier origin.[59] In 1623–4, the palms and garlands associated with the white and gold 'boyes' supporting the royal arms surmounting the new screen inserted across the west end of the Tudor chapel at Greenwich Palace were silvered and 'glassed with faire greene',[60] and a similar technique may have been used above parts of the gilding on the ironwork of James Wyatt's staircase at Frogmore House, Berkshire, in the mid-1790s.[61] In this connection, it is worthy of note also that carved elements including '4 very large Dragons' forming part of the curtain arrangement in the Music Room at the Brighton Pavilion were painted on silver 'in various colours and varnished' in 1820, a possible reference to glazing;[62] while another item in the accounts refers to '1 large Dragon silvered and painted in proper colours' in the Entrance Hall in 1815.[63]

Besides the varnishes, lacquers, or glazes just described, other special treatments could be given to gilding. After burnishing the carved parts of work which had been water-gilded. Stalker & Parker described the 'matting' of the remainder by means of a coat of size or lacquer. Following this, the work could be further 'set off or repossed' with an orange-coloured lacquer used to 'touch the hollownesses' of the carving in order to add depth to leaves and foliage.[64] Another method of heightening the effect of water-gilding was described by Félibien, who mentioned the use of vermilion applied in the crevices of the ornaments and sculpture to bring out the 'fire' of the gold.[65] On the other hand

Stalker & Parker remarked that although they knew some used vermilion in this way, they were 'not reconciled to it' since they did not feel it was so pleasant and agreeable to the eye as the method they had already described using a transparent lacquer.[66] Nevertheless, Dossie indicated the optional use of body colour in the hollow parts of the work, also calling this 'matting'. The colour chosen was, he said, to be near that of the gold, and could be made from red lead and vermilion ground in white of egg, although he felt that a mixture of yellow ochre and Dutch pink would be better. Other suitable, and more permanent, combinations were provided by slightly burnt *terra di Siena* or by a mixture of raw sienna and red lead. Isinglass size was, he added, as good for the purpose as white of egg.[67]

It seems doubtful that such refinements would have been commonly practised on ordinary architectural oil gilding, although glazes were undoubtedly used in *trompe l'oeil* work. Thus John Smith indicated that after gilding had been completed it was possible to 'Diaper or flourish on it with thin burnt Umber . . . tempered but thin, so that the Gold may appear through it';[68] and Gerbier gave a price for 'Painting in white and gold, upon flat moulding, and set off with shadowing, like carving'.[69] An instance dating from the late 1630s is to be seen in the Hall at the Queen's House, Greenwich,[70] while a later example apparently survives on a doorcase in the Tapestry Room at West Wycombe Park, Buckinghamshire.[71]

The practice of 'party gilding', in which only the highlights of carving were gilded, seems likely to have been developed in order to meet the need felt during the second half of the eighteenth century for greater 'variety' than was provided by unrelieved areas of solid gilding, and is discussed in the companion volume to this study. Other variations too were developed, including that described by the early nineteenth-century upholsterer George Smith, which he termed *rehaussée d'or*, where hatched areas of gold were employed on a dark ground;[72] but these too were, perhaps, more generally a matter of style and taste than technique.

Turning finally to prices charged for gilding, Pratt remarked: 'They ordinarily demand 8 groats a foot square gilding. Or 8*d.* a yard one inch broad', adding that both represented the same rate, which works out at 2*s.* 8*d.* per square foot.[73] This is borne out by prices charged for gilding at the Queen's House, Greenwich in November 1677 (widths of 1", $1\frac{1}{4}$", $1\frac{1}{2}$", $1\frac{3}{4}$", $2\frac{1}{2}$" and $10\frac{1}{2}$" all reducing to the same figure),[74] and by advice given by Christopher Wren to Dr Gardiner (Sub-Dean, and later Bishop) at Lincoln Cathedral. Wren's note is of particular interest:

> A fillet of Gilding flat halfe an inch broade at iiij^{d} p. yard running measure and soe proportionably for broader worke
>
> A foot square gilded flat is – 2^{s}. 8^{d}.
>
> Carved worke such as the inrichments of members in Cornices & mouldings is measured as flat worke & halfe as much more.
>
> Round Carving such as Maske heads & festoons is reckoned as double worke.
>
> Very hollow worke such as Corinthian Capitells is reckoned as trebble worke.
>
> All this is understood in the best gold comonly used.[75]

It is also of interest that in 1662, Gerbier observed, 'rich carved frames, painted and gilded, the gold fifteen Inches broad, the ground a fair white colour cost five shillings a [linear] foot'.[76] The rate of 4*s.* per square foot to which this reduces had, of course, to cover the cost of paint and the extra cost of gilding carved work.

Just over a century later, in 1776, the first edition of the *Builders Price-Book* quoted a rate of 3*s.* 9*d.* per square foot for 'Gilding with Gold', a figure similar to that given by Gerbier; and the same price appears too in later eighteenth-century copies, such as those of 1787 and 1794.[77] Confirmation of this rate for oil gilding in the 1770s and 1780s is provided by a number of building accounts, including David Adamson's bill for work carried out in the Drawing Room at Osterley Park, Middlesex, between 1772 and 1774. The majority of prices for enriched mouldings, both solid and partly gilt, whose girths varied between half an inch and six inches, work out at exactly 4*s.* per square foot, although there are small variations, the lowest being 3*s.* 6*d.* and the highest 4*s.* $3\frac{1}{2}$*d.*[78] Similar figures were charged by Charles Catton for work in the apartments of the Royal Academy at Somerset House in 1780. In the Library certain items of 'very rich Ornament' were party gilt in green gold at a rate of 4*s.* per square foot, and a similar rate was charged for oil-gilding on similar areas. Mouldings in oil-gilding were charged for at 3*s.* 6*d.* per square foot, and the same rate applied to the gilding of mouldings in the Council Room in both ordinary and green gold.[79]

By the time the 1810 and 1813 editions of the *Builder's Price-book* were published, however, these prices had increased, although, perhaps, to a lesser extent than those of house-painting in general; and for ordinary gilding figures of 4*s.* to 5*s.* 6*d.* were suggested. Early nineteenth-century copies, moreover, also show a rise in the price of water-gilding, which had been priced in the 1787 and 1794 editions at a minimum of 5*s.* per square foot, rising to 8*s.* on 'Enriched carved work'. In 1810 and 1813 these figures were revised to show a range of rates running from 5*s.* to 8*s.* for straightforward burnished gilding, and 6*s.* to 12*s.* per square foot for enriched carved work.[80]

Finally, it remains to note that gilding may not always have been priced by the superficial area, since the *Builders Price-Book* contained also the following note:

> *Gilders often charge in the following manner*:
>
> 3*s.* 6*d.* per book for oil gold, and labour to plain work.
>
> 5*s.* ditto, for burnished gold ditto, and from five to eight shillings ditto, carved work.[81]

Curiously, these prices appear unchanged in the early nineteenth-century editions mentioned above.[82]

CHAPTER 20

GRAINING, MARBLING, AND OTHER IMITATIONS

A considerable part of the house-painter's skill, especially during the seventeenth, early eighteenth, and nineteenth centuries, lay in the imitation of various fine materials, especially different varieties of marble and the finer cabinet timbers. Indeed, Nicholson listed graining as one of the four branches of house-painting;[1] and, in addition to marbles, such materials as bronze, tortoise-shell, and mother-of-pearl were imitated by painters. During the latter part of the eighteenth and early nineteenth centuries such tradesmen were employed also to provide ceilings representing a cloudy sky, as inclusion of this skill among those listed on the trade card of the London grainer William Davies makes clear.[2]

The techniques used for graining and marbling developed considerably during the period covered by this book, particularly during the early nineteenth century; and by the 1860s, when the Bolton grainer, Thomas Kershaw, won first prize at the International Competition in Paris, he could grain a piece of slate to look like oak, and transform a piece of oak to the appearance of marble with such complete success as to fool even the most critical modern eye. His work, recently exhibited at the Victoria and Albert Museum,[3] is an impressive tribute to the advances of skill which became possible as a result of technical improvement, said by Nathaniel Whittock to have taken place within the ten years prior to the publication in 1827 of his book on decorative painting, a large part of which is devoted to the subject.[4] Interestingly, in 1818 Laxton had referred to 'the late Mr Samuel Platt, well known to all painters, and admitted to be the first who brought imitation to perfection';[5] while in 1813 Martin had noted that the best London 'artists' in the field were Mr Harman of Chelsea and Mr Willement of Green Street, Grosvenor Square.[6] Whoever was responsible for the introduction of the new techniques, however, it seems clear from Whittock's descriptions that they lay in the use of a system whereby transparent darker glazes applied over a lighter ground would be manipulated and 'wiped out' to imitate the highlights of the figure, in place of the more laborious building up of the work in body colour. Such a method allows for great subtlety, and practice based on it was so fully described by Whittock and Vanherman that an extremely clear picture of early nineteenth-century technique may be obtained. Information on earlier practice is, however, scattered and fragmentary, and much has to be inferred from the briefest references. For this reason the later techniques will first be described in order that those which were to become obsolete may be compared with them, graining being dealt with before marbling since it was in this field that glazes were of greatest importance. Attention will then be turned to the evidence for seventeenth- and eighteenth-century methods, and a general summary made of costs for graining and marbling during the entire period. Techniques and rates for the imitation of individual varieties of timber and marble, however, are considered in Appendices B and C, and the present chapter will conclude with consideration of the methods used for reproducing the appearance of freestone, bronze, and other materials whose imitation formed part of the house-painter's repertoire, including the preparation of clouded ceilings.

EARLY NINETEENTH-CENTURY GRAINING METHODS

In principle, although less use is made today of an aqueous medium, the graining techniques employed by the 1820s will be familiar to many modern exponents of the art, the first step being the preparation of an oil ground, whose colour was that of the lightest part of the timber to be imitated.[7] It was necessary that this should be particularly smooth, Vanherman stipulating that the ground should be prepared in the same way as a coach panel, and meticulously rubbed down with glass-paper between coats.[8] Laxton indicated that an extra 3*d.* per square yard should be charged in the case of 'Colours for grounds for imitations' although a few years later Skyring suggested 2*d.*[9] On this prepared ground a glaze of more or less transparent colour was laid, which, while still wet, was modified and manipulated with various tools so as to allow the lighter ground to show through in places, imitating the natural highlights of the grain typical of the timber in question. This was called by Vanherman the 'stry' (no doubt a corruption of the French adjective *strié*).[10] Once dry, darker veins could be added, hard edges throughout the process frequently being 'softened' with a large dry brush. When completed, the work was generally, but not invariably, varnished, both to protect the surface and to give the imitation the apparent depth of polished timber.

The glazes used could be prepared either in an oil or an aqueous medium, in both cases the more transparent varieties of pigment finding particular employment. Whittock mentioned, for example, lake, Prussian blue, umber, and sienna as frequently used without white lead as glazing pigments,[11] and others will be found in the various detailed recipes for imitating the different timbers and other materials described in the glossaries below. Taking the oil mediums first, two varieties are mentioned in contemporary literature. The simpler, the normal linseed oil and oil of turpentine vehicle, was employed by Whittock to a very limited extent, but was mentioned also by Nicholson, whose graining method described in the *New Practical Builder* (1823–5) was rather different from that outlined above, and will receive attention below in connection with earlier techniques. The second, which, at least among the specialists, was probably in more general use, was known as *megilp*,[12] and was described by Whittock as being not a fluid 'but a compound of various ingredients mixed together to the consistence of a thick treacle'. The main reason for the use of megilp was to prevent the glaze, when figured in imitation of the timber grain, from running together again and obscuring the effect thus created; but a megilp could serve also to retard the speed at which a glaze dried in order to allow a greater working time. Although he indicated that formulae varied according to the fancy of the individual painter, to prepare a typical megilp glaze for use in the imitation of oak, Whittock directed that 8 ounces of sugar of lead and 8 ounces of rotten stone should be ground together in linseed oil as stiffly as possible. At the same time, 16 ounces of white wax should be dissolved in 8 ounces of oil of turpentine by means of gentle heat, and when cool ground into the first preparation.[13]

Turning to aqueous mediums, that used universally by Whittock for graining 'in distemper' was beer or ale. The main reason for the employment of this water and alcohol mixture was undoubtedly the effect the latter constituent had in eliminating the effects of any slight oiliness there may have been in the prepared oil ground which might have prevented the glaze from taking evenly. Both Whittock and Vanherman stressed the need to remove any greasiness of this nature, which Vanherman called the 'sessing' (now generally spelt *cissing*), before applying the first glaze: Whittock recommended washing with soap and water, laying emphasis on this in several places; while Vanherman used beer alone, rubbed over the ground.[14] When working in distemper, the glazing pigments were, Whittock indicated, to be ground in beer to the consistence of a thick paste, and thinned with more beer for use. In addition to beer, he also mentioned a second variety of megilp, which, he said, was used by some painters. It was designed to slow down the rate at which distemper glazes would dry, and was made up from soap, wax, and turpentine.[15]

With regard to the choice between an oil or distemper medium in any particular instance, it is evident that one or more practical reasons might constrain this, although no doubt the preference of the individual painter always played a large part. Thus Whittock, discussing the imitation of oak using his first megilp formula, regarded this oil medium as providing an easier method than the use of distemper;[16] but Vanherman indicated that the imitation of 'bulbous oak' was not easy in oil, and gave only a method for its execution in distemper.[17] The nature of the timber to be imitated was not, however, the only factor to be taken into consideration, and Vanherman suggested distemper possessed the considerable advantage that it was possible to wash off the glazes and to start again from scratch, should one not be satisfied with the effect at first obtained.[18]

The tools used for the application and manipulation of the graining glazes would depend on the effect required. If in the first instance the glaze was to be applied evenly over the surface of the ground, flat (or 'varnish') brushes would commonly be employed, leaving a more or less gently striated effect of grain in the glaze. Thus, for the imitation of mahogany, William Butcher indicated that the glaze should be applied 'with a flat brush, waving and imitating the veins as they run in any fine piece of mahogany';[19] while Whittock used a 'flat varnish brush' to spread the dabs of glaze first applied to the ground in the imitation of pollard oak in distemper.[20] On occasion too, an ordinary hog's-hair tool might be used, and, although Whittock at first directed that in imitating walnut in distemper a flat brush should be used to apply the glaze, he suggested that if a large area had to be covered 'a large tool, nearly worn out' could be used instead. In the imitation of oak, again in distemper, a 'large tool' was to be employed for the purpose, 'letting the hand press heavily on the brush so that the hairs may spread', in which case it would, he said, produce the same effect as the use of a graining comb in oil. In the imitation of rosewood in distemper a 'common tool' was to be used.[21]

More usually, where a more markedly grained effect was required, special 'graining tools' of various sizes,[22] having separated tufts of hair, were used to lay on the first and subsequent glazes. These were apparently made to fit into a special handle (probably similar to that provided for the combs) (fig. 38), and could be of several grades. Whittock illustrated a typical specimen (fig. 39) and described its use to apply the first glaze in the first method he gave for the imitation of bird's eye maple in distemper, referring to it as 'the flat hog's-hair brush'.[23] A softer version was, he indicated, required for the application of the second glaze, and a third variety having fine hog's hair was needed to apply the first glaze in the imitation of watered damask coral wood in distemper. The hairs of the brush in this case, Whittock directed, 'must be very thin and cut away in unequal distences, as in the former example [i.e. that in his illustration] . . . but the spaces must be narrower and more frequent'. He also used a 'flat brush, containing very few hairs, and some of these cut quite away' to add darker veins (in this case while the first glaze was still wet) in the imitation of pollard oak in distemper; while in the third method for imitating rosewood 'a flat brush with the hairs cut away till it has the appearance of a wide toothed comb' was employed, and in the fourth method 'a flat hog's-hair brush, cut very square at the end, and the hairs cut away at unequal distances'.[24] On other occasions, however, he merely referred to 'the flat brush with the hairs separated'.[25]

Occasionally resort might be had to other means of applying a glaze, and for the imitation of bulbous oak Vanherman eschewed the use of a brush altogether, using instead a 'good sized bladder' to dab the colour, which had been ground in beer or weak size, on the ground, in order to produce the special effect needed.[26]

Once the glaze had been applied by the methods described, it could be modified by the use of one of a

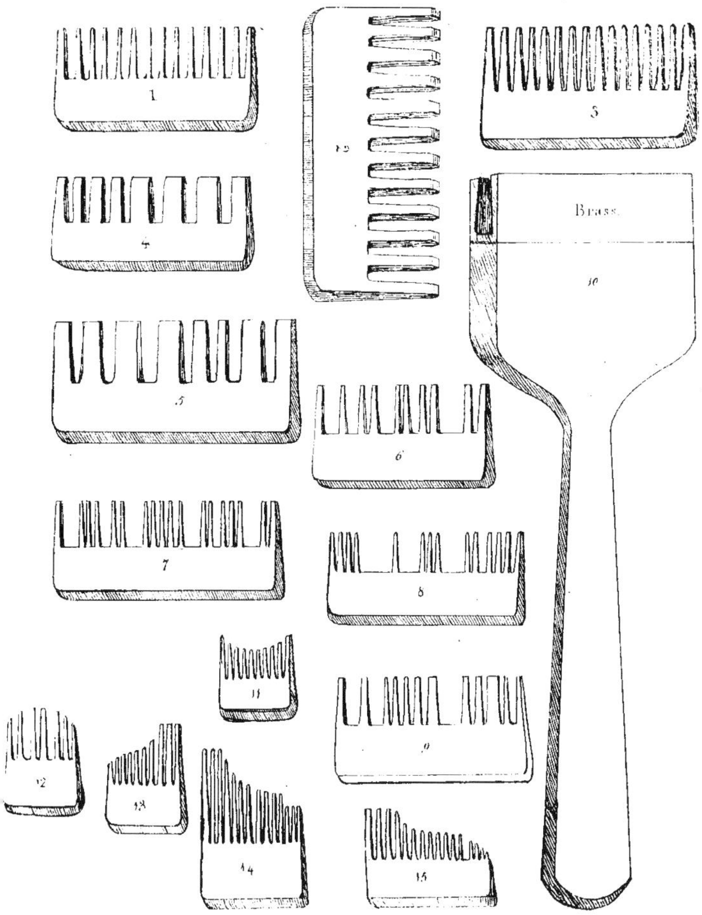

38. Early nineteenth-century graining combs and handle.

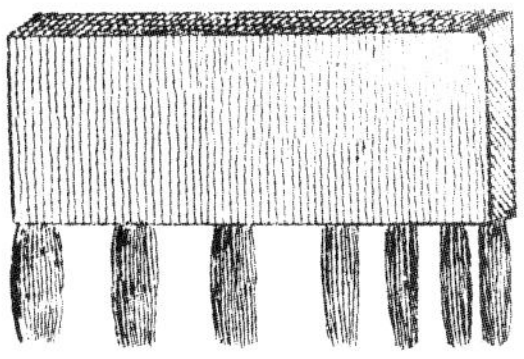

39. Early nineteenth-century graining tool fitting into handle shown at fig. 38.

number of different dry tools, ranging from specially made graining combs to a variety of everyday objects forming improvised implements. The combs, Vanherman indicated, were made from ivory,[27] and Whittock illustrated a number of specimens together with the handle into which they were inserted for use (fig. 38). Nos. 1, 2, and 3 were those generally used on plain surfaces, but it was, he suggested, better if the teeth were irregularly spaced, and Nos. 4, 5, and 6 would produce a more natural effect. Nos. 7, 8, and 9 were ordinary hair-combs adapted for graining purposes by the removal of groups of teeth, while Nos. 11 to 14 were combs for use on mouldings.[28] Although he described the method of using the combs in particular connection with the imitation of oak in oil (Vanherman too used a comb for this timber),[29] these implements could be used in distemper graining also and Whittock, for example, suggested the use of No. 3, his finest, in the imitation of red satin wood, and also in the third method he described for rosewood.[30]

A feather provided another ready means for the modification of the wet graining glaze, and in connection with the imitation of bird's eye maple in distemper by the first method he described, Whittock directed that the veins produced at first by the graining tool should be split into a variety of forms by passing 'the feather of a quill' over the work 'in the same direction that the flat brush was used, giving a sharp turn occasionally, and then proceeding over the lines again'. He used a feather also in the second method for the imitation of rosewood in a distemper medium, in this case giving the hand 'a light tremulous motion in the part where the grain appears wavy'.[31]

In some instances, once the basic effect of grain had been produced by the methods described above, it was necessary to break it by beating across it using either an ordinary dusting brush or the 'softener' to be described below. To effect this, either type of brush would be held flat (that is, in the plane of the imitation) with its bristles lying at right angles to the direction of the grain, and the surface beaten over with it. In the first methods he described for the imitation of rosewood and birds eye maple in distemper, Whittock, for example, suggested using the softener for the purpose, directing in the former instance that it should be applied 'against the grain, that is in an opposite direction to the way in which it was laid on', and in the second that it should again be used to beat the work 'the contrary way of the grain'. For the imitation of other timbers, however, a dusting brush was to be used, being applied for oak in distemper 'with the point of the hairs the reverse way from that in which the colour is laid on'. The same tool was used in the imitation of bird's eye maple by the second method he gave and in the reproduction of rosewood by his fourth.[32] In the case of oak in oil, Vanherman too used a comparable technique for simulation of the 'short grain', obtaining the necessary effect by dabbing the 'points of the duster' on the glaze.[33]

In the reproduction of certain timbers, resort might be had to a sponge which would be applied to the wet glaze in such a way as to provide a suitably dappled surface. Whittock suggested, for example, that the first glaze laid in the imitation of Honduras mahogany should be modified by dabbing a sponge on it 'with great freedom', a similar technique being used in the imitation of Spanish mahogany by the second method he described, the sponge in this case being 'dropped on it in quick succession and quite accidentally'. In the case of satin wood too, the first glaze (laid in distemper) was dappled with a small piece of sponge dropped 'accidentally on various parts of the work'; and a sponge was also used to take out the light areas in the imitation of red satin wood.[34]

Although Vanherman suggested the use of a sponge among a number of alternatives to wipe out the medullary rays in the imitation of oak in oil,[35] Whittock seems to have preferred the use of a wash-leather for this purpose, either doubled to a point or, for finer lines, placed on the end of a stick. He suggested the same procedure in the imitation of Spanish mahogany by the first method he described, to 'take out the lights that appear in small streaks either side of the vein'; and again used a piece of wash leather to take out the strong lights in his fourth method for the imitation of mahogany. A wash-leather also formed part of the system he described for the imitation of rosewood by his first and second methods.[36] In addition, Vanherman described a special leather tool 'for forming the short waves' in mahogany. This was a 'piece of stiff leather, about three inches in length and half an inch in breadth, to be fixed in the handle of a graining tool instead of the hair, and to project only a quarter of an inch from where it is inserted'. He used the 'graining tool prepared with leather' in this way in the imitation of mahogany in distemper, to 'express and mark the waves at the sides of the panel', and also mentioned the use of a piece of leather to take out the medullary rays in the imitation of oak in oil.[37] For the latter purpose, besides the sponge, he also suggested using a piece of cork, having indicated that among the tools required for graining were several of these 'cut chisel shape, and points, &c.'.[38]

An important accomplishment of the grainer lay in the imitation of knots. The light circle forming these could be made by a number of methods, and Whittock variously indicated the use of a camel-hair pencil held perpendicular to the work and turned between finger and thumb, a sponge used in a similar way, a piece of wash leather turned on the end of a finger, and use of the tips of the fingers, which were to be dabbed on the wet glaze.[39] To add darker spots, veins, and other touches, generally once the glaze beneath was dry, a camel- or sable-hair pencil could be used, although the tips of the fingers could also be employed to this end.[40]

During progress of the work, the veins and other markings made on the glaze would often be blended into each other using special badger-hair brushes of different sizes. These were known as 'softeners' and were passed dry across the work. Whittock mentioned this in connection with the imitation of several timbers, including pollard oak in distemper and Honduras mahogany;[41] while Vanherman indicated the use of a badger-hair softener in the imitation of oak in oil, and mahogany in distemper.[42] An ordinary dusting brush, however, could also be used for this purpose on occasion, and Whittock mentioned its employment, for example, in the imitation of Honduras mahogany, Spanish mahogany (by the second method he described), and walnut in distemper; while in order to soften the completed first glaze in the imitation of oak in oil, he directed that the end of a 'hard tool' should be dabbed over it.[43]

Other exponents of graining would no doubt have extended the range of tools described by Whittock and Vanherman, and probably a great deal of improvisation took place, so that each craftsman would have his own favourite for any given subject. Indeed, Whittock observed that every 'experienced grainer forms for himself a variety of tools that are useful in his peculiar style of painting'.[44] Considerable artistry was required in their use and, as Whittock remarked elsewhere, 'it is not the excellence of the tools, but the skill of the hand that wields them, that gives most effect'.[45] It is almost impossible to convey in words the curious dexterity of touch needed to achieve a successful imitation, a fact acknowledged by John Smith, who remarked that the method for the imitation of timbers and marbles,

> must be attained by ocular Inspection, it being impossible to deliver the manner of the operation by precept without Example, and I am bold to affirm, that a Man shall gain more knowledge by one days Experience, than by a hundred spent to acquire it some other way.[46]

Whittock too indicated that it was 'difficult to express in words the precise movements and the various ways of handling the different tools';[47] but something of these will be found in the rather fuller descriptions of the methods used for the imitation of the different timbers contained in Appendix B below. Apart from his detailed directions, however, Whittock offered important general advice, insisting firstly on the need for the aspiring grainer to study for himself natural speciments of the materials he was learning to imitate. He should also, he said, be familiar with the way a joiner worked, how he would select the best figured timber for the panels of a door, and the way in which a wide panel would be made up from carefully matched pieces of timber, in order that in the imitation the joiner's work should be represented naturally as well as the wood. For the same reason he laid stress on the order in which the different parts of a door should be grained, the panels coming first, followed by the horizontal and then the vertical members, a logical sequence, which, it will be appreciated, allows the joints to be reproduced properly.[48]

EARLY-NINETEENTH-CENTURY MARBLING METHODS

Methods used for the reproduction of marble during the nineteenth century were generally similar to those for graining, although certain modifications of the techniques already described were employed, and, other than softening, little if any manipulation of large areas of glaze was needed. Glazes in both oil and distemper mediums were again in use, but an important variation was the use of a distemper rather than an oil ground, made possible where the imitation was to be applied to plaster, rather than, as in the case of graining, almost exclusively to timber. Thus Whittock, for example, used two coats of 'common whitewash' followed by a third made from whiting and milk as the ground for veined white marble. In this case, and in that of his second variety of 'Florentine' marble, he also employed milk as the medium for the veining, but for darker marbles, such as *verde antico* and Siena, an ordinary size-distemper was used for the ground, beer being used for the veining in the latter instance.[49] Whether the reason for use of milk in the case of the white marble was to minimise any tendency to yellowing in the medium, or for any special characteristics it may have possessed in terms of flow across the surface to achieve a better imitation of the veining peculiarly required, he did not, however, make explicit; but it would not, of course, have enjoyed the water-resistent quatities of the milk/lime formulations described in Chapter 17.

With regard to the basic choice between an oil or distemper medium in the case of marbling, considerations additional to those mentioned above in connection with graining were present. Whittock, for example, remarked that since imitations of marble were 'generally painted where they are exposed to the weather, oil is usually preferred to distemper'. On the other hand, he observed that although oil marbling lasted longer, walls executed in this medium could soon become soiled, and for this reason in halls, passages, bars of coffee-houses, and the like he preferred the use of distemper, since the work could last two seasons well, and could be 'done cheap and quick, without any disagreeable smell'; while the rooms would always have a light, fresh appearance.[50]

Another variation in method, mentioned by Whittock in connection with the reproduction of veined white marble in both oil and distemper, was the application of the veins while the ground beneath was still wet; and he used a similar technique in other instances.[51] In oil he spoke of veins being *scumbled* onto the surface, indicating that by this expression he meant they were to be 'spread very thinly over the ground'.[52] Such features were generally applied, as in graining, by means of camel- or sable-hair pencils,[53] although, in the case of the second method for the imitation of *verde antico* in distemper, Whittock suggested the use of 'the flat brush with the hairs separated' described in connection with graining.[54] Many other tools were common to both techniques, Whittock calling for the use of feathers, a wash leather, and a cork for certain imitations, besides the employment of the softener.[55] The only additional item he mentioned was a mahl stick 'to rest the arm upon while penciling the small veins'.[56] By way of general advice on veining, he described the way in which in all marbles (except, perhaps, black and gold, and Florentine marble) it was necessary that the veins should 'all appear to be travelling to the same point by different roads', cautioning that 'nothing can be more contrary to nature than those violent and eccentric breaks which painters of veined marble usually practise'.[57]

All the techniques so far described in connection with both graining and marbling have involved the building up of darker, more or less transparent glazes on a prepared ground of light colour, and follow Vanherman's general advice that in marbling one should look first for the ground colour, laying on it the lightest followed by the darker tints of the veins. For certain marbles, however, it was necessary to reverse this order. Thus, Vanherman indicated, where marbles presented dark areas 'to a great depth, in appearance' this was copied by laying the darkest colour on first, and filling in between with the general, or middle, tint, finishing off with the lighter veins in due order. Working in this way it would, of course, be necessary to apply body colour rather than transparent glazes; and the example of marble he used to illustrate the point had dark brown-red patches, between which were areas of light red containing yellow areas 'running out in points of various lengths and thickness', with lighter yellow and white finishing touches.[58] Whittock followed a similar procedure in the case of the green marbles such as *verde antico*, Egyptian green, and the serpentines, all of which, he observed, required a black ground, as also, of course, did black and gold marble. Porphyry too was prepared in a comparable way, in this case the white spots being sprinkled rather than painted on the dark red ground.[59]

GRAINING AND MARBLING BEFORE THE EARLY NINETEENTH CENTURY

As already mentioned, seventeenth-century authors gave little information concerning the techniques then in use for graining or marbling, and even the normally exhaustive John Smith, for example, merely described the imitation of 'Walnut-Tree' as effected by means of a ground of 'burnt Umber, and white[,] vein'd over with the same Colour alone, and in the deepest places with Black'.[60] In 1706, however, Evelyn noted that graining was effected 'with a slight of the *Pensil*', a technique seemingly confirmed by an account for finishing the Dining Room at the Earl of Danby's lodging in Whitehall Palace 'wallnuttree colour pencoll grained' in 1674–5.[61] Taken together, these references appear to indicate that seventeenth-century graining would be built up by the addition of veins, rather than by the manipulation of an evenly applied glaze; and the general appearance of the graining recently discovered on the stiles and rails of a room in Apartment 29 at Hampton Court, Middlesex, tallies with this suggestion. Here, unfortunately, the panels and mouldings were removed, probably during the eighteenth century, to permit the walls to be hung with paper or fabric; but Streeter's account of 1674, containing a number of items for 'wallnut tree Colo:r', survives,[62] and technical examination has confirmed the authenticity of that remaining.[63] Earlier accounts too appear to reflect a technique in which veins were added above a prepared ground, notably an entry for 'painting wallnuttree cullor & graining' a wainscot at Richmond Palace in 1639–40;[64] and it is significant that a similar method was described in some detail by the early nineteenth-century American author Hezekiah Reynolds, who even employed the seventeenth-century terminology discussed below, by then virtually obsolete in England, referring to the imitations as 'mahogany colour' and 'cedar colour'. His methods for the reproduction of these timbers and 'cherytree wood' called in each case for the application of a primer, undercoat, and finish of appropriate colour, 'shading' in a darker tint being added while the last of these was still wet, using a 'graining or flat brush'.[65]

The obsolescent nature of such a method in early nineteenth-century England is made clear by Whittock, who, describing a comparable way used for the cheap imitation of mahogany in which the graining was built up by the painting on of veins in a linseed oil and oil of turpentine mixture, observed:

> The common error in this sort of graining, is that of having the ground a dark red, and forming (or rather trying to form, for it never succeeds) the strong lights with opaque colour instead of wiping them out: the consequence is that it is either left an unseemly lump, or it mixes with the red and black, spoiling the whole mass.[66]

The wiping out of wet paint to reveal the ground to which it had been applied does not seem, however, to have been an entirely new development during the early nineteenth century, since this formed a part of the 'old method' of imitating oak in oil which Whittock said was 'still practised by country painters'. In this case the effect of the grain was achieved by painting the work over with the requisite colour in a linseed oil medium to which the necessary driers had been added. This was then worked over with a large dry brush to give the appearance of the veins, after which the lighter markings were taken out with the end of a stick 'cut thin for the purpose', or by means of a small piece of cork.[67] A comparable method, also using body colour, was mentioned by Nicholson, who indicated that the ground should be laid in white lead tinted to the required depth and diluted with oil of turpentine. The shades and graining were then to be produced by dipping a flat hog's-hair brush in a mixture of linseed oil and oil of turpentine, and drawing it down the newly laid colour. A camel-hair pencil was later used to add further features.[68]

In distemper too, Whittock described the 'old style' of working, emphasising that this also was a poor method. The colour was spread evenly on the ground, and when dry a flat varnish brush dipped in spirits of salts (hydrochloric acid) diluted with water to the strength required was 'drawn over the work in a variety of forms'. The wet streaks thus made were brushed across with a dusting brush, the action of the acid being to 'loosen the colour and give the effect of grain where it was taken away upon the duster'.[69] How far this method was in common use is uncertain, but that on occasion a distemper medium was employed at an earlier date is clear from a reference to four picture frames at Oatlands being painted 'lute colour in distemper grained and varnished' in 1637–8.[70]

Turning to seventeenth- and eighteenth-century methods for the imitation of marble, references to both oil and distemper may be found in pre-Civil-War accounts. In 1620–1, oil was used at Whitehall for the imitation of rance; in 1622–3, distemper was employed at the same place for 'marble colour'; and in 1637–8 'marble colour' was executed in oil at Somerset House.[71] Again, however, only limited details of technique emerge from contemporary literature, but these are nevertheless significant. The method of imitating veined white marble described by Stalker & Parker, for instance, corresponds almost exactly with the early nineteenth-century procedure already described, the veins being laid (using a camel-hair pencil) in diluted size-colour on a damp white ground, commencing with 'the faintest large clouds', and finishing with the finest dark veins;[72] while in 1706 Evelyn directed:

> To *vein* and *wave* on *White*, temper a little *Lamp-black* and *white* exceedingly thin with *Nut-Oyl* and *Terpentine*, and then dipping a gentle flexible *Feather*, *vein* and *undulate* your work with a light hand, as naturally as you can, to express the *Veins* of *Marble*, &c, either on *Black* or any other.[73]

Félibien too described the addition of white veins to a black ground, here in distemper by means of a small brush;[74] and coloured marbling again seems to have been executed by the addition of colour, rather than by wiping out glazes. Cross-sections of paint from the panelling in the Balcony Room at Dyrham Park, Gloucestershire (now Avon), for example, indicate that the pink and orange marbling applied to it in 1694, for which the painter Hauduroy's account survives, was built up starting from a white ground by applying body colour in oil, probably worked wet-into-wet;[75] and this technique, still in use for some marbles in the early nineteenth century, thus appears to represent normal early practice.

IMITATIONS ON A GROUND OF METAL LEAF

To conclude general discussion of the techniques used for imitations, it remains to note the occasional use of silver or gold leaf as a ground. The graining probably dating from the 1670s in the Ante-room to the Queen's apartment at Ham, which is highlighted in this way, is well known;[76] and in the second half of the seventeenth century, Stalker & Parker described the imitation of tortoise-shell by the application of glazes on a ground of silver leaf.[77] In the 1820s, Vanherman gave a comparable method for the imitation of mother-of-pearl,[78] and Whittock indicated that areas of gold leaf could be used in the reproduction of black and gold marble, a black ground being laid over the areas of metal, which was re-exposed by means of a pointed bodkin or piece of wash-leather.[79] Further details of these will be found in the relevant places below.

PRICES

Prices for different imitations could vary between quite wide limits. The marbling in the Balcony Room at Dyrham Park, for example, was billed at a rate of 3*s.* per square yard in 1694, while that in the Summer House cost only 1*s.*;[80] and an estimate of 1705 for marbling at Stoke Edith, Herefordshire, included as the most expensive item lapis lazuli at 5*s.*[81] Variations may be seen too in seventeenth-century prices for graining, certain items at Kensington Palace in the early 1690s, for example, being 1*s.* 2*d.* per square yard, and others 1*s.* 8*d*[82] In this connection, it is of particular interest that Christopher Wren noted in a memorandum: 'Veined like Walnuttree or indian Woods well performed' should cost 1*s.* 6*d.*; whereas 'Ranse Marble & indian woods extraordinarly well don soe as to deceive the Eye & be taken for naturall may be worth 4 shillings the Yarde or more according to the Judgement of the painter'.[83]

By the early nineteenth century, imitations were charged for by the square foot. Laxton, for example, gave a range of prices for graining extending from 4*d.* to 1*s.* per foot, while different varieties of marbling could cost between 2*d.* and 1*s.* 6*d.* In addition, he indicated, the value of the imitation depended on the quality of its execution.[84] Prices noted for individual varieties will be found in the appended glossaries of timbers and marbles imitated.

OTHER IMITATIONS: FREESTONE

To complete this survey of imitations, six further subjects remain to be considered from a technical viewpoint: freestone; tortoise-shell; mother-of-pearl; bronze; ceilings painted to represent a cloudy sky; and imitation damask. The aesthetic use made of these and other *trompe l'oeil* effects is discussed in the companion volume.

Looking first at the imitation of freestone, in 1625–6 the cornices of the Presence and Privy chambers and other lodgings at Dover Castle were painted 'like Stoneworke in distemper'; while in 1629–30 the walls of the chapel at Montague House, London, were painted 'in likenesse of stoneworke' in oil, although this may refer to external work.[85] Whether either instance involved the painting of false joints to resemble ashlar (as often the case in exterior examples) is unclear from the references, but stone-like plain paintwork of early date is still extant behind eighteenth-century joinery on a window splay at the Queen's House, Greenwich.[86]

During the eighteenth century certain exterior timber elements of buildings, such as cornices, were commonly 'sanded' to look like stone. The process simply involved the dusting of sand onto the surface of wet paint, and often had to be repeated in order to obtain an even finish.[87] In his 'DIRECTIONS for PAINTING' of the 1730s, Alexander Emerton stipulated that for '*painting and covering* Weather-boarded *House Tops*' one should: 'PAINT the Boards twice over with the Composition; and the second Time, while it is wet, sift dry Sea Sand upon it, and when it is thorough dry sweep the loose Sand off, and paint it again and sift Sand upon it as before'. For the imitation of Portland stone on doorcases, sculpture, and other elements, on the other hand, he directed 'white or writing Sand' should be substituted.[88] The process seems also to have been used on interior cornices on at least two occasions. John Spinnage's account for painting the Great Hall at Bowood in 1765 notes that the entablature was painted '5 times in Oyl and Sanded';[89] and a sanded finish has been found at the bottom of cross-sections of paint taken from James Wyatt's plaster cornice in the Staircase at Frogmore House, Berkshire dating from the mid-1790s.[90]

By the beginning of the nineteenth century, a technique known misleadingly as 'fresco' had been developed for the purpose of making Roman cement (patented in 1796) look like ashlar masonry.[91] It was used by Henry Holland on the exterior of the Royal Pavilion, Brighton, in 1802 and 1803,[92] and the process was described a few years later by both Martin and Nicholson.[93] On Roman cement, the latter directed:

> So soon as finished, it should be *frescoed* with colour, composed of five ounces of copperas [ferrous sulphate] to every gallon of water, mixed up with as much cement and fresh lime as will produce the effect required. When the entire of the work is thus covered, and has assumed an uniform colour, it should then be *frescoed*, or tinted, in imitation of Portland, Bath, or such description of Free-stone as may be required to represent the most scientific or well-bonded masonry.

Besides the use of different tints to suggest separate blocks in an ashlar wall (to which Martin too had referred), Whittock also described the way in which the divisions between them could be 'promiscuously touched with rich tints of umber' to enhance the effect.[94] Whether the technique was ever practised internally is unclear, but it seems possible that the methods used to produce the stone-like effect in St James's church, Great Packington, Warwickshire (by Joseph Bonomi and the 4th Earl of Aylesford, 1789–90) and Monkstown church, Dublin (*c.* 1830), are comparable. Examination of cross-sections from the Chapel Royal in Dublin Castle (by Francis Johnston, 1807–14) has shown that the masonry effect shown on the walls and vault on a contemporary watercolour was produced in distemper, probably with the use of water-based semi-glazes, the technique perhaps being similar to those described above which Whittock gave for the imitation of marble. The joint-lines incised in the plaster had been marked by dark grey.[95] Soon, a proprietary paint for the purpose seems to have been available; and a contract of 1823 with the plasterer George Smith stipulated that the walls in the new Court House erected in the castle at Lincoln were 'to be coloured twice over with the lithic paint in imitation of Stone'.[96] The cost of 'Lithic' was given by Bennett in 1833 as £1 15*s.* per cwt.[97] Such finishes remained popular throughout the nineteenth century, and may often be seen in early photographs of country-house entrance halls, including, for instance, a view of *c.* 1890 of the Hall at Temple Newsam, Leeds, Yorkshire.[98]

TORTOISE-SHELL

Tortoise-shell is obtained from the hawk's-bill turtle, *Eretmochelys imbricata*, found in most tropical and sub-tropical seas, and was used during the late seventeenth century for the inlay of such furnishings as mirror frames. Naturally enough it seems to have been pressed into use as an imitation in an architectural context: it was used, for instance, on the columns and friezes of Wren's altarpiece in the Tudor Chapel at Whitehall Palace in 1676; and a room at Tredegar House, Newport, Monmouthshire (now Gwent), was painted to represent 'gray Marble & Tortell shell' in 1688.[99] In the same year, discussing the imitation of tortoiseshell, Stalker & Parker observed:

> House-Painters have of late frequently endeavoured it, for Battens, and Mouldings of Rooms; but I must of necessity say, with such ill success, that I have not to the best of my remembrance met with any that have humour'd the Shell so far, as to make it look either natural, or delightful.

They therefore suggested two methods by which this imitation could be properly effected. Both required a ground of silver leaf, and may, perhaps, have been more appropriate to furniture than to large areas of wainscot. In their first method, Vandyke brown finely ground and diluted with either common size or water in which gum arabic had been dissolved was used to 'spot the darkest of your Shell'. Once this was done, the reddish tones which appear on the edges of these areas, together with those which form streaks on the transparent parts, were put in with dragons blood. This was to be finely ground in gum water, and applied using a small pencil,

> flushing it in and about the dark places more thick, but fainter, thinner, and with less colour towards the lighter parts of the shells; sweetening it so, that by degrees it may loose its strength of red, being intermixt with, and quite lost in the silver, or more transparent part.

The work was next varnished using six coats of seed lac varnish, and a lacquer made from equal parts of dragons blood and gamboge applied, using as many coats as necessary to make the silver appear gold in colour. The work was finally polished.[100]

Their second method called for the use of burnt umber, Vandyke brown, brown pink, and lake, thickly ground in drying oil and placed on a palette. A coat of turpentine varnish was applied to the silver leaf, and the brown pink and lake thinly mixed with more varnish used to lay in all the 'faintest clouds or spots'. These could then be softened and, once the work had dried, a second coat of varnish was applied. The umber and Vandyke brown were next used in the same way to lay in the 'clouds more warm and dark' than those at first applied, sweetening these 'so that you cannot perceive where either of them begin or end'. This could be repeated if necessary, and the work completed by glazing with brown pink to which, they observed, the addition of 'a little tincture of Verdigreas' would not be amiss. Alternatively, the lacquer used in the first method could be substituted.[101]

MOTHER-OF-PEARL

Mother-of-pearl may be obtained from many shells, but in *Ure's Dictionary* it was suggested that only the 'large oysters of the Indian seas' secrete a coat of sufficient thickness to be of commercial use.[102] A method for the imitation of 'mother-o'-pearl' was described by Vanherman, who introduced it to his readers as 'a new ornament of decoration'. Its execution required, he indicated, an artist of no mean ability, so that, he warned, the employer would find such work was 'not performed for a trifle'. The ground was carefully prepared in the same way as for graining, the outlines of the mother-of-pearl motifs next sketched on, and silver leaf applied to them using a gold-size. Lake, Prussian blue, and yellow lake ground in oil and thinned for use with mastic varnish and oil of turpentine were then to be laid on the surface of the leaf 'in masses, as you see them in nature', and their edges blended and softened, so that the red mass would 'unite with the blue imperceptibly, and the blue with the yellow, and the green and purple the same'. Artfully combined in this way the colours would, he said, 'produce that changeable appearance so much admired in this beautiful production of nature'; but, he warned, the imitations could display a meagre, flat, and poor effect unless given shadows 'to relieve and raise them from the ground'.[103]

BRONZING

Various qualities of metal powder were used in the reproduction of oriental lacquer-work during the later seventeenth century and beyond, but were also employed in connection with the imitation of bronze, both new and patinated. Stalker & Parker described the colours and varieties available, listing brass dust, silver dust, green gold, 'dirty' gold, powdered tin, and copper, noting the criteria for their selection together with details of their respective prices, which ran from 4*s.* to over 16*s.* per ounce.[104] Dossie too listed the range available, mentioning true gold powder, 'German gold' (which was made from Dutch metal), 'aurum Mosaicum' (tin sulphide), silver powder, 'argentum musivum' (which seems to have been a tin-mercury amalgam), and copper powder.[105] During the early nineteenth century Lewis Berger had fairly substantial stocks of bronze powders, listing pale bronze, silver bronze, copper bronze, pale gold bronze, and deep gold bronze in his annual stocktakings at prices ranging from 10*s.* to 15*s.* 6*d.* per pound.[106]

Dossie described the process of bronzing as 'colouring by metallic powders, plaister, or other busts and figures in order to make them appear as if cast of copper or other metals'. Although silver or gold powders could be used for the purpose, proper bronzing was, he said, of a deeper and redder colour achieved either by grinding red lead with the metals or by the use of copper powder. While of old the powder had been laid on in a gum or size medium, he believed it was better to apply it to a japanner's gold-size in a tacky state, using a wash-leather or camel-hair brush.[107] The use of both mediums had been described by Stalker & Parker in connection with japanning;[108] but although both they and Dossie indicated that for this purpose vermilion should be added to japan gold-size, it seems likely this would often have been omitted in the case of bronzing.

The imitation of bronze was also discussed by D'Aviler, who mentioned use of the technique on plaster, wood, iron, or lead, and described how its colour could be varied so as to have a reddish, yellowish, or greenish cast. Although the colour of the copper powder could be deepened by means of heat, he indicated that use of *rouge brun* in execution would also have this effect; while to make the bronzing of a yellowish colour, the undercoat should be made of pure yellow ochre. For a greenish colour, yellow ochre was used with bone black.[109]

The extent to which these techniques were applied to architectural ornament as distinct from sculpture in English interiors of the seventeenth century and majority of the eighteenth is not very clear, but at the end of the latter century a fashion arose for the imitation of green patinated bronze on such elements as doors and the enrichments of mouldings. Several methods by which this could be effected were published during the first half of the nineteenth century, including that for bronzing plaster figures suggested in the *Painter's . . . Pocket Manual*:

> For the ground, after it has been rubbed down, take Prussian blue, verditer, and spruce ochre. Grind them separately in water, turpentine, or oil, according to the nature of the work, and mix them in such proportions as are required to produce the colour desired. Then grind Dutch metal in a part of this composition, laying it with judgement on the prominent parts of the figure, so as to produce the best effect.[110]

In addition Whittock described a means by which *trompe l'oeil* effects of light and shade could be achieved in the bronzing. Insisting on the use of a distemper medium, he directed that the ground be first laid in a middle tint of king's yellow, blue, and black. On this the shades were to be applied using a mixture of black and red. The strong lights were then added using king's yellow and a little Indian red, and could be further heightened by dusting powdered bronze onto wet size applied to them.[111] A further refinement for such a distemper-based bronzed finish, this time composed of about fifty per cent pipe-clay, with Prussian blue, patent yellow, raw umber, and lamp black, was described in the *Painter's, Gilder's, and Varnisher's Manual.* This lay in a final polishing of the surface after coating with a thin lather of castile soap, allowing this to dry before it was rubbed off.[112]

Cross-sections of bronzing from the caryatides in the Breakfast Room at Pitzhanger Manor, designed by John Soane in 1802, confirm the use of a green ground in the imitation of patinated bronze in the early nineteenth century.[113] The same is true of samples from the bead mouldings surrounding the door and window openings in the front Drawing Room on the first floor of 13 Lincoln's Inn Fields, designed by Soane a decade later.[114] In both cases, the metal powder appears to have been applied to the surface of a dark green oil paint, probably by dusting onto a tacky unpigmented japan size, the whole imitation being finished with a coat of varnish.

CLOUDED CEILINGS

Ceilings painted to look like a cloudy sky were extremely popular during the late eighteenth and early nineteenth centuries. To prepare them, it appears that a ground of uniform blue was first applied; and the Crace accounts for the Royal Pavilion. Brighton, contain a number of references showing that the clouding followed as a separate operation. Thus, in the accounts of 1802, the section relating to the Saloon contains an item for 'Three times fine Sky colour distemper' followed by another for 'Clouding the doom [dome] ceiling';[115] and that relating to the Billiard Room includes an entry for 'Twice sky colour to ceiling' followed by one for clouding it.[116] Similar pairs of entries follow for the Music Room and Breakfast Room in 1803,[117] while in 1815 the process in the Hall was described as 'Preparing and coloring the ceiling sky color and clouding Do.'[118] There is also a similar item in the same year relating to the Small Drawing Room.[119] Other clouded ceilings in the Pavilion were painted by Louis Barzargo.[120]

For the blue ground, it seems likely blue verditer would generally have been employed, since Watin observed that *cendre bleue* was much used in distemper, especially for painting skies in the theatre.[121] The operation of adding the clouds, on the other hand, appears to have been a 'trick of the trade', since Vanherman, the only writer encountered to give more specific technical directions, remarked that one should use red orpiment and blue verditer for the 'shade tint', adding that these 'mixed either separately or together with whiting, constitute the whole of this process, which has been and is still accounted a great secret'.[122] Perhaps the 'red grey' suggested by Whittock for the larger masses of cloud in his design for a ceiling for a concert hall reflects this technique;[123] and this and other examples of the *genre* are discussed in the companion volume.

IMITATION DAMASK, GOLD BROCADE, AND MOROCCO

In 1826, by his own account, D.R. Hay of Edinburgh patented a method for the imitation of damask, and later published two processes by which the effect was produced. In the first, a plaster wall which had received four or five coats of oil paint, on the dry surface of which the pattern was outlined, was coated with a thick substance composed of oil, mastic varnish, bees-wax, sugar of lead, and umber (or another tinting pigment). While wet, this was combed to produce a texture, which was then selectively smoothed to differentiate the pattern from its ground. Once dry, the wall was painted in the colour desired, and varnished with copal varnish.

In the second method, the ground was similarly prepared, here in the chosen colour. The pattern alone was filled in using the 'thick tenacious substance' employed in the first, to which white lead might be added to render it opaque. While still wet, sieved fine dry sand was thrown upon it, any excess not properly adhering being brushed off after a few days when the whole had hardened. A flatting coat matching the ground was then applied to complete the effect.

The same or a similar composition was used in the imitation of 'gold embroidery', presumably brocade. This was manipulated using a fine-toothed ivory graining-comb drawn successively from top right to bottom left, from top left to bottom right, and finally vertically. When after eight to ten days it had hardened, it was overpainted with a coat of flat paint in the chosen colour. The pattern was pounced onto the dry surface, and oil-gilded.

Imitation morocco-leather could be produced like the varnished imitation of damask by manipulating the 'thick tenacious paint' using a toothed instrument of ivory or steel. This too was covered with a coat of paint and finished with one of varnish.[124]

CHAPTER 21

COLOUR MIXING

To complete this survey of house-painting from a technological viewpoint, attention may finally be turned to the tinting of paint. In doing so, one point must first be emphasised: during the period under review, very little use was made of transparent glazes, except in graining, marbling, and other imitations, or in specialised decorative work such as arabesque. Instead, as will be appreciated from Chapters 15 to 17, house-paints were generally opaque in character; and, unless made solely from coloured pigments in order to provide a particularly intense or dark colour, were made starting from a base of opaque white.

In addition, a clear distinction must be made between pigment names and paint-colour names. Hence, 'Prussian blue' is the name of a pigment which may be mixed with white to produce a whole range of blues, to which names such as 'sky blue' or 'navy blue' might be applied; and it is with the latter, often subjective terms which were employed to describe paint-colours that this chapter is concerned. The distinction is, however, often blurred by use of pigment names for paint colours. Thus the term 'Prussian blue' is commonly employed to describe a dark blue colour reflecting that of the pigment in dry powder form, and during the period being considered, names such as *umber colour* or *verditer green* were also used to describe paint-colours rather than pigments. The employment of such terms did not necessarily imply, however, that the pigment lending its name to the paint-colour was inevitably used in its mixing; and Tingry, for example, suggested a method for matching the colour of green verditer in distemper by the use of verdigris in oil.[1]

In the Introduction to Part I, the imperfect nature of the pigments available to the early house-painter was mentioned, and even by the end of the period covered by this study there were still very great deficiencies in the range of those available for house-painting. In the seventeenth century, prior to the invention of Prussian blue, and in the eighteenth, prior to the introduction of pigments such as chrome yellow and French ultramarine, these were inevitably greater, with consequent implications for colour mixing. In particular, it was not necessarily possible to match the colour of a textile or ceramic in house-paint. Indeed, each technology had its own range of colours and, although there was some overlap, these could not all be transposed in interior decoration. To reproduce the colour of an eighteenth-century silk brocade for wallpaper, or 'Wedgwood blue' for paint, is, therefore, a most unsafe way to embark on restoration of the historic palette.[2]

Even within the sphere of house-painting itself, moreover, the range of colours available was not always of universal application, since each of the pigments in use had a character of its own. Most importantly, some were unsuited to employment in all the mediums employed; and because each medium was often more appropriate for certain parts of a room than others, the ranges of colour which might be applied to different elements were accordingly constrained. Oil, of course, was of universal application, but (at least by the latter part of the seventeenth century) distemper was rarely applied to joinery. Thus, prior to the availability of Naples yellow in the mid-eighteenth century, although plaster walls could easily be distempered a bright yellow, to produce large expanses of the same colour in oil was attended with some difficulty, since, as will be remembered from Chapter 4, king's yellow was highly toxic and singularly unpleasant in use, and the organic yellows were best suited to glazing or distemper. Accordingly, although small areas of bright yellow may be found in heraldry or arabesque, the colour is not generally encountered on joinery elements such as doors. Once available, moreover, Naples yellow was costly and of only moderate tinting strength; and while it and patent yellow (made from the 1770s) went some way to alleviating the problem, this was not completely overcome until chrome yellow became available about 1820.

On acount of such considerations, certain paint colours came to be commonly associated with the particular tasks to which they were suited, whether application to plastered surfaces, joinery, or decorative picking-out. This is well illustrated by the range of proprietary 'WATER COLOURS' sold by John Pincot during the early nineteenth century, which was intended for the decoration of walls and, at least in one case, ceilings.[3] It included French green, green verditer, blue verditer, golden yellow, Dutch pink, and English pink, all but one of these, it will immediately be realised, taking their names from pigments appropriate to an aqueous medium, and thus commonly to be found on plaster rather than joinery elements. Nevertheless, it has to be said that there also existed a wide range of colours available with facility in all mediums; and Pincot's range contained also French grey, while Nicholson gave directions for mixing straw colour, fine and inferior greys, pea greens, and fawn in distemper, all of which could be prepared equally successfully in oil.[4]

One specific instance of the manner in which the character of a pigment acted to constrain the way in which colour could be used must also be mentioned. During the seventeenth century, smalt was used to provide brilliant blue grounds or highlights, generally on comparatively small or broken areas; but for this it had to be applied by the special technique of strewing described in Chapter 2. It was not very practical, therefore, to apply it to large expanses of plain plaster wall, where blue verditer in distemper would instead have been easily employed. The hue of the latter is, however, very different from that of smalt, and for its part is unlikely to have been very satisfactory in oil when applied to large expanses of wainscoting. It thus seems clear that when Roger Pratt remarked of blues, greens, and yellows, 'naught which works in the panels etc.' it was as a reflection of the fact that by no means all of the already limited range of paint colours available could be used with equal facility on all parts of an interior.[5]

A further significant limitation on the use of colours was imposed by the relative instability of some pigments when exposed to daylight. The organic reds and yellows were particularly prone to fading, but were more or less essential in the production of bright clean colours; and the prudent would accordingly have reserved their use for rooms not exposed to the sun or those which, being used only occasionally, were kept shut up for most of the time. Common corridor walls are therefore unlikely to have been painted very often in bright yellow or delicate pink; and, in an analogous way, John Rutter expressed surprise at the use of yellow fabric hangings in a room at Fonthill Abbey, Wiltshire, which had windows to the south and west, on account of the amount of light to which they were thus exposed.[6]

Intimately bound up with the question of physical practicality was the matter of cost. Even to the artist working on a limited area of canvas, the expense of a pigment such as ultramarine at several pounds per ounce was significant, but to the house-painter it virtually precluded its use. So large, moreover, were the areas with which the latter was generally concerned that cost differences between much cheaper pigments were of considerable significance; and the effect may be seen in the earliest price-list for ready-mixed tints so far encountered, that of Alexander Emerton, which was published in 1734:[7]

Pearl colour Lead colour Cream colour Stone colour Wainscot or oak colour	4*d.* and 5*d.* per pound
Chocolate colour Mahogany colour Cedar colour Walnut tree colour	6*d.* per pound
Gold colour	8*d.* per pound
Olive colour Pea colour Fine sky blue mixed with Prussian blue	8*d.* to 1*s.* per pound
Orange colour Lemon colour Straw colour Pink colour Blossom colour	1*s.* per pound
Fine deep green	2*s.* 6*d.* per pound.

The extremes of price resulting from the cost and proportion of the staining pigments may appear surprising in the present day, when it is possible to buy (if not to manufacture) an extremely wide range of paint colours at a uniform rate. Naturally this had a considerable impact on their use in interiors, the cheapest being used where expensive colours were unnecessary, while the latter had the capacity to imply wealth and status when used in important rooms or apartments. Undoubtedly the greatest use was made of colours from the most economical end of the scale, both in interiors and especially for exterior work; and lightfast varieties of these inevitably made up the everyday background against which the finer, more expensive, but often more fragile and fugitive colours were set. They were known, appropriately, as *common colours*, a group defined in late eighteenth-century editions of the *Builders Price-Book* as including all those listed by Emerton in his cheapest category together with chocolate, and, presumably, by extension the remainder of those in his second price bracket.[8] Such dull but stable browns, greys, and off-whites thus formed, together with white, the backbone of 'vernacular' colour, used ubiquitously on exteriors; and it is important to recognise the fact as highlighting the contrast between the exterior elevations of town houses, the rustic landscape, and the interiors of humble dwellings, and the fine rooms of a richly appointed aristocratic house. In dealing with the painting of exterior work, the seventeenth-century writer John Smith, for example, mentioned the use of stone colour, timber colour, lead colour and Spanish brown;[9] while in the early nineteenth century Pincot and Vanherman too mentioned similar colours in an exterior context, together with olive green.[10] This is not to say, of course, that certain expensive colours were not also used externally on occasion, especially in connection with prestigious buildings on which, most importantly, blue ironwork was seen for a long period as a mark of status.[11]

Blues (made using smalt in the seventeenth century, or Prussian blue in the eighteenth) were, of course, reasonably stable in historic terms, and could thus be employed out of doors; but the same did not apply to the majority of expensive colours available to the house-painter. Turning to these with reference to their cost, it is worth noting that in early nineteenth-century editions of the *Builders Price-Book* blues, greens, and the finer varieties of grey were described as 'rich clours'.[12] Pincot, on the other hand, ranged French grey, olive greens, and buffs together in a middle category, while including 'Verdigrease Green', vermilion, dark blue, and purples with 'very extravagant colours';[13] and Skyring mentioned French green, deep blue, and scarlet as 'superior colours'.[14] All three authors, together with John Philips and Laxton, gave lists of the prices applicable to such special tints, ranging up to an extra 9*d.* per square yard above the cost of common colours,[15] their suggestions perhaps based on rates laid down from time to time by the Painter-Stainers Company;[16] but the figures they gave at a time of changing monetary values were not entirely consistent, and it is impossible to reduce them to a simple table. Much of the time, in fact, it seems quite probable that every painter would strike his own bargain for such work, especially outside London; but in general, it can be seen that prices increased depending on the cost and proportion of the staining pigments required. This may be broadly summarised in ascending order of cost as follows:

(1) Colours in which the moderately priced staining pigments, such as the better quality ochres, were used, or tints in which only small quantities of more expensive varieties, such as Prussian blue or the more moderately priced red lakes, were needed. Examples would include olive green, buffs, drabs, fawn, warm tints, and French grey.

(2) Deeper colours, such as greens, lilac, and peach colour, needing a greater addition of the more expensive pigments, in particular the lakes, Prussian blue, or vermilion.

(3) The most saturated colours of all, needing very large proportions of expensive pigment or the use of extremely costly varieties such as distilled verdigris, vermilion, or the higher-grade lakes. These would have included verdigris greens, dark blue, purple, patent greens, and scarlet.

The colours mentioned above (all of which were cited as examples illustrating different costs in the early nineteenth-century lists of Pincot, Laxton and Skyring) do not, of course, exhaust the range available, and were simply instanced by these authors in order to convey the broad principles which lay behind pricing to those who, through familiarity with the implications of general practice, would have an immediate grasp of their significance. The tradition is lost today, when cost has ceased to be a factor in the design of a colour scheme, but throughout the period under consideration it was undoubtedly of considerable importance.

In an age accustomed to opening a paint tin and applying a ready-mixed colour where fancy dictates, the constraints imposed by cost and the limitations of historic technology may seem complex. Beyond those listed above, there were, however, further matters which had to be borne in mind. Some pigments were incompatible with each other and could not be combined, so that king's yellow, for example, could not be used with white lead, nor Prussian blue with lime. In addition, skill was required in choosing between different varieties of the same pigment, a matter often also having cost implications. Between the red ochres, for instance, lie significant differences when they are used for tinting, samples which look identical in powder or paste form producing quite varied effects when mixed with white. Legislation too could have its effect, notably the requirement of the 1603 Act which allowed the plasterers to use nothing except 'Whiting, Blacking, Red-lead, Red-oker, Yellow-oker, and Russet, mingled with Size only, and not with Oil'.[17] Altogether such constraints resulted in a system of colour mixing in which certain tried and tested combinations played a prominent part, while others were used in circumstances where a particular effect was required. Above all, historic colour-mixing was not simply a question of taking the first pigments to hand, but an art which required application, experience, and an eye to economy if success was to be achieved.

In approaching particular ways of mixing colours, it is important to appreciate that advice given in the books forming the basis of the present study is generally couched in very broad terms. Only rarely were quantified formulae given; and even where these do appear, it is important to recognise that it is not possible to reconstruct a colour exactly. Different samples of white lead or chalk vary in their whiteness and reducing power, and coloured pigments in their brilliancy of hue, tinting power, and even colour itself, so that seemingly definitive formulae are of less absolute help than might at first be supposed. More often, in fact, directions for mixing merely give the names of the pigments to be combined, or at best indicate only in principle the quantities to be employed. Thus, for example, Vanherman suggested that *French grey* should be prepared by adding Prussian blue to white until a sufficient depth of colour was achieved, followed by as much organic red 'as will bestow on it a faint bloom'.[18]

This state of affairs reflects, though, the essential nature of the historic approach to colour and its mixing. In an age without universally laid down national standards, colours were inevitably conceptual in nature, and the various colour names in use never represented exact tints. The Edinburgh house-painter D.R. Hay, for example, remarked of *pomona green* that it took its name from the colour of an apple, 'and consequently admits of ample latitude as to variety of tone'.[19] There was, therefore, neither a definitive pomona green nor French grey, but the terms were understood between architect and house-painter as implying an area of colour which the latter could mix, often within quite wide limits, to meet the particular circumstances in which it was required. At a time in which on-site mixing was the norm, account could thus be taken of the subjective colour shift present when such a colour as French grey was seen against red damask, for example, and more red added to the paint to compensate for this; while if the damask was blue, less red would be required to give the desired 'bloom'; and a parallel situation prevailed with other colours.

In addition, of course, colours might occasionally be greyed, an operation normally carried out by the addition of black rather than by mixture with a complementary hue as is often advocated today.[20] In Appendix A are given references to all the colour names and mixing methods advocated for them encountered to date, and the remainder of this chapter will be devoted to consideration of the ways in which broad categories of different colours were generally prepared. In this connection it should be noted, however, that although on the basis of the evidence currently available all the commonly employed mixtures are probably included, it is quite possible that others were occasionally used, even if only on an *ad hoc* basis.

WHITES

The use of white in interiors was of fundamental importance throughout the period being considered. During the second half of the sixteenth century, William Harrison had commented on the 'delectable whitenesse' of plaster ceilings, a preference shared in the mid-seventeenth by Pratt;[21] while by the second half of the eighteenth white had come to form the essential foundation for the use of colour in all parts of the interior. Although the pigments available, notably chalk and white lead (samples 1 & 2), were rather duller in tone than titanium white, which forms the basis of many paints today, the great defect of early whites was not so much the difficulty of obtaining a modern brilliance, but their tendency to yellow, both in oil and distemper. Indeed, only one author, Tingry's later editor, referred directly to a dullness of tone, merely observing in passing that in distemper whiting produced a duller colour than lime, without suggesting that this was necessarily any disadvantage.[22] Instead, writers from Watin onwards were unanimous in condemning too great a brilliance in whites, so that Pincot, for example, recommended the addition of a little black to oil paint for interior work, observing that it 'takes off the rawness of the white', and the addition of a little blue black to distemper in order to make it 'cover better, and look sound'.[23]

There was, moreover, another reason for the greying of whites. Vanherman, who recommended the addition of a litle vine black, remarked that white 'by itself, has been of late years universally disused, for two principal reasons – first its staring, glaring colour; second its fugitive quality'.[24] This remark has, of course, to be placed in the context of an age when colour theory had led to the tinting of whites with colour,[25] but it seems clear that Vanherman was also referring to the tendency of oil to discolour in interior conditions. No doubt part of the attraction of the flatted oil finishes discussed in Chapter 15, which became increasingly used in high-class interiors from the 1740s, was their reduced tendency to yellow on account of the lower oil content in the finish; and, as discussed in Chapter 10, walnut oil had been used to the same end in the seventeenth century and early part of the eighteenth. In distemper, the latter was paralleled by occasional use of one of the better qualities of size, or its complete omission, a topic dealt with in Chapters 14 and 17.

Even so, these practices did not completly alleviate the problem, especially in everyday work where cost precluded their employment. Thus, in 1788 Charles Seguin noted that a little lamp or charcoal black should be added to distemper to prevent yellowing;[26] and in 1819 Nicholson advised that the finishing coat of white in oil should have a little ivory or lamp black added in order to reduce the whiteness and preserve the colour from changing owing to discolouration in the oil. (Later he recommended blue-black.)[27] Watin too, remarking on the tendency to yellow in whites, either in oil or distemper, recommended the addition of a little blue or charcoal-black;[28] and, probably for the same reason, in a 'receipt for painting rooms' in her notebook of 1756–70, Elizabeth Raper included a small quantity of blue-black in oil undercoats and a little Prussian blue in the finish.[29] In flatting, Pincot advocated 'a little tint of Prussian blue',[30] and Butcher recommended the addition of black or Prussian blue 'to clear the white';[31] while Tingry remarked that white was usually 'heightened' with blue,[32] and his later editor noted this was often done with Prussian blue in smoky towns such as London.[33] At first, the common use of black rather than blue may seem surprising, but experiment has shown that the practice, which was clearly widespread, is sound.

GREYS

Although exceptions, such as the suggestion made by Reynolds for mixing pearl colour by the combination of white with Prussian blue and yellow ochre,[34] may be found, the formulae given for greys by the various authors noted fall generally into three groups: simple mixtures of white with black, to which blue might also be added; mixtures of blue and white; and mixtures of blue, white, and red.

The first (samples 7, 10) is the commonest method described, lamp, ivory, and charcoal blacks being generally employed, although the first of these, being rather greasy in nature, was not very well suited to distemper. Such simple greys were proposed by D'Aviler, while John Smith suggested the use of lamp black to mix ash colour in oil.[35] Of authors recommending the inclusion of blue in greys based on the addition of black to a white base, Watin suggested the use of Prussian blue in *gris perle* and indigo in *gris argentin*;[36] while Tingry, no doubt basing his advice on Watin, suggested that a mixture of blue and black could be used in silver or pearl grey, and the author of the *Painter's . . . Pocket Manual* suggested a combination of indigo and black for these and a dark lead colour.[37] Apart from Watin, who noted that his formulae could also be used in distemper, the only writer to make a specific suggestion of this type for the latter medium was Nicholson, who proposed the use of indigo with black in inferior greys.[38] It must be remembered, however, that charcoal blacks were often marketed with an admixture of Prussian blue (see Chapter 9), and the inclusion of blue in greys may, therefore, often have been unwitting.

Only two oil formulae employing blue alone have been encountered, both dating from the seventeenth century. John Smith's lead colour (in contrast to later suggestions for its mixing) contained indigo (sample 11), and Bullet's *gris perle*, smalt (sample 9).[39] The latter combination has been found on one of the lower layers on a mid-seventeenth-century doorcase now in the Banqueting Hall at Tamworth Castle, Staffordshire,[40] and also formed one of the early finishes applied to the wainscot in the Marble Hall at Petworth, Sussex, which was first painted in 1692.[41] In distemper, Bullet indicated that *gris perle* was mixed using indigo (sample 8),[42] and blue verditer too was advocated for greys in this medium, refiner's verditer being mentioned by Nicholson for the preparation of fine greys,[43] and verditer of unspecified type, but most probably blue, in connection with French grey by Skyring and another early nineteenth-century writer, A.G. Cook.[44] The latter, however, were not giving complete mixing directions, and may have intended the colour should also contain other pigments.

The most subtle greys were made by the third method described, generally in oil by the combination of white with Prussian blue and a carmine lake (sample 12). Such mixtures seem absent from the early literature, but were described by Watin, Tingry, Nicholson (who incorporated ivory black), Butcher, the author of the *Painter's . . . Pocket Manual*, and Vanherman,[45] and, although also called simply grey or flaxen grey, were generally known in

England as French grey. In addition, Nicholson gave a similar formula for pearl colour, substituting Indian red for the lake;[46] while Whittock used Venetian red in a grey distemper.[47] It seems possible too that in distemper rose pink might have been used in this way.

BLACK

From an early date, intensely black paints could be prepared, notably for application to chimney-backs, the walls of tennis courts, or, in a varnish medium, for ironwork. Evidence for their formulation is reviewed in the glossary of colour names forming Appendix A.

BRIGHT PURPLES AND LILAC COLOURS

The first formula for a purplish colour in house-painting which has been encountered is that suggested by Watin, who gave directions for the preparation of *violet*.[48] He and the authors of subsequent recommendations for similar colours (such as lavender, lilac, and purple) are virtually unanimous in advocating the use of an organic red lake and (where a particular blue pigment is specified) Prussian blue, with white (samples 37, 38);[49] but the author of the *Painter's . . . Pocket Manual* suggested the employment of vermilion or red lead with black or blue for violet colour, and added 'dark red' (presumably a red ochre) to this to make purple.[50] The mixture of lake with Prussian blue is, of course, related to methods for the preparation of French grey discussed above; but obviously the more deeply tinted versions were considerably more expensive, and Pincot included purples in his list of 'very extravagant colours',[51] while Laxton illustrated the costliness of lilac compared with others.[52]

BRIGHT REDS AND PINKS

It will be remembered from the discussion of red pigments in Chapters 6 and 7 that, of the durable colours, the iron oxides were generally dull in tone, while vermilion was much more expensive; and red lead, although bright, was thought by some to blacken with age when used in oil. The organic pigments were transparent in the latter medium, and even the very expensive grades were fugitive, the cheaper varieties being extremely so. The problem to be faced in the production of red and pink paint was therefore to reconcile these constraints and achieve a compromise between cost, the desirable brightness of colour, and durability. In general, this seems often to have been effected in oil by means of a mixture of vermilion (sample 13) and carmine lake (sample 16), the latter giving life to the otherwise heavy, though bright, red of the former, and the vermilion tempering the purplish tendency of the carmine while imparting greater stability to the depth of colour. In this connection the common manufacturing practice of precipitating carmine onto vermilion will be remembered. Against such mixtures the red ochres (sample 31) are very brown in colour, and dull reds containing them will be discussed in due course.

Looking first at methods for formulating bright reds in oil, Reynolds mentioned the use of vermilion, red lead, and rose pink in making reds for interior purposes,[53] and Tingry referred to the use of vermilion to make a red varnish for *buffets*.[54] Between 1812 and 1817, John Soane used vermilion in oil on the walls of the Study at 13 Lincoln's Inn Fields, London, the finish including a little black and being varnished;[55] but in eighteenth-century interiors such intense colours seem generally to have been reserved for small discrete elements. Instances include the grounds of paterae in a number of ceiling designs,[56] and the pink and green ribbons on a ceiling design by James Wyatt which were to be 'touch'd with Carmine'.[57] Watin, indeed, warned against the more general use of the colour, remarking of red pigments: 'Les Peintres d'impression n'en sont guère usage, que pour les carreaux d'appartemens; l'uniformité d'une teinte rouge ne flatte pas assez la vue.'[58]

Turning to the pigments employed for red and pink distempers, the exclusion of vermilion from the list of those the plasterers to the City of London were permitted to use in this medium under the 1603 Act is important. Instead, they were allowed only red lead, red ochre, and 'Russet' (sample 17), a limitation which would have effectively precluded the preparation of the most intense reds.[59] Given the cost and nature of vermilion, these are more likely in any case to have been produced in oil; but for pinks, red ochres or combinations of red lead and the cheaper organic reds would have sufficed, the latter probably being employed in a way comparable with vermilion and carmine mixtures in oil.

In oil, John Smith recommended the use of lake with white (sample 16) to mix carnation, a suggestion copied by Nicholson and the author of the *Painter's . . . Pocket Manual*.[60] It seems to have been more common, however, to include vermilion in the mix, and to produce pinks (such as apricot, flesh colour, peach, and rose) by mixtures of carmine lake (or cheaper varieties) with vermilion and white in varying proportions (sample 14). Although duller pinks can be made by mixing red ochre with white, such a combination being suggested by Nicholson for flesh colour,[61] the former seems to have been the more usual method in better-class work; and it is significant in this connection that in the price lists of Emerton and the *Builders Price-Book* pink and blossom colour appear in the more expensive categories.[62]

DULLER REDS, BROWNS, AND PURPLES

In considering bright reds and pinks, reference has been made to the duller, brownish red of the ochres (samples 31, 39). The commonest of those in use was Spanish brown, whose name, like that of purple brown and other ochres, came also to be applied as a paint colour. Often, however, the more expensive grades, such as Venetian red, were used in interiors where their qualities in producing a more delicate and subtle colour were important. Vanherman, for example, used the latter in a red he recommended for picture galleries, noting that used with white and a little black it would produce a 'dark blotting-paper colour'.[63] Alternatively, the colour of red ochres could be heightened, and Reynolds, for example, added a proportion of red lead in a formula for an exterior red.[64] In making dark browns such as chocolate, rather than use umber (sample 34), which was more expensive, red ochre would generally be combined with larger quantities of black, often without the use of white (samples 32, 33); and for lighter tones such as chestnut and walnut, yellow ochre might also be added (sample 36) or used in combination with umber (sample 35).

YELLOWS

Until the introduction of chrome yellow in the early nineteenth century, production of yellow paint by the house-painter was subject to particularly significant constraints imposed by the character of the other pigments reviewed in Chapters 4 and 5. Yellow ochre (sample 19) was cheap, but although it provided stable colours when used in oil or distemper, either on its own or mixed with white, these were rather dull in tone. Nevertheless, Tingry noted its employment for yellows,[65] and both John Smith and Reynolds suggested that it should be combined with white to make straw colour.[66]

Reynolds, however, had an exterior context in mind, and for interior purposes a brighter colour was often required. This need was commonly met by the use of organic yellows in distemper (sample 21), and, taking his cue from Watin's formulae for *jonquille* and *citron*,[67] Tingry indicated that jonquil was made using Dutch pink, noting that it was prepared only in distemper, although a varnish medium could also be used. The same was true of lemon yellow, in which Dutch pink was combined with Naples yellow.[68] As usual, the author of the *Painter's . . . Pocket Manual* copied Tingry, indicating that the two colours could be produced only in distemper;[69] and Nicholson used Dutch pink in a distemper medium for straw colour.[70] Although in his formulae for *jonquille* and *citron* Watin does not appear to rule out use of an oil medium with *stil de grain*, and Butcher certainly seems to have suggested the use of Dutch or English pink for fine yellow in oil,[71] there is little doubt that organic yellows were probably less satisfactory in oil, except where applied as a glaze to small details; and for purposes of the application of bright yellow to larger areas, a distemper medium seems undoubtedly to have been the norm.

Organic yellows were, of course, extremely fugitive; but the alternative inorganic pigments each had other disadvantages. Thus, although Watin suggested the use of orpiment in conjunction with realgar for *citron*,[72] Tingry noted that the combination was out of favour on account of its toxicity;[73] and Vanherman warned against the use of king's yellow in the strongest possible terms.[74] The use actually made of these pigments accordingly remains obscure; and the same is true of massicot (lead-tin yellow), which John Smith mentioned only in connection with the colouring of prints.[75] It seems quite likely, though, that the latter was too expensive for general use, and, as indicated in Chapter 4, had become obsolete by the mid-eighteenth century. Thus Nicholson's proposal of 1819 for employment of massicot in straw-coloured distemper seems questionable, especially since it appears likely that by then the name was being applied to canary litharge, which is of pale colour and has a marked tendency to blacken.[76]

With the availability of Naples yellow for house-painting in the mid-eighteenth century and the introduction of patent yellow in the 1770s, the position was only partially ameliorated, since the former was comparatively expensive and of only moderate staining power, and the latter could discolour rapidly in oil and distemper. Nevertheless, Watin used Naples yellow (sample 22) in a formulae for *citron*, and Tingry too mentioned its use in mixing yellows in oil, varnish, or water.[77] There seems, however, to have been a tendency to strengthen its character by the addition of other pigments. For *couleur d'or*, for example, Watin combined it with yellow ochre;[78] while as already noted Tingry mixed it with Dutch pink in lemon yellow distemper, a formula copied by the author of the *Painter's . . . Pocket Manual*, who suggested too the use of Naples yellow and realgar in gold colour.[79]

Patent yellow (sample 23) was recommended by Tingry for yellows, including gold colour, instancing its general use in oil, distemper, or varnish.[80] The pigment was also advocated by Butcher for use in fine yellows, presumably in oil;[81] but it will be recalled that it had a tendency to discolour, and Vanherman recommended that it should be varnished,[82] a treatment found during technical investigation of the first-floor drawing rooms at the Soane Museum.[83]

Leaving aside the combinations of Naples yellow with ochre, realgar, or an organic yellow mentioned above, yellow pigments seem often to have been combined singly with white, although Tingry did suggest the use of realgar with yellow ochre in a method for mixing a golden yellow.[84] It thus appears to have been recognised that the defects of the yellows available could not generally be overcome by mixing; and it was only about 1820, at the very end of the period being considered, when chrome yellow (sample 24) became cheap enough for house-painting, that the problem of bright yellow oil paint was really solved. Vanherman was then able to recommend this pigment for mixing straw colour;[85] but until then painters had only been able to accept the limitations of contemporary technology, and, of all the colours, yellow undoubtedly illustrates best the way in which design could be constrained by the materials available.

ORANGES

The basic method for mixing orange colours seems to have been by combining red lead and yellow ochres, with or without white (sample 15). John Smith used this for both orange and brick colour,[86] a suggestion copied by the author of the *Painter's . . . Pocket Manual* and employed too by Reynolds in an orange for exterior work.[87] Exceptionally, Vanherman suggested the use of vermilion with ochre in his orange 'aromatic' paint for interiors.[88] Curiously, a mixture of red and yellow ochres (sample 18) does not seem to have been mentioned, and produces by comparison a rather brownish tone, but may have been employed during the first half of the seventeenth century to produce lute colour.

Tingry alone proposed the use of orpiment, suggesting it should be slightly calcined to make marigold, although this advice seems highly unsafe.[89] Interestingly, no recommendations for the employment of the organic reds and yellows have been noted until after the introduction of chrome yellow; but in the late 1820s Vanherman suggested that this immediately popular pigment could be mixed with an organic red to make brilliant orange.[90]

OFF-WHITES

Little need be written concerning the pale off-white colours used by the house-painter. For making buffs, creams, drabs, fawns, quaker tints, and, above all, stone colours, the ochres, umbers, and blacks rank above all others in importance (samples 3 to 6), although brighter reds were often added (sample 20); and for particularly clean tints others, such as the organic yellows, may occasionally have been pressed into service.

GREENS

Although green verditer (sample 46) allowed the production of brilliant greens in distemper throughout the period under consideration, the preparation of bright greens in oil undoubtedly provided the house-painter with more of a challenge. Verdigris (sample 41) was, of course, extensively used, often combined with a little yellow to remove its bluish cast; but it was expensive and, even where employed in the form of a copper resinate (sample 42), tended to discolour. Once Prussian blue became available in the early eighteenth century, it also became feasible to mix greens by combining it with organic yellows or yellow ochres (sample 43), but such combinations were either fugitive or comparatively dull in colour; and it was not until the commercial availability of Naples yellow (sample 44) that the position improved. However, the latter was quite costly; and, although patent yellow (sample 45) soon provided a cheaper (but less stable) alternative, the matter was fully resolved only by the arrival of chrome yellow (sample 48) during the 1820s.

At the end of the seventeenth century, John Smith, writing in connection with oil paint, dismissed green bice (malachite) and verditer as seldom used. The best and most useful pigment was, he indicated, verdigris (sample 41), which he described as 'a delicate Green inclining to a Bluish, but with a little Pink-Yellow, it makes the delicatest Grass-Green in the World'.[91] His greens for house-painting were willow green, which was pure verdigris (a light variety was made with the addition of white lead), and grass green, which included the organic yellow pigment, pink.[92] These formulae were copied by the author of the *Painter's . . . Pocket Manual*,[93] but other more independent writers throughout the period being considered mentioned the use of verdigris; and as late as 1830 Tingry's editor remarked that it was used for green of the finest kind.[94] Its expense has been mentioned in Chapter 3, and the very high price of Emerton's fine deep green, which may have contained verdigris, will be remembered.[95] Use of distilled verdigris in the form of a copper resinate will also be recalled, either as a green glaze or mixed with white lead to produce a paler green paint (sample 42).

John Smith's suggestion that yellow could be combined with verdigris is echoed in advice given by other writers. Nicholson and the author of the *Painter's . . . Pocket Manual*, of course, both copied directly from Smith;[96] but Reynolds added yellow to verdigris to make sea-green paint for interiors and parrot-green for exterior purposes;[97] Watin and Tingry suggested its mixture with yellow ochre and a little black to make olive colour in oil;[98] and the author of the *Painter's . . . Pocket Manual* provided a related formula for the same colour using organic yellow.[99] Watin also suggested the combination of verdigris with organic yellow and Prussian blue to make *vert-pomme* and *vert-Saxe*;[100] while Bullet had earlier used it with *vert de montagne* (malachite) and white lead to make a green paint for garden furniture.[101] Undoubtedly, therefore, verdigris was of prime importance for the manufacture of bright greens in oil from early times, and its colour was often modified by the use of yellow and blue pigments.

John Smith's rejection of malachite and green verditer in oil has already been mentioned; and although 'Best green verditer' is included in the list of prices for oil colours in the *Builders Price-Book*,[102] it will be remembered that Tingry and the author of the *Painter's . . . Pocket Manual* showed that its colour could be obtained in that medium by the use of verdigris rather than verditer.[103] The only author encountered to mention the use of copper carbonate in oil is D'Aviler, who employed *vert de montagne* in his finishing coat for garden furniture;[104] but this seems to have been a specialised application. In distemper, however, verditers and related copper carbonate pigments (sample 46) undoubtedly enjoyed considerable use throughout the period under review. Watin combined *vert de montagne* and ceruse in *vert d'eau*;[105] Laxton listed pea-green distemper 'with verditter';[106] Nicholson mentioned 'pea green in distemper with French green' (the latter a copper carbonate pigment produced by Lewis Berger's company);[107] and Pincot retailed French green and green verditer 'Water colours'.[108] Evidence for the contemporary use of copper chloride pigments has been reviewed in Chapter 3.

Combinations of blue verditer and organic yellow to make green distemper were recommended by Watin, who remarked that *vert d'eau* made in this way had more life than that made from pure *vert de montagne*, and was less likely to change colour with time.[109] He also suggested the employment of organic yellow with Prussian blue in preparing *vert de composition*, which could be used in distemper; while to make olive-green distemper both he and Tingry advocated the mixture of yellow ochre with indigo.[110]

Turning to blue and yellow pigments available during the seventeenth century for use in oil, it is notable that, despite his reservations about blue verditer in this medium, John Smith noted that it made a good green with yellows;[111] and such combinations have been found in late eighteenth-century oil paint at Somerset House and Frogmore House, illustrating their practical service a hundred years later.[112] Interestingly, John Smith only suggested use of indigo in oil to make French green in the colouring of mezzotints, but Tingry suggested its employment with an organic yellow in turpentine varnish for one of his compound greens for rooms.[113] Nor is king's yellow advocated in early literature, although in the early nineteenth century Whittock mentioned its use with blue, suggesting in particular its combination with verditer, Prussian blue, and whiting to mix a light delicate green in distemper; and its combination with indigo has been noted in a distemper of unknown but probably very early date.[114] Besides such bright greens, extremely dull tones were commonly used during the earlier part of the period being considered, and D'Aviler referred to *couleur d'olive* as being made by mixing yellow ochre with black (sample 40); while a similar mixture was later mentioned by Vanherman in connection with drab greens.[115]

With the discovery of Prussian blue, a new range of greens which did not place reliance on the use of verdigris became available in both oil and distemper, and were probably especially important in the former medium. They may be divided into two categories: those in which Prussian blue was combined with yellow ochres (sample 43); and those in which organic yellows were used. The latter brighter but far less lightfast alternative was mentioned only by Watin and Tingry, Watin suggesting it for *vert de mer* and *vert de composition* (the latter being translated into the English edition of Tingry as 'compound green'); but, although Watin noted that the latter colour could be used in oil or distemper, it seems questionable if either would have been extensively used for house-painting in oil.[116] For some reason, both authors neglected the use of ochre with Prussian blue, but English references to this combination are abundant, common appellations including 'inferior green', 'olive', or simply 'green'; and it is significant that in accounts for the purchase of painting materials at Osterley Park between 1779 and 1781 quantities of Prussian blue are often associated with items for stone ochre.[117] Of particular interest as reflecting early nineteenth-century practice are Vanherman's remarks concerning pea (probably a misprint for tea), sage, and drab greens. There were, he indicated, made from spruce ochre and Prussian blue, lowered with white. He noted, however, that raw umber could be substituted for the ochre, or black for the blue to obtain further varieties of green. All were chosen, he added, 'on account of their repose to the sight, and their solid and quiet tone.'[118] Prussian blue and yellow ochre were described by Tingry's editor as being used for inferior greens,[119] and the combination was probably standard from the early eighteenth century for the majority of instances where a green was required.

From about the middle of the eighteenth century, it seems clear that Naples yellow came into use for mixing greens with Prussian blue (sample 44), although no published formulae for this have been noted. Nevertheless, the pigment has been found in greens forming part of the original scheme of decoration dating from 1768–9 in the Drawing Room from Lansdowne House (now in the Philadelphia Museum of Art),[120] and has also been identified in a green of 1780 at Somerset House.[121] It seems likely, therefore, that the 'Naples green' used in 1786 in the Long Bow Room at Gordon Castle, Morayshire, may have contained this pigment.[122]

The use of patent yellow with Prussian blue to produce a green (sample 45) was recommended by Butcher and Nicholson,[123] and an example of this combination has been found in a green probably forming part of the original scheme of the mid-1780s in the Outer Library at Attingham Hall, Shrophire.[124] Despite the instability Vanherman later attributed to such mixtures,[125] these and other references to use of the pigment (see Chapter 4) suggest its fairly widespread employment from the 1780s.

The extent to which Scheele's green (sample 47), which became available in the 1780s, was used in house-painting remains enigmatic, although it probably enjoyed particular favour in the printing of wallpaper, often, perhaps, combined with blue. Like the copper chloride greens, which were possibly available from the mid-1760s, its principal use seems more likely to have been in distemper in than oil, and references supporting this contention have been discussed in Chapter 3.

Once chrome yellow (sample 48) became available for house-painting, however, its advantages seem quickly to have been taken up. As will already be clear from Chapter 3, Vanherman and Lewis Berger's sons made extensive use of chrome yellow Brunswick green, and in addition both combined chrome yellow with various other pigments including black (Berger's quaker green),[126] copper carbonate pigments (Berger's Persian green),[127] copper carbonate and Prussian blue (Vanherman's Berlin, olive, and Saxon greens),[128] and with verditer and Scheele's green (Berger's American green).[129]

The other new pigment, emerald green, seems also to have enjoyed application, Berger's sons using it with chrome yellow to make permanent pea green,[130] and adding this to Prussian blue to make aquatic and marine greens;[131] while indigo was substituted for Prussian blue in Chinese green.[132] Emerald green has been identified in decorative painting on the throne in the House of Lords, Palace of Westminster, dating from 1847.[133]

BLUES

The two principal pigments used for the production of blue paint during the eighteenth and early nineteenth centuries were blue verditer and Prussian blue. The former (sample 27) was best suited to a distemper medium, in which it produced a distinctive bright blue of slightly greenish cast. This may be seen, for example in Pyne's early nineteenth-century illustration of an ante-room at Carlton House, which was, he noted, decorated in blue distemper;[134] and it will be recalled in this connection that Pincot produced a proprietary 'WATER COLOUR' which he called 'blue verditter'.[135] The pigment was used to a limited extent in oil, both with white lead for the production of paler tints, and to produce an intense blue on small decorative elements. An instance of the former has been found, for example, on the frieze in the Mary Moser Room at Frogmore dating from the mid-1790s;[136] and blue verditer with linseed oil in deep blue touches on enrichments of white-painted joinery mouldings in the Saloon at the Casino, Marino, about 1770.[137] Prussian blue, on the other hand, was better suited to oil, and could produce a wide range of tints from pale to very deep blue (samples 28, 29). Thus, in the 1730s, Emerton retailed 'Fine Sky Blue mixed with Prussian Blue, ground in Oil';[138] and Watin recommended the use of Prussian blue with ceruse in mixing *bleu tendre, bleu céleste, bleu de Roi,* and *bleu turc.*[139] The pigment also worked well in distemper, but was subject to discolouration in alkaline conditions, such as those presented by fresh lime plaster. Nevertheless, special varieties of 'wet blue' were made for use in distemper, and these and instances of its employment in this medium have been discussed in Chapter 2. In addition, it may be noted that a mixture of Prussian blue and blue verditer has been found in the ground of a wallpaper of about 1780, possibly used with the intention of reducing the greenish tone of the verditer;[140] and it is thus possible that similar combinations may have been used for house-painting in distemper.

Prior to the invention of Prussian blue in the early eighteenth century, blues in oil were more difficult to produce. Of the two blue pigments which worked well in the medium, natural ultramarine was far too expensive for application to large areas, and indigo (sample 11) produced a dull greyish colour (called by John Smith lead colour and discussed above in connection with greys).[141] Blue verditer, which was available from the beginning of the seventeenth century, was accordingly pressed into service, as in the 'fair blew in Oylle' used in the Dining Chamber (now the Round Gallery) at Ham House in 1638;[142] and azurite (sample 26) was probably used in the same manner. The brightest blue obtainable was that produced by strewing smalt on a ground of wet white lead in the way described in Chapter 2 (sample 25) and found on the entabature and enriched ceiling beams of the late 1630s in the Queen's Cabinet at the Queen's House, Greenwich.[143] There is also evidence suggesting that azurite too was employed in this way before the Civil War, and a fuller discussion of the use of these pigments will be found in Chapter 2.

At the very end of the period under consideration, French ultramarine (sample 30) became available. From then on, it is commonly encountered as a constitutent in oil and distemper; and was used, for example, for the blue in the ground of the frieze beneath the timber roof in Lincoln's Inn Hall, dating from 1843–5,[144] and at the end of the decade on the throne in the House of Lords.[145]

APPENDICES

NOTES

SOURCES

INDEX

APPENDIX A

GLOSSARY OF COLOUR NAMES

The Glossary below is designed to record all the colour names encountered in the course of research, and, as far as practicable, to define the nature of the hues, tints, and shades which they represented. In some cases this remains enigmatic, but in others it is possible to obtain a fairly good idea of the colour concepts they conveyed, principally through the formulae recorded for their mixing. Sometimes, of course, colours were intended for exterior purposes, and authors did not always make the context in which they were to be employed clear, so that some colours or formulations listed may not have been used indoors. Pigment names are included only where applied to paint colours or for a commercial blend.

The entries are arranged in alphabetical order, rather than by colour groups. Where an ordinary name such as 'green' was frequently qualified, for example as 'pea green', this will be found under 'Green, pea'. It should also be noted that, especially during the earlier part of the period under review, a colour such as 'pearl grey' was often known as 'pearl colour', and for the majority of these the latter mode of expression has been used, with a corresponding cross reference. In general, no account has been taken of adjectives such as bright, dark, deep, dull, fair, fine, finest, light, pale, rich, sad, superior, or superfine, except where the qualification seems to have had implications for formulation.

Aerial tints. In 1819 Pyne described the ceiling of the Lower Vestibule at Carlton House as painted in 'aerial tints', by which, his illustration shows, he meant a clouded ceiling.[1] The term seems, on the other hand, also to have been used for ordinary paint colour, since Vanherman recommended that in planning the colour scheme for a house, as one advanced higher in the building 'the aerial tint' should be adopted.[2] This was, no doubt, an allusion to the aerial perspective of landscape painters, in which the receding planes of a composition are rendered successively more bluish to reproduce the effect of distance; and the term thus seems to have implied a bluish cast.

Amaranthe. Rondelet noted that *amarante* was available with a matt finish in the range of *couleurs lucidoniques* which had been manufactured in Paris since 1803.[3]

Apricot. Nicholson suggested apricot (and peach) could be mixed in oil by the combination of lake, Chinese vermilion, and white (cf. sample 14).[4]

Ash colour. John Smith described ash colour as a mixture of white with lamp black (sample 10), indicating it could be made darker or lighter as required.[5] In the early nineteenth century Nicholson copied his formula.[6] Other names for such cheap, basic greys will be found below.

Black. Apart from Vanherman and Tingry's later editor, who suggested the use of mineral black and black wadd respectively in cheap exterior paints (considered below), writers from the late seventeenth century to the early nineteenth seem virtually unanimous in stating that lamp black was the pigment employed in making black paint. The other exception noted is Butcher, who suggested that either lamp black or ivory black could be used,[7] but the latter would have possessed less body in oil although it might have been better in distemper. Otherwise, Bullet, Stalker & Parker, Watin, Tingry, Reynolds, and Nicholson all stipulated the use of lamp black in oil and varnish formulae.[8] In oil, Bullet combined it with a little white lead, which might have given the black a slightly greyish tendency; but Reynolds suggested the use of Spanish white, which would have acted merely as an extender. For a better colour and improved durability, however, he advocated the use of lamp black alone, and this too seems to have been Watin's invariable practice for finishes; although in a black undercoat for exterior ironwork he used a little umber, presumably as a drier. Bullet and Watin both stipulated the use of boiled oil, the latter combining it with three parts of raw linseed oil for use, no doubt because this would add both to the gloss of the paint and to its speed of drying.

For both interior and exterior work a varnish medium could also be used. Stalker & Parker described the preparation of black japan (a product sold by the Ripon varnish-maker Williamson during the eighteenth century),[9] and black was also available in the range of *couleurs lucidoniques* manufactured in Paris from 1803, being one of the colours advertised as drying with a gloss.[10] Watin's two formulae for black varnishes, spirit-based for interior work and oil-based for exteriors, have been described in Chapter 18, the latter being used on the black oil undercoat already mentioned; and Vanherman's black varnish formula has also been discussed. Evidence for the use of a distemper medium for black is provided by Gerbier's inclusion of a price of 1*d.* per square yard for: 'Walls done in faire black for a Tennis-Court' among others which relate to whitening and plasterwork.[11]

For exterior purposes, Vanherman gave directions for the preparation of a black 'IMPENETRABLE, OR ANTI-CORROSIVE PAINT' containing equal proportions of mineral black and crotia which he suggested was particularly suitable for the protection of ironwork;[12] and Tingry's later editor mentioned that black wadd was used with tar for the same purpose.[13] The London Patent Colour-Works advertised a black in their range of 'MINERAL, OR REFINED COAL-TAR PAINTS' for common outside work at a price of 20*s.* per cwt., a price which may be compared with that of the black in their range of 'IMPENETRABLE PAINTS IN LINSEED-OIL' at 52*s.* A second list printed by the same company gave the price of the latter as 56*s.*, which coincides exactly with the rates given by two other early nineteenth-century paint manufacturers, Crease and Bentley, for black in their ranges of oil paint and 'ANTI-CORROSIVE PAINT' respectively.[14] Vanherman, on the other hand, claimed that his black could be manufactured at a cost of approximately only 9*s.* 4*d.* per cwt.

For interior house-painting, black found a particular use on chimney-backs, references to this being found, for example, in accounts relating to the Queen's House at Greenwich, where an entry occurs in November 1677 'ffor 24 yds whited and blacked in size in 3 stone chimney peices',[15] and another in August 1711 'for blacking Chimnys'.[16] Items at Ditton Park in 1705 included '14 Chimney Backs done black';[17] in 1748 a total of sixteen rooms on the ground and first floors and in the attics at Henry Pelham's house in Arlington Street had their 'Chimneys black'd';[18] while in 1763 two chimneys at Egremont House (now the Naval and Military Club), Piccadilly, were 'plaister.[d] and Blackt'.[19] At Ditton and in the two London houses the unit cost was 12*d.*, but in 1794 a price of 9*d.* for 'Chimneys prepared and blacked' was suggested in the *Builders Price-Book*.[20] It is interesting to note that this entry is in the section on plasterer's prices, and the work at Arlington Street and Egremont House was performed by the plasterer. Other instances of a plasterer blacking chimneys are found at the Mansion House in London in 1748 and 1779;[21] in attic rooms at Osterley Park, Middlesex, in 1764;[22] and in smaller London houses in 1765.[23] The practice seems also to have persisted into the nineteenth century, and in 1827 it was ordered that the 'fire boards' in all the rooms at Dunham Massey were to be painted black.[24] In this connection, it is also worth noting that Watin described the use of powdered graphite in vinegar for polishing fireplace ironwork, a procedure copied by the author of the *Painter's . . . Pocket Manual*, although he mistranslated 'mine de plomb' as 'powdered lead ore'. After application of the wet suspension, the work was finished by rubbing with dry powdered graphite.[25]

Besides chimney-backs, black was used on other interior elements, including doors and skirting fascias. In 1662, for example, an item appears for 'blacking the bottom of the walls underneath the hangings' in the Queen's Chapel at St James's;[26] and in the early eighteenth century Moxon referred to 'blacking the bottom, or lower ports [sic] of rooms'.[27] A black door and skirting fascia are shown in Soane's 1823 perspective of the Old Board Room of the Board of Trade;[28] while a few years earlier Pyne recorded that the doors and window shutters in the Dining Room, and the surbase, plinth, stiles of the doors, and window shutters in the Lower Vestibule at Carlton House were similarly coloured.[29] Other examples may also be found.[30] Smaller details too could be coloured black, and in 1778 Adam annotated his design for the ceiling of the Lady's Dressing Room at Mellerstain, Berwickshire, to indicate its use.[31] At Osterley, 212 ft. run of 'cut fillet' were painted black in 1787;[32] and in 1802 the surveyor William Pepper drew an enriched cornice in a room at Milton Park, Buckinghamshire, in which the grounds between the flowers in the guilloche of the soffit were 'blacked in oil for effect at 1*d.*', flowers in a moulded ceiling frame being similarly treated.[33]

Finally, the use of black in connection with mourning formalities must be noted. The practice of hanging rooms with black fabric and painting furniture within the room black has been described in some detail by John Fowler & John Cornforth,[34] but it is clear that on such occasions architectural elements too might be painted in this way. When the Duchess of York died in 1671 her bedchamber was not only hung with black, but the doors and doorcases were coloured black to match;[35] and it seems likely that the Amber Room at Nostell Priory, Yorkshire, was similarly treated at some date during the nineteenth century since a layer of black was found on cross sections of paint from the joinery, but not on the entablature or ceiling.[36]

Blossom colour. Alexander Emerton's list of oil colours, which was published by Salmon in 1734 contained blossom colour.[37] The price of 1*s.* per pound, against 4*d.* for white lead, suggests that it was made using the expensive pigments vermilion and/or a carmine lake (cf. sample 14); and the colour name again appears in an expensive category of oil finishes at 10*d.* to 1*s.* per square yard in the 1787 and 1794 editions of the *Builders Price-Book*.[38] See also *Peach-blossom colour* below.

Blue. Methods of mixing blue have been reviewed in Chapter 21. The terms by which the colour name was qualified often reflected the addition of different quantities of staining pigment, a good example of this being provided by Reynolds for interior work in oil. To a basic quantity of 5 pounds of white lead, he suggested, $\frac{1}{2}$ ounce of Prussian blue should be added to make 'sky blue'; 1 ounce to make 'Prussian blue'; and 2 ounces to make 'navy blue'.[39] Watin too indicated that a whole range of blues, including *bleu tendre* and others discussed below, could be made in this way but did not give quantified formulae (cf. samples 28, 29).[40] The price of the paint would obviously depend on the amount of comparatively expensive staining pigment added to the white base, so that Phillips, for instance, listed a whole range of blues, probably made using Prussian blue, in ascending order of price. In 1812, fine sky blue cost 1*s.* 6*d.* per pound, a darker version 1*s.* 10*d.*, another blue suitable for balusters and railings 2*s.* 5*d.*, a darker variety 3*s.* 7*d.*, and one still darker 4*s.* 9*d.*[41] It is difficult, therefore, to make a detailed analysis of rates encountered for blue paintwork, but prices charged for several different blues are noted below; and Salmon indicated that the cost of 'Fine Sky Blue' in oil, made with Prussian blue, would vary between 10*d.* and 1*s.* per yard, against 4*d.* for common colours.[42] This figure was repeated in the 1787 and 1794 editions of the *Builders Price-Book*,[43] and is roughly comparable with the rate of 9*d.* per yard charged for painting iron railings at Somerset House from 1785 to 1793 '3 times done finish[d] Blue', '3[ce] in oil Blue' and so on. In 1780, however, 'five times done finished Blue' had been priced at 2*s.* per yard,[44] a rate roughly comparable with that of 2$\frac{1}{2}$*d.* per square foot for painting the staircase ironwork at Osterley 'fine blue' in 1772–4.[45] In the 1810 and 1813 editions of the *Builders Price-Book* the price of 'Twice in oil blue' was given as 11*d.*, 'Three times in oil ditto' as 1*s.* 1*d.*, and 'Four times in oil ditto' as 1*s.* 5*d.* These rates may be compared with the contemporary cost of two, three, and four coats of common colour at 8*d.*, 11*d.*, and 1*s.* 2*d.* respectively. Blue, as an expensive colour, could also be flatted, and prices for this are also given: 'Twice in oil and flated blue' cost 1*s.* 6*d.*; 'Three times in oil ditto' 1*s.* 9*d.*; and 'Four times in oil ditto' 2*s.*, against 1*s.* 3*d.*, 1*s.* 6*d.*, and 1*s.* 9*d.*, for two, three, and four times in oil 'flated dead white'.[46] These prices are consistent with the rate of an extra 3*d.* per square yard laid down for blue by the Painter-Stainers Company of London in 1803,[47] while in the early 1830s Skyring suggested that deep blue would cost an extra 4*d.*[48]

In some cases, rather than oil, a distemper medium would be preferred, both Prussian blue and blue verditer (sample 27) being used for tinting. Only one quantified formula for a distemper blue has been encountered, calling for the addition of 6 ounces of Prussian blue (costing 9*d.* per ounce) to a stone of Paris white;[49] but as in oil there is no doubt that widely varying quantities of staining pigment could be added to produce a whole range of tints. Information on prices too is limited, but in 1812 Phillips noted that blue distemper cost 8*d.* per yard (against $4\frac{1}{2}$*d.* for common colours) and in 1821 revised this rate to 7*d.*, although in 1818 Laxton had suggested a rate of 1*s.* 2*d.* (against 4*d.* for common colours).[50]

Before the Civil War, blue was used extensively in royal buildings, instances including the bice (sample 26) employed on the ground within the ribs of the apse in the Banqueting House in 1622–3 and on the columns of the chimneypiece in the Queen's New Cabinet Room at Somerset House in 1629–30.[51] Blue was also employed during the seventeenth century on interior and exterior ironwork, strewn smalt (sample 25) being superseded for the purpose by Prussian blue (sample 28) in the eighteenth, when the fashion continued.[52] By the 1730s, pale blues (sample 29) were among the staple interior colours. The 'Fine Sky Blue' marketed by Emerton in the 1730s is discussed below, and in 1752 Blondel listed *blue tendre* among other 'tons uniformes' used in house-painting.[53] Manuscript notes indicating the use of blue occur on a number of ceiling designs by Robert Adam,[54] and other instances of its employment in the eighteenth and early nineteenth centuries are plentiful.

Blue, etherial. A colour of this name appeared in the list of 'IMPENETRABLE PAINTS IN LINSEED-OIL' designed for interior or exterior use sold by the London Patent Colour-Works in 1816 at a cost of 1*s.* per pound.[55]

Blue, fair. A number of elements including the frieze, cornice, and door (with its jambs) in the Bedchamber, and entablature, door and its architraves, and wainscot 'under and about the Windoes' in the Dining Chamber at Ham House, Surrey, were painted 'fair blew' in 1638. The majority of the work was varnished, and received two, three, or four undercoats. One item (the entablature in the Dining Chamber) is noted as having been executed in oil,[56] but although recent analysis has shown that the pigment used in the work was blue verditer, the medium used on the remainder has not been confirmed.[57] References to fair blue may also be found in Royal buildings before the Civil War. In 1629–30 the ground of the frieze in the Queen's Bedchamber at St James's was painted 'faire blewe', and an item at Whitehall refers to 'divers tymes pryming payntinge and guildinge wth fyne gold and strewinge wth fayre blew'.[58] The latter technique suggests the use of smalt or azurite (samples 25, 26); and it is notable that the term 'faire' had been applied to bice used in the ceiling of the Chapel at Whitehall in 1621–2 and apse in the Banqueting House in 1622–3, perhaps suggesting that at this date it was particularly associated with azurite or blue verditer (sample 27).[59] In 1731, the term 'fair Blew' was used to describe the colour in which the study of Set 6 in the Gibbs building at King's College, Cambridge, was painted.[60]

Blue, French. In 1804, an item appears in the accounts for painting the Prince's Bedroom at the Royal Pavilion, Brighton, comprising 108 square yards 'Twice distemper french blue cut to borders' at 2*s.* 6*d.* per yard.[61]

Blue, garter. In 1787 the ironwork of the staircase at Osterley was re-painted 'fine garter-blue' at a cost of $3\frac{1}{2}$*d.* per square foot.[62]

Blue, navy. Reynolds recommended that navy blue should be mixed for interior purposes in oil using 2 ounces of Prussian blue to 5 pounds of white lead, both in paste form (cf. sample 28).[63]

Blue, Prussian. Although the term 'Prussian blue' was generally used to describe the pigment of that name, it appeared in the 1787 and 1794 editions of the *Builders Price-Book* to describe a variety of oil colour which was priced at 10*d.* to 1*s.* per yard.[64] Reynolds recommended that Prussian blue should be mixed for interior purposes in oil by combining 1 ounce of best quality Prussian blue with 5 pounds of white lead. Both pigments were measured in paste form, but if the blue was of poor quality, he noted, more would have to be added (cf. sample 28).[65]

Blue, royal. *Bleu de Roi* was included among the colours with a matt finish in the range of *couleurs lucidoniques* manufactured in Paris from 1803.[66]

Blue, sky. In the eighteenth century, sky blue appears often to have been made by the mixture of Prussian blue with white (sample 29). Emerton's fine sky blue oil paint, which sold at 8*d.* to 1*s.* per pound (against 4*d.* for white), was specifically noted to have been made using Prussian blue;[67] and Watin used the same pigment to make *bleu céleste* in both oil and distemper.[68] No doubt, however, blue verditer would also have been used, especially, perhaps, in distemper and in grounds for the clouded ceilings discussed in Chapter 20. The name 'sky blue' seems to have been used to imply a fairly light tint, and had been defined during the late seventeenth century by Holme as 'a light welmish Blew'.[69] Reynolds's formula contained the smallest amount of Prussian blue ($\frac{1}{2}$ ounce in 5 pounds white lead paste) among those forming his range of blues;[70] and a comparatively small quantity of staining pigment is implicit in the position of fine sky blue as the cheapest of the blues listed by Phillips in 1812 at 1*s.* 6*d.* per pound, deeper varieties costing up to 8*s.* 8*d.* As with all colours, however, variation in strength was possible, and Phillips noted a darker variety of sky blue was available at 1*s.* 10*d.*[71] *Bleu céleste* was one of the matt range of *couleurs lucidoniques* manufactured in Paris from 1803,[72] and sky blue appeared in the range of 'Anticorrosion paints' listed by Bennett in 1833 at a price equivalent to 3*s.* per pound.[73] When applied as an oil colour, the 1787 and 1794 editions of the *Builders Price-Book* indicated that sky blues (which were coupled with Prussian blues) would cost from 10*d.* to 1*s.* per square yard.[74]

The term sky blue may also be encountered in eighteenth-century correspondence, accounts, and designs. It was used by Chambers, for example, in writing to the Earl of Charlemont over alternative colour schemes for the Saloon in the Casino at Marino, Dublin, in 1767;[75] while Adam's design of 1766 for the ceiling of the Library at Nostell Priory, Yorkshire, has a manuscript note on it indicating the use of 'Skie Blue'.[76] It appears too in the 1772–4 account for painting the ceiling in the Drawing Room at Osterley,[77] and from the second quarter of the eighteenth century it was obviously an extremely popular colour. Notable examples of the use of 'sky colour' in the early nineteenth century may be found in the accounts for painting at the Royal Pavilion, Brighton, between 1802 and 1821, where it often formed the ground for clouded ceilings.[78]

Blue verditer. As already mentioned, *blue verditer* (sample 27) is properly the name of a pigment particularly suited to use in distemper. It was, nevertheless, used as a colour name by Pincot, who marketed a blue verditer 'WATER COLOUR' for house-painting,[79] and by Laxton who included it in a list of oil colours.[80] It seems likely, however, that in the latter medium Prussian blue would often have been added or preferred, possibly explaining Phillips's reference to 'Blue verditor . . . by mixture'.[81]

Brasil colour. In 1618–19 the 'Bearers for the Close Chair' at Royston, Hertfordshire, were distempered 'Brasill Cullor'.[82] This seems likely to have reflected the tint of the brasil wood lakes (sample 17) discussed in Chapter 7.

Brick colour. John Smith recommended a mixture of red lead, a little white, and yellow ochre (sample 15) to produce brick colour in oil, a suggestion copied by Nicholson and the author of the *Painter's . . . Pocket Manual* a century and a half later.[83]

Brimstone (sulphur) colour. Set 18 in the Gibbs Building at King's College, Cambridge was partly painted 'Brim Stone' in 1731,[84] while *jaune soufre ou paillé* was one of the range of *couleurs lucidoniques* manufactured with a matt finish in Paris from 1803.[85] Its tint may therefore have been seen as close to that of straw colour (q.v.).

Brown. Nicholson remarked that this colour contained no white lead whatsoever, and suggested that it was made using either raw or burnt umber (sample 34), or by mixing red and dark ochres with black (samples 32, 33).[86] The latter method was commonly recommended for other browns, notably chocolate colour (q.v.), but Nicholson appears to stand alone in proposing the use of umber, which would have been comparatively expensive, for an ordinary brown. Seventeenth-century references to 'umber colour' may be encountered, however, and these are discussed below. In another formula without parallel, Whittock suggested the use of Venetian red, yellow ochre, and a little Vandyke brown to mix a dark warm brown distemper.[87]

In 1618–19, the repaired roof and ceiling boards in the Hall at Somerset House were painted brown in oil,[88] and the upper part of the partition in the Parliament House at Oxford was similarly coloured in 1624–5.[89] Brown, often qualified as dark brown, was used by Adam in several ceiling designs;[90] and a brown 'Coal tar' paint, presumably for exterior use, was priced by Bennett in 1833 at 18*s.* per cwt.[91]

Brown, cinnamon. See *Cinnamon colour.*

Brown, clove. Nicholson mentioned 'clove brown' in a list of common varieties of the colour, but gave no specific details of its particular shade or formulation.[92]

Brown, Etruscan. 'Etruscan Brown' appears (together with 'Etruscan yellow') as a colour name in a manuscript note on Adam's design of 1773 for the ceiling of the Second Drawing Room at Ashburnham House[93] and is clearly related to his series of 'Etruscan' rooms discussed in the companion volume. It was also mentioned by Hay in 1828.[94]

Brown, London. Nicholson mentioned 'London brown' in a list of common varieties of the colour, but, as with others he noted, gave no specific details of its particular shade or formulation.[95]

Brown, olive. In 1808 Crease advertised a cheap 'Olive Brown' paint, probably intended for exterior purposes, at 3*d.* per pound.[96]

Brown, purple. See *Purple brown.*

Brown, quaker. In 1771 Mrs Powys described the stucco in the Eating Room at Fawley Court, Buckinghamshire, as painted 'Quaker brown'.[97] For a discussion of *quaker tints* see entry below.

Brown, sad. Nicholson mentioned 'sad brown' in a list of common varieties of the colour, but, as with others he noted, gave no specific details of its particular shade or formulation.[98] The adjective 'sad' is discussed, however, under *sad colour* below.

Brown, Spanish. Although properly the name of a red ochre (cf. sample 31), 'Spanish brown' was included by Nicholson in a list of common varieties of brown;[99] and a colour of this name was available in the range of 'IMPENETRABLE PAINTS IN LINSEED-OIL' advertised for interior or exterior use by the London Patent Colour-Works in 1816 at 32*s.* or 36*s.* per cwt.[100]

Brown, tawny. Nicholson included 'tawny brown' in a list of common varieties of the colour, but, as with others he noted, gave no specific details of its particular shade or formulation.[101]

Brown, warm. See under *Brown.*

Buff. John Smith, in a formula copied a century and a half later by Nicholson and the author of the *Painter's . . . Pocket Manual,* described buff in oil as made simply from yellow ochre and white lead (samples 4, 19);[102] but later authors seem to have been unanimous in recommending the addition of a little red. Vanherman, for example, observed that vermilion was mixed with yellow to make buffs, elsewhere noting the use of spruce ochre in this connection (cf. sample 20);[103] while Tingry suggested the employment of yellow and a little red lead to make buff or *chamois* in any medium.[104] Watin, however, had based his mixture for *chamois* on Naples yellow, directing that one should combine 'ceruse, beaucoup de jaune de Naples, une pointe de vermillon & un peu de jaune de Berry', again in all media.[105] Curiously, Butcher seems to have omitted yellow altogether, simply adding vermilion, orange lead, rose pink, or any other rose colour alone to white lead, a combination which would not produce buff as the term appears to have been generally understood during the eighteenth century or as thought of today; but this perhaps reflected fashionable usage in the 1820s, since the dull pink shown by Britton and Rutter on the walls in St Michael's Gallery at Fonthill Abbey, Wiltshire, was described by the latter as 'plain buff'.[106]

In a letter of 1770, William Chambers recommended to Gilbert Meason, a Leith merchant, that for a neat effect in his parlours he could use 'Buff colour' among a number of alternatives;[107] and in 1780 part of the interior stucco of Somerset House, London, was painted 'five times . . . finished Buff Colour' at a rate of 1*s.* 4*d.* per square yard.[108] Pincot indicated that buff oil paint would cost 6*d.* per yard above the cost of common colours;[109] the 1810 and 1813 editions of the *Builders Price-Book* indicated that it would cost 4*d.* per yard in distemper, against 3*d.* for common colours;[110] and Laxton a few years later gave a price of 5*d.* for buff in the same medium, against 4*d.* for common colours.[111] It may be noted also that *chamois* was one of the colours available in a matt finish which was included in the range of *couleurs lucidoniques* manufactured in Paris from 1803.[112]

Carmine. A drawing by James Wyatt calls for pink and green ribbons forming part of the decoration of a ceiling to be 'touch'd with Carmine'.[113] It is unclear, however, whether this was a technical direction requiring employment of the pure dyestuff, or whether the painter would have substituted a cochineal lake.

Carnation. John Smith, in a formula copied by Nicholson and the author of the *Painter's . . . Pocket Manual* a century and a half later, indicated that carnation for house-painting in oil was made from lake and white (sample 16).[114] Cf. *Flesh colour,* below.

Cedar colour. As with other names taken from timbers, the term 'cedar colour' could imply either graining or a plain paint finish, and, as pointed out in the introductory text to Appendix B, it is often difficult to know to which any given instance refers. An unambiguous example is provided, however, by certain elements in the Sheldonian Theatre, Oxford, which were painted 'cedar color . . . not being veined' at 1*s*. per square yard in 1669;[115] and it is notable that Emerton sold cedar colour oil paint at 6*d*. per pound (against 4*d*. for white lead), implying application of a plain finish.[116] Other instances are less certain, but the oak battens of the fret ceiling in the Queen's New Bedchamber at Whitehall were painted cedar colour in distemper in 1639–40;[117] various rooms at Dyrham Park, Gloucestershire (now Avon), were painted (or grained) cedar colour in 1694 at 10*d*. per square yard;[118] and Robert Abbott's tender for interior painting at Greenwich Hospital of about 1696 quoted a price of 8*d*. per yard for cedar colour and others 'Substantially Done 3 times in Oyle'.[119] About the same time Celia Fiennes noted that the Parlour at Broadlands, Hampshire, belonging to Sir John Barbe was 'wainscoated and painted a cedar coullour';[120] and an estimate for painting at Stoke Edith, Herefordshire, of 1705 quoted a price of 1*s*. per yard.[121] Although cedar colour appears in Leadbeater's reprint of Emerton's list in 1770, it seems fairly likely that the term had by then become archaic, and no later references to it have been encountered.[122]

Cerulian colour. In the *City & Country Purchaser & Builder*, published in 1667, Stephen Primatt quoted a price of 1*s*. 6*d*. per square yard for 'Painting the best *Cerulian* or Blew colour in Oyl' against 9*d*. to 1*s*. for a number of common colours including 'a fair Stone-colour laid in Oyl . . . being coloured over thrice' at 1*s*.[123] He gave no clue, however, as to how it was to be formulated.

Chestnut. To mix *marron foncé* Watin recommended a combination of English red, 'ochre de rue', and ivory black in either oil or distemper, advice repeated by Tingry in the English translation of his book for chestnut colour.[124] The author of the *Painter's . . . Pocket Manual* gave a similar mixture, suggesting that red ochre and black should be combined to make a dark chestnut, but added that yellow ochre could be added to make it lighter (cf. sample 36).[125] Earlier, to make chestnut colour japan Stalker & Parker had used Indian red or red-brown ochre with lamp black and a little white,[126] and for colouring prints John Smith had suggested the use of umber, lake, and white;[127] but it is unlikely that the latter combination would have been used for house-painting.

Chocolate colour. Those authors who give mixtures for chocolate colour are unanimous in making it from red ochre and black (sample 33). Nicholson, for example, suggested a mixture of Indian red and black, and stated that the colour contained no white lead whatsoever.[128] Reynolds (in a formula specifically for interior purposes), Butcher, and the author of the *Painter's . . . Pocket Manual* all combined lamp black with Spanish brown;[129] while Tingry's later editor mentioned the use of Venetian red.[130] Vanherman too used Spanish brown in making his chocolate 'IMPENETRABLE, OR ANTI-CORROSIVE PAINT' for exterior purposes, giving the following alternative quantities:[131]

1	whiting	224 lb.
	Spanish brown	112 lb.
	mineral black	112 lb.
	crotia	224 lb.
2	whiting	56 lb.
	Spanish brown	56 lb.
	mineral black	56 lb.
	crotia	84 lb.

Altogether, therefore, it is clear that the colour was generally darker than chestnut colour discussed above, and, lacking the addition of yellow ochre common in this colour, was colder in tone. Samples of chocolate paint from two rooms at Somerset House painted in 1780 were close in colour to Munsell references 2.5 YR 3/2 and 5 YR 2.5/1.[132]

Chocolate colour appears in Emerton's list at a price of 6*d*. per pound (against 4*d*. for white lead),[133] and was described in the *Builders Price-Book* as one of the common colours, a category in which it was also included by Laxton.[134] A large part of its employment was for exterior purposes, Pincot remarking that it was one of the five colours in general use for such work;[135] and Vanherman advocated his own colour as particularly suitable for timber fences.[136] The front gates of Egremont House (now the Naval and Military Club) in Piccadilly, London, were painted chocolate in 1760;[137] and in 1808 Crease observed that it was preferable to Spanish brown for exterior items.[138] Although 8*d*. per pound was paid in 1793 for a quantity of chocolate paint supplied to Tredegar House, Newport, Monmouthshire (now Gwent), Crease advertised his oil paint of this colour at a much cheaper rate, equivalent to 42*s*. per cwt.[139] This was matched by Lingard in his 'Invulnerable oil Paint' in 1825,[140] although in 1816 the London Patent Colour-Works had sold the chocolate in their range of 'IMPENETRABLE PAINTS IN LINSEED-OIL' for 52*s*.[141] Even cheaper varieties were, however, available for exterior use, including the chocolate in the latter's 'MINERAL OR REFINED COAL-TAR PAINTS' at 18*s*.;[142] while Vanherman suggested that his chocolate 'IMPENETRABLE OR ANTI-CORROSIVE PAINT', the formula for which has been given above, could be manufactured for as little as 9*s*. 4*d*. per cwt.[143] Bentley, on the other hand, had been selling his chocolate 'ANTI-CORROSIVE PAINT' for exterior purposes at 46*s*. in 1817, and Bennett noted in 1825 that chocolate 'Coal tar' paint would cost 52*s*.[144] In addition, chocolate was available in the London Patent Colour-Works range of 'ANTIQUE ORNAMENTAL PAINTS' for interior and exterior application at 6*d*. per pound, the equivalent of 56*s*. per cwt.[145]

In interiors chocolate had a particular use, being applied as an almost standard finish on softwood doors and often on skirtings during the mid-eighteenth century. Many of the doors in the Gibbs Building at King's College, Cambridge, for example were painted in this colour between 1731 and 1734;[146] while Philip Yorke of Erddig directed that the door of a room should be painted chocolate in 1772.[147] In this case the skirting was to be white, but investigation has shown that both the door and skirting in the rooms of the Royal Society's Housekeeper, and the Secretary of the Society of Antiquaries at Somerset House, were painted chocolate in 1780;[148] and it seems most likely that these were the areas to which $9\frac{1}{2}$ square yards of chocolate were applied in the Dining Room of Henry Pelham's house in Arlington Street, London, in 1745.[149] In addition it may be noted that a staircase handrail at Osterley, Middlesex, was painted chocolate between 1772 and 1774.[150]

Cinnamon colour. In 1692 it was recorded that one of the rooms at Erddig was 'but ordinary . . . and plane, ether a dark brown or sumewhat like a sinnimone culor'.[151] Over a century and a quarter later, Whittock directed that a light cinnamon brown distemper should be made using Vandyke brown, king's yellow, Venetian red, and whiting. The result was, he indicated, a delicate orange-grey tint; and he illustrated the use of cinnamon on trellis work in his Chinese apartment.[152] Within the previous decade two tints of 'cinnamon coloured brown' had been used in the Top Hall at Nostell Priory, Yorkshire;[153] and the colour was later mentioned by the eminent Edinburgh house-painter, D.R. Hay.[154]

Claret colour. Reynolds recommended that a claret colour for interior use should be mixed using 3 parts of white lead with 1 of Spanish brown, tinged with a small quantity of lamp black.[155] This may be compared with the red for the walls of a picture gallery advocated by Vanherman discussed below.

Clay colour. In 1809, the Entrance Hall at the Royal Pavilion, Brighton, was described as being 'a warm clay, with blue and red mouldings'.[156] A design of 1802 appears to relate to this scheme, and shows walls of a deep yellow-cream the niches and alcove in which are surrounded with blue and red lines.[157] It will be remembered that gilders often refer to yellow ochre as 'clay', and in 1686, Waller noted that yellow ochre was 'Clay Col.', giving also the latin 'luteus'.[158] At this date, clay colour was thus probably synonymous with *lute colour* (q.v.), and it is probably significant that in 1688 Holme included it in a list of those derived from red, possibly with the slightly orange cast of the latter in mind.[159]

Common colours. Common colours, an expression used by Salmon in 1734,[160] were later defined in the *Builders Price-Book* as including white lead, stone colour, lead colour, cream colour, pearl colour, wainscot colour, and chocolate colour.[161] The first six of these formed the cheapest range of paints sold by Emerton in the 1730s, while chocolate colour was only a little more expensive.[162] Alongside it Emerton listed mahogany colour, cedar colour, and walnut-tree colour, the last two of which seem to have gone out of use by the latter part of the century, but the first of which was also priced in the *Builders Price-Book* 'twice done' at 4*d.* per square yard, the same price as the other common colours there mentioned.[163] Its inclusion in this class may therefore be presumed. In the early nineteenth century Laxton too instanced lead, stone, chocolate, and white as common colours.[164] The term is frequently met in painting accounts, including, for example those for Henry Pelham's house in Arlington Street (1745–50); Egremont House, Piccadilly (1759); Osterley Park (1772–4); and Somerset House (1780).[165] The last of these illustrates well the common practice of abstracting all the items for common colours throughout the entire building and placing them at the head of the account, more expensive items alone being listed room by room.

Copper colour. The London colourman, Charles Hodgkin, advertised copper-colour 'Anticorrosion paint' at 54*s.* per 100 pounds,[166] a price repeated by Bennett, who may have been quoting from Hodgkin's trade card.[167]

Cream colour. Alexander Emerton advertised cream colour in the cheapest range of his ready-mixed tints,[168] and it was included with the common colours in the 1787 and 1794 editions of the *Builders Price-Book.*[169] For exterior purposes Reynolds indicated that it was prepared by mixing 1 pound of spruce yellow or English ochre with 30 pounds of white lead prior to grinding (cf. sample 4), but, he observed, the tint could be altered by using more or less yellow.[170] The lobby leading to the Old Parlour at Dyrham Park, Gloucestershire (now Avon), had been painted 'creami colour' in 1694, and the Library walls at Gordon Castle, Morayshire, cream colour in 1782.[171]

Crimson. Although Watin described *cramoisi* as made from carmine lake, carmine, and a very little white lead (sample 16),[172] it could be made also by mixing these with other pigments, in particular vermilion (sample 13). Thus, while Waller used carmine alone to define crimson in his chart intended to provide a set of colour standards for scientific use,[173] suggesting that a purplish hue was generally implied by the term, John Smith, who mentioned crimson only in connection with colouring prints, directed that it should be prepared using vermilion, lake, and white.[174] Vanherman gave a similar formula, suggesting that a crimson for use in libraries should be mixed using 1 pound of rose pink, 1 packet of Chinese vermilion, and $\frac{1}{4}$ pound of satin white. He gave this formula, which he noted 'agrees with books and their bindings', in connection with his 'AROMATIC PAINT', and observed interestingly: 'Some gentlemen prefer having the colour subdued, by the addition of a small portion of black'. It was applied over an undercoat made from rose pink and Venetian red.[175] Fine dark crimson was also used for the ground of the frieze in the Drawing Room at Osterley Park in 1772–4, and, among other colours, crimson was also used at the same date in the cabin of the 'San Pan' mentioned in the same account.[176] In 1823 Rutter recorded that the ground of the vault in the Oratory at Fonthill Abbey was deep crimson;[177] in 1817 it had been recommended that the walls in the Drawing Room at Towneley Hall, Lancashire, by Jeffry Wyatt should be crimson, gold, and white;[178] and the colour was mentioned by Hay in 1828.[179]

Dove colour. In 1780, parts of the ceiling in the Council Room of the Royal Academy at Somerset House, London, were painted dove colour,[180] and in 1803 and 1816 the Painter-Stainers Company listed it as commanding a price of 2*d.* per yard extra.[181] No contemporary suggestion for mixing this colour has been encountered; and, although John Smith noted that it could be made from white, a little lake and a little smalt, his formula was given in connection with the colouring of prints and would in any case have been obsolete by the latter part of the eighteenth century.[182]

Drab. Vanherman remarked that spruce ochre combined with reds or brown produced countless tints of pleasant drabs (samples 6, 20), and that Venetian red 'with white and black, vermillion and ochre . . . produces a variety of tints, particularly of the drab kind, which are always admired, for thir solid appearance and quiet tone'. For warm drabs he mentioned that burnt umber (sample 3) was employed.[183] He also applied the adjective to greens (q.v.), while Hay later indicated that tints of citrine (a tertiary colour he defined as made by combining orange and green) were called drab. The samples he gave correspond roughly with Munsell references 2.5 GY 7/2, 2.5 GY 6/2, and 7.5 Y 5/3.[184] In 1816, the Painter-Stainers Company listed drab as costing 2*d.* extra per yard,[185] and a couple of years later Laxton noted that drabs would cost 3*d.* per square yard over the rate for common colours.[186] In 1823 an intention was expressed to paint the walls of five privies in the garden at Dunham Massey, Cheshire, drab;[187] about the same time two tints of drab were used on the walls of the Top Hall at Nostell Priory, Yorkshire;[188] in his *Cabinet-Maker and Upholsterer's Guide* published in 1826 George Smith instanced the use of a very pale drab in the decoration of the walls of a room;[189] and in 1846 Bartholomew specified a light drab for the external painting of window sashes.[190] The term appears, therefore, to be one generally associated with the early nineteenth century, although a room at Erddig in which the wainscot seems to have been grained in imitation of a variety of timbers in 1691 was referred to the following year as 'the drab roome'.[191]

Fawn. Nicholson described the production of fawn colour distemper and fine yellow-fawn oil paint from burnt sienna, or burnt umber and white (sample 3).[192] Butcher, and the author of the *Painter's . . . Pocket Manual* (perhaps copying him), however, described a rather different tint made by combining white lead, stone ochre, and a small quantity of vermilion (sample 20).[193] The samples given by Hay in 1846 correspond roughly with Munsell references 7.5 R 7/2 and 7.5 R 6/2.[194] In 1816, the Painter-Stainers Company fixed its price at 2*d.* per square yard extra;[195] and Laxton and Skyring respectively indicated that fawn oil paint would cost an extra 5*d.* and 4*d.* over the rate for common colours.[196] Fawn was used in several rooms at the Royal Pavilion, Brighton, in 1803.[197]

Flesh colour. John Smith (Butcher and the author of the *Painter's . . . Pocket Manual* copying him) proposed a mixture of lake, white lead, and a little vermilion to make flesh colour, but Nicholson suggested the combination of Indian red with white.[198] Pincot described a flesh colour for priming made from 14 pounds of white lead and 1 pound of red lead;[199] and *couleur de chair* appears in the list of *couleurs lucidoniques* available in a matt finish which had been manufactured at Paris from 1803.[200]

Glass colour. In 1759 a blank window at Egremont House, Piccadilly, was painted a 'dark Glass colour'.[201] Earlier, Waller had used a mixture of ochre and ultramarine to prepare the sample of glass colour in his chart of standards for scientific use, but such a combination would not have been used for house-painting.[202]

Gold colour. Watin indicated that *couleur d'or* was made in oil or distemper from ceruse, Naples yellow and 'ochre de Berry'.[203] Tingry, however, altered this in his formula for golden yellow, suggesting the alternatives of Naples or Montpellier (patent) yellows (samples 22, 23) with Spanish white, or the use of realgar with ochre of Berry and white of Morat in all media.[204] The author of the *Painter's . . . Pocket Manual* revised this in turn, suggesting the use of massicot (then probably obsolete for house-painting) or Naples yellow with a small quantity of realgar and very little Spanish white.[205]

In 1629–30, the gilded pendants in the cockpit at Whitehall were washed and repaired in gold colour;[206] and in the 1730s Emerton was selling gold-colour oil paint at 8*d.* per pound.[207] In neither case, of course, could this have been made in any of the ways listed above, except by using massicot (lead-tin yellow), realgar, or yellow ochre; but although John Smith suggested the combination of red orpiment and white massicot in equal parts to imitate gold in the colouring of prints, this does not necessarily confirm that such mixtures were in use for house-painting.[208] The early formulations employed are thus uncertain.

Jaune d'or was one of the *couleurs lucidoniques* manufactured at Paris from 1803 with a gloss finish;[209] and about 1811 Pincot was marketing a 'bright Golden Yellow' in his range of 'WATER COLOURS' for the decoration of rooms at 1*s.* 6*d.* per pound,[210] the latter probably based on an organic yellow (sample 21).

Green. Methods for mixing different types of green have been reviewed in Chapter 21. Details of the formulae will be found under the various qualified names for greens below, but the word was often used on its own, such recipes being given by Watin, Nicholson (a 'good' green), Butcher, and Vanherman.[211] Their methods ranged from the use of verdigris (samples 41, 42) to the combination of blue verditer or Prussian blue with yellow ochre (sample 43), or employment of Prussian blue with patent yellow or chrome yellow (samples 45, 48). This wide variety of suggestions shows that the unqualified term did not necessarily imply any particular mixing method, although it was suggested in Chapter 21 that the most satisfactory for ordinary use in oil during the eighteenth century would have been to combine yellow ochre with Prussian blue.

On account of the widely varying cost and proportion of the possible constituents, prices for different types of green covered a broad spectrum. Emerton, it will be remembered, retailed his 'Olive Colour' and 'Pea Colour' at 8*d.* to 1*s.* per pound against 2*s.* 6*d.* for 'Fine deep Green';[212] and prices noted by Bennett a century later included 'common invisible green' oil paint at 7*d.* per pound, olive at 9*d.*, a 'good' green at 1*s.*, a 'superior' green and pomona green at 1*s.* 6*d.*, Roman green at 1*s.* 9*d.*, Saxon green at 2*s.*, Spanish olive green at 2*s.* 6*d.*, and patent grass green at 3*s.*[213] This makes comparative analysis of the prices encountered in painting accounts virtually impossible, but it is useful to note that in the 1794 edition of the *Builders Price-Book* 'Common greens' were priced at 10*d.* to 1*s.* per square yard against 'Fine deep greens' at 1*s.* to 1*s.* 2*d.*[214] In later editions the distinction was dropped and the following prices were given:

Twice in oil green	1*s.*
Three times in oil ditto	1*s.* 2*d.*
Four times in oil ditto	1*s.* 6*d.*
Twice in oil and flatted green	1*s.* 7*d.*
Three times in oil ditto	1*s.* 10*d.*
Four times in oil ditto	2*s.* 1*d.*
Ditto with verdigris green	2*s.* 6*d.*

At this date prices for two, three, and four coats of common colours were 8*d.*, 11*d.*, and 1*s.* 2*d.* respectively; and for twice, three times, and four times in oil flatted dead white 1*s.* 3*d.*, 1*s.* 6*d.*, and 1*s.* 9*d.*[215] These figures are more or less consistent with Laxton's suggestion that light greens would cost an extra 5*d.* per square yard over common colours.[216]

It may be noted also that proprietary green paints produced in the early nineteenth century included the 'Dull dead greens by mixture' which Phillips indicated were sold in 1812 at 1*s.* 2½*d.* per pound, the deep green in the range of 'IMPENETRABLE PAINTS IN LINSEED-OIL' for interior or exterior application manufactured by the London Patent Colour Works in 1816 and sold at 1*s.* 6*d.* per pound, and the light and deep greens in their range of 'ANTIQUE ORNAMENTAL PAINTS' sold at 1*s.* 3*d.*[217] Other greens in these ranges are referred to under the appropriate headings below.

It is clear from documentary references that in the seventeenth century green paint, both in oil and distemper, was often varnished. The Queen's Long Gallery at Oatlands, for example, was painted green in distemper and varnished in 1636–7, repairs being executed in the same manner in 1638–9;[218] and the cornice in the Green Parlour at Ham House was painted three times in oil in 1638 and 'layde greene and varnished', a door and two areas of wainscoting elsewhere in the house being similarly treated.[219] Similarly, the 1649 inventory of Wimbledon House noted that the wainscots in the Lower Spanish Room and Stone Gallery were varnished green;[220] and in 1663 Gerbier gave a price of 1*s.* per yard for 'Painting of the fairest green, that can be in distemper, and varnisht'.[221] Varnish does not seem invariably to have been applied, though, and there is no reference to it in connection with the four doors at Theobalds, Hertfordshire, painted green in distemper in 1619–29, the chamber and doors in the Lord Steward's lodging at Whitehall similarly treated in 1622–3, the green paint used in the King's Privy Chamber at Whitehall in 1624–5, the slit deal ceiling painted green in distemper in a closet at Whitehall in 1629–30, or a cornice at Whitehall painted green in the same medium in 1631–2.[222] The wainscot in the Buttery and entablature in the Closet of the Garden Chamber at Ham were finished 'greene in

Oylle' and 'fair greene' in 1638, both at a rate of 1*s.* 8*d.* per square yard, although the first had three and the second two oil undercoats;[223] while later in the century limited areas of green at 2*s.* per yard appear without mention of varnish in the accounts for Hampton Court, Whitehall Palace, and Kensington Palace.[224] The colour was also used on the Members' seats and a doorcase in the House of Commons at Westminster in February 1670;[225] and seems too to have been popular for similar furniture externally. Items for painting garden furniture and rails green appear in the accounts for Boughton House, Northamptonshire, and Montagu House, London, in the 1700s at the lower rates of 1*s.* 4*d.* and 1*s.* respectively, suggesting that a cheaper variety may have been employed in such situations.[226]

References to green paint in the second half of the eighteenth century, when it had come to be used on all coloured elements in a room including ceilings, skirtings, walls, and shutters, are too common to mention individually, but an indication of its popularity is given by its occurrence, often qualified as dark or light green, in over forty manuscript notes on the Adam ceiling designs in the Soane Museum.[227] By this date it was, of course, often flatted, and instances may be found in accounts for Osterley Park (1772–4 and 1787), Somerset House (1781–93), and notes for redecoration at Dunham Massey in 1823.[228] Undoubtedly, green was an extremely important and popular colour, a circumstance reflected in the wide range of adjectives listed below by which it was qualified.

Green, American. *Vert Américan* was one of the *couleurs lucidoniques* available in a semi-gloss finish which were manufactured at Paris from 1803;[229] while in 1841 Lewis Berger's successors used a commercial recipe for American green containing verditer, chrome yellow, and Scheele's green.[230]

Green, apple. See *Green, pomona.*

Green, aquatic. In 1831 Lewis Berger noted a manufacturing formula for this colour which contained 92 lb. emerald green, 8 lb. Antwerp blue, and 1 lb. 'pale' chrome yellow.[231]

Geen, Berlin. Vanherman suggested that Berlin green should be made from 1 pound of wet refiners verditer, 1 pound of wet chrome yellow, $13\frac{1}{2}$ pounds of wet blue, and 8 pounds of wet white lead. After passing the mixture through a 60-hole wire sieve and allowing it to dry it was ground into linseed oil for use.[232]

Green, bottle. In 1808 Crease retailed a 'Rich Bottle Green' oil paint at 1*s.* per pound, although in 1812 Phillips indicated that a bottle green 'by mixture' would cost 3*s.* 7*d.* per pound, a price amended to 3*s.* 6*d.* in 1821.[233]

Green, bronze. *Vert bronze* was one of the *couleurs lucidoniques* available with a semi-gloss finish manufactured in Paris from 1803.[234] The colour was, perhaps, related to those used in the imitation of patinated bronze (see Chapter 20).

Green, Brunswick. This pigment name was used by Vanherman to describe a colour in his range of 'Impenetrable or anti-corrosive paints'. It was made using equal parts of whiting, chrome yellow Brunswick green, and crotia, and could be manufactured, he claimed, for about 2*d.* per pound.[235]

Green, Chinese. In 1844 Lewis Berger's successors noted a manufacturing formula for this colour which contained 3 cwt. emerald green, 22 lb. indigo, and 8 lb. 'Super Pale' chrome yellow.[236]

Green, common. See *Green, inferior.*

Green, compound. Watin gave a formula (later transcribed by Tingry and published in English as a 'compound green' for rooms) under the heading *vert de composition.* It contained 1 pound of ceruse, 2 ounces of Dutch pink, and $\frac{1}{2}$ ounce of Prussian blue, although, he indicated, the quantity of pink could be varied. It could be used in oil or distemper, and Tingry added also directions for its employment in varnish.[237]

Green, drab. Vanherman discussed the preparation of drab greens from spruce ochre and Prussian blue with white (sample 43), suggesting as variations the substitution of black for the blue and raw umber for the ochre. The term *drab* (q.v.) has been discussed above, and Vanherman remarked that such greens were reposeful, solid, and of quiet tone.[238]

Green, duck-egg. In 1803, part of the Hall at the Royal Pavilion, Brighton, was painted 'Twice in oil and flatted duck egg green' at a cost of 1*s.* 4*d.* per square yard.[239]

Green, fine. The most expensive colour in Emerton's colour list of the 1730s was 'Fine deep Green' at 2*s.* 6*d.* per pound against 4*d.* for the cheapest and 8*d.* to 1*s.* for other greens.[240] As suggested in Chapter 3, it was probably based on verdigris (cf. samples 41, 42). As late as 1830 Tingry's editor indicated that green of the finest kind was made from that pigment,[241] but whether the term *fine green* invariably implied its use seems uncertain. In the 1794 edition of the Builders Price-Book, fine deep greens were listed at 1*s.* to 1*s.* 2*d.* per yard, a price not much higher than common greens at 10*d.* to 1*s.*;[242] and in 1803 the Painter-Stainers Company determined it should cost 3*d.* more per square yard than common colours.[243] These prices suggest that constituents cheaper than verdigris may have been employed, and it is useful to recall that between 1811 and 1815 Lewis Berger's company was using the name 'fine green' for a variety of Scheele's green which the family manufactured.[244] Nevertheless, it is clear the expression was generally used to imply one of the better-quality greens, and Bennett, for example, suggested that fine deep green coal-tar paint (presumably for exterior use) would cost 1*s.* 6*d.* per pound against 10*d.* for dark olive.[245] The term may be found also in eighteenth-century manuscripts, including Adam's estimate of 1771 for painting the Council Room at the Shire Hall, Hertford,[246] and the painting account for Gordon Castle, where the beading of the window shutters and doors of the Duchess's Bedroom was painted fine green in 1782;[247] while some of the grounds in the ceiling of the Drawing Room at Osterley Park were painted 'superfine' green between 1772 and 1774.[248]

Green, Fowler's patent. See *Green, patent.*

Green, French. The term *French green* was in use during the seventeenth century, John Smith recommending a combination of pink and indigo in its preparation for colouring prints.[249] The first mention of it so far encountered in connection with house-painting, however, is the French green 'Water colour' retailed by Pincot about 1811;[250] and in connection with this it is useful to recall that Lewis Berger's sons manufactured a copper carbonate pigment called 'French green' in 1816 (cf. sample 46), while at the same date 'second French green' was a variety of Scheele's green (sample 47).[251] Both Laxton and Skyring referred to French green oil paint as costing an extra 9*d.* and 4*d.* over the price of common colours respectively, the latter listing it with 'other superior colours'.[252]

Green, garden. On the Continent it seems the practice of painting garden furniture in green was well established by the closing years of the seventeenth century, and two early eighteenth-century English instances of this have been noted under *Green* above. D'Aviler described the 'green with which one paints trellis work, doors, grilles and garden benches' as made with 'verd de montagne' (malachite) the pure pigment being used for the finishing coat, which was laid on a ground made from equal parts of ceruse and 'verd de montagne'. The first coat was of pure ceruse. The colour, he observed, became more beautiful with time and did not blacken like verdigris, which was, he said, cheaper.[253] Bullet, on the other hand, recommended the use of equal parts of 'vert de montagne' and verdigris in the finishing coat, noting too that the addition of an equal part of ceruse would produce a beautiful colour.[254] For *vert de treillages* Watin simply used 1 pound of ordinary verdigris mixed with 2 pounds of ceruse, but in town recommended the use of 3 pounds of the latter on account of the blackening effect impure air had on it.[255] This suggestion was endorsed by Tingry, who copied his formula (cf. sample 41).[256]

In 1808 Crease was selling 'Garden Green' oil paint at 8*d.* per pound, a price which suggests that a far humbler green than those described by the French authors was commonly used in this country.[257] This is apparent too from the 'Receipt for a Green Paint proper for Rails &c' discussed below under *Green, invisible* (q.v.) and the use of olive green (q.v. also) for exterior work.

Green, granite. In 1819 Pyne recorded that the walls of the Great Hall, Vestibule, and Staircase at Carlton House were painted 'granite-green', a colour which, he remarked, 'accords admirably with the effect of the Sienna marble, the verd antique, porphyry, and the several imitations of these costly materials'.[258]

Green, grass. John Smith described the combination of a little pink-yellow with verdigris as making a delicate *grass green*, a suggestion copied by Nicholson and the author of the *Painter's . . . Pocket Manual.*[259] Elsewhere, however, Nicholson proposed only the use of verdigris, while Reynolds indicated that a grass green for exterior use should be made from equal portions of verdigris and white lead (cf. sample 41).[260] Smith, however, had regarded such a tint as *willow green* (q.v.). *Vert pré* appears among the range of *couleurs lucidoniques* available with a glossy finish which were manufactured at Paris from 1803;[261] and in 1812 Phillips indicated that grass green, the most expensive of the greens he listed, would cost 4*s.* 10*d.* per pound (presumably in oil), but in a spirit medium 6*s.* 10*d.*, and in varnish up to 8*s.* 4*d.* It seems likely that they contained verdigris since he preceded them with a 'Light verdigris' colour at prices between 3*s.* and 4*s.* 3*d.*[262] In 1816 the London Patent Colour-Works patriotically marketed 'Waterloo Grass-Green' in their series of 'IMPENETRABLE PAINTS IN LINSEED-OIL' for interior or exterior use at 2*s.* 6*d.* per pound, again the most expensive colour in their range;[263] and in 1833 Bennett indicated that 'Royal' grass green 'anticorrosion' paint would cost roughly the equivalent of 3*s.* 2½*d.* per pound (16*s.* per 5 pounds).[264] The expense of all these strongly suggests the use of verdigris, and as far as it is possible to link any particular green with a pigment, grass green does seem often to have implied its employment.

Green, immarcessible bright. The most expensive colour in Lingard's 1825 list of his 'Invulnerable Oil Paints' he called 'Immarcessible Bright Green'. It retailed at 2*s.* 6*d.* per pound (against about 4*d.* for invisible green) and he described it as,

> the most beautiful bright Colour ever yet offered for Ornamental Painting, such as Virandas, Garden-Chairs, Flower-Stands, Windows, Doors, &c. &c. It will keep its original colour, in the hottest sun, for a number of years, without blistering or fading, as may now be seen in London, where it has stood nearly seven years. Its brilliancy is also particularly adapted for beautifying the Interior of Public Buildings, or Private Drawing-Rooms.[265]

Green, inferior. Tingry's later editor described *inferior greens* as made from ochre and Prussian or other blues (sample 43).[266] Presumably it was greens of this kind which were referred to in late eighteenth-century editions of the *Builders Price-Book* as 'Common greens'.[267]

Green, invisible. *Invisible green* seems to have been the cheapest generally employed for exterior work, and appears in a large number of early nineteenth-century price lists. Crease described it as preferable to Spanish brown for exterior use, and explained that it,

> is so denominated, from its being proper for covering gates and rails, in parks, pleasure grounds, &c. by rendering them in a measure invisible at a distance, on account of its approximation to the hue of the vegetation.[268]

Earlier, in the *English Garden*, the poet William Mason had given a description in verse of how to prepare a dark green oil paint based on ochre and black with white lead (cf. sample 40), whose 'shadowy hues/Tinging thy fence may lose it in the lawn'; and concluded on a triumphant note:

> The paint is spread; the barrier pales retire,
> Snatch'd, as by magic, from the gazer's view.[269]

Vanherman gave two formulae for mixing the colour in his range of 'IMPENETRABLE, OR ANTI-CORROSIVE PAINTS', remarking that it was,

> one of the most pleasant colours for fences, and all work connected with buildings, gardens, or pleasure grounds, as it displays a richness and solidity, and also harmonises with every object, and is a background and foil to the foliage of fields, trees, and plants, as also to flowers.

His formulae were:

1	Whiting	112 pounds
	Bristol ochre	224
	Damp blue	112
	Crotia	112
	Mineral black	28
	English umber	14
2	Whiting	56 pounds
	Yellow ochre	56
	Mineral black	28
	Brunswick green	28
	Crotia	112

The first could, he claimed, be prepared for less than 2*d.* per pound, and the latter for not more than 1½*d.*[270]

Nicholson too gave a formula for invisible green, recommending the combination of dark ochre, blue, and a little black;[271] while a manuscript 'Receipt for a Green Paint proper for Rails &c so as to mix with Herbage or Trees', probably dating from the latter part of the eighteenth century, reads as follows:

> Take the palest yellow Oker, and mix it up with a small quantity of Ivory Black so as to produce a light Olive. – In finer Work use Prussian Blue in place of the Ivory Black which will

produce a light Green Colour, – and in either case if a Light Colour is required add White Lead. – The proper Tint must be chosen by the Eye at a due distance.[272]

Prices for proprietary invisible green paints in oil given by Crease (1808), Pincot (*c.* 1811), the London Patent Colour-Works (1816), and Lingard (1817) ranged from 40*s.* to 56*s.* per cwt., although Bennett (1833) suggested 7*d.* per pound (equivalent to 65*s.* 5*d.* per cwt.); while the London Patent Colour-Works 'ANTI-CORROSION' exterior paint was priced at 42*s.* and Bentley's 'ANTI-CORROSIVE PAINT' at 56*s.* in 1817. The London Patent Colour-Works also sold invisible green 'ANTIQUE ORNAMENTAL PAINT' suitable for interior or exterior use at 6*d.* per pound (equivalent to 56*s.* per cwt.), and 'MINERAL, OR REFINED COAL TAR PAINT' for exterior use at 20*s.* per cwt., although Bennett suggested that coal-tar invisible green would cost £3 per cwt. Bentley noted his product should be applied on an undercoat of lead colour, and Pincot recommended his colour particularly for 'field fences, ha ha fences, Park Railings or Inclosures', noting that it was 'agreeable when relieved by verdure and vegetation'.[273] Such dull greens as those represented by the formulae for invisible green described above may be compared with the greens for gardens recommended by Continental authors discussed under *Green, garden* above, and more particularly with those for olive green below to which family they seem often to have belonged.

Green, Japan. In 1833 Bennett noted that *Japan green* 'for fenders, &c.' would cost 1*s.* 9*d.* per pound.[274] This may have been related to the green japan used on furniture during the latter half of the eighteenth century, such as the two *bergères* 'Japan'd Green & White' supplied for the Drawing Room at David Garrick's house in the Adelphi, London, in 1772, and bedroom furniture in his house at Hampton, Middlesex, made about 1775 by Thomas Chippendale which was similarly treated.[275] A sample taken from one of the *bergères* suggests that a copper resinate (sample 42) was used to produce the green, which was close in colour to Munsell reference 7.5 GY 6/4.[276]

Green, marine. In 1841 the Berger firm noted a commercial production formula for a colour of this name which contained 150lb. emerald green, $\frac{1}{4}$lb. Antwerp blue ('Deep Chinese Blue'), and 1lb. 'Super Pale' chrome yellow, and was extended with 50lb. barytes.[277] (Cf. *Green, sea* below.)

Green, mineral. Although Scheele's green and copper chloride pigments were often known as 'mineral green', the name seems also to have been used to describe a paint colour. In his patent of 1812, Parker, for example, described the way in which 1 pound of Scheele's green could be combined with 1 pound of a copper carbonate pigment, $1\frac{1}{2}$ pounds of refiners' blue verditer, and 3 pounds of white lead to produce a 'bright mineral pea green';[278] while in the same year Phillips indicated that light mineral green would cost from 3*s.* to 4*s.* 10*d.* per pound, or 5*s.* if in a spirit medium.[279]

Green, Naples. In 1786 the walls of the Long Bow Room at Gordon Castle were painted 'Naples Green', but whether this was made using Naples yellow (cf. sample 44) is not clear.[280]

Green, olive. Writing before the invention of Prussian blue, D'Aviler indicated that *olive colour* was made from yellow ochre, white, and charcoal black (cf. sample 40);[281] and a manuscript formula of about a century later for 'a green Paint proper for Rails &c' directed that the palest yellow ochre should be mixed with a small quantity of ivory black to produce a 'light olive'. For finer work Prussian blue could be substituted for the black to produce a 'light Green Colour',[282] but by the early nineteenth century such a colour was known also as *olive green* (cf. sample 43). Thus Nicholson combined Prussian blue with Oxford ochre, although elsewhere he suggested the use of light ochre, Prussian blue, and a little black;[283] while the author of the *Painter's . . . Pocket Manual* also gave a formula in which black was combined with a little blue and yellow.[284] In 1824 Berger noted a formula for a compound 'olive green' pigment in which Prussian blue was formed in the presence of yellow ochre;[285] and a little later Vanherman gave the following three formulae, the first two of which were intended for his exterior 'IMPENETRABLE, OR ANTI-CORROSIVE PAINT', and the last to be ground into oil after drying.[286]

1	Whiting	112 pounds
	Bristol ochre	224
	Damp blue	112
	Raw Devonshire umber	14
	Crotia	112
2	Whiting	28 pounds
	Yellow ochre	28
	Crotia	14
	Prussian blue: 'till the green is to your mind'.	
3	Refiners' verditer, wet	1 pound
	Chrome yellow	$2\frac{3}{4}$
	Wet blue	10
	White lead	16.

Vanherman's use of chrome yellow in the last of these is interesting, and provides an indication of the importance this pigment was to assume later in the nineteenth century.

Watin's formula for *olive green* oil paint may be compared with the earlier ochre and black mixtures. Both he and Tingry, who drew heavily on his book, suggested that the colour should be made from French yellow ochre mixed with a little verdigris and lamp black;[287] but although the second pigment would impart a noticeable brightening of tone, it seems possible that it was being used more as drier than for this purpose. It is likely that it was Tingry's book which prompted the suggestion made by the author of the *Painter's . . . Pocket Manual* for the combination of yellow pink with a little verdigris and lamp black.[288] In distemper, Watin and Tingry recommended the use of French ochre with indigo and white.[289]

Olive was clearly one of the staples of the house-painter's trade. It occurs in Emerton's price list of colours ready-mixed and ground in oil published in the 1730s at 8*d.* to 1*s.* per pound,[290] and in several early nineteenth-century lists. In 1816 the London Patent Colour-Works were selling 'IMPENETRABLE PAINT IN LINSEED-OIL' of this colour for interior or exterior use at prices from 1*s.* per pound upwards, while in 1825 Lingard marketed his 'INVULNERABLE OIL PAINT' at 1*s.* 3*d.* to 2*s.* In 1833, however, Bennett indicated that olive green oil paint could be obtained for only 9*d.* per pound, although he also listed *Spanish olive green* at 2*s.* 6*d.* The most expensive prices were given by Phillips in 1812, who listed *light olive green* 'by mixture' at 2*s.*, a darker variety at 2*s.* 5*d.*, and a *good olive green* 'by mixture, with Oxford stone ochre' at no less than 3*s.* This wide range of prices perhaps reflects not only a differing depth of tint, but also the alternative ways of mixing the colour suggested in the formulae reviewed above. Other proprietary varieties noted include the 'ANTI-CORROSIVE' paint of Bentley which he sold in 1817 at a rate approximately equivalent to 8*d.* per pound, against the cost price of 2*d.* claimed by Vanherman for his variety a few years later; while Bennett indicated that *fine olive green* 'anticorrosion' paint would cost 1*s*. 8*d*. The London Patent Colour-Works also marketed an olive green 'ANTIQUE ORNAMENTAL PAINT' for interior or exterior application in 1816 at 10*d*. per pound, the same price, curiously, as that at which Bennett priced *dark olive* coal-tar paint. Both Bentley and Vanherman indicated that their products should be applied on a lead colour undercoat.[291]

Together with the price of the paint, rates for its application also varied and analysis is difficult. It is worth recording, however, that for exterior work at Osterley Park between 1772 and 1774 6*d*. per yard was paid for 2 coats of olive green in oil, 9*d*. for 3, and 1*s*. for 4; while internally an area 'of Stucco Round foot of Stairs 2ce done Olive Color' cost 8*d*. per yard, and another '5 oil on Stucco finished olive Green flatted' was priced at 1*s*. 7*d*.[292] In the 1794 edition of the *Builders Price-Book olive colour* was priced at 9*d*, or 10*d*. per yard, against 'Common greens' at 10*d*. to 1*s*. and 'Fine deep greens' at 1*s*. to 1*s*. 2*d*., illustrating clearly the relationship it enjoyed with other colours.[293] Pincot indicated that it would cost 6*d*. per yard above the cost of common colours, and Phillips 5*d*.;[294] but these rates seem a little high, and in 1803 and 1816 the Painter-Stainers Company fixed a figure of 4*d*. extra, while both Laxton and Skyring indicated an addition of 3*d*.[295]

The earliest instance noted to date in which olive colour was used in an interior is in the painting account of 1729 for the Mansion House in York, where the Best Lodging Room and doors in the Great Room or Gallery were painted this colour.[296] A few years later, between 1731 and 1734, it was extensively used in the Gibbs Building at King's College, Cambridge;[297] while Mrs Powys recorded in 1760 that the Saloon at Eastbury, Dorset, was painted olive, and in 1781 that the Ballroom at Wanstead, Essex, had an 'olive and gold' wainscot.[298] As already noted, olive colour was used in the staircase at Osterley, and also in the Vestibule between 1772 and 1774,[299] while an item for olive green on stucco appears in the Somerset House accounts for 1780.[300] *Vert olive* was one of the *couleurs lucidoniques* manufactured with a semi-gloss finish at Paris from 1803.[301]

Green, Olympian. In 1819, William Stitt gave rates of 6*d*. to 7*d*. per yard for one coat of distemper in 'Olympian green', against $3\frac{1}{2}$*d* to 4*d*. for Portland stone colour. Two coats, he indicated, would cost 7*d*. to 8*d*., three 8*d*. to $9\frac{1}{2}$*d*, and four 9*d*. to $10\frac{1}{2}$*d*.[302] It will be recalled that in the late eighteenth century and early nineteenth, Berger was applying the name 'Olympian green' to varieties of Scheele's green (sample 47) which he manufactured, and it seems possible that it was these which lay behind Stitt's expression, especially since he also lists 'French green', another name applied by Berger to green pigments.[303]

Green, parrot. Reynolds gave a formula for preparing *parrot green* for exterior use. It contained 5 pounds of white lead, 1 pound of verdigris, and 4 ounces of spruce ochre.[304]

Green, patent. In 1803 and 1816, the Painter-Stainers Company fixed a rate of 9*d*. per yard extra for 'patent green' in oil.[305] Laxton too gave a figure of 9*d*., although Phillips suggested 8*d*., and Skyring quoted 5*d*.[306] In 1816 the London Patent Colour-Works were selling *patent light green* 'IMPENETRABLE PAINT IN LINSEED OIL' for interior or exterior use at 2*s*. per pound,[307] and in 1833 Bennett suggested that *patent grass green* oil paint would cost 3*s*.[308] It will be remembered that the Berger company was manufacturing a copper carbonate pigment called 'patent green' from 1811 until at least 1831, but references are also encountered to 'Fowler's patent green'. In 1812, Phillips indicated it would cost 5*s*. 5*d*. per pound; while Butcher later suggested its employment for making *green*.[309] It is not clear, however, whether the name was being given to a pigment, or to a proprietary mixture for a particular paint colour, perhaps containing patent yellow.

Green, pea. Documents relating to Somerset House suggest that the colour names *pea green* and *green verditer* (q.v.) were interchangeable, although the latter is, of course, properly the name of a pigment. Indeed, in distemper pea green seems generally to have been made using green verditer (sample 46). Phillips, for example, gave a price of 11*d*. per square yard for 'pea green, with verditor' in 1812, rising to 1*s*. in 1821;[310] and Laxton, who priced it at 1*s*. 2*d*., included the same item in 1818.[311] Nicholson noted that pea green was made in distemper with French green, a name used by the Berger firm for a related copper carbonate pigment at about the same date, but also suggested the use of Olympian green, the name of a variety of the pigment Scheele's green (cf. sample 47) also made by Berger.[312] It seems clear, therefore, that the colour would have been fairly bright in tone, a conclusion borne out by the sample of pea green in Hay's book of 1846 (which is rather yellowish but corresponds approximately to Munsell reference 10 GY 7/5)[313] and by formulae for its preparation in oil.

To make pea green for exterior purposes in the latter medium, Reynolds proposed the use of 1 pound of verdigris with 10 pounds of white lead, a combination which, as Tingry and the author of the *Painter's . . . Pocket Manual* pointed out, could be used to match the colour of green verditer in distemper (cf. samples 41, 46).[314] Nicholson, on the other hand, suggested the use of 'mineral green' (probably Scheele's green) or the mixture of Prussian blue and white with 'fine yellow', perhaps Naples yellow or patent yellow (cf. samples 44, 45).[315] Confirmation that the latter method was in use has been provided by the oil-based 'Pea Green' used in 1780 on the ceiling of the meeting room of the Royal Society at Somerset House, London, examination of which has indicated that it was made by tinting white lead with Prussian blue and Naples yellow, the colour (perhaps slightly degraded) stabilising a little brighter than Munsell reference 5 G 7/2 after treatment to remove discolouration in the oil medium.[316] It seems likely, therefore, that in the eighteenth century, various mixing methods were in use. In addition, Vanherman suggested that pea green was made from spruce ochre and Prussian blue (sample 43), but it seems likely this is a misprint for *tea green* (q.v.), and a much brighter colour than this combination would produce seems generally to have been implied by the name.[317] Thus, by 1831, the Berger firm, taking advantage of developments in pigment manufacture, made a 'Permanent' pea green using 128 lb. emerald green and 1 lb. 'Pale' chrome yellow extended with 128 lb. barytes, the qualification possibly reflecting a tendency to discolouration in earlier oil formulae.[318]

'Pea colour' was sold by Emerton in the 1730s at between 8*d*. and 1*s*. per pound of paste;[319] while in 1816 the London Patent Colour-Works sold pea green 'ANTIQUE ORNAMENTAL PAINT' at 1*s*. 6*d*., a second variety specifically for interior purposes costing 2*s*.[320] In addition, the London colourman, Charles Hodgkin, sold pea green 'Anticorrosion' paint at 2*s*. 6*d*. per pound.[321]

In 1759 Lady Caroline Fox had her Dressing Room painted pea green,[322] and in 1768 Lady Shelburne agreed with Adam that the furniture in the Painted Antechamber at Shelburne House Berkeley Square, London, should be upholstered in pea green satin spotted with white.[323] In the 1770s many references to the colour are made in accounts, letters, and diaries, including, for example, a letter of 1770 from Chambers to Gilbert Meason, a Leith merchant, in which he gave it among a number of alternatives for his parlours,[324] and another of 1771 to Robert Gregory concerning his house in Berners Street, London, where he again proposed to paint the Parlour in pea green with white mouldings and ornaments.[325] In the same year, Mrs Powys noted that the stucco in the Breakfast Parlour at Fawley Court, Buckinghamshire, was pea green with a gilt border, and James Adam estimated for its use in the Assembly Room at the Shire Hall, Hertford;[326] while by 1772 the Gallery at Osterley was hung with pea green paper.[327] In 1775 Chambers recommended the use of 'pea green in oil' for an unidentified room belonging to the Earl of Charlemont,[328] and in 1780 the colour was used as part of his scheme for the Ante-room shared by the Society of Antiquaries and Royal Society, and the Meeting Room of the latter body at Somerset House.[329] It was also proposed for picking out enriched mouldings in a note on a drawing by Chambers which is now at Newby Hall, Yorkshire.[330] Altogether, therefore, it appears to have been an extremely fashionable and popular colour.

Green, Persian. In 1831 Berger was making a colour of this name by combining his copper carbonate pigment, French green, with chrome yellow.[331]

Green, pistachio. *Vert pistache* was one of the *couleurs lucidoniques* available with a gloss finish which were manufactured in Paris from 1803.[332]

Green, pomona. *Pomona green* was defined by Hay as 'the popular name of all full-toned greens in which yellow predominates. This of course means the colour of an apple, and consequently admits of ample lattitude as to variety of tone'.[333] Watin indicated that *vert pomme* was made from blue, distilled verdigris, and more yellow, and the colour was one of the *couleurs lucidoniques* available in a matt finish made at Paris from 1803.[334] Bennet noted that pomona green oil paint would cost 1*s.* 6*d.* per pound.[335]

Green, quaker. In 1840 Berger noted a manufacturing formula for *quaker green*, which contained 1 cwt. 1 qr. 21 lb. 'Com.ⁿ Orange' chrome yellow, 2 cwt. 2 qrs. blue black, and 2 cwt. barytes.[336] *Quaker tints* in general are discussed below.

Green, rainbow. *Rainbow green* was the most expensive of the green oil colours manufactured by Crease in 1808 and retailed at 3*s.* 6*d.* per pound.[337]

Green, rich. *Rich green* appears in the list of 'ANTIQUE ORNAMENTAL PAINTS' manufactured for interior and exterior use by the London Patent Colour-Works in 1816 and was sold at 1*s.* 8*d.* per pound.[338]

Green, Roman. Bennett indicated that *Roman green* oil paint would cost 1*s.* 9*d.* per pound.[339]

Green, royal grass. See under *Green, grass.*

Green, sage. Nicholson indicated that *sage green* oil paint was made from white, Prussian blue, and 'fine yellow',[340] the latter perhaps implying the use of patent yellow or one of the organic pigments. Neither would have been particularly satisfactory, and Vanherman's suggestion seems much more sound. He used spruce ochre with Prussian blue and white (cf. sample 43), and noted that black could be used instead of the blue or raw umber in place of the ochre to produce further varieties.[341] Hay's sample of sage green corresponds approximately with Munsell reference 10 GY 7/2.[342]

Green, Sardinian. Crease listed light and deep *Sardinian greens* in his range of proprietary oil paints and sold them at 2*s.* and 1*s.* 8*d.* per pound respectively.[343]

Green, Saxony. Watin suggested that *vert Saxe* should be made from white, distilled verdigris, yellow, and a preponderance of blue;[344] while Vanherman gave the following formula for an oil paint:

Refiners verditer, wet	1	pound
Chrome yellow, wet	$2\frac{3}{4}$	
Wet blue	24	
White lead	16.	

After screening and drying, the mixture was ground into linseed oil.[345] Bennett indicated that 'Saxon' green oil paint would cost 2*s.* per pound.[346]

Green, sea. In 1752, Blondel listed 'verd d'eau, ou céladon [sea greenl]' among colours used in house-painting,[347] and a few years later Watin gave two formulae for the preparation of *vert d'eau* in distemper. The first called for the combination of ceruse and 'verd de montagne' (malachite); and the second, which, he noted would produce a more lively colour less liable to change, employed ceruse, blue verditer, and pink.[348] These formulae were repeated by Tingry for the production of 'sea green'.[349] For *vert de mer*, however. Watin had recommended the use of ceruse with Prussian blue and pink,[350] a formula not found in Tingry, but comparable with the combination of white with Prussian blue and 'fine yellow' proposed by Nicholson for sea green in oil (cf. samples 44, 45).[351] In varnish, Watin noted, *vert d'eau* was made using verdigris, a suggestion copied by Tingry;[352] while Reynolds indicated that a sea green oil paint for interior purposes should be made from 1 pint of white lead, 1 tablespoonful of verdigris, and 1 tablespoonful of spruce ochre.[353] *Vert d'eau* was one of the *couleurs lucidoniques* manufactured at Paris from 1803 and was available in a matt finish.[354]

Green, Spanish olive. See *Green, olive.*

Green, stucco. Bennett noted that *stucco green* oil paint would cost 2*s.* per pound.[355]

Green, superior. Bennett noted that *superior green* oil paint would cost 1*s.* 6*d.* per pound.[356]

Green, tea. Vanherman mentioned that spruce ochre was used in mixing *tea green*, almost certainly with Prussian blue (sample 43) since it seems most likely that his later reference to the mixing of 'pea' green by this means was a misprint and that tea green was intended.[357] The name was, no doubt, taken from the greyish green of the dried leaves of imported green tea. In 1823 it was proposed to paint the walls of the Map Gallery at Dunham Massey, Cheshire, tea green in oil.[358]

Green, verdigris. The term *verdigris green* seems to have been used generically to cover the whole family of greens made using the pigment (samples 41, 42), and would thus have included *grass green* and *willow green* (q.v.). Pincot observed that he had known 7*s.* per pound given for verdigris green,[359] while Phillips priced 'Light verdegris mixed' at 3*s.* and 4*s.* 3*d.* He also suggested that four coats of oil finished with verdigris green would cost 2*s.* 6*d.* per yard in 1812, a rate modified in 1821 to 2*s.* 3*d.* and probably copied from an early nineteenth-century edition of the *Builders Price-Book.*[360] In the 1810 and 1813 editions of this a price of 2*s.* 6*d.* per yard for 'Four times in oil [and flatted green] with verdigrease green' is given.[361] In 1803 and 1816, the Painter-Stainers Company fixed the price of verdigris green as 9*d.* per yard above the cost of common colours.[362]

Green, verditer. In 1782 the walls of the Duchess's Bedroom at Gordon Castle were painted 'Verditer Green',[363] a colour whose name no doubt reflected that of the pigment (sample 46) and with which *pea green* (q.v. above) appears to have been synonymous. The latter, it will be recalled, was often formulated in distemper using green verditer; while verdigris or mixtures of bright blue and yellow were employed in oil. It thus seems likely that Pincot's proprietary *green verditer* 'Water colour' for rooms was formulated using that very pigment,[364] but unlikely that this was necessarily the case where the name was applied to oil paint, especially bearing in mind Tingry's advice (reiterated by the author of the *Painter's . . . Pocket Manual*) that green verditer should not be used in oil, but that 2 or 3 parts of verdigris to 1 of white lead could be used instead.[365]

Confirmation of this is provided by documents relating to the decoration of Somerset House in 1780. In the painting accounts, *green verditer* occurs several times as a colour name, and formed part of the decorative scheme in the Royal Academy's Library and Exhibition Room, together with the Ante-chamber to the latter. It was used also in the cove of the Ante-room shared by the Royal Society and Society of Antiquaries, where it was described in the Deed of Transfer the following year as 'Pea green'. The rates allowed seem generally to have been for four coats on stucco 'finished Green Verditer' at 1*s.* 2*d.*, five coats finished in the same way costing 1*s.* 6*d.*[366] These prices and the use of four or five coats suggest the use of oil rather than distemper, and it seems significant that a sample from the wall in the Ante-room of the Royal Society and Society of Antiquaries, which were also described as 'Pea green' in the Deed of Transfer of 1781, has shown that they were painted in oil using a green probably formulated using Naples yellow and Prussian blue.[367]

Green, water. See *Green, sea.*

Green, Waterloo grass. See *Green, grass.*

Green, willow. John Smith recommended the use of verdigris alone to produce *willow green*, adding that the addition of white would make a *light willow green* (cf. sample 41).[368] The latter suggestion was copied a century and a half later by Nicholson and the author of the *Painter's . . . Pocket Manual.*[369] Willow green was defined by the late seventeenth-century writer Holme as a 'whitish Green'.[370]

Grey. Methods for mixing greys have been reviewed in Chapter 21 and specific varieties are discussed below. The term was, however, commonly used without qualification, and in such cases it is often difficult to assess the family to which the colour belongs. Thus Nicholson indicated that ceruse, Prussian blue, ivory black, and lake were used in mixing greys,[371] although at a much earlier date D'Aviler had mentioned black pigments alone, listing bone black, charcoal black, and lamp black (cf. samples 7, 10).[372] Certainly by the second half of the eighteenth century it seems likely that the unqualified term could represent one of the finer varieties, in particular *French grey* (q.v.) or a derivative such as the pale grey distemper Whittock suggested should be made using a small quantity of Venetian red with Prussian blue or indigo and whiting.[373] (This may be compared with Nicholson's formula for *pearl colour*, q.v.) On the other hand, this cannot always be assumed; and instances where reference is made simply to 'grey', such as the occasional manuscript notes on the Adam drawings at the Soane Museum or in the accounts for Somerset House, must be approached with an open mind.[374] In the latter, however, the rates for both 'grey' and 'French grey' (q.v.) are identical, suggesting here at least that the former colour was one of the more expensive varieties. Again, early nineteenth-century editions of the *Builders Price-Book* list 'grey' under 'Rich colours in oil' and in the equivalent list for 'Rich colours flated' qualify it as 'French grey'. The price per yard for 'Twice in oil grey' was 10*d.*, three times 1*s.*, and four times 1*s.* 4*d.*; while 'Twice in oil and flated French grey' was 1*s.* 5*d.*, three times 1*s.* 8*d.*, and four times 1*s.* 11*d.* In the case of distemper, 'Wash stop and grey' would, it was indicated, cost 5*d.* per yard, a price revised to 7*d.* by Laxton a few years later.[375] In 1803 the Painter-Stainers Company fixed the price of grey oil paint at 2*d.* per square yard above the cost of common colours.[376]

Grey, dove. See *Dove colour.*

Grey, fine. In distemper, Nicholson indicated that *fine greys* were made from white and refiners verditer (cf. *Grey, inferior* below).[377]

Grey, flaxen. Watin indicated that *gris de lin* was made in oil or distemper from ceruse, lake, and a very little Prussian blue, a formula repeated by Tingry for *flaxen grey*.[378] The author of the *Painter's . . . Pocket Manual*, however, indicated the use of white lead, Prussian blue, and a small quantity of lake,[379] making the colour more akin to French grey (q.v.) as described by Vanherman (cf. sample 12).

Grey, French. The most explicit directions for mixing *French grey* were given by Vanherman in connection with his 'Aromatic Paint' to which, he directed, one should, 'put as much ground Prussian blue as shall make it to your mind, then add as much lake, or rose pink, as will bestow on it a faint bloom'. The colour should, he noted, 'neither be dark not yet too light, but a middle tint' (cf. sample 12).[380] This formula is, of course, close to that given by Watin and Tingry for *flaxen grey* (q.v.), although this seems to have been more pinkish in tone, and for French grey Butcher regarded the addition of red pigment (he recommended lake or vermilion) as an improvement 'to make a more beautiful and pleasant colour' than that provided by blue alone.[381] No doubt, therefore, the term might also be applied to the other greys Watin described such as *gris argentin* and *gris perle* (*silver grey* and *pearl grey* – q.v.), which contained blue without the red. Butcher indicated this could be either Prussian blue or blue verditer,[382] but the latter was probably used more generally in distemper than oil. Watin noted that his formulae could be used in either medium, but evidence that verditer was used in distemper is provided by two early nineteenth-century price-lists, those of Cook and Skyring, in which there are items for French grey 'with verditer' at 10*d.* and 9*d.* per yard respectively.[383] The latter indicated that an ordinary variety would cost 5*d.* but did not state how it differed, and it is possible this was an inaccuracy or uncritical acceptance from an earlier text or edition. The 1794 edition of the *Builders Price-Book* suggested that French grey distemper would cost 3*d.* per yard, a price reported by Phillips to have been current from 1760 to 1790, rising to 4½*d.* between 1790 and 1803 and 9*d.* in 1812, before falling back to 6*d.* in 1821.[384]

Turning to look at prices for French grey in oil, 10*d.* per yard was charged between 1772 and 1774 for '3 oil on Stucco finished french Gray', and 1*s.* 4*d.* per yard for 'Stucco Walls 5 oil flatt french Gray' in the Gardener's House at Osterley Park.[385]

The latter is matched by the price for '5 times french grey [to Stucco]' at Somerset House in 1787, where in 1789 and 1790 1*s.* per yard was paid for 'Stucco 4 times French Grey' and '4 times in oil on [Stucco] flatted french Grey'.[386] This is the same rate as that suggested in the 1787 edition of the *Builders Price-Book* for flatted 'French greys four times in oil', although this was modified to 10*d.* in 1794.[387] In the 1810 and 1813 editions the comparable figure was 1*s.* 11*d.*, representing together with those of 1*s.* 5*d.* for two and 1*s.* 8*d.* for three times in oil an extra of 5*d.* per yard over the cost of dead white, the figure given by Phillips.[388] Pincot, however, suggested the slightly higher difference of 6*d.*, but Laxton proposed 3*d.*, and in 1831 Skyring gave 2*d.*, which seems rather low.[389] In conclusion it may be noted that a quantity of 'Dead French Gray' was supplied at Dyrham Park in 1781 at a cost of 1*s.* per pound, while Pincot marketed his French grey 'WATER COLOUR' at 1*s.* 4*d.* per pound.[390]

In 1771 Mrs Powys described the stucco in the Hall at Fawley Court, Buckinghamshire, as painted French grey,[391] and the following year the walls of the Dining Room at Gordon Castle were painted this colour.[392] Besides the item for the Gardener's House already mentioned, French grey was used on the shutter-framing and panels and on the grounds of the friezes above the doors in the Hall at Osterley in the work done between 1772 and 1774, and also for the panel grounds in the soffit of the portico. In 1787 further items in the Hall, including the ceilings and plinth, were painted this tint.[393] In 1775 Adam proposed its use for the ceiling of the Oval Room at Great Saxham House, Suffolk;[394] while further instances of its intended employment are found in connection with a staircase in Arlington Street, London, in the same year,[395] and for the walls of the Best Staircase at Dunham Massey, Cheshire, in 1821.[396] Items in the accounts for Somerset House, where Chambers used French grey in the ceiling of the Ante-room shared by the Royal Society and Society of Antiquaries in 1780, have already been noted.

Grey, inferior. In distinction to *fine greys* (q.v.), Nicholson indicated that *inferior greys* were made in distemper using blue black or bone black and indigo.[397] Such a combination is similar to that which Watin suggested for *gris argentin* (discussed under *Grey, silver* below) and may be compared with that for his *gris ordinaire* in oil or distemper which contained white and charcoal black alone (see *Grey, ordinary* below).

Grey, iron. See *Iron colour.*

Grey, light. Tingry indicated that *light grey* was much used for rooms, especially those exposed to strong sunlight.[398] He suggested the use of white lead and lamp black in oil, a formula probably copied by the author of the *Painter's . . . Pocket Manual.*[399] Soane intended the use of light grey on the ceiling of the Staircase at Pitzhanger Manor, Ealing, in 1802.[400]

Grey, mouse. *Gris souris* was one of the *couleurs lucidoniques* manufactured at Paris from 1803 with a matt finish.[401]

Grey, ordinary. Watin indicated that *gris ordinaire* was made in oil or distemper by combining charcoal black with white (sample 7), a formula which may be compared with those for *inferior grey* given above.[402]

Grey, Paris. In writing to Gilbert Meason, a Leith merchant, in 1770 Chambers recommended the use of *Paris grey* among a number of alternatives for painting his parlours.[403] It seems likely that this represented one of the French greys (q.v.).

Grey, pearl. See *Pearl colour.*

Grey, silver. Watin indicated that *gris argentin* was made in oil or distemper from white and indigo (sample 8), 'noir de composition' (the charcoal made from the residue from the manufacture of Prussian blue), or vine black (sample 7) in very small quantities.[404] Tingry, on the other hand, observed that *pearl grey* (q.v.) made from white and blue (or blue with black) was also called *silver grey*;[405] while the author of the *Painter's . . . Pocket Manual* suggested silver grey should be made from white lead, indigo, and a very small portion of black.[406] In 1786 the panels of the windows and dado in the Drawing Room at Gordon Castle were flatted silver grey with white mouldings.[407]

Grey, slate. See *Slate colour.*

Hazel nut. *Noisette claire ou foncée* appeared in the range of *couleurs lucidoniques* manufactured at Paris from 1803 with a matt finish.[408]

Hydrangea. *Hortensia* was one of the *couleurs lucidoniques* manufactured at Paris from 1803 with a matt finish.[409]

Ice colour. Reynolds gave the following formula for *ice colour* oil paint intended for interior use: 'To one pint of white lead, add one teaspoonfull Rosin; one teaspoonfull Verdigris; and half a teaspoonfull of Lamp-black'. As usual the pigments were combined in paste form.[410]

Iron colour. Bullet indicated that *couleur de fer* for ironwork was made from ceruse and lamp black (sample 10).[411] In 1630–5 iron colour was used on the saddle-bars of the windows in the Chapel formed out of the tennis court at Somerset House;[412] and in 1694, among other exterior items four doors and two arbours at Dyrham Park were painted iron colour at a cost of 9*d.* per yard.[413] *Couleur de fer* was one of the *couleurs lucidoniques* manufactured at Paris from 1803 with a glossy finish.[414]

Jonquil. Tingry, copying Watin's formula, noted that *jonquil* was mixed from white lead and Dutch pink, adding that it was used only in distemper or occasionally in varnish.[415] The author of the *Painter's . . . Pocket Manual* also repeated the suggestion, but remarked it was 'only proper in distemper' (sample 21).[416] Nevertheless, in 1737 Blondel noted the use of *jonquille* on panelling, and again referred to its use in house-painting in 1752.[417]

Lake. Although properly the name for a type of pigment, generally red (cf. sample 16), and used in this sense by John Smith,[418] Laxton mentioned that 'lake colours' would cost an extra 9*d.* per yard over the cost of common colours.[419] *Laque carminée* also appears among the list of *couleurs lucidoniques* manufactured at Paris from 1803 in a matt finish.[420]

Lavender colour. In interesting contrast to the method for making *French grey* (q.v.), in which the blue was added first, Vanherman indicated that *lavender colour* was made by mixing 'lake, or rose pink, with a good portion of white, to bring it to a peach-blossom colour; you then add a little Prussian blue, sufficient to give it a cast' (sample 38). It was, he noted, an elegant tint for a drawing room, and would add an illusion of height to ceilings on account of its 'retiring appearance'.[421] A light lavender tint was used in the ground of the cornice and architrave in the Circular Room at Carlton House.[422]

Laylock. See *Lilac.*

Lead colour. Referred to in late eighteenth-century editions of the *Builders Price-Book* and by Laxton as one of the common colours, and appearing in Emerton's range of the 1730s in the cheapest range of colours at 4*d.* or 5*d.* per pound, *lead colour* was often mentioned by authors throughout the period being examined.[423] By the early nineteenth century it seems clear it was made by a simple mixture of white and black (usually lamp black – sample 10), and was therefore a neutral grey similar to *ash colour* (q.v.) as defined by John Smith in the late seventeenth century, or *iron colour* discussed above. Formulae employing lamp black were given by Pincot (who included it as one of the five colours used for finishing exterior work and advocated it as an undercoat for olive, chocolate, and invisible green), Butcher, Nicholson, and Tingry's later editor.[424] Vanherman, however, used mineral black in his 'IMPENETRABLE, OR ANTI-CORROSIVE PAINT', giving the following formulae:[425]

1	Whiting	224 pounds
	Dry white lead	224
	Mineral black	56
	Crotia	112
2	Whiting	56 pounds
	Dry white lead	56
	Mineral black	28
	Crotia	14

Earlier, John Smith had advocated a mixture of white with indigo, which would have produced a rather bluish grey (sample 11);[426] and his formula was repeated by Butcher, Nicholson, and the author of the *Painter's . . . Pocket Manual*, all of whom copied, often uncritically, from his by then obsolete work.[427] In the seventeenth century, therefore, lead colour probably reflected more accurately the bluish tinge of metallic lead, although indigo was a comparatively expensive pigment and it is possible that black was often substituted or mixed with the indigo in the way mentioned by the author of the *Painter's . . . Pocket Manual*, who recommended this as a way of mixing dark lead colour.[428]

Primatt mentioned that lead colour would cost 9*d.* or 10*d.* per yard in oil,[429] while a century and a half later Crease and Lingard sold their lead colour oil paints at 42*s.* per cwt.,[430] and the London Patent Colour-Works theirs at 52*s.* and 56*s.*[431] Vanherman noted that his 'ANTI-CORROSIVE' paint would cost the equivalent of 18*s.* 8*d.* per cwt. to manufacture; Bentley sold his at 46*s.* per cwt.; and Hodgkin his product at the equivalent of 50*s.* 6*d.*[432] The latter price was repeated by Bennett, who also mentioned a lead-colour coal-tar paint, indicating that it was available at 52*s.* per cwt.[433]

Lead colour was used on two parts of the walls in the Privy Chamber at Hampton Court which the hangings did not cover in 1617–18; on the window bars in the Prince's New Lodging at Newmarket, Suffolk, in 1620–1; on the rails and ballusters of two staircases (and probably also a doorcase) in the Banqueting House at Nonsuch in 1621–2; and in connection with the conversion of the tennis court at Somerset House into a chapel in 1630–5.[434] In 1671 the 'Iron raile that goes up the round Staires' (i.e. the Tulip Staircase) at the Queen's House, Greenwich, was painted lead colour;[435] two barrels at Montagu House, London, were painted lead colour in 1704;[436] and lead colour was used in the back stairs of the east wing of Somerset House (probably on the ironwork) in 1780.[437] In addition, a 'Very light Lead Colour' is mentioned in an alternative scheme for a ceiling on the reverse of an undated design by George Dance the younger.[438]

Lemon colour. *Lemon colour* appears in the most expensive category of Emerton's ready-mixed oil-paints at 1*s.* per pound,[439] while *jaune citron* was one of the *couleurs lucidoniques* available in a glossy finish which were manufactured in Paris from 1803.[440] To make *jaune citron* Watin advocated the use of more or less yellow and red orpiment, adding that the mixture was generally used only in oil. As a substitute avoiding the use of these extremely unpleasant pigments he proposed ceruse with an organic yellow or Naples yellow (sample 22), a method repeated by Tingry for making *lemon yellow* in distemper and varnish. The mixture of yellow and red orpiment was, he indicated, the way in which the colour was made of old;[441] but both were repeated by the author of the *Painter's . . . Pocket Manual*, who again stated that pink and Naples yellow mixtures were used only in distemper.[442]

Late eighteenth-century editions of the *Builders Price-Book* suggest a price of 10*d.* to 1*s.* per yard for lemon colour in oil: 'Distemper on stucco with enriched mouldings, grounds . . . lemon . . . and the mouldings white', however, would cost 6*d.* per yard.[443] For lemon-colour distemper Laxton too indicated a rate of 6*d.* per yard, but Skyring 5*d.*[444] In 1737, Blondel referred to the use of *citron* on panelling;[445] 'Limon Colour' is mentioned on a drawing by William Chambers now at Newby Hall, Yorkshire;[446] and the latter used lemon in the oval surrounding the central area of the ceiling of the Royal Academy's Exhibition Room at Somerset House in 1780.[447] It was also mentioned by Hay in the late 1820s.[448]

Lilac. In 1752, Blondel included *lilas* in a list of colours used in house-painting,[449] and the colour appears among the *couleurs lucidoniques* with a matt finish which were manufactured in Paris from 1803.[450] The only author noted who gave a formula was Watin, who suggested it should be made by combining lake, carmine, and a little blue (sample 37).[451] In 1803 the Painter-Stainers Company fixed the price of *lilac* as 6*d.* per yard above the rate for common colours,[452] Laxton later reducing this to 5*d.*[453] In late eighteenth-century England it seems often to have been called *laylock*, since this term was used in the Somerset House accounts to describe the paint applied to parts of the ceiling of the meeting room of the Royal Society itemised the following year in the Deed of Transfer as 'light purple'.[454] 'Laylock' was also used on the ceiling of the Antique Academy of the Royal Academy in the same building,[455] and 'laylock' appears as a manuscript note on drawings by Adam (dated 1768 and 1770) and George Dance the younger, the latter noting that a 'faint laylock' was to be used.[456] In 1819 Pyne recorded the 'small stiles' surrounding the door panels in the Throne Room at Carlton House were painted lilac.[457]

Liver colour. The wainscot in the Marble Parlour at Wimbledon House was described as varnished *liver colour* in the inventory of 1649,[458] and Pratt observed that burnt umber was almost of this hue.[459]

Lute colour. It seems most likely the term *lute colour*, to which references are found in pre-Civil-War documents, was used to signify a dull warm yellow or orange. This may have been synonymous with 'clay colour' (q.v.) and could have been mixed in oil or distemper using red and yellow ochres (cf. sample 18). The name appears to derive from the Latin adjective *luteus*, which was applied to yellows of red or orange cast, or to the noun *lutum* meaning mud or clay. Thus, in the sixteenth century, Mercato noted in connection with a specimen in the Vatican mineral collection: 'Ochra terra glebosa est coloris lutei'; in 1686 Waller described the colour of *ochra* as 'luteus' or 'Clay Col.'; and in the mid-eighteenth century Dr Johnson gave the meaning of 'lutarious' as 'of the colour of mud'.[460] Indicating its orange cast, Holme noted in 1688 that in describing the colours of birds, naturalists used 'luteous' for 'yellow like the yolk of an Egg'.[461] It is thus possible to suggest that the dull orange-yellow shown on walls forming the setting for Daniel Mytens's portrait of Alatheia Talbot, dating from about 1618 may represent lute colour.[462] This is comparable with a dull brownish yellow approximating to Munsell reference 10 YR 5/6 found on a seventeenth-century window splay in the north-east ground-floor room in the Queen's House, Greenwich, which has been obscured by eighteenth-century joinery. The pigments used to formulate the latter have been found by optical examination to be yellow and red ochres in oil.[463]

References to lute colour at Whitehall Palace include its use, apparently as an undercoat for walnut colour, on cupboards in the King's Closet in 1625–6.[464] It was used also on the linenfold panelling in the Tiltyard Gallery in 1627–8 (where it was executed in distemper and varnished);[465] and on the frieze and cornice in the Lord Chamberlain's Cabinet in 1629–30 (again in distemper and varnished), the chimneypiece also being painted lute colour.[466] In 1631–2 it was used on the wainscot in the Long Gallery leading to the Privy Lodging (where it was varnished); on the doors and other elements in Mr Taverner's bedchamber (in distemper); and on a wainscot partition in the Long Gallery adjoining the King's Withdrawing Room (where it was varnished).[467] In addition, it was employed in the wainscoted room in the garden at St James's Palace in 1629–30.[468] It is also worth noting that references are found in the Exchequer rolls to the use on picture frames of *sad lute colour*.[469]

Mahogany colour. No formulae for *mahogany colour* have been encountered in the course of research, although methods for imitation of the timber have been reviewed in Chapter 20. It is clear, however, that, as with similar colour names, graining was quite often not implied, and Emerton sold a *mahogany colour* paint at 6*d*. per pound in the 1730s.[470] The most likely constituents are red ochre and lamp black (sample 32), and eighteenth-century editions of the *Builders Price-Book* indicated that two coats would cost 4*d*. per square yard, putting it firmly in the realm of prices for common colours;[471] but Phillips gave prices for two qualities in 1821, a 'good' mahogany colour costing 3*s*. per pound, and a better, brighter variety 5*s*., rates well above those for the majority of browns he listed.[472] In the early 1730s mahogany colour had been used on doors in several of the sets in the Gibbs Building at King's College, Cambridge, including in one instance the shutters also;[473] and was applied too to the stair rail at a house associated with the Osterley Park estate between 1772 and 1774.[474] *Acajou* was one of the *couleurs lucidioniques* manufactured at Paris from 1803 with a semi-gloss finish.[475]

Marigold. Tingry indicated that *marigold* was made using slightly calcined orpiment, but this seems anachronistic and by the early nineteenth century less toxic pigments were available.[476]

Morocco. *Maroquin* was one of the range of *couleurs lucidoniques* manufactured at Paris from 1803 with a semi-gloss finish.[477]

Mouse colour. See *Grey, mouse.*

Myrtle. The mid-nineteenth-century writer Hay illustrated a sample of *myrtle* which approximates in colour to Munsell reference 5 G 4/4.[478]

Naples yellow. See *Yellow, Naples.*

Oak colour. John Smith indicated that a colour resembling new oak timber was made from umber and white (cf. sample 3),[479] but Watin included ochres in his formulation. *Bois de chêne* was, he suggested, to be mixed in oil or distemper using $\frac{3}{4}$ part of ceruse combined with $\frac{1}{4}$ part of a compound made from 'ochre de rue', umber, and yellow ochre of Berry. By varying the proportions of the last three pigments, the colour could be adjusted to the tint required (cf. sample 35).[480] Tingry and the author of the *Painter's . . . Pocket Manual* repeated his formula.[481] *Wainscot colour* was presumably more or less the same as *oak colour*, but the only information on mixing is given by Nicholson, who suggested that it contained no white lead and gave no further details.[482]

Prices encountered for wainscot colour during the late seventeenth century vary widely, probably depending on the number of coats applied in any given instance. Only in the account of 1705 for Ditton, Buckinghamshire (demolished 1812), where three are specified at a cost of 9*d*. per yard, is a number mentioned.[483] Neve remarked merely that wainscot colour on new work would cost 8*d*. per yard and on old work 7*d*.,[484] but it seems likely that new work would have required three coats including the primer, and old work probably two with an allowance for preparation. Figures of 8*d*. and 9*d*. were quoted in the tenders for Greenwich Hospital about 1696;[485] 8*d*. was charged at Montagu House, London, in 1706;[486] and 10*d*. was paid at Kensington Palace a few years earlier.[487] Both here and at Dyrham in 1694, however, other items are priced at 1*s*. 2*d*., suggesting that more coats were involved;[488] while for painting the doorcase on the best staircase in the Mansion House, York, oak colour in 1729 6*d*. per yard was paid, a rate suggesting this may have been by way of redecoration.[489]

Emerton sold his *wainscot or oak colour* oil paint at 4*d*. or 5*d*. per pound in the 1730s[490] showing that, as indicated by the author of the *Builders Price-Book* later in the century, it was one of the common colours;[491] and in the early nineteenth century Bentley sold oak colour 'ANTI-CORROSIVE PAINT' for exterior purposes at 46*s*. per cwt.[492]

References to wainscot colour are found before the Civil War. These include three areas of wall in the Cross Gallery at Hampton Court in 1621–2 (in distemper); a similar exercise in the King's Gallery at Whitehall in 1624–2, various doors elsewhere in the palace being painted this colour at the same date; and the deal partitions and window shutters in Mr Porter's lodging at the same in 1625–6 (in distemper), where sundry window lights and bars were similarly coloured.[493] As already seen from the data on prices given above, in the later seventeenth century wainscot and oak colour were used on panelling, and continued to be employed on doors. At Dyrham, for example, the doors of the Hall and Pavilion, and sashes of the former were painted wainscot colour in 1694; while at Montagu House, London, the hinges and bars of five windows were similarly coloured in 1705.[494] In addition to the other instances of its use mentioned in connection with the review of prices above, an intention was expressed to paint the Great Stairs at St James's Palace wainscot colour in 1723;[495] and the first-floor Lodging Room at the Mansion House, York was painted oak colour in 1729.[496] Almost a century later, in 1821 it was decided to paint the wainscot in the Hall at Dunham Massey 'rather light oak', in 1823 the woodwork of five privies in the garden 'Oak', and in 1829 the wainscot of the Billiard Room 'new Oak Colour'.[497]

Olive colour. See *Green, olive.*

Orange. John Smith suggested that yellow ochre should be mixed with red lead to make an orange colour oil paint.[498] His *brick colour* (q.v.), on the other hand, contained these pigments with white, as indeed did Reynolds's formula for an orange colour for exterior purposes (cf. sample 15). The latter called for the addition of 1 pound of red lead to 10 pounds of a straw colour made from 10 pounds of white lead and 1 pound of spruce or English ochre, the constituents being mixed dry before being ground into the oil.[499] Smith's formula was repeated by Nicholson and the author of the *Painter's . . . Pocket Manual* and was probably in common use,[500] but Vanherman noted in connection with his 'AROMATIC PAINT' that vermilion and yellow should be combined to make orange, a rather more expensive method which probably offered few advantages. In addition, he also suggested that brilliant oranges of various gradations could be made from lake with chrome yellow.[501] Although no distemper formulae have been noted, it is clear from the priced items reviewed in the next paragraph that orange was often prepared in this medium, and it will be recalled that both yellow ochre and red lead were contained in the list of pigments the plasterers were permitted to use under the 1603 Act.[502] There seems to be no reason, therefore, why the same formula as that for oil paint should not have been used; while to produce a duller and cheaper colour red ochre might be substituted for red lead (sample 18), the product perhaps being known in the seventeenth century as *lute colour* (q.v.).

In the 1730s Emerton sold his orange colour oil paint at 1*s.* per pound, and in 1821 Phillips noted that orange colour 'by mixture' would cost 1*s.* 2*d.*, the same price being charged for a reddish variety.[503] *Orange* was also available in the range of *couleurs lucidoniques* manufactured at Paris from 1803 with a glossy finish.[504] In oil, the compiler of the late eighteenth-century editions of the *Builders Price-Book* suggested that orange would cost from 10*d.* to 1*s.* per yard; while in distemper the same colour on stucco would cost 3*d.*[505] Phillips showed how the price of the latter had risen to 4½*d.* by 1803, rose further to 9*d.* in 1812, and fell back to 6*d.* in 1821.[506] By 1831 Skyring indicated that it stood at 5*d.*[507]

The way in which orange was used in interiors is unclear, and it seems doubtful that it can always have been a very popular colour on large areas of wall in rooms. The only eighteenth-century references to its employment encountered to date are in connection with small discrete areas on neo-classical ceilings: a note on Adam's design of 1778 for that of the Lady's Dressing Room at Mellerstain, Berwickshire, which was probably painted in 'Etruscan' colours, shows it applied to the central flower;[508] and an undated ceiling design by James Wyatt for an unknown location is annotated to show that the ground of the central flower was to be orange, this and other comparable areas on the drawing being tinted accordingly.[509] In the nineteenth century, both Whittock and Vanherman used orange in colour schemes reflecting contemporary ideals of colour harmony.[510]

Party colours. Laxton defined the term *party colours* as being applied 'where the framing is of one colour, and the pannels another'.[511] It was used in the 1755 account for Norfolk House, where many interior items including ceilings, shutter panels, window soffits and architraves, and an entablature were picked in with 'Party colours'.[512] In 1831, Skyring indicated that this treatment would cost an extra 3*d.* per square yard.[513]

Pea colour. See *Green, pea.*

Peach colour. In 1688 Holme indicated that *peach colour* was 'a more light bright coloured Violet';[514] and in the early nineteenth century Nicholson suggested that *peach* should be mixed using lake, white, and Chinese vermilion (cf. sample 14).[515] Laxton noted that in oil it would cost 5*d.* per square yard more than common colours, but Skyring quoted 2*d.*, a rate which suggests that it was often light in tone and much the same as peach-blossom colour (q.v.).[516]

Peach-blossom colour. In giving directions for the mixing of lavender colour, Vanherman indicated that the first stage was to prepare a *peach-blossom colour* by combining lake or rose pink with a good portion of white.[517] This suggestion may be compared with that made by Nicholson for making peach colour (q.v.) which may have been identical in concept. A few years later, Hay illustrated a sample of peach blossom which corresponds approximately with Munsell reference 2.5 RP 7/5.[518] George Smith suggested the use of peach blossom on the walls of a room reflecting a 'very chaste style of decoration';[519] while Pyne recorded that the areas of wall surrounding the velvet panels, the doors, dado, and skirting in the Blue Velvet Room at Carlton House were painted in a light peach-blossom.[520] In addition, a 'light peach blossom colour' was also used in the Octagon Hall at the Royal Pavilion, Brighton, in 1820.[521] It will be remembered that the unqualified term 'blossom colour' (q.v.) was in use in the eighteenth century, and it seems possible that this cluster of references in the early nineteenth to peach blossom may be traced to Goethe, who included it as one of the prismatic colours in 1791.[522]

Pearl colour. French formulae for *pearl colour* suggest it was seen as having a bluish cast. In distemper, Bullet suggested that indigo should be combined with Spanish white (sample 8), and in oil that as much smalt as necessary to produce the colour required should be added to white lead (sample 9).[523] The latter combination has been found on a mid-seventeenth-century doorcase now in the Banqueting Hall at Tamworth Castle, Staffordshire; and in one of the lower layers on the late seventeenth-century wainscot in the Marble Hall at Petworth, Sussex.[524] By the second half of the eighteenth century, other methods seem to have been employed, and in both oil and distemper Watin advocated the use of Prussian blue with white, suggesting also the addition of the charcoal pigments 'noir de composition' or vine black.[525] Tingry too indicated that white was mixed with blue or a blue-black mixture.[526] In 1819, Stitt gave prices for 'Verditer . . . pearl colour' and 'Indigo pearl colour' in distemper, the former costing 6*d.* or 7*d.* for a single coat (probably including preparation) and the latter 4*d.* or 4½*d.*, the price difference seeming to confirm employment of these pigments for mixing the colour.[527] The author of the *Painter's . . . Pocket Manual* too referred to the use of indigo and white, with or without the addition of a small proportion of black.[528] This formula, it will be remembered, Watin had reserved for silver grey (q.v.) but Tingry had since remarked this was synonymous with pearl grey. In contrast to all these formulae, the American author Reynolds seems to have had a greenish tinge in mind, directing that for interior purposes pearl grey should be made from 1 pint of white lead, a teaspoonful of Prussian blue, and a similar quantity of spruce ochre.[529] Nicholson too gave it a variant tint, suggesting a mixture of black, blue, white, and a little Indian red, a combination which would have resulted in a colour rather similar to French grey (q.v.), but, perhaps, lacking its refinement.[530]

Emerton sold pearl-colour oil paint in the 1730s at his cheapest rate of 4*d.* or 5*d.* per pound,[531] and in the *Builder's Price-Book* it was indicated as one of the common colours.[532] It was available also in the range of *couleurs lucidoniques* manufactured at Paris from 1803 in a matt finish.[533] In 1706 an appreciable yardage in an apartment at Montagu House, London, was painted pearl colour at 9*d.* per square yard, suggesting that it was applied to the wainscot;[534] and it was used also in the early 1730s in eleven of the sets in the Gibbs Building at King's College, Cambridge, no doubt for the same purpose.[535] In 1759 Chambers mentioned its use on ceilings, and in 1770 wrote to one of his clients suggesting it could be used among a number of alternatives for painting his parlours if he intended them to be 'very neat'.[536] A few years later it was used in the Hall and Staircase together with rooms on the 'bedchamber story' of a house attached to the Osterley Park estate.[537]

Pink. Although one of the most commonly encountered colour names, only one specific formula for mixing pink, that for a 'delicate pink' distemper made, Whittock suggested, from lake and white (cf. sample 17), has been noted.[538] Not to be confused with the organic yellow pigment, pink, the term seems to have been in use in its modern sense of rose pink by the beginning of the eighteenth century, and Emerton was selling pink oil paint at 1*s.* per pound in the 1730s.[539] The price suggests, of course, that it contained one or both of the comparatively expensive tinting pigments, lake and vermilion, and the colour was probably made using these in the way discussed in Chapter 21 in connection with general methods for mixing pink and bright reds (sample 14). Late eighteenth-century editions of the *Builders Price-Book* indicate pink would cost 10*d.* to 1*s.* per yard in oil, and mention also its use in distemper 'on stucco . . . and the mouldings white' at 6*d*;[540] while in 1803 the Painter-Stainers Company fixed the price of pink in oil as 6*d.* extra per square yard above the cost of common colours amending this to 4*d.* to 6*d.* in 1816.[541]

The name appears in manuscript notes on a large number of the Adam ceiling designs at the Soane Museum dated between 1766 and 1773, often qualified as light or dark in colour;[542] and in their *Works in Architecture* the fact that pink was used as part of the colour scheme for the ceiling of the Library at Kenwood was specifically mentioned.[543] It appears also in James Adam's estimate of 1771 for painting the Assembly and Council Rooms in the Shire Hall at Hertford.[544] It was used in ceiling grounds in the Drawing Room at Osterley between 1772 and 1774, and at the same time the stucco frames surrounding the wall panels in the Dining Room at the latter were painted '5 oil finished Pink Colour' at 1*s.* 6*d.* per yard: later, in 1787, items appear in connection with the house for 'three times in oil & flatted fine pink' at 1*s.* 9*d.*, and for picking panel grounds in a ceiling.[545] Naturally, Chambers too used pink, the Deed of Transfer of 1781 showing that it was employed as part of the colour schemes in the common Ante-room shared by the Royal Society and Society of Antiquaries, and in the ceilings of the Meeting Rooms of the two bodies at Somerset House.[546] It was used too at Fonthill, since Rutter recorded in 1823 that it was to be seen in the South Entrance Hall, on the ceilings in the Oak Parlour and Vaulted Library, and on the walls of an Ante-chamber.[547]

Pink, Dutch. Although properly the name of a yellow pigment, Pincot sold one of his proprietary 'WATER COLOURS' as *Dutch pink* in the early years of the nineteenth century. Its price was 1*s.* per pound (cf. sample 21).[548]

Pink, English. Again properly the name of a yellow pigment, Pincot sold a 'WATER COLOUR' called *English pink*, this time at 6*d.* per pound, suggesting that it was paler in colour than his Dutch pink (cf. sample 21).[549]

Pink, red. A 'Red Pink' was used by Adam in a design for the Drawing Room ceiling at Whitehaven dated 1769.[550]

Plum colour. Whittock suggested that a light *plum colour* distemper should be made from Indian red, blue, a little lake, and whiting. Both he and Vanherman illustrated its use in colour schemes reflecting contemporary ideals of colour harmony.[551]

Pompadour. Tingry's later editor indicated that the pigment commonly called purple brown was a purple iron oxide (cf. sample 39), and noted it was used to make *pompadour*.[552]

Portland stone colour. See *Stone colour, Portland* below.

Princes-wood colour. In 1694 the joinery in the Tapestry Bedroom at Dyrham Park was painted *princes-wood colour* at 1*s.* 2*d.* per square yard.[553] It is possible, however, that the finish was grained.

Puce. *Puce foncé* was one of the *couleurs lucidoniques* manufactured at Paris from 1803 with a glossy finish.[554]

Purple. Pincot observed that purple was an extravagant colour and would cost 8*d.* per yard over the cost of common colours.[555] For interior applications in oil, it was made, Reynolds indicated, by combining rose pink and Prussian blue in equal parts; and Nicholson used a similar method, mixing lake with blue and white, while Vanherman observed that lake would harmonise with Prussian blue to produce a variety of beautiful purples (cf. sample 37).[556] The name appears in nearly a score of manuscript notes on ceiling designs by Adam at the Soane Museum dated between 1768 and 1780,[557] and dark purple was used in some of the grounds of the Drawing Room ceiling at Osterley Park between 1772 and 1774.[558] Chambers too advocated the colour on a ceiling he had designed for the Earl of Charlemont, suggesting in 1775 that a little purple might be introduced in some areas.[559] In 1780, he employed it too at Somerset House in the ceiling and frieze of the Royal Academy's Exhibition Room, and in the ceiling and wall-panels of their Library.[560] In the Deed of Transfer of the following year, parts of the ceiling of the Meeting Room of the Royal Society (mentioned in the accounts as 'Laylock' – described under *lilac* above) were noted as being light purple, for pale tints of which the latter was an obvious synonym;[561] while in 1766 the Duchess of Northumberland had recorded the use of light purple in the ground of the ceiling of the Dining Room at Kedleston Hall, Derbyshire.[562]

Purple brown. Although properly the name of a dark iron-oxide pigment (cf. sample 39), the term *purple brown* was also applied to a paint colour, no doubt of a dark purple hue and probably identical with *pompadour* (q.v.). In 1816 the London Patent Colour-Works marketed a purple brown 'IMPENETRABLE PAINT IN LINSEED-OIL' for interior and exterior use at 42*s.* per cwt.,[563] and thirty years later Bartholomew specified the colour for painting sashes externally.[564]

Quaker tints. In 1828, Vanherman noted that mixture of raw umber with white would produce a number of pleasant *quaker tints*. The addition of a little black would provide more, while if any of the reds was mixed in this would increase the number still further.[565] It seems likely, therefore, that quaker tints were seen as dull off-whites; and by extension that quaker brown and quaker green mentioned above were similarly subdued in tone.

Reds. Methods for mixing reds have been reviewed in Chapter 21, where two categories were considered, the bright colours (samples 13, 16) and the darker tones (samples 31, 39). The range of hues in the first category is probably bounded on the one hand by *crimson* (q.v.), made using carmine, and on the other by *scarlet* (q.v.), made using vermilion; although Butcher noted that vermilion might be combined (or, perhaps, sophisticated) with red lead to make a red, which would thus have had a more orange cast. He also observed, however, that the latter pigments and lakes were generally used separately.[566] Reynolds too listed red lead, vermilion, and rose pink for use internally in a way which suggests he saw them as alternatives.[567] Against this, Nicholson (having noted that lakes had to be mixed with white for use, since unlike red lead, vermilion, purple brown and Indian red, they were not body colours) recommended that vermilion too might be added according to the tone desired.[568] It will be remembered that Watin proposed a similar mixture for crimson, and was often used in the case of pink colours; while for a dark red distemper Whittock combined Venetian red, vermilion, lake, and a little whiting.[569]

In general, the expensive pigments such as vermilion or lake were not used for red paint externally. Vanherman, for example, gave the following formulae for red in his 'IMPENETRABLE OR ANTI-CORROSIVE PAINT' intended for exterior use:

1	Spanish brown	224 pounds
	Crotia	224
2	Whiting	56 pounds
	Spanish brown	56
	Crotia	84.

This colour was, he indicated, 'a most excellent and durable covering for barns, sheds, cart and waggon wheels, implements of husbandry, tiles, &c.'.[570] Reynolds too used Spanish brown in his red oil formula for exterior use, combining 8 pounds of it with 4 pounds of red lead before grinding the mixture into oil, although he also indicated that Venetian red on its own would provide a richer colour and be more durable.[571] It was, perhaps, a red of this nature that was used on a ladder at Whitehall Palace in 1631–2.[572]

In addition, such duller reds could occasionally be used internally. Vanherman, for example, gave directions for mixing a colour for a picture gallery which would, he observed, harmonise with paintings and gilt frames. It was made from Venetian red, white, and a little black with the addition of a little turpentine varnish. The tint needed was, he indicated, 'the dark blotting-paper colour', and use of a colour based on this formula in redecorating the Dulwich Picture Gallery has shown that it can be extremely subtle for the purpose, the small quantity of black playing a vital role in removing any tendency to crudeness.[573] It may be compared with the *claret colour* (q.v.) mentioned by Reynolds.

Vanherman observed that his red 'ANTICORROSIVE PAINT' would cost about 9*s.* 4*d.* per cwt. to manufacture,[574] but prices charged commercially seem to have been much higher. Bentley sold his equivalent product at 37*s.* in 1817 and Bennett indicated a rate equivalent to over 71*s.* 8*d.* in 1833, although he listed dark red coal-tar paint at 42*s.*[575] Lingard sold his dark red 'INVULNERABLE OIL PAINT' in paste form at 26*s.* in 1825 (35*s.* diluted ready for use), and a bright red at 32*s.* (39*s.* diluted).[576] Such relative terms must, of course, be approached with caution; and it will be appreciated that 'bright red' in an outdoor context would be very different from the colour the term could imply internally.

Adam indicated his intention to use 'red' on part of the ceiling for the Library at Kenwood in 1767, and 'dark red' on two other ceilings three years later.[577] In 1827 John Britton recorded that a 'deep red colour, in imitation of the walls at Herculaneum and Pompeii' had been used in the Library and Dining Room at Sir John Soane's house in Lincoln's Inn Fields;[578] while Prince Pückler-Muskau described the colour on the walls in the Gallery of John Nash's house in Regent Street as 'pale red'.[579]

Red, Chinese. In 1802 and 1803 various elements at the Royal Pavilion, Brighton, were painted 'Chinese Red',[580] and in 1841 the Berger company was manufacturing a variety of chrome red by this name.[581]

Red, French. In 1802 Soane noted his intention to paint the upper part of the Staircase at Pitzhanger Manor, Ealing, 'French rouge'.[582]

Red, Pompeian. The term 'Pompeian red' has not appeared in any of the literature examined in connection with the present study; but Soane's use of a 'deep red colour, in imitation of the walls at Herculaneum and Pompeii' at Lincoln's Inn Fields has been mentioned in connection with reds in general (q.v. immediately above).

Red, walnut. See *Walnut* below.

Rose. Watin recommended a mixture of a little carmine, 'une pointe' of vermilion, and ceruse to make *couleur de rose* (cf. sample 14).[583]

Russet. A rate of 6*d.* per square yard was quoted for *russet* in oil in connection with the conversion of the tennis court at Somerset House into a chapel in 1630–35.[584] In 1648, Henry Henham translated the term into Dutch as meaning rose colour.[585]

Sad colour. In 1633–4 a door in Lady Mary's Gallery at Whitehall Palace was painted *sad colour* in distemper, and in 1637–8 the wainscot in the Cross Gallery at Somerset House was painted similarly in oil.[586] Pre-Civil-War references may be found also to its use on picture frames, the colour on one occasion being veined over to look like walnut.[587] In 1706, the Sad Colour Room at Montagu House was painted this colour.[588] References to *sad brown, sad green, sad lute, sad stone, sad timber,* and *sad walnut* colours will be found elsewhere in this Glossary, all no doubt reflecting the association with dark or dusky tones with which sad colour was aligned in Henry Henham's Dutch/English Dictionary of 1648.[589] Today, the term survives in connection with the dyeing of cloth, successive immersions in an iron mordant serving to dull the colour and increase its resistance to fading; but it seems otherwise to have passed from common usage.

Salmon colour. Whittock indicated that a light *salmon colour* distemper was made using Venetian red, a small quantity of yellow, and whiting,[590] although in 1803 the Painter-Stainers Company had determined that it would cost an extra 2*d.* per square yard above the price of common colours, suggesting the use of more expensive pigments when it was mixed in oil.[591] In 1826 an intention was expressed to paint some of the passages at Dunham Massey in distemper of a warm salmon colour.[592]

Scarlet. In connection with his 'AROMATIC PAINT' for interior application, Vanherman noted that vermilion with lake (cf. samples 13, 16) made a bright *scarlet.*[593] As might be expected, therefore, it was not a cheap colour, and it was indeed included in the most expensive category of hues by Laxton, who indicated in 1818 that it would cost 9*d.* per yard above the rate for common colours.[594] In 1831, however, Skyring reduced this figure to 4*d.*, including it nevertheless in his list of 'superior colours'.[595] In 1774 Lady Louisa Conolly coloured the ceiling of the Gallery at

Castletown, Co. Kildare, which dated from the 1730s, 'scarlet & grey & white & gold';[596] scarlet was used on various elements at the Royal Pavilion, Brighton, in 1802 and 1803;[597] and in 1826 Buckler described the walls of the Dining Room at Eaton Hall, Cheshire, as being scarlet, though whether painted or hung with fabric is not clear.[598]

Sky blue. See *Blue, sky* above.

Slate colour. Reynolds indicated that a *slate colour* oil paint for exterior purposes was made by adding a 'paper' of lamp black to 10 pounds of white lead and 10 pounds of Spanish white (cf. sample 10).[599] *Gris ardoise* was available with a glossy finish in the range of *couleurs lucidoniques* manufactured at Paris from 1803;[600] Lingard sold *slate* 'Invulnerable Oil Paint' at 42*s.* per cwt. in 1825;[601] and in 1833 Bennett suggested that coal-tar paint of this colour would cost 56*s.* per cwt.[602]

Steel colour. In 1638, eight large double casements at Ham House were painted *steel colour.*[603] It seems likely that at this date it may have been similar to *iron colour* (q.v.), although in the second half of the eighteenth century Watin indicated that for interior work *couleur d'acier* in oil was commonly mixed using ceruse, charcoal, and Prussian blue. This was, he indicated, a cheaper method than the first he gave, in which ceruse, Prussian blue, fine lake, and distilled verdigris were employed in a varnish medium, but would produce a less beautiful colour.[604]

Stone colour. *Stone colour* seems generally to have been used to describe a fairly pale off-white, standing in contrast to the darker shade which today might be expected. John Smith described it as made from spruce ochre and white (sample 4),[605] a suggestion copied by the author of the *Painter's . . . Pocket Manual,*[606] although Nicholson substituted stone ochre.[607] Vanherman, however, used spruce ochre in his 'Aromatic' paint for interior application, but Bristol ochre in the first formula for his 'Impenetrable or anti-corrosive' paint for exterior purposes. Significantly, the quantity of ochre in this formula was very small, the ingredients being:

Dry (white) lead	224 pounds
Whiting	224
Crotia	112
(Bristol) yellow ochre	8.

In his second formula he omitted even this small amount, combining:

Dry (white) lead	56 pounds
Whiting	56
Crotia	28.[608]

It is therefore of great interest to recall John Smith's remark that when posts and rails (in an external context) were painted white, the finish was called *stone colour.*[609] For the type of oil paint he had in mind, boiled oil would probably have been used in its dilution, imparting a slight yellowing to the paint; while in Vanherman's formulae, the crotia would probably have had the same effect. Thus, stone colour was clearly not far removed from white; and, indeed, George Smith specified the use of a variety 'decreasing in force to almost a white, and approaching nearly to a cream colour'.[610] This is borne out by samples taken from two rooms at Somerset House which, after treatment to remove yellowing in the oil medium, were close in colour to Munsell references 2.5 Y 9/1 and 5 Y 9/1.[611]

In other instances stone colour may have been given a slightly warmer tint. Nicholson, for example, suggested the use of umber with white (cf. sample 3) for its preparation,[612] although this combination was employed by John Smith for oak timber colour, and by other authors for fawn, warm drabs, and quaker tints (q.v.). Pincot used both umber and stone ochre in stone colour, adding $\frac{1}{4}$ pound of the former and $\frac{1}{2}$ pound of the latter to 28 pounds of white lead (all in paste form). He observed that it was one of the colours commonly used for finishing outside work, adding, 'it covers better than White has a warm and finished look and lasts clean longer than a white',[613] a remark which may be compared with Chambers's sentiment that in rooms for common use, stone colour would last best and was cheapest.[614] Butcher and the author of the *Painter's . . . Pocket Manual,* probably copying him, also used umber with yellow ochre, calling the result *Portland stone colour.*[615] White lead, stone ochre, and burnt umber, the first of these authors directed, should be 'mixed by degrees to the colour required' (cf. sample 6); and Vanherman too suggested the use of umber to make a warm stone colour, combining it with white and spruce ochre. It was, he said, an excellent colour for entrance halls and staircases, having a cheerful appearance and solid texture.[616]

Two further formulae for stone colours were given by Reynolds, both for interior use. *Dark stone colour* contained 6 pounds of white lead, 8 ounces of yellow ochre, and $\frac{1}{2}$gill of lamp black, a combination which, as its name implies, would produce a much darker colour than those so far reviewed, and which may have had something in common with the sad stone colour (q.v.) encountered in early eighteenth-century documents (cf. sample 5). His *light stone colour,* on the other hand, contained 1 pint of white lead, 2 teaspoonsful of Prussian blue, 4 teaspoonsful of spruce yellow, and a teaspoonful of umber.[617] Such a greenish tinge finds no parallel in the English formulae mentioned above. No formulae specifically for distemper have been encountered, but it seems likely that the same tinting pigments would have been employed in such cases (including, perhaps, the walls of the Great Stairs at Kensington Palace, which, it was directed in 1723, were to be 'whitened with stone colour in the size').[618] In oil, stone colour was occasionally flatted, an instance being found in the 1787 accounts for Osterley Park, where 'Twice in oil. & flatted Stone colour' appears at a rate of 1*s.* per yard.[619]

With the curious exceptions of Watin and Tingry, stone colour is mentioned by the vast majority of authors, and is a common item in painting accounts. It was clearly one of the most frequently employed and basic tints, and was accordingly instanced in the *Builders Price-Book* together with that of Laxton as being one of the common colours.[620] Emerton sold his stone colour oil paint at 4*d.* or 5*d.* per pound in the 1730s,[621] the latter (equivalent to 46*s.* 8*d.* per cwt.) being also the price charged by Crease in 1808.[622] The London Patent Colour-Works sold their stone colour 'Impenetrable paint in Linseed-oil' at 56*s.* per cwt. in 1816,[623] and Lingard his 'Invulnerable Oil Paint' at prices from 42*s.* to 56*s.*, depending on its quality and readiness for use, in 1825.[624] The 'Anti-corrosion' paint of the London Patent Colour-Works retailed at 42*s.* per cwt.,[625] while Bentley sold his 'Anti-corrosive paint' at 46*s.* in 1817;[626] although Vanherman later claimed that his 'Impenetrable or anti-corrosive paint', the formulae for which have been described above, could be manufactured for as little as the equivalent of 18*s.* 8*d.* per cwt.[627] Hodgkin sold his stone colour 'Anticorrosion' paint at the equivalent of 60*s.* 6*d.* per cwt.,[628] a figure repeated in 1833 by Bennett, who indicated also that stone-colour coal-tar paint would cost 56*s.* per cwt.[629] *Teinte de pierre* was one of the *couleurs lucidoniques* with a matt finish manufactured at Paris from 1803.[630]

Naturally, the rates encountered for stone colour in oil are generally consistent with its status as a common colour. In 1667, for example, Primatt indicated that three coats would cost 1*s.* per yard, the rate mentioned by Gerbier in 1663 without specifying the number of applications, and found too in the 1669 accounts for the Sheldonian Theatre in Oxford, although other items there were priced at 1*s.* 2*d.*[631] In the early eighteenth century, prices had fallen slightly, three coats of sad stone colour at Ditton Park costing 9*d.* in 1705, and two coats 6*d.*[632] At Egremont House, Piccadilly, about 1764, four coats of stone colour cost 8*d.* and two 5*d.*;[633] while at Somerset House rates of 9*d.* and 10*d.* per yard were paid for four coats on stucco between 1780 and 1790, and 1*s.* for five coats on stucco in 1785.[634]

Stone colour was a tint of such general application throughout the period covered in this study that it is needless to list all the instances in which it is known to have been used. References to special varieties will be found below, but, leaving aside its application to wainscots and walls, the following are of particular interest in illustrating the variety of ways in which it was employed. In 1620–1 it was applied to a chimneypiece in the Lord Steward's Bedchamber at Whitehall Palace, and to the cornices in the Prince's Presence Chamber and Withdrawing Room at Newmarket, together with a number of doorcases.[635] In 1624–5 it was used on the rails, ballusters, and columns of the Great Staircase at Whitehall; and in 1629–30 on the lights of a window in the King's Withdrawing Chamber.[636] In the early 1690s it was employed on two 'raised figures' at Kensington Palace,[637] and in about 1700 on six chimneypieces at Boughton House.[638] The painter's tenders and agreement of 1751 for decoration of the Mansion House in London required the application of 'a Beautiful Stone colour', and the same tint was called for on the walls in the Egyptian Hall in 1757.[639] In 1775, Adam proposed the use of 'Stone Colours of a Yellowish cas[t]' on a ceiling for the Eating Room at Great Saxham Hall, Suffolk;[640] and in 1786 the dome ornaments of the Register House, Edinburgh, were painted white picked in with stone colour.[641] In 1821 an intention was expressed that the Hall chimney and window at Dunham Massey should be painted a good stone colour, while the wainscot in the Tea Room was to be painted stone colour and white.[642] It was used too on the ceilings of the Oak Library and Vaulted Library at Fonthill Abbey;[643] and in 1836 it was recorded that the walls and woodwork of the Library at Audley End, Essex, were painted stone colour.[644]

Stone colour, brown. In 1705 an appreciable area of *brown stone colour* totalling 220 yards was used at Ditton Park in several unidentified rooms.[645]

Stone colour, dark. The formula given by Reynolds for *dark stone colour* oil paint for interior application has been discussed under *Stone colour* above.

Stone colour, fine. In 1771 James Adam provided an estimate for painting work at the Shire Hall, Hertford, which included the use of *fine stone colour* in the Ante-room;[646] and in the same year Chambers wrote to Robert Gregory concerning his house in Berners Street, 'if you have any Particular fancy about the Painting your principal Rooms be pleased to let me know[.] my intentions is to finish the whole of a fine stone colour as us[u]al excepting the Eating Parlour'.[647]

Stone colour, light. The formula given by Reynolds for *light stone colour* oil paint for interior application has been discussed under *Stone colour* above. A very considerable area of light stone colour amounting to 2545 square yards was used in a number of rooms at Montagu House, London, in 1706, where two years later it was also used in 'Mr Antonies Room'.[648]

Stone colour, Portland. The formulae given by Butcher and the author of the *Painter's . . . Pocket Manual* for *Portland stone colour* have been discussed under *Stone colour* above.

Stone colour, sad. At Ditton Park in 1705 the rooms adjoining the Saloon and Vestibule, certain rooms, stairs, and passages on the north side of the house, the Writing Room next to the Duke's Bedchamber, and another 'Where the Billiard Room was' were painted *sad stone colour*, the total area running to nearly 2000 square yards of work.[649] This may, perhaps, have been comparable with the *dark stone colour* discussed above.

Stone colour, warm. Vanherman's formula for *warm stone colour* and his comments on its general character have been discussed under *Stone colour* above. In 1819 Pyne recorded that the framework of the ceiling in the Great Hall at Carlton House was 'a warm stone colour'.[650]

Stone colour, white. In 1705 several window boards at Ditton Park were painted *white stone colour*, and the same was used in the passage next to the Duke's Closet at Montagu House in 1706.[651]

Straw colour. John Smith recommended a mixture of white with a little yellow ochre to make *straw colour*,[652] and Reynolds directed that for an exterior oil paint 10 pounds of dry white lead were to be mixed with 1 pound of spruce yellow or English ochre (sample 19).[653] Whittock spoke of 'yellow, subdued by White to a straw colour',[654] and such mixtures would conform well with Holme's definition of straw colour as a 'weak or imperfect Yellow'.[655] However, Emerton sold his straw colour oil paint at 8*d.* or 1*s.* per pound, suggesting that it contained a more expensive tinting pigment; and it seems likely that a rather cleaner colour than ochre would provide was sometimes implied.[656] Vanherman, for example, proposed the use of chrome yellow;[657] and in distemper Nicholson recommended the use of massicot or Dutch pink, the latter, perhaps, the more reliable suggestion.[658]

Phillips indicated that *straw yellow* would cost 1*s.* 10*d.* per pound in 1812,[659] and *jaune paillé* appears in the list of *couleurs lucidoniques* manufactured at Paris from 1803 with a matt finish.[660] In 1785, 1*s.* per yard was paid for four coats of oil paint on stucco at Somerset House finished straw colour;[661] and in late eighteenth-century editions of the *Builders Price-Book* it was indicated that straw colour oil paint would cost 10*d.* to 1*s.* per yard, while prices also appear for straw colour in distemper.[662] In the 1810 and 1813 editions the rate per yard for the latter was given as 4*d.*,[663] but in 1812 Phillips suggested the much higher figure of 9*d.*, recording earlier that the rate had been 3*d.* between 1760 and 1790, and 4½*d.* from then until 1803. By 1821 he indicated it stood at 6*d.*, while in 1818 Laxton quoted 5*d.*, and the same rate was given by Skyring in 1831.[664]

In 1752 *couleur de paille* was listed by Blondel amongst others in use for house-painting,[665] and straw colour is fairly commonly encountered in designs and accounts dating from the second half of the eighteenth century. A note on the reverse of a ceiling design by George Dance the younger, for example, shows his intention to use a bright straw colour in the guilloche of the members forming a frame to the panels;[666] and on four of the ceiling drawings at the Soane Museum Adam proposed the use of straw colour.[667] In 1771 James Adam provided an estimate including its use in the Grand Jury Room at the Shire Hall, Hertford,[668] and in 1782 the walls and parts of the ceiling and cornice in the Hall at Gordon Castle, together with the ground of the frieze in the Staircase, were painted straw colour.[669] It is mentioned also in the 1787 account relating to Osterley Park.[670]

Sulphur colour. See *Brimstone* above.

Timber colour. John Smith's colour resembling new oak timber made from umber and white has been described above (s.v. *Oak colour*), but he also included *light timber colour* in his list, made from spruce ochre, white, and a little umber (cf. sample 35).[671] The end product seems, therefore, to be similar to some of the suggestions for mixing stone colour (q.v.) but is likely to have been rather darker in tone. Smith's formula was copied a century and a half later by Nicholson and the author of the *Painter's . . . Pocket Manual*, by when it was probably obsolete.[672] In contrast, Bullet suggested the combination of ceruse and a little umber with either red or yellow ochre, according to the different colours desired.[673]

Gerbier, who mentioned its use as a ground colour for gilding, noted that timber colour would cost 10*d.* per square yard in 1663, but in 1667 Primatt gave a rate of 9*d.*[674] Timber colour was used extensively before the Civil War, especially on doors and windows. In 1620–1 the doors in Lady Buckingham's new lodging at Whitehall Palace were thus coloured, as were the panels under the windows; in 1629–30 the door and doorcase in the Queen's stoolhouse at Greenwich were painted this colour both sides with size (i.e. in distemper); and in 1637–8 it was used on the doors and doorcases in the Backstairs, Gallery, and New Presence Chamber at Somerset House.[675] Among windows at Whitehall painted this colour internally were those in the new Banqueting House in 1619–22; a great light in the King's Presence Chamber in 1624–5; the windows and 'shutting windows' (presumably casements) in the King's Presence Chamber in oil in 1625–6; and the 'shutting windows' in the Marquis of Hamilton's Bedchamber in 1635–6.[676] In 1639–40, it was also used on two windows in the Queen's Old Bedchamber at Oatlands, where it had also been used in 1638–9 on the window 'soiles' (sills) in the Gallery.[677] Other elements on which it was used include the old wainscot in one of the bedchambers at Dover Castle, Kent, in 1625–6 (in distemper); part of the cornice in the Lord Chamberlain's Closet at Whitehall in 1637–8 (the rest simply being refreshed); and on the chimneypiece in the Cross Gallery at Somerset House in the same year.[678] It is also of interest that in 1638 the wainscot in the Little Hall and Passage at Ham House was 'twise coullored over with Umber in Oylle, and then with light Timber cullo^r^' at 1*s.* 4*d.* per yard;[679] and that sad timber colour was used on a large picture frame at Whitehall in 1631–2, the whole being varnished and gilded.[680]

Later references include use of timber colour on wainscots in the new Volary Building at Whitehall in 1667–8;[681] and in 1674 in a number of rooms in the Lodgings of the Duke and Duchess of York (now Apartment 29) at Hampton Court, the total yardage being 1639½, charged at 1*s.* per yard.[682] As late as 1737, Blondel referred to the use of *couleur de bois* on panelling.[683]

Turquoise. Watin indicated that *bleu turc* was made in oil or distemper using ceruse and Prussian blue (cf. samples 28, 29),[684] and *bleu Turquoise* appears in the list of *couleurs lucidoniques* manufactured with a matt finish at Paris from 1803.[685]

Umber colour. In 1694 four rooms in the Nursery, the Servants Hall and Parlour, and the Common Waiting Room at Dyrham Park were painted *umber colour* at 9*d.* per yard.[686] Whether this contained umber (sample 34) is not clear, but the undercoat of 'Umber in Oylle' applied beneath the light timber colour (q.v.) at Ham House in 1638 suggests that this may have been the case.[687] *Terre d'ombre* appears in the range of *couleurs lucidoniques* manufactured with a glossy finish at Paris from 1803.[688]

Vermilion. *Vermillon pur* was one of the *couleurs lucidoniques* manufactured at Paris from 1803 with a glossy finish.[689] Vermilion is, of course, properly the name of a pigment (sample 13).

Violet. Watin advocated a combination of lake, Prussian blue, a little carmine, and a very little white lead to make *violet* in oil or distemper (cf. sample 37).[690] Nicholson, on the other hand, merely suggested that it was made by mixing red and blue pigments;[691] but the author of the *Painter's . . . Pocket Manual* gave vermilion or red lead as the red pigments, expressing a preference for the former, and indicating that these were to be mixed with either blue or black and a very little white.[692] Adam proposed the use of violet in his ceiling design of 1773 for the Second Drawing Room at Lord Stanley's in Grosvenor Square, London, and 'Violáceo' in 1770 for that in the Drawing Room at Luton Hoo, Bedfordshire.[693] *Violet foncé* was one of the *couleurs lucidoniques* manufactured at Paris from 1803, and was available in a matt finish.[694]

Virgin tints. The author of the *Painter's . . . Pocket Manual* noted: 'Compound colours which are formed by the mixture of *only two colours* are called by the Painters *virgin tints*'.[695]

Wainscot colour. See *Oak colour*, above.

Walnut-tree colour. Watin proposed a combination of ceruse, 'ochre de rue', and umber with red and yellow Berry ochre to mix *bois de noyer* in size or oil.[696] Tingry repeated this for *walnut tree wood*, noting that 2 parts of white lead should be added to 1 part of the combined tinting pigments.[697] The author of the *Painter's . . . Pocket Manual* repeated this, but omitted any reference to the particular varieties of ochre (cf. sample 35).[698]

Walnut-tree colour (often spelt 'wallnuttree') was in use before the Civil War. Examples noted include its employment in oil on the chimneypiece in the Lord Steward's Withdrawing Room at Whitehall Palace in 1619–20; on the walls of the closets next to the Prince's Bedchamber and Presence Chamber at St James's in 1623–4; on the entablature and jambs of two windows in the Queen's Closet at Somerset House in 1626–7; and in oil for repainting the ceiling and windows in the Banqueting House at Whitehall in 1637–8, following arrival of the ceiling paintings by Rubens.[699] References may be found also to the use of sad walnut-tree colour on picture frames.[700]

In 1663, Gerbier noted that 'Wainscot put into a Wale-nut red colour, in distemper' would cost 6*d.* per yard;[701] and in the 1730s Emerton was selling his walnut-tree colour oil paint at 6*d.* per pound, a rate slightly higher than that for the cheapest colours in his range.[702] Widely varying prices may be found for paintwork, and Neve, for example, remarked that walnut-tree colour 'is worth 10*d.* say some, others say 16 or 18*d.* *per* Yard'.[703] Perhaps the most likely explanation is that the term could often imply graining, as was probably the case in the Duchess of York's Lodging (now Apartment 29) at Hampton Court, where Streeter was paid 1*s.* 6*d.*, 2*s.*, and 2*s.* 6*d.* per yard in 1674 and walnut graining has recently been found.[704] At Kensington Palace, too, rates of 1*s.* 6*d.*, 1*s.* 8*d.*, and 2*s.* were paid in the early 1690s, graining being mentioned in one or two instances.[705] In 1694 the Pavilion, Family Parlour, Slope Room, Great Parlour, Great Stairs, Slope Chamber and Closet, the Chamber over the Servants' Parlour, and the Dressing Room at Dyrham Park were painted walnut colour at 1*s.* 2*d.* per yard;[706] but tenders for Greenwich Hospital of about 1696 quote only 8*d.* or 9*d.*, three coats of oil being specified in the first instance.[707] An estimate for work at Stoke Edith, Herefordshire, of 1705 gives a figure of 1*s.*;[708] while at Montagu House, London, 9*d.* was charged for a smallish yardage in the following year.[709] Altogether, walnut-tree colour seems to have been fashionable during the seventeenth century, but like other similar colours had probably gone out of fashion in England by the second half of the eighteenth. Significantly, it is not mentioned in the *Builders Price-Book*; although, as already seen, in France Watin provided a formula for its preparation, and *couleur de bois de noyer* was one of the *couleurs lucidoniques* available with a matt finish made at Paris from 1803.[710]

Warm tints. Laxton and Skyring respectively priced *warm tints* at 5*d.* and 2*d.* above the cost of common colours.[711]

White. The pigments in use, cost, and methods for preparing white paint have been described in Chapters 1, 15, 16, and 17, and special methods for minimising its tendency to discolouration have been reviewed in Chapter 21. It was, of course, commonly used in both oil and distemper throughout the period being considered, and both the author of the *Builders Price-Book* and Laxton included it in the group of common colours.[712]

White, blue. See *White, milk,* below.

White, dead. The adjective *dead* refers to provision of a matt finish by the method of flatting described in Chapter 15, and is not primarily a qualification of the tint used.

White, fair. In 1686, 509 square yards of 'faire white' were applied in Lady Tirconnell's Lodging at Whitehall Palace at a rate of 1*s.* 2*d.* per yard.[713] It seems possible that the use of walnut oil was implied by the term.

White, fine. The term 'fine white' is to be found in the 1772–4 and 1787 accounts for Osterley Park, perhaps implying a special finish.[714]

White, French. In a remark repeated by Tingry's later editor, Hay defined *French white* as the lightest 'shade' of purple, a comment which indicates it belonged to the same family as French grey (q.v.).[715] Vanherman also used the term to describe one of his proprietary paint mediums, observing that it 'does not produce a perfect white, but inclines to what is called a French white.'[716] The London painter and gilder, George Hutchison, advertised that he 'finishes French White in a peculiar and new Method in Varnish, so that the Lustre is little inferior to the best Japanning'.[717]

White, milk. *Blanc de lait ou azuré* was one of the *couleurs lucidoniques* with a matt finish manufactured at Paris from 1803.[718] In 1688 Holme had defined *milk white* as 'a blewish White'.[719]

White, rose-tinted. In 1833 an intention was expressed to paint the ceilings in the Dining Room, Drawing Room, and Breakfast Room at Dunham Massey in a 'Rose tinted White'.[720] This could have been prepared in the way suggested by Watin for *rose* (q.v.).

White, royal. This was not a colour, but a type of distemper advocated by Vanherman which, together with Watin's *blanc de Roi,* has been described in Chapter 17.

White, silver. Watin indicated that *blanc argentin* for his special 'chipolin' distemper should be made using indigo and vine black with the white.[721] It must, therefore, have been a pale version of his *gris argentin* (silver grey – q.v.).

White stone colour. See *Stone colour, white,* above.

Willow colour. See *Green, willow,* above.

Wood colour. The London painter and gilder George Hutchison indicated that he 'perform'd' *wood colour* 'in the Highest Perfection'.[722] No doubt it was similar to timber colour (q.v.).

Yellow. Methods for mixing various types of yellow paint have been reviewed above. Tingry indicated that Naples yellow, Montpellier (patent) yellow, or yellow ochres could be used in distemper or varnish;[723] while Butcher suggested the use of patent yellow and a small quantity of white lead, or alternative employment of Dutch or English pink, to make 'fine yellow' (cf. samples 19, 21–23).[724] In 1819, Stitt gave prices of 6*d.* to 8*d.* per yard for one coat of fine yellow in oil, two coats costing between 10½*d.* and 1*s.* 0½*d.*, three between 1*s.* 2*d.* and 1*s.* 4½*d.*, and four from 1*s.* 5½*d.* to 1*s.* 9*d.* In distemper, one coat cost from 6*d.* to 7*d.*, two from 7½*d.* to 9*d.*, three from 9*d.* to 10½*d.*, and four from 11*d.* to 1*s.* 1*d.*[725] Taken with the others in his list these appear to confirm the use of more expensive pigments than yellow ochre.

In 1628–9, a new pendant in the Queen's Presence Chamber at Hampton Court was painted yellow and blue;[726] and yellow was used on the ironwork of the Great Staircase at Henry Pelham's House in Arlington Street, London, in 1748, although this may have been intended as an undercoat for gilding.[727] Its use was proposed too in manuscript notes on four of the Adam ceiling designs in the Soane Museum dated between 1768 and 1773,[728] and in 1782 the walls of the Barrack Room at Gordon Castle were painted yellow in distemper.[729] Between 1789 and 1791 the mouldings and two members of an enriched cornice in one of the rooms at Woburn Abbey were picked in yellow;[730] in 1815 the walls of the Yellow Drawing Room at the Royal Pavilion, Brighton, were coloured 'bright yellow and high varnished' at a price equivalent to 5*s.* per square yard;[731] and in 1823 Rutter described the ceiling of the Oak Parlour at Fonthill Abbey as having pale yellow mouldings.[732] In 1817 Bentley was selling his yellow 'ANTI-CORROSIVE PAINT' for exterior purposes at 46*s.* per cwt.,[733] and in 1833 Bennet quoted a figure equivalent to 71*s.* 8*d.* per cwt. for 'Anticorrosion paint' of this colour.[734]

Yellow, chrome. In 1819, the walls of the Yellow Drawing Room at the Royal Pavilion, Brighton, were repainted 'light Chrome yellow' and varnished, a possible early reference to use of this pigment (sample 24) in house-painting.[735]

Yellow, Etruscan. In 1773 Adam proposed the use of 'Etruscan yellow' in a manuscript note on his design for the ceiling of the Second Drawing Room at Ashburnham House.[736]

Yellow, golden. See *Gold colour,* above.

Yellow, Italian. *Jaune d'Italie* was one of the *couleurs lucidoniques* available in a glossy finish which were manufactured at Paris from 1803.[737] The name seems likely to allude to the yellow lake known as 'Italian pink'.

Yellow, lemon. See *Lemon colour,* above.

Yellow, Naples. Between 1772 and 1774 certain elements in the Dining Room of Mr Manwaring's House at Norwood, Middlesex, relating to the Osterley Estate, were painted in 'naples Yellow': the cost of '4 oil finished naples Yellow flatted' was 1*s.* per square yard, and that of 'Stucco walls 5 oil naples Yellow flatt' 1*s.* 4*d.*[738] In 1774 it was ordered that the plain parts of the ceiling and walls in the Chapel at Queens' College, Cambridge, were to be painted 'a Naples yellow'.[739] Although it is uncertain whether or not employment of the pigment of that name (sample 22) is implied by either reference, this does not seem unlikely.

Yellow ochre. Although properly the name of a pigment (sample 19), *ocre jaune* was one of the *couleurs lucidoniques* with a glossy finish which were manufactured in Paris from 1803.[740]

Yellow, patent. An item for 'once in oil & twice patent yellow' appears in the 1787 account for Osterley Park at a rate of 1*s.* per yard, together with another relating to a plinth (i.e. skirting).[741] In 1816 the London Patent Colour Works were selling patent yellow 'IMPENETRABLE PAINT IN LINSEED-OIL' at 1*s.* 6*d.* per pound;[742] while Laxton and Skyring indicated that patent green or yellow oil paint would cost 9*d.* and 5*d.* per square yard respectively over the rate for common colours.[743] That the paint contained this pigment (sample 23) seems likely, since Soane used it for the yellow on the walls in the North and South Drawing Rooms at the Soane Museum, where it was varnished.[744]

Yellow, sulphur. See *Brimstone colour*, above.

APPENDIX B

GLOSSARY OF TIMBERS IMITATED

In dealing with references in early painting accounts it is important to note that the employment of a term such as 'wainscot colour' during the seventeenth and eighteenth centuries did not necessarily imply that the finish was grained to imitate the natural timber. Thus, in the Kensington Palace accounts a clear distinction was made between ordinary painting and graining, items for both 'Wallnutt Tree' at 1*s.* 6*d.* per square yard, and 'Wallnutt Tree grained' at 1*s.* 8*d.* being present, for example, in Robert Streeter's bill for March 1692;[1] and John Smith gave instructions for mixing 'timber colour' without mentioning the addition of veins, apparently showing that this term was commonly used simply to convey a plain paint of timber-like tone.[2] Again, Alexander Emerton advertised a range of ready-mixed tints during the 1730s which contained such items as 'wainscot colour' together with others which demonstrate the point.[3] Nevertheless, unqualified references to such timber colours can be ambiguous, and in the account of 1669 for painting the Sheldonian Theatre at Oxford a large number of items for 'Cedar colour' at 1*s.* 2*d.* per square yard are followed by a single item for 'cedar colour . . . not being veined' at 1*s.*, showing that here the term was being used without special qualification in connection with graining.[4] References to seventeenth-century examples in this glossary have therefore necessarily been restricted to those in which no ambiguity is present.

Air wood. See *Harewood.*

Amboyna. The timber known as *amboyna* (fig. 40) may be identified with that of *Lingosum indicum* (also known as *Pterocarpus indicum*), native to the East Indies. The name is applied to the burr rather than to the ordinary wood, and veneers of this became popular in Sheraton and Regency furniture.[5] Its colour ranges between orange and chestnut brown. Both Laxton and Skyring included the timber in their lists of imitations, the former giving a price of 1*s.* per square foot, and the latter 9*d.*[6]

Ash. The timber of the English ash, *Fraxinus excelsior* (fig. 41), is almost white in colour. In 1692 the Doctor's Chamber at Erddig, Denbighshire (now Clwyd), was described as 'prety well don sumewhat like Ash . . . and grained much like the Hall'.[7]

Bamboo. Imitation bamboo was used extensively as a part of the oriental décor at the Royal Pavilion, Brighton, in the early nineteenth century. In 1802, for example, the Saloon was provided with 7228 ft. run of 'Bamboo Shadowed spotted and varnished' at 3*d.* per ft.; and in 1803 the 'Bamboo railing' above the cornice was '3 times painted etc. and spotted'.[8] Among later items may be mentioned the iron balustrades of the staircases at the ends of the New Corridor (Gallery) painted 'in imitation of bamboo and varnished',[9] and three chimneypieces in the Gallery itself, which were similarly painted and varnished in 1815.[10]

Birds eye maple. This light-coloured timber with its distinctive small 'birds eye' knots (fig. 42) comes from the tree *Acer campestre* native to Britain. Whittock gave two methods for its imitation, directing first that the ground colour should be the same as that for oak (a mixture of rotten stone and white). The graining glaze was to be made from umber ground in ale, and applied by means of 'the flat hog's-hair brush' which he illustrated, having separated tufts of bristle (fig. 39). This was to be well loaded with colour, and with it one was to 'draw the veins very much curled, letting them wave in every direction', immediately passing the feather of a quill over the work 'in the same direction that the flat brush was used, giving a sharp turn occasionally, and then proceeding over the lines again'. This would 'split them into a variety of forms', and while still wet the work was to be beaten with the softener 'the contrary way of the grain'. The knots were next taken out by placing the point of a camel-hair pencil, held upright, on the work, and turning it between

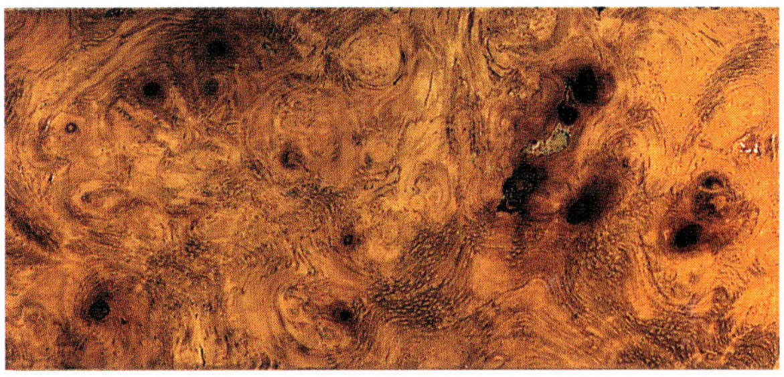

40. Amboyna.

41. Ash.

42. Birds eye maple.

finger and thumb to take a spot of colour off the ground. The work was allowed to dry, and a thin glaze of burnt umber 'drawn over it in veins', this time using a softer version of the flat brush with separated tufts of bristle he had illustrated, and, once this was dry, the work was varnished.[11]

The above method was, he indicated, to be followed where the work needed to be finely executed, but for shop fronts, halls, and so on greater rapidity and boldness were necessary. In this case the veins were again to be drawn on the ground with 'the flat hog's-hair brush'[12] in umber, and immediately beaten with a large duster 'in a contrary direction'. Once dry, veins were to be drawn all over the work 'in every variety of curl' using a thin glaze of Vandyke brown. While this was still wet, the tips of the fingers were dabbed on the surface, ensuring their configuration was properly varied, to produce the knots, and the whole allowed to dry. In addition a sparing number of dark knots could be made by the same method.[13]

Cedar. Where 'cedar' or 'red cedar' are mentioned in seventeenth- or early eighteenth-century documents it appears problematical whether the term was applied to the timber of the Spanish cedar, *Cedrela odorata*, which grows in tropical America and the West Indies, or to the American red cedar, *Juniperus virginiana*. The latter, known also as 'pencil cedar' (fig. 43), was being imported into England during the seventeenth century, and was much prized for use in panelling on account of its fragrant scent.[14] The architect Sir Roger Pratt mentioned the imitation of cedar in his notebooks,[15] and there are many items for 'cedar colour' at a rate of 1*s.* 2*d.* per square yard in the account receipted by Richard Hawkins in 1669 for painting work at the Sheldonian Theatre, Oxford. This also includes an item for 'cedar colour . . . not being veined' at 1*s.*, implying, presumably, the use of veining on the remainder.[16] Also, in 1687, the two doors either side of the altar in the Chapel at Whitehall Palace were painted 'like Cedar'.[17]

Directions for painting 'red cedar color' were given by the early nineteenth-century American author Hezekiah Reynolds. By European standards these seem to have been archaic, and, as suggested in the general discussion of graining methods in Chapter 20, may well reflect seventeenth-century technique. The ground was to be primed and undercoated with a mixture of red and white lead in equal quantities, while for the third coat 2 ounces of vermilion were to be mixed with 4 pounds of white lead. The 'shading' was to be added immediately, before the paint had dried, using well ground Indian red 'placed on a pallet or pane of glass, that it may take easily with the brush'.[18]

In 1815, varnished cedar graining was used on doors and skirtings in two bedchambers and on the woodwork of the water-closet adjoining the Glass Passage at the Royal Pavilion, Brighton.[19]

Cherry. Another timber for whose imitation Reynolds gave directions was 'cherytree wood', presumably the American *Prunus serotina* (fig. 44), a type not encountered in any of the European material which has formed the basis of the present study. Again, the method seems to reflect seventeenth-century British practice rather than that of the early nineteenth. White lead and yellow ochre in equal quantities were used for the first three coats, and umber 'shading' added on the surface of the last while it was still wet.[20]

Coral wood. See *Red sandal wood.*

Coromandel wood. Trees of the genus *Diospyros* growing in South India and Ceylon produce a group of timbers including all the truly black ebonies together with those streaked in brown or reddish hazel tones (fig. 45). The major species is *D. quaesita*. The timber was used extensively in Regency furniture, and by at least the mid-1850s three subdivisions were recognised by the trade, depending on the proportion of dark veins present.[21] Pyne described the doors and window shutters in the Crimson Drawing Room at Carlton House, London, as painted black in imitation of ebony;[22] and both Laxton and Skyring listed coromandel wood among those imitated, the former giving a price of 9*d.* per square foot, and the latter 6*d.*[23]

Ebony. See *Coromandel wood.*

Flother wood. An account of 1597–8 for painting in the Gallery at Oatlands, Surrey, includes an item for 'leying the pannells and battens of the same with soundry cullours curyously grayned wth a grayne called flother woode'.[24] Commenting on this, Edward Croft-Murray suggests that a flecked or speckled effect was intended, deriving from the word *flother*, meaning a snowflake;[25] but whether the term was applied to a specific timber having this type of figure is not clear.

Grey satin wood. See *Harewood.*

Harewood. Harewood was the name given to sycamore, *Acer pseudoplatanus* (fig. 46), altered in colour 'by staining it to a soft, clear green tone, which appears in old furniture as a pleasant gray-green hue' (fig. 47).[26] Vanherman observed that 'air wood' was 'reckoned one of the simplest of the graining subjects', indicating that the ground for the imitation should be laid in a very light grey, on which 'after being brushed over with a some-

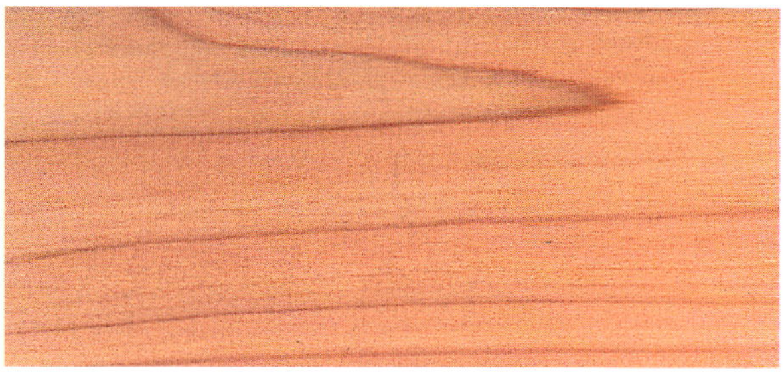

43. Pencil cedar.

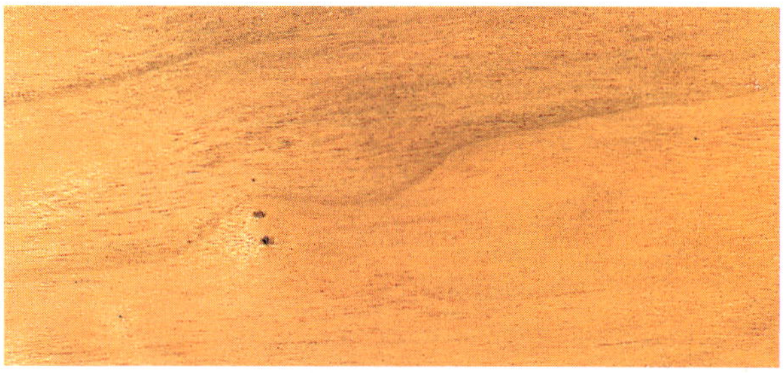

44. American cherry.

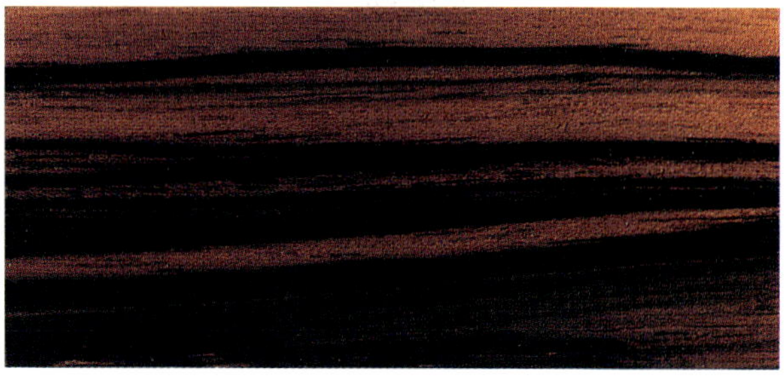

45. Coromandel ebony.

what darker grey, you imitate the stry with the graining tool, the[n] lengthways, with a still darker waving . . . with the same tool cross this first stry, which finishes the work'.[27] A comparable formula was given by Butcher under the heading 'satin wood', and that this timber was also artificially stained blue, green, or grey seems confirmed by a reference to 'Grey satin wood imitated and high varnished' at a cost of 2*s.* per square foot in the Saloon at the Royal Pavilion, Brighton, in 1802.[28] Butcher's instructions called for the first coat to be white, and the second light blue; and the work was to be finished with either dark blue or dark green as desired.[29] This formula for 'satin wood' was repeated by the author of the *Painter's . . . Pocket Manual.*[30] Nicholson gave a price of 5*d.* per square foot for 'Hare or satin wood' in the *New Practical Builder,* while Laxton listed 'Air wood' at 6*d.* per square foot, and Skyring 'Hair' wood at the same rate, varnish in all cases being extra.[31] In 1815, a pair of folding doors in the Small Drawing Room at Brighton were provided with '13 pannels of fret ornament red on hair wood ground'.[32]

Indian woods. In 1676, Christopher Wren noted in a memorandum: 'Veined like Walnuttree or indian Woods well performed' should cost 1*s.* 6*d.* per square yard; whereas 'Ranse Marble & indian woods extraordinarly well don soe as to deceive the Eye & be taken for naturall may be worth 4 shillings the Yarde or more according to the Judgement of the painter'.[33] The precise timber he had in mind is unclear, but he no doubt intended an allusion to an exotic species.

Kingwood. See *Princeswood.*

Lignum vitae. In 1685 *Lignum vitae* was priced at 1*s.* 6*d.* per square yard in connection with painting work at Combe Abbey, Warwickshire, the cost suggesting the finish was grained.[34] The timber is that of *Guaiacum officinale* or *G. sanctum* native to the West Indies and the coastal regions of tropical America (fig. 48).

Mahogany. Two distinct species of mahogany, which is often cut to show a distinctive figure (fig. 49), were commonly used in cabinet-making: Spanish mahogany, *Swietenia mahogani* (fig. 50), from the West Indies, including the islands of Cuba, Jamaica, and Hispaniola, that from the island of Santo Domingo being particularly noted; and Honduras mahogany, *S. macrophylla* (fig. 51), from the Central American mainland. The former timber is generally darker in colour, and often contains chalky markings in the pores of the grain, in distinction to the grey or black specks and lines of the Honduras;[35] but few eighteenth- or early nineteenth-century documents indicate the specific imitation of one or other variety, and the majority of references are simply to 'mahogany'. To this, however, Whittock provides a notable exception, describing methods for the reproduction of each. Honduras was, he indicated, the easier, and, being capable of

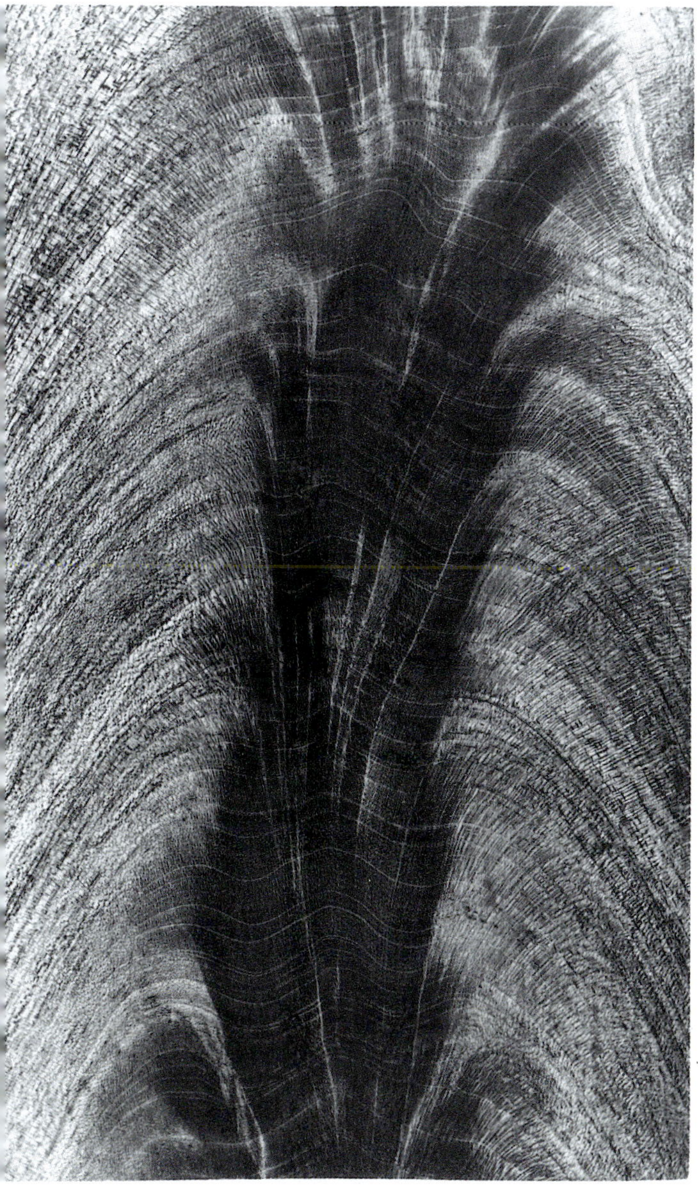

49. Mahogany (feather veneer).

46. Sycamore, unstained.

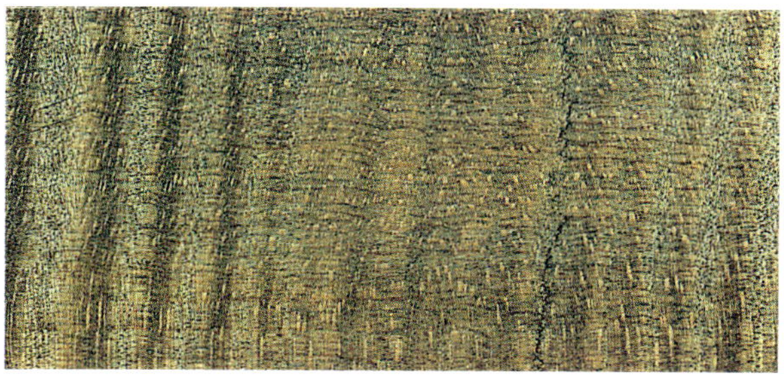

47. Harewood (stained sycamore).

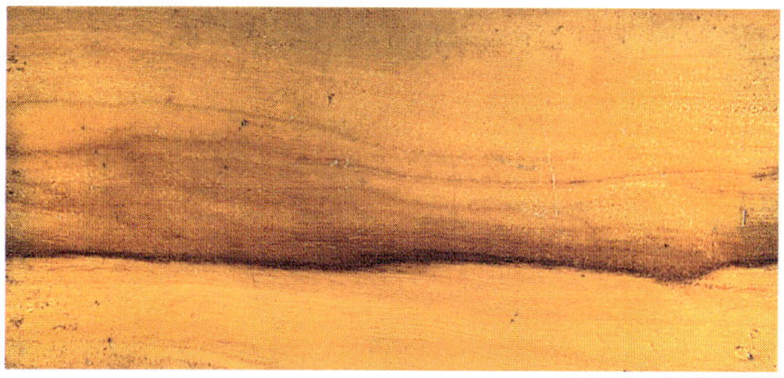

48. Lignum vitae.

execution with 'quickness and spirit', was the proper mahogany for street doors, shutters, and the like (fig. 52). The ground was laid in white lead in oil stained to the required colour with Venetian red, and the first glaze to be applied was of Vandyke brown. This was figured by means of a sponge, which was dabbed on the surface 'with great freedom' to take out the light areas, hard edges being blended using a softener in the direction in which the dark veins were to run. When this coat was dry, a deeper tint of Vandyke brown was used to form the lightest of the dark veins, which were to run 'in the direction of the light, both above and below it'. Some of the touches were to be darker than others, and, he added, 'just under the light a dab of colour must be laid on nearly opaque'. All this was to be blended and softened with the dusting brush 'handled in the same direction given to the colour' and finally blended with a badger-hair softener moved 'from right to left'.[36]

Whittock regarded Spanish mahogany, on the other hand, as 'the highest test of the grainer's art', and described two methods for its imitation (fig. 53). In the first, the ground was to be laid on in a much 'richer' and 'finer' red than that used for the Honduras mahogany, made by the additional use of a little crimson lake. The first graining glaze, made from lake and Vandyke brown ground in ale, was spread with 'the flat brush with the hairs separated', so as to leave the light grain uncovered. In the particular specimen he illustrated, he was at pains to point out that 'the flower runs in a slanting direction across the wood, and in the centre appears as if suddenly separated'. This effect was, he indicated, 'produced by checking the hand at the end of the first sweep taken with the flat brush, and at the same time bearing harder upon it', a technique which would 'spread the hairs, and give a greater quantity of colour'. While the glaze was still damp, darker veins were added using the same pigments and technique, after which a piece of wash leather 'either placed on a stick, or folded to a point' was used quickly, with a light hand, to 'take out the lights that appear in small streaks on either side of the vein'. Finally the work was softened.[37]

For the second variety of Spanish mahogany, which, he observed, was time-consuming to imitate and could therefore only be applied to the best work, the ground colour was prepared from Indian red, lake, and white lead. On this was laid a thin glaze of rose pink ground in ale, which was manipulated by means of a thin piece of sponge 'dropped on it in quick succession and quite accidentally'. This was allowed to dry without softening, varnished, and a distemper glaze of lake and Vandyke brown applied in 'short thick touches' with a small brush. The sponge was then applied in 'nearly the same places as it was on the first ground' to produce the 'second tint of light', and the work softened and allowed to dry. The 'flat brush with the hairs separated' was next used to apply a glaze of thin Vandyke brown, 'crossing the touches on the dark side'. When dry, the imitation was varnished.[38]

For common work, such as shop fronts, Whittock described a fourth method for the imitation of mahogany, by means of which, he indicated, many yards could be completed with good effect in the course of a morning. The technique was similar to the 'old' methods of graining, discussed in Chapter 20, of which he was extremely critical, the ground in this case being laid in a mixture of white lead and Indian red, and the graining built up by means of brushes separately charged with Indian red and black ground in boiled oil and turpentine with the necessary driers, large veins being formed 'according to fancy'. When the surface was nearly covered, the strong lights were taken out with a wash leather, and the whole softened with a large dusting brush.[39]

An even simpler method was suggested by Butcher, who ob-

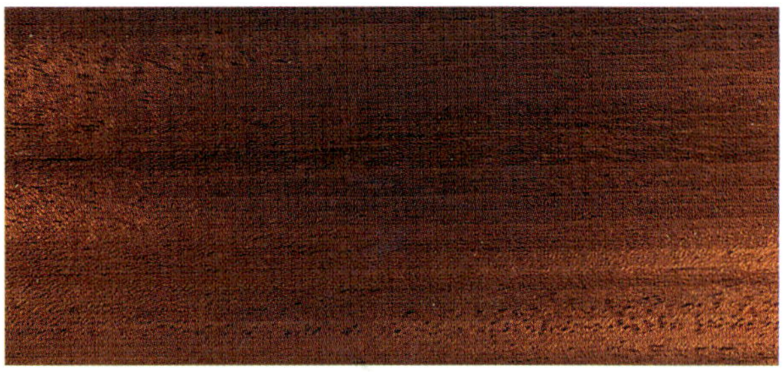

50. Spanish (or 'Cuban') mahogany.

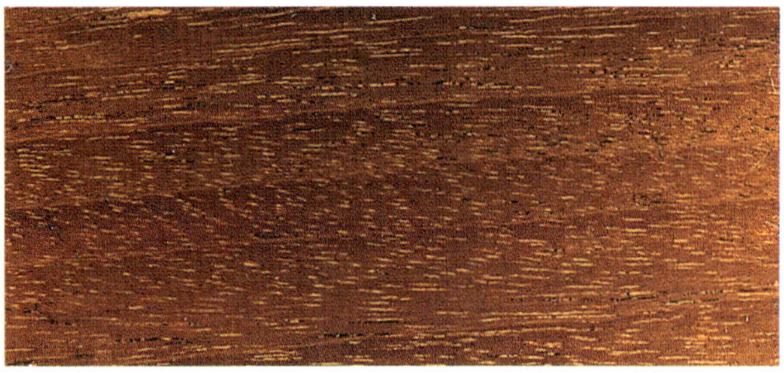

51. Honduras Mahogany.

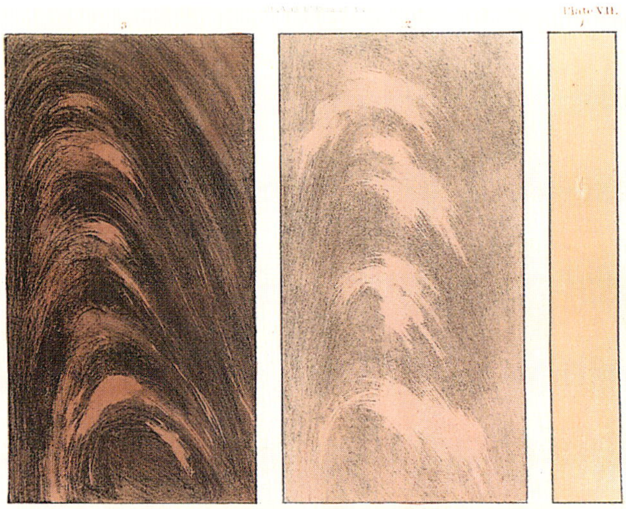

52. Stages shown by Whittock in the imitation of Honduras mahogany.

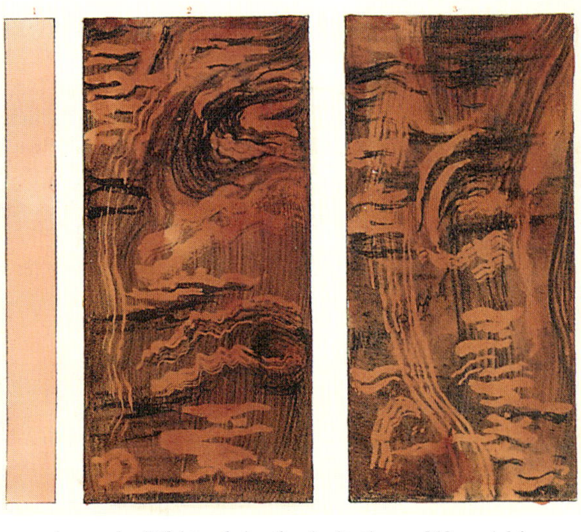

53. Stages shown by Whittock in the imitation of 'Spanish' mahogany.

served that mahogany colour thus 'properly managed, will have the effect of fine-grained wood itself': the first coat was laid in white lead, and the second in an orange colour made using orange lead, after which the work was finished with burnt sienna 'with a flat brush, waving and imitating the veins as they run in any fine piece of mahogany'.[40] The author of the *Painter's . . . Pocket Manual* followed the same suggestions for pigments, but gave burnt umber as an alternative for the sienna.[41] These latter methods seem in many ways to reflect earlier practice in their simplicity, having little of the subtlety possessed by those suggested by Whittock; and that suggested by Reynolds also falls into this category. The work was primed using spruce ochre, and an undercoat containing 4 ounces of white lead to a pound of the latter provided. On this a layer of burnt ochre ground in 'clarified or boil'd oil' was laid and 'shaded' with burnt umber while still wet 'that the colors may more easily blend together'. For this a 'graining or flat brush' was used, and the work varnished on completion.[42]

The lack of refinement inherent in such methods is obvious in comparison with those of Whittock and Vanherman, the latter of whom too described methods for the imitation of mahogany in both oil and distemper. For the latter the ground could, he indicated, be either buff, or dark or light orange according to fancy or situation. If the latter, it seems likely that he had a mixture containing red lead in mind, since he had remarked earlier in his book that it was seldom used in house-painting except as a ground for mahogany graining. Once the ground was dry, and had been washed with beer, a glaze of burnt sienna was laid on, after which, he directed, the painter was to,

> imitate all turns and wavings of the curl, or flower, with the large graining tool, and take care not to destroy or stop out the lights, for every rich curl has a dark and a light side. The graining tool, prepared with leather, is suitable to express and mark the waves at the sides of the panel. You then sweeten the whole gently with the badger, and, when dry, varnish.

In oil, the process was, he said, nearly the same, although some grainers would add finishing touches with lake, and also strengthen the shades with lake and black, a refinement which would, he noted, bestow great brilliancy on the work.[43]

The Norfolk House accounts of 1755 contain a single item for four square yards of 'mahogany' graining at a cost of 1*s*. 6*d*. per yard, but it is not clear whether this price included the necessary undercoats or varnishing.[44] Later eighteenth-century sources, however, are generally more specific. At Osterley Park, Middlesex, for example, just over five yards of work were painted '4 oil Graind Mahogany Colour' in 1772–4 at a rate of 1*s*. 9*d*. per yard;[45] while the Somerset House accounts of 1780 contain items for 'Painting Twice done Extra to Doors, finished Grain'd Mahogany & Varnished' at 1*s*. 6*d*. per yard. Subsequent work at the latter, the last entry being dated 1791, was priced at the same rate, an extra 2*d*. per yard being included for each additional undercoat.[46] In price-books, however, the rate for graining is clearly separated from that for the grounds, so that in the 1776, 1787, and 1794 editions of the *Builders Price-Book* 'Mahogany grained' cost 1*s*. per yard, and mahogany 'grained and varnished' 1*s*. 2*d*.[47] These, it will be seen, are precisely comparable with the rates allowed at Somerset House. The same prices are given in William & James Pain's *British Palladio* (1786), but in the schedule of prices appended to the fifth edition of William Pain's *Practical House Carpenter* published in 1794 they were increased to 1*s*. 4*d*. and 1*s*. 6*d*. respectively, marking the beginning of the inflation occasioned by the wars with France.[48] As a result of this, in the 1810 and 1813 editions of the *Builders Price-book* 'Twice in oil grained mahogany' had become 2*s*. per square yard, the same varnished being 2*s*. 6*d*.[49]

The same development may be traced through various editions of *Crosby's Builder's New Price-book*, which throws further light on the additional cost of varnish. In the 1804 edition, for example, it was noted that the cost of 'Mahogany colour grained' had been 1*s*. per yard between 1760 and 1790, but had increased to 1*s*. 1½*d*. by 1803; while prices at the same periods if the work was varnished were 1*s*. 2*d*. and 1*s*. 3*d*. respectively, or, if two coats of varnish were applied, 1*s*. 4*d*. and 1*s*. 6½*d*.[50] In the 1812 edition the pricing method was changed, so that for the graining an addition of 1*s*. 6*d*. per yard had to be made to the basic cost of the ground; and assuming this to be 7*d*. (the cost of common colours twice in oil) the total of 2*s*. 1*d*. is very close to that of 2*s*. given in the 1810 and 1813 editions of the *Builders Price-book* already mentioned. If the work was varnished the addition was 2*d*., but in the 1821 edition both figures had again risen, this time to 2*s*. 9*d*. and 3*s*. 6*d*. respectively.[51]

Other early nineteenth-century price-lists priced imitations by the square foot rather than by the yard, Skyring, for example, quoting 4*d*. per square foot for 'mahogany', the equivalent of 3*s*. per yard.[52] A few years earlier, however, Laxton gave a figure of 10*d*. per foot for 'Hispaniola mahogany', reflecting no doubt Whittock's comment already noted on the superiority of this timber.[53] A similar but less marked difference appears in the 'Perpetual Price Book' which formed an appendix to Nicholson's *New Practical Builder*, where a figure of 5*d*. was suggested for 'Honduras mahogany', and 7½*d*. for 'Hispaniola mahogany'.[54] In all these instances varnish was separately billed as an extra.

Oak and wainscot. Imitations of oak were ubiquitous during the late seventeenth and the early nineteenth centuries. As will be seen from the discussion of prices below, it was used extensively by Wren in several of the Royal Palaces, and apparently by James Wyatt in a number of ceilings at Fonthill;[55] while Whittock remarked that it was the grain preferred for exterior work, such as street doors and shutters.[56] Although it has been suggested that the term 'wainscot' was used in cabinet work to indicate the use of timber imported from the Continent,[57] the name seems to have been used as a matter of course in the years between 1660 and the early eighteenth century, and it is doubtful whether in painting the distinction, if maintained at this period, was of any importance. The two principal species of oak used in joinery, *Quercus robur* (otherwise known as *Q. pedunculata*) and *Q. sessiliflora*, produce timber of almost indistinguishable character, one of the main delights of which is the fine figure made by the medullary rays when the boards are 'quarter sawn', that is, cut on the diameter of the log (fig. 54). These, having the advantage also, in a timber notorious for its instability, of being less liable to bow with changes in moisture content, were often selected for the panels of doors and wainscoting.

Whittock provided detailed directions for the imitation of oak in both oil and distemper, remarking that the former (fig. 55) was the easier. The ground was laid in a mixture of rotten stone

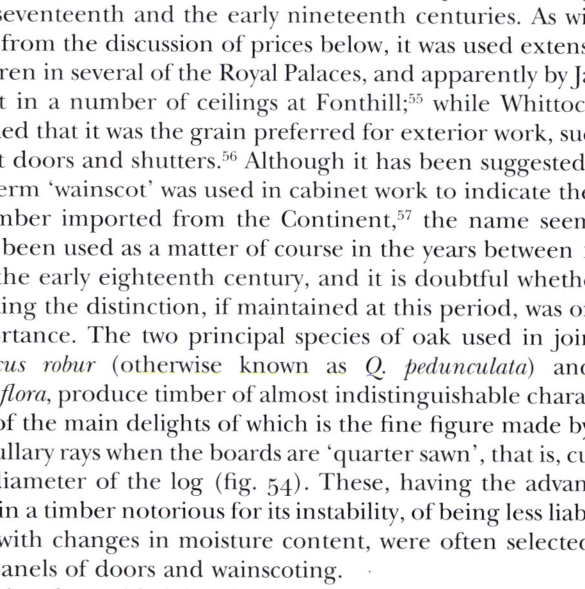

54. English oak (quarter sawn).

and white, and the first glaze, composed of the megilp formula described in Chapter 20, applied a square yard at a time at the most. A few minutes were allowed to elapse, and a large comb (No. 1 on his plate) (fig. 38) then used to produce the grain, being drawn over the work in such a way as to make it 'slant or look wavey'. This was followed by a second comb (No. 2 on his plate) drawn 'over the whole, letting the arm in parts bear lighter than in others, and sometimes giving the hand a very tremulous motion'. By this means the coarse lines were broken, and a third comb (No. 3 on his plate) used to produce the finest grain 'nearest the centre of the tree'. After this the medullary rays were taken out with a piece of wash leather, doubled to a point, or, for finer lines, put on the end of a stick, and the whole softened by 'dabbing the end of the brush [a 'hard tool'] all over the work'. Once the glaze had hardened, the dark touches were put in using Vandyke brown ground in ale. Later, he indicated, a thin glaze of burnt umber ground in ale could be applied, if desired, to darken the whole. Burnt umber was used in this way, he said, for the reproduction of 'old wainscot oak', the method being otherwise identical with that already described. The completed work was varnished.[58]

For distemper work, the same ground was used, and, this having been well washed with soap and water, a wash of burnt or raw umber ground to the consistence of a thick paste in beer, and thinned with more beer for use, was laid on with a 'large tool'. This was to be drawn over the panel, 'not in a straight line, but in a slanting and in some cases a wavy direction, letting the hand press heavily on the brush so that the hairs may spread'. In this case the brush would, he said, perform the same function as the comb in the oil method. The work was immediately beaten with a large dusting brush, 'with the points of the hairs the reverse way from that in which the colour is laid on', an operation which was, he indicated, to be done very quickly and with a light hand 'using proper judgement to vary the beating by turning the brush according to the various directions that the veins have taken when laid on first'. Once the colour was tacky, the lights were to be taken out using a damp wash leather, and, when dry, the dark veins crossing the grain added using burnt umber and a camel-hair or sable pencil. Knots were to be imitated by turning a piece of wash leather on the point of the finger, the same means being used to take out the light mark above and below the knot.[59] The 'old' methods given by Whittock for the imitation of oak in oil and distemper have already been discussed in Chapter 20.

Vanherman provided instructions only for the imitation of oak in oil, indicating that there were two principal colours used for grounds, one using orange lead, and the other buff in tone. These could be made darker or lighter to suit the wishes of the employer. The graining glaze was composed of either raw or burnt umber, and was laid on in such a way as to be thin in some places and more opaque in others. It could be manipulated using the comb or the graining tool, and in particular areas the short grain could be imitated by dabbing the glaze with the 'points of the duster'. The medullary rays crossing the grain in a serpentine form were 'shaped out' with a piece of sponge, leather, or cork 'observing to avoid any formality or redundance', after which the whole was tenderly sweetened using a large badger-hair brush; and lastly any 'dark serpentines' in the pattern put in across the grain.[60]

Although Whittock used rotten stone to stain the ground for imitations of oak, since, he believed, yellow ochre was too deep in colour and would impart an undesirable greenish hue to the work,[61] other authors seem to have been less apprehensive of this. Butcher suggested a coat of half white and half stone ochre as an undercoat for 'wainscot', which was to be finished with stone ochre alone, and shadowed in imitation of the wood with sienna or burnt umber.[62] This formula, which may, of course, owe something to John Smith's late seventeenth-century advice on the preparation of 'Timber Colour', was repeated by the author of the *Painter's . . . Pocket Manual*, who merely specified yellow ochre in place of stone ochre;[63] while Nicholson recommended the use of ochre, raw sienna, and umber in the ground, the glaze being made up from the same pigments, with the addition of burnt sienna.[64] Variations in practice of this nature are, of course, to be expected, since natural oak in joinery is quite commonly stained to a variety of shades, and indeed Laxton listed imitations of 'New wainscot', 'White oak', and 'Old or dark oak'.[65] In this connection it is interesting to note that, rather than vary the colour of the ground, Whittock appears to have preferred to darken oil oak-graining by glazing after completion, although this was not, he indicated, possible in distemper.[66]

Several items for 'wainscott colour grained' appear in late seventeenth-century accounts for Whitehall Palace, Hampton Court, and Kensington Palace at a consistent price of 1*s.* 2*d.* per square yard.[67] Although some entries for the last of these buildings also mention varnish, apparently without variation in the rate, it is possible that the yardages for these were simply added together, since an item for varnish alone at Hampton Court also works out at 1*s.* 2*d.* per yard.[68] The explanation for this discrepancy is otherwise elusive. Late eighteenth-century editions of the *Builders Price-Book* do not include items for oak graining, but the 1810 and 1813 editions gave rates of 1*s.* 6*d.* per yard for 'Twice in oil grained wainscot', and 2*s.* for the same varnished.[69] The same rates were given in the 1812 edition of *Crosby's Builders' New Price Book*, although as with mahogany these were in addition to the basic paintwork, suggesting that one or other may be inaccurate. By 1821 they had risen to 2*s.* 3*d.* and 3*s.* respectively.[70] The rates given in the 1818 edition of Laxton, in which, as already mentioned, several varieties of oak are listed, are still higher, 4*d.* per square foot being quoted for 'New wainscot' and 'Old or dark oak', while 'White oak' was 5*d.*, varnish in all cases being extra.[71] For 'Wainscot or oak', 'scientifically performed', Nicholson indicated a rate of 3½*d.* per foot in the 'Perpetual Price Book' attached to the *New Practical Builder*,[72] and a further reduction in price seems to have taken place by 1831, when *Skyring's Builder's Prices* suggested 3*d.* as the appropriate rate, varnish in both instances being separately billed.[73]

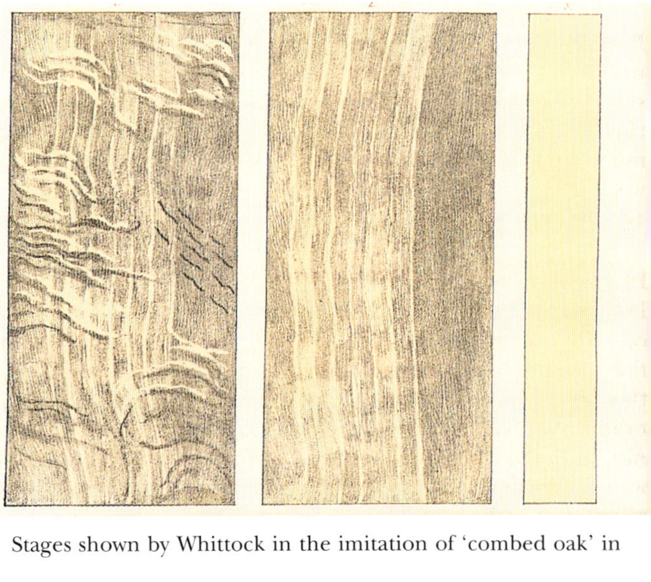

55. Stages shown by Whittock in the imitation of 'combed oak' in oil.

Oak, pollard or bulbous. Whittock defined 'pollard oak' (fig. 56) as 'the lower end of the trunk of the oak tree, near and under the surface of the earth . . . cut directly across', and recommended it as a 'fit colour for hall chairs, tables, &c.' as it was easily repaired.[74] Vanherman, who referred to it as 'bulbous oak', also mentioned its origin as the root of the tree, remarking that he had 'grained drawing-room door panels and styles in this way, and added gilt mouldings, which produced a rich and superb display'. He indicated that it was not the easiest grain to imitate in oil, but a good resemblance could be obtained in watercolour by a simple process. Burnt umber was first ground in beer or weak size:

> Then . . . having a good-sized bladder, made wet (but partially dried with a cloth), you dip it in the burnt umber, and apply it to the . . . ground . . . and . . . endeavour to imitate all the curls and zigzags you perceive in the pattern, by turning and twisting the bladder in every direction – by sometimes dabbing, sometimes trailing, pressing hard and gentle.

Two coats of varnish completed the work.[75] Whittock, on the other hand, using a brush, first dabbed umber ground in beer on the centre of the panel, after which a flat varnish brush was used to 'spread the colour thinly from the mass in the centre in rays in every direction, taking care that the rays are not straight, like rays from the sun, but irregularly curled and wavy'. Small touches of Vandyke brown were then added at various points and blended with a badger-hair softener. A 'flat brush, containing very few hairs, and some of them cut quite away' dipped in burnt umber was then drawn lightly over the work, and, when dry, the imitation finally varnished. Dark knots could be added before varnishing by the same means as those in birds eye maple.[76]

In 1820 the door and window joinery in the Hall and Octagon Vestibule at the Royal Pavilion, Brighton, were grained in imitation of 'Pollard oak'.[77]

Olive. The olive, *Olea europaea*, grows in southern Europe, and its timber, light greenish yellow in colour, was used in England for cabinet-work during the latter part of the seventeenth century (fig. 57).[78] John Smith indicated that: 'Olive-Wood is [i]mitated with Oaker, and a little White[,] veined over with burnt Umber';[79] and there is an item for a small quantity of 'olive colour grained' in an account for Hampton Court dated 1690, the rate being 1*s.* 6*d.* per square yard.[80]

Pine. Edward Croft-Murray notes a first-floor room at 'Thurnalls' in Melbourne Street, Royston, Hertfordshire, in which the wainscot is, he indicates, painted to represent pine.[81] He suggests that this finish may date from about 1635, the date on two carved mantelpieces in the house, in which other decorative paintings were found under later coatings of paint at some time prior to 1910.[82]

Pink wood. In 1815 the joinery of the doors and windows in the Hall at the Royal Pavilion, Brighton, were grained in imitation of 'pink wood' and varnished.[83] A contemporary design for the room, probably by Frederick Crace, appears to show this, the timber having a bold dark pink grain resembling that of tulip wood.[84] The latter (q.v. below) is known in French as *bois de rose*, and the two are, therefore, probably synonymous. 'Pink wood' graining was also used in other rooms at the Pavilion in 1815.[85]

Pollard oak. See *Oak, pollard or bulbous.*

Princeswood or kingwood. The imitation of 'princeswood' was mentioned by Sir Roger Pratt in his notebooks;[86] and at Erddig, Denbighshire (now Clwyd), the Drab Room was reported in 1692 to have contained elements 'painted . . . resembling . . . prince wood'.[87] Hinkley indicates that the term is found in English seventeenth-century furniture accounts, and gives two identifications for the timber. The first is that of the Spanish elm, *Cordia gerascanthus*, native to the West Indies and Central America, and the second a timber known as 'violet wood', which, he indicates, comes from an unidentified species of the genus *Dalbergia*, native to the Guianas and Brazil.[88] Rosewoods, too, belong to the latter genus, and can be of a dark purplish hue, so that it seems more than likely the name was applied by the seventeenth-century tradesman indiscriminately to a whole group of timbers of this colouration. Hinkley also identifies kingwood (fig. 58), the imitation of which was mentioned by Nicholson,[89] as synonymous with violet wood; and early nineteenth-century references to the imitation of 'black rosewood' will be found under that timber below.

Red sandal wood and coral wood. Directions for the imitation of at least two types of red sandal wood were given by Whittock under the names *red satin wood* and *coral wood.* The use of *Pterocarpus santalinus* in connection with the preparation of lacquers has already been mentioned, Tingry's later editor referring to it as *red saunders* or *red sandal wood;*[90] and Hinkley notes also employment of the names *rubywood* or *santal* for the timber, indicating that it is native to South India and the East Indies. It is, he observes, dark claret red to almost black in colour, with a

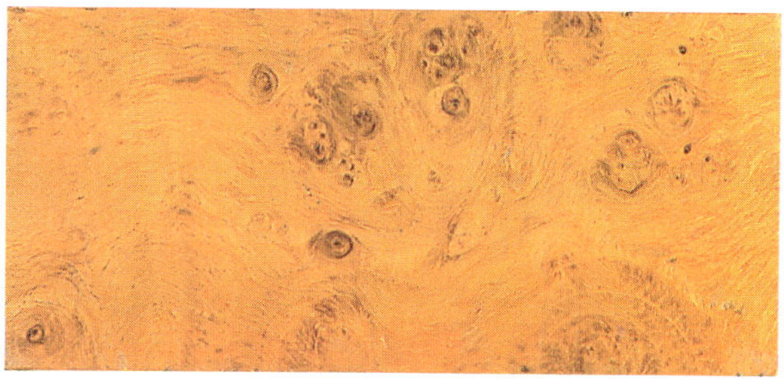

56. Pollard oak.

57. Olive.

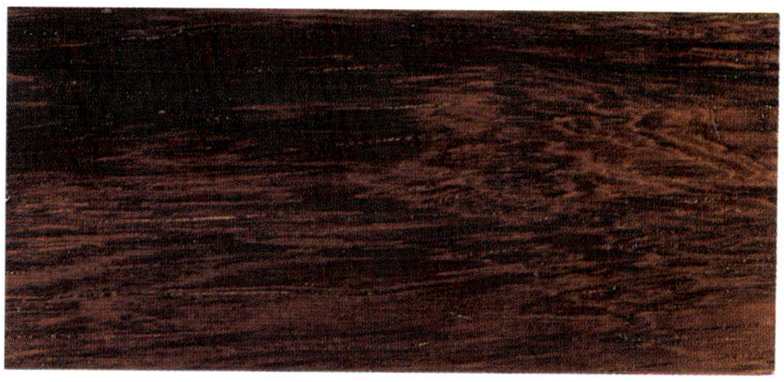

58. Princeswood (Kingwood).

figuring of darker stripings in the lighter varieties, radial sawing sometimes bringing out a darker stripe.[91]

Coral wood, on the other hand, he identifies as the timber of *Adenanthera pavolina*, native to India, Burma, and the Andaman Islands, and naturalised in the West Indies. Although it is yellow when first cut, the colour changes to a fine red or coral colour.[92] Whittock described coral wood as coming from Ceylon, and, since it was rare and valuable, 'a fit wood for the grainer to imitate, particularly in shop fronts that require glare and show, such as oilmen, hatters, and others', adding that it could be produced at a trifling expense (fig. 59). The ground for the imitation was to be laid in white lead tinted with vermilion, and the first glaze, in which the broad veins were to be worked, was made from vermilion, rose pink, and, in good work, one of the more expensive (drop) lakes ground in beer. This was to be laid on with 'the flat camel-hair brush',[93] imitating the graceful curve of the veins, which were to run in an upright direction, and the edges softened. When dry, a second glaze composed of Vandyke brown was drawn over the veins with 'the flat hog's-hair brush',[94] taking care to handle this tool 'so that it may bring the dark shade off with a point'. Immediately, a comb (No. 3 in his plate) (fig. 38) was to be applied so as to 'give the effect of the dark vein running into the other' and the whole softened.[95]

Whittock also described a method for the reproduction of 'watered damask coral wood', which he illustrated as showing a figure similar to that of watered silk (fig. 60). For this, the ground was to be more pink than in the ordinary variety, and should, he indicated, therefore contain rather more lake. The graining glaze was made from a mixture of vermilion and rose pink ground in beer and applied by means of a hog's-hair brush whose hairs, he stipulated, 'must be very thin and cut away in unequal distances as in the former example [i.e. that which he illustrated (fig. 39)] . . . but the spaces must be narrow and more frequent'. The brush was to be well filled with colour, and 'drawn over the panel to be painted in graceful curls, sometimes using a tremulous motion of the hand'. Dark veins were subsequently added in Vandyke brown, although, he said, these were 'little seen in this sort of wood, as it is rather a continuance of the red in deeper shades', and would not require softening.[96]

For the imitation of 'red satin wood' (fig. 61), on the other hand, which, he noted, came from the West Indies (suggesting either that both species had been naturalised there, or that he was confusing the two), Whittock indicated that the ground was to be laid in a mixture of vermilion, lake, and white, and the graining glaze made from a drop lake ground in ale, the lights being taken out with a sponge. A comb (No. 3 in his plate) (fig. 38) was then passed lightly across the work, and the colour allowed to dry. The broad veins were formed with rose pink and vermilion, to which a little crimson lake could be added to give brilliancy, 'laid on with the flat brush, leaving the light parts in the centre'.[97] When dry, small spots of black were touched in with a sable pencil, and the work completed by varnishing.[98]

No documentary references to the use of red sandal wood graining have been encountered to date, but the shop counter in the painting 'Choosing the Wedding Gown' by William Mulready (1786–1863) in the Victoria and Albert Museum appears as if grained a bright red colour, and it seems quite possible that this is a representation of either coral wood or the 'red satin wood' described by Whittock.[99]

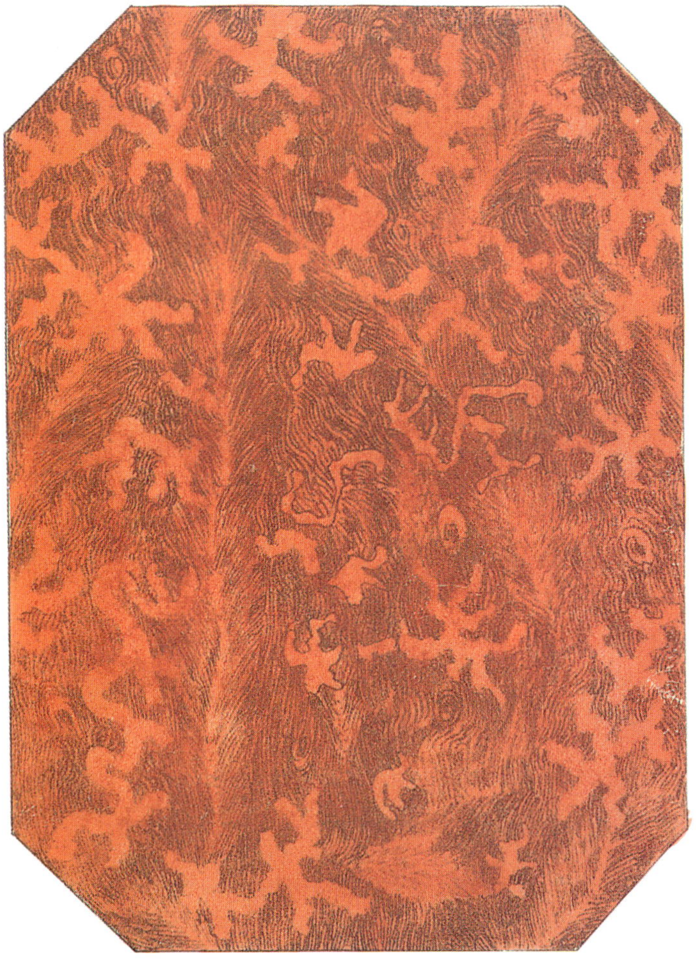

59. Specimen of 'coral wood' illustrated by Whittock in 1827.

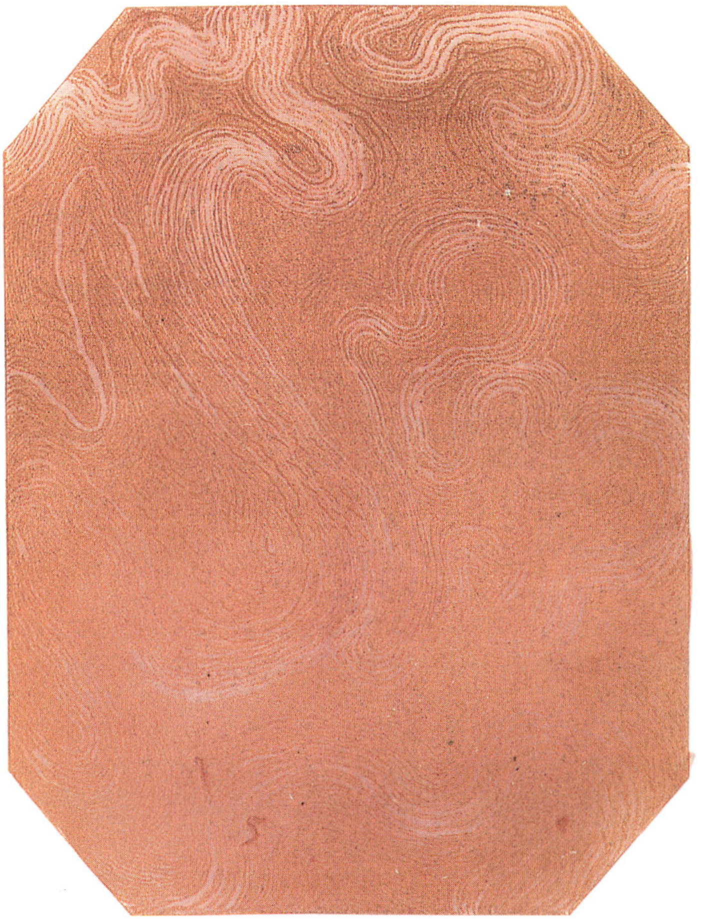

60. Specimen of 'watered damask coral wood' illustrated by Whittock.

Red satin wood. See *Red sandal wood.*

Rosewood. Two species of rosewood (fig. 62) are recognised, the American, *Dalbergia nigra*, which varies from yellowish to dark purple in colour, and Indian rosewood, *D. latifolia*, from the East Indies, of a medium or dark purplish brown. It seems likely that the darker purple varieties may have been used in the trade under the name *princeswood* (q.v.) during the seventeenth century, and *kingwood* by the early nineteenth, while the term 'black rosewood' is also encountered. Pyne described the frieze in the Golden Drawing Room at Carlton House, London, as painted in imitation of rosewood,[100] and both Vanherman and Whittock suggested methods by which this could be effected.

Vanherman indicated that the ground was prepared in the same way as that for mahogany (viz. either buff, or dark or light orange) followed by a light, transparent tint of lake, on which, he directed,

> with your graining tool, you lay in the large masses of stry with brown red, not too heavy, and then strengthen the shades with a mixture of lake and black, observing to keep the lights clean, and well defined.

In blending or softening, he added, care had to be taken to avoid losing the character of the timber.[101]

Whittock, on the other hand, provided no fewer than four different methods, observing that there was 'so great a variety of form in the grain and colour of this most elegant wood, that it is almost impossible to find two specimens alike'. The ground could not, he said, be too brilliant, vermilion, lake, and flake white being mixed to 'a beautiful rose red letting it partake more of the pink than the scarlet'. In the first method, nearly opaque Vandyke brown was spread over the ground in various directions, and then beaten 'against the grain, that is in an opposite direction to the way in which it was laid on'. A piece of wash leather on the point of a stick was next used 'with great freedom [to] take out the light veins that appear to be part of the veins formed by a knot'. Free and strong touches of the darkest tint of Vandyke brown were put in under these using a sable pencil, and also applied to other parts where the ground was thinly covered. The whole was then softened, and eventually varnished.[102]

For the second variety, which he considered very fit for bookcases, cabinets, and other work that was likely to be much handled, since it would not soil quickly, the grain was formed using Vandyke brown and rose pink ground in beer, laid on with a 'common tool'. The feather of a quill was then drawn over the colour, giving the hand 'a light tremulous motion in the part where the grain appears wavy'. The small bright lights were next taken out with the wash leather, and the work softened and allowed to dry. The very dark touches under the light parts were added using the same pigment 'nearly opaque'.[103]

The third variety he described as 'the light rose wood', and required the same pigments for the glaze. In this case, however, it was 'put on not in a mass . . . but with a flat brush, with the hairs cut away till it has the appearance of a wide toothed comb . . . [and] spread on in strokes in a curled direction as if winding round a knot'. When dry, a comb (No. 3 in his plate) (fig. 38) was applied directly across the grain, and a dark vein put in with Vandyke brown 'laid on nearly opaque'.[104]

Lastly, he described the variety 'now so fashionable for shop fronts', which was, he said, the common kind. The ground in this case could be less brilliant, and formed merely with Indian red and white lead as if for mahogany. Long streaks of glaze were irregularly laid on in nearly parallel lines, which waved and varied in thickness, and the graining produced between these using a 'flat hog's-hair brush, cut very square at the end, and the hairs cut away at unequal distances', knots and fissures being formed. The knots were then painted in with a large camel-hair pencil, and the work beaten against the grain with a duster to complete the imitation.[105]

In 1802, Crace billed for materials used at the Royal Pavilion, Brighton, 'consisting of fine colors for the Patterns [i.e. samples] of Rose wood: Vermillion, purple brown, yellow Lake, Best Lake, Pattent yellow, and other expensive colors'.[106] The same year he charged 2*s.* per square foot for 'Rose wood imitated and high varnished', and in 1803 1*s.* 6*d.* per square foot for 'Rose wood two colors and shadowed'.[107] Later, in the schedule of prices appended to the *New Practical Builder*, Nicholson gave a rate of 10*d.* per square foot for the imitation of rosewood; while Laxton listed 'black rosewood' at 10*d.*, and Skyring the same at 6*d.*, varnishing in all cases being separately billed.[108]

Sandal wood. See *Red sandal wood.*

Satin wood. Vanherman observed that satin wood 'is a most elegant and delicate subject for the grainer, and requires all his

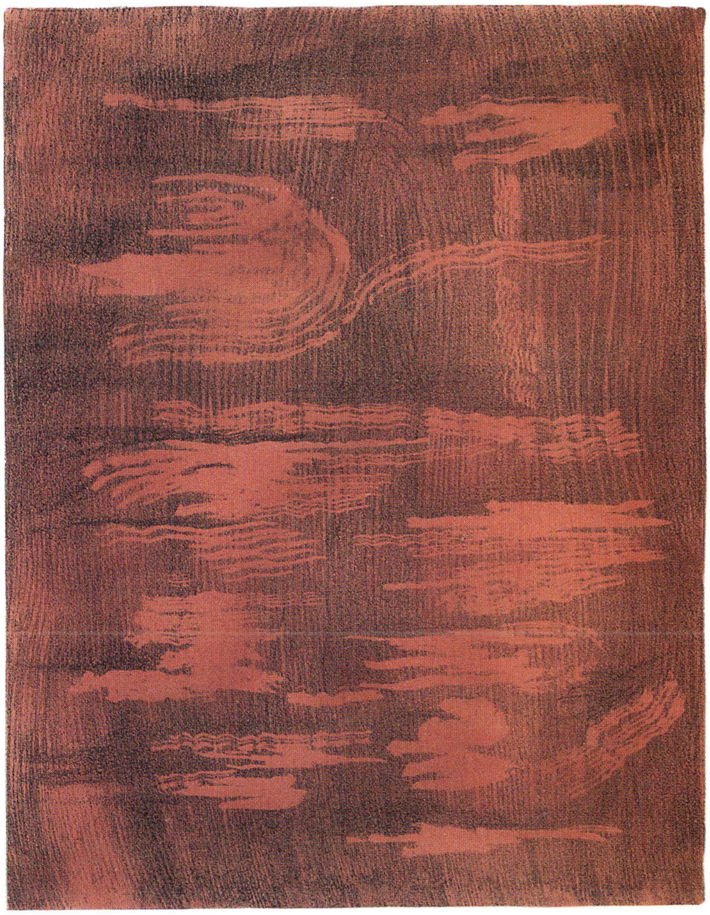

61. Specimen of 'red satin wood' illustrated by Whittock.

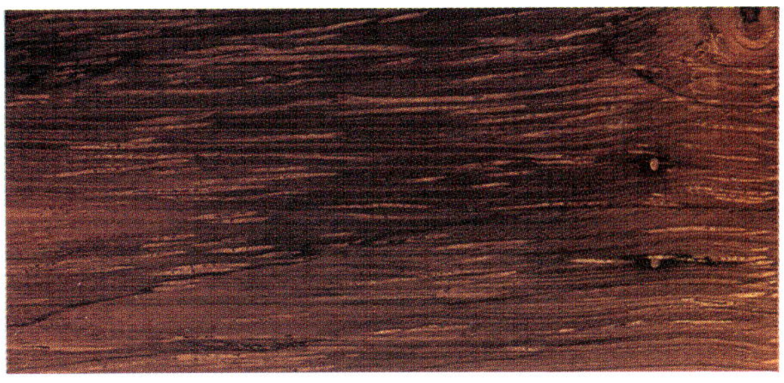

62. Rosewood.

skill to render it a perfect representation of nature'.[109] Two types are recognised, that from the East Indian species, *Chloroxylon swietenia* (fig. 63), and West Indian timber from various species of *Zanthoxylum*, the commonest being *Z. flavum*. Both are yellow in colour and can be cut to show a well-marked figure. Whittock described a method for the imitation of satin wood in distemper (fig. 64), the oil ground for which was to be the same as that he had indicated should be used for the lightest variety of oak (rotten stone and white). On this a wash of yellow Oxford ochre ground in pale ale was to be laid, dappled with a small piece of sponge dropped 'accidentally on various parts of the work' to produce the characteristic markings, and softened with the badger-hair softener. A second glaze of umber and raw sienna in ale was then applied with 'the flat brush with the hairs separated', passed 'over the work lightly, in a wavy direction'. This was softened in turn, letting the softener 'touch a little harder upon the bright lights than in the other parts, to remove the vein just laid on from it', and the work finally varnished.[110]

Vanherman too specified a pale yellow ground, this time made by mixing chrome yellow and white. Various shades of spruce ochre could, he said, be used for the glaze, in which one was directed, 'with the graining tool, to express the stry from the top to the bottom, waving occasionally, as you perceive in your pattern'.[111] Nicholson, on the other hand, recommended that the ground should be laid in a mixture of ceruse and Naples yellow, the graining glaze being made of raw and burnt sienna and Vandyke brown.[112] The formulae given for 'satin wood' by Butcher and the author of the *Painter's Pocket Manual*, however, were for the imitation of a timber stained blue or green, and have been discussed in the entry on harewood above.

In 1802, Crace provided 'Chinese Satin wood imitated 2 colors and high varnished' in the Billiard Room at the Royal Pavilion, Brighton at a cost of 1*s*. 2*d*. per square foot,[113] although the 'Satin Wood' in the Dining Room cost 1*s*. and 'Satin wood two colours' in the Ante-room 1*s*. 6*d*. (in neither case is varnishing mentioned).[114] In 1803, however, 'yellow Satin wood imitation and varnished' in the Prince's and other bedrooms cost only 9*d*.[115] Further references to yellow satin wood occur in 1815,[116] the term perhaps distinguishing timber from the West Indies, since satin wood from this source was, apparently, also known as yellow wood.[117] A few years later, Laxton gave a price of 8*d*. per square foot for the imitation of 'satin wood', and Skyring a rate of 6*d*. for 'Hare or satin wood'.[118]

Satin wood, grey. See *Harewood*.

Satin wood, red. See *Red sandal wood*.

Teawood. In 1803 the ceiling of the Glass Passage at the Royal Pavilion, Brighton, was 'grained Tea wood . . . to imitate boards'.[119] This and further items for the imitation of tea wood on the stiles of the Saloon doors and in other rooms in the same and the following year were all charged at a rate of 1*s*. per square foot, two of the entries specifically including varnish.[120] Contemporary designs for the Glass Passage and Saloon show a blue-coloured timber on the ceiling and door stiles respectively,[121] and it thus seems likely that the wood was one stained in a manner similar to those discussed in the section on Harewood above.

Tea wood graining is again mentioned in 1818,[122] but later references are to 'pink tea wood'. In 1819, for instance, the doors and other elements in the bed- and dressing-rooms of the Dukes of York and Clarence were painted 'in imitation of pink tea wood and highly varnished',[123] and similar entries occur in 1820 and 1821.[124]

Tulip wood. In 1803, parts of the ceiling and frieze, the skirting, columns, and column bases in one of the circulation areas of the Royal Pavilion, Brighton, were painted in imitation of tulip wood.[125] The timber (fig. 65) is obtained from Brazil, although similar timber has been imported from the East Indies and Madagascar, and is probably from one or more trees belonging to the species *Dalbergia*. It has pinkish red streaks on a yellowish ground, and is known in French as *bois de rose*.[126] Possibly, therefore, items for 'pink wood' (q.v. above) may also refer to it.

Wainscot. See *Oak and wainscot*.

Walnut. A drawing by John Smythson dated 1618 shows a grained panel in the lower part of the wainscot in the Great Chamber at Theobald's Park as 'wallnuttree Cullor',[127] and references to imitation of walnut are common in seventeenth-century accounts. In 1639–40, for example, an item appears for 'wallnuttree cullo^r & graining' on the wainscot in the Prince's New Closet at Richmond Palace,[128] and the imitation of walnut was mentioned by Sir Roger Pratt.[129] The tree, *Juglans regia*, which produces this greyish brown timber, grows in many

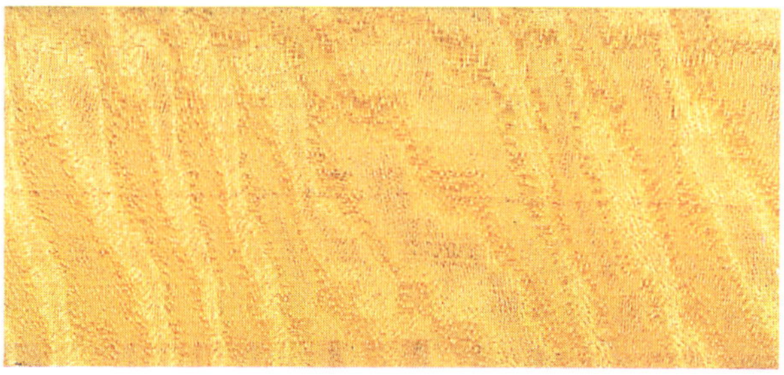

63. East Indian satin wood.

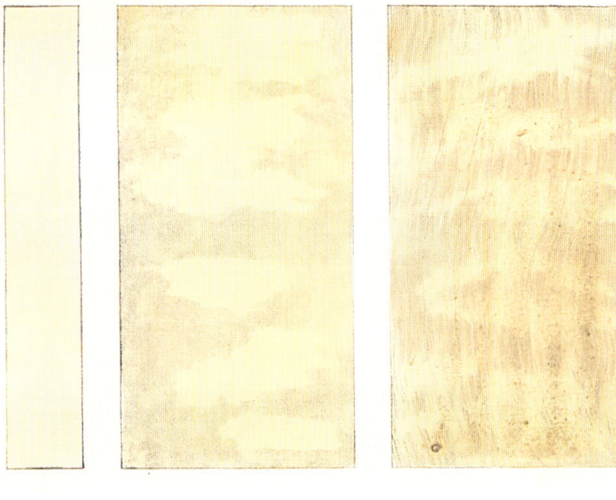

64. Stages shown by Whittock in the imitation of satin wood.

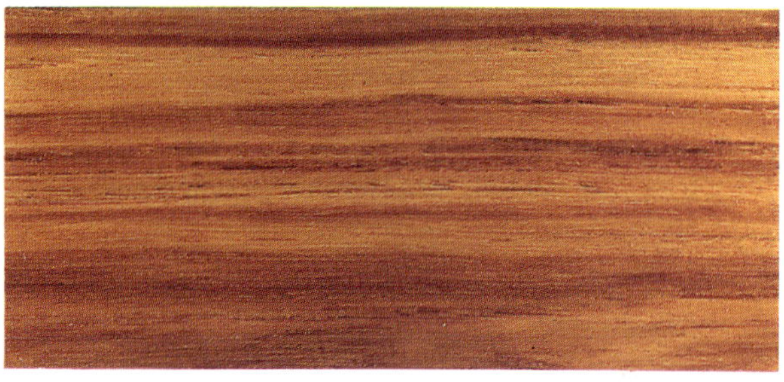

65. Tulip wood.

European countries, but the English wood (fig. 66) is most highly regarded for the beauty of its grain and tone.

Little technical information is available regarding early methods of imitating the wood, but in 1632–3 a large picture frame at Somerset House was painted 'with sad colour vained like walnuttree',[130] and, writing after the Civil War, John Smith indicated that 'Walnut-Tree is [i]mitated with burnt Umber, and White[,] vein'd over with the same Colour alone, and in the deepest places with Black.'[131] In the early nineteenth century, Whittock described a method for imitating Walnut, but observed that it was then not much used 'as a fancy wood'. The ground was to be laid in a mixture of yellow ochre, a little umber, and white; and the graining glaze was made from raw umber ground in beer applied with 'the flat brush',[132] or, if a large area was to be covered, with 'a large tool, nearly worn out'. If desired a knot could be added by placing a sponge on the wet glaze, 'and turning it round with the finger and thumb'. The light parts above and below the knot were also 'wiped out' with the sponge, and the work allowed to dry. The darkest veins were next added with 'the flat brush',[133] taking care that these followed roughly the grain already laid on, and the dark parts of the knot, and the touches above and below it put in. The work was softened with a dusting brush, and finally varnished.[134]

At Ham House, Surrey, in 1638 an item for 'painting . . . once over, Walnuttree coullour Vayned and Varnished' was priced at 8*d.* per square yard; while others for 'thrise primed and layde Walnuttree coullo[r] in Oyll and Vayned' were charged for at 1*s.* 6*d.* and 1*s.* 8*d.*[135] In 1676, Christopher Wren noted that 'Veined like Walnuttree . . . well performed' should cost 1*s.* 6*d.* per square yard,[136] but an item for 'Wallnutt Tree grained' in the Kensington Palace Pay Book dated 1692,[137] and another in the accounts for Hampton Court in 1690,[138] were both charged at the rate of 2*s.* per square yard.

Yew. The English yew, *Taxus baccata*, provides a warm brownish yellow timber, often containing small 'birds eye' knots (figs. 67, 68). In 1692 the panels in the Drab Room at Erddig, Denbighshire (now Clwyd), were described as painted 'resembling Yew';[139] while during the early nineteenth century Laxton listed the imitation at 1*s.* per square foot, Nicholson gave a rate of 10*d.*, and Skyring quoted 9*d.*[140] In 1686 'Yew Root' was included in an account for painting at Combe Abbey, Warwickshire, perhaps imitating a burr form of the timber.[141]

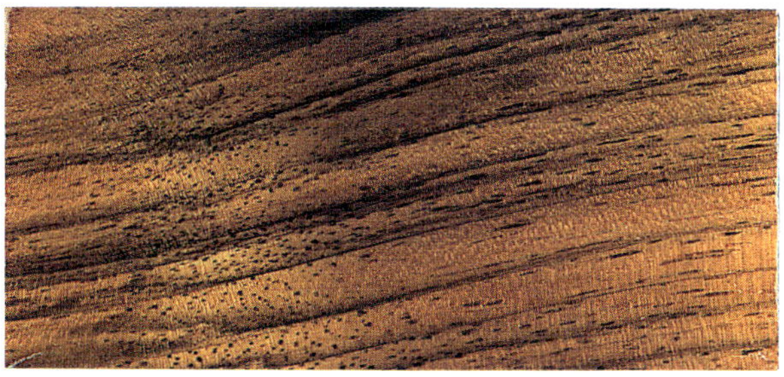

66. English walnut.

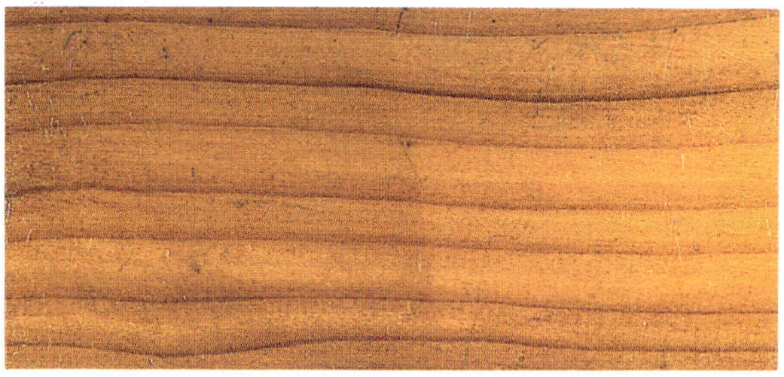

67. Yew.

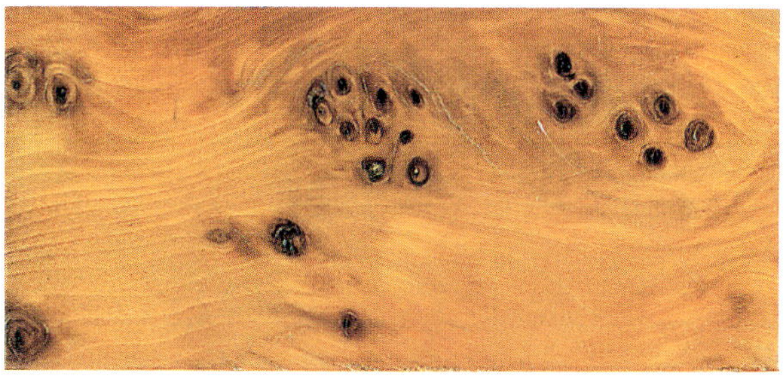

68. Birds eye yew.

APPENDIX C

GLOSSARY OF MARBLES AND DECORATIVE STONES IMITATED

Naturally it is the architectural use of genuine marbles and decorative stones which provides the key to an understanding of their imitation in paint. During the seventeenth century, as in the Middle Ages, considerable use was made of native English 'marbles' in architecture, fireplaces of Derbyshire fossil limestone, for example, being fairly common in interiors of the period; while in addition Rance and Namur marbles were extensively imported from Belgium, besides other European varieties. In the eighteenth century it was natural that the use of Italian marbles should increase, both new stone and pieces robbed from the ruins of classical antiquity providing supplies for architectural use. In the latter instance, the locations of many of the quarries from which the different marbles had originally been obtained had been forgotten, and specimens accordingly were particularly highly prized. As no doubt did a number of his contemporaries, William Chambers possessed a considerable number of both antique and currently quarried samples;[1] and other systematic collections came to be assembled, Nathaniel Whittock referring, for example, to that made by J. Scott which was being catalogued for deposit in the Ashmolean at Oxford.[2] The contemporary importance attached to the use of marbles is emphasised by a favourite method used for their display by the inlaying of small pieces to form chequered table-tops; and a useful example dating from about 1820 and formerly belonging to George Gwilt may be seen, together with its manuscript index, in the furniture galleries at the Victoria and Albert Museum.[3]

Such collections are of obvious importance as working references, but the architectural classification of the various marbles they contain is a matter of considerable complexity, since, although with cabinet timbers it is possible in the majority of instances to identify the botanical species associated with the common name, this facility finds no comparison in the case of decorative stones. Indeed, strictly scientific criteria reflect a need very different from that of the practising architect; and, while to the building trade any decoratively figured stone which will take a polish is a 'marble', to the geologist the term has a precise technical meaning, being restricted to certain metamorphic rocks, so that many of those found listed below belong, in fact, to other geological classifications. Moreover, even among the true marbles, similarly coloured and marked specimens may be procured from widely separated quarries, but may nevertheless share a common trade name; and conversely, different names, sometimes misleading as far as their geographical origin is concerned, have been applied to similar material from a single quarry. During the nineteenth century much effort was expended on research into the subject, but the topic is one which has recently been much neglected, at least from the point of view of architectural history; and much remains to be done in making it accessible to the architectural historian in a way immediately relevant to his needs. A significant number of questions concerning the identification of marbles in paint therefore remain unanswered, and the glossary which follows is almost inevitably based primarily on the terms used by the trade during the period covered by this book.

Aragon. Whittock included the marble of 'Arragon' in his list of yellow marbles which, he said, were 'usually known by the name of Sienna' in painting, adding that all these had 'nearly the same appearance';[4] while Vanherman described 'Aragon' as yellow and orange in colour.[5] Possible sources include both the region of Aragon in Spain, which lies adjacent to Catalonia whence brocatello (q.v.) is obtained, and Aragona in Sicily, Hull noting varieties of yellow marbles from Castelnuovo and Segesta in the island.[6]

Bardiglio. Grey marbles (fig. 69), often bluish in tone, are found in a number of places besides Burdilla in Italy, and exhibit a range of different figures. In particular Whittock included 'bardiglio from Carrara' among those which were, he noted, 'called in painting dove-coloured marble', providing a formula for the imitation of a grey marble with broad veins of white and black.[7] Vanherman, however, described bardiglio as blue;[8] and, writing early this century, Renwick clearly separated the two categories, dove, he indicated, being a soft grey marble with light patches, while he defined bardiglio as having 'a light blue ground with fine pencil veinings of deep purple'.[9] Hull also described bardiglio as grey or bluish in colour traversed by dark veins,[10] but in Gwilt's *Encyclopaedia* it was simply described as a 'dark grey marble with black veins',[11] and Burnham indicated that bardiglio was 'pure flesh-white or gray, covered with veins, spots, or clouds of very deep purple tending to black'.[12] Any distinction between bardiglio and dove-coloured marble (q.v.) does not seem, therefore, to have commanded universal acceptance; and the terms were probably regarded as interchangeable by many house-painters, the two sharing a common price of 4*d.* per square foot in the price-books of Laxton and Skyring.[13]

Black marble. Black marbles, often containing white veins or fossil-like markings, are obtainable from several sources in Italy, and also from the counties of Galway, Limerick, Carlow, Kilkenny, Mayo, and Waterford in Ireland, and from the province of Namur in Belgium.[14] In 1703, Neve noted the use of 'black fleak'd Marble' for chimneypieces,[15] and in Gwilt's *Encyclopaedia* it is suggested that Wren used Galway marble for steps at St Paul's Cathedral, Marlborough House, Hampton Court, and Kensington Palace;[16] while towards the end of the eighteenth century Sir William Chambers employed black Namur marble at Somerset House.[17]

Félibien described a method for the imitation of black marble by grinding calcined lamp black and a little graphite with olive oil and soapsuds. Two or three coats were to be applied and the surface burnished when dry. If desired, white veins could be added with a small brush before burnishing.[18] An estimate dated 1705 for painting at Stoke Edith, Herefordshire, included 'Black marble' at 1*s.* 6*d.* per square yard.[19]

Black and gold marbles, including Portoro. In 1803 Soane expressed his intention to paint the 'Basem!.' of the staircase at Pitzhanger Manor, his villa at Ealing, in imitation of 'black marble & gold veins'.[20] Black marble with 'yellow, white, and brown' figuring was mentioned by Vanherman,[21] and Whittock described 'Black and gold marble' as 'in great use for superior chimneypieces'.[22] Marbles having this colouration (fig. 70) are also known as *Portoro,* a corruption of Port d'Oro, and are obtained from Porto Venere on the southern extremity of the peninsula protecting the Gulf of Spezia,[23] similarly coloured stone being found at Ormea in Piedmont.

To imitate black and gold marble, Whittock indicated the ground should be prepared in black, and that 'the large spots from which the fibrous veins run' were to be of yellow ochre and white, mixed with a little vermilion to give them a golden tinge. The masses were to be 'dabbed with freedom upon the ground with the brush full of colour, and while quite fluid, small threads . . . drawn from it in all directions, some larger than others'. For quick work, where durability was not an object, distemper could be used, but oil was, he indicated, better. In cabinet work, he added, gold and silver leaf could first be applied in certain areas, the black ground then put on rather thickly, and the veins and large areas taken out with a round-pointed bodkin and a wash leather on the point of a stick. When dry, other white and yellow veins could be added as before, and the work finally varnished.[24]

British 'marbles'. Having completed his list of marbles suitable for imitation, Vanherman observed: 'The above are foreign, but there is a great variety of the Irish and Scotch marbles, which do not yield, in beauty and diversity of colours, to any.'[25] Many stones, of a wide range of colours, capable of receiving a polish have been quarried in the British Isles for use as 'marble', and were used extensively for fireplaces, especially during the seventeenth century. They also enjoyed a vogue for ecclesiastical work during the nineteenth. Besides those mentioned by Hull, an exhaustive list appeared in Gwilt's *Encyclopaedia*;[26] but Whittock mentioned specifically only a variety of a deep grey colour, interspersed with black veins, besides the Cornish and Anglesey serpentines, adding that some specimens of the latter were in his opinion 'equal in brilliancy of colour and variety of figure, to verde antique or Egyptian green'.[27] The methods he described for their imitation will be found in the articles on serpentine and dove-coloured marble below.

Brocatello. Whittock listed 'Brocatello' (fig. 71) as 'a breccia limestone, composed of fragments of a yellowish red and purple colour, which are cemented by a semi-transparent white calcarious spar', adding that it was little used in England.[28] The term is, nevertheless, encountered in several contemporary price-books; and, for example, the marble itself was used by Chambers (who referred in his *Treatise* to the 'brocatello of Spain')[29] for a fireplace at Somerset House.[30] Renwick described 'Spanish brocatelle' as a 'shell marble of brilliant appearance, quarried near Tortosa (Catalonia)'. The ground is, he noted, 'deep red, and is almost covered with small yellow, grey, and white crystals'.[31] Burnham gave a similar description, adding that the name 'Brocatello di Spagna' was applied to those varieties in which a violet colouration was present, but that when all the

69. Bardiglio or dove grey.

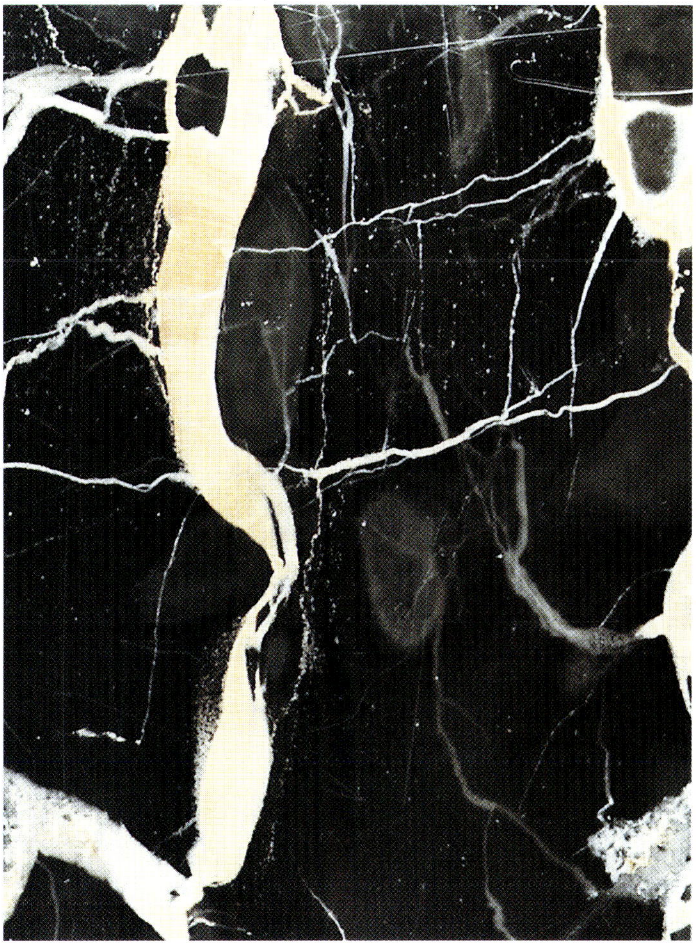

70. Black and gold or 'Portoro'.

colours were yellow, the marble was called 'Orientale'.[32] 'Rose brocatelle di Centro' was, on the other hand, Renwick observed, a selected variety of Verona red having bands of a deeper shade than the ground of the marble traversing the formation,[33] but it seems unlikely that it was to this that Whittock referred.

Laxton listed the imitation of 'brocattelli' at 6*d.* per square foot, Nicholson 'Brocatella' at the same rate, and Skyring 'Brocatella' at 7*d.*[34]

Campan. Vanherman listed Campan (fig. 72), describing it as a green marble.[35] Renwick defined the term as a distinctive name given to French variegated marbles quarried in the Campan district of the Hautes Pyrenées, adding that these could be identified by their peculiar mottled markings. *Campan vert* was, he indicated, a light-green marble with white markings occasionally tending to flesh colour, having white crystalline veins, although he also gave details of other varieties having chocolate or reddish brown markings.[36]

Carrara. Marble is quarried extensively from the range of the Apennines overlooking the bay of La Spezia in Italy, especially in the vicinity of Carrara, Massa, and Seravezza, a range of colours and figures being obtained. Vanherman mentioned the pure white marble of 'Carura', and Whittock bardiglio (q.v.) from the same source.[37]

Chinese marble. References occur in the accounts for painting at the Royal Pavilion, Brighton, to the imitation of various colours of 'Chinese' marble, probably stylisations of marbles depicted in oriental pictures rather than specific geological types. In 1803, for example, an entry for the Hall mentions '2 Chinese Pedestals for Figures 4 oils and flatted and veined in imitation of blue Chinese Marble and varnished',[38] and another for the Prince's Staircase and associated spaces 'Cove and pilasters . . . veined white and red Chinese marble' followed by a large area of 'green, blue, white and red Chinese marble to represent sunk panels and raised stiles', no doubt on the walls.[39] The following year 'green Chinese marble' was imitated in the Eating Room Lobby, and similar entries may be found in 1815.[40]

Cipolin. Whittock used the term 'cipolin' for 'the statuary [i.e. white] marble, traversed by veins of mica' the imitation of which was, he said, commonly called by the painters 'white-veined marble'.[41] The term is, however, generally applied to marbles having typical onion-skin-like markings. Burnham listed several of these, including varieties from France and Saxony,[42] but the best-known stone of this type in undoubtedly the classical *cipollino*, a marble from Euboea in Greece (fig. 73), which had

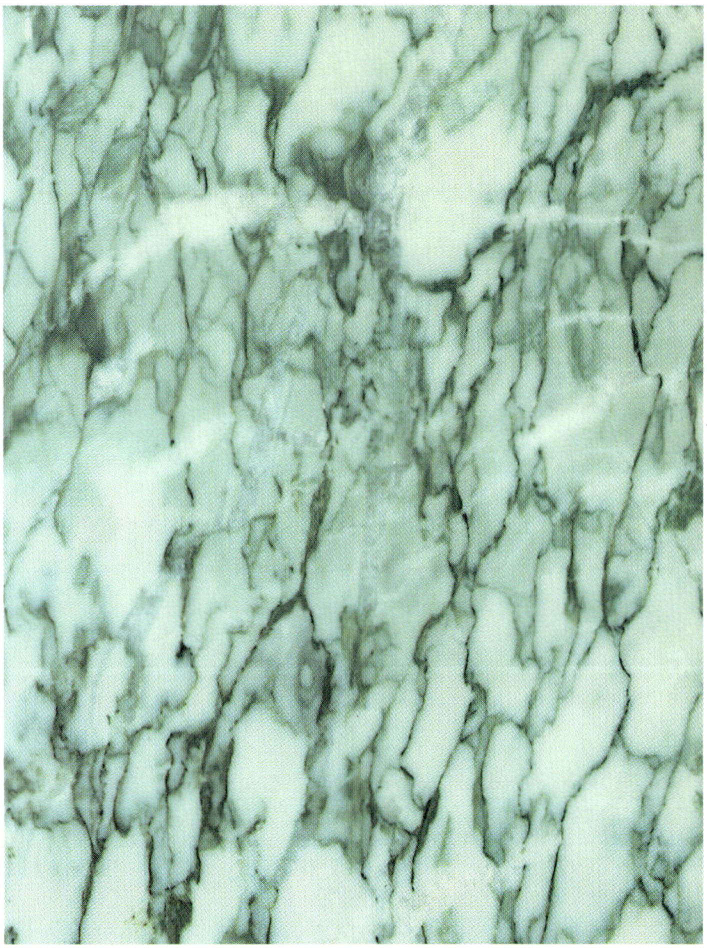

72. Campan vert.

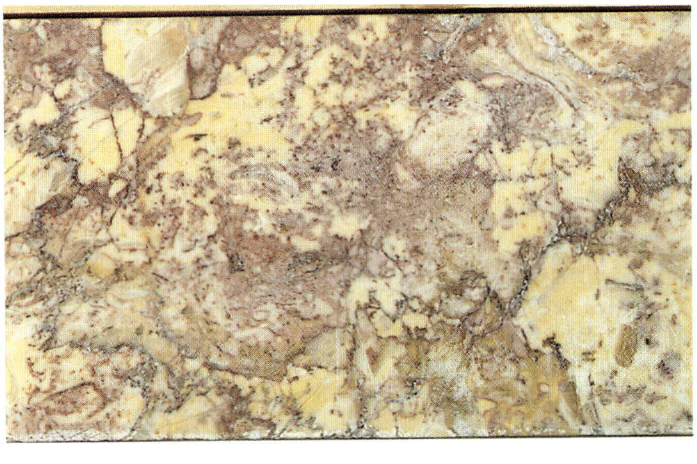

71. Spanish brocatello.

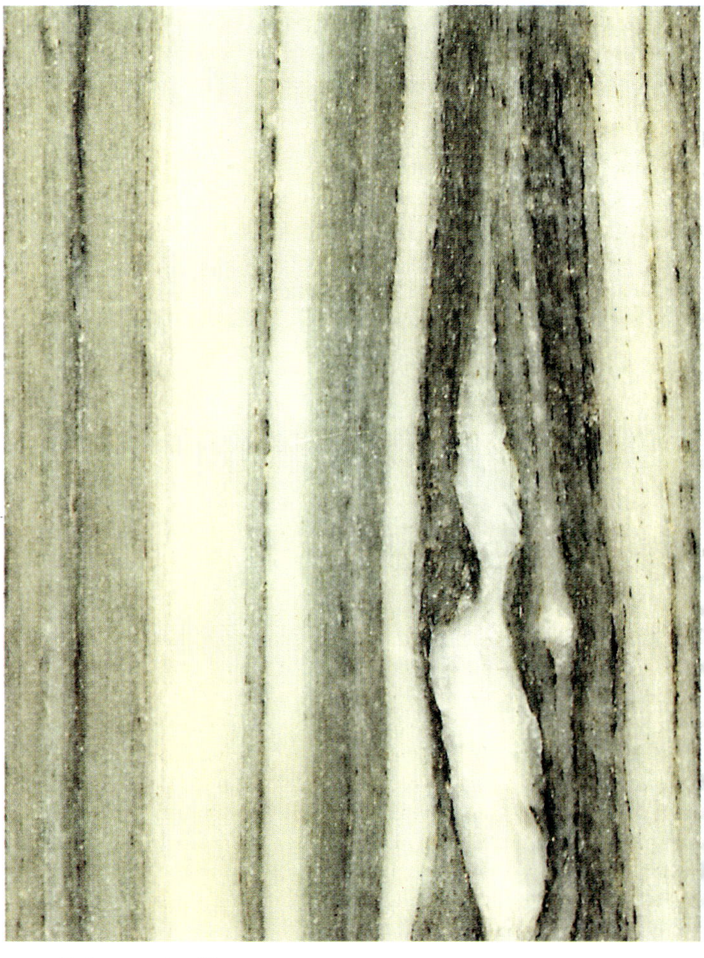

73. Euboean cipollino.

been quarried in classical times. Although the quarries had been lost, and were not rediscovered until the late nineteenth century, ancient pieces were known to Regency architects, and Jeffry Wyatt, for example, incorporated columns of antique cipollino in the Sculpture Gallery he formed for the Duke of Bedford from Henry Holland's Greenhouse at Woburn Abbey on which work started in 1816.[43] It is quite likely, therefore, that imitations of the true cipolins were also carried out.

Dolomite. Vanherman listed 'Dolomite' as a pale red marble, with 'small globules'.[44] Although *dolomite* itself is a term reserved by geologists exclusively for magnesian limestones, Burnham observed: 'Many species of marbles are derived from the Swiss limestones and dolomites, including those valued for their qualities as an ornamental stone'. It is possible, therefore, that Vanherman may have had such a stone in mind, and Burnham continued by describing a specimen which was a,

> Coralline marble of light-brown, enclosing the Madrepora vermicularis, of pale yellow, glittering spar, exhibiting large stars with a variable number of rays, [forming] a compact marble receiving a medium polish. Another kind of Madrepore appears like a gray, semi-pellucid flint, resembling the Indian agate; the color varies from ash-gray to grayish-black tinged with red, while the coral consists of white pentagonal columns crowned with a star.

A similar variety, known as 'Feather Stone', was, he noted, found in England.[45]

Dove-coloured marble. Whittock described 'Dove-coloured marble' as including the 'bardiglio from Carrara', and other marbles 'of a deep grey colour, interspersed with black veins, found in Britain'.[46] As already noted in the entry above on bardiglio, however, Renwick differentiated between dove and bardiglio, describing the former as an Italian marble, soft grey in tone, with occasional light patches, as distinct from the latter which had darker veins on a grey ground. It was, he said, quarried at Carrara, Massa, and Seravezza, and sometimes known as 'Blue Turquoise'.[47] For the imitation of dove-coloured marble, Whittock indicated that the ground should be prepared in a light lead colour on which broad veins of white and black were irregularly scumbled in oil, and blended together with the duster, 'so laid on that when they mix together they appear to form light and dark veins of grey, and not a decided black or white'. He added that some specimens were more mottled than others, but the marble was, he indicated, too dark to be required often in distemper.[48]

Laxton and Skyring both listed 'Dove, or burdilla' at 4*d.* per square foot, although Nicholson gave a price of 3½*d.* for 'Dove marbling'.[49]

Egyptian green marble. In 1686 'Egiptian Marble' was included among other items in the painter's account for work at Combe Abbey, Warwickshire, the natural material being listed by Neve in 1703 as '*Egyptian* Marble vein'd with a variety of Greens'.[50] In the 1820s Whittock mentioned the imitation of 'Egyptian green' marble, indicating that the method of effecting this was the same as that he had described for *verde antico* (q.v.). It was, he said, a 'superior serpentine' and similar to *verd antique*, but differed slightly in the 'form of the veins, which run in a more horizontal direction, having a greater quantity of small fossil substances mixed with it, and the dark veins frequently running in streaks, which often appear as if broken by violence'. To this he added that there were 'many different sorts, which are distinguished by separate names', all of which, however, were generally, he said, called by this title.[51] Hull, writing later in the century, described the 'breccia di verde' from Egypt, which had been quarried by the ancients between the Nile and the Red Sea in latitude 26° 8' N., including it among a number of serpentines obtained from Egypt, Greece, and Italy which passed under the name of *verde antico*.[52]

Florentine marble. Whittock described methods for the imitation of two varities of 'Florentine marble', the first of which was 'seen to break suddenly into the form of rocks or ruins of houses' (fig. 74), the second being an 'Italian argillaceous limestone'.[53] This was known as *Pisana* by the late nineteenth century, and Burnham described the 'modern argillaceous marble of Pisa, called Lithomarge' in some detail, indicating that:

> The small fissures, filled with a ferruginous substance, often assume fantastic forms representing various objects; . . . if rocks, walls, and ruined castles are imitated, it becomes Ruin-marble; when the lines represent doubtful forms, it is said to be Varioform; and when unicolored, or simply veined, it is merely Lithomarge.[54]

To imitate the ruin variety, Whittock indicated that the ground should be prepared in a mixture of white, Indian red, and black, mixed to form a very light reddish neutral tint. Umber or burnt sienna were used for the veins and were to be laid on 'very irregularly' while the ground was still wet. However, although he observed that the imitation was of good effect in small spaces, he cautioned that 'the beauty of the work . . . will scarcely repay the great trouble there is in painting it'.[55]

The ordinary variety he recommended as being suitable for passages and halls, and was, he said, easy in distemper. Yellow ochre and red were added to whiting which had been mixed with milk 'to the consistence of thick cream' until it was of a delicate yellowish fawn colour, and, at the same time, Indian red and pure white were prepared in separate basins, presumably using a similar medium or perhaps beer. Some of the fawn colour was dabbed on in two or three places with apparent carelessness, letting some areas be larger than others. Immediately, using another brush, Indian red was washed with freedom between the dabs of fawn, and the edges between them blended together with a large dusting brush. White and red veins were then drawn on using camel-hair pencils.[56]

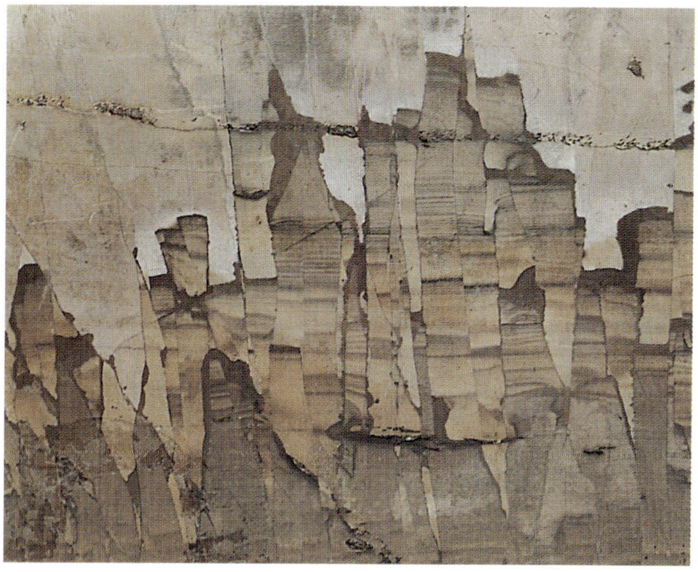

74. 'Florentine' ruin marble.

French marble. Both Laxton and Skyring listed the imitation of 'French' marble, the former quoting a rate of 8*d.* per square foot, and the latter 7*d.*[57] A large variety of different marbles is obtained from France, and, since neither writer offers any details of colour or markings, it is difficult to suggest which of these was implied.

Giallo antico. Renwick indicated that *giallo antico* (fig. 75) was obtained from the vicinity of Chemtou in the Medjera Valley, Tunisia, and described it as a 'marble of great beauty, having a rich yellow ground with a rose pink tint and occasional deep red markings'.[58] Burnham (who stated that the quarries were said to have been on Mount Maurasidus in Numidia) added that, while the base was always yellow, or yellowish, four varieties of this were recognised: *dorato*, or golden; *cupo*, or deep orange; *paglia*, or straw coloured; and *carnigione*, or flesh-coloured.[59]

Imitations of *giallo antico* were listed by both Laxton and Skyring at rates of 1*s.* and 10*d.* per square foot respectively.[60]

Granite. In 1829 it was noted that the chimneypiece in the Billiard Room at Dunham Massey, Cheshire, was to be painted in imitation of granite.[61]

Green stone. An item for 'Green stone' at 2*s.* per square yard is included in an estimate for painting at Stoke Edith, Herefordshire, dated 1705.[62] Hull indicated that this name was 'much used, but much abused', adding that it should strictly be applied only to the group of plutonic rocks, which included diorite (which occurs at Cader Idris and Penmaenmawr in North Wales, Bardon Hill in Leicestershire, and St Mewan in Cornwall), gabbro, and diabase (to which a number of British stones bear a resemblance).[63] It is almost impossible, therefore, to obtain a precise idea of what was intended at Stoke Edith.

Green verd. Both Laxton and Skyring listed 'green verd', the former at a rate of 1*s.* per square foot, and the latter at 7*d.*[64] In both cases the imitation of *verde antico* is separately given, showing that one of a number of other green marbles was intended.

Grey marble. Vanherman listed 'Grey' marble, describing it as 'Saxon blue' in colour.[65] Since he listed bardiglio (q.v.) separately, it seems likely that he was using the term 'grey' where others might have mentioned 'dove-coloured marble' (q.v.). An account of 1638 for painting in the Great Hall at Ham House, Surrey, contains an item for 'painting lyke gray Marble the Chimney peece';[66] in 1686–8 Streeter painted 'Gray Marble Coloure' on walls and other stonework in 'Henry VIII's Chapel' at Windsor Castle;[67] and an account of 1688 for painting at Tredegar House, Newport, Monmouthshire (now Gwent), has an entry for 'gray Marble & Tortell shell' at a rate of 1*s.* per square yard.[68]

Jasper. A number of sixteenth-century accounts apparently for the imitation of jasper exist, including one of 1592–3 for a bridge in the gardens at Greenwich Palace which involved 'jasperinge like a Rannce'.[69] This suggests that the term may sometimes have been used simply to convey the use of marbling, especially where the imitation was red in colour, as was the case with rance (q.v.). Although no references to the imitation of jasper during the period covered by this book have been encountered, natural Sicilian jasper, a red marble obtained from that island, some varieties of which contain greenish areas, was used extensively (examples appear, for instance, in chimneypieces by Chambers at Somerset House – fig. 76), and it is quite probable that its imitation was practised.[70]

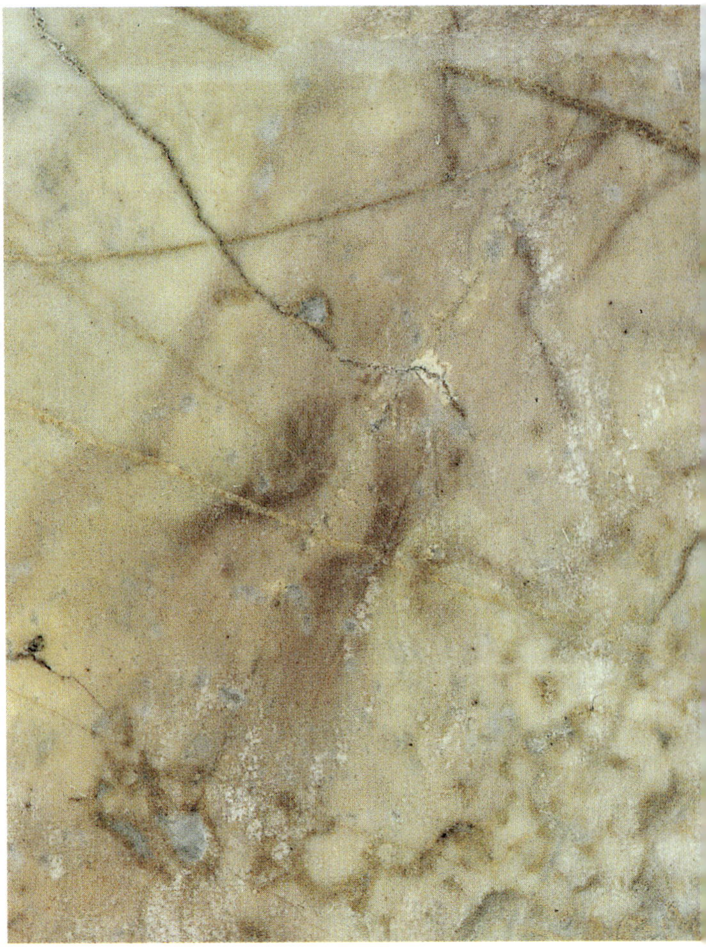

75. Giallo antico.

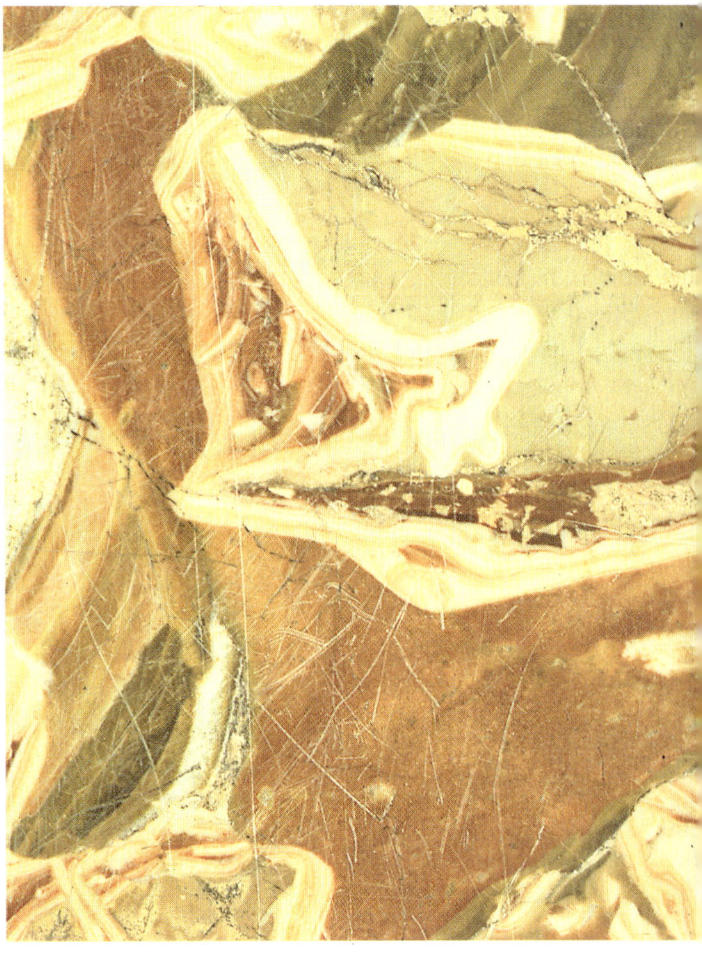

76. Sicilian jasper.

Lapis lazuli. The semi-precious mineralised limestone lapis lazuli (fig. 77) occurs in several parts of the world, and has been described in Chapter 2 in connection with the pigment natural ultramarine. The stone is a rich blue in colour, often with veins of white, containing gold-coloured flecks of iron pyrites. In 1672, Salmon gave instructions for its imitation, directing that an opaque blue ground made from ultramarine or other blue pigment should be laid in a varnish medium on a white undercoat also in varnish. Then, he continued,

> with wild irregular streaks (in resemblance of nature) with liquid or shell gold, run straglingly all over the blew, adding very small specks upon the blew part, of such various colours, as are usually to be seen upon this stone.[71]

In 1685, 'Lupis Lazuri' was included among other items in the painter's account for work at Combe Abbey, Warwickshire;[72] while an estimate of 1705 for painting at Stoke Edith, Herefordshire, contains an item for 'Lapus Lasure' at 5*s.* per square yard; and at Burley-on-the-Hill, Rutland (now Leicestershire), *trompe l'oeil* busts on the staircase were painted in imitation of lapis lazuli by Lanscroon at some date prior to 1700.[73] Lapis lazuli was also imitated on pedestals and other furnishings at the Royal Pavilion, Brighton, in 1803.[74]

Lumachella. The term lumachella is applied to a large number of different marbles containing fossil shells, deriving from the Italian *lumacha*, meaning a snail or slug, and William Chambers, for example, listed five different varieties in his series of marbles.[75] Whittock described lumachella as brownish grey containing shells, and Vanherman too stated that lumachelli consisted of 'Shells, united with brown'.[76] The specimens of 'Lumachelli antico' and 'Lumachelli di Spagna moderno' in a table-top of about 1820 in the Victoria and Albert Museum both conform to these descriptions.[77]

Marble colour, ordinary. The expression 'marble colour' is found from the beginning of the period covered by this study. In 1622–3, for example, the walls and doors of part of the Withdrawing Chamber of the Lord Steward's lodging at Whitehall Palace were painted 'marble colour in distember', and in 1637–8 the lower part of the wainscot in the Cabinet Room at Somerset House was painted 'in a marble cullo:r 'in oyle'.[78] In the early eighteenth century, Neve gave the price of painting 'ordinary Marble colour, on new Stuff' as about 1*s.* per square yard, adding that if painted on old colour the price was about 9*d.*[79] Thus qualified, it seems likely that veined white marble would have been the variety commonly implied; but the unqualified term could evidently be applied to more expensive imitations, such as the 'marble colour' directed to be used in the Great Room at Combe Abbey, Warwickshire, in 1685 at a cost of 2*s.* 4*d.* per yard, besides the 'marble Colour' applied in the Balcony Room at Dyrham Park, Gloucestershire (now Avon), in 1694 at 3*s.* per yard, the latter comprising simulated porphyry and an orange-pink marble.[80]

Mona marble. See *Serpentine.*

Oriental marble. Both Laxton and Skyring listed the imitation of 'oriental' marble, the former at a rate of 1*s.* per square yard, and the latter 10*d.*[81] The term is one commonly used in trade names of different colours of marble, for example, 'rosso orientale', and 'oriental alabaster'; but it seems quite possible that the completely yellow variety of Spanish brocatello (q.v.), which Burnham stated was called 'Orientale' was the one in question, although this is by no means certain.

Parian marble. Both Whittock and Vanherman referred to the pure white Parian marble.[82] The name is properly applied to that from the island of Paros, which, wrote the author of Stuart's *Dictionary of Architecture*, 'has always been celebrated', adding that the finest was that obtained from Mount Marpessus.[83] Whittock, however, simply regarded it as the 'pure delicate and translucent species of granularly foliated limestone . . . used by the ancient Greek sculptors', mentioning the group of the Laocoon (in the Vatican, Rome) and the sculpture in the pediment of the Parthenon (the latter, in fact, of Pentellic marble)[84] as examples. It was, he said, easily imitated by the painter as it was 'in its most perfect state . . . quite white'.[85]

Porphyry. References to the imitation of 'porphyry' are commonly encountered. An account dating from 1610–11 for painting a chimney-piece at Somerset House indicates that it was 'garnished with divers Culloured stones' including 'purfrire';[86] and Croft-Murray notes a chimneypiece of about 1635 at 'Thurnalls', Melbourne Street, Royston, Hertfordshire, on which a reputedly contemporary imitation of porphyry may be seen.[87] On 1 July 1664 John Evelyn visited Thomas Povey's house in Lincoln's Inn Fields, and recorded 'the perspective in his court, painted by Streeter . . . with the vasas in imitation of porphyrie'.[88] In the years around 1800, imitations of porphyry again became popular. Instances include a small area of 'Porphery Marble' in the Billiard Room at the Royal Pavilion, Brighton, in 1802,[89] and it appeared too in the Entrance Hall at Carlton House;[90] while an example, reputedly dating from about 1843, may apparently be seen on the overdoors in the Hall at Prestwold Hall, Leicestershire.[91]

In interpreting references to 'porphyry', however, it must be borne in mind that, although, as Hull remarked, the term was originally only applied to certain kinds of igneous rock of reddish or purplish tint, such as the red porphyry of Egypt (fig. 78), a green porphyry was quarried in antiquity from 'between Sparta and Marathon'.[92] This, he indicated, has a 'dark green felspathic base with imbedded light-green crystals of felspar';

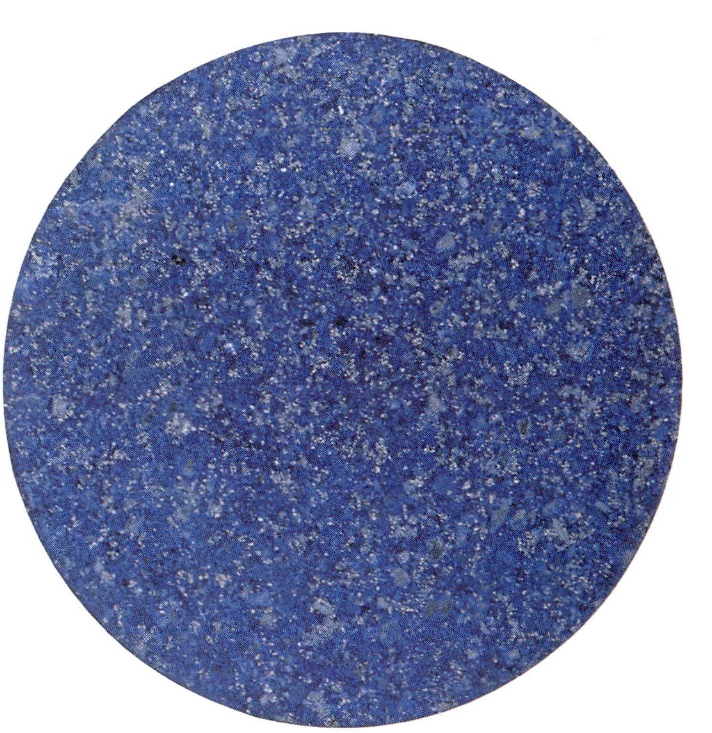

77. Lapis lazuli.

but, although known to the architects of the Regency, specific references to its imitation have so far proved elusive, and it is likely that the majority of unqualified references to 'porphyry' are to the more commonly encountered red variety. This, Hull indicated, has a 'reddish-brown or chocolate-coloured felspathic base, in which small crystals of nearly white felspar are abundantly distributed';[93] while Burnham recorded that the 'ancient quarries of red, antique porphyry were re-discovered by Burton and Wilkinson, in a district east of the Nile, in the mountains of Djebel Dakhan, twenty-five miles from the Red Sea'.[94]

Investigation of the paintwork in the Balcony Room at Dyrham Park, the account of 1694 for painting which 'marble Colour' survives,[95] revealed that it had originally been decorated in imitation of red porphyry and a pink-and-orange marble.[96] In 1803 Soane painted the skirting and other elements in the Breakfast Room at Pitzhanger Manor, Ealing in imitation of red porphyry,[97] having recorded his intention of using this treatment for the skirting, both on a drawing and in his notebook, each of which refer to 'porphyry'.[98] Neither example is visible today, although the scheme in the latter room was re-created in 1986, but an imitation of red porphyry executed at some date after 1795, and possibly dating from this period, has been recorded as extant on the overdoors in the Dining Room at Southill, Bedfordshire.[99]

Whittock described the imitation of red porphyry, indicating that the ground was to be composed of Venetian red and white together with a little vermilion. On this a layer of spots was sprinkled by striking against the back of an old knife a brush which had been dipped in a mixture of the ground colour and a greater quantity of white, and wrung out. This was allowed to dry and the process repeated using a slightly darker mixture made with Indian red and a very little white, taking care to apply the spots sparingly 'and rather more in some parts than others'. Finally white was sprinkled on, holding the stick against which the brush was to be struck at least a yard above the work, and, when dry, a narrow, opaque white vein added using a sable pencil, transparent threads being drawn from it in various directions using a feather.[100]

Portoro. See *Black and gold marbles.*

Rance. This 'Belgian fossiliferous marble having a reddish-brown ground and large white markings, presenting a handsome though rather massive effect' (fig. 79) was quarried, Renwick indicated, at Rance in the province of Hainaut. He also mentioned that the quarry had been re-opened in 1900 after nearly two hundred years of disuse.[101] Examples of its imitation before the Civil War include 'jasperinge like a rannce' on a bridge at Greenwich Palace in 1592–3;[102] its employment on a 'little arbor' in the garden of Whitehall Palace in 1593–4;[103] and its use in 1610–11 on a chimneypiece at Somerset House, which by this means was 'garnished with divers Culloured stones as rance' and several others.[104] In addition, an item appears in 1620–21 for 'twice priming stopping and Painting Rance colour in oil the pillars Rails and the ballusters of the new gallery at the lower end of the lower house of Parliament' at Whitehall.[105] In 1676, Christopher Wren noted in a memorandum that 'Ranse Marble . . . extraordinarly well don soe as to deceive the Eye & be taken for naturall may be worth 4 shillings the Yarde or more according to the Judgement of the painter', although it seems that everyday prices would probably have been lower.[106] In 1703, Neve mentioned use of the marble itself on chimneypieces,[107] and its continued imitation in the early eighteenth century therefore seems likely.

78. Egyptian porphyry.

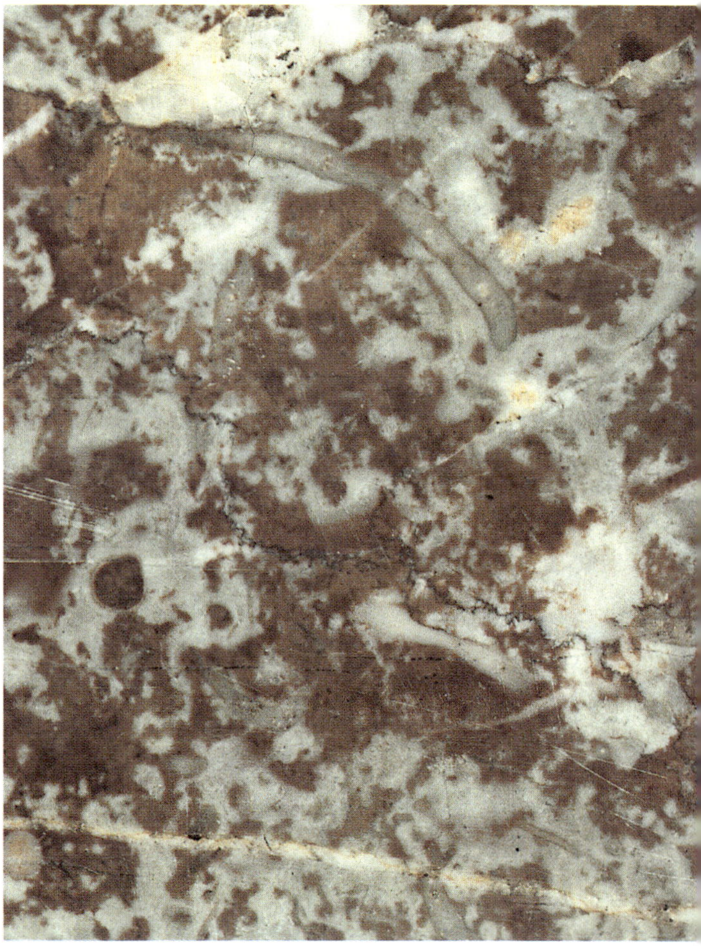

79. Rance.

Rock stone. An estimate for painting work at Stoke Edith, Herefordshire, dated 1705 contains an item for 'Rock stone' at a price of 3*s.* 6*d.* per square yard.[108] It is difficult to suggest an identification for this, but it seems most probable that a conglomerate or breccia was intended, or possibly an imitation of oriental rock-work.

Ruin marble. See *Florentine marble.*

Schiola. Vanherman included 'schiola' in his list of marbles for imitation, indicating that it was 'White, orange, light and dark brown, and brown red'.[109] Possible identifications might include the marble known as Escalette from the département of Ariège in the French Pyrenées, or marble from the Greek island of Skyros.

Serpentine. Serpentine was one of the 'divers Culloured stones' imitations of which were used in 1610–11 to decorate a chimneypiece at Somerset House.[110] Whittock mentioned varieties from Germany, Russia, and both Cornwall and Anglesey (now Ynys Môn) in Britain, indicating that the noble, or precious, serpentine (in distinction to the common variety which was found in great abundance on Anglesey (fig. 80), and often known during the early nineteenth century as Mona marble), had nearly the same appearance as Egyptian green marble. Its green, he indicated, was 'generally the cold colour of the leek, but varies in shades, some appearing the darkest olive', while the black veins sometimes ran 'in an horizontal direction, and then suddenly break and appear nearly upright'. In other cases, he added, they seemed 'to have undergone a violent concussion, and become broken and shivered to small pieces'. The common serpentine, on the other hand, was, he said, not so bright and varied, the dark shades of green being much broader, and the light veins not so fine and reticulated, while the black veins were so mixed with the darkest shades of green as to be scarcely perceptible in some instances, so that the marble was, he concluded 'dull, and unfit for ornamental painting'.[111]

Hull mentioned the 'rich oil-green colour' of noble serpentine from Prussia, and went into considerable detail over the various varieties of common serpentine found in the British Isles. In particular he described two varieties from Anglesey, a greenish, or sometimes reddish, variety which occurs at Llanfechell and Ceryg-moelion, and a brecciated serpentinous marble, with veins of white calcspar found at Tre-gala.[112] Besides those mentioned by Whittock, it may be noted that *verde antico* (q.v.) is classed geologically as a serpentinous marble.

Siena marble. True Siena marble (fig. 81) was described by Renwick as an 'Italian variegated marble, having a yellow ground with deep purple veins' which was quarried at Siena and Montarenti. A variety without the distinctive veinings, the ground colour being of a lighter tint, was, he indicated, known as pale Siena.[113] Whittock, however, remarked that in painting all the yellow marbles were usually known by the name of 'Sienna marble', and listed varieties from Syria, Aragon, and Siena, remarking that all three were nearly the same in appearance. Its imitation was, he indicated, 'used with good effect for door posts, halls, passages, and in furniture painting',[114] and he gave methods for effecting this in both oil and distemper.

For the first medium, the ground was laid in pure yellow ochre; and the 'varied tints' which were first laid on it made from yellow ochre and white, together with raw and burnt sienna. These were put on very thickly with a brush and blended with the softener. While still wet the 'veins that are more removed from the surface' were to be put on with a sable pencil, using Venetian red and Prussian blue, running the lines 'in the same direction as the shade'. The darker veins 'nearer the surface' were carefully drawn using lake, Venetian red, and blue 'mixed to the tint required', after which the work was allowed to dry. The original shading could then be improved if necessary, and the darkest veins added using 'lake and Prussian blue, letting them run in small threads over those previously put on'.[115]

For distemper work, yellow ochre and whiting mixed with size were used for the ground, and separate basins provided containing raw and burnt sienna, Indian yellow ochre, whiting,

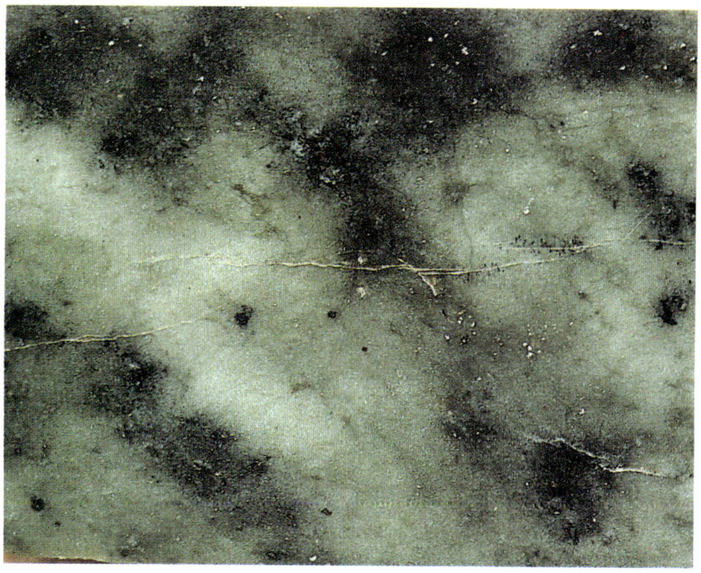

80. Mona marble.

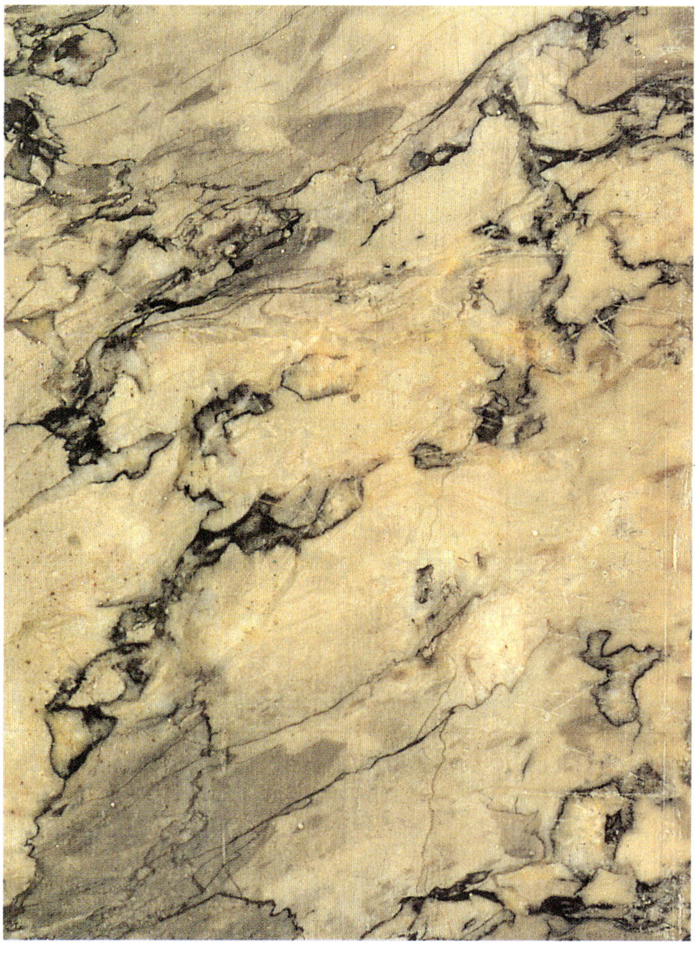

81. Siena.

lake, and damp blue, all ground in beer except for the whiting, which was instead 'mixed very thickly with milk'. Separate brushes were used with great freedom to paint on large broad veins of yellow ochre mixed with a little white. Next to these, small areas of raw sienna were added, followed by 'a dash of white by itself, and near that some burnt sienna'. When one or two yards had been covered in this way, the brush used for the whiting was dabbed over the work in four or five places, and a large dusting brush dipped in size alone and squeezed out used to soften and blend the different shades together. Small veins of Indian red and blue, and a small vein of lake and blue were added while the work was still wet to complete the imitation.[116]

An item for 'Ionic pilasters . . . in Sienna' is included among others executed in distemper in the 1787 edition of the *Builder's Price-Book*,[117] and Pyne mentioned the imitation of Siena marble in the Entrance Hall at Carlton House, London.[118] Laxton gave the price for the imitation of 'Sienna' as 6*d.* per square foot;[119] Nicholson gave the same figure;[120] but Skyring suggested a rate of 7*d.*[121] Varnish was extra in all cases.

Speckled marble. An item for 'speckled marble cullor' in oil appears in accounts relating to the Cross Gallery at Somerset House in 1614–15,[122] but it is uncertain whether this was intended to imitate any specific marble.

Statuary marble. See *White marbles.*

Syrian marble. Whittock included marble 'of Syria' in his list of yellow marbles which were, he said, usually 'known by the name of Sienna' (q.v.) in decorative painting, adding that all these 'have nearly the same appearance'.[123] A yellow marble has been obtained from the Lebanon Mountains,[124] and it may have been to this that Whittock was referring.

Touch. Croft-Murray notes an account of 1610–11 for the imitation of 'divers Culloured stones' on a fireplace at Somerset House, London, including an item for 'touch'. He suggests that this may be identified with touchstone (basanite).[125]

Valencia. Vanherman described 'Valentia' as a violet marble, and it seems possible that he had the yellowish-cream marble containing pink with reddish purple veins from Valencia, Spain, in mind.[126]

Venetian marble. Laxton, Nicholson, and Skyring all referred to 'Venetian' marble, the first giving a price of 8*d.* per square foot, the latter two suggesting a rate of 7*d.*[127] The identification of 'Venetian' marble presents something of a difficulty, since, as Hull observed, it 'is scarcely necessary to add that all the stones used in Venice have been brought from long distances'. However, he also mentioned the extensive use of Verona marble at Venice,[128] and, since this well-known variety seems otherwise to be missing from the literature of the Regency period, it is just possible it was to this that the term 'Venetian' was applied. Many varieties of Verona marble have been worked, but these are of two basic colours, being either red or yellow. Renwick described the former (fig. 82) as a fossiliferous marble, brick red in colour, with small markings of lighter tone, while the latter, he indicated, is of similar character and formation, but has a more yellow colour.[129] It is much more likely, though, that the term 'Venetian' was used simply to imply a veined white marble, since Skyring, whose price for 'Venetian' marble has been mentioned above, also quoted a rate of 3*d.* for 'Venetian marbling on dead white ground'.[130]

Verde antico. Pyne mentioned the use of 'verd antique' together with other marbles, several of which were imitated, in the Entrance Hall at Carlton House.[131] Whittock indicated that since it was scarce and expensive it was considered greatly desirable, and described it as containing fossils;[132] but Vanherman simply observed that 'verde antique' had 'white and black patches, dark green, &c.'[133] The true *verde antico* (of which, he observed, there were light, medium, and dark varieties) was described by Renwick as a 'brecciated serpentine of great beauty, made up of angular fragments of light and dark green serpentines and pure white marble'. 'The colouring matter,' he continued, 'has penetrated the white fragments during the process of cooling down, giving the marble its distinct markings'; and he mentioned the rediscovery in 1886 of the ancient quarries worked by the Romans near Lárissa in Thessaly (fig. 83).[134] A few years before this event, however, Burnham had mentioned that *verde antico* had been quarried near Atrax (an ancient city approximately 10 miles west of Lárissa) on the river Peneus in Thessaly, describing one variety as having 'a foundation of lively green with spots of deeper shade passing to blue', while another, he said, 'exhibits marks of snow-white or clear black'. This so nearly resembled a green stone quarried in Piedmont, that it was, he said, only with difficulty that the ancient was distinguished from the modern;[135] and in earlier years it is clear that many other green marbles were variously referred to as *verde antico*. Thus Hull wrote that 'vert antique' was 'probably of no special description, but the name applies to many varieties of green serpentinous rock used by the ancient Romans, sometimes brecciated, or variously veined, and derived from various

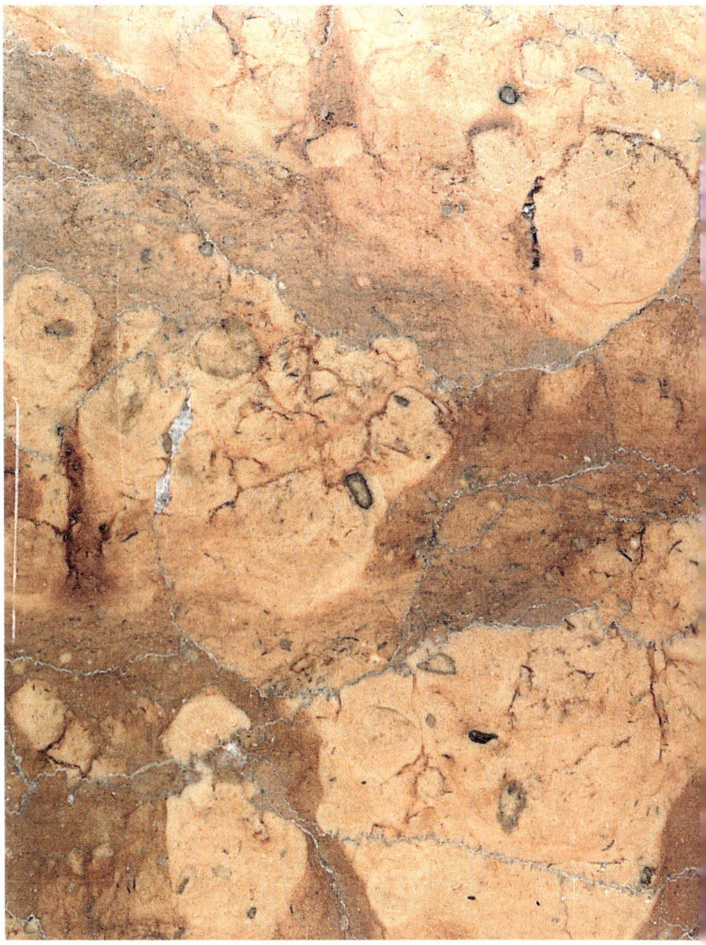

82. Verona red.

sources, both those of Italy, Greece, and Egypt', on all of which he enlarged.[136]

Whittock gave methods for the imitation of 'verd antique' in both oil and distemper. The ground, as for all green marbles, was prepared in black, and on this, using a hog's-hair tool, white lead was scumbled 'so thin in places that the white is scarcely perceptible, and in others nearly opaque'. While this was still wet, the colour was rubbed off with a piece of wash leather 'in the shape you wish the shells or other fossil remains to appear'. Other shells could be formed by pressing hard on the work with a square piece of cork notched in one or two places, and turning it between finger and thumb. A partly cut away goose-quill was then passed over the white, which would 'take it out in small irregular veins over the black'. By 'suddenly checking the hand, and making it take an angular direction', he indicated, 'the veins will break and curl as they do in nature, appearing with more freedom, fineness, and variety, than they would in some hours painting with the sable pencil, the usual mode of drawing veins in this marble'. The work was allowed to dry before localised glazing with Prussian blue and raw sienna, parts being left uncoloured. For this he recommended distemper colour, since this would dry quickly, although most painters, he intimated, used oil. When dry, a feather similar to that already used was dipped in whiting ground very finely in milk and used to add the light veins and thicker white veins; and a few dark veins of Prussian blue, 'made to curl lightly over the strong lights', added with a sable pencil. When this in turn was dry, a final oil glaze of Prussian blue mixed with a preponderance of raw sienna to produce a 'fine warm green' was applied overall.[137]

Where durability was unimportant, such as in the interiors of 'theatres, ball and concert rooms, &c. where pilasters of this elegant marble are introduced' it could, Whittock indicated, be imitated in distemper. Lamp black ground in size was first laid on in 'large veins or streaks' with a large brush, and a second brush used to 'dash in' white between these. A large dusting brush was used to blend these 'making the veins imperceptibly run into each other'. Smaller tools were used to dab white figures on the black, and black spots 'of various sizes, to represent the shells, &c.' on the white. The 'flat hog's-hair brush with the hairs separated' (the tufted brush he had illustrated (fig. 39)) was then used to draw small irregular veins over the black; and, while the work was drying, a vein of pure black, 'formed in a zig-zag, wavy direction', 'laid over that part which has become grey from its incorporation with the white'. When dry, a thin glaze of king's yellow ground in thin size was to be laid on quickly 'with a light hand' in order to prevent the distemper colour from absorbing the varnish. This was to be the common spirit varnish in which a little Prussian blue and raw sienna had been ground to form a green glaze.[138]

For tabletops or slabs which could be laid flat, a third method provided 'the most perfect imitation that can be produced'. The ground was laid in common stone colour in oil, and lamp black ground in thin size applied with a large brush 'leaving spaces in various parts of the work'. Whiting ground in milk was then poured upon the black in thin streams, and the table or slab . . . moved in various directions to let the white run in veins among the black, which by this means floats and branches out into more natural and foliated veins than it is possible to produce with a brush'. A wet feather could next be used to draw small threads from the wet masses of white over the dark parts that had dried, and when the whole had been allowed to dry the fossil figures were drawn in with a camel-hair pencil. When again dry, a coat of spirit varnish was applied, on which a few bright lines and thin glazes 'of oil colour of various tints placed where required'. A green glaze of Prussian blue and raw sienna was then applied, and the work finally varnished.[139]

Laxton, Nicholson, and Skyring all listed imitations of 'verd antique' at rates of 1*s.* 6*d.*, 1*s.* 2*d.*, and 10*d.* per square foot respectively, exclusive of varnish.[140]

Verde di Corsica. Whittock referred to *verde di Corsica* among the other green marbles,[141] and a sample of 'Verde di Corsica moderno' is contained in a table-top of about 1820 in the Victoria and Albert Museum.[142]

Verona marble. See *Venetian marble.*

White marbles. Several instances of the use of imitations of white marble before the Civil War may be noted. At Sir Thomas Cawarden's house in Whitefriars, London, 253 square yards of 'whyt marbyll' were executed prior to 1544;[143] parts of the chimneypiece and the doorcase in the Queen's New Cabinet Room at Somerset House were painted 'like white Marble' in 1629–30;[144] the lower part of the wainscot in the King's Attiring Room at the latter was similarly treated in 1637–8, as were the jambs of several windows in the privy lodgings;[145] and in the same year a chimneypiece at Oatlands was painted in a 'white marble cullo:r'.[146] All these examples have been destroyed together with an early eighteenth-century instance which occurs as an item in an account for work at St Mary Redcliffe, Bristol, in 1710, when 'all the in Side of the Partition Windows in the Midle Chancill' was painted 'with White Marble Colour'.[147] Such references may, however, imply a veined rather than pure white marble, since an item in the accounts of 1638 for painting at Ham House, Surrey, is for certain elements 'Likewise painted like white Marble', the

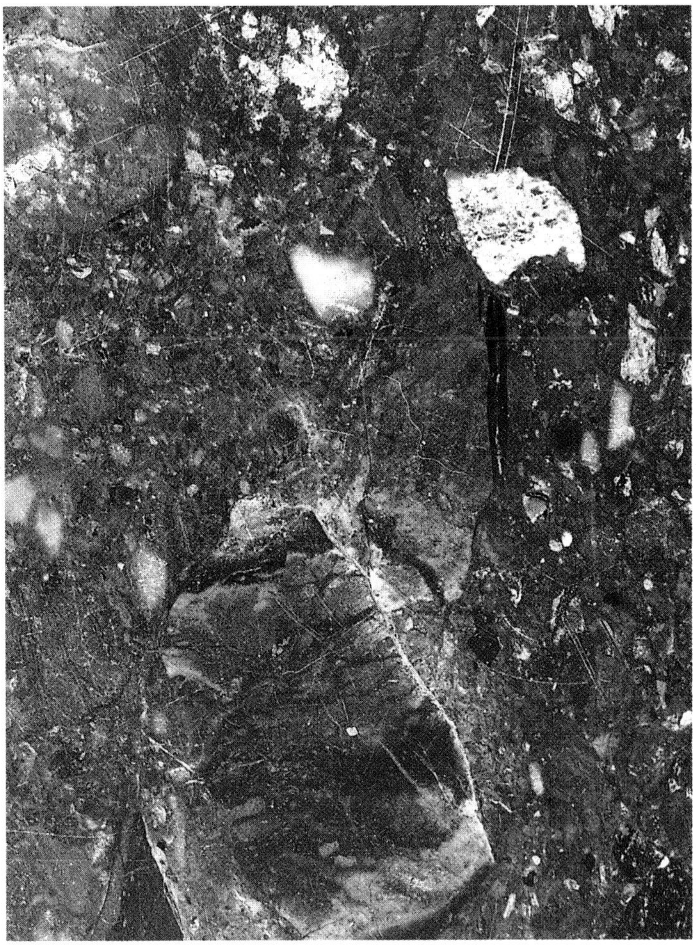

83. Thessalonian verde antico.

preceding item having been varnished and 'veyned'.[148] In an estimate dated 1705 for painting work at Stoke Edith, Herefordshire, on the other hand, an item for 'White in nutt oil' at a rate of 1*s.* 6*d.* per square yard appears between 'Black marble' and 'Green stone',[149] suggesting perhaps that this too was seen as one of a number of 'marbled' finishes, and that plain white paint was indeed used in this context.

Writing in the early nineteenth century, both Whittock and Vanherman mentioned the imitation of the white Parian marble (q.v.) from the Greek island of Paros, while the latter also mentioned the Italian white Carrara marble (q.v.).[150] White marbles occur in several other locations, including France, but these two were undoubtedly the best known for purity of colour. The early twentieth-century author Renwick noted that although the term *statuary marble* was a general name given to all pure white marbles free from markings, the name was generally understood as meaning the best qualities of Italian white, the principal supplies of which were obtained from Carrara, Massa, and Seravezza.[151]

White marble, veined. In 1638 the 'great Arch' through which the Staircase at Ham House, Surrey, was entered was 'layde over twise wth whit lead in Nutt Oyll and varnished and veyned as polished Marble';[152] and in 1626–7 the altar rails and balusters together with the columns flanking the altar, the cornice above them, and a 6 ft. high candlestick in the Queen's Chapel at Somerset House were laid 'wth faire white and Marbling'.[153] In 1676, Wren noted the price of 'Veined Worke like black or white Marble' as 1*s.* 4*d.* per square yard;[154] and references to 'white and veined' may be found in several later seventeenth-century painting accounts. These include, for example, an item for 171 square yards in the Priest's Lodging over the Ante-chapel at Whitehall Palace in 1687,[155] and another for 114 yards at Hampton Court, Middlesex, in 1690[156] at rates of 2*s.* and 1*s.* 6*d.* per square yard respectively. A number of similar items occur in the Kensington Palace accounts between 1692 and 1693 at rates of 1*s.* 8*d.* or 2*s.* per yard, the first also being the rate for 'White & veined in nutt Oile' and for 'White colo[r]: veined'; while another entry refers to 'White & veined and varnished' at a rate of 3*s.* 3*d.* per yard.[157] In the early nineteenth century Laxton gave a rate of 2*d.* per square foot for 'Veined on a dead white ground', and Nicholson a price of 3½*d.* per foot for 'Veined' marbling.[158] Suggesting a price of 3*d.*, however, Skyring seems to have adapted Laxton's text, quoting for 'Venetian marbling on dead white ground'.[159] It is likely, therefore, that, as noted above in connection with Venetian marbling (q.v.), the latter term was applied in the trade to white veined marbles (fig. 84).

The late seventeenth-century writers Stalker & Parker described a method for imitating a marble of this type, which, they claimed, 'if neatly done, well polisht, and varnisht, will not only exceed any Marbling in oyl, but will in beauty and gloss equal the real stone'. Their method seems to have been conceived in terms of small boxes or furniture, a white gesso ground, the last few coats of which were based on white lead, first being provided. 'Two or three degrees' of vine black were then mixed with white lead and a very weak warm size to the colour intended for the 'clouds and veins', the work wetted, and the palest colour laid on with 'a great Camels-hair-pencil'. While the work was still damp, but not too wet, a smaller pencil was used to touch in the lesser veins, using a colour one degree darker than the first, and lastly the deepest colour applied with a small, pointed feather, in such a way as to 'touch and break all your suddain or smaller veins, irregular, wild, and confused, as you have them in the natural Marble', the completed imitation eventually being varnished.[160]

A comparable method for imitating 'marble color', this time in oil, was described by the American author Hezekiah Reynolds. The work was primed and undercoated in white paint containing half white lead and half Spanish white, the third coat being laid in pure white lead. While this was still wet, one was directed to: 'Shade with Prussian blue, ground and mixed with oil, and laid on with a graining brush while the third coat is green; in imitation of clouded marble'. The work was to be finished with copal varnish.[161]

The early nineteenth-century writer Nathaniel Whittock, in discussing 'Cipolin, or white, veined marble' provided both oil and distemper formulae for its imitation. The ground for the former was to be white, prepared perfectly smooth and the first broad, feint veins 'scumbled, or spread very thinly over the ground' using a mixture of white, black, and Indian red, since he observed: 'The shadows of white always partake of a yellow hue, and thus the faint veins will appear of a reddish grey'. The veins nearer the surface were to be made a little more grey by adding black, and applied 'sometimes making them form angles and then letting the lines seem to float away in a zig-zag direction'. The veins 'nearest the eye' were, he said, of course darker than the others, and it was necessary to add a little lake to the black and white, while in some specimens a little blue would be required. These were to be drawn sparingly 'with a fine sable pencil very thin, and made to take nearly the direction of the last veins'. In all cases the veins were 'put on one upon another while wet, and blended together with the badger-hair softener'. Once dry, the dark veins could be partially retouched.[162]

To imitate white veined marble in distemper, Whittock directed, the walls were first prepared in size and two coats of

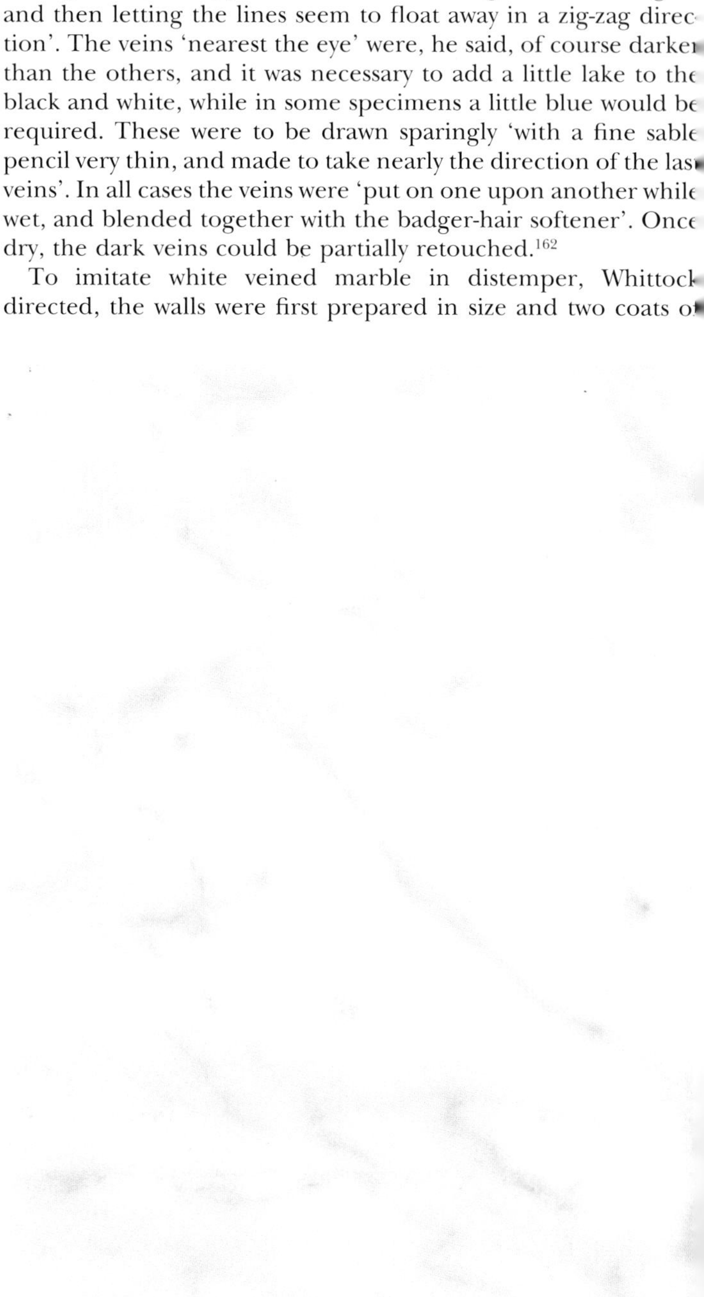

84. White with grey veins.

common whitewash, a third coat being added made from whiting mixed with milk. Lamp black, Indian red, and damp blue were separately ground in milk, and, everything being to hand (since, he indicated, the whole had to be finished while the work was wet), one commenced at the top of the room by laying at the most a yard or two with a very thin coat of the white ground in milk. Immediately, a little black, Venetian red, and whiting were quickly mixed using 'another brush kept on purpose for this tint' and the broad veins drawn on and softened with 'the large brush used for the white'. Slightly darker, narrow veins were superimposed on this, and then a few veins were drawn very thinly with the blue and Indian red 'always inclining the same way that the large vein is made to run'. Finally, using a camel-hair pencil, a thin white vein was 'made over the blue veins'. In conclusion, he stressed the need to keep the edges of the work always damp, and observed that if the work was varnished it would have the effect of oil colour, while if left unvarnished the milk would be quite adequate as a binder.[163]

Nicholson too provided a formula for the imitation of a marble of this nature, indicating that the ground was to be laid in white lead diluted in $\frac{2}{3}$ linseed oil and $\frac{1}{3}$ oil of turpentine, a mixture of blue-black and a little Prussian blue being used for the veins.[164]

APPENDIX D

PAINTED FLOORS AND FLOORCLOTHS

Although it is clear that in the eighteenth century timber and stone floors were commonly left in their natural state,[1] a few references may be found to their colouring or waxing. Thus, in 1724 the anonymous author of an 'Explanation of the Draughts of a House *Proposed for a Merchant*', deprecated the use of wax on oak since it made the floor slippery;[2] and Watin included descriptions of the staining and waxing of parquet, the colour being provided by decoctions of yellow berries, turmeric, and safflower mixed with size.[3] His directions were repeated by Tingry, who added that the lemon yellow, often used for staining oak, could also be used to good effect on plaster floors.[4] (Presumably, though, the grey and red plaster floors to which reference is made in the *Builders Price-Book* were self-coloured.)[5] In addition, references may be found to the colouring of stone floors. The use of Indian red on Bremen paving is mentioned in accounts for painting at Henry Pelham's house in Arlington Street in 1747–8,[6] and in this connection it is worth mentioning Hannah Glasse's advice that brick hearths should be coloured with red lead mixed with milk.[7] Watin, moreover, gave detailed directions for the colouring of tiles with red ochre: a coat of *gros rouge* in glue-size was first laid on very warm; the second coat consisted of *rouge de Prusse* in linseed oil; and the third employed the latter pigment in warm glue-size. The whole was finished with wax.[8] Tingry repeated this method, suggesting also employment of red ochre in ox-blood serum or the use of madder with alum, the tiles again being finished by waxing.[9] That ordinary timber floors were sometimes stained in England is shown by John Wood the elder, who noted that in Bath about 1727 'the Boards of the Dining Rooms and most other Floors were made of a Brown Colour with Soot and small Beer to hide the Dirt';[10] while in 1760 Hannah Glasse indicated that the use of tansy, mint, and balm in the rubbing of floors would render them a fine brown colour like mahogany.[11]

During the eighteenth century and much of the nineteenth, floors were often covered either in whole or in part by painted or printed floorcloths. These are frequently mentioned in inventories, and many accounts for their supply survive. They also feature in a number of trade-cards, which show the types of designs available, many imitating chequered paving. At first, they seem to have been prepared by a simple process of painting canvas, often on site; but by the second half of the eighteenth century, they were commonly made in factories, and various improvements were made including the giving of greater substance to the ground and the introduction of printing for the pattern.

One of the best accounts of the method for preparing simple painted floorcloths was given by the American writer Hezekiah Reynolds, who noted that 'Floor Carpets or Oil'd Cloth' were made as follows:

> Canvas or common tow cloth is sewed with a flat seam, of the dimensions required; and nailed firm upon a floor; then wet with water even, and thoroughly; and before dry, is primed with any common colour. When this coat is dry, a second coat is laid with the same—The third coat is painted with a stone colour; and when dry, the carpet is turned and painted with any convenient color on the other side—When dry, the carpet is turned back, and any flaws or cracks which appear are filled with putty, and the surface is made smooth and even.
>
> With a chalk line a Margin six or eight inches wide is struck; and the remaining part is divided into squares or diamonds of which one half . . . are painted white; and the other half black.

The squares, he added, could be 'clouded' or marbled as desired, and an ornamental border provided.[12]

A British example of provision of a floorcloth by a painter in this way is provided by an account of October 1773 in connection with work at Gordon Castle, Morayshire.[13]

> Paid for 54. yards Sail Duck, & Making for a floor Cloth Sent to Gordon Castle 3. 17. 6
>
> To Painting D:° Chocolate Coll:r One side & marble Pavement the other measuring $44\frac{1}{2}$ Sq:r Y:ds a 2/2
> Includ: Excise 5. 7. $6\frac{1}{2}$.

The origin of painted floorcloths is obscure, but it is clear that in the seventeenth century timber floors had sometimes been painted to look like stone or marble. The Parliamentarian inventory of Wimbledon House, Surrey, which was taken following the execution of Charles I in 1649, for instance, records that the Green Chamber had a deal floor 'paynted cheker worke, red, blacke, and whyte'; while the steps of the east staircase were 'varnished black and whyte, and cheker worke'.[14] That cloth was painted in oil during the preceding decade is shown by a patent granted to Richard and Edward Greenbury in 1637 'for painting with oyle culler upon wollen cloath, kerseys and stuffes';[15] and the waterproofing of cloth with an oil and resin mixture for use in tents and waterproof garments was described by John Smith in 1687.[16] There is, however, no suggestion that any of these had floor-coverings in mind; and the first seemingly unequivocal reference to a floorcloth so far encountered is a painting bill of 1710 in connection with Captain Hoskins's apartment at Greenwich Hospital, which includes '32 y.ds in a Cloth imitating black and white marble' and '32 y.ds on y.e backside of ditto 3 times done in plain Colour'.[17]

The types of pavement which could be imitated were quite elaborate, twenty-four, including many giving illusory effects of three-dimensional blocks, being illustrated by John Carwitham in his *Various Kinds of Floor Decorations . . . whether in Pavements of Stone or Marble or wth Painted Floor Cloths* (1739). Other designs, including a variety of fret and guilloche borders, were published by Batty Langley in 1740. In addition, references are found to the imitation of carpets and woven mats: Biggerstaff & Walsh's later eighteenth-century trade card, for instance, lists 'all sorts of Painted Floor Cloths Such as Plain, Ornamented, Check, Matt and Carpet Patterns' (fig. 85). A variety of colours too could be used, and at Appuldurcombe House, Isle of Wight, (which, now ruined, had been remodelled internally by Sir Richard Worsley in the 1770s) the inventory of *c.* 1780 records floorcloths 'in Imitation of India Matt' and, in the Library: 'A Square floor cloth painted green & white', no doubt to accord with the furniture and upholstery, which were in the same colours. In the housekeeper's room was a 'plain red floor cloth'.[18]

An account of making a floorcloth which appears to have been painted to resemble a carpet is contained in the following charming reminiscence by Lyman Beecher, which shows also the luxurious nature of the commodity on the eastern coast of the United States as late as 1800. On setting up home in East Hampton, Long Island, following his marriage, he recalled:

> We had no carpets: there was not a carpet from end to end of the town. All had sanded floors, some of them worn through. Your mother introduced the first carpet. Uncle Lot gave me some money and I had an itch to spend it. Went to a vendue, and bought a bale of cotton. She spun it, and had it woven; then she laid it down, sized it, and painted it in oils, with a

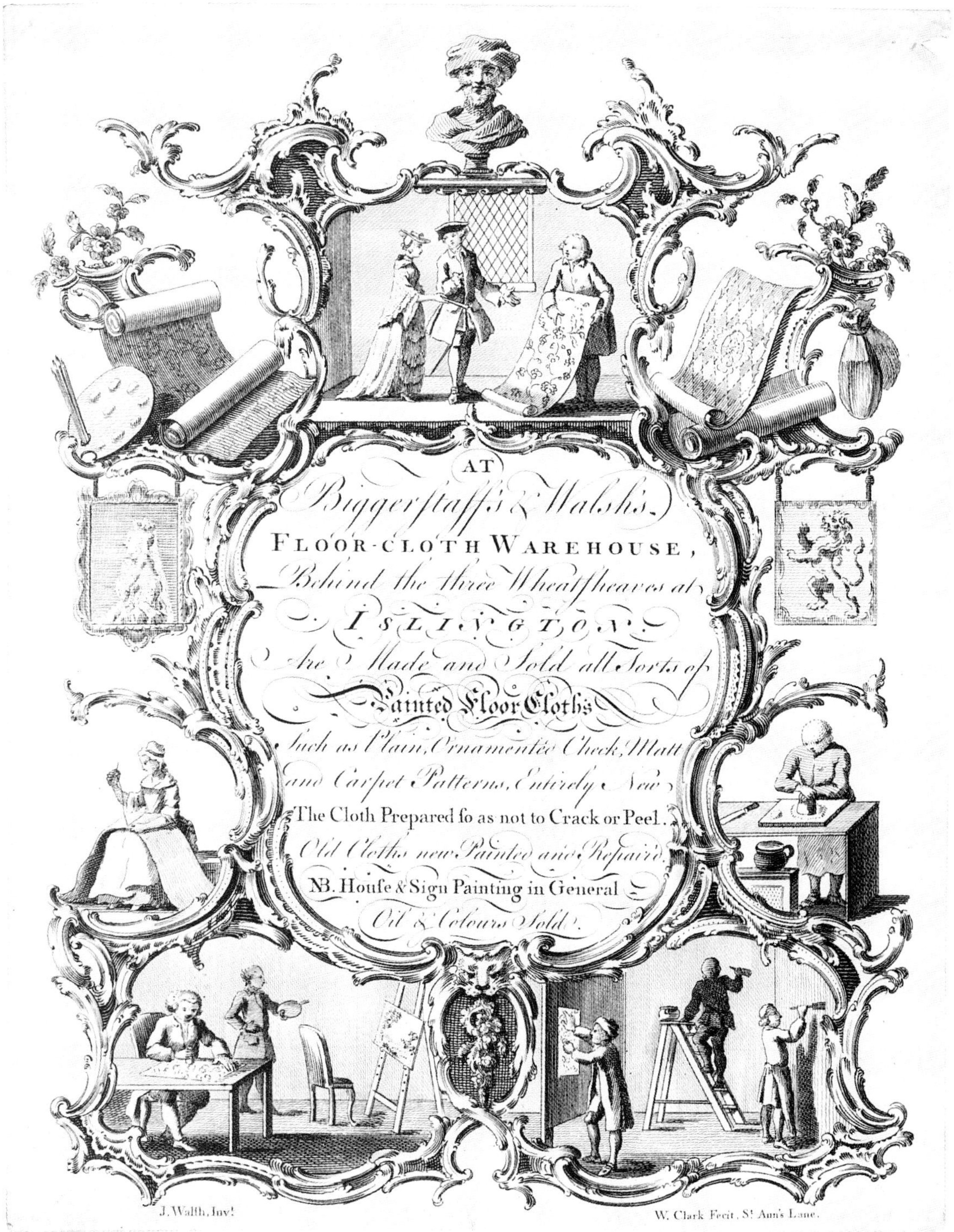

85. Late eighteenth-century trade card of Biggerstaff & Walsh, Islington, showing processes in the manufacture of floor-cloth.

border all around it, and bunches of roses and other flowers over the centre. She sent to New York for her colours, and ground and mixed them herself. The carpet was nailed down on the garret floor, and she used to go up there and paint.[19]

Painted floorcloths are probably to be seen in many eighteenth-century pictures, although they are easily taken for paving or carpeting. The jointless dull red of the floor seen in *The Marriage Contract* from the series *Marriage à la mode* by William Hogarth (painted about 1750),[20] and that surrounding the carpet in Arthur Devis's portrait of the Rev. Streynsham Master (*c.* 1742–3),[21] may well depict floorcloth; and there may be a similar explanation for the seeming flatness of what otherwise appears to be a carpet in Arthur Devis's portrait of John Bacon and his family (also of *c.* 1742–3).[22] Certainly, the apparently paved floor in a late eighteenth-century watercolour of the chapel at Audley End, Essex (fig. 86), is but a floorcloth, since this was supplied to Sir John Griffin Griffin by Nathan Smith in 1781, his bill noting a 'Paintd Cloth for the Chapple at Audley End in Squares to Imitate Portland and Breming Stone Pavement'.[23]

The floorcloth manufacturer Nathan Smith seems to have been one of the early entrepreneurs in production of the commodity. His works in Knightsbridge, London, were founded in 1754, but were burnt down in the mid-1790s and rebuilt.[24] Later the firm became Smith & Baber, and, besides 'Plain Red', by 1821 they were offering: 'Yellow Mat', 'Clermont', 'Hampton', 'Alex. Pavement', 'Green Mat', 'Palmyra Marble', 'Octagon Marble', 'Patera', 'Bringull', 'Tesselated mble.', 'Fancy Flower', 'Carlton', 'Large Oak', 'Oak Leaf', 'Foliage', 'Green Cluster', 'Imperial', 'Turkey', and 'Persian' floorcloths.[25] By this date production of such elaborate designs had been facilitated by the introduction of a printing process for the pattern, a development which may have taken place about 1770. Evidence for this is not complete, but it is noteworthy that in 1747, Robert Campbell had noted simply that floorcloths were 'painted in Oil Colours, which is performed by a Class of Painters who do little else';[26] and in 1763 Nathan Smith had taken out a patent for a composition to be used in preparing an improved ground for floorcloths without mentioning the use of a printing process for the design. This comprised a liquid mixture of rosin, pitch, and Spanish brown, to which beeswax and linseed oil might also be added, the cloth being impregnated with it by means of a heated iron roller.[27] It seems likely too, that the introduction of printing was preceded by use of stencilling or by the painting in of designs pounced through using a pricked paper. The latter process appears to be illustrated on Biggerstaff & Walsh's late eighteenth-century trade card (fig. 85), and may also explain the 'paper patterns' to which Reynolds referred in 1812.[28]

The design of what is said to be the earliest block for printing floorcloth was illustrated in the *Penny Magazine* in 1842. The article 'A Day at a Floor-Cloth Factory' was based on a visit to Smith & Baber's works, and gives credit to Nathan Smith for the introduction of printing, suggesting that he used the block, which produced a mat-like pattern, in secret without revealing the process to his workers.[29] This story was apparently current too in the 1820s, since Robert Barnes, another manufacturer of the commodity, noted a discussion he had had with James Baber (who was Smith's son-in-law) in 1825, recording of the latter:

He remarked that Mr Smith in conversation had often related that he struck an impression of his first pattern . . . one

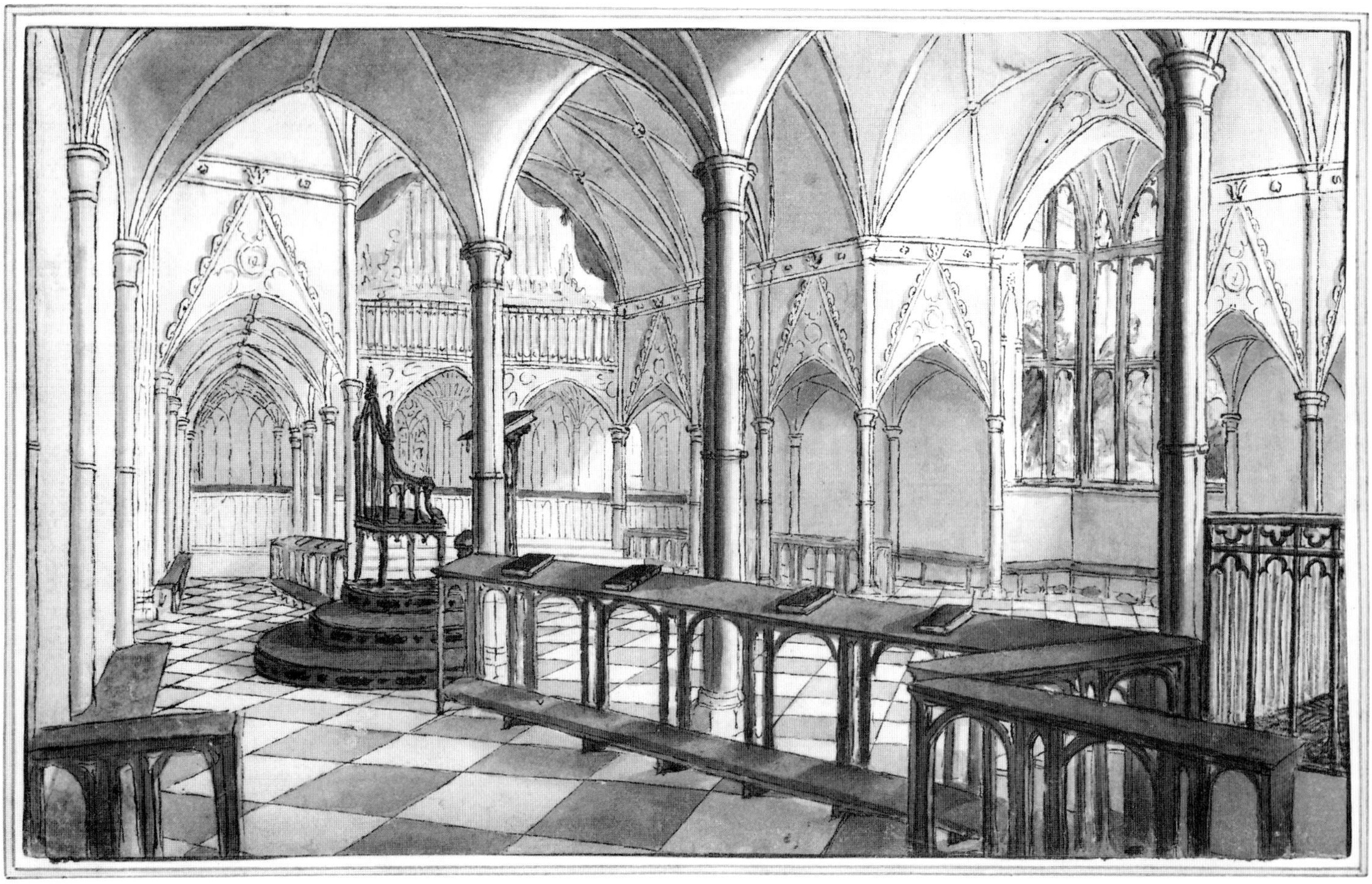

86. Late eighteenth-century watercolour showing floorcloth in the Chapel at Audley End, Essex.

> evening after the men had left work. & that the men next morning on seeing the impression were struck with astonishment not imagining how the work could have been done.

In the scrapbook which he compiled in 1857, he included a drawing of the same block, but seems to ascribe credit for its introduction to his grandfather, Joseph Barnes, the event taking place 'during the period of Mr Ruer's apprenticeship & consequently between the years 1766 & 1773'.[30]

Whatever the truth of the matter, it is clear that by 1842 floorcloth was not only printed, but had become a much more substantial material. The *Penny Magazine* relates how the ground coats were applied to the fabric, which had been stretched on a vertical frame, by means of a trowell, providing an illustration of the process;[31] and in 1847 it was said that good floorcloth weighed up to $4\frac{1}{2}$ pounds per square yard.[32] The need for improvement in manufacture had earlier been indicated by Smith, who noted in his patent specification of 1763 that 'the Damps from Water used in Clearing [sic] Painted Floor Cloths, as then made in common, occasioned the Size or Glew used in the Groundwork of such Cloths to Swell, grow Soft, and by Means thereof Peel or Scale off, so that the Coth [sic] became Bare, void of Paint, and soon rendered Unserviceable'.[33] The instructions given by Hannah Glasse to her 'little young House-maid' reflect this, together with the care needed to prevent any tendency to curling at the edges. 'To clean Oil-cloths that lie on the Floors', she directed:

> DRY-RUB them every Day, its soon done, and both cleans and preserves them far beyond any other way; the mopping of them, wears them out soon, and makes them turn up at the Sides. But Oil-cloths should lie on the wrong-side upwards, once a Week, to keep them from turning. Once a Year, if you would have them look like new, first clean them with Milk, and when dry, dry-rub them, and they will look very well.[34]

The rather fragile nature of painted floorcloths was pointed out by J.C. Loudon in 1833. He noted that in cottages they were 'not economical articles, where there is much going out and coming in of persons generally employed in the open air, and of course wearing strong shoes, probably with nails in the soles'.[35] Even in less demanding situations, it is clear the pattern tended to wear through, and the repainting of floorcloths is a feature of several eighteenth-century trade cards. Biggerstaff & Walsh, for example, advertised: 'Old Cloths new Painted and Repair'd' (fig. 85); and the need for occasional repainting may be reflected in the references to painting 'Checkers' which occur in eighteenth-century builders' price-books.[36] Inevitably, few examples survive today, although a number of late eighteenth- and early nineteenth-century specimens were recently exhibited at Temple Newsam House, Leeds;[37] and others are preserved in the United States, including a much repainted area of chequered floorcloth now at Winterthur.

APPENDIX E

NOTE ON THE BERGER ARCHIVE

Since its postwar alienation from the family, the firm of paint manufacturers founded by Lewis Berger in the 1760s, which traded as Lewis Berger and Sons, has passed through several hands, and is now part of Crown Berger Europe Limited, based in Darwen, Lancashire. For about two centuries, however, the company occupied its early premises at Homerton in the East End of London, the site now marked by Berger Road, E. 9. When production at this location ceased, the survival of the early records of the firm was, apparently, a matter of pure chance; but at the time they were consulted in connection with the present study they were kept by Berger Paints at Berger House in Berkeley Square. They are now lodged at the Hackney Archives Department. The records cover a period extending well beyond the terminal date of covered in this book, and from the total of just over two dozen volumes available (together with several maps and nineteenth-century photographs), ten were selected as relevant for detailed examination.

In 1766 Louis Steigenburger (1741–1814) entered into a partnership with two others for the manufacture of 'a certain blue colour for paints', and by 1772 was described as 'Blue Maker' in an order from Dublin addressed to 'Louis Bergers' of Narrow Street, Limehouse, London.[1] By the late 1770s, his output seems to have been extended to include a pink lake pigment apparently based on cochineal, samples of which are contained in a leather-bound quarto volume bearing a paper label identifying it as the 'Sample Book'. This seems to have started life as an account book, one entry for 1778–9 surviving, but during 1779 and 1780 it was used to record batches of pigment under the headings: 'to whom sold', 'price', 'quantity', 'when sold', 'coch'l [i.e. cochineal]', and 'quality'. Under the last heading in each case there is a smear of pigment. From 1789 to 1795 the book was also used to record samples of 'wett blue', and a few further entries occur up to 1802. The latter seem to be a record of samples sent out and the prices quoted for each rather than a record of pigments sold, and the volume is altogether fascinating as showing the many different qualities of Prussian blue manufactured and the prices relevant to each (fig. 3, p. 99).

Contemporary with this volume is a letter book of similar size and binding. The copy letters are divided into two series, running from 1785 to 1788, and from 1778 to 1788. At this period the company seems to have been acting also as merchants, only manufacturing a proportion of the pigments they sold, and (as was usual at that time for a colourman) their wares included anchovies, capers, and emery paper, besides other commodities. Business extended to Dublin, Exeter, Bristol, and Newcastle, as well as to Ostend, Danzig (now Gdansk), and Bordeaux. Several letters are of particular moment since they contain price lists.

Of especial importance are the five formula books, two of which seem to have been used to record pigments in production, and the other three for experiments. The earliest is a tall vellum-bound volume labelled in ink: 'Lake & Carmine Book' (fig. 4, p. 27). Entries commence in 1787 as a priced record of batches of carmine and cochineal lakes, but from 1 February 1788 the pricing is omitted. From October 1792 the batches were numbered, and in 1793 the first reference to a yellow lake occurs. From 1803 a new format was adopted with the recipes for the various qualities of carmine written at the head of succeeding pages, and a record of each batch below. A new series in this format was commenced in 1811, by which time the manufacture of other pigments seems to have been well established. The formulae were again transcribed in 1815, and for some reason which is not apparent this is followed by a second transcription of the same date. Various notes dating between 1821 and 1829 follow, and at the end of the volume are a few miscellaneous items. In 1831 the 'Lake & Carmine Book' was superseded by another formula book of similar size and binding, into which all the current formulae were transcribed. Dated modifications and notes continued to be made well beyond the middle of the nineteenth century, all the formulae being given in great detail including quantities of materials and procedure, and all the products were costed out. Of the experimental notebooks, the first is a quarto, half-bound volume labelled (on the back cover) 'Recipes & Experiments Various', and covers a period between 1815 and 1818. The second is also a quarto volume of similar size but bound in vellum, and contains notes and formulae dated between 1819 and 1831, with a final item dated 1840; while the third is again similar and contains formulae dated between 1830 and 1846 together with a quantity of loose papers covering the same period.

Last to be mentioned are the annual accounts and stocktaking lists forming a series of volumes running from 1801 to 1810. From these, three were selected for detailed analysis. The first contains summarised extracts from the accounts for 1801 together with a detailed list of the company's stock on 1 January 1802, the second deals in the same way with 1805–6, and the third 1809–10. All are of particular value in showing not only the cost of virtually the complete range of house-painting pigments, but also the quantities in stock, giving a fairly clear picture of those in common use and those whose employment was more limited.

Following Lewis Berger's death in 1814, the business was run by his two surviving sons (the eldest, Lewis Berger, who was born in 1770, having died in 1800). Samuel, the youngest, who was born in 1776, died in 1855; and the middle son John in 1860. John's sons Capel Berrow (b. 1809) and Lewis Curwood (b. 1814) carried on the firm in their turn.[2]

APPENDIX F

PREFACE TO COMPANION VOLUME

'Taste is not hereditary; no one has yet been found to possess this talent by intuition. On the contrary, it is to be acquired by gaining a competent knowledge of the old.'[1]

The foundations of this study were laid during the three-year duration of the Berger Research Fellowship which I held at the Institute of Advanced Architectural Studies from May 1975. My resulting D.Phil. thesis 'Interior House-painting from the Restoration to the Regency' was presented to the University of York in 1983. At the time of my appointment, such information as had been published on the role of paint colour in interiors consisted mainly of occasional references scattered throughout a wide range of books, although in 1914 and 1922 Margaret Jourdain had devoted a certain amount of space to the subject in her important books *Decoration in England from 1660 to 1770* and *English Decoration and Furniture of the Later XVIIIth Century (1760–1830)*. More recently, Edward Croft-Murray had produced his important survey *Decorative Painting in England 1537–1837*, published in two volumes in 1962 and 1970; but this was virtually confined to artistic and semi-artistic matters. In 1974 John Fowler & John Cornforth's *English Interior Decoration in the 18th Century* made a noble start at rectifying matters with a chapter on 'Colour and the Painter's Craft', in which many useful references were collated, but the authors indicated that their writing was tentative and in particular they felt it would 'be rash to try to differentiate between, let us say, a Palladian and a neo-classical way of painting a room . . . as our knowledge stands at present it is impossible to give precise guidelines'.[2]

Since John Fowler's death in 1977 interest in the subject of historic interiors has not only been sustained, but has benefitted from the publication of detailed studies by a number of individuals. In 1978, Mark Girouard published *Life in the English Country House* and Peter Thornton his *Seventeenth-century Interior Decoration in England, France and Holland*; while more recently Florence Montgomery's *Textiles in America 1650–1870* has added notably to literature on this aspect of decoration. Probably the most comprehensive book is Peter Thornton's *Authentic Décor* (1984), whose perceptive text is illustrated by a splendid series of early paintings and watercolours; while further informative reproductions are contained in John Cornforth's *English Interiors 1790–1848* (1978), Susan Lasdyn's *Victorians at Home* (1981), and Caroline Davidson's *The World of Mary Ellen Best* (1985). John Morley too has contributed much with *The Making of the Royal Pavilion at Brighton* (1984), and the major exhibitions of pictures by Arthur Devis and Francis Hayman held in 1983 and 1987 respectively have added greatly to appreciation of mid-eighteenth-century interiors.[3]

Undoubtedly, however, the most tantalising aspect of the whole subject has been that of architectural paint colour, the essential background against which fine fabrics, pictures, and furniture were often set. My own study is accordingly dedicated to this, and is now published in two separate but related volumes: one [the present volume] deals with paint technology and the preparation of the colours and effects available historically; while the other [the companion volume][4] considers the use made of paint colour in interiors dating broadly from the appointment of Inigo Jones as Surveyor of the King's Works to the end of the decade which saw the death of John Soane.

On starting work in 1975 it quickly became clear that while a certain amount had been done in collating documentary references to architectural paint colour and the examination of pictures and drawings having a bearing on this, their correct interpretation was often problematical. There was, moreover, no coherent framework within which such information as had been accumulated could be set. The technical study of historic house-paint had not, however, been attempted in Britain;[5] and it seemed obvious that it was this which could provide the key to a proper understanding of historic practice.

Accordingly, the first year of research was taken up by the examination of technical treatises and manuscripts with a view to determining how different types of house-paint were made and applied. In this connection, Rosamond Harley's book *Artists' Pigments* c. *1600–1835* (1970) was an indispensable guide, since there was a considerable overlap between the pigments used by the painter and house-painter (although employment of certain expensive and exotic varieties was restricted to the former, and certain crude grades to the latter, to whom cost was vitally important). Once a good body of data had been assembled, specimens of historic materials were obtained or, in many cases, specially prepared to contemporary formulae, a process which itself required careful research. Using these, samples of colour were mixed in accordance with the practices revealed by the documents, and the ranges of tints available established. The end-product of this was not, however, merely a series of colour charts, but also an intimate knowledge of the working characteristics of each pigment and paint formulation, and of the limitations these imposed on their usefulness for different purposes. Some, for example, were suitable for employment in only one of the two common mediums (oil and distemper); while a series of fading tests quickly showed up inadequacies in stability. Throughout, it was a delight to see how closely such characteristics matched those described by authors two centuries or more ago.

The second phase of research concentrated on the technical investigation of paintwork surviving in a series of interiors. This work was inspired by that of Morgan Phillips at the Society for the Preservation of New England Antiquities, Boston,[6] and the cross-section technique in use by Josephine Darrah in the Department of Conservation at the Victoria and Albert Museum for the series of studies she had commenced at Ham House and

Osterley Park for the Department of Furniture and Woodwork (then under the Keepership of Peter Thornton). Needless to say, the information gained in the first year of research was a vital element in developing the interpretation of cross-sections under the microscope. The rooms chosen for examination were all carefully selected to represent as wide a range of dates as possible, and for the initial series only examples for whose original treatment documentary evidence survives were tackled.

The importance of this exercise cannot be sufficiently stressed. In the first place it quickly showed up the inadequacies of the traditional 'scrape', the exposure of paint with a knife or chemical paint stripper, which was proved to have been highly inaccurate and thus misleading in several instances.[7] It was also possible to show that a number of interiors hitherto thought to exhibit their original painted finishes had in fact been redecorated, and perception of these as historical evidence had, therefore, to be reviewed.[8] On the positive side, these studies also showed that the conclusions reached by compilation of the technical treatises were broadly sound; and, most importantly, provided a series of accurately determined and documented colour schemes of known date, establishing a fixed series of references (since supplemented by many further similar studies) to which more general historical information could be related. In addition, the technical research had elucidated much of the historical colour nomenclature, making more precise interpretation of documents possible.

Thus prepared, it was possible to embark on collation and ordering of the more conventional art-historical evidence for colour usage, the current fruits of this forming the subject of the [companion] volume.

Altogether, the most fundamental fact to emerge from this study has been that it is impossible to approach the understanding of historic interiors through modern concepts of colour and taste in their redecoration. Modern thinking on the matter is separated from that of the eighteenth century by the theories of the nineteenth, which are described in Chapter 7 [of the companion volume] and still inform many of the preconceptions which characterise present-day opinion. Just as the study of early music has reduced the scale of the orchestra, and removed many rich Victorian sonorities together with the hitherto ubiquitous vibrato from authentic performance, so too early interiors as originally seen might appear today rather strait and lacking in the plump fullness which has come to be expected. Exactly like early music, however, they gain in clarity and, once the conventions of the earlier age have become familiar, in architectural expression and interest. This is most noticeable, perhaps, in the case of the earlier interiors here considered, those pre-dating the mid-eighteenth century, which seem in the majority of cases to have been conspicuously drab in terms of paint. In many, dull tones and whites or off-whites predominated, used in a way reflecting fairly formal ideas of architectural organisation; and where brighter colours were used, they were commonly positioned in such a manner that they were set off by these cheaper shades. With the advent of the Rococo, however, brighter paint colours came into vogue, and by about 1750 a fashion had started for the employment of pastel tints on ornamented ceilings. This idea was seized enthusiastically by neo-classical architects, and, combined with the study of antique survivals, was developed during the second half of the eighteenth century, most notably by Robert Adam. In the early nineteenth century the development of a coherent colour theory led to an entirely new approach to colour, which, added to an interest in the new historical models provided by increasing knowledge of antique and other styles, and coupled with contemporary changes in life style, culminated in a revolution of taste, superseding and soon causing to be forgotten the earlier ideas of interior paint colour with which much of this study of concerned.

Also of importance is the link which emerged and may now be seen clearly to have existed between technology and the aesthetic use of colour. The influence of cost has already been touched on, and its fundamental significance will immediately be appreciated when it is realised that whites, browns, and other ordinary or 'common' colours were being sold at 4*d.* per pound in the 1730s, while pinks and some greens were two or three times that price, and the best deep green seven-and-a-half times that of white, at 2*s.* 6*d.*[9] Technology also directly established the limits of what could be achieved in paint colour. It was, as one eighteenth-century writer implied by the title of his book (reviewed below), the 'handmaid to the arts', and house-painting was very much an 'art' of the possible. Architects were certainly familiar with the best way to achieve architectural effect through exploitation of the materials and techniques of the day, and William Chambers, for example, gave detailed technical directions to the Earl of Charlemont over the materials to be used in painting the Saloon at the Casino, Marino, Dublin.[10]

Although study has been directed primarily to the subject of house-painting, it has naturally been necessary also to consider at certain key points the relationship between it and the work of the decorative painter and the upholsterer. With the former in particular there was often some overlap; and in 1665, for example, when Robert Streeter, the King's Sergeant Painter, contracted for work at Clarendon House, Piccadilly, London, besides the rates to be paid for ordinary paint-work it was agreed that *trompe l'oeil* roses were to be painted between the modillions of the exterior cornice at 2*s.* each, with the proviso that these were 'not to be painted by any of his Seruants, but by himself to be touched and Finished'.[11] It is clear, therefore, that throughout the period being considered a number of painters would do both ordinary and decorative painting in this way; and this was evidently regarded as a common skill exhibited by several members of the the Painter Stainers Company of London, including, notably, Charles Catton, whose work at Somerset House is mentioned in Chapter 4 [of the companion volume]. On occasion, of course, especially at times when Italian or French styles were being introduced, artists from abroad would be employed for specific exercises. Thus in the late seventeenth and early eighteenth centuries Louis Laguerre and Antonio Verrio, for example, were much employed on ceilings and architectural schemes in the great houses and palaces of England; in the 1760s Adam was employing Italians such as Giovanni Battista Cipriani, Michelangelo Pergolesi, Antonio Zucchi and Biagio Rebecca to paint arabesque and medallions in his interiors; and, a little later, artists such as John James Boileau were associated with schemes by Henry Holland in the French style. The relationship between their work and that of the house-painter is discussed again in Chapter 4 [of the companion volume].

Considering the role of the architect *vis à vis* that of the upholsterer, it seems clear that the choice of paint colour in new buildings was commonly regarded as the province of the former. In the mid-seventeenth century, Sir Roger Pratt, for example, noted: 'Mem. Leaves to be brought to the architect whereof to make his choice as to the colour', relating the latter firmly to architectural considerations such as the sizes of rooms and the amount of light within them;[12] while even at the very end of the period under consideration, at a time when upholstery probably played its greatest part in interiors, the architect Sir Jeffry Wyatville carefully defined his responsibility at Windsor Castle, Berkshire, as including the painting and gilding, mentioning particularly the shutters, ceilings, and doors as his concern. The gilded 'framing to the silk-work and glasses', he indicated on the other hand, formed part of the furniture and thus lay outside his province.[13] Clearly, painting and upholstery were and remained separate trades, and in his book *The London Tradesman* (1747) were described as such by Robert Campbell, who made no mention of the painter's work as comprising any part of the activities of the upholsterer. Perhaps studied co-ordination of paint and upholstery colours had been less necessary during the first half of the century, since most rooms were painted a uniform brown, some other drab colour, or white, which would suit almost any textile; but after the mid-1760s, when more complex colour schemes began to be widely used, architectural paint often took the lead, especially in rooms with elaborately tinted ceilings. In this connection, it is notable that Adam, an architect well known for his furniture and carpet designs, was consulted over the choice of upholstery fabric by Lady Shelburne;[14] while at Osterley he noted a colour for the taffeta to be used in the Etruscan Room.[15] In the early nineteenth century, on the other hand, with the advent of a fashion for elaborate draperies the balance shifted, and these furnishings often came to dominate the work of the architect, particularly in existing rooms being redecorated. Thus, views of the interiors of Carlton House show clearly how Walsh Porter's upholstery overlaid the architecture of Holland;[16] and similar effects were no doubt to be seen in many lesser interiors. Nevertheless, although Wyatville excluded the upholstery from his remit at Windsor, in the early nineteenth century John Nash had sent sketches for curtains to Mrs Stewart at Killymoon Castle, Co. Tyrone (which he had designed in 1801–3), and discussed these in a covering letter;[17] Soane too seems from many of his drawings to have been greatly concerned with the form and colour of curtains and other furnishings in the rooms which he designed (figs. 191, 192, 193 [in the companion volume]); while Decimus Burton provided variant designs for curtains in his coloured schemes for the Drawing Room at the Athenaeum Club, London.[18] It is thus clear that in new buildings the architect's work not only continued to embrace the matter of paint colour, but could also extend beyond it into the field of upholstery.

Another facet of architectural paintwork which must be stressed is the difference between the colours which could be used in interiors and those suited to and generally employed for exterior work. The physical demands made on exterior paint were obviously much more severe than those provided by interior conditions, most notably in the need for a much higher degree of freedom from fading when exposed to strong sunlight; while questions of economy were often also more pressing, especially where large areas of paintwork, which would need comparatively frequent renewal, were involved. For this reason, with the notable exception of the use of blue for prestige purposes on ironwork (discussed in Chapter 5 [of the companion volume]) and other occasional excursions into more assertive hues, 'common colours' made using earth pigments and black provided the everyday norm in town and country. These included browns, greys, dull greens, white, and off-whites, besides the dull red paint made from red ochre which T.H. Vanherman, whose book is reviewed below, described as 'a most excellent and durable covering for barns, sheds, cart and waggon wheels, implements of husbandry, . . . &c.'[19] At the end of the eighteenth century, moreover, figures such as Sir Uvedale Price and, a few years later, Humphry Repton actively discouraged the use of white out-of-doors, preferring instead such colours as 'invisible green', which, James Crease commented in 1808, was 'so denominated, from its being proper for covering gates and rails, in parks, pleasure grounds, &c. by rendering them in a measure invisible at a distance, on account of its approximation to the hue of the vegetation.'[20]

Special finishes such as 'sanding' and 'fresco' were often employed to give a dull, stone-like finish to joinery and stucco;[21] and against the general background of such 'vernacular' paint colours the interiors of country houses would have scintillated. Apart from the richness of their upholstery and gilding, in the best apartments of the later eighteenth century the eye would have been beguiled by delicate and fresh tints of paint colour, in which the brilliance and luminosity of the more expensive pigments were exploited. At every stage, therefore, cost and the limitations of technology provided an essential framework for the use of paint colour; and the often dull setting in both town and country of the houses containing the interiors discussed in this study was an important reflection of this.

SOURCES

In reviewing the sources used for study it is convenient to discuss them under two headings, although it will be obvious that aesthetic information is often present in a work dealing primarily with technique, and, to a lesser extent, technical information in a text whose main aim is aesthetic. This is especially true of the notebooks of the gentleman architect Sir Roger Pratt (1620–85), which were published by R.T. Gunther as *The Architecture of Sir Roger Pratt* in 1928. In these is to be found a mixture of technical and aesthetic information, ranging from ways of designing and embellishing ceilings to the fairly detailed information contained in the 1665 painter's agreement for Clarendon House already mentioned, besides a number of other memoranda. It is not, however, a coherent account of contemporary painting practice, and with literature of an aesthetic nature this remains true of all the sources examined until the 1800s are reached. To begin with, the material used primarily in the initial technical studies will be considered.

The first English book on painting technique was the anonymous quarto entitled *A Very Proper Treatise, wherein is briefly sett forthe the Arte of Limming* published in 1573. It and the other printed books which followed over the next century, including John Bate's *Mysteries of Natvre, and Art* (1633 and later editions) were concerned with the use of paint by artists, and contain little of direct relevance to house-painting, although the Devon plasterer John Abbott copied extensively from both these works in the 1660s.[22] Not until the 1670s did the first two specialised texts so far identified appear: in the second edition of his *Sylva, or a Discourse on Forest Trees* (1670), John Evelyn added a few paragraphs on house-painting; and in 1676 John Smith published *The Art of Painting wherein is included the Whole Art of Vulgar Painting*. Smith's main interest was in sun-dials, as the superscription of the pages throughout the book 'The Art of Painting/Sun-Dials' makes clear; but he made a detailed review of the methods and materials of the painter and provided a special chapter on 'The Practice of Vulgar Painting', dealing with both interior and exterior house-painting work.

Smith's book was soon developed, and in 1687 a second, much enlarged edition appeared under the title *The Art of Painting in Oyl*, in which further pigments were added and some of the earlier instructions revised. Unfortunately, though, in this it is far less obvious when discussion relates to interior as distinct from exterior work; and it is clear too that much of the time the author still had sundials in mind, and did not expect that all the pigments he listed should necessarily be used in house-painting. As his title implies, he was concerned only with oil paint, and gave no information at all on the other medium extensively employed in interiors of the period, distemper. Nevertheless, it is extremely fortunate that such an excellent book, albeit needing careful interpretation, was published during the first century covered by this study – although this seems inevitably to have resulted in a reciprocal disadvantage, since with such a good text already available there was little incentive for anyone in Britain to produce another for many years, in fact until the early nineteenth century, by which time techniques had changed considerably. Further editions of Smith were published in 1701, 1705, 1723, 1738, 1753, and 1788, but (at least up to the 1753 edition) only very minor alterations were made and, most notably, no account was taken of the introduction of the important pigment Prussian blue in the first quarter of the eighteenth century, or the taste for flat oil finishes from the 1740s. It remained, therefore, a book reflecting late seventeenth-century ideas until crudely revised and re-issued as *Smith's Art of House-Painting* by William Butcher in 1821 (second edition 1825). Even so, Butcher did little more than remove certain parts of the text while adding some new material and allowing other parts of Smith's original work to stand without critical revision, so that by this stage the work, in part completely obsolete, was highly misleading as a statement of contemporary practice.

For information on eighteenth-century developments one has therefore to look elsewhere. The most important English work in this connection is *The Handmaid to the Arts* by Robert Dossie, the first edition of which appeared in 1758 (followed by a second, which contains some additional material, in 1764). Although Dossie was not primarily concerned with house-painting, he discussed gilding in some detail, and his book is of particular significance for its descriptions of the materials used by painters in general, on whose manufacture it offers substantial information. Nevertheless, it must constantly be remembered that Dossie dealt with many substances which were far too specialist or costly for use by the house-painter, and care must be taken not to be beguiled by these.

Otherwise, to bridge the gap in printed books between the original appearance of John Smith's volume and the early nineteenth century, recourse may be had to works published in France. In Paris in 1691, for example, the architect A.C. D'Aviler published the two volumes of his *Cours d'architecture*, devoting three pages to 'La Peinture ou impression dans les bastimens'. In these, he described a number of colour mixtures, giving an interesting insight into French taste; and more limited information of the same kind is to be found in Pierre Bullet's *L'Architecture pratique*, also published in Paris in 1691. Most importantly, in 1772 the Parisian painter and colour-merchant J.F. Watin published a major work, the third (much enlarged) edition of which appeared in Paris in 1776 as *L'Art du peintre, doreur, vernisseur*, with a fourth following in 1785. In this he described the materials and paint finishes used, including distemper, together with a range of colour mixtures reflecting clearly those employed by Adam and his contemporaries. It is therefore of considerable significance for the study of British practice, although it must be approached with caution in many respects. Watin described, for example, a number of varnish mediums at great length; but although these were used in both countries on furniture, they seem also to have been used in France for the decoration of *boiserie* or wainscot, which had largely fallen from favour in English interiors by that date. In addition, he described with great enthusiasm a number of highly elaborate finishes employing up to twenty coats, but it seems doubtful if these were greatly used, even in France. His book formed the foundation of that by P.F. Tingry of Geneva, first published in 1803 as *Traité théoretique et pratique sur l'art de faire et appliquer les vernis*, translated into English the following year as *The Painter and Varnisher's Guide*. This is again of major importance to the present study, but as with Watin's book has to be approached with care. Like Watin, Tingry gave a comprehensive account of painting materials together with oil, distemper, and varnish formulae and methods of colour mixing, but these are seen again from a Continental point of view. A second, edited, English edition followed in 1816; and a third, anonymously but extensively 'corrected and improved by a practical chemist' in 1830, under the title *The Painter's & Colourman's Complete Guide*. The latter is of especial interest for its account of the new pigments introduced in the first three decades of the nineteenth century.

By the 1830s, however, English house-painting literature had expanded enormously. About 1811, the Hackney colourman John Pincot (whose premises were at 'The Rainbow') produced *Pincot's Treatise on the Practical Part of Coach & House Painting*. In contrast to the often rarefied ideas and highly cultured exposition of house-painting given by Watin, Pincot's down-to-earth language is practical and obviously trustworthy as reflecting everyday practice. As his title implies, besides dealing with the varnish-painting of coachwork, he gave a clear exposition of interior and exterior house-painting, and also described the use of distemper. It is interesting to compare this with the virtually contemporary American book by Hezekiah Reynolds, published at New Haven in 1812, *Directions for House and Ship Painting*, in which interior and exterior technique and colours are also clearly divided. Although his directions are fairly minimal and much less full than those of Pincot, Reynolds's work is valuable for the colour mixtures it contains. These seem, however, rather old-fashioned by European standards, and this is certainly the case with his graining methods which, though possibly still practised by provincial house-painters in Britain, had been superseded in fashionable work. His text probably represents, therefore, the best description of seventeenth- and eighteenth-century methods so far located.

Both these books were obviously written by practical men well versed in their trade, but the encyclopaedic works of the next decade must be approached more carefully. In 1813, Thomas Martin (now believed to be a pseudonym for John Farley) published *The Circle of the Mechanical Arts* dealing in detail with a large number of trades, among them house-painting. Much of the chapter he devoted to this subject seems reasonably reliable, and could, perhaps, have been based on material communicated by a house-painter; but other parts, notably his descriptions of materials, seem to have come from other sources. His mention of fish oil, a substance promoted by Vanherman, but then generally unknown in common practice, is one instance;[23] but it was in taking the complete list of pigments from Dossie, whose descriptions of over half a century earlier he abridged, that the editor betrayed his lack of intimate knowledge of the field by continuing to include many of these which would never have been used for house-painting. Also, of course, he omitted to notice certain important pigments such as patent yellow or Scheele's green which had been introduced since the late 1750s. The whole of Martin's text must therefore be examined critically in a way which Peter Nicholson failed to realise when he plagiarised it in his *New Practical Builder* (1823–5). Nicholson's chapter on house-painting is taken virtually entirely from Martin, although he removed one or two passages and made two or three other minor alterations. Most notably, however, he made the text even more of a trap for the unwary by adding a list of colour mixtures taken from Smith's seventeenth-century work (possibly using Butcher's 1821 re-issue) many of which were archaic. In general, by contrast, the entry in Nicholson's *Architectural Dictionary* of 1819 under the heading 'PAINTING, *Economical*' and the chapter 'Painting in Oil' in his *Mechanic's Companion* (published in

Oxford in 1825) seem rather more dependable; but the chapter on house-painting in the 1834 edition of the *Builder's and Workman's New Director* is based on that in the *New Practical Builder*. Another work obviously compiled from a variety of sources is the *Painter's and Varnisher's Pocket Manual*, published by Knight & Lacey in 1825. This relies heavily on Butcher's edition of Smith and also on Tingry, although it contains additional material of interest; and further new information is present in an edition of about 1830 published by M. Taylor as *The Painter's, Gilder's, and Varnisher's Manual*.

Finally, in the late 1820s two important new books appeared. The first was *The Decorative Painters' and Glaziers' Guide*, published in 1827 by Nathanial Whittock. From a technical point of view, Whittock's main contribution was a fairly accurate assessment of the pigments and other materials employed by the house-painter, together with detailed descriptions of the improved methods of graining and marbling then in use. The second work is *The Painter's Cabinet, and Colourman's Repository*, published in 1828 by T.H. Vanherman and reprinted the following year as *Every Man His Own House-Painter and Colourman*. Vanherman, who described himself on the title-page of the 1829 edition as an artist and house-painter (mentioning his experience as having been acquired in the course of fifty years) seems to have been an interesting figure, and his main concern was 'amelioration of the noxious quality of common paint'. He therefore described two new types of paint, 'Impenetrable or Anti-Corrosive' for exterior use, and 'Aromatic' for interiors, but gave besides a great deal of other useful and accurate information on a host of practical matters. His book had been preceded by a number of pamphlets and trade cards issued by others in the house-painting field, some merely listing the wares or accomplishments of their progenitors, but others being of greater substance. Of these the 'DIRECTIONS for PAINTING' issued by Alexander Emerton during the 1730s are of particular interest as going a little way towards filling the otherwise long gap in British house-painting literature during the eighteenth century;[24] while his brother Joseph issued a slightly amended, handsomely engraved version, some time in or before 1744 [fig. 1].[25] These contain a number of useful points on technique, as do also a group of rather later pamphlets: *Hints for the Preservation of Wood-Work Exposed to the Weather* (1808) by James Crease; the description of *The Antique Ornamental Paints* (1816) issued by the Patent Colour-Works;[26] the *Prospectus of the Various Paints . . . Manufactured exclusively by Thos Bentley* (1817); and *A Comparative View of the . . . Invulnerable Oil Paint, prepared by John Lingard, Jun.*, the second edition of which appeared in 1825. Bentley's document is of especial importance as containing a series of colour samples, most now completely discoloured but interesting as the earliest such colour card so far discovered.

Throughout the period covered by this study, a plethora of architectural books was published; but in almost every case where house-painting is mentioned the author's concern was primarily with the prices applicable to different items of work. Occasionally a small amount of practical information was included, notably by Thomas Wilsford in his *Architectonice: the Art of Building* (1659); Sir Balthazar Gerbier, *Counsel and Advise to all Builders* (1663); William Leybourn (clearly paraphrasing Wilsford), *A Platform for Purchasers, a Guide for Builders, a Mate for Measurers* (1668) and *Architectonicae: or, A Compendium of the Art of Building* (1700); and Richard Neve (under the pseudonym of T.N. Philomath, and quoting from Leybourn's later work), *The City and Countrey Purchaser, and Builder's Dictionary* (1700). Others, notably Stephen Primatt in *The City & Country Purchaser & Builder* (1667); J. Leadbeater, *The Gentleman and Tradesman's Compleat Assistant* (3rd edn, 1770); William and James Pain, *Pain's British Palladio* (1786); and William Pain, *The Practical House Carpenter* (5th edn, 1794), were simply concerned with prices; but even from such books a great deal of information can be gleaned, since different rates were charged for different colours, and those listed give a good insight into taste and technical development of the day. This is especially true of William Salmon's *Palladio Londinensis: or, the London Art of Building* (1734) in which he reprinted the complete priced colour list of Alexander Emerton, whose 'DIRECTIONS for PAINTING' have just been mentioned. Further editions, including the third (1755) and fifth (1773), also contain this; and his article was plagiarised by James Aheron in his *General Treatise of Architecture* published in Dublin in 1754.[27] A comparable trade list, this time of Madame Cosseron's 'Couleurs Lucidoniques' was published by J. Rondelet in the fifth volume of his *Traité théoretique et pratique de l'art de bâtir* (Paris, 1812-n.d.). From 1776, when I. Taylor published *The Builders Price-Book*, whole books were devoted exclusively to prices. Later editions include the 4th (1787), 11th (1794), and further editions of 1810 and 1813. In 1804 John Phillips produced *Crosby's Builder's New Price-book*, partly based on Salmon, later editions including the 19th (1812) and 31st (1821). In 1811 Z. Skyring published the first edition of *Skyring's new and complete List of Builder's Prices*, the 21st edition of which was published by his son W.H. Skyring in 1831 under the shortened title *Skyring's Builder's Prices*. Also noteworthy are *The Improved Builder's Price Book* by W.R. Laxton (2nd edn, 1818), and William Stitt's *Practical Architect's Assistant*, published in Dublin in 1819.

Technical understanding of the house-painting literature so far reviewed is greatly aided by correlation with information from contemporary works dealing with the use of the same or similar materials for fine-art purposes, and also with purely scientific works. Among the first may be mentioned André Félibien's *Des principes de l'architecture, de la sculpture, de la peinture* published at Paris in 1676 which is of particular interest in connection with gilding, together with Dossie's *Handmaid to the Arts* already noted. During the early years covered by this study, the scientific works largely reflect the interest taken by members of the Royal Society in manufacturing processes: in 1678, for example, articles were published in the *Philosophical Transactions* of that body by David Colwall, Christopher Merret, and Sir Philiberto Vernatti dealing respectively with the manufacture of ferrous sulphate (important in connection with the making of artificial red ochres), silver refining (important in connection with the preparation of blue and green verditers), and the manufacture of white lead. Earlier, another Fellow of the Royal Society, John Ray, had published descriptions of the manufacture of verdigris in his *Observations Topographical, Moral, & Physiological* (1673), and of silver refining and the manufacture of red lead in his *Collection of English Words* (1674); while Robert Plot described a number of ochre deposits and the strata within which they were found in his *Natural History of Oxford-Shire* (1677). Between 1692 and 1703, John Houghton published a series of articles under the general title *A Collection for Improvement of Husbandry and Trade* which included a significant amount of material (often taken from other publications) useful in connection with botanical products; and in 1724 John Woodward published in the *Philosophical Transactions* his well-known description of the manufacture of Prussian blue. In 1746, John Hill translated the geological work of the ancient writer Theophrastus, providing in his commentary to the latter's *History of Stones* a number of interesting observations on eighteenth-century pigments; but in the second half of the eighteenth century scientific interest in this field seems to have moved, at least temporarily, to France. In 1766, Auguste Fougeroux de Bondaroy published an article on

Naples yellow in the *Histoire de l'Académie Royale des Sciences*; in 1783 Guyton de Morveau's paper on white pigments appeared in the *Nouveaux Mémoires de L'Académie de Dijon*; and in 1792 Bertrand Pelletier's article in the *Annales de chimie* described alternatives to the secret English method for the manufacture of blue verditer. This was followed by another work of some interest, *Chimie appliquée aux arts* by J.A.C. Chaptal, published (together with its English translation *Chemistry Applied to Arts and Manufactures*) in 1807. Nearly two decades later, in 1825 the German writer J.C. Leuchs published *Anleitung zur Bereitung aller Farben und Flüssigkeiten*, a valuable encyclopaedic work which was translated into French with a commentary by M.E. Peclet under the title *Traité complet des . . . couleurs* in 1829. In the intervening years, a number of English books containing useful information were published, but it will suffice to mention finally Andrew Ure's *Dictionary of Arts, Manufactures, and Mines*, which drew extensively on Leuchs and other writers, and first appeared in 1839. To these sources should be added the host of patent specifications entered with ever-increasing frequency throughout the period studied, which contain much data useful relating to the manufacture of pigments.

A detailed account of technical literature relating to fine art is contained in the chapter 'Sources for the History of the Colour Trade' in Rosamond Harley's *Artists' Pigments*. In it, she also reviews the work of the Society for the Encouragement of Arts, Manufactures, and Commerce (now the Royal Society of Arts) in the years around 1800. Further discussion of this material is accordingly unnecessary here, although in extending the present research into the subject of natural resins recourse has also been had to a number of early botanical works. Another important addition to the references Dr Harley discusses has been provided by the manuscript records of the firm of paint manufacturers founded by Lewis Berger. These hitherto virtually untapped documents contain much that is important for the history of pigment manufacture and marketing, and cover a period extending from the last quarter of the eighteenth century to the First World War. Their relevance thus extends beyond this study, but material up to about 1840 has been analysed in detail, and the volumes in which it is contained are described in an appendix to the companion volume [viz. Appendix E in the present book].

Another notable group of manuscripts comprises the notebooks of the early nineteenth-century writer George Field, now at the Courtauld Institute of Art.[28] These include a number of watercolour samples which were invaluable for comparison with some of the pigments made in accordance with early formulae for purposes of the colour-mixing trials described above; and in this connection the specimens of British earth pigments at the Institute of Geological Sciences, South Kensington, London, were of similar help in understanding references to such material in the early literature.

Finally reference must be made to the later and more modern books on paint technology and related matters which have been found particularly valuable in the course of research. General works include *The Chemistry of Paints and Painting* by A.H. Church (2nd edn, 1892); *Painters' Colours, Oils, and Varnishes* by George H. Hurst (1892; 2nd edn, 1896); *A Treatise on Colour Manufacture* by George Zerr and R. Rübencamp (tr. Dr Charles Mayer, 1908); and *Outlines of Paint Technology* by Noël Heaton (2nd edn, 1940), which is largely based on Hurst. While not reflecting up-to-date knowledge amd scholarship, the information they contain on obsolete materials and processes is invaluable. Of more specialised works, that on pigments by Dr Harley has been mentioned more than once, but to it should be added the *History of Seed Crushing in Great Britain* by H.W. Brace (1960) – a work frustrating for its lack of references – and *Vegetable Gums and Resins* by F.N. Howes (1949). The latter subject still offers considerable obscurities, but present-day knowledge has been carefully surveyed by John Mills & Raymond White in their article 'Natural Resins of Art and Archaeology' published in *Studies in Conservation* in 1977. With reference to the study of timbers imitated in graining, the *Directory of the Historic Cabinet Woods* by F. Lewis Hinkley (1960) has been found useful; but little has recently been published for marbles, and the best information on historic varieties and nomenclature has been found in *A Treatise on the Building and Ornamental Stones of Great Britain and Foreign Countries* by Edward Hull (1872); the *History and Uses of Limestones and Marbles* by S.M. Burnham (1883); *Marble and Marble Working* by W.G. Renwick (1909); and *Marble, a Handbook* by Ian Cater [1933]. Again, the study collections at the I.G.S. have proved invaluable, supplemented by those at the Natural History Museum, South Kensington, and, most importantly, by the named specimens in the table formerly belonging to George Gwilt now at the Victoria and Albert Museum, South Kensington.[29]

The above sources were primarily of use in the preliminary technical studies, and in considering aesthetic aspects of the way colour was used in interiors over the period covered by the present study it has, of course, been necessary to turn to a much wider range of evidential material, especially since during the seventeenth and eighteenth centuries very little was published on this subject. Books have, therefore, been found less useful than tradesmen's accounts, architectural drawings, and pictures of interiors, besides the technical studies of surviving rooms mentioned above.

The published sources examined may be divided roughly into four classes: architectural and design books; books dealing with colour theory; books devoted to the description of a particular house; and published letters and diaries. All have, however, considerable limitations. As already mentioned, a certain amount of information about the colours used in late seventeenth-century France may be gleaned from the books published in 1691 by D'Aviler and Bullet; and further information concerning colours used in later French interiors is given by Jacques-François Blondel in his *De la Distribution de maisons de plaisance* (1737–8) and his continuation of Jean Mariette's *Architecture françoise* (1752–6). In addition, Marc-Antoine Laugier was clearly concerned with colour as an integral part of architectural composition, and in his *Essai sur l'architecture* (1753) devoted two or three sentences to it, commenting especially on the use of different coloured marbles. Comparable references seem lacking, though, from English books of the period, and even in his *Complete Body of Architecture* (1756) Isaac Ware provided only a few oblique allusions to colour, notably in connection with the measurement of painters' work for pricing. In 1759, rather more precise references to the colours used on ceilings were given by William Chambers in his *Treatise on Civil Architecture*, but neither these nor the few allusions to colour in the first two volumes of Robert and James Adam's *Works in Architecture* (1773–9) add up to more than a few small pieces needing to be set into the much larger context of the whole jigsaw puzzle; and the same is true of the comments on colour contained in *The Exhibition . . . being Remarks on the Principal Works to be Exhibited . . . at the Royal Academy* published by Robert Smirke under the pseudonym of Roger Shanhagan in 1779, and in *Οἰκίδια, or Nutshells* published by James Peacock under the pseudonym Jose Mac Packe in 1785.

After 1800, however, a profound change in English architectural literature took place with the advent of a series of copy books in which colour was discussed as an integral part of a scheme, rather than its provision simply being assumed. In 1801

Rudolph Ackermann published his *Designs for Architects, Upholsterers, Cabinet-Makers, &c.* in which were described the various rooms of a house, complete with their furnishings and paint and fabric colours; and in 1807 Thomas Hope included a revealing description of the colours used in the interior of his house in Duchess Street, London, in his *Household Furniture and Interior Decoration.* Other design books, notably by George Smith (1808 and 1812) followed, but of particular interest is the latter's *Cabinet-Maker and Upholsterer's Guide* (1826). This is paralleled by Whittock's *Decorative Painters' and Glaziers' Guide* (1827) which has already been mentioned, and ultimately by *The House Decorator and Painter's Guide* (1840) by H.W. & A. Arrowsmith. In all these, the drawings of rooms, some of which are coloured are accompanied by written descriptions giving a clear impression of the way in which colour was now conceived and organised in a domestic interior.

Again, few references to architectural colour have been encountered in early art-theory publications, although the Flemish artist Gerard de Lairesse considered the use of coloured marbles in *Het groot schilderboeck* published at Amsterdam in 1707 and translated into English as *The Art of Painting* (1738). The mid-eighteenth century, however, saw the careful application of purely abstract theory concerning colour following the appearance of Edmund Burke's *Philosophical Enquiry into the Origin of our Ideas of the Sublime and Beautiful,* first published in 1757; while at the end of the century and beginning of the nineteenth the ideas of the German philosopher J.W. Goethe, set out firstly in his *Beiträge zur Optik* in 1791 and in fully developed form in his *Zur Farbenlehre* of 1810, wrought a revolution in outlook. His work influenced a whole generation of writers, most notably David Ramsay Hay, the content of whose book, *The Laws of Harmonious Colouring* (1828 and later editions), which is of special importance for its application of colour theory to the interior, is described in Chapter 7 [of the companion volume].

During the second half of the period covered by this study, a handful of books was published describing specific buildings. Most notable in the present connection for the eighteenth century are Horace Walpole's *Aedes Walpolianae* which first appeared in 1747 and his *Description of. . . Strawberry-Hill* published at Strawberry Hill in 1784. In the former, while noting the colours and types of hangings in each of the rooms at Houghton Hall, Norfolk, he furnished no details of paint colour; but in the latter he gave more attention both to this and to the furnishings. The same type of information is contained in several books published in the first quarter of the nineteenth century, including John Britton's *Graphical and Literary Illustrations of Fonthill Abbey, Wiltshire* and John Rutter's *Delineations of Fonthill,* both published in 1823; while a limited amount of information on paint colour is contained in *Views of Eaton Hall* in Cheshire published by J. & J.C. Buckler in 1826. Towering over all these is the lavishly illustrated *History of the Royal Residences* published in 1819 by W.H. Pyne. Many copies were issued with coloured plates, and for Carlton House, London, in particular, these are matched by detailed descriptions of the colours employed together with other aspects of the *décor.* Amongst contemporary publications, the plates are fully equalled only by those in John Nash's account of the *Royal Pavilion at Brighton* (1826). These few books cannot, however, be said to present a general cross-section of typical interiors, since every one of them was clearly exceptional.

Outside the field of purely architectural publications, diarists and letter-writers also often described the different houses they visited or in which they stayed; but such references are scattered through many volumes and, though sometimes valuable, are time-consuming to locate. Two ladies in particular, Celia Fiennes in the late seventeenth century and Mrs Lybbe Powys in the second half of the eighteenth, seem to have taken a consistent interest in the interiors of a house, and the *Journeys* of the former (ed. R. Morris in 1947) together with the *Passages from the Diaries* of the latter (ed. E.J. Climenson in 1899) make particularly rewarding reading.

The relevant manuscripts fall into three groups: notes prepared by architects and others, and further documents in which intentions for paintwork were expressed; tradesmen's accounts, which form by far the largest number of sources in this category; and a few inventories. The latter, including for example the mid-seventeenth-century series relating to Ham House, Surrey,[30] and that of 1754 for Henry Pelham's house in Arlington Street, London,[31] generally concentrate on moveable furniture, of which curtains and wall-hangings were regarded as part, but remain silent concerning paintwork. A notable exception is provided, however, by the inventory of Wimbledon House, Surrey, taken in 1649 following the execution of King Charles I, which was later published by the Society of Antiquaries of London.[32] An altogether unusual document of similar character is the 'Deed of Transfer' signed by the officers of the latter body when they took up residence in their new rooms at Somerset House, London, in 1781, which offers considerable data on both paint and furnishings.[33] Notes and letters giving details of interior colour schemes have been found useful for the second half of the period considered, notably the letter books of Sir William Chambers preserved at the British Library, London,[34] and his letters to the Earl of Charlemont now at the Royal Irish Academy, Dublin.[35] Examples of other items of interest include, for instance, notes for gilding at James Wyatt's Thirkleby Park, Yorkshire;[36] Soane's notes for the decoration of his villa, Pitzhanger Manor, at Ealing, Middlesex;[37] and a series of memoranda on paintwork it was intended to carry out at Dunham Massey, Cheshire, in the 1820s.[38] In general, though, such documents contain fairly abbreviated information, so that often it is simply the salient points of a scheme which are noted, while the general context into which they were to be fitted is taken for granted. One noteworthy instance of detailed discussion is provided, however, by the letter sent in 1769 by Chambers to the Earl of Charlemont arguing the relative merits of two schemes for the Saloon at the Casino, Marino, Dublin.[39]

Undoubtedly, painters' accounts have proved to provide the best and fullest technical detail of colour schemes. They generally offer a precise date with virtual certainty that the work they describe was carried out. Landowners, their agents, and their architects seem to have been as assiduous in checking tradesmen's bills as any modern employer could wish; and indeed at Dyrham Park, Gloucestershire (now Avon), and Boughton House, Northamptonshire, corrections were made to the measurements for which Hauduroy and Dandridge respectively attempted to charge.[40] Where in an account items are broken down into units to which differing rates were applicable, their precise, technical language is a delight to read, and it is here that the primary decision to base the present study firmly on a thoroughly investigated foundation of early paint technology has proved of fundamental importance. In the past, such documents have frequently been misinterpreted, and significant points passed over without understanding, although it would be invidious to cite specific instances here.

Accounts do, however, present particular problems of their own. While many are related to named rooms, in other instances no locations are given; and it is frustrating to encounter items for an unspecified site such as the '99 Yards three oyl & flatted. Moulding on pannells and styles pickd in yellow' among items in John Crace's bill for painting at Woburn Abbey, Bedfordshire, under Henry Holland.[41] It was also common practice to sum the total yardages of the same or similar colours used in a whole house or suite of rooms, so that an item for several hundred square yards of green or dead white, for example, could be abstracted from a number of interiors. Such items were often placed at the head of a ledger, followed by room-by-room bills covering only areas for which special rates were chargeable. The accounts for the Strand block at Somerset House provide a good instance of this, where William Evans's account of 1780 contains first a summary of common colours and general items applied to large areas, and goes on to mention selected items in connection with particular interiors. Thus, in the Meeting Room of the Society of Antiquaries, for instance, he noted that the Ionic cornice, ceiling ornaments, and mouldings were dead white, while the ceiling grounds were pea green, pink, and lilac; but he did not include the walls. The 'Deed of Transfer' indicates, however, that the latter were green, and it appears, therefore, that this item is included in the $409\frac{1}{3}$ square yards of 'Green Verditer' listed along with the common colours and others at the head of his account.[42]

Even within a room, accounts do not always identify the disposition of the different colours, but by looking carefully at the yardages mentioned it is often possible to go at least part of the way in reconstructing a scheme. The Somerset House accounts again provide a good instance of this, but in many cases it is necessary to take and examine a series of paint samples to obtain definitive data. Thus at first the location of $9\frac{1}{2}$ square yards of chocolate mentioned in a context of nearly 300 square yards of dead white in the 1745 bill for the Dining Room at Henry Pelham's house in Arlington Street, London, was enigmatic;[43] but examination of paint samples from another room in the house (the Dining Room is no longer extant) showed that this was almost certainly applied to the door and skirting fascia.[44]

A final problem in dealing with accounts is the common difficulty of identifying rooms to which reference is made. The names given to these could change with surprising frequency, often depending on fairly short-lived functions or occupancy: at Ham, for example, the room called Mrs Henderson's Chamber in the 1677 inventory had by 1679 become the Chaplain's Chamber, and by 1683 was known as My Lord Maynard's Chamber.[45] Such ephemeral changes are often difficult to unravel, and it is sometimes necessary to stray well beyond the immediate topic of painting-work in order to make sense of a tradesman's bill.

In connection with the study of accounts, it should be noted in addition that distemper (water-based paint), which would commonly form an important part of a colour scheme, especially on ceilings, was often applied by the plasterer. As with the documents relating to work carried out at Ham House in the 1630s and Dyrham Park in the 1690s, reference has, therefore, to be made not only to the painter's account but also to that of the plasterer.[46] Likewise, a separate tradesman would sometimes be employed for gilding, as at Henry Pelham's house in Arlington Street, London;[47] but this was not invariable, and at Osterley Park, Middlesex, in the 1770s David Adamson was responsible for both painting and gilding in the Drawing Room.[48] Often, too, the woodcarver would be responsible for the gilding, this being the case in the 1750s at Norfolk House, London.[49]

Although a good spread of accounts of varying dates is available for study, a very different picture is presented by architectural drawings. Very few coloured designs dating from before the 1750s survive, and those that do generally relate to exceptional projects. Thus, the coloured, late seventeenth-century elevations for Queen Mary's Closet at Hampton Court show an extremely sumptuously furnished room (figs. 32, 33, [in the companion volume]), and the early eighteenth-century designs by John Talman for a Trianon in the grounds of the same building are also notably rich in conception (fig. 78 [in the companion volume]). Such drawings have therefore to be set into a context established by the use of other material, but once the latter half of the eighteenth century is reached it is largely the architectural drawings which provide the main basis for research. This is owing in large measure to the well-known collection of drawings from the Adam practice which was acquired by Soane in the nineteenth century; but many drawings by Adam's contemporaries also survive, although these often have to be sought more assiduously.

The collections of drawings consulted in the course of research are listed at the end of this volume. Those at the Royal Institute of British Architects, Victoria and Albert Museum, and Soane Museum are naturally pre-eminent; but other collections have not been neglected, and include a number of country-house archives together with material in the National Library of Ireland, Dublin, and in New York at the Metropolitan Museum of Art, Cooper-Hewitt Museum, and Pierpont Morgan Library. At Eton College, Buckinghamshire, the Topham collection was found to be of particular importance in connection with the study of antique precedents for Adam's neo-classical designs; and in this connection should also be mentioned such books as *Le Pitture antiche* (1680) and *Gli Antichi Sepolcri* (1727) by G.P. Bellori, both published in Rome, together with the *Recueil de peintures antiques trouvées à Rome* published by the Comte de Caylus and Pierre Jean Mariette in Paris in 1757 (2nd edn, 1783). These contain illustrations of similar antique examples, those in the latter volume being coloured; while the *Specimens of Ancient Decorations from Pompeii* published by John Goldicutt in 1825 are also important in the study of antique models from that site.

The principal difficulty with architectural drawings is one of interpretation, the use of yellow as a convention to represent gold (discussed in Chapter 5 [of the companion volume]) being a particular example which can give rise to ambiguity. Also, it cannot always be assumed that a plain tinted wash on a wall implies a plain colour, and Columbani's *post facto* (*c.* 1780) elevations of the Drawing Room at Audley End, for example, show a plain pink wash on walls in fact hung with a patterned fabric.[50] In addition, timber was commonly washed in brown, and it is not always clear whether polished hardwood or brown paint was intended. Similarly, with early nineteenth-century drawings it is often impossible to know whether timber or marbled elements on which naturalistic veining is shown were to be executed in the genuine material, or whether they were to be imitated in paint. This is, perhaps, less important than it seems, since the tonality of the drawing would be carried through into execution; but much more tricky are those instances where receding planes in a design are rendered in increasingly deeper tints on the drawing in order to express their depth. In 1826, George Smith suggested that this could actually be done on walls where *trompe l'oeil* panels were to be painted, so that 'the style [stile] of the panel may be of a similar colour as the ground, but worked darker for the purpose of giving the appearance of projection to the panel itself';[51] but whether three-dimensional panels or other architectural elements were ever 'helped' in this way, as often done today, is not immediately clear. Thus, although in 1787 the coffers in the semi-domes of the apses at either end of the Hall at Osterley were 'minutely pick'd in with three tints of grey',[52] on the basis of Adam's drawing for the coffered ceiling of the Eating Room at 20 St James's Square the account seems equally likely to represent a fairly bold colour contrast between their planes rather than a subliminal playing up of their depth (fig. 120 [in the companion volume]). Similarly, although on drawings the different planes of architectural mouldings may be washed in different depths of grey to give the illusion of depth, the evidence from painting accounts and technical studies indicates that a uniform tint was the norm during the eighteenth century, allowing the architecture to read naturally, rather than the 'shades of white' and other colours popularly favoured today in the redecoration of historic interiors. A similar finding applies to the decoration of panelling, and this is more fully discussed in Chapter 3 [in the companion volume].

To complete this review of the evidence presented by architectural drawings, it is apparent that schemes could be changed in execution, as is evident from notes giving an alternative set of colours on the reverse of a tinted ceiling design by George Dance the younger (fig. 142 [in the companion volume]); and the existence of a coloured design cannot be taken as unequivocal evidence for the finished work. There is even a significant discrepancy between Adam's drawing for the ceiling of the Music Room at 20 St James's Square, London, labelled quite unequivocally 'as executed', and the version in the coloured copy of the *Works* in the Soane Museum, which (with others), the text indicates, shows 'the tints used in the execution'.[53]

Turning to depictions of rooms, a number of difficulties of interpretation also initially arise, particularly in the case of mid-eighteenth-century conversation pieces whose backgrounds often seem at first glance to be an indeterminate drab. Even so, once examined carefully in the light of information from other sources, it seems clear the artists were generally representing common practice rather than simply providing a *sotto voce* backdrop to their sitters; and this is discussed fully in Chapter 3 [of the companion volume]. In the early nineteenth century, watercolours of rooms come to the fore, particularly valuable series being the perspectives at the Soane Museum of many of Soane's schemes; the noteworthy album of watercolours painted in the early 1840s by the amateur artist Charlotte Bosanquet which is now at the Ashmolean; and the now dispersed work of Mary Ellen Best, Caroline Davidson's publication on which has already been mentioned.

To these and all the other sources of evidence reviewed above, including that from the technical investigation of rooms, should finally be added a host of standard modern architectural works, each generally containing very little directly on colour, but providing comprehensive information of a more general nature. These include many of the splendid series of biographies of architects which have appeared since the Second World War, together with broader studies such as Sir John Summerson's *Architecture in Britain 1530 to 1830* (1953 and later editions); the *History of the King's Works* (1963–82) edited by Howard Colvin; and the latter's *Biographical Dictionary of English Architects* 1660–1840 (1954) and its successor the *Biographical Dictionary of British Architects* 1600–1840 (1978). A number of articles in *Country Life* are also useful, besides the various guidebooks provided by the National Trust, Victoria and Albert Museum, and others responsible for the maintenance and presentation of different buildings. Lastly, mention must be made of the *History of the Painter-Stainer's Company* by W.A.D. Englefield, which first appeared in 1923 and reveals much about the organisation of the painting trade in London, to the labours of whose members and provincial colleagues much of the present study is devoted.

NOTES

Abbreviations used are to be found in the bibliography and lists of other sources below.

1. White pigments, extenders, and adulterants

1 Hurst (1896), p. 84; Heaton (1940), p. 107.
2 Heaton (1940), p. 113.
3 Hurst (1896), pp. 84–5; Heaton (1940), p. 107.
4 1 Jac. I, c. 20.
5 Chester MS.
6 Tingry (1804), pp. 286–7; (1816), p. 181.
7 Butcher (1825), p. 6.
8 P.R.O. MSS., E. 351/3249–72; AO. 1/2422/49; AO. 1/2429/71.
9 Gunther (1928), pp. 67, 80.
10 Leyburn (1700), p. 71.
11 Reynolds (1812), pp. 9, 12.
12 Berger MSS.; stock 1801–2, pp. 47, 58, 63; stock 1805–6, pp. 4, 35.
13 Hurst (1896), p. 84.
14 Heaton (1940), p. 106.
15 Watin (1785), p. 20.
16 Tingry (1804), pp. 280–1; (1816), pp. 178–9.
17 Watin (1785), p. 21.
18 Nicholson (1819), s.v. 'PAINTING, *Economical*', vol. II, p. 417.
19 Tingry (1830), p. 53.
20 D'Aviler (1691), vol. I, p. 228; vol. II, p. 514.
21 Bullet (1691), p. 284.
22 Tingry (1804), p. 294; (1816), p. 187.
23 Tingry (1804), p. 295; (1816), p. 188.
24 Tingry (1830), p. 53.
25 Watin (1785), p. 21.
26 Tingry (1804), pp. 285–6; (1816), pp. 181–2.
27 Tingry (1804), p. 289; (1816), p. 184.
28 Tingry (1804), pp. 280–1.
29 Hurst (1896), p. 94; Heaton (1940), p. 111.
30 Watin (1785), p. 20.
31 Tingry (1804), pp. 281, 295; (1816), pp. 178, 188.
32 Berger MSS., stock 1805–6, p. 31.
33 Dossie (1758), vol. I, p. 127; (1764), vol. I, pp. 136–7.
34 Dossie (1758), vol. I, p. 128; (1764), vol. I, p. 138.
35 Martin (1813), p. 462; Nicholson (1823–5), p. 412.
36 Whittock (1827), p. 8.
37 Boughton MS., vol. III, p. 158.
38 Soane MSS., 'Ealing'.
39 Berger MSS., stock 1801–2, pp. 47, 58, 63; stock 1805–6, pp. 4, 35; stock 1809–10, p. 37.
40 Stapleton & *al.* (1975), pp. 57, 58. The prices in pence given by the London surveyor John Phillips (Phillips (1812), pp. 212–13) are enigmatic, being:

Whiten in water, 2*s.* 6*d.* a dozen pounds, and at	10
Paris white, in water pound	$2\frac{1}{2}$
Paris white, in oil, do.	7
Water white, do.	$7\frac{1}{2}$.

The first works out at a rate of £1 3*s.* 4*d.* per cwt., which seems astonishingly high, especially since most of the weight would presumably have been that of the water; and the use of Paris white ground on its own in oil is mysterious (unless intended for use as an extender with white lead), as is the nature of 'water white'. The prices for the same materials in the 31st. edition (Phillips (1821), pp. 170–1) had fallen to 9*d.*, 2*d.*, 6*d.*, and 7*d.* respectively.
41 Hill (1746), pp. 150–1 (footnote y).
42 Hurst (1896), pp. 79, 81.
43 Britton & Brayley (1802), p. 334.
44 Hurst (1896), pp. 79, 80.
45 Tingry (1804), pp. 287–8, 295–6; (1816), pp. 183–4, 189.
46 Whittock (1827), p. 9.
47 Neve (1703), pp. 197–8.
48 Berger MSS., 'Lake & Carmine Book', p. 368.
49 Vanherman (1828), p. 17.
50 Phillips (1812), p. 196.
51 Neve (1703), pp. 197–8.
52 Kendall (1809), vol. II, p. 234.
53 Gottesman (1954), p. 345.
54 Tingry (1830), p. 60.
55 Phillips (1812), p. 196.
56 Hurst (1896), p. 81.
57 Peacham (1606), p. 56.
58 Waller (1686), p. 24.
59 Dossie (1758), vol. I, pp. 127–8; (1764), vol. I, pp. 137–8.
60 Martin (1813), p. 463; Nicholson (1823–5), p. 416.
61 Whittock (1827), p. 9.
62 D'Aviler (1691), vol. I, p. 228.
63 Félibien (1676), p. 293.
64 Heaton (1940), p. 194.
65 Vanherman (1828), p. 17.
66 Tingry (1830), pp. 48–9.
67 Berger MSS., 'Lake & Carmine Book', pp. 132, 212, 261; 1831 formula book, p. 62. Both satin white formulae in the former MS are dated 1815, the second (which is a slightly expanded version of the first) being as follows:

Cwt. qr. lb.
0. 1. 21 or 49^{lbs} Picked Chalk Lime ab^{t} a B[arre]l
0. 3. 20 or 104 [lb.] Powdered Alum –
['About' – struck out] 2 butter boats full of Orchill –

Slack the Lime with about 2 pails warm Water & then mix it well with the Alum. Divide it into five parts and knead each for half an hour and make into three lumps. Divide the lumps and knead again for half an hour 3 at a time – Tread[in]^{g} from 9 til 6[,] 1 man & horse.

Put four lumps into the Barrel with 18 pails of water and turn an hour let it out of the barrel through a corn sieve into the back – Repeat the barrelling until the lumps are all used & then turn the barrel an hour with 14 pails ['warm water' – struck out] to wash it out – Then add the Orchill stir it well together and fill [filter] it out through a 68 Sieve.
68 Berger MSS., stock 1801–2, p. 56; stock 1805–6, pp. 24, 29, 34; stock 1809–10, pp. 27, 37.

69 John Smith (1676), p. 11.
70 Vitruvius, *l.* 7, *c.* XII ((1826), p. 223).
71 Vernatti (1678), pp. 935–6.
72 Hurst (1896), p. 10.
73 No. 1581 (1787).
74 Hill (1746), p. 133 (footnote n); Dossie (1758), vol. I, p. 123; (1764), vol. I, p. 133; Tingry (1804), pp. 290–1; (1816), p. 186.
75 Tingry (1830), p. 267.
76 Birch (1756–7), vol. III (1757), p. 517.
77 Robert Campbell (1747), p. 107.
78 Trade cards of John G. & Jeremiah Pilcher, Colour Merchants, Morgan's Lane, Tooley Street, London; and of Cox's & Poyser, Lead Merchants, Derby.
79 John Smith (1687), p. 14.
80 Watin (1785), pp. 17–18.
81 Nicholson (1823–5), p. 410.
82 Nicholson (1825), p. 407.
83 Smith (1676), p. 11; (1687), p. 15.
84 Dossie (1758), vol. I, p. 123; (1764), vol. I, p. 132; Nicholson (1819), s.v. 'PAINTING, *Economical*', vol. II, p. 415.
85 Tingry (1830), p. 50.
86 Caylus (1755), p. 92.
87 Watin (1785), pp. 17–19.
88 Butcher (1825), p. 7.
89 Nicholson (1823–5), p. 410; Watin (1785), p. 18.
90 Dossie (1758), vol. I, pp. 123–4; (1764), vol. I, p. 133.
91 Butcher (1825), p. 6.
92 Vanherman (1828), pp. 26–7.
93 Reynolds (1812), p. 9.
94 Leuchs (1829), vol. II, pp. 31–2. That this explains the nature of the 'Dutch lead' of which Lewis Berger made extensive use in pigment manufacture seems questionable. Many references to the latter are to be found among the Berger MSS. On 1 January 1802, for example, he had a stock of 40 cwt. 'Dutch Lead' valued at 5*s.* per cwt. (stock 1801–2, p. 63); on 1 January 1806 this had risen to 138 cwt. at the same price, together with 26 cwt. 'common' Dutch lead at 2*s.* 8*d.* (stock 1805–6, p. 34); while on the same date in 1810 he had in stock just over 241 cwt. 'Dutch Lead' at 4*s.* 6*d.* per cwt., 189 cwt. of 'Dutch Lead Hansons' at 4*s.* 9*d.* per cwt., and $157\frac{1}{2}$ cwt. of 'Com^{n} Dutch Lead' at 2*s.* 8*d.* per cwt. (stock 1809–10, pp. 4, 37, 38). The substance was used by the Berger company for certain lake pigments, appearing in a number of formulae, including, for example, one dated 1815 in the 'Lake & Carmine Book' (p. 202) for Dutch pink in which both 'fine' and 'sandy' varieties were mixed; and it was also employed in the preparation of refiners (blue) verditer (q.v.), which suggests it was a carbonate. The formula for the latter in the 1831 formula book (p. 185) calls for the use of 'Pinnings D. Lead' which then (1834) cost 4*s.* 8*d.* per cwt., and a loose MS. inserted at that page refers to 'Dutch Lead (Pinnings make of Hull)'. Both the price and uses to which the substance was put make it seem unlikely that it contained much, if any, white lead, especially since the better qualities were comparable in price with Paris white; and it seems possible that it may have been barium carbonate (q.v.).
95 Ure (1839), s.v. 'WHITE LEAD', pp. 1297–8.
96 Stalker & Parker (1688/1971), p. 70.
97 Smith (1687), p. 16.
98 Watin (1785), p. 16.
99 Dossie (1758), vol. I, pp. 121–2; (1764), vol. I, p. 131.
100 Martin (1813), p. 462; Nicholson (1819), s.v. 'FLAKE WHITE', vol. II, p. 4; Nicholson (1823–5), p. 416; Whittock (1827), p. 8.
101 Butcher (1825), p. 7; Tingry (1830), p. 50.
102 Petworth MSS., PHA 6614, No. 219, p. [12].
103 Osterley MSS., Burchett (1779); Burchett (1780); Burchett (1781a).
104 Op. cit., p. 68.
105 Field (1835), p. 69.
106 Op. cit., p. 8.
107 *Builders Price-Book* (1810), p. 83; (1813), p. 126.
108 Phillips (1812), p. 209; (1821), p. 167.
109 Martin (1813), p. 460.
110 Nicholson (1823–5), p. 410; Nicholson (1825), p. 408.
111 Butcher (1825), p. 30.
112 Pat. No. 651 (1749); Hurst (1896), pp. 18–19.
113 Watin (1785), p. 19.
114 Field (1835), p. 69.
115 Hurst (1896), p. 25.
116 Leuchs (1829), vol. II, p. 6.
117 Tingry (1804), pp. 281–7; (1816), pp. 180–1.
118 Pat. No. 2189 (1797); Hurst (1896), p. 36.
119 Pat. No. 3099 (1808); Hurst (1896), p. 25.
120 Pat. No. 4254 (1821); Tingry (1830), pp. 51–2.
121 Vanherman (1828), pp. 81–3.
122 Pat. No. 7521 (1837); Ure (1839), s.v. 'WHITE LEAD', p. 1299; Hurst (1896), p. 41.
123 Ure (1839), s.v. 'WHITE LEAD', p. 1298.
124 Tingry's later editor, for example, referred (Tingry (1830), pp. 51–2) to two patents, the first (No. 5377) awarded to John Ham of Bristol in 1826, the second (No. 5383) awarded to Peter Groves in the same year. Groves treated galena (lead sulphide) with potassium nitrate and sulphuric acid, the product, as Tingry's editor pointed out, being lead sulphate rather than white lead. Although the latter was 'not prepared to state that sulphate of lead is equally useful as a pigment with the carbonate', Hurst ((1896), p. 50) referred to its unsatisfactory nature when used alone, but described various combinations in which it had come to be used by the late nineteenth century. It had, however, been used as a watercolour pigment at the end of the eighteenth century (Harley (1970), p. 160). Also, Vanherman (Vanherman (1828), pp. 81–3) described a method of making white lead by grinding granulated lead with white sand to produce 'a white oxide of lead' which was carbonised by the same means as that employed in the other methods he described. It is possible that this was related to the process proposed by Torassa & Wood, which Hurst discussed (Hurst (1896), p. 40) and was, he considered, 'of interest on account of its novelty only, not from any practical value it may possess'.
125 Heaton (1940), pp. 65–6.
126 Chester MS.
127 Neve (1703), p. 197.
128 Boughton MS., vol. III, p. 158.
129 Stalker & Parker (1688/1971), p. 70.
130 Salmon (1734), p. 57.
131 Dyrham MSS., D.1799, A141.
132 Tredegar MSS., 68/76.
133 Soane MSS., 'Ealing'.
134 Phillips (1812), p. 213:

Second lead for priming, per pound			$8\frac{1}{2}$[*d.*]	[8*d.*]
Do. White lead, do			$9\frac{1}{2}$[*d.*]	[9*d.*]
Best white lead, do.	1	–	10 [*d.*]	
Do. in spirits, do.	1	–	0	
Nottingham lead, do	1	–	1	
Flake white, do	1	–	10	[1*s.* 9*d.*]
Do. a fine sort, do.	2	–	0 '.	

The prices shown in the second column within square brackets are those which appear in the 31st edition ((1821), p. 171) where these differ from the rates of 1812. The nature of the white lead 'in spirits' is not clear, but it could possibly represent a ready-mixed 'flatting' finish of the type discussed in Chapter 15 (q.v.).
135 Vanherman (1828), p. 9. It is also interesting to note an early nineteenth-century price list (Rondelet (1812–n.d.), vol. V, p. 221) in which *céruse* (*2me qualité*) was 70c. per lb., *céruse* (*1er qualité*) was 80c., *plomb en écailles* was 1 fr. 25, and the same 'en trochisques' 2 fr. 26. The last must have been a very special quality of pigment, perhaps related to that prepared by the refining process described by Watin ((1785), p. 17).
136 Guyton de Morveau (1783), pp. 22–3.
137 Nos. 1996 (1794), 2094 (1796).
138 Vanherman (1828), pp. 49–51.
139 Op. cit. (1795), p. 243.
140 Watin (1785), p. 20.
141 Berger MSS.

142 Vanherman (1828), pp. 49, 51.
143 Op. cit. [1859], pp. xxi, 813.
144 Heaton (1940), p. 102.
145 Hurst (1896), p. 74.
146 Harley (1970), p. 165.
147 Vanherman (1828), p. 99.
148 Berger MSS., first experimental notebook, Nos. 42–7 of 1816; second experimental notebook, p. 7.
149 Tingry (1830), p. 58; Patent No. 5258 (1825).
150 Heaton (1940), p. 105.
151 Vanherman (1828), pp. 99–101.
152 Tingry (1830), p. 58.
153 Dossie (1758), vol. I, p. 124; (1764), vol. I, p. 133.
154 Félibien (1676), p. 292.
155 Vanherman (1805).
156 Vanherman (1828), p. 21.
157 Pincot [*c.* 1811], p. 39.
158 Martin (1813), p. 461; *Painter's . . . Pocket Manual* (1825), pp. 184–5; Tingry (1830), p. 277.
159 Dossie (1758), vol. I, p. 125; (1764), vol. I, pp. 134–5; Martin (1813), p. 461; Nicholson (1823–5), p. 412.
160 Whittock (1827), p. 8.
161 Martin (1813), p. 461; Nicholson (1823–5), p. 412.
162 Tingry (1830), p. 61.

2. Blue pigments

1 Tingry (1804), p. 324; (1816), pp. 207–8.
2 Tingry (1830), pp. 128, 130–1.
3 Harley (1970), pp. 62–3.
4 John Smith (1687), p. 25.
5 Tingry (1804), p. 324; (1816), pp. 207–8.
6 Op. cit. [*c.* 1830], pp. 4–6.
7 D'Aviler (1691), vol. I, pp. 228–9.
8 John Smith (1687), p. 26.
9 Church (1892), p. 202.
10 John Smith (1676), p. 20.
11 Harley (1970), pp. 60–1.
12 Fiennes (1947), p. 31.
13 PRO. MSS., E. 351/3264, M. iv[r]; AO. 1/2429/71, f. xi[v].
14 Evelyn (1670), p. 196.
15 John Smith (1687), p. 51.
16 Watin (1785), pp. 31, 41.
17 Caylus (1755), p. 104.
18 Butcher (1825), pp. 23, 24; Nicholson (1823–5), p. 416; *Painter's . . . Pocket Manual* (1825), p. 104.
19 Butcher (1825), pp. 12, 31.
20 Bullet (1691), p. 284.
21 Watin (1785), pp. 41, 46.
22 Stapleton & *al.* (1975), p. 58.
23 Nicholson (1819), s.v. 'PAINTING, *Economical*', vol. II, p. 417.
24 Berger MSS., 1831 formula book, p. 113. Tingry's later editor (Tingry (1830), p. 129) indicated that indigo was combined with starch to form *fig-blue* or *queen's-blue*, which were sold in cakes and lumps for use in 'domestic economy'. On 1 January 1806 Lewis Berger had a stock of 1 cwt. of the latter valued at 1*s.* per lb., and in 1810 173 lb. at 11*d.* together with 14 lb. 'Flat figg Blue' at 1*s.* 4*d.* It is also possible that the 'Cake Blue' of which he had 2 cwt. in 1806 valued at 1*s.* per lb., and the 'Princes blue' of which he had 426 lb. valued at 10*d.* per lb. in 1810, were similar preparations of indigo. (Berger MSS., stock 1805–6, pp. 21, 31; stock 1809–10, pp. 10, 11, 26.)
25 Berger MSS., stock 1805–6, p. 27; stock 1809–10, pp. 21–2.
26 Phillips (1812), p. 212; Harley (1970), p. 63.
27 Harley (1970), pp. 58–9.
28 Tingry (1804), pp. 356–7; (1816), pp. 237–8.
29 Ure (1839), s.v. 'ARCHILL', p. 52.
30 Tingry (1830), p. 137.
31 Berger MSS., stock 1801–2, p. 48.
32 Addy (1898), pp. 71, 91, 123.
33 Leuchs (1829), vol. II, p. 183; Harley (1970), p. 51.
34 Tingry (1830), p. 64; Ure (1839), s.v. 'COBALT', p. 301.
35 Harley (1970), pp. 51–2, 183–7; Hurst (1896), pp. 219–24.
36 John Smith (1687), p. 26; Watin (1785), p. 32.
37 John Smith (1723), pp. 69–71.
38 Ibid., p. 26.
39 Dossie (1758), vol. I, p. 89; (1764), vol. I, p. 95; James Smith (1815), vol. II, p. 733.
40 John Smith (1723), p. 26.
41 Stalker & Parker (1688/1971), p. 71.
42 Walpole, 'Anecdotes', *Works* (1798), vol. III, p. 336.
43 In 1802 Berger's stock of strewing smalt stood at 168 lb. valued at 1*s.* 6*d.* per lb.; in 1806, 1082 lb. at 1*s.* 7*d.*; and in 1810 87 lb. at 1*s.* $9\frac{1}{2}$*d.*, plus 820 lb. 'Smalts HFE' at 2*s.* 9*d.* per lb. In addition, he possessed small stocks of 'Smalt Royal', these standing at $8\frac{3}{4}$ lb. valued at 52*s.* 6*d.* per lb. in 1802; $6\frac{3}{4}$ lb. at the same price in 1806, and just over $2\frac{3}{4}$ lb. at 84*s.* in 1810. Although it is not clear why this variety was so much more expensive, it may be doubted that it was destined for house-painting purposes. (Berger MSS., letter book, pp. 249, 261; stock 1801–2, pp. 52, 60; stock 1805–6, pp. 3, 22; stock 1809–10, pp. 10, 24, 28.) Classifications such as 'HFE' were discussed briefly by Hurst, who observed that the letters varied with different makers and represented no particular standard (Hurst (1896), p. 224).
44 Bristow (1990), pp. 70–1; Bristow MSS., Queen's House (1986), pp. 40–8.
45 P.R.O. MSS., E. 351/3270, M. viii[r].
46 Ibid., 3263, M. vi[r].
47 Bristow MSS., thesis (1983), vol. II, pp. 820–1.
48 Abbott MS.; Chenevix Trench (1987), p. 26.
49 Evelyn (1670), p. 196.
50 John Smith (1687), pp. 26, 61, 75.
51 Soane MSS., Martin, loose ff. inserted between pp. 133 and 134, f. [2][r].
52 Bristow MSS., notes, C. 40.
53 Ham MSS., Moore's account.
54 P.R.O. MSS., WORK. 5/48, f. 172[v].
55 *Vide* n. 43 to this chapter.
56 Martin (1813), p. 461; Nicholson (1823–5), pp. 412, 414.
57 Butcher (1825), pp. 12–14.
58 D'Aviler (1691), vol. I, pp. 228–9.
59 Bullet (1691), p. 284.
60 Bristow MSS., thesis (1983), vol. II, pp. 820–1.
61 P.R.O. MSS., WORK. 5/46, f. 206[v]; Bristow (1990), pp. 69–70; Bristow MSS., reports, Queen's House (1986), pp. 26–32.
62 Bristow MSS., thesis (1983), vol. II, pp. 822–3.
63 Dossie (1758), vol. I, p. 89; (1764), vol. I, p. 95.
64 Watin (1785), p. 32.
65 Tingry (1804), p. 302; (1816), p. 193.
66 Hill (1746), pp. 102–3 (footnote o); Leuchs (1829), vol. II, p. 163.
67 Harley (1970), pp. 44–8.
68 Bristow MSS., thesis (1983), vol. II, p. 820.
69 P.R.O. MSS., E. 315/3255, M. v[v].
70 Ibid., 3256, M. v[v].
71 Ibid., 3254, M. v[r].
72 Ibid., 3263, M. xi[r].
73 Evelyn (1670), p. 196.
74 P.R.O. MSS., E. 351/3250, MM. vii[r], ix[r].
75 Ibid., AO. 1/2422/49, M. xiv[v]; E. 351/3253, MM. xii[r], xii[v], xiii[r]; 3256, M. v[v]; 3265, M. xvii[r].
76 Painter-Stainers MS., vol. I, p. 53 (for a poor transcription of the full account, see Englefield (1936), pp. 98–9).
77 John Smith (1687), p. 24.
78 Harley (1970), p. 46.
79 Stalker & Parker (1688/1971), p. 71.
80 D'Aviler (1691), vol. I, pp. 228–9.
81 Watin (1785), pp. 30–1.
82 Harley (1970), pp. 48, 50.
83 Watin (1785), p. 31; Vitruvius, *l.* 7, *c.* xi ((1826), p. 222).
84 Leuchs (1829), vol. II, p. 163.
85 Harley (1970), p. 4.

86 Ibid., pp. 47, 48.
87 P.R.O. MSS., E. 351/3258, M. v[r].
88 John Smith (1676), p. 19; (1687), p. 25.
89 Merret (1678), pp. 1048–9.
90 Neri (1662), p. 292.
91 MacTaggart (1980).
92 For 'Dutch lead', see note 94 to Chapter 1.
93 Berger MSS., 1831 formula book, pp. 185–6.
94 Berger MSS., stock 1801–2, p. 45; Vanherman (1828), pp. 26, 86.
95 No. 3594 (1812).
96 Nicholson (1819), s.v. 'PAINTING, *Economical*', vol. II, p. 417.
97 *Encyclopaedia Britannica* (1810), s.v. 'CHEMISTRY', vol. V, p. 554b, para. 901.
98 Dossie (1758), vol. I, pp. 86–7; (1764), vol. I, p. 92.
99 Pelletier (1792), pp. 47 sqq.
100 Chaptal (Paris, 1807), vol. III, pp. 415–19; (London, 1807), vol. III, pp. 401–5.
101 Berger MSS., 'Lake & Carmine Book', p. 216. The process is given as follows in the 1831 formula book:

> 72lb Roman Vitriol [copper sulphate] dissolved in 18 Pails (ab[t]. 3 Galls each) boiling Water. 50lb Pearl Ash dissolved in 9 Pails (ab[t]. 3 Gall[s]. each) boiling Water.
>
> Let down $\frac{1}{3}$ of Roman Vitriol into the Tub & add to it 6lb Cream Tartar. Then strike the Ash upon it till it ceases to effervesce make two more strikings of the Roman adding to each of them as before 6lb Cream Tartar –
>
> Let it stand till next day when fill up with Lime Water (without drawing off upper liquor as formerly did) once – fill [filter] out thro' a 68 Sieve – laid on [the chalkstones used for drying] in *thin* Cakes & dried in moderate heat.

The production cost was 1*s.* 2*d.* per lb., and the formula should be compared with that for Berger's 'French green' discussed in Chapter 3 in connection with green verditer. Although not explicitly stated in the manuscripts, experiment indicates that to obtain a blue pigment the solutions had to be mixed cold (Berger MSS., 1831 formula book, p. 75).

102 Berger MSS., 'Lake & Carmine Book', p. 236. The 1818 formulation (ibid., p. 368) was as follows:

> Solution of Vitriol to Strike with. Take a pail full of Roman Vitriol [copper sulphate] which is about 36lb. & add it to 9 pails of water when dissolved & cold it will produce 9 pails of the Solution.
>
> 10lb. Plymouth Stone Lime [a supplementary note added later suggests the substitution of 12lb. chalk lime]
> 2lb. Com[n] Salt [sodium chloride]
> 200 pails of water used over again
> ab[t]. 7 & $\frac{1}{2}$ pails of Sol[n] Vitriol
>
> Levigate the Lime & Salt together & wash into the Water then strike with the Sol[n] of Vitriol – when dry shoot it off the Racks into a tub of water.

Berger's 1831 product was similar to that of 1818, and cost 45*s.* per cwt. to produce dry, or 36*s.* 6*d.* damp, the yield being 2 cwt. dry or $2\frac{1}{2}$ cwt. wet. A note adds that the solutions were to be quite cold for use; and from 1836 it appears that an addition of 1 lb. tartaric acid was made to each hundredweight of completed verditer where a deeper tint was required, although this was omitted after 1839 (Berger MSS., 1831 formula book, pp. 119–22.)

103 Tingry (1804), pp. 315–16 (quoting Pelletier); (1816), pp. 199–200; Mackenzie (1825), p. 154; Leuchs (1829), vol. II, pp. 160–1, 164–9; Ure (1839), s.v. 'VERDITER, OF BLUE VERDITER', pp. 1274–5.
104 Hurst (1896), p. 227.
105 Berger MSS., letter book, pp. 11, 19, 24, 29, 30, 249; stock 1801–2, p. 45; stock 1805–6, pp. 24, 31; stock 1809–10, p. 25. Elsewhere, the sale of blue verditer some time after 1781 at 4*s.* per lb. is recorded (Wilson (1960), pp. 27–8); while Phillips gave the price of a pound of 'Blue verditor' as 10s. (Phillips (1812), p. 212; (1821), p. 170). Prices in contemporary France were cited as 9fr. per lb. for first quality *cendre bleue*, the second grade being 6fr. (Rondelet (1812–n.d.), vol. V, p. 222).
106 See notes 101 and 102 to this chapter.
107 Berger MSS., stock 1801–2, p. 54; stock 1805–6, pp. 8, 29, 32; stock 1809–10, pp. 26, 34, 36, 37.
108 Ham MSS., Gooderick's account; MacTaggart (1980), p. 42; Bristow MSS., notes, CS. 21. (I am most grateful to Miss Jo Darrah, who produced an internal Victoria and Albert Museum report on this important paintwork in 1977, for providing a small reference sample of the blue.)
109 Bristow (1985), p. 41; Bristow MSS., reports, Casino Marino (1980), p. 5; thesis (1983), vol. II, p. 775.
110 John Smith (1687), p. 25.
111 Examples include paint probably dating from the mid-1770s in the South Passage and Long Gallery at Osterley Park (both green), and paint of the mid-1790s in the Staircase (green) and Mary Moser Room (blue) at Frogmore House, Berkshire (Bristow MSS., reports, Osterley (1989), pp. 24, 34; Frogmore (1986), pp. 89, 90).
112 Vanherman (1828), p. 26.
113 No. 3594 (1812).
114 Butcher (1825), p. 30.
115 Watin (1785), p. 31.
116 Tingry (1804), p. 317; (1816), p. 200.
117 Whittock (1827), p. 11.
118 Op. cit. (1825), p. 101.
119 Laxton (1818), p. 96.
120 Phillips (1812), p. 212; (1821), p. 170.
121 Op. cit. (1795), p. 65.
122 Pincot [*c.* 1811], p. 22.
123 Nicholson (1819), s.v. 'PAINTING, *Economical*', vol. II, p. 417.
124 Watin (1785), pp. 30, 43.
125 Harley (1970), pp. 65–7.
126 Woodward (1724), pp. 15–17.
127 Salmon (1734), pp. 56, 57, 58.
128 P.R.O. MSS., T. 1/241, f. 382[r].
129 Dossie (1758), vol. II, pp. 387–91; (1764), vol. II, pp. 424–7.
130 Hurst (1896), p. 214.
131 Robert Campbell (1747), p. 106; Watin (1785), p. 33.
132 Dossie (1758), vol. I, pp. 77, 82; (1764), vol. I, pp. 82, 88.
133 Phillips (1812), p. 212; (1821), p. 170; Whittock (1827), p. 11.
134 Vanherman (1828), p. 86.
135 Berger MSS. The formulae in the 'Lake & Carmine Book' at pp. 242–56, dated 1816, are numbered '34', '$38\frac{3}{4}$', '$42\frac{1}{2}$', '$44\frac{1}{4}$', '57', '65', and '$67\frac{1}{2}$', but in later entries at pp. 376–96, dated 1816, 1818, and 1826, this system of classification is replaced by 'Deep Prus[n] Blue', '2nd Deep Pruss[n]. Blue', 'No 3', 'No 4 Wet Blue', 'No 5', and 'No 7' Prussian blues. 'Chrome Blue' was a special variety made with the addition of barium sulphate and sulphuric acid for use in the manufacture of 'Chrome Green', known today as Brunswick green (pp. 408, 409). Experimental notes are plentiful in the second experimental notebook, in which names such as 'Cranes Pale Dry Pruss.[n] Blue', and 'Mineral Blue, Celestial Blue or Meggitts' Blue for Sale in Powder' are found (p. 5, f. 21[r]). In the third experimental notebook a loose sheaf of manuscripts recording experiments carried out between 1829 and 1830 is preserved at p. 87, together with other notes of a later date. The 1831 formula book shows that the range of pigments manufactured in that year, cost prices per pound also being given, was:

> Antwerp blue @ $11\frac{1}{2}$*d.*
> Prussian magnesian blue @ 2*s.* $2\frac{1}{2}$*d.*
> Deep Prussian blue @ 2*s.* $4\frac{1}{2}$*d.*
> Second deep Prussian blue @ 2*s.* 1*d.*
> No. 3 Prussian blue @ 1*s.* 9*d.*
> No. 4 Prussian blue @ 1*s.* 7*d.*
> Crane's pale Prussian blue @ 1*s.* 8*d.*
> New Prussian blue @ 3*s.* 2*d.*
> Wet blue @ 23*s.* per cwt.

'New Prussian blue' was later deleted, and seems to have been superseded by the pale and deep 'Chinese blue' formulae dated 1836, while an extra-deep Chinese blue was added in 1838. 'Celestial blue' was made in 1831 as a mixture of Antwerp and Prussian blues with barytes and sulphuric acid. (1831 formula book, pp. 111, 115, 125, 126, 127, 129, 195, 197, 198.)

136 Berger MSS., letter book, pp. 11, 24, 29, 30.
137 Ibid., stock 1801–2, pp. 50, 58, 60, 61; stock 1805–6, pp. 3, 4, 28, 35; stock 1809–10, pp. 15, 21, 24, 36.
138 Vanherman (1828), pp. 25–6.
139 Berger MSS., letter book, pp. 19, 24, 30, 249; stock 1801–2, p. 44; stock 1805–6, p. 18; stock 1809–10, pp. 16, 37.
140 B.M. trade cards, Heal 89.89, MS. bill dated 13 June 1776 on reverse; Vanherman (1828), pp. 7, 8.
141 Tredegar MSS., 68/76.
142 Stapleton & *al.* (1975), p. 58.
143 Soane MSS., 'Ealing'.
144 Phillips (1812), p. 212; (1821), p. 170.
145 Bristow MSS., thesis (1983), vol. II, pp. 784–8.
146 Vanherman (1828), p. 28.
147 Whittock (1827), p. 19.
148 Harley (1970), pp. 41–3; Church (1892), p. 188; Cennini, c. 62 ((1844), pp. 33–6; (1930), pp. 47–51).
149 Stalker & Parker (1688/1971), p. 71.
150 Walpole, 'Anecdotes', *Works* (1798), vol. III, pp. 333, 334.
151 John Smith (1687), p. 25.
152 D'Aviler (1691), vol. I, pp. 228–9.
153 P.R.O. MSS., T. 1/241, f. 382[r].
154 Watin (1785), p. 32; Tingry (1804), p. 399; (1816), p. 280.
155 Martin (1813), p. 461; Nicholson (1823–51), pp. 412, 414; Dossie (1758), vol. I, p. 8; (1764), vol. I, p. 8.
156 Whittock (1827), p. 11.
157 Phillips (1812), p. 212; (1821), p. 170.
158 Heaton (1940), p. 152.
159 Harley (1970), p. 54.
160 Tingry (1830), p. 65.
161 Berger MSS., second experimental notebook, f. [32][r] (a note headed 'Trials for Smalts March 1831' together with a loose MS. inserted at that page).
162 Heaton (1940), p. 162; Harley (1970), pp. 53–5.

3. Green pigments

1 John Smith (1687), pp. 23–4; Ray (1673), pp. 454–6.
2 Tingry (1804), pp. 373–4; (1816), pp. 254–5.
3 John Smith (1687), p. 24; Tingry (1804), pp. 374–5; (1816), p. 255.
4 Stalker & Parker (1688/1971), p. 71; Evelyn (1670), p. 197.
5 Berger MSS., letter book, pp. 29, 30, 249 (letters dated 14 June and 20 August 1780, and 20 June 1788); stock 1801–2, pp. 44, 57, 58, 60; stock 1805–6, pp. 9, 17, 26, 28; stock 1809–10, pp. 15, 17, 19, 29.
6 Dossie (1758), vol. I, p. 104; (1764), vol. I, p. 112.
7 For other pigments known as 'English verdigris' or 'British verdigris' see articles on green verditer and copper chloride Brunswick green below. In addition the name was applied to a pigment manufactured by Berger's sons in 1819 containing a complex of copper carbonate and copper acetate. Their 'English Verdigrease' was made as follows:

28 lb Roman Vitriol Dried }
28 lb Sugar Lead Powdered } well mixed under stone
7 lb Pot Ash = desolved in 2 Pails Water and reduced to 1 Pail & ¼ then let it stand 12 Hours to settle put the Dregs in a Cloth to run of[f] then put it to the ingredients to be well mixed to stand abt 6 Hours then well mixed and laid on [chalkstones].

From 1811 the firm had been making a pigment called *patent green* by a similar method, although this contained almost equal weights of the three ingredients; and by 1816 it contained also a proportion of verditer. In that year it was renamed *azure blue*, but in 1817 the formula for this too was changed, and it was made from copper sulphate, pearl ash, and cream of tartar until after 1831. The name *patent green* (which is discussed in connection with Scheele's green, q.v.) also occurs in one of the experimental notebooks in an entry dated 1821, where a formulation (given below in the section on copper chloride Brunswick green – q.v.) containing French green (a variety of green verditer (q.v.) described below), lime, 'salt tartar', and sal ammoniac appears. (Berger MSS., 'Lake & Carmine Book', pp. 135, 216, 343; 1831 formula book, p. 75; second experimental notebook, f. 12[r].)
8 Tingry (1830), p. 91 (first and second formulae); Vanherman (1828), p. 88.
9 John Smith (1676), p. 22; (1687), pp. 24, 51–2; Watin (1785), pp. 43–5.
10 Smith (1687), p. 52; Bullet (1691), p. 285; Watin (1785), pp. 43–5; Reynolds (1812), pp. 11, 15, 16.
11 Tingry (1804), pp. 317–18, 404–5; (1816), pp. 201, 285–6; *Painter's . . . Pocket Manual* (1825), p. 103.
12 Butcher (1825), p. 30.
13 Tingry (1804), pp. 404–5; (1816), p. 286; Evelyn (1706), p. 272.
14 John Smith (1687), pp. 51–2; Bullet (1691), p. 285.
15 D'Aviler (1691), vol. I, p. 229.
16 Dossie (1758), vol. I, p. 104; (1764), vol. I, p. 112; Watin (1785), p. 29; Tingry (1830), p. 88.
17 Watin (1785), pp. 43, 44; Pincot [*c.* 1811], p. 23.
18 Evelyn (1670), p. 196.
19 Soane Museum pictures.
20 Clark-Morgan House, Salem, Massachusetts (*c.* 1737); North Parlor, Webb House, Wethersfield, Connecticut (*c.* 1752); 'Guest Chamber Suite', Jeremiah Lee Mansion, Marblehead, Massachusetts (1768). I am grateful to Morgan Phillips of the Society for the Preservation of New England Antiquities, Boston, for describing his work on verdigris glazes to me, and showing me the original and restored paintwork in the last of these houses, and to Sara Chase of the same organisation for correspondence.
21 B.M. trade cards, Heal 89.53.
22 I am indebted to Dr John Mills for this suggestion.
23 Salmon (1734), p. 58.
24 Bristow MSS., thesis (1983), vol. II, pp. 834–5.
25 Phillips (1812), p. 210; (1821), p. 168; *Builders Price-Book* (1810), p. 84; (1813), p. 127.
26 Whittock (1827), p. 12.
27 Leuchs (1829), vol. II, p. 307; Hurst (1896), p. 171.
28 Tingry (1830), p. 88; Watin (1785), p.29.
29 Mercato (1717), p. 23; Brignoli de Brunnhoff (1820), pp. 355–7.
30 Hill (1746), p. 142 (footnote r).
31 Hurst (1896), p. 183; Church (1892), p. 175.
32 Boughton MS., vol. III, p. 158.
33 Martin (1813), p. 461; Nicholson (1823–5), pp. 412, 415; Dossie (1758), vol. I, pp. 9, 110; (1764), vol. I, pp. 9, 118.
34 Watin (1785), p. 30; Tingry (1804), p. 369; (1816), p. 249.
35 Rondelet (1812–n.d.), vol. v. p. 222.
36 *Painter's . . . Pocket Manual* (1825), p. 102.
37 Berger MSS., stock 1809–10, p. 18.
38 Dossie (1758), vol. I, p. 108; (1764), vol. I, p. 116; Watin (1785), p. 29.
39 Watin (1785), p. 29.
40 Tingry (1804), p. 376; (1816), p. 257.
41 Watin (1785), pp. 43, 44, 46.
42 Martin (1813), p. 461; Nicholson (1823–5), pp. 412, 415.
43 Berger MSS., stock 1801–2, p. 56; stock 1805–6, p. 26; stock 1809–10, p. 18.
44 Rondelet (1812–n.d.), vol. v. p. 222.
45 Phillips (1812), p. 214; (1821), p. 172.
46 John Smith (1687), p. 24.
47 D'Aviler (1691), vol. I, p. 229; Bullet (1691), p. 284; Watin (1785), p. 30; Rondelet (1812–n.d.), vol. v. p. 222; Tingry (1804), p. 402; (1816), p. 283.
48 Agricola (1546), p. 221; Watin (1785), p. 30; Tingry (1804), p. 369; (1816), p. 249.
49 Leuchs (1829), vol. II, pp. 288–9.
50 John Smith (1687), p. 24.
51 *Builders Price-Book* (1787), p. 138; (1794), p. 150; Tingry (1816), p. 201.
52 *Painter's . . . Pocket Manual* (1825), p. 103.
53 Pincot [*c.* 1811], p. 21.
54 Patent No. 3519 (1812); Tingry (1830), p. 91. For use of such

terms for other pigments, *vide* section above dealing with verdigris, and section below on copper chloride Brunswick green.
55 Berger MSS., 'Lake & Carmine Book', p. 218.
56 Berger MSS., stock 1801–2, pp. 51, 55.
57 Berger MSS., 'Lake & Carmine Book', p. 131.
58 Berger MSS., 1831 formula book, p. 77.
59 Berger MSS., stock 1801–2, pp. 51, 55; stock 1805–6, p. 9; stock 1809–10, pp. 24, 25, 30, 36. The prices ranged from 1*s.* $2\frac{1}{2}$*d.* to 1*s.* 10*d.* per lb.
60 Berger MSS., letter book, pp. 11, 24, 249.
61 Nicholson (1819), s.v. 'PAINTING, *Economical*', vol. II, p. 417.
62 Pincot [*c.* 1811], p. 21.
63 Claydon MS.
64 Vanherman (1828), p. 88.
65 No. 3594 (1812).
66 Leuchs (1829), vol. II, p. 273.
67 Ibid., pp. 274–5.
68 Ure (1839), s.v. 'GREEN PAINTS', p. 619.
69 Leuchs (1829), vol. II, p. 275.
70 Op. cit. (1795), p. 33.
71 Chaptal (Paris, 1807), vol. III, p. 420; (London, 1807), vol. III, p. 406.
72 James Smith (1815), p. 733.
73 Leuchs (1829), vol. II, p. 276.
74 Hurst (1896), p. 167.
75 Tingry (1830), p. 91.
76 Berger MSS., second experimental notebook, p. 7.
77 Vanherman (1828), pp. 87–8.
78 Ure (1839), s.v. 'VERDITER OF BREMEN GREEN', pp. 1275–6.
79 Chaptal (Paris, 1807), vol. III, p. 420; (London, 1807), vol. III, p. 406.
80 Leuchs (1829), vol. II, p. 275, 281.
81 Ibid., pp. 273–92.
82 See note 7 to this chapter. The term *patent green* is also discussed in the section on Scheele's green.
83 Berger MSS., 'Lake & Carmine Book', p. 345.
84 Berger MSS., 1831 formula book, p. 79.
85 Davy (1815), p. 122.
86 Private communication of 15 July 1985 from Morgan W. Phillips, Society for the Preservation of New England Antiquities, Boston. The distemper was partly sandwiched between the first and second schemes on the woodwork, and identified at the Fogg Museum of Art, Harvard.
87 Hurst (1896), p. 167.
88 Harley (1970), pp. 75–6.
89 Hurst (1896), p. 176.
90 Leuchs (1829), vol. II, p. 293; Tingry (1830), pp. 86–7; Ure (1839), s.v. 'SCHEELE'S GREEN', p. 1094. Leuchs (p. 276) noted, however, that Mittis green (put on the market in 1814 by M. de Mittis of Vienna) was arsenate of copper obtained by warming Scheele's green with tartar, common salt, or sal ammoniac, the colour being changed in varying degrees. Elsewhere (p. 294), he suggests this was similar to that of emerald green, although the latter was stronger and more pure.
91 No. 3594 (1812).
92 It was, for example, applied by Hurst to malachite (Hurst (1896), p. 180), and also to copper chloride Brunswick green (q.v.).
93 Harley (1970), p. 76; Butcher (1825), p. 11.
94 See note 7 to this chapter.
95 Butcher (1825), p. 30.
96 Phillips (1812), p. 213; (1821), p. 171.
97 Englefield (1936), p. 185; Laxton (1818), p. 96; *Painter's . . . Pocket Manual* (1825), p. 103; Skyring (1831), p. 88.
98 Berger MSS., 'Lake & Carmine Book', p. 134; letter book, pp. 11, 19, 29, 30.
99 Nicholson (1819), s.v. 'PAINTING, *Economical*', vol. II, p. 417.
100 Stitt (1819), pp. 349.
101 Berger MSS., 'Lake & Carmine Book', pp. 132, 134, 127.
102 Berger MSS., 1831 formula book, p. 81. For the other formulae, see n. 104 to this chapter.
103 Mérimée (1839), pp. 177–8.
104 Berger MSS., 1831 formula book, pp. 83, 85, 86, 91, 93, and 95. The most notable changes were omission of Dutch lead from the mineral greens, and substitution of the same quantities of whiting. Barytes was added to the formula for Olympian green, and second French green was now made without the addition of the copper carbonate pigment also made by the company under that name.
105 Berger MSS., stock 1801–2, pp. 52, 53, 54, 55, 56, 61, 62; stock 1805–6, pp. 2, 6, 8, 9, 28, 29, 30, 31, 34; stock 1809–10, pp. 15, 26, 28, 29, 36, 38.
106 Hurst (1896), p. 176.
107 Leuchs (1829), vol. II, p. 294.
108 Harley (1970), pp. 76–7; Tingry (1830), p. 93.
109 Hurst (1896), p. 179.
110 Op. cit. [*c.* 1830], p. 43.
111 Berger MSS., second experimental notebook, ff. 19^{r}, 22^{r}. The formula at the first of these is headed 'M Bracannot's Blue' and is noted as extracted from the *Edinburgh Journal of Science*, No. 20, for April 1829. At the second is a note dated 4 February 1830 for the formulation of a compound pigment containing emerald green, which was called 'Permanent Pea Green', marked 'Sample Green made to send to Graves', suggesting that the firm was producing emerald green commercially by that date. For details of this and similar compound pigments containing emerald green marketed by Berger, see Appendix A, s.vv. 'Green, Aquatic', 'Green, Chinese', 'Green, Marine', and 'Green, Pea'.
112 Berger MSS., 1831 formula book, p. 97.
113 Bristow MSS., reports, Westminster (1985–6).
114 Bristow MSS., notes, C. 55B.
115 Church (1892), p. 182; Hurst (1896), p. 179.
116 Vanherman (1828), p. 109.
117 Heaton (1940), pp. 144, 145.
118 Vanherman (1828), pp. 109, 14.
119 Berger MSS., second experimental notebook, p. 7 (note dated 11 October 1824); 'Lake & Carmine Book', pp. 408–9; 1831 formula book, p. 103. A specially reduced Prussian blue known as *chrome blue* or *mineral blue* was at first used, although during the 1830s this ceased to have a particular identity and Chinese blue was employed directly, barytes being added to the chrome yellow instead. The 1831 formula for chrome blue directed:

> Take 28 lb Deep Pruss^{n} Blue – Cranes & powder it fine then add to it 8 cwt Sulphate Barytes mix well & levigate three times, after which add 8 lb Sulphuric Acid, stir same well together – put in pans to dry.

At this date 'Deep' Brunswick green, which contained 1 part of yellow to 10 of blue, cost 25*s.* per cwt. to produce; 'Middle' Brunswick green, containing 1 part of yellow to 7 of blue, cost 28*s.* 5*d.*; 'Pale' Brunswick green, containing 1 part of yellow to 8 of 'Pale Chrome blue' (made in the same way as the ordinary variety, but with only half the quantity of Prussian blue), 23*s.* 3*d.*; while in addition a variety known as 'Yellow pale' Brunswick green was also made at a cost of 29*s.* per cwt. (1831 formula book, pp. 103, 117, 118).
120 Hurst (1896), p. 135.
121 Martin (1813), p. 461; Nicholson (1823–5), pp. 412, 415; Dossie (1758), vol. I, pp. 9, 108–9; (1764), vol. I, pp. 9, 116–17.

4. Inorganic yellow pigments

1 P.R.O. MSS., E. 351/3253, M. iv^{v}; 3266, M. iv^{v}; 3267, M. iv^{v}.
2 Osterley MSS., Burchett (1779); Burchett (1780).
3 Heaton (1940), p. 166.
4 I.G.S. samples Nos. MI. 16468 (Vale of Avoca); 14689–90 (Winford, Somerset); 24245–7 (Axbridge, Somerset); 24248–51, 24254–5 (Wick, Gloucestershire – now Avon); 27395 (Chillaton Barton, nr. Tavistock, Devon); 14696–8 (Gwennap Adit, Cornwall).
5 Hurst (1896), pp. 141, 148; Hurst (1902), p. 315.
6 Powle (1678), p. 932; Waller (1686), p. 27.
7 Reynolds (1812), p. 10.
8 Berger MSS., letter book, p. 135.

9 Pincot [*c.* 1811], p. 31; Vanherman (1828), p. 6.
10 Tingry (1830), p. 74.
11 Hill (1746), p. 122 (footnote f).
12 Berger MSS., stock 1809–10, p. 5.
13 John Smith (1687), p. 22.
14 Plot (1677), pp. 55–7.
15 Osterley MSS., Burchett (1779); Burchett (1780); Burchett (1781a).
16 Soane MSS., 'Ealing'.
17 Pincot [*c.* 1811], pp. 8, 28.
18 Butcher (1825), pp. 30, 34.
19 Berger MSS., stock 1801–2, p. 49; Phillips (1812), p. 212; (1821), p. 170.
20 Crease (n.d.), p. 28.
21 Nicholson (1825), p. 412; Nicholson (1819), s.v. 'PAINTING, *Economical*', vol. II, p. 417.
22 Berger MSS., stock 1801–2, p. 46; stock 1805–6, p. 31; stock 1809–10, pp. 2, 3.
23 Berger MSS., stock 1809–10, p. 5; Vanherman (1828), pp. 7, 8.
24 Berger MSS., stock 1801–2, pp. 49, 56; stock 1805–6, pp. 10, 18; stock 1809–10, pp. 10, 18.
25 John Smith (1676), p. 22; (1687), p. 22.
26 Harley (1970), pp. 82–3; Tingry (1830), p. 74.
27 Op. cit., No. 128 (1697).
28 Harley (1970), pp. 83–4.
29 Berger MSS., letter book, p. 249; stock 1801–2, p. 51; stock 1805–6, pp. 1, 13; stock 1809–10, pp. 6, 11, 12.
30 Caylus (1755), p. 94.
31 Rondelet (1812–n.d.), vol. V, p. 221.
32 Watin (1785), pp. 42, 43, 45; Tingry (1804), pp. 394, 395, 397, 398; (1816), pp. 275, 276, 278, 279; Harley (1970), p. 83.
33 Boughton MS., vol. III, p. 158.
34 Berger MSS., letter book, pp. 29, 30.
35 Whittock (1827), pp. 56–7.
36 Caylus (1755), p. 94.
37 Berger MSS., stock 1801–2, p. 56; stock 1805–6, p. 26; stock 1809–10, p. 20.
38 Harley (1970), p. 83.
39 Dossie (1758), vol. I, p. 100; (1764), vol. I, p. 107; Watin (1785), p. 34.
40 Whittock (1827), pp. 19, 38, 55–61 *passim*; Butcher (1825), p. 32; Vanherman (1828), p. 30; Nicholson (1834), pp. 160–1.
41 Whittock (1827), p. 12.
42 Osterley MSS., Burchett (1780).
43 Berger MSS., letter book, p. 249; stock 1801–2, pp. 47, 51, 56; stock 1805–6, pp. 5, 19; stock 1809–10, p. 16.
44 Berger MSS., stock 1801–2, p. 44; stock 1805–6, p. 5; stock 1809–10, pp. 2, 6.
45 1 Jac. I, c. 20.
46 Vanherman (1828), p. 29.
47 Pincot [*c.* 1811], p. 8; Tingry (1830), p. 273.
48 P.R.O. MSS., E. 351/3253, M. vii^r^.
49 Stalker and Parker (1688/1971), p. 70.
50 Berger MSS., letter book, p. 249; stock 1801–2, p. 58; stock 1805–6, p. 13; stock 1809–10, p. 14.
51 Stapleton & *al.* (1975), p. 57.
52 Soane MSS., 'Ealing'; Tredegar MSS., 68/76.
53 Stapleton & *al.* (1975), p. 57; Soane MSS., 'Ealing'.
54 Boughton MS., vol. III, p. 158.
55 Phillips (1812), p. 212; (1821), p. 170.
56 Harley (1970), p. 89.
57 Church (1892), p. 143.
58 Berger MSS., stock 1809–10, p. 19; second experimental notebook, p. 6 (formula headed 'York Brown from Martin Bentzing George Gardens Bethnal Green Road'); 1831 formula book, p. 163.
59 In connection with pigments of this type, it is worth bearing in mind that they were often prepared *in situ* as part of the process known as 'fresco' practised during the early nineteenth century for the colouring of exterior stucco. The method was mentioned by Martin ((1831), p. 490) and Nicholson ((1823–5), p. 137), and is discussed in Chapter 20 (see too Bristow (1980)).
60 Hill (1746), pp. 103–4 (footnote r), p. 121 (footnote o).
61 Dossie (1758), vol. I, pp. 90–1, 98; (1764), vol. I, pp. 97–8, 105.
62 Watin (1785), pp. 36–7.
63 Tingry (1804), p. 358; (1816), p. 238.
64 Op. cit. (1825), p. 98.
65 Butcher (1825), p. 2.
66 Dossie (1758), vol. I, p. 90; (1764), vol. I, p. 97.
67 John Smith (1687), p. 23.
68 Vanherman (1828), p. 26.
69 Harley (1970), p. 87.
70 Watin (1785), pp. 36–7, 42–3.
71 Tingry (1804), p. 396; (1816), p. 277.
72 Tingry (1804), p. 397; (1816), pp. 278–9.
73 Op. cit. (1825), p. 105.
74 Berger MSS., stock 1801–2, pp. 56, 57; stock 1805–6, pp. 25, 27; stock 1809–10, pp. 19, 20.
75 Berger MSS., letter book, pp. 29, 30; stock lists, *ut supra*. Other early nineteenth-century prices noted are those given by Phillips, his orange orpiment and king's yellow relating unusually well to those of Berger's stock at between 1*s.* 10*d.* and 2*s.* 5*d.*, and 7*s.* and 8*s.* 8*d.* per lb. respectively; although the price of 6*s.* given for yellow orpiment is rather higher (Phillips (1812), p. 212; (1821), pp. 170, 171). Stalker & Parker ((1688/1971), p. 71) gave a price of 2*d.* per oz. (equivalent to 2*s.* 8*d.* per lb.) for red orpiment.
76 Whittock (1827), pp. 60, 132, 133.
77 Ibid., p. 12; Dossie (1758), vol. I, p. 90; (1764), vol. I, p. 97.
78 Merrifield (1849), vol. I, pp. clvi–clxiii; Harley (1982), pp. 95–6.
79 Waller (1686), p. 27.
80 Kühn (1968), pp. 20–30; Feller & *al.* (1986), p. 223b.
81 John Smith (1687), pp. 93, 94.
82 Stalker & Parker (1688/1971), p. 71.
83 V.A.M. MSS., L. 1774–1935, f. 62^r^.
84 John Smith (1687), pp. 23, 93, 94.
85 Dossie (1758), vol. I, p. 97; (1764), vol. I, p. 104.
86 Watin (1785), p. 37.
87 Tingry (1804), pp. 344–6; (1816), pp. 226–7.
88 Martin (1813), p. 461; Nicholson (1823–5), pp. 412, 415; Butcher (1825), p. 15 (his suggestion for roasting flake white probably emanating from Watin's *teinte-dure* (Watin (1785), p. 97)); Ure (1839), s.v. 'MASSICOT', p. 802.
89 Phillips (1812), p. 212; (1821), p. 170.
90 Nicholson (1819), s.v. 'PAINTING, *Economical*', vol. II, p. 417; *Painter's . . . Pocket Manual* (1825), p. 106.
91 Berger MSS., stock 1801–2, p. 56.
92 Harley (1970), p. 86.
93 Courtauld MS., p. 369.
94 Field (1835), p. 79.
95 Piccolpasso (1934), pp. 33, 37, 47.
96 Feller & *al.* (1986), pp. 219–23.
97 Ibid., p. 230.
98 Félibien (1676), p. 400.
99 Caylus (1755), p. 93.
100 For translation of 'antimoine diaphorétique', see Feller & *al.* (1986), p. 234, notes c and e.
101 Fougeroux de Bondaroy (1766), pp. 60–4, 303–14.
102 Tingry (1804), pp. 320–1; (1816), pp. 203–5.
103 Mérimée (1839), pp. 100–1. Curiously, both Tingry and Mérimée give the date of Fougeroux de Bondaroy's paper as 1772, but there does not appear to be anything further by him on the same subject in the *Histoire de l'Académie* in that or the intervening years since 1766.
104 Feller & *al.* (1986), pp. 232–3.
105 Dossie (1758), vol. I. pp. 91–2; (1764), vol. I, pp. 98–9.
106 Church (1892), p. 144.
107 Hurst (1896), p. 153.
108 Watin (1785), pp. 26, 42–3.
109 Tingry (1804), pp. 395–7; (1816), pp. 276–8.
110 Op. cit. (1825), p. 106.
111 Osterley MSS., Thorogood (1774); Burchett (1775); Burchett (1779); Burchett (1780).

112 Bristow MSS., notes, C. 104A.
113 Osterley MSS., Adamson (1772–4).
114 Willis & Clarke (1886), vol. II, p. 42.
115 Gordon Castle MS., p. 7.
116 Berger MSS., stock 1801–2, p. 57; stock 1805–6, p. 27; stock 1809–10, p. 19.
117 Phillips (1812), p. 212; (1821), p. 170.
118 Martin (1813), pp. 462, 464; Nicholson (1823–5), pp. 412, 414; Nicholson (1834), p. 160.
119 Butcher (1825), p. 2.
120 Whittock (1827); Vanherman (1828).
121 Harley (1970), pp. 91–2.
122 Patent No. 1281 (1781).
123 Chaptal (Paris, 1807), vol. IV, p. 309; (London, 1807), vol. IV, pp. 317–18.
124 Mérimée (1839), pp. 96–7.
125 Courtauld MS., p. 357.
126 Tingry (1804), pp. 322–3; (1816), pp. 205–6.
127 Lelièvre & *al.* (1794), pp. 129–31.
128 Tingry (1804), pp. 322–3; (1816), pp. 205–7.
129 Field (1835), p. 78.
130 Butcher (1825), pp. 10, 30, 31.
131 Nicholson (1825), pp. 411, 412.
132 Pincot [*c.* 1811], p. 28.
133 Vanherman (1828), p. 29.
134 Osterley MSS., Adamson (1787).
135 Bristow MSS., notes, C. 83.
136 Harpur-Crewe MS.
137 Vanherman (1828), p. 29.
138 Brighton/Crace MS., p. 6.
139 Soane Museum MSS., Crace (1807).
140 Bristow MSS., reports, Soane Museum (1986a & b).
141 Vanherman (1828), p. 26.
142 Laxton (1818), p. 96; Skyring (1831), p. 88.
143 Vanherman (1828), p. 29. In 1788 Berger was offering patent yellow at 1*s.* per lb., but in 1802 had only a small stock of just over $\frac{1}{2}$ cwt. valued at £5 per cwt. By 1806, however, this had risen to a total of nearly $17\frac{1}{2}$ cwt., although the price had fallen to 72*s.* per cwt.; in 1810 he had over $31\frac{1}{4}$ cwt. in stock valued at 70s. per cwt. together with more than $4\frac{1}{4}$ cwt. of 'Bad' pigment at 28*s.* (Berger MSS., letter book, p. 249; stock 1801–2, p. 48; stock 1805–6, pp. 6, 31; stock 1809–10, p. 18.) In 1803 Soane settled an account for the supply of various pigments including 1 lb. of patent yellow at 1*s.* 6*d.* and 1 lb. of the same ground into oil at 2*s.* (Soane MSS., 'Ealing'); and Phillips quoted a price of 2*s.* 5*d.* per lb. in 1812, reducing this slightly to 2*s.* 3*d.* in 1821 (Phillips (1812), p. 212; (1821), p. 170).
144 Tingry (1830), pp. 107–8.
145 Hurst (1896), p. 152.
146 Vauquelin (1797); Vauquelin (1798); Harley (1970), p. 93.
147 Vauquelin (1809), pp. 71, 93–4.
148 Feller & *al.* (1986), p. 188b.
149 Hibbert (1821).
150 Davy (1815), p. 122.
151 Harley (1979), pp. 78–80, 82–3.
152 Harley (1970), pp. 92–3.
153 Brighton/Crace MS., pp. 94, 106.
154 Berger MSS., second experimental notebook, pp. 3, 9; 'Lake & Carmine Book', p. 408; 1831 formula book, pp. 171–81, 225, 226.
155 Hurst (1896), p. 135.
156 Vanherman (1828), pp. 28–9, 38, 87, 89. His instructions for manufacture of the pigment are as follows:

> To one pound of chromate of iron, dissolved in warm water (two gallons), add two pounds of white lead, ground in water; stir and mix it up well, and throw in one pound of sugar of lead [lead acetate]; stir all up again and suffer to precipitate, and then you will obtain a deep chrome, which may be put on the filter and afterwards dried.

157 Tingry (1830), pp. 107–8.
158 Harley (1970), pp. 93–4.
159 Op. cit. [*c.* 1830], p. 33.
160 Nicholson (1834), p. 155.
161 Whittock (1827), pp. 21, 22, 38.

5. Organic yellow pigments and dyestuffs

1 Harley (1970), pp. 97–8.
2 Dossie (1758), vol. I, pp. 111–12; (1764), vol. I, pp. 119–20.
3 John Smith (1687), p. 41.
4 Stalker & Parker (1688/1971), p. 63; Tingry (1804), pp. 358–9; (1816), pp. 239–40; Vanherman (1828), p. 77.
5 Tingry (1804), p. 365; (1816), p. 246.
6 James Smith (1815), p. 734.
7 Berger MSS., 'Lake & Carmine Book', pp. 149, 320.
8 Heaton (1940), p. 186.
9 Harley (1970), pp. 103–4.
10 Berger MSS., 'Lake & Carmine Book', p. 400. In 1824, however, it is recorded that the firm had 'bo[t]. fine Bark at 11/6 duty paid', and in 1825 the price of the latter is given as 12*s.* per cwt. (ibid., pp. 400, 402). Prices found in Lewis Berger's stock-books covering the first decade of the century (which also show considerable fluctuations in the quantities he possessed) are sometimes much higher than these. Thus, for example, in 1802 he had 5 cwt. 'Bark' valued at 35*s.* per cwt., but in 1810 valued his stock of nearly 10 cwt. at 59*s.* In 1806, however, he had nearly 364 cwt. of 'Quercitron Bark' at the lower price of 17*s.* per cwt. together with another 77 cwt. at 18*s.* (Berger MSS., stock 1801–2, p. 63; stock 1805–6, pp. 20, 35; stock 1809–10, p. 37).
11 Berger MSS., 'Lake & Carmine Book', p. 196. For variations on names quoted see also, e.g. ibid., pp. 113, 199, 310, 335, 402.
12 Stalker & Parker (1688/1971), p. 63.
13 Ure (1860), vol. III, s.v. 'SAFFRON', p. 618.
14 Dossie (1758), vol. I, p. 94; (1764), vol. I, p. 101.
15 Stalker & Parker (1688/1971), p. 63; Vanherman (1828), p. 77.
16 Watin (1785), pp. 26, 69.
17 Rondelet (1812–n.d.), vol. V, p. 222.
18 *Painter's . . . Manual* [*c.* 1830], p. 36.
19 Tingry (1803), vol. II, p. 106; (1804), p. 363; (1816), pp. 244, 245.
20 Berger MSS., stock 1801–2, p. 63; stock 1805–6, p. 32; stock 1809–10, p. 36.
21 Dossie (1758), vol. I, pp. 94–6; (1764), vol. I, pp. 101–3; James Smith (1815), p. 734.
22 Watin (1785), p. 27; Tingry (1804), p. 364; (1816), p. 244.
23 Rondelet (1812–n.d.), vol. V., p. 222.
24 Berger MSS., stock 1801–2, p. 56; stock 1805–6, p. 18; stock 1809–10, p. 12.
25 Berger MSS., 'Lake & Carmine Book', p. 334.
26 Ibid., pp. 208, 320, 334, 531.
27 Berger MSS., stock 1809–10, p. 12.
28 Berger MSS., 1831 formula book, p. 65.
29 Berger MSS., 'Lake & Carmine Book', p. 313; 1831 formula book, pp. 65, 139.
30 Berger MSS., stock 1801–2, p. 63; stock 1805–6, p. 32.
31 Stalker & Parker (1688/1971), p. 70.
32 John Smith (1676), p. 23; (1687), pp. 23, 52.
33 Dossie (1758), vol. I, p. 94; (1764), vol. I, p. 101.
34 Watin (1785), pp. 27, 44.
35 Tingry (1804), pp. 363–6, 405; (1816), pp. 244–7, 286–7. 'Woad' on the first group of pages in each edition is a mistranslation of *gaude* (weld) in the first edition (1803), vol. II, p. 106.
36 Berger MSS., 'Lake & Carmine Book', pp. 113, 133, 134, 148, 149, 202, 203, 320–1, 324, 402–3, 531.
37 Ibid., pp. 201, 316, 404–5, 538.
38 See note 94 to Chapter 1.
39 Berger MSS., 'Lake & Carmine Book', pp. 206, 330. Phillips referred to '[Dutch pink] and part masticot', perhaps suggesting a similar combination (Phillips (1812), p. 212; (1821), p. 170).
40 Berger MSS., 'Lake & Carmine Book', pp. 202, 321, 402.
41 Berger MSS., 1831 formula book, pp. 67, 139–41.

42 Berger MSS., stock 1801–2, pp. 49, 56, 63; stock 1805–6, pp. 14, 31; stock 1809–10, pp. 25, 37.
43 Berger MSS., stock 1801–2, p. 56; stock 1805–6, pp. 25, 30; stock 1809–10, p. 20.
44 Berger MSS., stock 1801–2, p. 48; stock 1805–6, p. 8; stock 1809–10, p. 6.
45 Berger MSS., letter book, pp. 19, 24, 29, 30, 249.
46 Stapleton & *al.* (1975), p. 58.
47 Phillips (1812), p. 212; (1821), p. 170.
48 Dossie (1758), vol. I, p. 94; (1764), vol. I, p. 101.
49 Nicholson (1819), s.v. 'PAINTING, *Economical*', vol. II, p. 417.
50 Pincot [*c.* 1811], p. 22.
51 Whittock (1827), p. 12.
52 Butcher (1825), p. 31.
53 Stalker & Parker (1688/1971), p. 26; Dossie (1758), vol. I, p. 95; (1764), vol. I, pp. 101–2.
54 Dossie (1758), vol. I, pp. 95–6; (1764). vol. I, pp. 102–3.
55 Op. cit. (1795), p. 39.
56 Martin (1813), p. 461; Nicholson (1823–5), p. 415.
57 Tingry (1830), p. 149.
58 Berger MSS., 'Lake & Carmine Book', pp. 204, 326, 400–1.
59 Berger MSS., 1831 formula book, p. 143.
60 Berger MSS., letter book, pp. 19, 24, 29, 30, 249.
61 Berger MSS., stock 1801–2, pp. 47, 61, 62, 63, 64; stock 1805–6, pp. 23, 29; stock 1809–10, p. 26.
62 Pincot [*c.* 1811], p. 22.
63 Butcher (1825), p. 31.
64 Berger MSS., 'Lake & Carmine Book', pp. 132, 318; 1831 formula book, p. 69.
65 Neri (1662), p. 334.
66 Berger MSS., 'Lake & Carmine Book', p. 193 (typical formula).
67 Ibid., pp. 69, 113, 196, 197, 308, 472, 310, 312–13; 1831 formula book, pp. 63, 65.
68 Berger MSS., letter book, pp. 29, 30.
69 Berger MSS., stock 1801–2, pp. 56, 59; stock 1805–6, p. 21; stock 1809–10, p. 23.
70 Berger MSS., 1831 formula book, pp. 63, 65.
71 Brighton/Crace MS., p. 6.
72 Stalker & Parker (1688/1971), p. 70; Dossie (1758), vol. I, p. 115; (1764), vol. I, p. 123.
73 Berger MSS., 'Lake & Carmine Book', pp. 127, 133, 208, 335.
74 Berger MSS., stock 1801–2, p. 59; stock 1805–6, p. 21; stock 1809–10, p. 23.
75 Berger MSS., 'Lake & Carmine Book', pp. 148, 198, 335.
76 Martin (1813), p. 462; Nicholson (1823–5), pp. 412, 415.
77 Rondelet (1812–n.d.), vol. v., p. 222; Phillips (1812), p. 213; (1821), p. 171.
78 Soane MSS., 'Ealing'.
79 Whittock (1827), pp. 8–13.
80 Dossie (1758), vol. I, pp. 111–12; (1764), vol. I, pp. 119–20; Martin (1813), p. 461; Nicholson (1823–5), pp. 412, 415.
81 Berger MSS., 'Lake & Carmine Book', p. 81.
82 Berger MSS., stock 1801–2, p. 59.

6. Inorganic red pigments

1 Powle (1678), p. 932.
2 Hill (1746), p. 123 (footnote g).
3 Heaton (1940), p. 116.
4 I.G.S. samples Nos. MI. 14685–6 (Crawshay red, St Annal's Mine); 14853–4 (Robin Hood Mine); 16055–7 (Highmeadow Mine, near Coleford).
5 Hill (1746), p. 125 (footnote h).
6 Waller (1686), p. 28.
7 Tingry (1830), p. 74.
8 Heaton (1940), p. 116; I.G.S. samples Nos. MI. 24256–7 (Wick); 8483, 14687–8 (Winford).
9 Heaton (1940), p. 117.
10 Hurst (1896), p. 116. He gave also (ibid.) an assay of a sample of red chalk from Speeton, Yorkshire; while Church (1892, p. 169) mentioned Hunstanton, Norfolk, as a source of this material. Ure ((1860), s.v. 'REDDLE OR RED CHALK', vol. III, p. 574) mentioned the employment of such substances for marking sheep in some of the western counties; while a fine variety found near Rotherham, Yorkshire, was, he stated, used in grinding spectacle lenses at Sheffield. There seems no especial reason to assume, therefore, that Berger's stocks of, for example, nearly $16\frac{3}{4}$ cwt. of 'Cutt Red Chalk' in 1802 valued at 25*s.* per cwt. or his stocks of nearly $1\frac{1}{2}$ cwt. in 1810 valued at 55*s.* per cwt. imply that the substance was used in house-painting (Berger MSS., stock 1801–2, p. 51; stock 1809–10, p. 11).
11 I.G.S. samples Nos. MI. 32161 (Scandalbeck, nr. Crosby Garth, Westmoreland (now part of Cumbria); 27386 (Burley Ironstone Pit, near Oakham, Rutland (now Leicestershire)); 32720 (Co. Antrim).
12 Dossie (1758), vol. I, p. 50; (1764), vol. I, p. 53; I.G.S. sample No. MI. 14683.
13 Church (1892), p. 167.
14 Nicholson (1823–5), p. 413; Nicholson (1834), p. 157.
15 Berger MSS., stock 1805–6, p. 23.
16 Merrifield (1849), p. clxx.
17 Heaton (1940), p. 120.
18 Dossie (1758), vol. I, p. 52; (1764), vol. I, pp. 54–5.
19 Soane MSS., Martin, loose ff. inserted between pp. 133, 134, f. [2]^{r}.
20 Heaton (1940), p. 117.
21 John Smith (1676), p. 14.
22 PRO. MSS., C. 66/2357/3.
23 Ibid., E. 351/3253, M. xiv^{v}.
24 No. 1996 (1794).
25 Dossie (1758), vol. I, p. 52; (1764), vol. I, p. 55; Whittock (1827), p. 10; Tingry (1830), p. 73.
26 Berger MSS., stock 1805–6, p. 18.
27 Dossie (1758), vol. I, pp. 52, 118–19; (1764), vol. I, pp. 55, 127; Stalker & Parker (1688/1971), p. 70.
28 Watin (1785), pp. 42, 45; Tingry (1804), p. 409; (1816), p. 290.
29 Berger MSS., stock 1801–2, p. 53.
30 Hurst (1896), p. 108; Church (1892), p. 169.
31 Hill (1746), p. 103 (footnote q).
32 Ibid., p. 129 (footnote k).
33 Tingry (1830), p. 73.
34 Waller (1686), p. 27.
35 Hill (1746), pp. 129–30 (footnote l).
36 Reynolds (1812), p. 18; Dossie (1758), vol. I, p. 66; (1764), vol. I, p. 69; Martin (1813), p. 461; Nicholson (1823–5), p. 414; Whittock (1827), p. 11.
37 Watin (1785), p. 22.
38 Stalker & Parker (1688/1971), p. 70; Dossie (1758), vol. I, pp. 52, 391; (1764), vol. I, pp. 55, 427–8.
39 Berger MSS., stock 1801–2, p. 57.
40 Dossie (1758), vol. I, p. 53; (1764), vol. I, p. 56; Rondelet (1812–n.d.), vol. v, p. 222.
41 Berger MSS., stock 1801–2, p. 57; stock 1805–6, p. 27; stock 1809–10, p. 19.
42 Butcher (1825), p. 31; Whittock (1827), pp. 55–7 *passim*; Vanherman (1828), pp. 30, 61; Nicholson (1834), pp. 160–1 *passim*; Soane MSS., 'Ealing'.
43 Lomazzo (1598), p. 99.
44 Dossie (1758), vol. I, pp. 49–51; (1764), vol. I, pp. 51–4.
45 Op. cit. (1795), p. 41.
46 Watin (1785), p. 22.
47 Colwall (1678).
48 Pozzo (1693–1700), vol. II.
49 Tingry (1804), pp. 354–5; (1816), pp. 235–6; Ure (1839), s.v. 'SULPHATE OF IRON', p. 1214.
50 Rondelet (1812–n.d.), vol. v, p. 221; Watin (1785), pp. 22–3.
51 Tingry (1804), p. 356; (1816), p. 237.
52 No. 1996 (1794).
53 Berger MSS., stock 1801–2, pp. 45, 46, 47, 48, 50; stock 1805–6, pp. 9, 18, 19, 27, 31; stock 1809–10, pp. 4, 5, 10.
54 Ure described a method used to separate the dross containing iron from Cornish copper ore (Ure (1860), s.v. 'COPPER', vol. I,

pp. 821–3), and Atkinson may well have been using the former for his process. At the end of the century, Hurst remarked that the use of Spanish cupreous pyrites in the manufacture of sulphuric acid, and the extended use of wet processes for extraction of the copper from the residual oxide after the sulphur had been burnt off, had placed at the disposal of the colour-maker new and cheap sources of waste iron liquors (Hurst (1896), p. 114).

55 Berger MSS., letter book, p. 249; stock 1801–2, p. 47; stock 1805–6, pp. 13, 31; stock 1809–10, pp. 8, 9.
56 1 Jac. I, c. 20.
57 John Smith (1676), pp. 14, 15; (1687), p. 21.
58 Leyburn (1700), p. 71; Dossie (1758), vol. I, p. 52; (1764), vol. I, p. 55.
59 Op. cit. (1808), pp. 11–12.
60 Vanherman (1828), pp. 10, 15, 16.
61 Berger MSS., stock 1801–2, pp. 45, 46; stock 1805–6, pp. 19, 31; stock 1809–10, p. 5.
62 Berger MSS., stock 1801–2, p. 55; stock 1805–6, p. 11; stock 1809–10, p. 14.
63 Reynolds (1812), p. 12.
64 Vanherman (1828), pp. 28, 38–9.
65 Dossie (1758), vol. I, p. 52; (1764), vol. I, p. 55; Whittock (1827), pp. 34, 52, 55, 64.
66 Berger MSS., stock 1801–2, pp. 47, 48, 50; stock 1805–6, pp. 9, 27; stock 1809–10, pp. 4, 10.
67 Berger MSS., stock 1801–2, p. 55; stock 1809–10, p. 14.
68 Phillips (1812), pp. 213, 214; Soane MSS., 'Ealing'.
69 Tredegar MSS., 68/76.
70 Nicholson (1825), pp. 411, 412.
71 Reynolds (1812), p. 19; Whittock (1827), pp. 36, 37, 42, 50, 52, 54, 57, 64.
72 Phillips (1812), p. 214; (1821), p. 172.
73 Ibid.
74 Nicholson (1819), s.v. 'PAINTING, *Economical*', vol. II, p. 417.
75 Greninger & *al.* [1975], p. 70.
76 Vitruvius, *l.* 7, *c.* XII ((1826), p. 223).
77 John Smith (1687), p. 21; Ray (1674), p. 138.
78 Campbell (1747), p. 107; Watson (1781–8), vol. III (1782), pp. 338, 339.
79 Cennini, cc. 41, 72 ((1844), pp. 25, 47; (1930), pp. 35, 67).
80 1 Jac. I, c. 20; Dossie (1758), vol. I, pp. 47–8; (1764), vol. I, p. 50; Watin (1785), p. 37.
81 Whittock (1827), p. 10.
82 Dossie (1758), vol. I, pp. 47–8; (1764), vol. I, p. 50; Whittock (1827), p. 10.
83 John Smith (1687), p. 21.
84 Vanherman (1828), p. 29.
85 John Smith (1687), p. 21.
86 Nicholson (1834), p. 154; Bartholomew (1846), para. 1931.
87 Dossie (1758), vol. I, p. 48; (1764), vol. I, p. 50.
88 Tingry (1804), pp. 346, 408; (1816), pp. 228, 289; Pincot [*c.* 1811], p. 26; Vanherman (1828), p. 29.
89 Reynolds (1812), p. 19.
90 Vanherman (1828), p. 29.
91 Watin (1785), pp. 37, 42.
92 Tingry (1804), p. 346; (1816), p. 228; Reynolds (1812), pp. 10, 17; Nicholson (1825), p. 411.
93 Reynolds (1812), p. 10.
94 John Smith (1687), p. 52; Nicholson (1825), p. 412.
95 Tingry (1804), p. 398; (1816), p. 278; Watin (1785), p. 42; Butcher (1825), p. 30.
96 Butcher (1825), p. 31.
97 Rondelet (1812–n.d.), vol. V, p. 221. In England red lead is also sometimes known as *minium*, but this can be a source of confusion since Pliny had applied the term primarily to vermilion, calling red lead *secundarium minium* (Pliny, *l.* 33 ((1938–62), vol. IX (1952), pp. 84–95). This is discussed more fully by Harley ((1970), pp. 112–13).
98 Berger MSS., stock 1801–2, pp. 54, 57; stock 1805–6, pp. 24, 25; stock 1809–10, pp. 20, 27.
99 Hurst (1896), p. 106.
100 Vanherman (1828), p. 29.
101 Chester MS.; Boughton MS., vol. III, p. 158; Soane MSS., 'Ealing'. As usual, the prices given by Phillips are rather higher than those found elsewhere for red lead, being at rates of 7½*d.* per lb. ((1812), p. 214) and 7*d.* per lb. ((1821), p. 172).
102 Ure (1860), s.v. 'CINNABAR', vol. I, p. 689.
103 Leuchs (1829), vol. II, p. 121.
104 Harley (1970), p. 115; Watin (1785), p. 23; Rondelet (1812–n.d.), vol. V, p. 221.
105 Hill (1746), p. 137 (footnote o).
106 John Smith (1687), p. 19; Dossie (1758), vol. I, pp. 42–3; (1764), vol. I, pp. 44–5.
107 Heaton (1940), p. 126.
108 Harley (1982), p. 127 (citing A.F.E. van Schendel, 'Manufacture of Vermilion in 17th-century Amsterdam: the Pekstok papers', *Conservation*, vol. XVII (1972), pp. 70–82).
109 Ure (1860), s.v. 'VERMILION', vol. III, pp. 965–6 (taken from Tuckert, 'Mémoire sur la fabrication du sulfure de mercure sublimé (cinnabre du commerce), à Amsterdam', *Annales de chimie*, vol. IV (1790), pp. 25–30).
110 Hurst (1896), pp. 96, 97–8 (citing *Oil and Colourman's Journal* (1883), p. 86; *Chemical News* (1884), vol. 50, p. 77).
111 Harley (1970), p. 116; (1982), p. 127.
112 Tingry (1804), p. 318; (1816), p. 202.
113 Nicholson (1834), p. 156.
114 Courtauld MS., pp. 310, 354.
115 Berger MSS., 'Lake & Carmine Book', p. 8.
116 Vanherman (1828), p. 27.
117 Dossie (1758), vol. I, p. 44; (1764), vol. I, p. 46; Butcher (1825), p. 9; Whittock (1827), p. 9; Vanherman (1828), p. 27.
118 Watin (1785), p. 23.
119 Leuchs (1829), vol. II, pp. 121–2.
120 Berger MSS., second experimental notebook, f. 14r.
121 Berger MSS., 1831 formula book, p. 151.
122 Stalker & Parker (1688/1971), p. 71.
123 Berger MSS., letter book, pp. 29, 30, 249.
124 Berger MSS., stock 1801–2, p. 57; stock 1805–6, p. 25; stock 1809–10, pp. 21, 36.
125 Berger MSS., stock 1801–2, p. 60; stock 1805–6, p. 23; stock 1809–10, p. 24. Although John Payne suggested that each packet of Chinese vermilion should weigh fourteen ounces (Payne (1798), p. 11), applying this to the valuations of Berger's stocks in the years mentioned above produces figures equivalent to 6*s.* 7*d.*, 11*s.* 6*d.*, and 5*s.* 2*d.* per lb. respectively. In view of these wide fluctuations it seems possible that the size of the packets may not have been constant. Furthermore, in the formula of 1787 to which n. 127 refers, the contents of ten 'papers' of Chinese vermilion are given as weighing 12¼ oz.
126 Phillips (1812), p. 214; (1821), p. 172.
127 Berger MSS., 'Lake & Carmine Book', p. 8.
128 Leuchs (1829), vol. II, p. 109; Kopp (1843–7), vol. IV, p. 187.
129 Gillespie (1970–80), vol. VII, p. 378; Zerr & Rübencamp (1908), p. 279.
130 Hurst (1896), p. 98 (citing *Chemical News*, vol. V (1862), p. 247).
131 Zerr & Rübencamp (1908), pp. 279–80.
132 Ure (1860), s.v. 'VERMILION', vol. III, p. 966.
133 Berger MSS., second experimental notebook, f. 27r.
134 Armitage (n.d.), pp. 18–19.
135 Stalker & Parker (1688/1971), p. 71; Tingry (1830), p. 273; Vanherman (1828), pp. 25–6.
136 Whittock (1827), p. 9.
137 Nicholson (1823–5), p. 413.
138 Pincot [*c.* 1811], p. 35.
139 John Smith (1687), p. 51.
140 Tingry (1804), p. 408; (1816), p. 289.
141 Reynolds (1812), p. 17; Nicholson (1825), p. 411; Pincot [*c.* 1811], p. 27.
142 Bristow MSS., reports, Soane Museum (1988), p. 5.
143 Buckler (1826), p. 3.
144 Vanherman (1828), pp. 27, 38.
145 John Smith (1687), p. 51.

146 Watin (1785), p. 42.
147 Nicholson (1819), s.v. 'PAINTING, *Economical*', vol. II, p. 417.
148 Vanherman (1828), p. 27.
149 Watin (1785), p. 42.
150 Butcher (1825), p. 30.
151 Op. cit. (1825), p. 106.
152 Butcher (1825), p. 30.
153 Reynolds (1812), p. 19; Whittock (1827), pp. 40, 44–6, 63–5.

7. Organic red pigments and dyestuffs

1 Feller & *al.* (1986), pp. 255–8.
2 Harley (1970), p. 203, n. 203.
3 *Shellac* (1965), pp. 10, 34, 85.
4 Harley (1970), p. 123.
5 Ibid., p. 124.
6 B.L. MSS., Sloane 3292, f. 6.
7 Berger MSS., stock 1801–2, p. 61; stock 1805–6, p. 32; stock 1809–10, pp. 35, 36.
8 Harley (1970), pp. 132–3.
9 B.L. MSS., Sloane 2052, f. 62.
10 Ure (1860), s.v. 'BRAZIL WOOD', vol. I, pp. 397–8.
11 Ibid., s.v. 'LOGWOOD', vol. II, p. 735.
12 23 Eliz. I, c. 9.
13 13 & 14 Car. II, c. 11, s. 26.
14 Berger MSS., stock 1805–6, p. 30. While it is possible that his stock of 3 tons 'Peach Wood' on 1 January 1802 (stock 1801–2, p. 44), valued at the equivalent of £16 per ton, may also have been of *H. campeacheanum*, this name too seems subject to considerable confusion; and Dossie ((1758), vol. I, pp. 64–5; (1764), vol. I, p. 68), for example, suggested the use of 'Campeachy (commonly called Peachy wood)' in making rose pink, using it mixed with an equal part of brasil wood. This suggests that he had a timber yielding red dye in mind.
15 Hurst (1896), p. 269.
16 Berger MSS., stock 1805–6, pp. 18, 35; stock 1809–10, pp. 13, 38; 'Lake & Carmine Book', p. 336.
17 Berger MSS., 1831 formula book, p. 73.
18 Harley (1970), pp. 127–32.
19 Berger MSS., stock 1805–6, p. 20; 1831 formula book, p. 55.
20 Ure (1860), s.v. 'CARTHAMUS, OR SAFFLOWER', vol. I, p. 624.
21 Tingry (1830), p. 140.
22 Watin (1785), p. 27.
23 John Smith (1687), p. 20; (1701), p. 20; (1705), p. 20; (1723), p. 20.
24 John Smith (1687), p. 20.
25 Harley (1970), p. 124, citing as an example B.S. MS. Sloane 6284, f. 109.
26 Dossie (1758), vol. I, p. 54; (1764), vol. I, p. 57.
27 Berger MSS., 'Lake & Carmine Book', *passim.*
28 Field (1835), p. 99; Ure (1860), s.v. 'CARMINE', vol. I, p. 618.
29 Berger MSS., 1831 formula book, pp. 1, 3, 5, 7.
30 Berger MSS., letter book, pp. 11, 24, 29, 30; stock 1801–2, pp. 58, 59; stock 1805–6, p. 22; stock 1809–10, pp. 24, 36.
31 Watin (1785), p. 24.
32 Waller (1686), p. 28.
33 Watin (1785), p. 24.
34 Dossie (1758), vol. I, p. 55; (1764), vol. I, p. 59.
35 Dossie (1758), vol. I, p. 57; (1764), vol. I, pp. 60–1.
36 Tingry (1804), pp. 332–3; (1816), p. 215.
37 Ure (1860), s.v. 'LAKES', vol. II, p. 632.
38 Berger MSS., 'Lake & Carmine Book', p. 193 (typical formula).
39 Ure (1860), s.v. 'CARMINE', vol. I, p. 618; Berger MSS., letter book, p. 115.
40 Berger MSS., 'Lake & Carmine Book', *passim.*
41 Berger MSS., 1831 formula book, pp. 9, 11, 13, 15, 17, 19, 21, 23, 25, 27, 29, 31, 33, 37, 39, 41, 45.
42 Berger MSS., letter book, pp. 19, 24, 29, 30; stock 1801–2, pp. 58, 59; stock 1805–6, pp. 22, 30, 36; stock 1809–10, pp. 23, 36. In 1802 he had in addition $4\frac{1}{2}$ lb. of 'Blood Lake' valued at 15*s.* per lb. (stock 1801–2, p. 59), and in this and the other years quoted had also a small stock of purple lake amounting to $4\frac{1}{2}$ lb. in 1802, just over 6 lb. in 1806, and just over 14 lb. in 1810 at prices ranging from 12*s.* to 8*s.* per lb. (stock 1801–2, p. 59; stock 1805–6, p. 21; stock 1809–10, p. 23). Although no details of the former are to be found in the Berger MSS., a formula of 1809 for the latter ('Lake & Carmine Book', p. 133) indicates that it was made from 'Carmine Grouts' left over from the preparation of carmine from cochineal, with the addition of sal ammoniac (ammonium chloride) and pearl ash.
43 Butcher (1825), p. 31; Nicholson (1825), p. 411.
44 Laxton (1818), p. 96.
45 Vanherman (1828), pp. 27–8; Nicholson (1825), p. 412.
46 Philadelphia (1986), pp. 42, 43 (n. 13).
47 Tingry (1804), p. 392; (1816), p. 273 (flaxen grey); Nicholson (1819), s.v. 'PAINTING, *Economical*', vol. II, p. 417 (grey, apricot, and peach); Butcher (1825), p. 30 (French grey); Vanherman (1828), pp. 38, 39 (French grey, lavender).
48 Vanherman (1828), pp. 60–1.
49 Whittock (1827), pp. 35–57 *passim.*
50 Ibid., p. 10; Dossie (1758), vol. I, pp. 54–65 *passim*; (1764), vol. I, pp. 57–69 *passim*; Tingry (1804), pp. 334–43 *passim*; (1816), pp. 216–19 *passim.*
51 Berger MSS., 'Lake & Carmine Book', pp. 131, 210, 336; 1831 formula book, p. 73. The 1831 formulation was as follows:

> 3 cwt. Nicaragua Wood cut into Chips boil 1$^{cwt.}$ at a time with ab^{t} 300 Galls Water for One Hour: draw off thro' a Wicker Sieve fill up again & boil for 1 hour & 20 minutes – draw that off & then put in a fresh 1^{cwt} Wood repeat the boiling as before till all is boil'd – Dissolve 1^{cwt}. 2 [qrs]. 11 [lb.] Alum in a Copper of Water & add to the liquor & stir well together This liquor must remain 5 Days before it is struck – when ready for striking take 2^{cwt}. 0 [qrs]. 20 [lb.] Whiting & wash thro' a 68 Sieve then let half the liquor down on it & stirr well: next day draw off upper liquor & let down the remaining half upon the precipitate & stirr well as before – next day draw off & fill out The Whiting must be put into soak 2 or 3 days before it is used or the Color will be full of specks.

Powder crimson lake and violet lake, which appear for the first time in the 1831 formula book (pp. 47, 49), were similar pigments produced from Nicaragua wood, but contained vermilion and Antwerp blue respectively. Their cost prices were 1*s.* $9\frac{1}{2}$*d.* and 1*s.* 9*d.* per lb.
52 Berger MSS., letter book, pp. 19, 24, 29, 30, 249; stock 1801–2, pp. 44, 61; stock 1805–6, pp. 29, 34; stock 1809–10, pp. 25, 36.
53 Harley (1970), p. 133.
54 P.R.O. MSS., E. 351/3250 (1615–16), Newmarket, M. xx^{r}; 3252 (1617–18), Whitehall, M. iv^{r}; Greenwich, M. ix^{r}; Richmond, M. xii^{r}; Nonsuch, M. xiv^{v}; Newmarket, M. xv^{v} ($1\frac{1}{2}$*d.*/lb.); 3252 (1619–20), Whitehall, M. iii^{v}; Old Palace of Westminster. M. iv^{v}; Greenwich, M. vii^{r}; 3257 (1623–4), Whitehall, M. v^{v}; Greenwich, M. x^{v}; 3258 (1624–25), Newmarket, M. xiv^{r}; 3259, Whitehall, M. vi^{v}; 3261 (1627–28), Whitehall, M. v^{v}; 3263 (1629–30), Whitehall, M. v^{r}; St James's, M. vii^{v}; Hampton Court, M. xv^{r}; 3265 (1631–2), Hampton Court, M. xvi^{v}; 3266 (1632–3), Tower of London, M. iii^{r}; Whitehall, M. iv^{v}; 3267 (1633–4), Whitehall, M. iv^{v}; Somerset House, M. viii^{v}; Greenwich M. ix^{v}; 3269 (1635–36), Tower of London, M. iii^{r}; Whitehall, M. iv^{r}; Hampton Court, M. xii^{r}; 3271 (1637–8), Greenwich, M. viii^{v}; AO. 1/2429/71 (1639–40), Greenwich, f. xi^{v}.
55 1 Jac. I, c. 20.
56 P.R.O. MSS., AO. 1/2422/49, f. xxvi^{r}.
57 Dossie (1758), vol. I, p. 64; (1764), vol. I, p. 68.
58 Tingry (1830), p. 149.
59 Vanherman (1828), pp. 28, 38, 39.
60 Whittock (1827), pp. 36–46 *passim.*
61 Nicholson (1834), p. 161.
62 Reynolds (1812), p. 17.
63 Field (1835), p. 101.
64 Tingry (1804), pp. 334–6; (1816), pp. 217–18; (1830), pp. 120–1; Vanherman (1828), p. 84.

65 Op. cit. [*c.* 1830], p. 30.
66 Berger MSS., first experimental notebook, f. 7^{v}; 1831 formula book, p. 55.

8. Brown pigments

1 Gunther (1928), p. 282.
2 I.G.S. samples Nos. MI. 14701–2.
3 John Smith (1687), p. 27.
4 Plot (1677), pp. 57–8. These included 'a gritty sort of *Umbers*, found in all parts of the *County* where there are Quarries of Stone: a courser kind of them . . . met with near *Witney*, and a somewhat finer at *Bladen* Quarry [this was used in leather-dressing]; . . . a much finer than either of the former . . . lately . . . taken up at *Waterperry*, in the ground, and near the House of . . . Sir *Thomas Curson*, of so rich and beautiful a colour, that perhaps it might better have been placed among the *Ochres*'.
5 Vanherman (1828), p. 7.
6 I.G.S. samples Nos. MI. 14703–4.
7 Hurst (1896), pp. 234, 236.
8 Nicholson (1819), s.v. 'UMBER', vol. II, p. 799.
9 Courtauld MS., p. 382; Church (1892), p. 213; Heaton (1940), p. 166.
10 Tingry (1830), p. 75.
11 Ham MSS., Gooderick's account.
12 Dyrham MSS., D. 1799, A 141.
13 John Smith (1687), p. 51.
14 Watin (1785), pp. 33, 45; Tingry (1804), p. 394; (1816), p. 275.
15 Reynolds (1812), p. 15.
16 Nicholson (1819), s.v. 'PAINTING, *Economical*', vol. II, p. 417.
17 Butcher (1825), p. 30.
18 Vanherman (1828), pp. 7, 30, 39, 85.
19 John Smith (1687), p. 52; Reynolds (1812), pp. 18–19, 20; Whittock (1827), pp. 21–55 *passim*; Vanherman (1828), p. 59.
20 John Smith (1687), p. 27.
21 Soane MSS., Martin, loose ff. inserted between pp. 133, 134.
22 1 Jac. I, c. 20.
23 Whittock (1827), p. 13.
24 Berger MSS., letter book, pp. 29, 30, 249; stock 1801–2, p. 46; stock 1805–6, pp. 7, 14; stock 1809–10, pp. 1, 10.
25 Vanherman (1828), p. 7.
26 Berger MSS., stock 1801–2, p. 56; stock 1805–6, p. 25; stock 1809–10, p. 19.
27 Boughton MS., vol. III, p. 158; Tredegar MSS., 68/76; Soane MSS., 'Ealing'.
28 Harley (1970), pp. 139–40.
29 Berger MSS., stock 1801–2, p. 60; stock 1805–6, p. 27; stock 1809–10, p. 20.
30 Whittock (1827), p. 132.
31 Soane MSS., Martin, loose ff. inserted between pp. 133, 134.
32 Whittock (1827), pp. 21–46 *passim*; Nicholson (1834), p. 160.
33 Martin (1813), p. 462; Nicholson (1823–5), pp. 412, 415; Dossie (1758), vol. I, pp. 9, 118; (1764), vol. I, pp. 9, 127.
34 Martin (1813), p. 462; Nicholson (1823–5), pp. 412, 415; Dossie (1758), vol. I, pp. 9, 117; (1764), vol. I, pp. 9, 125–6.
35 Phillips (1812), p. 213; (1821), p. 171.
36 Martin (1813), p. 462; Nicholson (1823–5), pp. 412, 416; Dossie (1758), vol. I, pp. 9, 120; (1764), vol. I, pp. 9, 129.

9. Black pigments

1 John Smith (1687), pp. 16–17.
2 Stalker & Parker (1688/1971), p. 21; Dossie (1758), vol. I, p. 129; (1764), vol. I, pp. 138–9.
3 Tingry (1830), p. 274.
4 Vanherman (1828), p. 30.
5 John Smith (1687), p. 17.
6 Watin (1785), p. 35.
7 Vanherman (1828), p. 30.
8 D'Aviler (1691), s.v. 'COULEURS', vol. II, p. 514; Bullet (1691), p. 284.
9 Pincot [*c.* 1811], pp. 10–11; Tingry (1804), p. 388; (1816), p. 269.
10 Berger MSS., stock 1801–2, p. 46; stock 1805–6, p. 17; stock 1809–10, p. 16.
11 Stapleton & *al.* (1975), p. 58.
12 Soane MSS., 'Ealing'.
13 Tredegar MSS., 68/76.
14 Phillips (1812), p. 213; (1821), p. 171.
15 Watin (1785), p. 36; Tingry (1804), p. 347; (1816), p. 229.
16 Reynolds (1812), pp. 12, 15.
17 Ibid., pp. 17, 18.
18 Butcher (1825), p. 31; Tingry (1830), p. 275.
19 John Smith (1687), p. 51; Nicholson (1823–5), p. 416; Bullet (1691), p. 285; Reynolds (1812), p. 12; Watin (1785), p. 41.
20 Whittock (1827), pp. 52, 60.
21 D'Aviler (1691), vol. I, p. 228.
22 Tingry (1804), p. 350; (1816), p. 232.
23 John Smith (1687), p. 18; Butcher (1825), p. 8; Whittock (1827), p. 9.
24 Dossie (1758), vol. I, p. 130; (1764), vol. I, p. 139.
25 Watin (1785), p. 36; Hurst (1896), pp. 255, 258.
26 Berger MSS., letter book, pp. 11, 19, 24, 29, 30, 249; stock 1801–2, p. 45; stock 1805–6, pp. 11, 31; stock 1809–10, p. 6.
27 Berger MSS., 'Lake & Carmine Book', p. 406; 1831 formula book, p. 159.
28 Berger MSS., stock 1809–10, p. 33.
29 References as n. 26 to this chapter.
30 D'Aviler (1691), vol. I, p. 228; Nicholson (1819), s.v. 'PAINTING, *Economical*', vol. II, p. 417.
31 Watin (1785), p. 34.
32 Church (1892), p. 222.
33 John Smith (1676), p. 14; (1687), p. 18.
34 D'Aviler (1691), vol. I, p. 228.
35 Watin (1785), pp. 35, 41.
36 Dossie (1758), vol. I, p. 131; (1764), vol. I, p. 141.
37 Watin (1785), p. 35.
38 Tingry (1804), pp. 349–50; (1816), p. 231.
39 Vanherman (1828), p. 40.
40 Watin (1785), p. 36.
41 Tingry (1804), p. 349; (1816), p. 231; (1830), p. 133.
42 Berger MSS., stock 1801–2, pp. 47, 56; stock 1805–6, p. 6; stock 1809–10, p. 10.
43 Berger MSS., 'Lake & Carmine Book', p. 407; 1831 formula book, p. 161.
44 Vanherman (1828), p. 78.
45 Berger MSS., stock 1801–2, p. 46; stock 1805–6, p. 17; stock 1809–10, p. 9.
46 Berger MSS., letter book, pp. 11, 19, 24, 29, 30, 249.
47 Stalker & Parker (1688/1971), p. 71. The price, 3*d.* per oz., seems high for pigment destined for use in house-painting, as also (in common with those he gave for many other pigments) are those mentioned by Phillips of between 1*s.* and 1*s.* 10*d.* per lb. ((1812), p. 213; (1821), p. 171).
48 Berger MSS., stock 1801–2, p. 55.
49 Tingry (1804), p. 348; (1816), p. 230.
50 Vanherman (1828), p. 85.
51 Nicholson (1819), s.v. 'PAINTING, *Economical*', vol. II, p. 417; Nicholson (1825), p. 407.
52 Tredegar MSS., 68/76.
53 Vanherman (1828), p. 30.
54 Bristow MSS., thesis (1983), vol. II, p. 830.
55 Nicholson (1834), p. 161.
56 John Smith (1676), p. 14.
57 Vanherman (1828), pp. 6–16 *passim*.
58 Field (1835), p. 181.
59 Courtauld MS., p. 324.
60 Remington [1946], pp. 158–9.
61 Heaton (1940), p. 180.
62 Plot (1686), p. 124.
63 Phillips (1812), p. 213; (1821), p. 171.
64 Tingry (1830), p. 83.

65 Ure (1860), s.v. 'WADD', vol. III, p. 975.
66 Heaton (1940), p. 166.
67 Vanherman (1828), p. 91; Tingry (1830), pp. 83–4.

10. Driers, drying oils, and their preparation for use

1 Heaton (1940), p. 203.
2 Berger MSS., stock 1801–2, p. 57; stock 1805–6, p. 24; stock 1809–10, p. 20; Evelyn (1670), p. 196.
3 Ray (1674), p. 114.
4 Pliny, *l.* 33 (1938–62), vol. 9 (1952), pp. 106–7.
5 Tingry (1804), pp. 343–4; (1816), pp. 225–7.
6 Martin (1813), p. 460.
7 Watin (1785), p. 84.
8 Greninger & *al.* [1975], pp. 49–50.
9 John Smith (1687), p. 38; Nicholson (1819), s.v. 'PAINTING, *Economical*', vol. II, p. 416; (1823–5), p. 410.
10 Tingry (1804), p. 346; (1816), p. 225.
11 Stalker & Parker (1688/1971), p. 72; Tingry (1804), p. 346; (1816), p. 228.
12 Tingry (1830), p. 104.
13 Berger MSS., stock 1801–2, pp. 54, 57; stock 1805–6, pp. 24, 25; stock 1809–10, pp. 7, 25.
14 Dyrham MSS., D. 1799, A 141; Soane MSS., 'Ealing'.
15 Watin (1785), p. 87.
16 Osterley MSS., Burchett (1780); Burchett (1781a); Dyrham MSS., D. 1799, A 141.
17 Tingry (1830), p. 273.
18 Dossie (1758), vol. I, pp. 147, 152; (1764), vol. I, pp. 158, 162–3.
19 Berger MSS., letter book, p. 249; stock 1801–2, pp. 56, 61; stock 1805–6, p. 23; stock 1809–10, p. 19.
20 Osterley MSS., Burchett (1779); Burchett (1780); Soane MSS., 'Ealing'; Phillips (1812), p. 213; (1821), p. 171.
21 Pincot [*c.* 1811], p. 14; Nicholson (1819), s.v. 'PAINTING, *Economical*', vol. II, p. 416.
22 Dossie (1758), vol. I, p. 153; (1764), vol. I, p. 163.
23 Tingry (1830), pp. 56–7.
24 Berger MSS., letter book, p. 249; stock 1801–2, p. 47; stock 1805–6, p. 6; stock 1809–10, p. 11.
25 Hurst (1896), p. 418.
26 Watin (1785), p. 85.
27 John Smith (1687), p. 39.
28 Watin (1785), p. 85.
29 Butcher (1825), pp. 7, 29–30.
30 Dossie (1758), vol. I, pp. 147–8; (1764), vol. I, p. 158; Tingry (1830), p. 57.
31 Osterley MSS., Thorogood (1774), 4lb.; Burchett (1775), 4lb.; Burchett (1779), 4lb.; Burchett (1780), 6 lb.; Burchett (1781a), 9lb. The rates charged lie between 1*s.* and 1*s.* 4½*d.* per lb. and, being fairly consistent, appear to relate to material ground in oil, since this is specified in two of the entries.
32 Berger MSS., stock 1801–2, p. 58; stock 1805–6; p. 28; stock 1809–10, p. 15.
33 Vanherman (1828), p. 51; Tingry (1830), p. 57.
34 Hurst (1896), p. 418.
35 Berger MSS., stock 1801–2, pp. 47, 61, 63; stock 1805–6, pp. 11, 34; stock 1809–10, p. 7.
36 Dossie (1758), vol. I, pp. 51, 147–8; (1764), vol. I, pp. 53, 158.
37 Whittock (1827), p. 17.
38 Evelyn (1670), p. 196; John Smith (1705), p. 17; (1723), p. 17.
39 Watin (1785), p. 85; Tingry (1804), p. 80; (1816), p. 30.
40 Watin (1785), pp. 50, 85.
41 Brace (1960), pp. 17, 18, 25.
42 Diderot & D'Alembert (1754–72), vol. X (1765), p. 811 (s.v. 'MOULIN pour exprimer l'huile des graines').
43 Merret (1696), pp. 344–5.
44 French (1651), p. 39.
45 Dossie (1758), vol. I, p. 144; (1764), vol. I, p. 154.
46 Smeaton (1760).
47 Ure (1839), s.v. 'OILS', p. 899; (1860), s.v. 'OILS', vol. III, pp. 277–9.
48 Church (1892), pp. 36–7.
49 Theophilus, *l.* 1, *c.* XX ((1986), p. 18).
50 Chaptal (Paris, 1807), vol. II, p. 362; (London, 1807), vol. II, p. 302; Tingry (1804), pp. 77–9; (1816), pp. 29–30; (1830), p. 157.
51 Dossie (1758), vol. I, pp. 141–2; (1764), vol. I, pp. 152–3.
52 Chaptal (Paris, 1807), vol. II, pp. 366–7; (London, 1807), vol. II, p. 304; Martin (1813), p. 460.
53 Church (1892), p. 37.
54 Dossie (1758), vol. I, p. 142; (1764), vol. I, p. 153.
55 John Smith (1687), p. 40 (words in angle brackets added from 1705 edition, p. 39).
56 Watin (1785), p. 50; Martin (1813), p. 461 (quoting a formula given by Vanherman in an unidentified source); Whittock (1827), p. 18; Vanherman (1828), p. 66.
57 Brace (1960), p. 30.
58 Nicholson (1825), pp. 407, 409.
59 Dossie (1758), vol. I, p. 145; (1764), vol. I, p. 155.
60 Vanherman (1828), p. 67.
61 Martin (1813), p. 460; Nicholson (1823–5), p. 411.
62 Vanherman (1828), pp. 66–7; Tingry (1830), pp. 168–9; patent No. 4739 (1822).
63 Chaptal (Paris, 1807), vol. II, p. 367; (London, 1807), vol. II, pp. 304–5.
64 No. 631 (1748).
65 Pincot [*c.* 1811], p. 14; Butcher (1825), p. 32; Crease (1808), p. 14.
66 John Smith (1676), p. 16.
67 John Smith (1723), pp. 37–8 (cf. (1687), p. 38).
68 Stalker & Parker (1688/1971), p. 72.
69 Reynolds (1812), pp. [7], 13.
70 Dossie (1758), vol. I, p. 149; (1764), vol. I, pp. 159–60.
71 Tingry (1804), pp. 80–5; (1816), pp. 30–8; Nicholson (1825), p. 411; Whittock (1827), pp. 17–18.
72 Dossie (1758), vol. I, p. 149; (1764), vol. I, p. 160; Tingry (1804), p. 80; (1816), p. 30.
73 Nicholson (1834), p. 154.
74 Martin (1813), pp. 460–1.
75 Watin (1785), p. 85.
76 Nicholson (1823–5), p. 410.
77 Nicholson (1834), p. 154.
78 P.R.O. MSS., E. 351/3266, M. iv[r].
79 Stalker & Parker (1688/1971), p. 72.
80 Salmon (1734), p. 59; Salmon (1745), p. 48.
81 Petworth MSS., PHA 6614, No. 219, pp. [11], [12]; Tredegar MSS., 68/76.
82 Soane MSS., 'Ealing'.
83 Phillips (1804), p. 130; (1812), p. 210; (1821), p. 169.
84 Pincot [*c.* 1811], p. 35.
85 Berger MSS., stock 1805–6, pp. 12, 30.
86 Lingard (1825), p. 10.
87 Salmon (1734), p. 59; Petworth MSS., PHA 6614, No. 219, p. [12].
88 Tredegar MSS., 68/76.
89 Berger MSS., stock 1801–2, p. 55; stock 1805–6, p. 11; stock 1809–10, p. 27.
90 Phillips (1812), p. 211.
91 *Builders Price-Book* (1810), p. 86; (1813), p. 129.
92 Lingard (1825), p. 10.
93 John Smith (1687), p. 41.
94 Evelyn (1670), pp. 55–6 (quoted by Houghton (1692–1703), No. 433 (1700)), 196; (1706), pp. 271–2.
95 Hurst (1896), p. 386.
96 Dossie (1758), vol. I, pp. 145–6; (1764), vol. I, p. 156.
97 Tingry (1804), pp. 77–8, 80–4; (1816), pp. 29, 30–6.
98 John Smith (1687), pp. 40–1.
99 Gerbier (1663), p. 48.
100 Gunther (1928), p. 79.
101 P.R.O. MSS., WORK. 19/48/1, ff. 50(iv), 64(iii), 64(iv) (Kensington); Boughton MS., vol. I, p. 173 (Montagu House).
102 Rondelet (1812–n.d.), vol. V, p. 223.
103 Stalker & Parker (1688/1971), p. 72.

104 Berger MSS., stock 1805–6, p. 28; stock 1809–10, p. 28.
105 *Builders Price-Book* (1787), pp. 141, 142; (1794), p. 153; Butcher (1825), p. 30.
106 Nicholson (1819), s.v. 'FLATTING', vol. II, p. 4.
107 Tingry (1830), pp. 156–7; Whittock (1827), p. 17.
108 Church (1892), p. 44.
109 Mills & White, 'Analyses' (1977), p. 58.
110 Dossie (1758), vol. I, p. 146; (1764), vol. I, p. 157.
111 Church (1892), p. 44; Heaton (1940), p. 225.
112 Ure (1860), s.v. 'OILS', vol, III, p. 293; Church (1892), p. 44; Hurst (1896), p. 385; Watin (1785), p. 51.
113 Tingry (1804), p. 74; (1816), p. 27.
114 No. 583 (1742).
115 Castle Museum, York, tradecard.
116 Bullet (1788), p. 546.
117 Tingry (1804), pp. 76, 389, 391–3; (1816), pp. 27–8, 270, 272–4.
118 Rondelet (1812–n.d.), vol. V, p. 223.
119 Nicholson (1819), s.v. 'FLATTING', vol. II, p. 4.
120 Whittock (1827), p. 17.
121 Vanherman (1828), p. 65.
122 Hurst (1896), p. 386.
123 Vanherman (1828), p. 65.
124 Ure (1860), s.v. 'OILS', vol. III, p. 289.
125 Vanherman (1805), pp. 195–8.
126 Pincot [*c.* 1811], p. 39.
127 Martin (1813), p. 461.
128 Hurst (1896), p. 389.
129 Vanherman (1828), pp. 67–71.
130 Vanherman (1805), p. 199.
131 B.M. trade cards, Banks 89.28.
132 Ibid., 89.27.
133 Hurst (1896), p. 407.

11. Turpentines and their derivatives

1 Houghton (1692–1703), Nos. 414, 418 (1700). The original (Bent (1698)) differs slightly from Houghton's version.
2 Hurst (1896), pp. 391–3.
3 Ibid., pp. 393–6; Heaton (1940), p. 234.
4 Hurst (1896), p. 390.
5 Houghton (1692–1703), No. 414 (1700).
6 Op. cit., p. 17.
7 Watin (1785), p. 218.
8 Tingry (1804), pp. 38–9; (1816), p. 19.
9 Heaton (1940), pp. 232, 280.
10 Howes (1949), p. 107.
11 Watin (1785), p. 218; Tingry (1804), pp. 35–42; (1816), pp. 17–21.
12 Tingry (1804), pp. 38–9; (1816), p. 19.
13 Watin (1785), p. 218.
14 John Smith (1687), p. 41.
15 Dossie (1758), vol. I, p. 151; (1764), vol. I, p. 162.
16 Evelyn (1670), p. 107; Mills & White, 'Natural Resins' (1977), p. 17.
17 Houghton (1692–1703), No. 414 (1700).
18 Watin (1785), p. 218.
19 Heaton (1940), p. 280.
20 Tingry (1804), p. 37; (1816), p. 18.
21 Watin (1785), pp. 240, 252.
22 Mills & White, 'Natural Resins' (1977), p. 17.
23 Tingry (1804), p. 38; (1816), p. 19.
24 Watin (1785), p. 218.
25 Heaton (1940), p. 280.
26 Mills & White, 'Natural Resins' (1977), p. 17.
27 Houghton (1692–1703), No. 414 (1700).
28 Mills & White, 'Natural Resins' (1977), p. 17.
29 Tingry (1804), p. 43; (1816), p. 21.
30 Ure (1860), s.v. 'FRANKINCENSE', vol. II, p. 295. In this connection, however, it should be noted that Tingry identified incense with 'gallipot resinified and become friable by long exposure to the air' ((1804), p. 42, 'white incense'; (1816), p. 21, 'frankincense').
31 Ibid., s.v. 'BURGUNDY PITCH', vol. I, p. 468. In this connection, it is worth noting that Evelyn quoted information provided by John Winthrop the younger which indicated that a turpentine which became like Burgundy pitch on exposure to the air was produced in New England from the pitch pine (Evelyn (1664), p. 55).
32 Mills & White, 'Natural Resins' (1977), p. 21.
33 Watin (1785), p. 218.
34 Tingry (1804), p. 35; (1816), p. 17.
35 Stalker & Parker (1688/1971), p. 3.
36 Berger MSS., stock 1805–6, p. 15; stock 1809–10, p. 17.
37 The major constituents of all distilled oils of turpentine belong to the group of hydrocarbons known as *terpenes*, and form a series of isomeric compounds sharing the common formula $C_{10}H_{16}$. The most important in the present connection are *pinene*, *sylvestrene*, and *dipentine*, the first providing the main constituent of French and American oils, and the latter two being found in Russian and Swedish varieties, the sylvestrene predominating. In samples from the French *Pinus maritima* the greater proportion of the pinene is laevo-rotatory, so that a column of these of standard height rotates a beam of polarised light to the left by about 30°; while American products from *P. australis*, *P. taeda*, or *P. palustra* have a predominance of the dextro-rotatory form, causing opposite rotation within the approximate range of 8° to 16°. Sylvestrene, which exists in Russian and Swedish oil derived from the Scots pine, *P. sylvestris*, exists only in dextro-rotatory form, although the dipentene, also present in these varieties, is without optical activity. (Church (1892), pp. 85, 89–91; Hurst (1896), pp. 396–7; Heaton (1940), pp. 231, 234.)
38 Tingry (1804), p. 40; (1816), p. 20.
39 Hurst (1896), p. 396.
40 Martin (1813), p. 461.
41 Watin (1785), p. 51.
42 See, for example, references to 'Turps' in a bill for materials supplied in connection with work at Osterley Park in 1774 and in David Adamson's account for work at the house in 1788 (Osterley MSS., Thorogood (1774); Adamson (1788)).
43 Englefield (1936), p. 176.
44 Stalker & Parker (1688/1971), p. 72.
45 Salmon (1734), p. 59; Dyrham MSS., D. 1799, A 141.
46 Pincot [*c.* 1811], p. 35.
47 Phillips (1812), p. 211; (1821), p. 169.
48 Tredegar MSS., 68/76; Berger MSS., stock 1805–6, p. 30; *Builders Price-Book* (1810), p. 86; (1813), p. 129.
49 Lingard (1825), p. 10.
50 Watin (1785), p. 219.
51 Tingry (1803), vol. I, p. 49; (1804), p. 41; (1816), p. 20.
52 Nicholson (1823–5), p. 411.
53 Houghton (1692–1703), Nos. 414, 418 (1700); French (1651), p. 36.
54 Dossie (1758), vol. I, p. 161; (1764), vol. I, p. 172.
55 Stalker & Parker (1688/1971), pp. 12, 13–14.
56 Tingry (1804), p. 40; (1816), p. 20.
57 Ure (1860), s.v. 'ROSIN', vol. III, p. 605.
58 Hurst (1896), p. 435; Heaton (1940), p. 284.
59 Heaton, ibid.
60 Stalker & Parker (1688/1971), pp. 3, 4.
61 Tredegar MSS., 68/76; Berger MSS., stock 1805–6, p. 26.
62 Watin (1785), pp. 218–19.
63 Evelyn (1664), pp. 55–7.
64 Tingry (1804), pls. facing pp. 46, 48, and 50 (omitted in 1816 edition).
65 Clarke (1810–23), pt. III, vol. I (1819), p. 241.
66 Ibid., pp. 251–2.
67 Ure (1860), s.v. 'TAR, WOOD', vol. III, p. 852. The second and later paragraphs of this article are misplaced in the text, and appear s.v. 'TARTRATES' in the same volume, p. 854.
68 Dossie (1758), vol. I, pp. 397–8; (1764), vol. I, p. 434; Crease (1808), pp. 8–9.
69 Gunther (1928), p. 274 (see also reference at foot of p. 275).

70 Osterley MSS., Burchett (1781).
71 Ibid., Burchett (1780).
72 Soane MSS., 'Ealing'.

12. Solvents and thinners other than turpentine

1 French (1651), pp. 12, 26, 28.
2 Lull (1572), p. 1 ff.
3 French (1651), p. 45.
4 Ure (1860), s.v. 'ALCOHOL', vol. I, p. 43; Church (1892), pp. 83–4.
5 Boyle (1663–71), bk. II, pt. 2, essay V, pp. 10, 11.
6 Cooper (1760), p. 92; Watin (1785), p. 206.
7 Tingry (1816), p. 23. This does not appear in the 1804 edition.
8 Ure (1860), s.v. 'ALCOHOL', vol. I, p. 44.
9 Hurst (1896), p. 411.
10 Stalker & Parker (1688/1971), pp. 2–3.
11 Ure (1860), s.v. 'ALCOHOL', vol. I, p. 44; Hurst (1896), p. 411.
12 Watin (1785), pp. 206–7.
13 Tingry (1804), pp. 58–60; Boyle (1675).
14 Ure (1860), s.v. 'DISTILLATION', vol. II, p. 40; patent No. 5974 (1830).
15 Ure (1860), s.v. 'ALCOHOL', vol. I, p. 44.
16 Watin (1785), p. 206.
17 Vanherman (1828), p. 33.
18 Ure (1860), s.v. 'METHYLATED SPIRIT', vol. III, pp. 83–4; s.v. 'ALCOHOL', vol. I, p. 55.
19 Cadet-de-Vaux (1801), p. 413; Butcher (1825), p. 35; Vanherman (1828), p. 33.
20 Ure (1860), s.v. 'OILS, VOLATILE, ETHERIOUS, OR ESSENTIAL', vol. III, p. 308.
21 Tingry (1804), pp. 71, 73; (1816), pp. 25–6.
22 Ure (1860), s.v. 'OILS, VOLATILE, ETHERIOUS, OR ESSENTIAL', vol. III, p. 307.
23 Church (1892), pp. 91–2.
24 P.R.O. MSS., E. 351/3404, M. iv[v].
25 Gunther (1928), p. 147.
26 Félibien (1676), p. 412.
27 Op. cit., (1825), pp. 35–6.
28 Whittock (1827), p. 17.
29 Ure (1860), s.v. 'OILS, VOLATILE, ETHERIOUS, OR ESSENTIAL', vol. III, p. 308.
30 Gunther (1928), p. 147.

13. Resins and other substances used in varnish

1 Sabin (1904), p. 363.
2 Theophilus, *l.* 1, *c.* XXI ((1986), pp. 19–20).
3 Mills & White, 'Natural Resins' (1977).
4 Watin (1785), p. 247.
5 Tingry (1804), pp. 165–71; (1816), pp. 90–6.
6 Church (1892), pp. 50–2; Hurst (1896), pp. 425–8; Monardes (1577/1925), p. 12.
7 Mills and White, 'Natural Resins' (1977), pp. 18–19. The origin of amber as a pine-resin was suggested by Pliny *l.* 37 ((1938–62), vol. 10 (1962), pp. 194–5).
8 Salmon (1672), p. 215.
9 Watin (1785), pp. 221–2.
10 Church (1892), p. 51.
11 Vanherman (1828), p. 75.
12 *Painter's . . . Pocket Manual* (1825), p. 52; Vanherman, ibid.
13 Ure (1860), s.v. 'AMBER', vol. I, p. 128.
14 Hurst (1896), pp. 427–8.
15 Hurst (1896), pp. 445–6.
16 Watin (1785), p. 216.
17 Ure (1860), s.v. 'BENZOIN, OR BENJAMIN', vol. I, p. 294.
18 Hurst (1896), p. 446.
19 Watin (1785), pp. 215–16; Tingry (1804), pp. 3–4; (1816), p. 2.
20 Stalker & Parker (1688/1971), p. 4.
21 Vanherman (1828), p. 74.
22 Heaton (1940), p. 280.
23 Ure (1860), s.v. 'BALSAM OF COPAIVA', vol. I, p. 247.
24 Piso (1658), p. 118.
25 Howes (1949), p. 93.
26 Dossie (1758), vol. I, p. 213; (1764), vol. I, pp. 229–30.
27 Watin (1785), p. 243.
28 Tingry (1804), p. 14; (1816), p. 6.
29 Stalker & Parker (1688/1971), p. 4.
30 Barry (1932), p. 44 (quoting Fr. Stuhlman, *Deutsch Ost. Afrika*, p. 163).
31 Howes (1949), p. 96.
32 Mills & White, 'Natural Resins' (1977), p. 19.
33 Hurst (1896), pp. 428–30.
34 Heaton (1940), p. 272.
35 Guibourt (1836), vol. II, p. 526. In connection with resin from Madagascar, it is worth noting that it was to ambergris rather than amber from the island that Marco Polo referred, as is clear from his association of the substance with whales. Agricola, who was quoted in connection with amber by Mrs Merrifield, appears not to have understood this. Also, Mrs Merrifield's reference should be to the latter's *De Natura Fossilium* and not to 'De Metallicis.' (Marco Polo (1958), p. 299; Agricola (1546), p. 245; Merrifield (1849), vol. I, p. cclvii).
36 Agricola (1546), p. 245.
37 Amatus Lusitanus (1554), pp. 44–5.
38 Dossie (1758), vol. I, p. 213; (1764), vol. I, pp. 229–30.
39 Hurst (1896), p. 428; Heaton (1940), p. 272.
40 Tingry (1804), p. 21; (1816), p. 11.
41 Ure (1860), s.v. 'ANIMÉ', vol. I, p. 162.
42 Stalker & Parker (1688/1971), p. 28.
43 Tingry (1804), p. 120; (1816), p. 55; Whittock (1827), p. 88.
44 Hurst (1896), pp. 430–2; Church (1892), p. 53.
45 Heaton (1940), p. 273.
46 Howes (1949), p. 93.
47 Dossie (1758), vol. I, p. 213; (1764), vol. I, p. 230.
48 Amatus Lusitanus (1554), pp. 44–5; *Gazetteer* (n.d.), vol. III, p. 194.
49 Hurst (1896), p. 432.
50 Ure (1839), s.v. 'ANIMÉ', p. 47.
51 Ure (1860), s.v. 'ANIMÉ', vol. I, p. 162.
52 Tingry (1804), p. 21; (1816), p. 11.
53 Monardes (1577/1925), pp. 11–12.
54 Piso (1658), p. 118.
55 Stalker & Parker (1688/1971), p. 4.
56 Dossie (1758), vol. I, p. 213; (1764), vol. I, p. 230.
57 Watin (1785), p. 221; *Practical Treatise* (1795), p. 35.
58 Tingry (1804), pp. 12–14; (1816), pp. 6–7.
59 Ure (1860), s.v. 'COPAL', vol. I, p. 817.
60 *Encyclopaedia Britannica* (1810), s.v. 'CHEMISTRY', vol. V, p. 732a, para. 2469.
61 Church (1892), p. 54; Hurst (1896); Heaton (1940).
62 Howes (1949), p. 99ff.
63 Heaton (1940), p. 274.
64 Hurst (1896), p. 440.
65 Mills & White, 'Natural Resins' (1977), p. 18.
66 Ure (1860), s.v. 'COPAL', vol. I, p. 817.
67 Dossie (1758), vol. I, p. 213; (1764), vol. I, p. 230; Tingry (1804), p. 12; (1816), p. 6.
68 Mills & White, 'Natural Resins' (1977), p. 18.
69 Hurst (1896), p. 434.
70 Ure (1839), s.v. 'RESIN, KAURI', p. 1067; (1860), s.v. 'DAMAR GUM, OR DAMMARA RESIN', vol. II, p. 4.
71 Mills & White, 'Natural Resins' (1977), p. 21.
72 Church (1896), pp. 55–6; Hurst (1896), pp. 436–8.
73 Howes (1949), pp. 115, 117.
74 Mills & White, 'Natural Resins' (1977), p. 21.
75 Tingry (1804), pp. 22–3; (1816), pp. 12–13.
76 Mills & White, 'Natural Resins' (1977), pp. 21, 22.
77 Piso (1658), p. 122.
78 Watin (1785), p. 215.
79 *Encyclopaedia Britannica* (1810), s.v. 'CHEMISTRY', vol. V, p. 732a, para. 2471; Ure (1839), s.v. 'ELEMI', p. 422.

80 Ure (1860), s.v. 'Elemi', vol. II, p. 113.
81 *Encyclopaedia Britannica* (1810), s.v. 'Chemistry', vol. v, p. 732a, para. 2471.
82 Hurst (1896), p. 445.
83 Stalker & Parker (1688/1971), p. 4.
84 Tingry (1804), p. 18; (1816), p. 9.
85 Ure (1860), s.v. 'Lac', vol. II, p. 625.
86 Stalker & Parker (1688/1971), p. 3.
87 Dossie (1758), vol. I, p. 159; (1764), vol. I, p. 170.
88 Watin (1785), pp. 217–18.
89 Howes (1949), p. 138.
90 Houghton (1692–1703), No. 420 (1700).
91 Church (1892), p. 57.
92 Heaton (1940), p. 277.
93 Vanherman (1828), p. 75.
94 Stalker & Parker (1688/1971), p. 10.
95 Watin (1785), pp. 216–17, 250.
96 Berger MSS., stock 1809–10, p. 20.
97 Mills and White, 'Natural Resins' (1977), p. 18; Heaton (1940), p. 277; Church (1892), p. 56; Hurst (1896), p. 434; Ure (1860), s.v. 'Sandarach, or juniper resin', vol. III, p. 631.
98 Watin (1785), pp. 216, 234.
99 Stalker & Parker (1688/1971), p. 3.
100 Berger MSS., stock 1805–6, p. 27; stock 1809–10, p. 20.
101 Tingry (1804), p. 6; (1816), p. 3.
102 Ure (1860), s.v. 'Camphor, or camfire', vol. I, p. 565.
103 Watin (1785), p. 216.
104 Tingry (1804), pp. 7–8, 120, 133; (1816), pp. 3, 55, 68.
105 Vanherman (1828), p. 74.
106 Tingry (1830), p. 142.
107 Ure (1860), s.v. 'Alkanet', vol. I, p. 86.
108 Harley (1970), pp. 140–2.
109 Heaton (1940), pp. 290, 291.
110 Harley (1970), p. 140.
111 Church (1892), p. 215; Hurst (1896), pp. 435–6.
112 Dossie (1758), vol. I, p. 120; (1764), vol. I, p. 129.
113 Watin (1785), p. 223.
114 Tingry (1804), p. 2; (1816), p. 1.
115 Stalker & Parker (1688/1971), p. 28.
116 Dossie (1758), vol. I, p. 384; (1764), vol. I, p. 438.
117 Op. cit. (1825), pp. 61–2.
118 Vanherman (1828), p. 78.
119 Watin (1785), p. 249.
120 Howes (1949), pp. 139–40.
121 Hurst (1896), p. 454.
122 Stalker & Parker (1688/1971), p. 4.
123 Hurst (1896), pp. 454–5.
124 Watin (1785), p. 217.
125 Tingry (1804), pp. 25–6; (1816), pp. 15–16.
126 Harley (1970), p. 102.
127 Hurst (1896), pp. 453–4.
128 Tingry (1804), p. 23; (1816), p. 13.
129 Watin (1785), p. 215.
130 Stalker & Parker (1688/1971), pp. 4, 63; Watin (1785), p. 242; Vanherman (1828), p. 77.
131 Dossie (1758), vol. I, pp. 96–7; (1764), vol. I, p. 103.
132 Berger MSS., stock 1801–2, p. 57; stock 1805–6, p. 26; stock 1809–10, pp. 22, 23.
133 Phillips (1812), p. 212; (1821), p. 170.
134 Tingry (1830), pp. 141–2.
135 Ure (1860), s.v. 'Red sanders wood', vol. III, p. 575.

14. Sizes, casein, and water-soluble gums

1 Howes (1949), pp. 16, 17.
2 Church (1892), p. 69.
3 Hurst (1896), pp. 448–9.
4 Stalker & Parker (1688/1971), p. 3.
5 Tingry (1804), p. 16; (1816), p. 8.
6 Berger MSS., stock 1801–2, p. 50; stock 1805–6, p. 28; stock 1809–10, pp. 12, 13. In addition he held sizeable stocks of 'Com^{n} Gum' in both 1806 and 1810 (pp. 19 and 13 in their respective volumes), but although the 1810 entry is sandwiched between the gum arabic and gum Senegal entries, it is not possible to be certain that this was a related substance.
7 Dossie (1758), vol. I, p. 149; (1764), vol. I, p. 160.
8 Howes (1949), p. 39; Hurst (1896), p. 449.
9 Tingry (1804), p. 15; (1816), p. 7.
10 Ure (1860), s.v. 'Gum', vol. II, p. 425.
11 D'Aviler (1691), vol. I, p. 229.
12 Heaton (1940), p. 293.
13 Ure (1860), s.v. 'Glue', vol. II, pp. 376–9.
14 Dossie (1758), vol. I, p. 156; (1764), vol. I, p. 166.
15 Watin (1785), p. 49.
16 Tingry (1804), pp. 489–90; (1816), p. 370.
17 B.M. trade cards, Heal 89.53.
18 Reynolds (1812), p. 14.
19 PRO. MSS., E. 351/3261, M.xviii^{v} (Newmarket).
20 Ibid., 3249 (1614–15), M. xx^{v} (Newmarket); 3251 (1616–17), M. xiv^{r} (Theobalds); 3257 (1623–4), M. xv^{r} (Newmarket); 3267 (1633–4), M. xv^{r} (Royston); 3271 (1637–8), M. xiii^{v} (Holdenby).
21 Chester MS.
22 Stapleton & *al.* (1975), p. 58.
23 Claydon MS.
24 Salmon (1734), p. 59.
25 *Builders Price-Book* (1776), p. 83.
26 Op. cit. (1897–8), vol. II, p. 179.
27 Phillips (1804), p. 131.
28 Soane MSS., 'Ealing'.
29 Phillips (1812), p. 211; (1821), p. 169.
30 Dossie (1758), vol. I, p. 156; (1764), vol. I, p. 167.
31 PRO. MSS., E. 351/3271 (1637–8), M. xiii^{v} (Holdenby).
32 Watin (1785), p. 48.
33 Ibid., pp. 48–9.
34 Tingry (1804), p. 489; (1816), p. 369.
35 Watin (1785), pp. 66, 77, 79.
36 Tingry (1804), p. 489; (1816), p. 370; Nicholson (1819), s.v. 'Painting, *Economical*', vol. II, p. 417.
37 Church (1892), p. 66.
38 Dossie (1758), vol. I, p. 157; (1764), vol. I, p. 168.
39 Merrifield (1849), p. 192.
40 Stalker & Parker (1688/1971), p. 4.
41 Dossie (1758), vol. I, p. 168; (1764), vol. I, p. 181.
42 Tingry (1804), p. 487; (1816), pp. 367–8.
43 Nicholson (1819), s.v. 'Painting, *Economical*', vol. II, p. 417.
44 Dossie (1758), vol. I, p. 175; (1764), vol. I, p. 188.
45 R.I.A. MSS., Charlemont letters, second series, vol. I, letter 62 (22 March 1769).

15. Manufacture and formulation of oil paint

1 P.R.O. MSS., E. 351/3249 (1614–15) to 3272 (1638–9).
2 Ham MSS., Gooderick's account.
3 John Smith (1687), pp. 32–3.
4 Berger MSS., 1831 formula book, pp. 1, 9, 47, 75, 77, 163.
5 Vanherman (1828), pp. 5, 12, 24.
6 *Painter's . . . Pocket Manual* (1825), p. 12.
7 John Smith (1687), pp. 1–2, 3–4 (words in angle brackets added from 1705 edn, pp. 1–2).
8 John Smith (1687), pp. 33–4 (words in angle brackets added from 1705 edn, p. 33).
9 Tingry (1804), p. 441; (1816), p. 320.
10 *Repertory of Arts*, vol. v (1796), pl. VII (reproduced by Harley (1970), pl. 7).
11 No. 421 (1718).
12 B.M. trade cards, Heal 89.54 (newspaper cutting having the date 1741 added in manuscript).
13 Harley (1970), caption to pl. 2.
14 Dossie (1758), vol. I, p. 164; (1764), vol. I, p. 175.
15 Ure (1839), s.v. 'Paints, Grinding of', pp. 916–17; (1860), vol. III, pp. 374–5.
16 Coad (1983), p. 81, pls. 68, 78.

17 *Transactions of the Society . . . of Arts*, vol. XXII (1804), pl. VI (facing p. 256), fig. 3 (reproduced by Harley (1970), pl. 8).
18 Ure (1860), s.v. 'PAINTS, GRINDING OF', vol. III, p. 375.
19 Hurst (1896), p. 340ff.
20 No. 4891 (1824). In addition it may be mentioned that Reynolds ((1812), pp. 7–8) described the use of a crude ball-mill in the preparation of paint for exterior use; while Sabin ((1904), p. 137) referred to the 'Boston Stone', said to have been exported from England to America about 1700, as a reputed paint mill. One fragment of a trough originally capable of holding 75 or 100 gallons survived upon which the date 1737 had subsequently been carved, together with a stone ball two feet in diameter; but any suggestion of its employment in the dispersion of pigment in oil seems unsatisfactory. The stones were still in situ in 1983.
21 P.R.O. MSS., E. 351/3253, M. vii[r].
22 John Smith (1687), p. 35 (words in angle brackets added from 1705 edn, p. 35).
23 Salmon (1734), p. 57.
24 B.M. trade cards, Heal, 89.53.
25 Stalker & Parker (1688/1971), p. 71.
26 Pincot [*c.* 1811], p. 8.
27 Tingry (1830), p. 273.
28 John Smith (1687), pp. 4–5.
29 Dossie (1758), vol. I, p. 164; (1764), vol. I, p. 176.
30 B.M. trade cards, Heal 89.53.
31 Tingry (1830), p. 268.
32 John Smith (1687), p. 36; Pincot [*c.* 1811], p. 11.
33 John Smith (1687), p. 36.
34 Watin (1785), pp. 81–2; Tingry (1804), p. 462; (1816), pp. 341–2. This may be compared with Watin's advice that to take up varnish, one should just touch its surface with the brush, and on drawing back the hand should turn it two or three times to cut the thread which it brought after it. This was re-phrased by Tingry in connection with paste diluted with varnish or 'prepared oil': 'The colour on being taken from the pot ought not to drop from the brush when turned round two or three times in the hand, raising it obliquely to check the thread which is formed'. (Watin (1785), p. 285; Tingry (1804), pp. 442–3; (1816), p. 321.)
35 D'Aviler (1691), vol. I, p. 228.
36 Watin (1785), p. 88.
37 B.M. trade cards, Heal 89.53.
38 No. 3594 (1812).
39 Tingry (1830), p. 269.
40 Op. cit., p. 12, No. 4.
41 John Smith (1676), p. 12; Crease (1808), p. 13.
42 Evelyn (1706), p. 271.
43 D'Aviler (1691), vol. I, p. 228.
44 Dossie (1758), vol. I, p. 164; (1764), vol. I, p. 175.
45 Tingry (1830), p. 271.
46 B.M. trade cards, Heal 89.53.
47 Dossie (1758), vol. I, p. 151; (1764), vol. I, p. 161.
48 Crease (1808), p. 14.
49 Evelyn (1706), p. 271.
50 Butcher (1825), p. 34.
51 Reynolds (1812), p. 13.
52 Watin (1785), p. 53.
53 Ibid., pp. 92–5 *passim.*
54 Nicholson (1825), p. 407.
55 Butcher (1825), p. 29.
56 Pincot [*c.* 1811], p. 38.
57 Nicholson (1825), p. 407.
58 Pincot [*c.* 1811], p. 16.
59 John Smith (1687), p. 38; (1705), p. 38 (mentioning specifically red lead, verdigris, and umber as drying well by themselves); Watin (1785), p. 84.
60 Dossie (1758), vol. I, pp. 152, 153–4; (1764), vol. I, pp. 163, 164.
61 Tingry (1830), p. 273.
62 John Smith (1687), p. 39.
63 Watin (1785), p. 87.
64 John Smith (1687), pp. 38–9.
65 Crease (1808), p. 14.
66 Nicholson (1825), p. 409.
67 Pincot ([*c.* 1811], p. 8), for example, referred to 'Dryer ground'; and Lewis Berger's firm was manufacturing a dryer in this form from at least 1831. An experimental formula is noted in 1830, and a production formula in 1831 headed 'New Dryer for Aquatic Green &c'. This called for 90 lb. of 'Calcined Sulphate Barytes' and 126 lb. anhydrous 'Sugar Lead' (144 lb. hydrated weight) to be ground into about 46 lb. of oil (Berger MSS., second experimental notebook, f. 29[r]; 1831 formula book, p. 191).
68 Pincot [*c.* 1811], p. 16; Butcher (1825), pp. 29, 31; Nicholson (1825), p. 407.
69 John Smith (1687), p. 39; Dossie (1758), vol. I, pp. 153–4; (1764), vol. I, p. 164; Watin (1785), p. 87; Tingry (1804), p. 465; (1816), p. 344; Nicholson (1819), s.v. 'PAINTING, *Economical*', vol. II, p. 416; Butcher (1825), p. 29; Nicholson (1825), p. 410; Tingry (1830), p. 273.
70 Nicholson (1819), ibid.; (1825), ibid.
71 Watin (1785), p. 86.
72 Ibid., p. 87; Butcher (1825), p. 29; Tingry (1830), p. 274; *Specification for Repainting Work* (1939), *passim.*
73 Nicholson (1819), s.v. 'PAINTING, *Economical*', vol. II, p. 416.
74 Butcher (1825), p. 29.
75 Pincot [*c.* 1811], p. 16.
76 Watin (1785), p. 86.
77 Op. cit. (1659), p. 26.
78 John Smith (1687), pp. 37–8.
79 Op. cit., (1668), pp. 115–16.
80 Crease (1808), p. 12.
81 Pincot [*c.* 1811], p. 7; Nicholson (1819), s.v. 'PAINTING, *Economical*', vol. II, p. 416; Nicholson (1825), p. 407; Watin (1785), pp. 85–9, 92; Butcher (1825), p. 29.
82 Tingry (1804), pp. 463–4; (1816), p. 343.
83 John Smith (1687), pp. 54–5; Nicholson (1819), s.v. 'PAINTING, *Economical*', p. 417.
84 Félibien (1676), p. 405; Watin (1785), p. 92.
85 John Smith (1676), pp. 14, 69, 70; (1687), p. 45.
86 Dossie (1758), vol. I, p. 52; (1764), vol. I, p. 55.
87 Leyburn (1700), p. 71.
88 Dossie (1758), vol. I, p. 204; (1764), vol. I, p. 219.
89 Bristow MSS., reports, Ham (1984), p. 5.
90 Bristow MSS., thesis (1983), vol . II, p. 822.
91 Ibid., p. 823.
92 Neve (1703), p. 277.
93 Watin (1785), pp. 94–5.
94 P.R.O. MSS., WORK 19/48/1, f. 50(iv).
95 Watin (1785), p. 88.
96 Pincot [*c.* 1811], pp. 7, 39; Nicholson (1825), p. 407.
97 Bristow MSS., reports, Royal Academy (1988), pp. 6–9.
98 Bristow MSS., notes, C. 67C (draft report, February 1988).
99 Evelyn (1670), p. 196; (1706), p. 271.
100 Nicholson (1834), p. 154.
101 Bartholomew (1846), para. 1931.
102 Smith (1687), p. 53.
103 B.M. trade cards, Heal 89.53.
104 Pincot [*c.* 1811], p. 38.
105 P.R.O. MSS., WORK. 5/3 (August 1662).
106 Op. cit., (1776), p. 91; (1787), p. 135; (1794), p. 147; (1810) p. 81; (1813), p. 124.
107 Dossie (1758), vol. I, p. 204; (1764), vol. I, p. 219.
108 Pincot [*c.* 1811], p. 38.
109 Reynolds (1812), p. 14.
110 Stalker & Parker (1688/1971), p. 57.
111 Salmon (1745), p. 47; *Builders Price-Book* (1776), p. 90.
112 Martin (1813), p. 463.
113 Nicholson (1823–5), p. 417.
114 Pincot [*c.* 1811], pp. 18, 38.
115 Arundel MS., Evans's bill, *passim.*
116 Ibid., f. 1.
117 Pincot [*c.* 1811]. p. 38.
118 Gunther (1928), p. 282.
119 Vanherman (1828), p. 37.

120 Nicholson (1825), p. 410.
121 Pincot [*c.* 1811], p. 18.
122 Osterley MSS., Adamson (1772–4).
123 R.I.B.A. MSS., CHA 3/3, p. 67.
124 Evelyn (1670), p. 196.
125 Leyburn (1700), p. 71.
126 Bristow MSS., reports, Queen's House (1986), p. 29; Ham (1984), p. 3.
127 Evelyn (1706), p. 271.
128 Bristow MSS., thesis (1983), vol. II, p. 823.
129 Boughton MS., vol. I, p. 163; Bristow MSS., thesis (1983), vol. II, pp. 761–4.
130 Bristow (1979); Bristow MSS., thesis (1983), vol. II, pp. 752–60.
131 Watin (1785), pp. 44, 91.
132 Ibid., p. 59.
133 B.M. trade cards, Heal 89.53.
134 Bristow MSS., reports, Heveningham (1984b), p. 2.
135 Bristow MSS., reports, Heveningham (1984c), p. 3.
136 Pincot [*c.* 1811], p. 10; Bentley (1817), p. 6; Vanherman (1828), p. 15; Reynolds (1812), pp. 10–11.
137 Bristow MSS., thesis (1983), vol. II, p. 839.
138 Ibid., p. 792 (zone E).
139 Vanherman (1828), p. 89.
140 Pincot [*c.* 1811], p. 10.
141 Bristow MSS., reports, British Museum (1983); notes, C. 67E (Mansion House, London, exterior ironwork, draft report, June 1988).
142 Pincot [*c.* 1811], p. 13.
143 Butcher (1825), p. 30.
144 Tingry (1804), pp. 404–5; (1816), p. 286.
145 Crease (1808), p. 13.
146 Reynolds (1812), pp. 11–12.
147 Dossie (1758), vol. I, p. 48; (1764), vol. I, p. 50.
148 Pincot [*c.* 1811], pp. 26–7.
149 Vanherman (1828), p. 38.
150 Pincot [*c.* 1811], p. 28; Tingry (1804), p. 395; (1816), p. 276.
151 Vanherman (1828), p. 29.
152 Nicholson (1819), s.v. 'PAINTING, *Economical*', vol. II, p. 417.
153 Reynolds (1812), p. 10.
154 D'Aviler (1691), vol. I, p. 229.
155 Vanherman (1828), p. 38.
156 John Smith (1687), p. 41.
157 Ibid., p. 39.
158 Castle Museum, York, trade cards.
159 B.M. trade cards, Heal 89.53.
160 Dossie (1758), vol. I, p. 151; (1764), vol. I, p. 162.
161 John Smith (1687), pp. 41–2 (words within angle brackets added from 1705 edn, p. 40).
162 Tingry (1804), p. 101; (1816), pp. 33–4.
163 Reynolds (1812), p. 15.
164 Dossie (1758), vol. I, pp. 147–50; (1764), vol. I, pp. 158–60. Hurst ((1896), p. 434) indicated that sandarac resin is readily soluble in oil after fusing, but it is not clear what benefit the gum arabic would confer.
165 Félibien (1676), p. 406.
166 Raper (1924), p. 81.
167 Reynolds (1812), p. 13.
168 Tingry (1830), p. 271.
169 Watin (1785), pp. 96–9.
170 Soane MSS., Berkeley Square, f. 10; R.I.B.A. MSS., PEL/1, pp. 82–6, 154 *passim*; Arundel MS., Evans's bill, *passim*.
171 Watin (1785), pp. 92–6 *passim*.
172 *Builders Price-Book* (1776), p. 91.
173 Watin (1785), p. 95; Nicholson (1819), s.v. PAINTING, *Economical*', vol. II, p. 416.
174 Butcher (1825), p. 30.
175 Vanherman (1828), p. 34.
176 Tingry (1830), p. 271.
177 Skyring (1831), p. 88.
178 Butcher (1825), pp. 29–30.
179 Pincot [*c.* 1811], p. 17; Nicholson (1825), p. 408.
180 *Builders Price-Book* (1787), pp. 141, 142; (1794), p. 153; Nicholson (1819), s.v. 'FLATTING', vol. II, p. 4.
181 Nicholson (1819), s.v. 'PAINTING, *Economical*', vol. II, p. 416.
182 *Builders Price-Book* (1810), pp. 83, 84; (1813), pp. 126, 127.
183 Dyrham MSS., D. 1799, A141.
184 R.I.B.A. MSS., CHA 3/3, p. 192.
185 Nicholson (1819), s.v. 'PAINTING, *Economical*', vol. II, p. 416.

16. The application of oil paint

1 John Smith (1687), pp. 44–6.
2 B.M. trade cards, Heal 89.53.
3 Watin (1785), p. 83; Tingry (1804), p. 464; (1816), p. 344.
4 Nicholson (1819), s.v. 'KNOTTING', vol. II, p. 202; (1825), p. 406.
5 Butcher (1825), p. 29.
6 Bentley (1817), p. 11.
7 Tingry (1830), pp. 153–4.
8 Vanherman (1828), p. 33.
9 Nicholson (1819), s.v. 'KNOTTING', vol. II, p. 202; ibid., s.v. 'PAINTING, *Economical*', vol. II, pp. 415–16.
10 Nicholson (1825), p. 406.
11 Arundel MS., Evans's bill, *passim*.
12 Nicholson (1819), s.v. 'KNOTTING', vol. II, p. 202.
13 Bristow MSS., thesis (1983), vol. II, p. 834.
14 Bartholomew (1846), para. 1494.
15 Leybourn (1668), p. 116.
16 John Smith (1687), p. 45 (phrase within angle brackets added from 1705 edn, p. 43).
17 Pincot [*c.* 1811], p. 11.
18 Vanherman (1828), p. 20.
19 Evelyn (1670), p. 196; Tingry (1804), p. 393; (1816), p. 274.
20 Nicholson (1819), s.v. 'BADIGEON', vol. I, p. 42.
21 Watin (1785), p. 66.
22 Salmon (1734), p. 59; Leadbeater (1770), p. 46.
23 Tredegar MSS., 68/76; *Builders Price-Book* (1810), p. 86; (1813), p. 129.
24 Phillips (1804), p. 130; (1812), p. 211; (1821), p. 169.
25 John Smith (1687), pp. 5–7; (1705), p. 6.
26 Watin (1785), p. 10.
27 P.R.O. MSS., E. 351/3250, M. x[r].
28 Tingry (1830), p. 266.
29 Pincot [*c.* 1811], p. 9; Vanherman (1828), pp. 11, 25.
30 Tingry (1830), p. 266.
31 Berger MSS., stock 1801–2, p. 52; stock 1805–6, pp. 14, 31; stock 1809–10, p. 30. 'Brushes' were stocked in sizes 000, 00, 0, 1, 2, 3, and 4, and the 'Dusters' and 'Ground Brushes' in sizes 1, 2, and 3.
32 Ure (1860), s.v. 'BRUSHES', vol. I, pp. 466–7.
33 Tredegar MSS., 68/76.
34 Martin (1813), p. 463.
35 Nicholson (1823–5), p. 416.
36 Cennini, *c.* 65 ((1844), pp. 37–8; (1930), p. 54).
37 Watin (1785), p. 10.
38 Elliot (1924), pp. 18–19, 23.
39 John Smith (1687), p. 48; B.M. trade cards, Heal 89.53.
40 Pincot [*c.* 1811]. p. 9.
41 Ibid.
42 Tredegar MSS., 68/76.
43 Berger MSS., stock 1801–2, pp. 52–3; stock 1805–6, p. 16; stock 1809–10, p. 30. These were stocked in sizes 1, 2, 3, 4, 5, 6, 7, and 8, No. 3, for example, being valued at 4s. per dozen in 1806.
44 Stalker & Parker (1688/1971), p. 1; Nicholson (1823–5), p. 417; Berger MSS., stock 1801–2, p. 60; stock 1809–10, p. 24.
45 Watin (1785), p. 10.
46 *Painter's . . . Pocket Manual* (1825), p. 15.
47 Watin (1785), p. 10; John Smith (1687), p. 6.
48 Stalker & Parker (1688/1971), p. 1.
49 Berger MSS., stock 1805–6, p. 23; stock 1809–10, p. 24.
50 John Smith (1687), p. 6; Vanherman (1828), p. 25.
51 Berger MSS., stock 1805–6. p. 23.
52 Vanherman (1828), pp. 11, 12.

53 Pincot [*c.* 1811], pp. 6–7.
54 The use of matting by house-painters as a temporary protective floor-covering is mentioned in a bill of 1764 (Gilbert & *al.* (1987), p. 98a, citing North Yorkshire Record Office ZNK X 1/7/1–3).
55 Gunther (1928), pp. 147, 282.
56 During the opening years of the nineteenth century, Lewis Berger had large stocks of pumice stone. In 1802, for example, he had nearly 28 cwt. valued at 42*s.* per cwt., together with nearly 63 cwt. of 'Brown' pumice stone at only 6*s.* In 1806 he had over 37 tons and in 1810 15 tons at 15*s.* and 14*s.* per cwt. respectively. (Berger MSS., stock 1801–2, p. 50; stock 1805–6, p. 30; stock 1809–10, p. 31.)
57 Vanherman (1828), pp. 33–5.
58 Nicholson (1825), p. 407.
59 Vanherman (1828), p. 36.
60 Nicholson (1819), s.v. 'PAINTING, *Economical*', vol. II, p. 417.
61 Nicholson (1825), p. 407; John Smith (1687), pp. 44–5.
62 Bartholomew (1846), para. 1930.
63 Vanherman (1828), pp. 36–7; Pincot [*c.* 1811], pp. 15–16; Nicholson (1825), p. 408.
64 Nicholson (1823–5), p. 417.
65 B.M. trade cards, Heal 89.53.
66 Pincot [*c.* 1811], pp. 11, 15–16.
67 Donaldson [1859], vol. II, p. 818.
68 Laxton (1818), p. 96.
69 B.M. trade cards, Heal 89.53.
70 Bentley (1817), p. 11.
71 Vanherman (1828), p. 36.
72 Ibid., p. 34.
73 Pincot [*c.* 1811], pp. 9–10.
74 Tingry (1804), p. 461; (1816), p. 340.
75 Reynolds (1812), p. 16.
76 Op. cit. (1825), pp. 32–3.
77 Pincot [*c.* 1811], pp. 11–12.
78 Vanherman (1828), pp. 35–6.
79 B.M. trade cards, Heal 89.53.
80 Martin (1813), p. 463.
81 Nicholson (1819), s.v. 'PAINTING, *Economical*', vol. II, p. 417.
82 Ibid., p. 416; Hertford MS., p. 387; R.I.B.A. MSS., CHA 3/1, p. 247 ff.
83 Boughton MS., vol. I, p. 175.
84 R.I.B.A. MSS., WiR/1/1/1.
85 John Smith (1676), pp. 69–70.
86 Op. cit. [1667], p. 70.
87 R.I.B.A. MSS., WRE/2/19–21.
88 B.M. trade cards, Heal 89.53.
89 Boughton MS., vol. I, p. 163.
90 Pincot [*c.* 1811], p. 7.
91 Nicholson (1825), p. 409.
92 R.I.B.A. MSS., PEL/1, p. 84.
93 *Builders Price-Book* (1776), p. 91; (1787), pp. 135, 138.
94 Op. cit. (1786), p. 14.
95 Englefield (1936), p. 181.
96 *Builders Price-Book* (1787), p. 138.
97 Woburn MSS., box 394.
98 Op. cit. (1810), pp. 81, 83.
99 Laxton (1818), p. 96.
100 Martin (1813), p. 463.
101 Nicholson (1823–5), p. 417.
102 Op. cit. (1756), p. 743.
103 Wilsford (1659), p. 27; Leybourn (1668), p. 116; Leyburn (1700), p. 83.
104 Mandey (1717), p. 231.
105 Neve (1703), p. 215.
106 Ware (1756), p. 743.
107 Neve (1703), p. 215.
108 Leybourn (1668), p. 116.
109 Neve (1703), p. 22.
110 Gerbier (1663), pp. 84–5; Salmon (1734), p. 56.
111 Op. cit. (1776), pp. 90–2; (1787), p. 134.
112 Salmon (1734), p. 56; *Builders Price-Book* (1787), p. 134.
113 R.I.B.A. MSS., CHA 3/1, p. 247 ff.

17. Water-based paints

1 Robert Campbell (1747), p. 162.
2 Dossie (1764), vol. I, p. 177 (not in 1st edn (1758)).
3 R.I.B.A. MSS., WiR/1/1/1.
4 Op. cit. (1825), p. 114.
5 Op. cit. (1833), p. 263, para. 537.
6 R.I.B.A. MSS., PEL/1, pp. 74, 84.
7 Robert Campbell (1747), p. 163.
8 1 Jac. I, c. 20.
9 Englefield (1936), p. 129.
10 Op. cit. (1831), pp. 77, 88.
11 19 & 20 Vic., c. 64.
12 Vanherman (1828), p. 100.
13 Binders listed by Clough Williams-Ellis ((1919), pp. 113–15), which were taken from various sources, included, for example, skimmed milk, rye flour, size, and tallow; while Loudon ((1833), p. 262, para. 534) suggested the use of bullock's blood as a binder for exterior purposes. It seems most unlikely, however, that the latter would ever have been used to tint interior paint in the way suggested by Margaret Jourdain ([1914], p. 32); and John Smith ((1705), p. 52), for example, mentioned its employment only as a hardener in plaster for exterior clock-dials.
14 See, e.g., P.R.O. MSS., E. 351/3249, M. xvi[r] (1614–15, whitewash, Hampton Court); 3250, M. vi[r] (1615–16, distemper, Whitehall); and ibid., M. xviii[v] (whiting, Holdenby).
15 B.M. trade cards, Heal 89.53.
16 Neve (1703), p. 227; Salmon (1773), p. 44.
17 D'Aviler (1691), vol. I, p. 228; Watin (1785), pp. 60–79 *passim*.
18 Dossie (1758), vol. I, p. 174; (1764), vol. I, p. 188; Tingry (1804), pp. 495–6; (1816), pp. 375–6; Nicholson (1819), s.v. 'PAINTING, *Economical*', vol. II, p. 417.
19 R.I.B.A. MSS., CHA 3/1, p. 247.
20 Woburn MSS., box 394.
21 Gerbier (1663), pp. 80–2. A square was defined by Neve ((1703), p. 246) as containing 100 square feet; and this unit remained in everyday use for measuring tiling until the recent imposition of the metric system.
22 Dyrham MSS., D. 1779, A105.
23 Osterley MSS., Bacon (1779); (1780); (1781); (1784); (1785); (1788); (1789); (1791).
24 Salmon (1745), p. 46; *Builders Price-Book* (1776), p. 70; (1787), p. 114; (1794), p. 130.
25 *Builders Price-Book* (1810), p. 69; (1813), p. 111.
26 Laxton (1818), p. 88.
27 Skyring (1831), p. 77.
28 P.R.O. MSS., E. 351/3257, M. xiii[v].
29 Laxton (1818), p. 88.
30 P.R.O. MSS., WORK, 5/3, August 1662.
31 Ibid., E. 351/3249 to 3272, *passim*.
32 Gunther (1928), pp. 67, 68, 191.
33 Mansion House MSS., Downes (1748); Fewkes (1749); Fewkes (1755).
34 S.A.L. MS.
35 Gordon Castle MS., p. 2.
36 Wren Society, vol. XI (1934), p. 97.
37 Salmon (1745), p. 45.
38 Osterley MSS., Bacon (1780); (1784); (1785); (1789).
39 Woburn MSS., box 394.
40 *Builders Price-Book* (1776), p. 70; (1787), p. 114; (1794), p. 130; (1810), p. 69; (1813), p. 111.
41 Phillips (1804), p. 113; (1812), p. 196; (1821), p. 156.
42 Laxton (1818), p. 88.
43 Skyring (1831), p. 77.
44 D'Aviler (1691), vol. I, p. 228.
45 Félibien (1676), p. 293.
46 Op. cit. (1833), p. 137.
47 Watin (1785), pp. 61, 63.

48 Tingry (1804), pp. 493–5; (1816), pp. 373–6.
49 Bullet (1788), p. 547.
50 Pincot [*c.* 1811], pp. 14–15, 19.
51 Vanherman (1828), pp. 51–3.
52 D'Aviler (1691), vol. I, p. 228.
53 Tingry (1804), p. 492; (1816), p. 372.
54 Osterley MSS., Bacon (1788).
55 Mansion House MSS., Willmott (1779–81).
56 R.I.A. MSS., Charlemont letters, second series, vol. I, letter 62 (22 March 1769).
57 Nicholson (1819), s.v. 'PAINTING, *Economical*', vol. II, p. 417.
58 Skyring (1831), p. 77.
59 Tingry (1830), p. 60.
60 The only other reference encountered to the addition of 'turpentine' in this way is the item for: 'Ceilings and walls in distemper with white lead, turpentine, &c.' priced at 6*d.* per yard, given by Skyring ((1831), p. 77). Precisely what the author had in mind is not clear, but by the late nineteenth century a technique known as *bastard flatting* was in use. For this 'a little size, or raw oil well bleached' was added to the oil of turpentine with which the white lead paste was diluted in order to enable the paint to stand washing better (Seddon (1886), p. 295); and it may have been something of this nature to which he was referring.
61 Watin (1785), pp. 65–6.
62 P.R.O. MSS., E.351/3259, M.xxvi^{r}.
63 Ibid., WORK. 5/22, f. 114^{r}; 5/23, f. 64^{v}.
64 Ibid., E.351/3253, M. ix^{r}.
65 Ibid., 3256, M. v^{v}.
66 Ibid., 3257, M. xv^{r}.
67 Ibid., 3267, M. v^{v}.
68 Ibid., 3253, M. ix^{r}.
69 Ibid., 3263, M. xii^{v}.
70 Ibid., 3259, M. xxvi^{r}.
71 Bristow (1986), pp. 33–4.
72 Watin (1785), pp. 68–9.
73 Tingry (1804), pp. 501–5; (1816), pp. 382–5.
74 R.I.B.A. MSS., PEL/1, p. 86.
75 Watin (1785), pp. 66, 77, 79.
76 Nicholson (1819), s.v. 'PAINTING, *Economical*', vol. II, p. 417.
77 Dossie (1758), vol. I, p. 175; (1764), vol. I, p. 188.
78 Watin (1785), pp. 61–2.
79 Ibid., p. 61; Tingry (1804), pp. 491, 493, 494; (1816), pp. 371, 373, 374.
80 Gunther (1928), p. 67.
81 Fowler & Cornforth (1974), p. 179.
82 Ibid., p. 203.
83 Pincot [*c.* 1811], p. 19
84 Nicholson (1834), p. 161.
85 Pincot [*c.* 1811], p. 20.
86 Ibid., pp. 14, 15.
87 Op. cit. (1825), p. 114.
88 Vanherman (1828), p. 53.
89 Nicholson (1819), s.v. 'PAINTING, *Economical*', vol. II, p. 417.
90 D'Aviler (1691), vol. I, p. 228.
91 Watin (1785), p. 64.
92 Holme (1688), pp. 344, 396.
93 Moxon (1703), p. 249.
94 Vanherman (1828), p. 53.
95 Pincot [*c.* 1811], pp. 15, 20–1.
96 D'Aviler (1691), vol. I, p. 228; Bullet (1691), p. 284; Nicholson (1819), s.v. 'PAINTING, *Economical*', vol. II, p. 417.
97 Pincot [*c.* 1811], p. 19.
98 Watin (1785), p. 64.
99 Fowler and Cornforth (1974), p. 179.
100 Bowood MSS., Bowood bills, Spinnage's account. The four coats mentioned by Fowler & Cornforth ((1974), p. 205) were, in fact, probably of oil paint. Although the account is not specific, this is suggested both by the terminology 'finishd Dead Stone' and the rate of 11*d.* per yard against 6½*d.* for three coats of distemper and 4½*d.* for two.
101 Tingry (1804), p. 493; (1816), p. 374.
102 Watin (1785), p. 61; Tingry (1804), p. 493; (1816), p. 373; *Painter's . . . Pocket Manual* (1825), p. 114.
103 Watin (1785), pp. 78–9.
104 Bristow MSS., thesis (1983), vol. II, pp. 831–2.
105 Mansion House MSS., Willmot (1779–81).
106 Ibid., Willmot (1783–5).
107 Vanherman (1828), pp. 51–2.
108 Watin (1785), pp. 71–8.
109 P.R.O. MSS., E. 351/3261, M. vi^{v}.
110 Ibid., 3263, M. vi^{r}.
111 Ibid., 3270, M. viii^{r}; 3272, M. ix^{r}.
112 Gerbier (1663), p. 84.
113 Vanherman (1828), p. 52.
114 Tingry (1804), p. 492; (1816), p. 372.
115 Neve (1703), p. 143.
116 Watin (1785), pp. 106–7.
117 Cadet-de-Vaux (1801).
118 Candee (1965), pp. 124–8.
119 Butcher (1825), pp. 35–6; *Painter's . . . Pocket Manual* (1825), p. 137.
120 Vanherman (1828), pp. 18–19. He also gave (pp. 89–91) a formula for a 'Cement Paint' for exterior use. It was made simply by adding 'Incorporated oil' to Parker's cement (i.e. Roman cement), a material to which Tingry's later editor also referred (Tingry (1830), pp. 84–5), quoting Vanherman. In 1805, it will be remembered, he had used the term 'incorporated oil' to refer to fish-oil clarified using lime-water (see Chapter 10). This was no doubt an earlier version of his 1828 product.
121 Vanherman (1828), pp. 30–3.
122 Ibid., pp. 55–6. The drying linseed oil was to be prepared by shaking up 2 ounces of 'coarse' litharge with 1 pint of linseed oil put into a quart bottle of white glass, both night and morning for a week. The liquid was then decanted, the residue washed with oil of turpentine, and the oil returned to the bottle for a further week's treatment before use.
123 Ibid., pp. xii, xvii–xviii, 3–4, 24.

18. Varnishes, varnish-paints, and lacquers

1 Watin (1785), p. 291.
2 *Painter's . . . Pocket Manual* (1825), p. 80.
3 D'Aviler (1691), vol. I, p. 229; Blondel (1737), vol. I, p. 26.
4 Watin (1785), p. 240.
5 Caley (1792), p. 406.
6 Castle Museum, York, trade card of R.R. & T. Williamson.
7 P.R.O. MSS., WORK 19/48/1, ff. 50(iv), 56(iv), 79(iii).
8 R.I.B.A. MSS., CHA 3/1, pp. 247, 251
9 Brighton/Crace MS., pp. 15, 43, 67, 71 (discussed by Morley (1984), pp. 223, 85, 199, 110 respectively).
10 John Smith (1676), pp. 73–4.
11 Watin (1785), pp. 96–103; Tingry (1804) and (1816), *passim.*
12 Stalker & Parker (1688/1971), pp. xiv–xv.
13 Ibid., pp. 62–4.
14 Watin (1785), pp. 205, 234, 243, 250.
15 Stalker & Parker (1688/1971), pp. 9–10.
16 Watin (1785), p. 242; Vanherman (1828), p. 77.
17 Whittock (1827), p. 90.
18 Stalker & Parker (1688/1971), pp. 11–12.
19 Watin (1785), p. 239.
20 Ibid., pp. 239–40.
21 Ibid., p. 240.
22 Tingry (1804), pp. 122–3, 391; (1816), pp. 56–9, 272.
23 Watin (1785), p. 240.
24 Ibid., p. 239.
25 Tingry (1804), pp. 119, 389, 392; (1816), pp. 54, 271, 273.
26 Vanherman (1828), p. 79.
27 Whittock (1827), pp. 89–90.
28 Stalker & Parker (1688/1971), p. 11.
29 Tingry (1804), pp. 120, 391; (1816), pp. 55, 273.
30 Whittock (1827), pp. 88–9; *Painter's . . . Pocket Manual* (1825), p. 47.

31 D'Aviler (1691), vol. I, p. 229.
32 John Smith (1676), p. 79.
33 Whittock (1827), pp. 83–4.
34 Watin (1785), p. 243.
35 See discussion in Eastlake (1847), pp. 241–6, 288; and Merrifield (1849), vol. I, pp. cclxi–cclxxiv.
36 Salmon (1672), p. 215.
37 Watin (1785), pp. 247–8.
38 Vanherman (1828), pp. 73, 74, 75.
39 Whittock (1827), p. 84.
40 Hurst (1896), p. 434.
41 Watin (1785), pp. 233, 291.
42 Salmon (1672), p. 214.
43 Watin (1785), p. 250.
44 *Painter's . . . Pocket Manual* (1825), p. 53.
45 Ibid., p. 46.
46 Whittock (1827), p. 84.
47 Watin (1785), pp. 251–2.
48 Whittock (1827), p. 89.
49 Pincot [*c.* 1811], p. 24; Vanherman (1828), p. 79.
50 Watin (1785), pp. 78, 82–3, 289; Tingry (1804), p. 410; (1816), p. 291.
51 Watin (1785), pp. 96–8.
52 Tingry (1804), pp. 450, 524; (1816), pp. 329, 405.
53 Watin (1785), p. 287.
54 Vanherman (1828), pp. 79–80.
55 Vanherman (1828), p. 77.
56 Watin (1785), pp. 285–6.
57 Laxton (1818), p. 96.
58 Bartholomew (1846), para. 1500.
59 Pincot [*c.* 1811], p. 25.
60 Heaton (1940), p. 115.
61 Ure (1860), s.v. 'ROTTEN-STONE', vol. III, pp. 605–6; s.v. 'TRIPOLI', vol. III, p. 914.
62 Berger MSS., stock 1809–10, pp. 7, 33.
63 Stalker & Parker (1688/1971), pp. 2, 15, 16, 17.
64 Watin (1785), pp. 317–18.
65 Soane MSS., 'Ealing'; Pincot [*c.* 1811], p. 24.
66 Laxton (1818), p. 100; Skyring (1831), p. 91.
67 R.I.B.A. MSS., CHA 3/3, p. 69.
68 Boughton MS., vol. I, p. 181.
69 Wren Society, vol. IV (1927), p. 47 (Hampton Court); ibid., vol. VII (1930), p. 127 (Whitehall); P.R.O. MSS., WORK. 19/48/1, ff. 56(iv), 74(iii) (Kensington).
70 Tingry (1804), p. 445; (1816), p. 324.
71 Watin (1785), p. 102.
72 Stalker & Parker (1688/1971), p. xiv.
73 Ibid., pp. 8, 19–26.
74 Watin (1785), pp. 94, 241.
75 Ibid., p. 242.
76 Ibid., p. 93.
77 Ibid., pp. 249, 295.
78 Vanherman (1828), p. 78.
79 Watin (1785), p. 251.
80 Tingry (1804), p. 133; (1816), p. 68.
81 Tingry (1804), pp. 392, 395; (1816), pp. 273, 276.
82 Watin (1785), p. 252.
83 Tingry (1804), p. 139; (1816), pp. 74–5.
84 Tingry (1804), p. 136; (1816), pp. 71–3.
85 Watin (1785), pp. 98–9.
86 Ibid., pp. 100–2.
87 Tingry (1804), pp. 408, 446; (1816), pp. 289, 325.
88 Tingry (1804), p. 447; (1816), p. 326.
89 Watin (1785), p. 295.
90 Tingry (1804), pp. 448–9; (1816), pp. 327–8.
91 P.R.O. MSS., E. 351/3265, M. vi[v].
92 Dyrham MSS., D. 1799, E234.
93 Neve (1703), p. 216.
94 P.R.O. MSS., ADM. 68/683, August 1708.
95 Dossie (1758), vol. I, p. 208; (1764), vol. I, p. 224.
96 Dossie (1758), vol. I, p. 407; (1764), vol. I, p. 479.
97 Dossie (1758), vol. I, p. 138; (1764), vol. I, p. 149. The author of the *Practical Treatise* ((1795), p. 196) later mentioned that the 'Birmingham varnish' was the best for pictures.
98 *Adelphi Accounts* (1918), p. 8 (see further discussion in Bristow MSS., thesis (1983), vol. II, pp. 834–5).
99 Reynolds (1812), p. 13.
100 As noted above, Stalker & Parker mentioned the use of japan on coach-bodies, and Pincot discussed the techniques of varnish-painting in this respect at length (Stalker & Parker (1688/1971), p. 10; Pincot [*c.* 1811], pp. 23–33).
101 Rondelet (1812–n.d.), vol. V, pp. 233–7.
102 B.M. trade cards, Banks 89.28.
103 The method generally used by the Romans for painting plastered wall surfaces, such as those found at Pompeii, was true fresco, the surface being trowelled or otherwise worked while still wet to produce a glossy surface. The procedure was described by Vitruvius, and it appears that Pliny too was familiar with the use of fresco (Vitruvius, *l.* 7, *c.* iii; (1826), p. 205; Pliny, *l.* 33, *c.* lvi (resistence of an ochre to lime); *l.* 35, *c.* xxxi (pigments to which damp plaster is inimical); (1938–62), vol. 9 (1952), pp. 118–19, 296–7): for a discussion of this, see Laurie (1910), pp. 68–88.

In addition, Vitruvius described a method of protecting vermilion on walls from blackening by brushing them with a mixture of melted wax and oil, the surface then being heated using a pan of live coals and rubbed with a candle and clean cloth; and a similar process was described by Pliny (Vitruvius, *l.* 7, *c.* xi; (1826), p. 219; Pliny, *l.* 33, *c.* xl; (1988–62), vol. 9 (1952), p. 93).

Perhaps on this account (especially since it would readily explain the glossy surface of Roman murals) eighteenth-century interest centred on another technique mentioned by Pliny, that of wax-painting or 'encaustic', although he stated quite explicitly that it could not be used on walls. The information he gave concerning the method was, however, slight, although he noted that it was commonly used for naval and cargo ships, and also with an engraver for painting ivory. Evidently too, it was employed by artists for pictures. For ship-painting, the wax was melted by fire, while an Aegean artist had noted on a picture that the colours were 'burnt in'; and he listed the pigments which were used to colour the wax. (Pliny, *l.* 35, *cc.* xxxi, xxxix, xli; (1938–62), vol. 9 (1952), pp. 296–9, 350–1, 370–1.)

The principal mid-eighteenth-century study of the subject was undertaken by the Comte de Caylus, who published the results of experiments in the medium in his *Mémoire sur la peinture à l'encaustique et sur la peinture à la cire* in 1755 and an essay 'Du genre de l'espèce des peintures anciennes' in the *Mémoire de l'Académie des Inscriptions*, vol. XII (1771). In September 1758, Horace Walpole recorded in a letter to Sir Horace Mann: 'I have a painter in the house . . . We are just now practising, and have succeeded surprisingly in a new method of painting, discovered at Paris by Count Caylus, and intended to be the encaustic method of the ancients' (Walpole, *Letters* (1903–25), vol. iv, p. 185). The painter was the Swiss artist J.H. Müntz, who published his own work on the subject *Encaustic: or, Count Caylus's Method of Painting in the Manner of the Ancients* in 1760. Notes on wax painting were added by Dossie to the second edition of his *Handmaid to the Arts* (Dossie (1764), vol. i, p. 245ff); and the French writer Watin also commented on the subject (Watin (1785), pp. 106–8).

In his work of 1755, Caylus suggested four methods which would conform with Pliny's references: (1) grinding of pigments with melted wax and their application with the latter in a molten state; (2) forming droplets of molten wax into which pigments had been ground by beating with hot water, cooling them in suspension until solid, applying the resulting damp mass by brush in the normal way, and on completion applying heat to fuse the particles; (3) coating canvas, plaster, or a timber panel with wax, rubbing the surface with powdered chalk to counteract its greasiness, executing the painting in distemper, and on completion heating to allow the wax to impregnate the whole; and (4) painting in distemper in the normal way, covering the finished surface with wax, and heating as in the previous method. Although he did not believe the ancients would have dissolved wax in oil of turpentine, he nevertheless experimented with this technique too, but to make it work had to evolve a series of wax-varnish mixtures.

Encaustic is said to have been used some time before 1781 by the Italian artist Vincenzo Valdré at Stowe, Buckinghamshire (Raspe (1781), p. 33), although the precise method he adopted for the arabesque panels in the Music Room is unclear (Croft-Murray (1962–70), vol. II, pp. 55, 288–9, 310, pls. 94, 96). The ceiling-panels by J.F. Rigaud in the Library of 1787 at Packington Hall, Warwickshire, however, were executed on a black ground using the fourth method put forward by Caylus, being described by the artist as being in 'water and size colours', his son adding that they were: 'painted in Encaustic, the water colours being used with merely a sufficient quantity of fine thin size, made of glove leather, just strong enough to bind the colours to the stucco; and when the paintings were finished, they were sprinkled all over with melted wax, which being imbibed by the colours, was afterwards more equally diffused over the whole surface by a *salamander*, or heated iron being passed as near as possible to the pictures, without burning them' (Rigaud (1984), pp. 74–5). Although Croft-Murray believed the medium simply to have been 'glue tempera' (Croft-Murray (1962–70), vol. II (1970), pp. 55, 269, 310, pls. 101, 103), it was recorded in the 1950s that white waxy flakes were present above areas of black paint (Hey (1957–8), p. 188).

Although it seems unlikely that such methods were used other than exceptionally in the decoration of interiors, mid-nineteenth-century interest in the technique is found in the Entrance Hall of the British Museum, which was described in the early 1850s as having its ceiling 'painted in encaustic, in various colours, most harmoniously blended' (*London* (1851), p. 229). The scheme, designed about 1848 by Leonard Collmann (B.M. drawings, 1902-1-29-1) was of strongly archaeological character, and the idea of encaustic may well have been suggested by Michael Faraday's identification in 1837 of wax in samples of colour from the Acropolis at Athens ('Elgin Marbles', p. 106). Recent examination has indicated, however, that the work was probably executed in white lead in oil and varnished to give a glossy surface (Bristow MSS., reports, British Museum (1984)).

104 B.M. trade cards, Banks 89.27.
105 Watin ((1785), p. 248) did, however, include a formula for *vernis gras à l'or*; but, it will be remembered, he only advocated the use of oil varnishes for exterior purposes. The formula has been given above.
106 D'Aviler (1691), vol. I, p. 229.
107 Dossie (1758), vol. I, pp. 428–9; (1764), vol. I, p. 502.
108 Holme (1688), p. 425.
109 Stalker & Parker (1688/1971), pp. 63–4.
110 Ibid., p. 64.
111 Félibien (1676), p. 292; John Smith (1687), p. 73.
112 Watin (1785), p. 242.
113 Vanherman (1828), p. 77.
114 Tingry (1830), pp. 141–2.

19. Gilding and silvering

1 Gunther (1928), pp. 282, 283; John Smith (1687), pp. 71–2.
2 R.I.B.A. MSS., PEL/1, p. 154.
3 Berger MSS., stock 1805–6, p. 31; Félibien (1676), p. 279.
4 Wren Society, vol. XV (1938), p. 173; Osterley MSS., Adamson (1772–4).
5 Dautermann & *al.* (1964), p. 39a (quoting bill of Ince & Mayhew in possession of Croome Estate Trust, entry dated 5 October 1769).
6 Berger MSS., stock 1805–6, p. 31.
7 Gunther (1928), p. 283.
8 Dossie (1758), vol. I, p. 369; (1764), vol. I, p. 423.
9 Op. cit. (1825), p. 127.
10 P.R.O. MSS., E. 351/3450, M. xiii^{v}.
11 R.I.B.A. MSS., CHA 3/1, pp. 250, 251; Brighton/Crace MS., p. 74.
12 Dossie (1758), vol. I, p. 368; (1764), vol. I, p. 422.
13 John Smith (1687), p. 8; Stalker & Parker (1688/1971), pp. 55–6; Dossie (1758), vol. I, p. 370; (1764), vol. I, p. 424.
14 Stalker & Parker (1688/1971), p. 55.
15 John Smith (1687), p. 8.
16 Ibid., pp. 9–10.
17 Stalker & Parker (1688/1971), p. 55.
18 Dossie (1758), vol. I, pp. 370–1; (1764), vol. I, pp. 424–5.
19 John Smith (1687), p. 10.
20 Dossie (1758), vol. I, p. 371; (1764), vol. I, p. 425.
21 John Smith (1723), p. 10.
22 Dossie (1758), vol. I, p. 374; (1764), vol. I, p. 428.
23 Stalker & Parker (1688/1971), p. 54.
24 Félibien (1676), p. 293; Watin (1785), p. 160.
25 D'Aviler (1691), vol. I, p. 229.
26 John Smith (1687), p. 43.
27 Stalker & Parker (1688/1971), p. 54.
28 Dossie (1758), vol. I, pp. 372–4; (1764), vol. I, pp. 426–8. In addition, Vanherman ((1828), p. 78) suggested that his 'baked oil' (discussed in Chapter 18 above in connection with oil-varnish paints) would make an excellent gold-size if diluted with oil of turpentine.
29 For employment with gold powder, presumably in the reproduction of oriental lacquer objects, it was to be ground with enough vermilion to give it an opaque body, and diluted to a working consistency with oil of turpentine. This formula may be derived from Stalker & Parker ((1688/1971), pp. 28–9), who described a similar size based on identical quantities of the same constituents for the purpose of receiving metal powders. Vermilion and oil of turpentine were again added for use.
30 Dossie (1758), vol. I, pp. 374, 375, 384–5; (1764), vol. I, pp. 428, 429, 438–9.
31 Op. cit. (1825), pp. 60–2.
32 Bristow MSS., thesis (1983), vol. II, pp. 752–60; 765–8; 828–30; 835–6.
33 Stalker & Parker (1688/1971), p. 55.
34 John Smith (1687), pp. 69–70.
35 Stalker & Parker (1688/1971), p. 56.
36 Dossie (1758), vol. I, p. 371; (1764), vol. I, p. 425.
37 The use of chalk for the manufacture of gesso is in contrast to the practice of southern Europe, where gypsum was employed (see, for example, method for the preparation of gesso given by Cennini, *c.* 115ff ((1844), p. 68ff; (1930), p. 95ff).
38 Félibien (1676), pp. 281–91; Stalker & Parker (1688/1971), pp. 57–60; Dossie (1758), vol. I, pp. 377–83; (1764), vol. I, pp. 431–7; Watin (1785), pp. 162–78.
39 Stalker & Parker, ibid.
40 Félibien (1676), p. 291.
41 V.A.M. drawings, E. 3610–1911; Nostell Priory drawings, C3/1/4/170; Soane Museum drawings, Adam albums, vol. 54, No. 267.
42 Dossie (1758), vol. I, p. 377; (1764), vol. I, p. 431.
43 C.M. & G. MS.
44 Félibien (1676), p. 291; D'Aviler (1691), vol. I, p. 229; Watin (1785), pp. 172–3.
45 Op. cit. (1819), vol. III, p. 58.
46 Op. cit. (1823), p. 35.
47 Dossie (1758), vol. I, p. 403; (1764), vol. I, p. 474.
48 John Smith (1687), p. 43; (1705), p. 42.
49 Stalker & Parker (1688/1971), p. 58.
50 Watin (1785), p. 174.
51 Dossie (1758), vol. I, p. 401; (1764), vol. I, p. 471.
52 Beard (1968), p. 77.
53 Brighton/Crace MS., p. 1.
54 Dossie (1758), vol. I, pp. 401–2; (1764), vol. I, p. 472.
55 Dossie (1758), vol. I, p. 429; (1764), vol. I, pp. 502–3.
56 Stalker & Parker (1688/1971), p. 64.
57 John Smith (1687), p. 73.
58 P.R.O. MSS., WORK. 5/41 (extraordinary account).
59 Merrifield (1849), vol. II, p. 812.
60 P.R.O. MSS., E. 351/3257, M. xi^{r}.
61 Bristow MSS., reports, Frogmore (1986), p. 10.
62 Brighton/Crace MS., p. 117.
63 Ibid., p. 76.
64 Stalker & Parker (1688/1971), p. 60.

65 Félibien (1676), p. 290.
66 Stalker & Parker (1688/1971), p. 60.
67 Dossie (1758), vol. I, p. 382; (1764), vol. I, p. 436.
68 John Smith (1687), p. 71.
69 Gerbier (1663), p. 85.
70 Bristow MSS., reports, Queen's House (1986), pp. 26–32.
71 Illustrated in Fowler & Cornforth (1974), pl. XXXIII.
72 George Smith (1826), p. 165.
73 Gunther (1928), p. 283.
74 P.R.O. MSS., WORK. 5/29, f. 345v.
75 Lincoln Cathedral MS.
76 Gerbier (1663), p. 85.
77 *Builders Price-Book* (1776), p. 92; (1787), p. 140; (1794), p. 152.
78 Osterley MSS., Adamson (1772–4).
79 R.I.B.A. MSS., CHA 3/1, pp. 250, 251.
80 *Builders Price-Book* (1810), p. 86; (1813), p. 129.
81 Ibid. (1787), pp. 140–1; (1794), p. 152.
82 Ibid. (1810), p. 86; (1813), p. 129.

20. Graining, marbling, and other imitations

1 Nicholson (1823–5), p. 410.
2 B.M. trade cards, Heal 90.35.
3 Panels on loan from Bolton Museum and Art Gallery.
4 Op. cit. (1827), p. 20.
5 Laxton (1818), p. 99.
6 Martin (1813), p. 464.
7 Whittock (1827), p. 21.
8 Vanherman (1828), p. 58.
9 Laxton (1818), p. 96; Skyring (1831), p. 88.
10 Vanherman (1828), pp. 59, 60, 62.
11 Whittock (1827), p. 19.
12 For a discussion of megilp and related materials in fine art during the eighteenth and early nineteenth centuries, see Carlyle & Southall (1993).
13 Whittock (1827), pp. 21–2.
14 Whittock (1827), pp. 27, 30, 38; Vanherman (1828), p. 60.
15 Whittock (1827), pp. 27–8, 31.
16 Ibid., p. 21.
17 Vanherman (1828), p. 59.
18 Ibid., p. 61.
19 Butcher (1825), p. 31.
20 Whittock (1827), pp. 32–3.
21 Ibid., pp. 28, 39, 41.
22 Vanherman (1828), p. 58.
23 Whittock (1827), p. 43. Although on this occasion, since he specifically referred his readers to his illustration (fig. 39 in this volume), it is clear that 'the flat hog's-hair brush' was a tufted graining tool of this type, on other occasions he simply referred to 'the flat brush' (walnut and red satin wood in distemper, pp. 39, 46), 'the flat hog's-hair brush' (second method for birds eye maple and coral wood in distemper, pp. 43, 45), and 'the flat camel-hair brush' (coral wood in distemper, p. 45) making it ambiguous whether a graining tool or an ordinary flat brush was to be used.
24 Ibid., pp. 33, 41, 42, 43, 45.
25 Ibid., pp. 36, 38 (Spanish mahogany in distemper, first and second methods; satin wood in distemper).
26 Vanherman (1828), p. 60.
27 Ibid., p. 58.
28 Whittock (1827), p. 22.
29 Vanherman (1828), p. 59.
30 Whittock (1827), pp. 41, 46.
31 Ibid., pp. 41, 43.
32 Ibid., pp. 28, 40, 42, 43, 44.
33 Vanherman (1828), p. 59.
34 Whittock (1827), pp. 35, 36, 38, 46.
35 Vanherman (1828), p. 59.
36 Whittock (1827), pp. 23, 28, 36, 37, 40, 41.
37 Vanherman (1828), pp. 58, 59, 61.
38 Ibid., pp. 58, 59.
39 Whittock (1827), p. 43 (bird's eye maple, first method, in distemper), p. 39 (walnut in distemper), p. 29 (oak in distemper), p. 44 (birds eye maple, second method, in distemper), respectively.
40 Ibid.: camel or sable-hair pencil to add veins, p. 28 (oak in distemper); sable-hair pencil to add dark touches, p. 40 (rosewood, first method); sable-hair pencil to add spots, p. 46 (red satin wood); tips of the fingers to add knots, pp. 43–4 (bird's eye maple, second method).
41 Ibid., pp. 33, 35.
42 Vanherman (1828), pp. 59, 61.
43 Whittock (1827), pp. 23, 35, 36, 39.
44 Ibid., p. 42.
45 Ibid., p. 22.
46 John Smith (1687), p. 47.
47 Whittock (1827), p. 45.
48 Ibid., pp. 20, 24, 29–30.
49 Ibid., pp. 52, 54, 56, 57, 60.
50 Ibid., pp. 50, 53.
51 Ibid., pp. 50–1, 52–3. Other instances include: Florentine ruin marble (p. 54); Siena marble, first method, in oil (p. 55); *verde antico*, second method, in distemper (p. 60).
52 Ibid., p. 50.
53 Whittock (ibid.) mentioned sable pencils in connection with the veining of: porphyry (pp. 64–5); Siena, in oil (pp. 55–6); *verde antico*, first method, in oil (pp. 57–9); and white veined marble, first method, in oil (pp. 50–1). Camel-hair pencils were used to add veins in white veined marble, second method, in distemper (pp. 52–3); and to add fossils in *verde antico*, third method, in distemper (p. 61).
54 Ibid., p. 60.
55 Whittock (ibid.) called for use of a feather in the imitation of *verde antico* by the third method he described (p. 61), and a partly cut away goose quill in the first method for the same in oil (pp. 57–8). A wash leather was also to be used for the latter and in the imitation of black and gold marble on a ground of gold leaf (pp. 63–4). His first method for *verde antico* also required a square piece of cork, notched in one or two places, and a softener was to be used in connection with the imitation of Siena marble in oil (pp. 55–6). A dusting brush was employed for the latter purpose, however, in the cases of: dove coloured marble in oil (pp. 53–4); Florentine marble, ordinary variety, in distemper (p. 55); Siena marble, in distemper (pp. 56–7); *verde antico*, second method, in distemper (p. 60); and white veined marble, in oil (pp. 50–1).
56 Ibid., p. 52.
57 Ibid., p. 51.
58 Vanherman (1828), pp. 63–4.
59 Whittock (1828), pp. 57, 63, 65.
60 John Smith (1687), p. 52.
61 Evelyn (1706), p. 271; P.R.O. MSS., WORK. 5/23 (extraordinary account, Lord Treasurer's Building, second book).
62 P.R.O. MSS., WORK. 5/24 (extraordinary account).
63 Bristow MSS., thesis (1983), vol. II, pp. 821–2.
64 P.R.O. MSS., AO. 1/2429/71, M.xiiiv.
65 Reynolds (1812), pp. 18–21.
66 Whittock (1827), p. 37.
67 Ibid., p. 32.
68 Nicholson (1823–5), p. 417.
69 Whittock (1827), p. 32.
70 P.R.O. MS., E. 351/3271, M. xiir.
71 Ibid., E. 351/3254, M. vr; E. 351/3256, M. vv; E. 351/3271, M. viiv.
72 Stalker & Parker (1688/1971), p. 82.
73 Evelyn (1706), p. 271.
74 Félibien (1676), pp. 292–3.
75 Dyrham MSS., D. 1799, E234 (Hauduroy's account); Bristow (1979), p. 144; Bristow MSS., thesis (1983), vol. II, pp. 752–60.
76 Bristow MSS., reports, Ham (1989), pp. 19–21 (referring to five paint samples taken by Jo Darrah, Department of Conservation, Victoria and Albert Museum, in 1979–80).
77 Stalker & Parker (1688/1971), pp. 79–82.
78 Vanherman (1828), pp. 102–3.

79 Whittock (1827), p. 64.
80 Dyrham MSS., D. 1799, E234.
81 Croft-Murray, vol. I (1962), p. 217a (quoting letter from Isaac Bayley to Thomas Foley, 3 March 1705, in possession of Mr H.T.H. Foley, Stoke Edith, Herefordshire).
82 P.R.O. MSS., WORK 19/48/1, ff. 50(iv), 64(iii), 74(iii).
83 Lincoln Cathedral MS.
84 Laxton (1818), pp. 96, 99.
85 P.R.O. MSS., E. 351/3259, M. xxvi^{r-v}; E. 351/3263, M. xvii^{v}.
86 Bristow MSS., reports, Queen's House (1986), p. 23.
87 For a fuller discussion, see Bristow (1980) and Welsh & Grandquist (1983).
88 B.M. trade cards, Heal 89.53.
89 Bowood MSS., Bowood bills, Spinnage's account.
90 Bristow MSS., reports, Frogmore (1986), pp. 7–11.
91 For a fuller discussion, see Bristow (1980).
92 Roberts (1939), pp. 44, 46.
93 Martin (1813), p. 490.
94 Nicholson (1823–5), p. 379; ibid., 'The Practical Builder's Perpetual Price-book' (appendix to the main text), p. 137.
95 Bristow MSS., notes, C. 105 (watercolour in possession of John J. O'Connell, Dublin).
96 Lincoln Castle MS.
97 Bennett (1833), p. 295.
98 *Leeds Arts Calendar* (1983), pl. 43.
99 P.R.O. MSS., WORK. 5/27 (bound into Hampton Court account between January and February 1677, preceding joiner's and carver's accounts); Tredegar MSS., 102/98.
100 Stalker & Parker (1688/1977), pp. 79–81.
101 Ibid., p. 81. Salmon ((1672), pp. 220–2) also gave two methods for the imitation of tortoise-shell.
102 Ure (1860), s.v. 'MOTHER OF PEARL', vol. III, p. 207.
103 Vanherman (1828), pp. 102–3.
104 Stalker & Parker (1688/1971), pp. 5–6.
105 To make true gold powder, Dossie indicated, gold leaf was ground with virgin honey on a stone, and the resulting powder washed several times to free it from the latter before being dried (Dossie (1758), vol. I, p. 386).

German gold powder was made in the same way from Dutch gold, which he defined as gilded copper beaten into leaves (ibid., pp. 369, 386).

'Aurum Mosaicum' or 'aurum musivum' was prepared by grinding an amalgam of tin and mercury with sulphur and ammonium chloride, and heating the product to leave a residue of bright flaky tin sulphide (ibid., p. 387). For further information on preparation of the latter, see also: Leuchs (1829), vol. II, pp. 79–81; Zerr & Rübencamp (1908), p. 155.

Silver powder, Dossie notes, was made in the same way as gold powder (Dossie (1758), vol. I, p. 402).

'Argentum musivum' was prepared by dissolving 'bismuth or tin glass' in molten tin, amalgamating the product with mercury, and bruising the resulting paste into a flaky powder (ibid., pp. 402–3).

Copper powder was made by precipitation from a solution of copper nitrate on the addition of iron (ibid., p. 404).

See also Dossie (1764), vol. I, pp. 423, 440, 441, 472–3, 477.
106 Berger MSS., stock 1801–2, p. 59; stock 1805–6, p. 22; stock 1809–10, p. 24.
107 Dossie (1758), vol. I, pp. 404–5; (1764), vol. I, pp. 476–8.
108 Stalker & Parker (1688/1971), pp. 26–30.
109 D'Aviler (1691), vol. I, p. 230.
110 Op. cit. (1825), p. 135.
111 Whittock (1827), p. 153.
112 Op. cit. [*c.* 1830], pp. 151, 152.
113 Bristow (1987), p. 45; Bristow MSS., thesis (1983), vol. II, pp. 798–812.
114 Bristow MSS., reports, Soane Museum (1986b), pp. 2–3.
115 Brighton/Crace MS., pp. 1–2.
116 Ibid., p. 3.
117 Ibid., pp. 8, 11.
118 Ibid., p. 71.
119 Ibid., p. 69.
120 Morley (1984), p. 87 (quoting MS. in Royal Archive, No. 33529).
121 Watin (1785), p. 31.
122 Vanherman (1828), p. 45.
123 Whittock (1827), p. 142.
124 Hay (1847), pp. 168–74.

21. Colour mixing

1 Tingry (1804), pp. 317–18; (1816), p. 201. Copied as usual in *Painter's . . . Pocket Manual* (1825), p. 103.
2 A well-known example of this is the attractive volume of *Historical Colours* first published by Thomas Parsons & Sons Ltd in 1934 (4th edn, 1950).
3 Pincot [*c.* 1811], pp. 19–22.
4 Nicholson (1819). s.v. 'PAINTNG, *Economical*', vol. II, p. 417.
5 Gunther (1928), p. 282.
6 Rutter (1823), p. 51.
7 Salmon (1734), pp. 57–8.
8 Op. cit. (1787), p. 134; (1794), p. 146.
9 John Smith (1687), p. 46.
10 Pincot [*c.* 1811], p. 8; Vanherman (1828), pp. 8–16.
11 See discussion of this in Bristow (1996a), Chapter 5.
12 Op. cit. (1810), p. 83; (1813), p. 126.
13 Pincot [*c.* 1811], p. 35.
14 Skyring (1831), p. 88.
15 Phillips (1804), pp. 127–8; Laxton (1818), p. 96.
16 Englefield (1936), pp. 185–6, 190–1.
17 1 Jac. I, c. 20.
18 Vanherman (1828), p. 38.
19 Hay (1846), p. 44.
20 Black was used, for example, to grey the pink used in the frieze of the Gallery at Osterley Park, Middlesex, about 1770 (Bristow MSS., reports, Osterley (1989), p. 34).
21 Harrison (1577), bk. 2. ch. X. f. 84^{v}; Gunther (1928), p. 80.
22 Tingry (1830), p. 60.
23 Pincot [*c.* 1811], pp. 14, 18.
24 Vanherman (1828), pp. 39–40.
25 See discussion of this in Bristow (1996a), Chapter 7.
26 Bullet (1788), p. 546.
27 Nicholson (1819), s.v. 'PAINTING, *Economical*', vol. II, p. 416; Nicholson (1825), pp. 407–8.
28 Watin (1785), p. 41.
29 Raper (1924), p. 81.
30 Pincot [*c.* 1811], p. 17.
31 Butcher (1825), p. 29.
32 Tingry (1804), p. 389; (1816), p. 270.
33 Tingry (1830), pp. 270–1.
34 Reynolds (1812), p. 15.
35 D'Aviler (1691), vol. I, p. 228; John Smith (1687), p. 51.
36 Watin (1785), p. 41.
37 Tingry (1804), p. 392; (1816), p. 273; *Painter's . . . Pocket Manual* (1825), pp. 105, 108.
38 Nicholson (1819), s.v. 'PAINTING, *Economical*', vol. II, p. 417.
39 John Smith (1687), pp. 46, 52; Bullet (1691), p. 284.
40 Bristow MSS., thesis (1983), vol. II, pp. 820–21.
41 Ibid., pp. 822–3.
42 Bullet (1691), p. 284.
43 Nicholson (1819), s.v. 'PAINTING, *Economical*', vol. II, p. 417.
44 Skyring (1831), p. 77; Cook (1820), p. lxxxix.
45 Watin (1785), p. 41; Tingry (1804), p. 392; (1816), p. 273; Nicholson (1819), s.v. 'PAINTING, *Economical*', vol. II, p. 417; Butcher (1825), p. 30; Vanherman (1828), p. 38.
46 Nicholson (1825), p. 412.
47 Whittock (1827), p. 132.
48 Watin (1785), p. 45.
49 Watin (1785), p. 42; Reynolds (1812), p. 17; Nicholson (1825), p. 412; Vanherman (1828), pp. 28, 39, 42.
50 Op. cit. (1825), p. 106.
51 Pincot [*c.* 1811], p. 35.
52 Laxton (1818), p. 96.

53 Reynolds (1812), p. 17.
54 Tingry (1804), p. 408; (1816), p. 289.
55 Bristow MSS., reports, Soane Museum (1988), p. 5.
56 Scarlet paterae are shown, for example, on a ceiling design in the Kauffman album at the Pierpont Morgan Library, New York, (No. 1966.10.54), and a brightish red on paterae in Adam's design for the ceiling of Lloyd's Coffee House (Soane Museum drawings, Adam albums, vol. XII, No. 120).
57 N.L.I. drawings, uncatalogued Wyatt collection (sketch for V.A.M. drawings, No. 7231.38).
58 Watin (1785), p. 21.
59 1 Jac. I, c. 20.
60 John Smith (1687), p. 52; Nicholson (1823–5), p. 416; *Painter's . . . Pocket Manual* (1825), p. 106.
61 Nicholson (1825), p. 412.
62 Salmon (1734), p. 58; *Builders Price-Book* (1787), pp. 139, 141; (1794), p. 150, 153.
63 Vanherman (1828), pp. 38–9.
64 Reynolds (1812), pp. 11–12.
65 Tingry (1804), p. 395; (1816), p. 276.
66 John Smith (1687), p. 52; Reynolds (1812), p. 10.
67 Watin (1785), pp. 42–3.
68 Tingry (1804), pp. 395–6; (1816), p. 277.
69 Op. cit. (1825), p. 106.
70 Nicholson (1819), s.v. 'PAINTING, *Economical*', vol. II, p. 417.
71 Butcher (1825), p. 31.
72 Watin (1785), pp. 42–3.
73 Tingry (1804), p. 396; (1816), p. 277.
74 Vanherman (1828), p. 26.
75 John Smith (1687), p. 94.
76 Nicholson (1819), s.v. 'PAINTING, *Economical*', vol. II, p. 417.
77 Watin (1785), pp. 42–3; Tingry (1804), p. 395; (1816), p. 276.
78 Watin (1785), p. 43.
79 Op. cit. (1825), p. 106.
80 Tingry (1804), pp. 395, 397; (1816), p. 276, 278.
81 Butcher (1825), p. 31.
82 Vanherman (1828), p. 26.
83 Bristow MSS., reports, Soane Museum (1986a); (1986b).
84 Tingry (1804), p. 397; (1816), pp. 278.
85 Vanherman (1828), p. 38.
86 John Smith (1687), p. 52.
87 *Painter's . . . Pocket Manual* (1825), pp. 105, 106; Reynolds (1812), p. 10.
88 Vanherman (1828), p. 27.
89 Tingry (1804), p. 358; (1816), p. 238.
90 Vanherman (1828), p.28.
91 John Smith (1687), p. 24.
92 Ibid., pp. 51–2.
93 Op. cit. (1825), p. 107.
94 Tingry (1830), p. 275.
95 Salmon (1734), p. 57.
96 Nicholson (1823–5), p. 416; *Painter's . . . Pocket Manual* (1825), p. 107.
97 Reynolds (1812), pp. 11, 16.
98 Watin (1785), p. 46; Tingry (1804), p. 398; (1816), p. 279.
99 Op. cit. (1825), p. 106.
100 Watin (1785), p. 45.
101 Bullet (1691), p. 285.
102 Op. cit. (1787), p. 138; (1794), p. 150.
103 Tingry (1804), pp. 317-18; (1816), p. 201; *Painter's . . . Pocket Manual* (1825), p. 103.
104 D'Aviler (1691), vol. I, p. 229.
105 Watin (1785), p. 43.
106 Laxton (1818), p. 88.
107 Nicholson (1819), s.v. 'PAINTING, *Economical*', vol. II, p. 417.
108 Pincot [*c.* 1811], p. 21.
109 Watin (1785), p. 43.
110 Watin (1785), pp. 44, 46; Tingry (1804), pp. 398; (1816), p. 279.
111 John Smith (1687), p. 25.
112 Bristow MSS., notes, C. 104A (Somerset House); reports, Frogmore (1986), p. 89.
113 John Smith (1687), p. 93; Tingry (1804), p. 405; (1816), pp. 286–7.
114 Whittock (1827), pp. 12, 132; Bristow MSS., notes, C. 50.
115 D'Aviler (1691), vol. I, p. 228; Vanherman (1828), p. 39.
116 Watin (1785), p. 44; Tingry (1804), p. 405; (1816), pp. 286–7.
117 Osterley MSS., Burchett (1779); Burchett (1780); Burchett (1781a).
118 Vanherman (1828), p. 39.
119 Tingry (1830), p. 275.
120 Philadelphia (1986), p. 42.
121 Bristow MSS, notes, C. 104A.
122 Gordon Castle MS., p. 7.
123 Butcher (1825), p. 30; Nicholson (1825), p. 412.
124 Bristow MSS., notes, C. 83.
125 Vanherman (1828), p. 29.
126 Berger MSS., 1831 formula book, p. 213 (formula dated 1840).
127 Ibid., p. 78.
128 Vanherman (1828), p. 86.
129 Berger MSS., 1831 formula book, p. 217 (formula dated 1841).
130 Ibid., p. 101.
131 Ibid., pp. 105, 215 (latter formula dated 1841).
132 Ibid., p. 219 (formula dated 1844).
133 Bristow MSS., reports, Westminster (1985–6).
134 Pyne (1819), vol. III, p. 40, pl. facing p. 43 (illustrated in companion volume, Bristow (1996a).
135 Pincot [*c.* 1811], p. 22.
136 Bristow MSS., reports, Frogmore (1986), p. 90.
137 Bristow (1985), p. 41; Bristow MSS., thesis (1983), vol. II, p. 775.
138 Salmon (1734), p. 58.
139 Watin (1785), p. 45.
140 Bristow (1983), p. 19 (wallpaper from Frognal House, London); Bristow MSS., notes, CS. 30.
141 John Smith (1687), p. 51.
142 Ham MSS., Gooderick's account; MacTaggart (1980), p. 42; Bristow MSS., notes, CS. 21 (my thanks are due to Jo Darrah of the Victoria and Albert Museum for samples of paint).
143 Bristow MSS., reports, Queen's House (1986), pp. 40–48.
144 Bristow MSS., notes, C. 69.
145 Bristow MSS., reports, Westminster (1985–6).

Appendix A. Glossary of colour names

1 Pyne (1819), vol. III, p. 52.
2 Vanherman (1828), p. 41.
3 Rondelet (1812–n.d.), vol. V, p. 236.
4 Nicholson (1819), s.v. 'PAINTING, *Economical*', vol. II, p. 417.
5 John Smith (1687), p. 51.
6 Nicholson (1823–5), p. 416.
7 Butcher (1825), p. 31.
8 Bullet (1691), p. 285; Stalker & Parker (1688/1971), pp. 19–21; Watin (1785), pp. 91, 94, 295; Tingry (1804), p. 388; (1816), p. 269; Reynolds (1812), p. 12; Nicholson (1825), p. 411.
9 Stalker & Parker (1688/1971), *ibid.*; Castle Museum, York, trade card of R.R. & T. Williamson.
10 Rondelet (1812–n.d.), vol. V, p. 236.
11 Gerbier (1663), p. 83.
12 Vanherman (1828), pp. 10, 16.
13 Tingry (1830), p. 84.
14 B.M. trade cards, Banks 89.27, 28 (London Patent Colour-Works); Crease (1808), p. [16]; Bentley (1817), p. 5.
15 P.R.O. MSS., WORK. 5/29.
16 Ibid., ADM. 68/686.
17 Boughton MS., vol. I, p. 181.
18 R.I.B.A. MSS., PEL/1, p. 76.
19 Petworth MSS., PHA 6615, No. 265.
20 Op. cit., (1794), p. 130.
21 Mansion House MSS., Downes (1748); Willmot (1779–81).
22 Osterley MSS., surveyor's notebook, p. 33.
23 Ibid., pp. 45, 48, 49.
24 Dunham Massey MSS.

25 Watin (1785), pp. 67–8; *Painter's . . . Pocket Manual* (1825), pp. 164–5.
26 P.R.O. MSS., WORK. 5/3 (September 1662).
27 Moxon (1703), p. 249.
28 Soane Museum drawings, Soane perspective albums, vol. VI, p. 119.
29 Pyne (1819), vol. III, pp. 52, 80.
30 See Bristow (1996a), chapters 2 and 5.
31 Soane Museum drawings, Adam albums, vol. XII, No. 64.
32 Osterley MSS., Adamson (1787).
33 G.L.R.O. MSS., Pepper.
34 Fowler & Cornforth (1974), pp. 170–3.
35 *History of the King's Works*, vol. V (1976), p. 234.
36 Bristow MSS., thesis (1983), vol. II, p. 840.
37 Salmon (1734), p. 58.
38 Op. cit., (1787), p. 139; (1794), p. 150.
39 Reynolds (1812), p. 16.
40 Watin (1785), p. 45.
41 Phillips (1812), p. 212.
42 Salmon (1734), p. 58.
43 Op. cit. (1787), p. 139; (1794), p. 150.
44 R.I.B.A. MSS., CHA 3/1, p. 253; 3/2, p. 211; 3/3, pp. 67, 122, 336.
45 Osterley MSS., Adamson (1772–4).
46 Op. cit. (1810), pp. 81, 83, 84; (1813), pp. 124, 126, 127.
47 Englefield (1936), p. 186.
48 Skyring (1831), p. 88.
49 Stapleton & *al.* (1975), p. 58.
50 Phillips (1812), p. 196; (1821), p. 156; Laxton (1818), p. 88.
51 P.R.O. MSS., E. 351/3256, M. v^{v}; 3263, M. xi^{r}.
52 See discussion of this in Bristow (1996a), Chapter 5.
53 Blondel (1752–6), vol. I, p. 167.
54 Soane Museum drawings, Adam albums, vol. XI, Nos. 112, 161, 262; vol. XII, Nos. 42, 90, 136.
55 B.M. trade cards, Banks 89. 28.
56 Ham MSS., Gooderick's account.
57 MacTaggart (1980), pp. 42, 44.
58 P.R.O. MSS., E. 351/3263, MM. viii^{v}, vi^{r}.
59 Ibid., 3255, M. v^{v}; 3256, M.v^{v}.
60 King's College, Cambridge MS.
61 Brighton/Crace MS., p. 41.
62 Osterley MSS., Adamson (1787).
63 Reynolds (1812), p. 16.
64 Op. cit. (1787), p. 139; (1794), p. 150.
65 Reynolds (1812), p. 16.
66 Rondelet (1812–n.d.), vol. V, p. 236.
67 Salmon (1734), p. 58.
68 Watin (1785), p. 45.
69 Holme (1688), p. 13.
70 Reynolds (1812), p. 16.
71 Phillips (1812), p. 212.
72 Rondelet (1812–n.d.), vol. V, p. 236.
73 Bennett (1833), s.v. 'PAINT', p. 295.
74 Op. cit. (1787), p. 139; (1794), p. 150.
75 R.I.A. MSS., Charlemont letter, first series, vol. II, No. 10 (25 August 1767).
76 Soane Museum drawings, Adam albums, vol. XI, No. 226.
77 Osterley MSS., Adamson (1772–4).
78 Brighton/Crace MS., pp. 1, 2, 3, 8, 11, 62, 63, 67, 69, 71, 85, 90, 98, 105, 106, 126.
79 Pincot [*c.* 1811], p. 22.
80 Laxton (1818), p. 96.
81 Phillips (1812), p. 212; (1821), p. 170.
82 P.R.O. MSS., AO. 1/2422/49, M.xxvi^{r}.
83 John Smith (1687), p. 52; Nicholson (1823–5), p. 416; *Painter's . . . Pocket Manual* (1825), p. 105.
84 King's College, Cambridge MS.
85 Rondelet (1812–n.d.), vol. V, p. 236.
86 Nicholson (1825), pp. 410, 412.
87 Whittock (1827), p. 132.
88 P.R.O. MSS., AO. 1/2422/49, M. xiv^{v}.
89 Ibid., E. 351/3258, M. vi^{v}.
90 Soane Museum drawings, Adam albums, vol. XI, No. 251; vol. XII, Nos. 24, 42, 76, 131.
91 Bennett (1833), s.v. 'PAINT', p. 295.
92 Nicholson (1819), s.v. 'BROWN', vol. I, pp. 137–8.
93 Soane Museum drawings, Adam albums, vol. XII, No. 131.
94 Hay (1828), p. 58.
95 Nicholson (1819), s.v. 'BROWN', vol. I, pp. 137–8.
96 Crease (1808), p. [16].
97 Powys (1899), p. 146.
98 Nicholson (1819), s.v. 'BROWN', vol. I, pp. 137–8.
99 Ibid.
100 B.M. trade cards, Banks 89.28.
101 Nicholson (1819), s.v. 'BROWN', vol. I, pp. 137–8.
102 John Smith (1687), p. 51; Nicholson (1823–5), p. 416; *Painter's . . . Pocket Manual* (1825), p. 105.
103 Vanherman (1828), pp. 27, 29.
104 Tingry (1804), p. 398; (1816), p. 278.
105 Watin (1785), p. 42.
106 Butcher (1825), p. 30; Britton (1823), pls. 9, 10; Rutter (1823), p. 54, pl. 7.
107 B.L. MSS., Add. 41133, f. 12^{v} (letter dated 5 May 1770).
108 R.I.B.A. MSS., CHA 3/1, p. 247.
109 Pincot [*c.* 1811], p. 35.
110 Op. cit., (1810), p. 69; (1813), p. 111.
111 Laxton (1818), p. 88.
112 Rondelet (1812–n.d.), vol. V, p. 236.
113 N.L.I. drawings, uncatalogued Wyatt collection.
114 John Smith (1687), p. 52; Nicholson (1823–5), p. 416; *Painter's . . . Pocket Manual* (1825), p. 106.
115 Wren Society, vol. XIX (1942), pp. 98–9.
116 Salmon (1734), p. 58.
117 P.R.O. MSS., AO. 1/2429, M. vii^{v}.
118 Dyrham MSS., D. 1799, E234.
119 R.I.B.A. MSS., WRE/2/20.
120 Fiennes (1947), p. 55.
121 Croft-Murray, vol. I (1962), p. 216b (quoting letter from Isaac Bayley to Thomas Foley, 3 March 1705, in possession of Mr H.T.H. Foley, Stoke Edith, Herefordshire).
122 Leadbeater (1770), p. 44.
123 Op. cit. [1667], pp. 70, 71.
124 Watin (1785), pp. 45–6; Tingry (1804), p. 409; (1816), p. 290.
125 Op. cit., (1825), p. 107.
126 Stalker & Parker (1688/1971), p. 25.
127 John Smith (1687), p. 94.
128 Nicholson (1825), pp. 410, 412.
129 Reynolds (1812), p. 18; Butcher (1825), p. 31; *Painter's . . . Pocket Manual* (1825), p. 108.
130 Tingry (1830), p. 275.
131 Vanherman (1828), pp. 10, 15.
132 Bristow MSS., thesis (1983), vol. II, pp. 796–7.
133 Salmon (1734), p. 58.
134 *Builders Price-Book* (1787), p. 134; (1794), p. 146; Laxton (1818), p. 96.
135 Pincot [*c.* 1811], p. 8.
136 Vanherman (1828), p. 10 (s.v. 'BLACK').
137 Petworth MSS., PHA 6614, No. 219, p. [10].
138 Crease (1808), p. 12.
139 Tredegar MSS., 68/76; Crease (1808), p. [16].
140 Lingard (1825), p. 10.
141 B.M. trade cards, Banks 89.28.
142 Ibid.
143 Vanherman (1828), pp. 10, 15.
144 Bentley (1817), p. 5; Bennett (1833), s.v. 'PAINT, p. 295.
145 B.M. trade cards, Banks 89.28.
146 King's College, Cambridge MS.
147 Fowler & Cornforth (1974), p. 206.
148 Bristow MSS., thesis (1983), vol. II, pp. 789–97.
149 R.I.B.A. MSS., PEL/1, p. 82.
150 Osterley MSS., Adamson (1772–4).
151 Cust (1914), vol. I, p. 42.
152 Whittock (1827), pp. 133, 153.

153 Nostell MSS., C3/1/5/6/2.
154 Hay (1828), p. 58.
155 Reynolds (1812), pp. 17–18.
156 Attree (1809), p. 6.
157 Cooper-Hewitt drawings, 1948-40-6 (reproduced by Morley 1984), pl. 150).
158 Waller (1686), pl. following p. 28.
159 Holme (1688), bk. I, ch. 2, p. 13.
160 Salmon (1734), p. 56.
161 Op. cit. (1787), p. 134; (1794), p. 146.
162 Salmon (1734), pp. 57, 58.
163 Op. cit. (1787), p. 138; (1794), p. 150.
164 Laxton (1818), p. 96.
165 R.I.B.A. MSS., PEL/1; Petworth MSS., PHA 6614, No. 219; Osterley MSS., Adamson (1772–4); R.I.B.A. MSS., CHA 3/1–3.
166 B.M. trade cards, Heal 89.75.
167 Bennett (1833), s.v. 'PAINT', p. 295.
168 Salmon (1734), p. 58.
169 Op. cit. (1787), p. 134; (1794), p. 146.
170 Reynolds (1812), pp. 9–10.
171 Dyrham MSS., D. 1799, E234; Gordon Castle MS., p. 1.
172 Watin (1785), p. 42.
173 Waller (1686), plate between pp. 26, 27.
174 John Smith (1687), p. 93.
175 Vanherman (1828), p. 38.
176 Osterley MSS., Adamson (1772–4).
177 Rutter (1823), p. 37.
178 Linstrum (1972), p. 84.
179 Hay (1828), p. 53.
180 R.I.B.A. MSS., CHA 3/1, p. 250.
181 Englefield (1936), pp. 186, 190.
182 John Smith (1687), p. 94.
183 Vanherman (1828), pp. 28, 29, 30.
184 Hay (1846), pp. 18, 50; pl. 21, Nos. 1–3.
185 Englefield (1936), p. 190.
186 Laxton (1818), p. 96.
187 Dunham Massey MSS.
188 Nostell MSS., C3/1/5/6/2.
189 George Smith (1826), p. 165.
190 Bartholomew (1846), para. 1934.
191 Cust (1914), vol. I, p. 41.
192 Nicholson (1819), s.v. 'PAINTING, *Economical*', vol. II, p. 417.
193 Butcher (1825), p. 30; *Painter's . . . Pocket Manual*, p. 108.
194 Hay (1846), pl. 22, Nos. 4, 5.
195 Englefield (1936), p. 190.
196 Laxton (1818), p. 96; Skyring (1831), p. 88.
197 Brighton/Crace MS., pp. 11, 13, 14, 26.
198 John Smith (1687), p. 51; Butcher (1825), p. 24; *Painter's . . . Pocket Manual* (1825), p. 107; Nicholson (1825), p. 412.
199 Pincot [*c.* 1811], p. 7.
200 Rondelet (1812–n.d.), vol. V, p. 236.
201 Petworth MSS., PHA 6614, No. 219, p. [10].
202 Waller (1686), plate between pp. 26, 27.
203 Watin (1785), p. 43.
204 Tingry (1804), p. 397; (1816), p. 278.
205 Op. cit. (1825), p. 106.
206 P.R.O. MSS., E. 351/3263, M. vi^{v}.
207 Salmon (1734), p. 58.
208 John Smith (1687), p. 93.
209 Rondelet (1812–n.d.), vol. V, p. 236.
210 Pincot [*c.* 1811], p. 22.
211 Watin (1785), p. 30; Nicholson (1825), p. 412; Butcher (1825), p. 30; Vanherman (1828), pp. 85–6.
212 Salmon (1734), p. 58.
213 Bennett (1833), s.v. 'PAINT', p. 295.
214 Op. cit. (1794), p. 150.
215 Ibid. (1810), pp. 81, 83, 84; (1813), pp. 124, 126, 127.
216 Laxton (1818), p. 96.
217 Phillips (1812), p. 213; B.M. trade cards, Banks 89.28 (London Patent Colour-Works).
218 P.R.O. MSS., E. 351/3270, M. viii^{r}; 3272, M. x^{r}.
219 Ham MSS., Gooderick's account.
220 Caley (1792), pp. 401, 402.
221 Gerbier (1663), p. 84.
222 P.R.O. MSS., E. 351/3253, M. ix^{r}; 3256, M. v^{v}; 3258, M. v^{v}; 3263, M. vi^{r}; 3265, M. vi^{v}.
223 Ham MSS., Gooderick's account.
224 Wren Society, vol. IV (1827), p. 53 – Hampton Court; ibid., vol. VI (1930), p. 130 – Whitehall; P.R.O. MSS., WORK. 19/48/1, f. 50(iv – Kensington.
225 P.R.O. MSS., WORK. 5/15, Westminster Palace, May 1670.
226 Boughton MS., vol. I, pp. 159, 175, 181.
227 Soane Museum drawings, Adam albums, vol. XI, Nos. 112, 160 161, 226, 240, 250, 251, 256, 261, 262; vol. XII, Nos. 1, 2, 24, 42 43, 60, 62, 63, 76, 97, 103, 114, 128, 131, 143, 151; vol. XIII, Nos 41, 42, 70, 104, 105, 128, 131, 139; vol. XIV, Nos. 7, 30, 31, 58, 71 72, 73, 74.
228 Osterley MSS., Adamson (1772–4); ibid. (1787); R.I.B.A. MSS. CHA 3/1–3; Dunham Massey MSS.
229 Rondelet (1812–n.d.), vol. V, p. 236.
230 Berger MSS, 1831 formula book, p. 217.
231 Ibid., p. 105.
232 Vanherman (1828), pp. 86–7.
233 Crease (1808), p. [16]; Phillips (1812), p. 213.
234 Rondelet (1812–n.d.), vol. V, p. 236.
235 Vanherman (1828), p. 14.
236 Berger MSS., 1831 formula book, p. 219.
237 Watin (1785), p. 44; Tingry (1804), p. 405; (1816), pp. 286–7.
238 Vanherman (1828), p. 39.
239 Brighton/Crace MS., p. 14.
240 Salmon (1734), p. 58.
241 Tingry (1830), p. 275.
242 Op. cit. (1794), p. 150.
243 Englefield (1936), p. 186.
244 See Chapter 3.
245 Bennett (1833), s.v. 'PAINT', p. 295.
246 Hertford MS., p. 387.
247 Gordon Castle MS., p. 2.
248 Osterley MSS., Adamson (1772–4).
249 John Smith (1687), p. 93.
250 Pincot [*c.* 1811], p. 21.
251 See Chapter 3.
252 Laxton (1818), p. 96; Skyring (1831), p. 88.
253 D'Aviler (1691), vol. I, p. 229.
254 Bullet (1691), p. 285.
255 Watin (1785), p. 44.
256 Tingry (1804), pp. 404–5; (1816), pp. 285–6.
257 Crease (1808), p. [16].
258 Pyne (1819), vol. III, p. 14.
259 John Smith (1687), p. 52; Nicholson (1823–5), p. 416; *Painter's . . . Pocket Manual* (1825), p. 107.
260 Nicholson (1825), p. 412; Reynolds (1812), p. 11.
261 Rondelet (1812–n.d.), vol. V, p. 236.
262 Phillips (1812), pp. 213–14.
263 B.M. trade cards, Banks 89.28.
264 Bennett (1833), s.v. 'PAINT', p. 295.
265 Lingard (1825), p. 10.
266 Tingry (1830), p. 275.
267 Op. cit., (1787), p. 139; (1794), p. 150.
268 Crease (1808), p. 12.
269 Mason (1783), pp. 44–5 (bk. II, lines 362–3, 367–80, 393–4).
270 Vanherman (1828), pp. 8, 13–14.
271 Nicholson (1825), p. 412.
272 S.R.O. MSS., GD 150/3396.
273 Crease (1808), p. [16]; Pincot [*c.* 1811], p. 8; B.M. trade cards, Banks 89.28 (London Patent Colour-Works); Bentley (1817), p. 5; Lingard (1825), p. 10; Bennett (1833), s.v. 'PAINT', p. 295.
274 Bennett, ibid.
275 Adelphi Accounts (1920), p. 10; V.A.M. MSS., L. 4631C-1970, pp. 5–6.
276 V.A.M. accession No. W. 41–1977; Bristow MSS., thesis (1983), vol. II, pp. 834–5.

277 Berger MSS., 1831 formula book, p. 215.
278 No. 3594 (1812).
279 Phillips (1812), p. 213.
280 Gordon Castle MS., p. 7.
281 D'Aviler (1691), vol. I, p. 228.
282 S.R.O. MSS., GD 150/3396.
283 Nicholson (1819), s.v. 'Painting, *Economical*', Vol. II, p. 417; Nicholson (1825), p. 412.
284 Op. cit. (1825), p. 106.
285 Berger MSS., second experimental notebook, p. 5.
286 Vanherman (1828), pp. 7, 14–15, 86.
287 Watin (1785), p. 46; Tingry (1804), p. 398; (1816), p. 279.
288 Op. cit. (1825), pp. 106–7.
289 Watin (1785), p. 46; Tingry (1804), p. 398; (1816). p. 279.
290 Salmon (1734), p. 58.
291 Phillips (1812), p. 213; B.M. trade cards, Banks 89.28 (London Patent Colour-Works); Bentley (1817), p. 5; Lingard (1825), p. 10; Bennett (1833), s.v. 'Paint', p. 295.
292 Osterley MSS., Adamson (1772–4).
293 Op.cit. (1794), p. 150.
294 Pincot [*c.* 1811], p. 35; Phillips (1812). p. 209; (1821), p. 167.
295 Englefield (1936), pp. 186, 190; Laxton (1818), p. 96; Skyring (1831), p. 88.
296 York City MSS., Mansion House painting account.
297 King's College, Cambridge MS.
298 Powys (1899), pp. 63, 205.
299 Osterley MSS., Adamson (1772–4).
300 R.I.B.A. MSS., CHA 3/1, p. 247.
301 Rondelet (1812–n.d.), vol. V, p. 236.
302 Stitt (1819), pp. 348–9.
303 See Chapter 3.
304 Reynolds (1812), p. 11.
305 Englefield (1936), pp. 186, 190.
306 Laxton (1818), p. 96; Phillips (1812), p. 209; (1821), p. 167; Skyring (1831), p. 88.
307 B.M. trade cards, Banks 89.28.
308 Bennett (1833), s.v. 'Paint', p. 295.
309 Phillips (1812), p. 213; Butcher (1825), p. 30.
310 Phillips (1812), p. 196; (1821), p. 156.
311 Laxton (1818), p. 88.
312 Nicholson (1819), s.v. 'Painting, *Economical*', vol. II, p. 417.
313 Hay (1846), pl. 6, No. 1.
314 Reynolds (1812), p. 11; Tingry (1804), pp. 317–8; (1816), p. 201; *Painter's . . . Pocket Manual* (1825), p. 103.
315 Nicholson (1825), p. 412; Nicholson (1819), s.v. 'Painting, *Economical*', vol. II, p. 417.
316 R.I.B.A. MSS., CHA 3/1, p. 255; Bristow MSS., notes, C. 104A.
317 Vanherman (1828), p. 39.
318 Berger MSS., 1831 formula book, p. 101.
319 Salmon (1734), p. 58.
320 B.M. trade cards, Banks 89.28.
321 Ibid., Heal 89.75.
322 Leinster (1949–57), vol. I (1949), p. 238.
323 Bowood MSS., diary, vol. IV, p. 119 (entry for 25 August 1768).
324 B.L. MS. Add. 41133, f. 12^{v}. (letter dated 5 May 1770).
325 Ibid., f. 52^{r}. (letter dated 31 August 1771).
326 Powys (1899), p. 147; Hertford MS., p. 387.
327 Osterley MSS., Beauchamp-Proctor (1772).
328 R.I.A. MSS., Charlemont letters, second series, vol. II, No. 5 (7 September 1775).
329 S.A.L. MS.
330 Cornforth (1979), p. 2008.
331 Berger MSS., 1831 formula book, p. 78.
332 Rondelet (1812–n.d.), vol. V, p. 236.
333 Hay (1846), p. 44.
334 Watin (1785), p. 45; Rondelet (1812–n.d.), vol. V, p. 236.
335 Bennett (1833), s.v. 'Paint', p. 295.
336 Berger MSS., 1831 formula book, p. 213.
337 Crease (1808), p. [16].
338 B.M. trade cards, Banks 89.28.
339 Bennett (1833), s.v. 'Paint', p. 295.
340 Nicholson (1819), s.v. 'Painting, *Economical*', vol. II, p. 417.
341 Vanherman (1828), p. 39.
342 Hay (1846), pl. 22, No. 1.
343 Crease (1808), p. [16].
344 Watin (1785), p. 45.
345 Vanherman (1828), pp. 86–7.
346 Bennett (1833), s.v. 'Paint', p. 295.
347 Blondel (1752–6), vol. I, p. 167.
348 Watin (1785), p. 43.
349 Tingry (1804), pp. 402–3; (1816), pp. 203–4.
350 Watin (1785), p. 44.
351 Nicholson (1819), s.v. 'Painting, *Economical*', vol. II, p. 417.
352 Watin (1785), p. 43; Tingry (1804), p. 403; (1816), pp. 283–4.
353 Reynolds (1812), p. 16.
354 Rondelet (1818–n.d.), vol. V, p. 236.
355 Bennett (1833), s.v. 'Paint', p. 295.
356 Ibid.
357 Vanherman (1828), pp. 28, 39.
358 Dunham Massey MSS.
359 Pincot [*c.* 1811], p. 13.
360 Phillips (1812), pp. 210, 213; (1821), pp. 168, 171.
361 Op.cit., (1810), p. 84; (1813), p. 127.
362 Englefield (1936), pp. 186, 190.
363 Gordon Castle MS., p. 2.
364 Pincot [*c.* 1811], p. 21.
365 Tingry (1804), pp. 317–8; (1816), p. 201; *Painter's . . . Pocket Manual* (1825), p. 103.
366 R.I.B.A. MSS., CHA 3/1, pp. 247, 248, 249, 251, 253; S.A.L. MS.
367 Bristow MSS., notes, C. 104B.
368 John Smith (1687), p. 52.
369 Nicholson (1823–5), p. 416; *Painter's . . . Pocket Manual* (1825), p. 107.
370 Holme (1688), p. 13.
371 Nicholson (1819), s.v. 'Painting, *Economical*', vol. II, p. 417.
372 D'Aviler (1691), vol. I, p. 228.
373 Whittock (1827), p. 132.
374 Soane Museum drawings, Adam albums, vol. XII, Nos. 64, 65, 151, 153; vol. XIII, Nos. 67, 139; vol. XIV, Nos. 51, 72, 73; R.I.B.A. MSS., CHA 3/1, pp. 247, 248, 251, 252, 253, 256; CHA 3/2, p. 212; CHA 3/3, p. 69, 147, 336.
375 *Builders Price-Book* (1810), pp. 69, 83, 84; (1813), pp. 111, 126, 127; Laxton (1818), p. 88.
376 Englefield (1936), p. 186.
377 Nicholson (1819), s.v. 'Painting, *Economical*', vol. II, p. 417.
378 Watin (1785), p. 41; Tingry (1804), p. 392; (1816), p. 273.
379 Op. cit. (1825), p. 105.
380 Vanherman (1828), p. 38.
381 Butcher (1825), p. 30.
382 Ibid.
383 Cook (1820), p. lxxxix; Skyring (1831), p. 77.
384 *Builders Price-Book* (1794), p. 130; Phillips (1804), p. 113; (1812), p. 196; (1821), p. 156.
385 Osterley MSS., Adamson (1772–4).
386 R.I.B.A. MSS., CHA 3/3, pp. 67, 122, 192.
387 Op. cit. (1787), p. 139; (1794), p. 150.
388 Ibid., (1810), p. 84; (1813), p. 127; Phillips (1812), p. 209; (1821), p. 167.
389 Pincot [*c.* 1811], p. 35; Laxton (1818), p. 96; Skyring (1831), p. 88.
390 Dyrham MSS., D. 1799, A141; Pincot [*c.* 1811], p. 21.
391 Powys (1899), p. 146.
392 Gordon Castle MS., p. 1.
393 Osterley MSS., Adamson (1772–4); (1787).
394 Soane Museum drawings, Adam albums, vol. XIV, No. 4.
395 Newcastle MS.
396 Dunham Massey MSS.
397 Nicholson (1819), s.v. 'Painting, *Economical*', vol. II, p. 417.
398 Tingry (1804), p. 391; (1816), p. 272.
399 Op. cit. (1825), p. 104.
400 Soane Museum MSS., 'Business', p. 18.
401 Rondelet (1812–n.d.), vol. V, p. 236.

402 Watin (1785), p. 41.
403 B.L. MSS. Add. 41133, f. 12^{v} (letter dated 5 May 1770).
404 Watin (1785), p. 41.
405 Tingry (1804), p. 392; (1816), p. 273.
406 Op. cit. (1825), p. 105.
407 Gordon Castle MS., p. 8.
408 Rondelet (1812–n.d.), vol. v, p. 236.
409 Ibid.
410 Reynolds (1812), p. 15.
411 Bullet (1691), p. 285.
412 P.R.O. MSS., E. 351/3404, M. iv^{v}.
413 Dyrham MSS., D. 1799, E. 234.
414 Rondelet (1812–n.d.), vol. v, p. 236.
415 Watin (1785), p. 42; Tingry (1804), pp. 395–6; (1816), p. 277.
416 Op.cit. (1825), p. 106.
417 Blondel (1737), vol. I, p. 26; Blondel (1752–6), vol. I, p. 167.
418 John Smith (1687), pp. 20, 52.
419 Laxton (1818), p. 96.
420 Rondelet (1812–n.d.), vol. v, p. 236.
421 Vanherman (1828), p. 39.
422 Pyne (1819), vol. III, p. 24.
423 *Builders Price-Book* (1787), p. 134; (1794), p. 146; Laxton (1818), p. 96; Salmon (1734), p. 57.
424 Pincot [*c.* 1811], pp. 8, 10–11; Butcher (1825), p. 31; Nicholson (1825), p. 412; Tingry (1830), p. 270.
425 Vanherman (1828), pp. 9, 12.
426 John Smith (1687), p. 51.
427 Butcher (1825), p. 23; Nicholson (1823–5), p. 416; *Painter's . . . Pocket Manual* (1825), p. 107.
428 Op. cit. (1825), p. 108.
429 Primatt [1667], p. 70.
430 Crease (1808), p. [16]; Lingard (1825), p. 10.
431 B.M. trade cards, Banks 89.28.
432 Vanherman (1828), pp. 9, 12; Bentley (1817), p. 5; B.M. trade cards, Heal 89.75 (Hodgkin).
433 Bennett (1833), s.v. 'PAINT', p. 295.
434 P.R.O. MSS., E. 351/3252, M. xiii^{r}; 3254, M. xvii^{r}; 3255, M. xvi^{r}; 3404, M. iv^{v}.
435 Ibid., WORK. 5/17, f. 318^{v}.
436 Boughton MS., vol. I, p. 175.
437 S.A.L. MS.
438 R.I.B.A. drawings collection, Dance/Leoni volume, No. 64 (Cat. C-F, George Dance the younger, 'Dance Leoni' 64).
439 Salmon (1734), p. 58.
440 Rondelet (1812–n.d.), vol. v, p. 236.
441 Watin (1785), pp. 42–3; Tingry (1804), p. 396; (1816), p. 277.
442 Op. cit. (1825), p. 106.
443 Op. cit. (1787), p. 139; (1794), p. 150.
444 Laxton (1818), p. 88; Skyring (1831), p. 77.
445 Blondel (1737), vol. I, p. 26.
446 Cornforth (1979), p. 2008.
447 R.I.B.A. MSS., CHA 3/1, p. 248.
448 Hay (1828), p. 45.
449 Blondel (1752–6), vol. I, p. 167.
450 Rondelet (1812–n.d.), vol. v, p. 236.
451 Watin (1785), p. 42.
452 Englefield (1936), p. 186.
453 Laxton (1818), p. 96.
454 R.I.B.A. MSS., CHA 3/1, p. 255; S.A.L. MS.
455 R.I.B.A. MSS., CHA 3/1, p. 250.
456 Soane Museum drawings, Adam albums, vol. XI, No. 161; vol. XIII, No. 2; R.I.B.A. drawings collection Dance/Leoni volume, No. 64 (Cat. C–F, George Dance the younger, 'Dance Leoni' 64).
457 Pyne (1819), vol. III, p. 26.
458 Caley (1792), p. 403.
459 Gunther (1928), p. 282.
460 Mercato (1717), p. 18; Waller (1686), plate following p. 28; Johnson (1755), vol. II, s.v. 'Lutarious'.
461 Holme (1688), bk. 2, ch. XIII, p. 312.
462 Arundel Castle pictures (reproduced in companion volume).
463 Bristow MSS., reports, Queen's House (1986), p. 24; notes, C. 63U.
464 P.R.O. MSS., E. 351/3259, M. vii^{r}
465 Ibid., 3261, M. vi^{v}.
466 Ibid., 3263, M. vi^{r}.
467 Ibid., 3265, M. vi^{v}.
468 Ibid., 3263, M. viii^{v}.
469 P.R.O. MSS., E. 351/3265. M. viii^{r} (1631–2, St James's Palace, varnished and gilded); 3266, M. v^{v} (1632–3, Whitehall, in varnish and gilded); 3267, M. v^{v} (1633–4, Whitehall, varnished and gilded); ibid., M. xi^{r} (Greenwich, in oil, varnished and gilded); 3269, M. viii^{r} (1635–6, in Long Gallery at Somerset House, in oil and gilded); 3270. M. viii^{r} (1636–7, Hampton Court, nine frames, varnished).
470 Salmon (1734), p. 58.
471 Op. cit., (1776), p. 92; (1787), p. 138; (1794), p. 150.
472 Phillips (1821), p. 172.
473 King's College, Cambridge MS.
474 Osterley MSS., Adamson (1772–4).
475 Rondelet (1812–n.d.), vol. v, p. 236.
476 Tingry (1804), p. 358; (1816), p. 238.
477 Rondelet (1812–n.d.), vol. v, p. 236.
478 Hay (1846), pl. 11, No. 4.
479 John Smith (1687), p. 51.
480 Watin (1785), p. 45.
481 Tingry (1804), p. 394; (1816), p. 275; *Painter's . . . Pocket Manual* (1825), p. 105.
482 Nicholson (1825), p. 410.
483 Boughton MS., vol. I, p. 177.
484 Neve (1703), p. 215.
485 R.I.B.A. MSS., WRE/2/20, 21.
486 Boughton MS., vol. I, p. 185.
487 P.R.O. MSS., WORK.19/48/1, ff. 50(iv), 93(iii).
488 Dyrham MSS., D. 1799, E234.
489 York City MSS., Mansion House painting account.
490 Salmon (1734), p. 58.
491 Op. cit. (1787), p. 134; (1794), p. 146.
492 Bentley (1817), p. 5.
493 P.R.O. MSS., E. 351/3255, M. xiv^{v}; 3258, M. v^{v}; 3259, M. vii^{r}.
494 Dyrham MSS, D. 1799, E. 234; Boughton MS., vol. I, p. 177.
495 Wren Society, vol. VII (1930), p. 222.
496 York City MSS., Mansion House painting account.
497 Dunham Massey MSS.
498 John Smith (1687), p. 52.
499 Reynolds (1812), p. 10.
500 Nicholson (1823–5), p. 416; *Painter's . . . Pocket Manual* (1825) p. 106.
501 Vanherman (1828), pp. 27, 28.
502 1 Jac. I, C. 20.
503 Salmon (1734), p. 58; Phillips (1821), p. 171.
504 Rondelet (1812–n.d.), vol. v, p. 236.
505 Op. cit. (1776), p. 70; (1787), pp. 114, 139; (1794), pp. 130, 150
506 Phillips (1804), p. 113; (1812), p. 196; (1821), p. 156.
507 Skyring (1831), p. 77.
508 Soane Museum drawings, Adam albums, vol. XII, No. 64.
509 M.M.A drawings, 34, 78.2(22).
510 Whittock (1827), p. 133; Vanherman (1828), p. 42.
511 Laxton (1818), p. 95.
512 Arundel MS., Evans's bill, pp. 5–8 *passim.*
513 Skyring (1831), p. 88.
514 Holme (1688), p. 13.
515 Nicholson (1819), s.v. 'PAINTING, *Economical,* vol. II, p. 417.
516 Laxton (1818), p. 96; Skyring (1831), p. 88.
517 Vanherman (1828), p. 39.
518 Hay (1846), p. 47; pl. 19, No. 1.
519 George Smith (1826), p. 165.
520 Pyne (1819), vol. III, p. 45.
521 Brighton/Crace MS., p. 119.
522 Matthaei (1971), p. 21 (Goethe (1791), para. 37) .
523 Bullet (1691), p. 284.
524 Bristow MSS., thesis (1983), vol. II, pp. 820–1, 822–3.
525 Watin (1785), p. 41.
526 Tingry (1804), p. 392; (1816), p. 273.

527 Stitt (1819), p. 349.
528 Op. cit. (1825), p. 105.
529 Reynolds (1812), p. 15.
530 Nicholson (1825), p. 412.
531 Salmon (1734), p. 57.
532 Op. cit. (1787), p. 134; (1794), p. 146.
533 Rondelet (1812–n.d.), vol. v, p. 236.
534 Boughton MS., vol, I, p. 187.
535 King's College, Cambridge MS.
536 Chambers (1759), p. 84; B.L. MSS., Add. 41133, f. 12v (letter dated 5 May 1770).
537 Osterley MSS., Adamson (1772–4).
538 Whittock (1827), p. 133.
539 Salmon (1734), p. 58.
540 Op. cit. (1787), pp. 139, 141; (1794), pp. 150, 153.
541 Englefield (1936), pp. 186, 190.
542 Soane Museum drawings, Adam albums, vol. XI, Nos. 160, 226, 250, 251, 256, 261, 262; vol. XII, Nos. 1, 2, 4, 42, 43, 76, 97, 114, 131, 147; vol. XIII, Nos. 41, 70.
543 Robert and James Adam (1773–1822), vol. I, No. II (1774), description of pl. vii.
544 Hertford MS.
545 Osterley MSS., Adamson (1772–4); (1787).
546 S.A.L. MS.
547 Rutter (1823), pp. 9, 11, 16, 17.
548 Pincot [*c.* 1811], p. 22.
549 Ibid.
550 Soane Museum drawings, Adam albums, vol. XI, No. 262.
551 Whittock (1827), p. 132; Vanherman (1828), p. 42.
552 Tingry (1830), pp. 208, 275.
553 Dyrham MSS., D. 1799, E. 234.
554 Rondelet (1812–n.d.), vol. v, p. 236.
555 Pincot [*c.* 1811], p. 35.
556 Reynolds (1812), p. 17; Nicholson (1825), p. 412; Vanherman (1828), pp. 28, 42.
557 Soane Museum drawings, Adam albums, vol. XI, Nos. 161, 240; vol. XII, Nos, 60, 62, 63, 65, 128, 151; vol. XIII, Nos. 70, 104, 128, 133, 139; vol. XIV, Nos. 31, 58, 71, 72, 74, 75.
558 Osterley MSS., Adamson (1772–4).
559 R.I.A. MSS., Charlemont letters, second series, vol. II, No. 5 (7 September 1775).
560 R.I.B.A. MSS., CHA 3/1, pp. 248, 249, 251.
561 S.A.L. MS.
562 Northumberland MS.
563 B.M. trade cards, Banks 89.28.
564 Bartholomew (1846), para. 1502.
565 Vanherman (1828), p. 30.
566 Butcher (1825), p. 31.
567 Reynolds (1812), p. 17.
568 Nicholson (1825), p. 411.
569 Whittock (1827), p. 133.
570 Vanherman (1828), pp. 10, 11, 16.
571 Reynolds (1812), pp. 11–12.
572 P.R.O. MSS., E. 351/3265, M.vi^{v}.
573 Vanherman (1828), pp. 38–9.
574 Ibid., pp. 10, 11, 16.
575 Bentley (1817), p. 5; Bennett (1833), s.v. 'PAINT', p. 295.
576 Lingard (1825), p. 10.
577 Soane Museum drawings, Adam albums, vol. XI, No. 112; vol. XII, Nos. 42, 76.
578 Britton (1827), p. 33.
579 Pückler-Muskau (1832). vol. IV, p. 86.
580 Brighton/Crace MS., pp. 1, 16.
581 Berger MSS., 1831 formula book, p. 205.
582 Soane MSS., 'Business', p. 18.
583 Watin (1785), p. 42.
584 P.R.O. MSS., E. 351/3404, M. iv^{v}.
585 Slive (1961), p. 380.
586 P.R.O. MSS., E. 351/3267, M. v^{v} 3271, M. vii^{v}.
587 Ibid., 3263, M. viii^{v} (1629–30, two large frames at St James's Palace); 3266, M. ix^{v} (1632–3), frame at Somerset House veined in imitation of walnut); 3269, M. v^{v} (1635–6, frame at Whitehall in distemper).
588 Boughton MS., vol. I, p. 185.
589 Slive (1961), p. 378.
590 Whittock (1827), p. 132.
591 Englefield (1936), p. 186.
592 Dunham Massey MSS.
593 Vanherman (1828), p. 27.
594 Laxton (1818), p. 96.
595 Skyring (1831), p. 88.
596 Fowler & Cornforth (1974), p. 207 (quoting MS. letter in possession of the Hon. Desmond Guinness).
597 Brighton/Crace MS., pp. 4, 15, 20.
598 Buckler (1826), p. 3.
599 Reynolds (1812), p. 12.
600 Rondelet (1812–n.d.), vol. v, p. 236.
601 Lingard (1825), p. 10.
602 Bennett (1833), s.v. 'PAINT', p. 295.
603 Ham MSS., Gooderick's account.
604 Watin (1785), pp. 93–4.
605 John Smith (1687), p. 52.
606 *Painter's . . . Pocket Manual* (1825), p. 107.
607 Nicholson (1823–5), p. 416.
608 Vanherman (1828), pp. 9, 15, 29.
609 John Smith (1687), p. 52.
610 George Smith (1826), p. 165.
611 Bristow MSS., thesis (1983), vol. II, pp. 796–7.
612 Nicholson (1825), p. 412.
613 Pincot [*c.* 1811], pp. 8, 13.
614 B.L. MSS., Add. 41133, f. 12 (letter dated 5 May 1770).
615 Butcher (1825), p. 30; *Painter's . . . Pocket Manual* (1825), p. 108.
616 Vanherman (1828), p. 39.
617 Reynolds (1812), pp. 15, 17.
618 Wren Society, vol. VII (1930), p. 193.
619 Osterley MSS., Adamson (1787).
620 *Builders Price-Book* (1787), p. 134; (1794), p. 146; Laxton (1818), p. 96.
621 Salmon (1734), p. 57.
622 Crease (1808), p. [16].
623 B.M. trade cards, Banks 89.28.
624 Lingard (1825), p. 10.
625 B.M. trade cards, Banks 89.28.
626 Bentley (1817), p. 5.
627 Vanherman (1828), pp. 9, 15.
628 B.M. trade cards, Heal 89.75.
629 Bennett (1833), s.v. 'PAINT', p. 295.
630 Rondelet (1812–n.d.), vol. v, p. 236.
631 Primatt [1667], p. 70; Gerbier (1663), p. 83; Wren Society, vol. XIX (1942), pp. 98–9 (Sheldonian).
632 Boughton MS., vol. I, pp. 177, 179, 181.
633 Petworth MSS., PHA 6614, No. 219, pp. 3, 4.
634 R.I.B.A. MSS., CHA 3/1, pp. 247, 253; CHA 3/2, p. 211; CHA 3/3, pp. 67, 122, 192.
635 P.R.O. MSS., E. 351/3254, MM. v^{r}, xvii^{r}.
636 Ibid., 3258, M. v^{v}; 3262, M. vi^{r}.
637 P.R.O. MSS., WORK. 19/48/1, f. 50(iv).
638 Boughton MS., vol. I, p. 161.
639 Mansion House MSS., Stock (1751); Rowe (1757).
640 Soane Museum drawings, Adam albums, vol. XIV, No. 5.
641 S.R.O. MSS., 4/62/4.
642 Dunham Massey MSS.
643 Rutter (1823), pp. 14, 17.
644 Braybrooke (1836), p. 116.
645 Boughton MS., vol. I, p. 177.
646 Hertford MS.
647 B.L. MSS., Add. 41133, f. 51^{v} (letter dated 31 August 1771).
648 Boughton MS., vol. I, pp. 187, 191.
649 Ibid., pp. 177, 179, 181.
650 Pyne (1819), vol. III, p. 14.
651 Boughton MS., vol. I, pp. 181, 187.
652 John Smith (1687), p. 52.

653 Reynolds (1812), p. 10.
654 Whittock (1827), p. 132.
655 Holme (1688), p. 13.
656 Salmon (1734), p. 58.
657 Vanherman (1828), p. 38.
658 Nicholson (1819), s.v. 'PAINTING, *Economical*', vol. II, p. 417.
659 Phillips (1812), p. 212.
660 Rondelet (1812–n.d.), vol. V, p. 236.
661 R.I.B.A. MSS., CHA 3/2, p. 211.
662 Op. cit. (1776), pp. 70, 114; (1787), pp. 139, 141; (1794), pp. 150, 153.
663 Ibid. (1810), p. 69; (1813), p. 111.
664 Phillips (1804), p. 113; (1812), p. 196; (1821), p. 156; Laxton (1818), p. 88; Skyring (1831), p. 77.
665 Blondel (1752–6), vol. I, p. 167.
666 R.I.B.A. drawings collection, Dance/Leoni volume No. 64 (Cat. C-F, George Dance the younger, 'Dance Leoni' 64).
667 Soane Museum drawings, Adam albums, vol. XI, Nos. 213, 262; vol. XII, No. 43; vol. XIV, No. 72.
668 Hertford MS.
669 Gordon Castle MS., pp. 1, 3.
670 Osterley MSS., Adamson (1787).
671 John Smith (1687), p. 52.
672 Nicholson (1823–5), p. 416; *Painter's . . . Pocket Manual* (1825), p. 107.
673 Bullet (1691), p. 285.
674 Gerbier (1663), p. 84; Primatt [1667], p. 70.
675 P.R.O. MSS., E. 351/3254, M. v^{r}; 3263, M. xii^{v}; 3271, M. viii^{r}.
676 Ibid., 3391, M. iv^{v}; 3258, M. v^{v}; 3259, M. xxvi^{v}; 3269, M. v^{r}.
677 P.R.O. MSS., AO.1/2429/71, M. xv^{v}; E. 351/3272, M. vi^{r}.
678 Ibid., E.351/3259, M. xxvi^{v}; 3271. M. v^{v}; 3271, M. vii^{v}.
679 Ham MSS., Gooderick's account.
680 P.R.O. MSS., E. 351/3265, M. vi^{v}.
681 Ibid., WORK. 5/12 (extraordinary account), ff. 428^{v}–429^{r}.
682 Ibid., WORK. 5/24 (extraordinary account).
683 Blondel (1737), vol. I, p. 26.
684 Watin (1785), p. 45.
685 Rondelet (1812–n.d.), vol. V, p. 236.
686 Dyrham MSS., D. 1799, E. 234.
687 Ham MSS., Gooderick's account.
688 Rondelet (1812–n.d.), vol. V, p. 236.
689 Ibid.
690 Watin (1785), p. 45.
691 Nicholson (1825), p. 412.
692 Op. cit. (1825), p. 106.
693 Soane Museum drawings, Adam albums, vol. XII, Nos. 24, 143.
694 Rondelet (1812–n.d.), vol. V, p. 236.
695 Op. cit. (1825), pp. 108–9.
696 Watin (1785), p. 45.
697 Tingry (1804), p. 394; (1816), pp. 275–6.
698 Op.cit. (1825), p. 105.
699 P.R.O. MSS., E. 351/3253, M. iv^{r}; 3257, M. ix^{r}; 3260, M. vi^{r}; 3271, M. xiv^{v}.
700 Ibid., 3265, M. viii^{r}; 3270. M. v^{v}.
701 Gerbier (1663), p. 84.
702 Salmon (1734), p. 58.
703 Neve (1703), p. 215.
704 P.R.O. MSS., WORK. 5/24, extraordinary account; Bristow MSS., thesis (1983), vol. II, pp. 821–2.
705 Ibid., WORK. 19/48/1, ff. 50(iv), 64(iii), 74(iii).
706 Dyrham MSS., D. 1799, E234.
707 R.I.B.A. MSS., WRE/2/20, 21.
708 Croft-Murray, vol. I (1962), p. 216b (quoting letter from Isaac Bayley to Thomas Foley, 3 March 1705, in possession of Mr H.T.H. Foley, Stoke Edith, Herefordshire).
709 Boughton MS., vol. I, p. 185.
710 *Builders Price-Book* (1776); (1787); (1794); Watin (1785), p. 45; Rondelet (1812–n.d.), vol. V, p. 236.
711 Laxton (1818), p. 96; Skyring (1831), p. 88.
712 *Builders Price-Book* (1787), p. 134; (1794), p. 146; Laxton (1818), p. 96; Pincot [*c.* 1811], p. 8.
713 Wren Society, vol. VII (1930), p. 116.
714 Osterley MSS., Adamson (1772–4); (1787).
715 Hay (1828), p. 41; Tingry (1830), pp. 33–4.
716 Vanherman (1828), p. 54.
717 B.M.trade cards, Heal 90.56*.
718 Rondelet (1812–n.d.), vol. V, p. 236.
719 Holme (1688), p. 13.
720 Dunham Massey MSS.
721 Watin (1785), p. 77.
722 B.M.trade cards, Heal 90.56*.
723 Tingry (1804), p. 395; (1816), p. 276.
724 Butcher (1825), p. 31.
725 Stitt (1819), p. 348.
726 P.R.O. MSS., E. 351/3262, M. ix^{r}.
727 R.I.B.A. MSS., PEL/1, p. 84.
728 Soane Museum drawings, Adam albums, vol. XI, No. 161; vol. XII, Nos. 24, 114, 131.
729 Gordon Castle MS., p. 2.
730 Woburn MSS., box 394.
731 Brighton/Crace MS., p. 67.
732 Rutter (1823), p. 11.
733 Bentley (1817), p. 5.
734 Bennett (1833), s.v. 'PAINT', p. 295.
735 Brighton/Crace MS., p. 106.
736 Soane Museum drawings, Adam albums, vol. XII, No. 131.
737 Rondelet (1812–n.d.), vol. V, p. 236.
738 Osterley MSS., Adamson (1772–4).
739 Willis and Clarke (1886), vol. II, p. 42.
740 Rondelet (1812–n.d.), vol. V, p. 237.
741 Osterley MSS., Adamson (1787).
742 B.M. trade cards, Banks 89.28.
743 Laxton (1818), p. 96; Skyring (1831), p. 88.
744 Bristow MSS., reports, Soane Museum (1986a); (1986b).

Appendix B. Glossary of timbers imitated

1 P.R.O. MSS., WORK. 19/48/1, f. 50(iv).
2 Smith (1687), pp. 46, 52.
3 Salmon (1734), pp. 58–9.
4 Wren Society, vol. XIX (1942), p. 98.
5 Hinkley (1960), p. 77.
6 Laxton (1818), p. 99; Skyring (1831), p. 91.
7 Cust (1914), vol. I, pp. 41–2.
8 Brighton/Crace MS., pp. 1, 19.
9 Ibid., p. 65.
10 Ibid., pp. 60, 74.
11 Whittock (1827), p. 43.
12 See n. 23 to Chapter 20.
13 Whittock (1827), pp. 43–4.
14 Hinkley (1960), pp. 86, 116–17.
15 Gunther (1928), p. 282.
16 Wren Society, vol. XIX (1942), p. 98.
17 Ibid., vol. VII (1930), p. 127.
18 Reynolds (1812), pp. 19–20.
19 Brighton/Crace MS., pp. 64, 71.
20 Reynolds (1812), p. 20.
21 Hinkley (1960), pp. 171–2.
22 Pyne (1819), vol. III, p. 22.
23 Laxton (1818), p. 99; Skyring (1831), p. 91.
24 P.R.O. MSS., E.351/3233, M. 9^{r}.
25 Croft-Murray, vol. I (1962), p. 27.
26 Hinkley (1960), p. 38.
27 Vanherman (1828), p. 62.
28 Brighton/Crace MS., p. 1.
29 Butcher (1825), p. 32.
30 Op. cit. (1825), p. 109.
31 Nicholson (1823–5), 'The Practical Builder's Perpetual Price-book', p. 152; Laxton (1818), p. 99; Skyring (1831), p. 91.
32 Brighton/Crace MS., p. 68.
33 Lincoln Cathedral MS.
34 Colvin (1984), pp. 289, 307.

35 Gwilt (1894), p. 499.
36 Whittock (1827), pp. 34–5.
37 Ibid., pp. 35–6.
38 Ibid., pp. 36–7.
39 Ibid., p. 37.
40 Butcher (1825), p. 31.
41 Op. cit. (1825), p. 109.
42 Reynolds (1812), pp. 18–19.
43 Vanherman (1828), pp. 29, 60–1.
44 Arundel MS., Evans's bill, f. 5.
45 Osterley MSS., Adamson (1772–4).
46 R.I.B.A. MSS., CHA 3/1, pp. 247, 254; 3/3, pp. 69, 122, 147, 244.
47 *Builders Price-Book* (1776), p. 92; (1787), p. 138; (1794), p. 150.
48 Pain (1786), p. 14; Pain (1794), p. 21.
49 Op. cit. (1810), p. 83; (1813), p. 126.
50 Phillips (1804), p. 127.
51 Ibid. (1812), p. 209; (1821), p. 167.
52 Skyring (1831), p. 91.
53 Laxton (1818), p. 99.
54 Nicholson (1823–5), 'The Practical Builder's Perpetual Price-book', p. 152.
55 Rutter (1823), pp. 18, 25, 29.
56 Whittock (1827), p. 20.
57 Hinkley (1960), p. 69.
58 Whittock (1827), pp. 21–4.
59 Ibid., pp. 27–9.
60 Vanherman (1828), p. 59.
61 Whittock (1827), p. 21.
62 Butcher (1825), pp. 30–1.
63 Op. cit. (1825), p. 109.
64 Nicholson (1834), p. 160.
65 Laxton (1818), p. 99.
66 Whittock (1827), p. 27.
67 Wren Society, vol. IV (1927), pp. 47, 53 (Hampton Court); vol. VII (1930), pp. 116, 130 (Whitehall); P.R.O. MSS., WORK. 19/48/1, ff. 50(iv), 56(iv), 64(iii) (Kensington).
68 Wren Society, vol. IV (1927), p. 47.
69 *Builders Price-Book* (1810), p. 83; (1813), p. 126.
70 Phillips (1812), p. 209; (1821), p. 167.
71 Laxton (1818), p. 99.
72 Op. cit. (1823–5), 'The Practical Builder's Perpetual Price-book', p. 152.
73 Skyring (1831), p. 91.
74 Whittock (1827), pp. 32, 34.
75 Vanherman (1828), pp. 59–60.
76 Whittock (1827), pp. 32–3, 44.
77 Brighton/Crace MS., pp. 119–20.
78 Hinkley (1960), p. 59.
79 John Smith (1687), p. 52.
80 Wren Society, vol. IV (1927), p. 47.
81 Croft-Murray, vol. I (1962), p. 212b.
82 *Hertfordshire* (1910), p. 175a.
83 Brighton/Crace MS., p. 72.
84 Cooper-Hewitt drawings, 1948–40–33 (reproduced in companion volume and by Morley (1984), p1. 161).
85 Brighton/Crace MS., pp. 62, 64–66.
86 Gunther (1928), p. 282.
87 Cust (1914), vol. I, p. 41.
88 Hinkley (1960), pp. 113–14, 154.
89 Nicholson (1823–5), p. 417.
90 Tingry (1830), pp. 141–2
91 Hinkley (1960), p. 152.
92 Ibid., p. 118.
93 See n. 23 to Chapter 20.
94 Ditto.
95 Whittock (1827), pp. 44–5.
96 Ibid., pp. 45–6, pl. XV.
97 See n. 23 to Chapter 20.
98 Whittock (1827), p. 46.
99 V.A.M. pictures, accession No. F.A. 145.
100 Pyne (1819), vol. III, p. 58.
101 Vanherman (1828), p. 62.
102 Whittock (1827), p. 40.
103 Ibid., p. 41.
104 Ibid.
105 Ibid., pp. 41–2.
106 Brighton/Crace MS., p. 6 (punctuation added).
107 Ibid., pp. 1, 24.
108 Nicholson (1823–5), 'The Practical Builder's Perpetual Price-Book', p. 152; Laxton (1818), p. 100; Skyring (1831), p. 91.
109 Vanherman (1828), p. 62.
110 Whittock (1827), p. 38.
111 Vanherman (1828), pp. 61–2.
112 Nicholson (1834), p. 160.
113 Brighton/Crace MS., p. 2.
114 Ibid., pp. 3, 4.
115 Ibid., p. 15.
116 Ibid., pp. 64, 67.
117 Hinkley (1960), p. 47.
118 Laxton (1818), p. 99; Skyring (1831), p. 91.
119 Brighton/Crace MS., p. 24.
120 Ibid., pp. 8, 11, 42.
121 Cooper-Hewitt drawings, 1948-40-50 (Glass Passage, reproduced by Morley (1984), pl. 91); 1948-40-25 (Saloon, reproduced by Morley (1984), pl. 50).
122 Brighton/Crace MS., p. 99.
123 Ibid., p. 103.
124 Ibid., pp. 125, 128, 129.
125 Ibid., p. 13.
126 Hinkley (1960), pp. 100–3.
127 R.I.B.A. drawings, Smythson collection, III/13 (Cat. S, Smythson, John [281]). Reproduced in companion volume.
128 P.R.O. MSS., AO. 1/2429/71, MM. xiii[v] to xiv[r].
129 Gunther (1928), p. 282.
130 P.R.O. MSS., E. 351/3266, M. ix[v].
131 John Smith (1687), p. 52.
132 See n. 23 to Chapter 20.
133 Ditto.
134 Whittock (1827), p. 39.
135 Ham MSS., Gooderick's account.
136 Lincoln Cathedral MS.
137 P.R.O. MSS., WORK. 19/48/1, f. 50(iv).
138 Wren Society, vol. IV (1927), p. 47.
139 Cust (1914), vol. I, p. 41.
140 Laxton (1818), p. 100; Nicholson (1823–5), 'The Practical Builder's Perpetual Price-book', p. 152; Skyring (1831), p. 91.
141 Colvin (1984), p. 307.

Appendix C. Glossary of marbles imitated

1 List in Chambers's sketchbook, V.A.M. drawings, 5712, ff. 126[v], 127[r], 127[v], 128[r].
2 Whittock (1827), p. 47.
3 V.A.M. accession No. W. 54-to-6-1953.
4 Whittock (1827), pp. 49, 55.
5 Vanherman (1828), p. 63.
6 Hull (1872), p. 141.
7 Whittock (1827), pp. 49, 53–4.
8 Vanherman (1828), p. 63.
9 Renwick (1909) pp. 190, 198.
10 Hull (1872), p. 126.
11 Gwilt (1894), p. 489.
12 Burnham (1883), p. 310.
13 Laxton (1818), p. 100; Skyring (1831), p. 91.
14 Gwilt (1894), p. 492.
15 Neve (1703), pp. 107, 201.
16 Gwilt (1894), p. 492.
17 R.I.B.A. MSS., CHA 3/1, p. 270.
18 Félibien (1676), pp. 292–3.
19 Croft-Murray, vol. I (1962), p. 216b (quoting letter from Isaac Bayley to Thomas Foley, 3 March 1705, in possession of Mr H.T.H. Foley, Stoke Edith, Herefordshire).

20 Soane MSS., 'Business', p. 18.
21 Vanherman (1828), p. 63.
22 Whittock (1827), p. 63.
23 Cater [1933], p. 59.
24 Whittock (1827), pp. 63–4.
25 Vanherman (1828), p. 63.
26 Gwilt (1894), p. 490ff.
27 Whittock (1827), p. 49.
28 Ibid.
29 Chambers (1759), p. 79.
30 R.I.B.A. MSS., CHA 3/1, p. 270.
31 Renwick (1909), p. 217.
32 Burnham (1883), p. 302.
33 Renwick (1909), p. 211.
34 Laxton (1818), p. 100; Nicholson (1823–5), 'The Practical Builder's Perpetual Price-book', p. 153; Skyring (1813), p. 91.
35 Vanherman (1828), p. 63.
36 Renwick (1909), p. 195.
37 Vanherman (1828), p. 63; Whittock (1827), p. 53.
38 Brighton/Crace MS., p. 22.
39 Ibid., p. 26.
40 Ibid., pp. 42, 66, 71.
41 Whittock (1827), p. 49.
42 Burnham (1883), pp. 144, 146, 157, 171.
43 Linstrum (1972), p. 121.
44 Vanherman (1828), p. 63.
45 Burnham (1883), p. 171.
46 Whittock (1827), p. 49.
47 Renwick (1909), p. 198.
48 Whittock (1827), pp. 53–4.
49 Laxton (1818), p. 100; Skyring (1831), p. 91; Nicholson (1823–5), 'The Practical Builder's Perpetual Price-book', p. 153.
50 Colvin (1984), p. 307; Neve (1703), p. 201.
51 Whittock (1827), pp. 61–2.
52 Hull (1872), pp. 107, 109, 148. By the early years of the present century, however, John Watson noted that 'Egyptian green' had no connection with Egypt, and was obtained from beds of serpentinous rock occurring in the vicinity of Genoa. He believed its name arose from its employment in Paris by Napoleon following his Egyptian campaign. (Watson (1916), pp. 427–8.) Hull had described this as 'Vert de Gênes' (op. cit., p. 108).
53 Whittock (1827), p. 54.
54 Burnham (1883), p. 311.
55 Whittock (1827), p. 55.
56 Ibid.
57 Laxton (1818), p. 100; Skyring (1831), p. 91.
58 Renwick (1909), p. 199.
59 Burnham (1883), p. 289.
60 Laxton (1818), p. 100; Skyring (1831), p. 91.
61 Dunham Massey MSS.
62 Croft-Murray, vol. I (1962), p. 217a (quoting letter from Isaac Bayley to Thomas Foley, 3 March 1705, in possession of Mr H.T.H. Foley, Stoke Edith, Herefordshire).
63 Hull (1872), p. 80.
64 Laxton (1818), p. 100; Skyring (1831), p. 91.
65 Vanherman (1828), p. 63.
66 Ham MSS., Gooderick's account.
67 P.R.O. MSS., E. 351/3453, M. xi^{v}.
68 Tredegar MSS., 102/98.
69 P.R.O. MSS., E. 351/3227, M. v^{v} (example cited). Others include: pillars of a conduit at Greenwich, 1532–3 (Kirby (1957), p. 45 – transcription of Bodleian Library MS. Western Rawl. D 775); panels in Sir Thomas Cawarden's house, Whitefriars, London, some time before 1544 (Croft-Murray, vol. I (1962), p. 163a – quoting Losely MS. 127 in Borough Museum, Guildford, Surrey); seats in St James's Park and at Greenwich, 1597–8 (P.R.O. MSS., E. 351/3233, MM. iii^{v}, v^{r}.)
70 R.I.B.A. MSS., CHA 3/1, p. 270.
71 Salmon (1672), p. 222.
72 Colvin (1984), p. 307.
73 Croft-Murray, vol. I (1962), p. 217a (quoting letter from Isaac Bayley to Thomas Foley, 3 March 1705, in possession of Mr H.T.H Foley, Stoke Edith, Herefordshire); p. 254b (Burley-on-the-Hill)
74 Brighton/Crace MS., pp. 16, 21, 22.
75 List in Chambers's sketchbook, V.A.M. drawings, 5712, f. 127^{r}.
76 Whittock (1827), p. 49; Vanherman (1828), p. 63.
77 V.A.M. accession No. W. 54-to-6-1953, Nos. 40, 71.
78 P.R.O. MSS., E. 351/3256, M. v^{v}; 3271, M. vii^{v}.
79 Neve (1703), p. 201.
80 Colvin (1984), p. 289 (Combe Abbey); Dyrham MSS., D. 1799 E234; Bristow (1979); Bristow MSS., thesis (1983), vol. II, pp 798–812.
81 Laxton (1818), p. 100; Skyring (1831), p. 91.
82 Whittock (1827), p. 48; Vanherman (1828), p. 63.
83 Meikleham [*c.* 1835], s.v. 'MARBLE', vol. II.
84 Burnham (1883), p. 136.
85 Whittock (1827), p. 48.
86 P.R.O. MSS., E. 351/3245, M. xiv^{v}.
87 Croft-Murray, vol. I (1962), p. 212b.
88 Evelyn (1870), p. 297.
89 Brighton/Crace MS., p. 3.
90 Pyne (1819), vol. III, p. 14.
91 Croft-Murray, vol. II (1970), p. 306a.
92 Hull no doubt refers to the town known today as Spáta, which is approximately 14 miles south of Marathon, and not to the better known ancient city of Sparta (modern Spárti) which is in the Peloponnese.
93 Hull (1872), pp. 63, 73, 75.
94 Burnham (1883), p. 276.
95 Dyrham MSS., D. 1799, E234.
96 Bristow (1979); Bristow MSS., thesis (1983), vol. II, pp. 752–60.
97 Bristow (1987); Bristow MSS., thesis (1983), vol. II, pp. 798–812
98 Soane Museum drawings, Soane collection, 31/4/26; Soane MSS., 'Business', p. 18.
99 Croft-Murray, vol. II (1970), p. 305a.
100 Whittock (1827), pp. 64–5.
101 Renwick (1909), p. 214.
102 P.R.O. MSS., E. 351/3227, M. v^{v}.
103 Ibid., E. 351/3228, M. iv^{v}.
104 Ibid., E. 351/3245, M. xiv^{v}.
105 Ibid., E. 351/3254, M. v^{r}.
106 Lincoln Cathedral MS.
107 Neve (1703), pp. 107, 201.
108 Croft-Murray, vol. I (1962), p. 217a (quoting letter from Isaac Bayley to Thomas Foley, 3 March 1705, in possession of Mr H.T.H Foley, Stoke Edith, Herefordshire).
109 Vanherman (1828), p. 63.
110 P.R.O. MSS., E. 351/3245, M. xiv^{v}.
111 Whittock (1827), p. 62.
112 Hull (1872), pp. 97–104.
113 Renwick (1909), p. 216.
114 Whittock (1827), pp. 49, 57.
115 Ibid., pp. 55–6.
116 Ibid., pp. 56–7.
117 Op. cit. (1787), p. 143; (1794), p. 155.
118 Pyne (1819), vol. III, p. 14.
119 Laxton (1818), p. 100.
120 Nicholson (1823–5), 'The Practical Builder's Perpetual Price book', p. 153.
121 Skyring (1831), p. 91.
122 P.R.O. MSS., E. 351/3249, M. ix^{v}.
123 Whittock (1827), pp. 49, 55.
124 Burnham (1883), p. 237.
125 P.R.O. MSS., E. 351/3243, M. xiv^{v}; Croft-Murray (1962–70), vol. I (1962), p. 199.
126 Vanherman (1828), p. 63.
127 Laxton (1818), p. 100; Nicholson (1823–5), 'The Practical Builder's Perpetual Price-book', p. 153; Skyring (1831), p. 91.
128 Hull (1872), p. 133.
129 Renwick (1909), p. 221.
130 Skyring (1831), p. 91.
131 Pyne (1819), vol. III, p. 14.

132 Whittock (1827), p. 57.
133 Vanherman (1828), p. 63.
134 Renwick (1909), p. 220.
135 Burnham (1883), p. 321.
136 Hull (1872), p. 107ff.
137 Whittock (1827), pp. 57–9.
138 Ibid., p. 60.
139 Ibid., p. 61.
140 Laxton (1818), p. 100; Nicholson (1823–5), 'The Practical Builder's Perpetual Price Book', p. 153; Skyring (1831), p. 91.
141 Whittock (1827), p. 49.
142 V.A.M. accession No. W. 54-to-6-1953, No. 9.
143 Croft-Murray (1962–70), vol. I (1962), p. 163a (quoting Losely MS. 127 in Borough Museum, Guildford, Surrey).
144 P.R.O. MSS., E. 351/3263, M. xi[r & v].
145 Ibid., E. 351/3271, MM. vii[v], viii[r].
146 Ibid., M. xii[r].
147 Croft-Murray (1962–70), vol. I (1962), p. 222b (quoting St Mary Redcliffe MS., 'The Queen Anne Restorations Book').
148 Ham MSS., Gooderick's account.
149 Croft-Murray (1962–70), vol. I (1962), p. 216b (quoting letter from Isaac Bayley to Thomas Foley, 3 March 1705, in possession of Mr H.T.H. Foley, Stoke Edith, Herefordshire).
150 Whittock (1827), pp. 48–9; Vanherman (1828), p. 63.
151 Renwick (1909), p. 218.
152 Ham MSS., Gooderick's account.
153 P.R.O. MSS., E. 351/3260, M. vi[r].
154 Lincoln Cathedral MS.
155 Wren Society, vol. VII (1930), p. 130.
156 Ibid., vol. IV (1927), p. 47.
157 P.R.O. MSS., WORK. 19/48/1, ff. 50(IV), 64(III), 74(III), 79(III).
158 Laxton (1818), p. 100; Nicholson (1823–5), 'The Practical Builder's Perpetual Price-book', p. 153.
159 Skyring (1831), p. 91.
160 Stalker & Parker (1688/1971), p. 82.
161 Reynolds (1812), p. 20.
162 Whittock (1827), pp. 50–1.
163 Ibid., pp. 52–3.
164 Nicholson (1834), p. 161.

Appendix D. Painted floors and floorcloths

1 For a discussion of this, see Fowler & Cornforth (1974), pp. 210–11.
2 Bold (1990), p. 81.
3 Watin (1785), pp. 69–70.
4 Tingry (1804), pp. 503–4; (1816), p. 384.
5 Op. cit. (1787), p. 118; (1810), p. 71.
6 R.I.B.A. MSS., PEL/1, f. 86.
7 Glasse (1760), p. 37.
8 Watin (1785), p. 68.
9 Tingry (1804), pp. 505–6; (1816), p. 385.
10 John Wood (1749), Preface.
11 Glasse (1760), p. 29.
12 Reynolds (1812), pp. 21–22.
13 S.R.O. MSS., GD 44/51/385/138.
14 Caley (1792), pp. 404, 408.
15 Patent No. 99 (1637).
16 John Smith (1687), c. xvii.
17 P.R.O. MSS., ADM. 68/685, July 1710.
18 Boynton (1965), pp. 43, 45, 46, 56.
19 Beecher (1863), vol. I, pp. 102–3.
20 National Gallery, London, No. 113.
21 Devis Exhibition (1983), No. 15 (private collection).
22 Ibid., No. 10 (Mellon Collection, Yale Center for British Art).
23 Gilbert & *al.* (1987), p. 101b (quoting MS. in Essex Record Office, D/DBy, A 30/11).
24 B.M. trade cards, Heal 30.21; Lysons (1792–6), vol. II (1795), p. 181.
25 V.A.M. MSS., L. 1911–1929, f. 42.
26 Robert Campbell (1747), p. 245.
27 Patent No. 787 (1763).
28 Reynolds (1812), p. 22.
29 *Penny Magazine* (August 1842), pp. 337–44.
30 V.A.M. MSS., L. 1911–1939, ff. 15, 26, 42.
31 *Penny Magazine* (August 1842), pp. 337–44.
32 Gilbert & *al.* (1987), p. 104a (quoting Thomas Webster, *Encyclopaedia of Domestic Economy* (1847), p. 299).
33 Patent No. 787 (1763).
34 Glasse (1760), pp. 23, 33–4.
35 Op. cit., p. 346, para. 678.
36 *Builders Price-Book* (1776), p. 92; (1787), p. 140; (1794), p. 151; (1810), p. 82; (1813), p. 125.
37 See Gilbert & *al.* (1987).

Appendix E. Note on the Berger archive

1 Armitage (n.d.), pp. 3–4, and Appendix [1].
2 Ibid., *passim.*

Appendix F. Preface to companion volume

1 Vanherman (1828), p. 48.
2 Fowler & Cornforth (1974), pp. 174, 180.
3 For the Devis exhibition (held in 1983–4 at the Harris Museum and Art Gallery, Preston, and at the National Portrait Gallery, London) see the catalogue (cited as Devis Exhibition (1983)); and for the Hayman exhibition (held in 1987 at the Yale Center for British Art, New Haven, Connecticut, and Kenwood, Middlesex) see Allen (1987).
4 Ian C. Bristow, *Architectural Colour in British Interiors 1615–1840* (1996).
5 In America, two theses had been devoted to the subject: Richard M. Candee, 'Materials Towards a History of Housepaints', Master's thesis, Cooperstown Graduate Program, State University of New York, 1965; and Theodore Z. Penn, 'Decorative and Protective Finishes, 1750–1850', Master's thesis, University of Delaware, 1966.
6 Phillips (1971).
7 The Music Room at Kedleston Hall, Derbyshire, is a typical example. Beneath the red thought by scraping to have been the original colour are several other much paler schemes. See Bristow MSS., thesis (1983), vol. II, p. 749.
8 These include the Balcony Room at Dyrham Park, Gloucestershire (now Avon); the Saloon at Uppark, Sussex; and the Boudoir at Attingham Hall, Shropshire. See Bristow MSS., thesis (1983), vol. II, pp. 752–60; pp. 832–4; and pp. 837–8, respectively. The first of these is reviewed also in Bristow (1979).
9 Salmon (1734), pp. 57–8.
10 R.I.A. MSS., Charlemont letters, second series, vol. I. No. 62 (22 March 1769).
11 Gunther (1928), p. 147.
12 Ibid., p. 282.
13 *Report from the Select Committee* (1830), p. 16.
14 Bowood MSS., diary, vol. IV, p. 119 (entry for 25 August 1768). For a transcription of the relevant passage, see Lees-Milne (1947), p. 113.
15 Soane Museum drawings, Adam albums, vol. XI, No. 212 (dated 1772).
16 Pyne (1819), vol. III.
17 N.L.I. drawings, No. 2131.
18 Athenaeum drawings.
19 Vanherman (1828), p. 11.
20 Price (1796), pp. 172–6; Repton (1816), pl. facing p. 76; Crease (1808), p. 12.
21 Bristow (1980).
22 These are reviewed in detail by Harley (1970), pp. 5–8, 16–18. John Abbott's design book is now at the Exeter Record Office (404M/B1). It is signed and dated 1665 on the flyleaves at each end, and the date 1662 appears on a sketch for a Charles II royal arms in the body of the book. Passages from the *Very Proper Treatise* are generally copied fairly closely, and very nearly all the

remainder of the text parallels passages on painting in the 1634 edition of Bate's *Mysteries*. For a transcription of the manuscript see Chenevix Trench (1987), although his commentary is based on the 1654 edition of Bate, which is much less close than that of 1634.

23 Vanherman (1805). See Chapter 10 of the present book above.
24 B.M. trade cards, Heal 89.53.
25 Ibid., Heal 89.55 (this has a bill on the reverse dated 6 July 1744).
26 Ibid., Banks, 89. 27, 28.
27 Salmon (1734) was also plagiarised by Leadbetter (1737), pp. 190–3. The preceding text (from p. 167) is copied from one of the editions of John Smith (1687, &c.).
28 For a full description, see Harley (1979).
29 V.A.M. accession No. W. 54-to-6-1953.
30 Published in Thornton & Tomlin (1980).
31 G.L.R.O. MSS., Arlington Street.
32 Caley (1792).
33 S.A.L. MS.
34 B.L. MSS., Add. 41133.
35 R.I.A. MSS., Charlemont letters.
36 Y.A.S. MS.
37 Soane MSS., 'Business', pp. 18, 19.
38 Dunham Massey MSS.
39 R.I.A. MSS., Charlemont letters, second series, vol. I, No. 62 (22 March 1769).
40 Dyrham MSS., D. 1799, E234; Boughton MS. vol. I, letter at p. 193.
41 Woburn MSS., box 394.
42 R.I.B.A. MSS., CHA 3/1, pp. 253–5; S.A.L. MS.
43 R.I.B.A. MSS., PEL/1, p. 82.
44 Bristow MSS., thesis (1983), vol. II, pp. 823–6.
45 Thornton and Tomlin (1980), p. 159.
46 Ham MSS., Gooderick's account and Kinsman's account; Dyrham MSS., D. 1799, A105 and E234.
47 R.I.B.A. MSS., PEL/1, p. 86.
48 Osterley MSS., Adamson (1772–4).
49 Arundel MS., Cuenot's bill.
50 Audley End drawings, No. 54.
51 George Smith (1826), p. 165.
52 Osterley MSS., Adamson (1787).
53 Soane Museum drawings, Adam albums, vol. XII, No. 47; Robert & James Adam (1773–1822), vol. I, part I (1773), preface; vol. II (1779), part II, pl. 7.

REFERENCES TO ILLUSTRATIONS

1 B.M. trade cards, Heal 80.55. (Copyright British Museum.)
2 Middleton (1915), fig. 176 (p. 345).
3 Berger MSS., 'Sample Book', f.6^{r}.
4 Berger MSS., 'Lake & Carmine Book', p. 127.
5 Diderot & D'Alembert (1754–72), plates, *tom.*I, *liv.*I (1762), 'Moulins pour exprimer le suc des fruits & l'huile des graines', pl. 2 (see also description on p. 5).
6 Ibid., pl. 3, fig. 2.
7 Ibid., pl. 3, fig. 3.
8 Ure (1860), fig. 1343 (vol. III, p. 279).
9 Clarke (1810–23), pt. III, vol. I (1819), pl. facing p. 252. (By permission of the British Library: 10024.l.3.)
10 French (1651), figure at foot of p. 28. (By permission of the British Library: 43.d.27.)
11 Tingry (1804), pl. iv (facing p. 168).
12 Ure (1860), vol. II, s.v. 'GLUE', p. 377.
13 B.M. trade cards, Heal 89.141. (Copyright British Museum.)
14 Ibid., Banks 90.25. (Copyright British Museum.)
15 Ibid., Banks 89.9. (Copyright British Museum.)
16 Ure (1860), figs. 1432–4 (vol.III, p. 374).
17 V.A.M. MSS., L.1911–1939, f.11^{r}. (Reproduced by courtesy of the Board of Trustees of the V&A.)
18 P.R.O. MSS., ADM.140/107, part 3.
19 B.M. trade cards, Banks 89.17. (Copyright British Museum.)
20 Ibid., Heal 89.148. (Copyright British Museum.)
21 Bristow MSS., notes, C.1, sample 3.
22 Ibid., C.39F, sample 90.
23 Ibid., C.63A, sample 5.
24 Ibid., C.13A, sample 12.
25 Castle Museum, York.
26 *New Decorators' Hand-book*, p. 37.
27 Holme (1688), bk. III, p. 364 (wrongly numbered 380), No. 33. (Society of Antiquaries of London.)
28 *New Decorators' Hand-book*, p. 23.
29 Holme (1688), bk. III, p. 330, No. 89. (Society of Antiquaries of London.)
30 Ibid., p. 391, No. 158. (Society of Antiquaries of London.)
31 Ibid., No. 159. (Society of Antiquaries of London.)
32 Moxon (1703), Bricklayer's Work, pl. 2.
33 *New Decorators' Hand-book*, p. 23.
34 Ibid.
35 Caylus (1755), frontispiece.
36 Diderot & D'Alembert (1754–72), plates, vol. II, 'Batteur d'Or', pl. 1.
37 Diderot & D'Alembert (1754–72), plates, vol. III, 'Doreur', pl. 4.
38 Whittock (1827), pl. II (facing p. 22).
39 Ibid., pl. V (facing p. 33).
40 Private collection.
41 Private collection.
42 Private collection.
43 Private collection.
44 Private collection.
45 Private collection.
46 Private collection.
47 Private collection.
48 Private collection.
49 Private collection.
50 Private collection.
51 Private collection.
52 Whittock (1827), pl. VII (facing p. 37).
53 Whittock (1827), pl. VIII (facing p. 35).
54 Private collection.
55 Whittock (1827), pl. I (facing p. 21).
56 Private collection.
57 Private collection.
58 Private collection.
59 Whittock (1827), pl. XIV (facing p. 44).
60 Whittock (1827), pl. XV (facing p. 45).
61 Whittock (1827), pl. XVI (facing p. 46).
62 Private collection.
63 Private collection.
64 Whittock (1827), pl. IX (facing p. 38).
65 Private collection.
66 Private collection.
67 Private collection.
68 Private collection.
69 Private collection.
70 Private collection.
71 By kind permission of the Administrator, Westminster Cathedral.
72 By kind permission of the Administrator, Westminster Cathedral.
73 By kind permission of the Administrator, Westminster Cathedral.
74 Author's photograph.
75 By kind permission of the Administrator, Westminster Cathedral.
76 By kind permission of the Director, Courtauld Institute Galleries.
77 Wallace Collection, London.
78 By kind permission of the Administrator, Westminster Cathedral.
79 Private collection.
80 Private collection.
81 By kind permission of the Director, Courtauld Institute Galleries.
82 Private collection.
83 By kind permission of the Administrator, Westminster Cathedral.
84 Private collection.
85 B.M. trade cards, Banks 30.1. (Copyright British Museum.)
86 Audley End drawings, No. 70. (English Heritage Photographic Library.)

SOURCES AND ABBREVIATIONS USED IN NOTES

1. BIBLIOGRAPHY

(N.B. Books were published in London unless otherwise stated.)

Acloque & Cornforth (1971) — G. Acloque & John Cornforth, 'The Eternal Gothic of Eaton', *Country Life*, vol. CXLIX (11 and 18 February 1971), pp. 304ff., 361ff.

Acts of Parliament — 23 Eliz. I, c. 9; 1 Jac. I, c. 20; 13 & 14 Car. II, c. 11, s. 26; 58 Geo. III. c. 28; 19 & 20 Vic., c. 64.

James Adam (1831) — 'Journal of a Tour in Italy', *Library of the Fine Arts* (1831–2), vol. II (1831), pp. 165–78, 235–45 (wrongly attributed to Robert Adam).

Robert & James Adam (1773–1822) — Robert & James Adam, *Works in Architecture* (1773–1822).

Addy (1898) — S.O. Addy, *The Evolution of the English House* (1898).

Adelphi Accounts (1920) — Victoria and Albert Museum, Department of Woodwork, *Accounts of Chippendale Haig & Co. for the Furnishing of David Garrick's House in the Adelphi* (1920).

Agricola (1546) — Georgius Agricola, *De Ortu et causis subterraneorum . . . De Natura fossilium* (Basle, 1546).

Aheron (1754) — James Aheron, *General Treatise of Architecture* (Dublin, 1754).

Allen (1987) — Brian Allen, *Francis Hayman* (1987).

Amatus Lusitanus (1554) — Amatus Lusitanus, *In Dioscorides anazarbei de medica* (Strasbourg, 1554).

A.P.S. (1852–92) — Architectural Publication Society, *The Dictionary of Architecture* (ed. Wyatt Papworth, 1852–92).

Arbuthnot (1950) — *The Journal of Mrs. Arbuthnot 1830–1832* (ed. Francis Bamford and the Duke of Wellington, 1950).

Architectural Drawings from Lowther Castle (1980) — *Architectural Drawings from Lowther Castle Westmorland* (ed. Howard Colvin, J. Mordaunt Crook, and Terry Friedman, Society of Architectural Historians of Great Britain, 1980).

Armitage (n.d.) — See MSS. sources.

Arrowsmith (1840) — H.W. & A. Arrowsmith, *The House Decorator and Painter's Guide* (1840).

Ashby (1916) — Thomas Ashby, 'Drawings of Ancient Paintings in English Collections', *Papers of the British School at Rome*, vol. VII (1914), pp. 1–62; vol. VIII (1916), pp. 35–54.

Attree (1809) — H.R. Attree, *Attree's Topography of Brighton* (1809).

Barry (1932) — T. Hedley Barry, *Natural Varnish Resins* (1932).

Bartholomew (1846) — Alfred Bartholomew, *Specifications for Practical Architecture* (2nd edn, 1846). (1st edn, 1840).

Bate (1634); (1654) — John Bate, *The Mysteries of Natvre, and Art* (1634); (3rd edn, 1654).

Beard (1966) — Geoffrey Beard, *Georgian Craftsmen and their Work* (1966).

Beard (1968) — Geoffrey Beard, ed., 'The Harewood Chippendale Account 1772–7', *Furniture History*, vol. IV (1968), pp. 70–80.

Beard (1978) — Geoffrey Beard, *The Work of Robert Adam* (1978).

Beecher (1863) — *Autobiography, Correspondence, &c. of Lyman Beecher* (ed. Charles Beecher, London, 1863).

Bellori (1680) — G.P. Bellori, *Le Pitture antiche* (Rome, 1680).

Bellori (1727) — G.P. Bellori, *Gli Antichi Sepolcri* (Rome, 1727).

Bellori (1728) — G.P. Bellori, *Veterum Sepulcra* (Rome, 1728).

Bellori & Causseo (1750) — G.P. Bellori & M.A. Causseo, *Picturae antiquae cryptarum Romanorum* (Rome, 1750).

Bennett (1833) — J. Bennett, *The Artificers Complete Lexicon* (1833).

Bent (1698) — Thomas Bent, 'The way of making Pitch, Tarr, Rosin and Turpentine near Marseilles', *Philosophical Transactions of the Royal Society*, vol. XX (1698), p. 291.

Bentley (1817) — *Prospectus of the Various Paints . . . Manufactured Exclusively by Thos. Bentley* (1817).

Berkeley and Percival (1914) — *Berkeley and Percival . . . the Correspondence of George Berkeley afterwards Bishop of Cloyne and Sir John Percival afterwards Earl of Egremont* (ed. Benjamin Rand, Cambridge, 1914).

Birch (1756–7) — T. Birch, *The History of the Royal Society* (1756–7).

Blondel (1737–8) — Jacques-François Blondel, *De la Distribution des maisons de plaisance* (Paris, 1737–8).

Blondel (1752–6) — Jacques-François Blondel, *Architecture françoise* (1752–6).

Bold (1990) — John Bold, 'The Design of a House for a Merchant, 1724', *Architectural History* (vol. 33, 1990), pp. 75–82.

Bolton (1922) — Arthur T. Bolton, *The Architecture of Robert and James Adam* (1922).

Boyle (1663–71) — Robert Boyle, *Some Considerations touching the Usefulnesse of Experimental Natural Philosophy* (Oxford, 1663–71).

Boyle (1664) — Robert Boyle, *Experiments and Considerations Touching Colours* (1664).

Boyle (1675) — Robert Boyle, 'A New Assay Instrument', *Philosophical Transactions of the Royal Society*, vol. x (1675–6), pp. 329–48.

Boynton (1965) — L.O.J. Boynton, 'Sir Richard Worsley's Furniture at Appuldurcombe Park', *Furniture History*, vol. I (1965), pp. 39–58.

Brace (1960) — H.W. Brace, *History of Seed Crushing in Great Britain* (1960).

Braybrooke (1836) — Richard Lord Braybrooke, *The History of Audley End* (1836).

Brayley (1838) — Edward Wedlake Brayley, *Illustrations of Her Majesty's Palace at Brighton* (1838).

Brignoli de Brunnhoff (1820) — Giovanni de Brignoli de Brunnhoff, 'Dissertation sur la chlorite ou terre verte de Vérone', *Journal de physique* (Paris [1794]–1823), vol. XC (1820), pp. 355–61, 423–42.

Bristow (1979) — Ian C. Bristow, 'The Balcony Room at Dyrham', *National Trust Studies 1980* (1979), pp. 140–6.

Bristow (1980) — Ian C. Bristow, 'Two Exterior Treatments used to Imitate Stone during the Eighteenth and early Nineteenth Centuries', *ASCHB Transactions 1979* (vol. IV, 1980), pp. 3–6.

Bristow (1982, interiors) — Ian C. Bristow, 'Repainting Eighteenth-century Interiors', *ASCHB Transactions 1981* (vol. VI, 1982), pp. 25–33.

Bristow (1982, Dulwich) — Ian C. Bristow, 'The Redecoration of the Dulwich Picture Gallery', *ASCHB Transactions 1981* (vol. VI, 1982), pp. 33–6.

Bristow (1983) — Ian C. Bristow, 'The Architect's Handmaid' (handlist for exhibition at R.I.B.A. Heinz Gallery, 9 November to 17 December 1983).

Bristow (1985) — Ian C. Bristow, 'The Casino, Marino: An Account of the Technical Investigation of the Paintwork and Redecoration of the Interior', *ASCHB Transactions 1984* (vol. IX, 1985), pp. 36–7, 40–4.

Bristow (1986) — Ian C. Bristow, 'The Great Drawing Room from Bowood', *ASCHB Transactions 1985* (vol. X, 1986), pp. 25–36.

Bristow (1987) — Ian C. Bristow, 'The Restoration of John Soane's Colour Scheme in the Breakfast Room at Pitzhanger Manor, Ealing', *ASCHB Transactions 1986* (vol. XI, 1987), pp. 43–8.

Bristow (1990) — Ian C. Bristow, 'Research into and Reconstruction of the Historic Paint Colours [at the Queen's House, Greenwich]', *ASCHB Transactions 1989* (vol. XIV, 1990), pp. 16, 65, 68–73.

Bristow (1996a) — Ian Bristow, *Architectural Colour in British Interiors 1615–1840* (1996).

Bristow (1996b) — Ian Bristow, *Interior House-Painting Colours and Technology 1615–1840* (1996).

Britton (1810) — John Britton, *The Beauties of Wiltshire* (1801).

Britton (1823) — John Britton, *Graphical and Literary Illustrations of Fonthill Abbey* (1823).

Britton (1827) — John Britton, *The Union of Architecture, Sculpture, and Painting* (1827).

Britton & Brayley (1802) — John Britton & E.W. Brayley, *The Beauties of England and Wales*, vol. III Derbyshire (1802).

Britton & Pugin (1825–8) — John Britton & Augustus Pugin, *The Public Buildings of London* (1825–8).

Buckler (1826) — J. & J.C. Buckler, *Views of Eaton Hall in Cheshire* (1826).

Builders Price-Book (1776) — *The Builders Price-Book* (I. Taylor, 1776).

Builders Price-Book (1787) — *The Builder's Price-Book* (4th edn, I. & J. Taylor, 1787).

Builders Price-Book (1794) — *The Builder's Price-Book* (11th edn, I. & J. Taylor, 1794).

Builders Price-Book (1810) — *Taylor's Builder's Price-book* (new edn 'Corrected to February, 1810', J. Taylor).

Builders Price-Book (1813) — *Taylor's Builder's Price-book* (new edn 'Corrected to January, 1813', J. Taylor).

Bullet (1691) — Pierre Bullet, *L'Architecture pratique* (Paris, 1691).

Bullet (1788) — Pierre Bullet, *Architecture Pratique . . . avec une explication . . . par M. Seguin* (Paris, 1788).

Burke (1757) — Edmund Burke, *A Philosophical Enquiry into the Origin of Our Ideas of the Sublime and the Beautiful* (1757).

Burnham (1883) — S.M. Burnham, *History and Uses of Limestones and Marbles* (Boston, U.S.A., 1883).

Butcher (1825) — William Butcher, *Smith's Art of House-Painting* (2nd edn, 1825). (1st edn, 1821).

Cadet-de-Vaux (1801) — Antoine Alexis Cadet-de-Vaux, 'Memoir on a Method of Painting with Milk', *The Repertory of Arts and Manufactures*, vol. XV (1801), pp. 411–21.

Caley (1792) — John Caley, 'A Survey of the Manor of Wymbledon', *Archaeologia*, vol. X (1792), pp. 399–448.

Cameron (1772) — Charles Cameron, *The Baths of the Romans* (1772).

Colen Campbell ([1715]–1771) — Colen Campbell & *al.*, *Vitruvius Britannicus* ([1715]–1771).

Robert Campbell (1747) — Robert Campbell, *The London Tradesman* (1747).

Carlyle & Southall (1993) — Leslie Carlyle & Anna Southall, 'No Short Mechanic Road to Fame' in Robin Hamlyn & *al.*, *Robert Vernon's Gift* (Tate Gallery, 1993), pp. 21–6.

Carwitham (1739) — John Carwitham, *Various Kinds of Floor Decorations . . . whether in Pavements of Stone or Marble or Wth Painted Floor Cloths* (1739).

Cater [1933] — Ian Cater, *Marble, a Handbook* [1933].

Caylus (1755) — Comte de Caylus, *Mémoire sur la peinture à l'encaustique* (Geneva, 1755).

Caylus & Mariette (1757); (1783) — Comte de Caylus & Pierre Jean Mariette, *Recueil de peintures antiques trouvées à Rome* (Paris, 1757). The second volume, together with a reprint of the first, was published in Paris in 1783.

Caylus (1771) — Comte de Caylus, 'Du Genre et l'espèce des peintures anciennes', *Mémoire de l'Académie des Inscriptions*, vol. XII (Paris, 1771).

Cennini (1844) — Cennino Cennini, *A Treatise on Painting* (tr. Mary Merrifield, 1844).

Cennini (1930) — *The Book of the Art of Cennino Cennini* (tr. Christiana J. Herringham, 3rd impression, 1930).

Chambers (1759); (1768) — William Chambers, *A Treatise on Civil Architecture* (1759); (2nd edn, 1768).

Chambers (1791) — Sir William Chambers, *A Treatise on the Decorative Part of Civil Architecture* (3rd edn of the above, 1791).

Chaptal (Paris, 1807)	J.A.C. Chaptal, *Chimie appliquée aux arts* (Paris, 1807).
Chaptal (London, 1807)	J.A.C. Chaptal, *Chemistry applied to Arts and Manufactures* (1807).
Chaptal (1809)	J.A.C. Chaptal, 'Sur quelques couleurs trouvées à Pompeïa', *Annales de chimie*, vol. LXX (Paris, 1809), pp. 22–31.
Chenevix Trench (1987)	John Chenevix Trench, 'John Abbott's Manual of Limming', *ASCHB Transactions 1986* (vol. 11, 1987), pp. 19–26.
Chettle (1937)	George H. Chettle, *The Queen's House, Greenwich* (14th Monograph of the London Survey Committee, 1937).
Church (1892)	A.H. Church, *The Chemistry of Paints and Painting* (2nd edn, 1892).
Clarke (1810–23)	Edward Daniel Clarke, *Travels in Various Countries* (1810–23).
Coad (1983)	Jonathan Coad, *Historic Architecture of the Royal Navy* (1983).
Coke (1889–96)	*The Letters and Journals of Lady Mary Coke* (Edinburgh, 1889–96).
Collections de Musée de l'Union Centrale	*Les Collections de Musée de l'Union Centrale des Arts Décoratifs*, série XXIII (Paris, n.d.).
Colvin (1954)	H.M. Colvin, *A Biographical Dictionary of English Architects 1660–1840* (1954).
Colvin (1978)	H.M. Colvin, *A Biographical Dictionary of British Architects 1600–1840* (1978).
Colvin (1984)	H.M. Colvin, 'Letters and Papers relating to the Rebuilding of Combe Abbey, Warwickshire, 1681–1688', *Walpole Society*, vol. 50 (1984), pp. 248–309.
Colwall (1678)	David Colwall, 'An Account of the Way of Making English Green-Copperas', *Philosophical Transactions of the Royal Society*, vol. XII (1687), pp. 1056–64.
Cook (1820)	A.G. Cook, *The New Builders' Magazine* (1820).
Cooper (1760)	Ambrose Cooper, *The Complete Distiller* (2nd edn, 1760).
Cornforth (1978)	John Cornforth, *English Interiors 1790–1848* (1978).
Cornforth (1979)	John Cornforth, 'Newby Hall, Yorkshire-III', *Country Life*, vol. 165 (21 June 1979), pp. 2006–9.
Crease (n.d.)	James Crease, *Elegance, Amusement, and Utility* (2nd edn. [*c.* 1800]).
Crease (1808)	James Crease, *Hints for the the Preservation of Wood-Work Exposed to the Weather* (1808).
Creevey (1948)	*Creevey* (selected and re-edited by John Gore, 1948).
Croft-Murray (1962–70)	Edward Croft-Murray, *Decorative Painting in England 1537–1837* (1962–70).
Cumberland (1806)	Richard Cumberland, *Memoirs* (1806).
Cummings (1971)	Abbott Lowell Cummings, 'Decorative Painters and House Painting at Massachusetts Bay, 1630–1725', *Winterthur Conference Report 1971: American Painting to 1776: a Reappraisal* (University of Virginia, 1971), pp. 71–125.
Cummings (1979)	Abbott Lowell Cummings, *The Framed Houses of Massachusetts Bay, 1625–1725* (1979).
Cust (1914)	Albinia Lucy Cust, *Chronicles of Erthig on the Dyke* (1914).
Dale (1956)	Antony Dale, *James Wyatt* (Oxford, 1956).
Dautermann & *al.* (1964)	Carl Christian Dautermann, James Parker, & E.A. Standen, *Decorative Art from the Kress Collection* (1964).
Davidson (1985)	Caroline Davidson, *The World of Mary Ellen Best* (1985).
D'Aviler (1691)	A.C. D'Aviler, *Cours d'architecture* (Paris, 1691).
Davy (1815)	Sir Humphry Davy, 'Some Experiments and Observations on the Colours used in Painting by the Ancients', *Philosophical Transactions of the Royal Society*, vol. CV, part I (1815), pp. 97–124.
Davy (1827)	Henry Davy, *Views of the Seats of the Noblemen and Gentlemen in Suffolk* (1827).
Defoe (1738)	Daniel Defoe, *A Tour Thro' the Whole Island of Great Britain* (2nd edn, 1738)
Delany (1861–2)	*The Autobiography and Correspondence of Mary Granville, Mrs. Delany* (ed. Lady Llanover, 1861–2).
Designs for Architects (1801)	*Designs for Architects, Upholsterers, Cabinet-Makers, &c.* (R. Ackermann, 1801).
Devis Exhibition (1983)	*Polite Society by Arthur Devis 1712–1787* (Harris Museum and Art Gallery, Preston, 1983).
Dickens (1965–)	*The Letters of Charles Dickens* (Pilgrim edn, Oxford, 1965–).
Diderot & D'Alembert (1754–72)	Denis Diderot & Jean le Rond D'Alembert, *Encyclopédie, ou dictionnaire raisonné des sciences, des arts et des métiers* (Geneva, 1754–72).
Donaldson [1859]	T.L. Donaldson, *Handbook of Specifications* [1859].
Dossie (1758); (1764)	Robert Dossie, *The Handmaid to the Arts* (1758); (2nd edn, 1764).
Downes (1979)	Kerry Downes, *Hawksmoor* (2nd edn, 1979).
Drossaers & Scheurleer (1974–6)	S.W.A. Drossaers & T.H. Lunsingh Scheurleer, ed., *Inventarissen van de Inboedels in de verblijven van de Oranjes . . . 1567–1795* (Rijks Geschiedkundige publication, The Hague, 1974–6).
Dyer (1875)	Thomas H. Dyer, *Pompeii. Its History, Buildings, and Antiquities* (new edn, 1875).
Eastlake (1847)	C.L. Eastlake, *Materials for a History of Oil Painting* (1847).
Eastlake (1868); (1872)	C.L. Eastlake, *Hints on Household Taste* (1868); (3rd edn, 1872).
Egger (1906)	H. Egger, *Codex Escorialensis* (Vienna, 1906).
'Elgin Marbles' (1842)	'Report of the Committee Appointed to Examine the Elgin Marbles', *Transactions of the Royal Institute of British Architects*, vol. I, part II (1842), pp. [102]–108.
Elliot (1924)	John Elliot, *Practical House Painting* (2nd edn, Glasgow, 1924).
Encyclopaedia Britannica (1810)	*Encyclopaedia Britannica* (4th edn, ed. J. Millar, Edinburgh, 1810).
Englefield (1936)	W.A.D. Englefield, *The History of the Painter-Stainers Company* (1936). Second binding of first edition (1923) with added introduction.
Englefield (1950)	W.A.D. Englefield, *The History of the Painter-Stainer's Company* (3rd edn, 1950).
Evelyn (1664); (1670); (1706)	John Evelyn, *Sylva, or à Discourse of Forest-Trees* (1664); (2nd edn, 1670); (4th edn, 1706).

Evelyn (1870) — *Memoirs . . . of John Evelyn* (ed. William Bray, 1870).

Farington (1922–8) — *The Farington Diary* (ed. James Grieg, 1922–8).

Félibien (1676) — André Félibien, *Des principes de l'architecture, de la sculpture, de la peinture* (Paris, 1676).

Feller & *al.* (1986) — Robert L. Feller (ed.), *Artists' Pigments A Handbook of their History and Characteristics* (vol. I, 1986).

Field (1817) — George Field, *Chromatics: or, An Essay on the Analogy and Harmony of Colours* (1817).

Field (1835) — George Field, *Chromatography* (1835).

Fiennes (1947) — *The Journeys of Celia Fiennes* (ed. Christopher Morris, 1947). Re-issue of 1949 has same pagination.

Finch (1901) — Pearl Finch, *History of Burley-on-the-Hill* (1901).

Fitz-Gerald (1973) — Desmond Fitz-Gerald, *The Norfolk House Music Room* (1973).

Fleming (1962) — John Fleming, *Robert Adam and his Circle* (1962).

Fougeroux de Bondaroy (1766) — Auguste Denis Fougeroux de Bondaroy, 'Sur le giallolino ou jaune de Naples', *Histoire de l'Académie Royale des Sciences année 1766* (Paris, 1769), pp. 60–4 (*Histoire*), 303–14 (*Mémoires*).

Fowler & Cornforth (1974) — John Fowler & John Cornforth, *English Decoration in the 18th Century* (1974).

French (1651) — John French, *The Art of Distillation* (1651).

Fresnoy (1783) — *The Art of Painting of Charles Alphonse du Fresnoy* (tr. William Mason, Dublin, 1783).

Friedman (1984) — Terry Friedman, *James Gibbs* (1984).

Gallet (1972) — Michel Gallet, *Paris Domestic Architecture of the 18th Century* (1972).

Gallet (1980) — Michel Gallet, *Claude-Nicholas Ledoux* (Paris, 1980).

Gartside (1805) — Mary Gartside, *An Essay on Light and Shade* (1805).

Gazetteer (n.d.) — *A Gazetteer of the World* (A. Fullerton & Co., London and Edinburgh, n.d.).

Gell (1835) — William Gell, *Pompeiana. The Topography, Edifices, and Ornaments of Pompeii, the Result of Excavations since 1819* (1835).

Gell (1852) — William Gell, *Pompeiana. The Topography, Edifices, and Ornaments of Pompeii* (3rd edn, 1852).

Gentleman's Magazine (1731–1868) — *Gentleman's Magazine* (1731–1868).

Gerbier (1663) — Sir Balthazar Gerbier, *Counsel and Advise to all Builders* (1663).

Gerbier (1664) — Sir Balthazar Gerbier, *A Brief Discourse Concerning . . . Magnificent Building* (1664).

Gilbert (1968) — Christopher Gilbert, 'Lady Hertford, John James Audubon and the Chinese Drawing Room at Temple Newsam', *Leeds Arts Calendar*, No. 61 (1968), pp. 14–17.

Gilbert & *al.* (1987) — Christopher Gilbert, James Lomax, & Anthony Wells-Cole, *Country House Floors 1660–1850* (Leeds City Art Galleries, 1987).

Gillespie (1970–80) — Charles Coulston Gillespie (ed.), *Dictionary of Scientific Biographies* (New York, 1970–80).

Girouard (1978) — Mark Girouard, *Life in the English Country House* (1978).

Girouard (1983) — Mark Girouard, *Robert Smythson & the Elizabethan Country House* (1983).

Glasse (1760) — Hannah Glasse, *The Servant's Directory* (1760).

Goethe (1791) — Johann Wolfgang Goethe, *Beiträge zur Optik* (Weimar, 1791).

Goethe (1810) — Johann Wolfgang Goethe, *Zur Farbenlehre . . . Nebst einem Hefte mit sechzehn Kupfertafeln* (Tübingen, 1810).

Goethe (1840) — *Goethe's Theory of Colours* (tr. C.L. Eastlake, 1840).

Goldicutt (1825) — John Goldicutt, *Specimens of Ancient Decorations from Pompeii* (1825).

Gottesman (1954) — Rita S. Gottesman, *The Arts and Crafts in New York 1777–1799* (New York, 1954).

Greninger & *al.* [1975] — Dorothy Greninger, Valerie Kollonitsch, & Charles H. Kline, *Lead Chemicals* (International Lead Zinc Research Organisation, New York, [1975]).

Grimaldi (1665) — P. Francisco Grimaldo, *Physico-Mathesis de Lvmine, Coloribvs, et Iride* (Bologna, 1665).

Guibourt (1836) — Nicolas Jean Baptiste Gaston Guibourt, *Histoire abrégée des drogues simples* (3rd edn, Paris, 1836).

Gunther (1928) — R.T. Gunther, *The Architecture of Sir Roger Pratt* (Oxford, 1928).

Guyton de Morveau (1783) — Guyton de Morveau, 'Recherches pour perfectionner la préparation des couleurs employées dans la peinture', *Nouveaux Mémoires de l'Académie de Dijon 1782* (Dijon, 1783), pp. 1–24.

Gwilt (1894) — Joseph Gwilt, *An Encyclopaedia of Architecture* (new edn, 1894, revised . . . with additions by Wyatt Papworth).

Haddon-Reece (1987) — David Haddon-Reece & *al.*, 'Tree-ring list 22', *Vernacular Architecture*, vol. 18 (1987), pp. 54–5.

Hakewill (1813) — James Hakewill, *The History of Windsor* (1813).

Ham House (1976) — *Ham House* (Victoria and Albert Museum guidebook, 1976).

Hamilton (1776–79) — William Hamilton, *Campi Phlegraei* (Naples, 1776–79).

Harley (1970); (1982) — R.D. Harley, *Artists' Pigments* c. *1600–1835* (1970); (2nd edn, 1982).

Harley (1979) — R.D. Harley, 'Field's Manuscripts', *Studies in Conservation* (1952-date), vol. XXIV (1979), pp. 75–84.

Eileen Harris (1967) — Eileen Harris, 'Burke and Chambers on the Sublime and Beautiful', *Essays in the History of Architecture presented to Rudolph Wittkower* (ed. Douglas Fraser, Howard Hibbard, & Milton J. Lewine, 1967), pp. 207–13.

Eileen Harris (1990) — Eileen Harris, assisted by Nicholas Savage, *British Architectural Books and Writers 1556–1785* (Cambridge, 1990).

John Harris (1970) — John Harris, *Sir William Chambers* (1970).

John Harris & *al.* (1973) — John Harris, Stephen Orgel, & Roy Strong, *The King's Arcadia* (Arts Council of Great Britain, exhibition catalogue, 1973).

Harris & Tait (1979) — John Harris & A.A. Tait, *Catalogue of the Drawings by Inigo Jones, John Webb and Isaac de Caus at Worcester College Oxford* (Oxford, 1979).

Leslie Harris (1987) — Leslie Harris, *Robert Adam and Kedleston* (1987).

Moses Harris (1963) — Moses Harris, *The Natural System of Colours* (facsimile edn with historical notes and commentary by Faber Birren, 1963).

Harrison (1577) — William Harrison, 'An Historicall Description of the Islande of Britayne' (printed in Raphael Holinshead, *Chronicles of England, Scotlande, and Irelande* (1577), vol. I).

Hatton (1708) — Edward Hatton, *A New View of London* (1708).

Hay (1828); (1829); (1847) — D.R. Hay, *The Laws of Harmonious Colouring adapted to House Painting* (Edinburgh, 1828); (2nd edn, Edinburgh, 1829); (6th edn, 1847).

Hay (1845) — D.R. Hay, *The Principles of Beauty in Colouring Systematised* (Edinburgh, 1845).

Hay (1846) — D.R. Hay, *A Nomenclature of Colours* (2nd edn, Edinburgh, 1846).

Heaton (1940) — Noël Heaton, *Outlines of Paint Technology* (2nd edn, 1940). (1st edn, 1928).

Hertfordshire (1910) — Royal Commission on Historical Monuments (England), *An Inventory of the Historical Monuments in Hertfordshire* (1910).

Hey (1957–8) — Margaret Hey, 'The Analysis of Paint Media by Paper Chromatography', *Studies in Conservation* (1952-date), vol. III (1957–8), p. 183ff.

Hibbert (1821) — Communications from Samuel Hibbert, Royal Society of Arts, *Transactions*, vol. XXXVIII (1821), pp. 23–26.

Hill (1746) — John Hill, *Theophrastus's History of Stones* (1746).

Hinkley (1960) — F. Lewis Hinkley, *Directory of the Historic Cabinet Woods* (New York, 1960).

History of the King's Works (1963–82) — *The History of the King's Works* (ed. H.M. Colvin, 1963–82).

Holme (1688) — Randle Holme, *The Academy of Armory* (Chester, 1688).

Hooke (1665) — Robert Hooke, *Micrographia: or some Physiological Descriptions of Minute Bodies* (1665).

Hope (1807) — Thomas Hope, *Household Furniture and Interior Decoration* (1807).

Houghton (1692–1703) — John Houghton, *A Collection for Improvement of Husbandry and Trade* (1692–1703).

Howes (1949) — F.N. Howes, *Vegetable Gums and Resins* (Waltham, Massachusetts, 1949).

Hull (1872) — Edward Hull, *A Treatise on the Building and Ornamental Stones of Great Britain and Foreign Countries* (1872).

Hurst (1896) — George H. Hurst, *Painters' Colours, Oils, and Varnishes* (2nd edn, 1896). (1st edn, 1892).

Hurst (1902) — George H. Hurst, *The Painter's Laboratory Guide* (1902).

Hussey (1967) — Christopher Hussey, 'Wimpole Hall, Cambridgeshire – III', *Country Life*, vol. CXLII (14 December 1967), pp. 1594–7.

Interiors (1981) — *Interiors* (1981) (catalogue of exhibition held by Hazlitt, Gooden & Fox, 38 Bury Street, St James's, London SW1Y 6BB, 6 November to 11 December 1981).

Jackson-Stops (1980) — Gervase Jackson-Stops, 'Broadlands, Hampshire – I', *Country Life*, vol. 168 (4 December 1980), pp. 2099–2102.

Jeans (1950) — Sir James Jeans, *The Growth of Physical Science* (1950).

Johnson (1755) — Samuel Johnson, *A Dictionary of the English Language* (1755).

Jourdain [1914] — Margaret Jourdain (pseud. Francis Lenygon), *Decoration in England from 1660 to 1770* [1914].

Jourdain [1922] — Margaret Jourdain, *English Decoration and Furniture of the later XVIIIth Century (1760–1820)* [1922].

Jourdain (1926) — Margaret Jourdain, *English Decorative Plasterwork* (1926).

Kendall (1809) — Edward A. Kendall, *Travels through the Northern Parts of the United States* (New York, 1809).

Kirby (1957) — J.W. Kirby, 'Building Work at Placentia 1532–1533', *Transactions of the Greenwich & Lewisham Antiquarian Society*, vol. V, No. 1 (1957), pp. 22–50.

Kopp (1843–7) — Hermann Kopp, *Geschichte der Chemie* (Brunswick, 1843–7).

Kühn (1968) — Hermann Kühn, 'Lead Tin Yellow', *Studies in Conservation* (1952-date), vol. XIII (1968), pp. 7–33.

Lairesse (1738) — Gerard de Lairesse, *The Art of Painting* (tr. John Fritsch, 1738). The first edition was published as *Het groot Schilderboeck* (Amsterdam, 1707).

Langley (1740) — Batty Langley, *The City and Country Builder's and Workman's Treasury of Designs* (1740).

Laugier (1977) — Marc-Antoine Laugier, *An Essay on Architecture* (tr. Wolfgang and Anni Herrmann, Los Angeles, 1977). The first edition was published as *Essai sur l'architecture* (Paris, 1753).

Laurie (1910) — A.P. Laurie, *Greek and Roman Methods of Painting* (Cambridge, 1910).

Laxton (1818) — W.R. Laxton, *The Improved Builder's Price Book* (2nd edn, 1818).

Leadbeater (1770) — J. Leadbeater, *The Gentleman and Tradesman's Compleat Assistant* (3rd edn, 1770).

Leadbetter (1737) — Charles Leadbetter, *Mechanick Dialling: Or, the New Art of Shadows* (1737).

Le Blon (n.d.) — James Christopher Le Blon, *Coloritto, or the Harmony of Colouring in Painting* (n.d.).

Le Camus de Mézières (1780) — Nicolas le Camus de Mézières, *Le Génie de l'architecture* (Paris, 1780).

Leeds Arts Calendar (1983) — *Leeds Arts Calendar*, No. 93 (Leeds, 1983).

Lees-Milne (1947) — James Lees-Milne, *The Age of Adam* (1947).

Leger Galleries (1983) — *Realism through Informality* (1983). (Catalogue of exhibition held at the Leger Galleries, Old Bond Street, London, from 12 October to 25 November 1983).

Leinster (1949–57) — *Correspondence of Emily, Duchess of Leinster (1731–1814)* (ed. Brian Fitzgerald, Dublin, 1949–57).

Lelièvre & *al.* (1794) — Lelièvre, Pelletier, D'Arcet, & Giroud, 'Rapport sur les divers moyens d'extraire d'avantage le sel de soude du sel marin', *Journal de Physique* (1794–1823), vol. II (1794), pp. 118–34 (August), 191–7 (September).

Leuchs (1829) — J. Ch. Leuchs, *Traité complet des proriétés, de la préparation et de l'emploi des matières tinctoriales et des couleurs . . . revu pour la partie chimique par M.E. Péclet* (Paris, 1829).

Leybourn (1668) William Leybourn, *A Platform for Purchasers, a Guide for Builders, a Mate for Measurers* (1668).

Leyburn (1700) William Leyburn, *Architectonice: or, a Compendium of the Art of Building* (1700). This was published as an addition to: John Brown, *The Mirror of Architecture: . . . by Vincent Scamozzi* (4th edn, 1700).

Liberate Rolls (1916–1964) *Calendar of the Liberate Rolls . . . Henry III* (1916–64).

Lingard (1825) *A Comparative View of the . . . Invulnerable Oil Paint, prepared by John Lingard, Jun.* (2nd edn, 1825).

Linstrum (1972) Derek Linstrum, *Sir Jeffry Wyatville Architect to the King* (Oxford, 1972).

Lomazzo (1598) G.P. Lomazzo, *A Tracte containing the Artes of Curious Paintinge* (tr. Richard Haydocke, Oxford, 1598). The first edition was published as *Trattato dell'arte de la pittura* (Milan, 1584).

London (1851) *London as it is To-day: Where to go, and what to see, during the Great Exhibition* (1851).

London Interiors (n.d.) *London Interiors with their Costumes & Ceremonies* (n.d.).

Loudon (1833) J.C. Loudon, *An Encyclopaedia of Cottage, Farm, and Villa Architecture* (1833).

Lull (1572) Ramón Lull, 'Testamentum novissimum' in *Libelli aliqot chemici* (Basle, 1572).

Luxborough (1775) *Letters written by the Right Honourable Lady Luxborough to William Shenstone, Esq.* (1775).

Lysons (1792–6) Daniel Lysons, *The Environs of London* (1792–6).

McCormick (1990) *Charles-Louis Clérisseau and the Genesis of Neo-Classicism* (Cambridge, Massachusetts, 1990).

Mackenzie (1825) Colin Mackenzie, *One Thousand Processes in Manufactures* (5th edn, 1825).

MacTaggart (1980) Peter and Ann MacTaggart, 'Refiners' Verditers', *Studies in Conservation* (1952-date), vol. XXV (1980), pp. 37–45.

Mandey (1717) Venterus Mandey, *Mellificium Mensionis: or the Marrow of Measuring* (3rd edn, 1717).

Manor House (1832) *Manor House, Great Ealing, Middlesex, Particulars* . . . (sale catalogue, 1832). Copy in Pitzhanger album at Soane Museum (see under Soane Museum drawings below).

Marco Polo (1958) *The Travels of Marco Polo* (tr. Ronald Latham, 1958).

Benjamin Martin (1747) Benjamin Martin, *Philosophia Britannica* (Reading, 1747).

Martin (1813) Thomas Martin (pseudonym for John Farley), *The Circle of the Mechanical Arts* (1813).

Mason (1783) William Mason, *The English Garden* (new edn, York, 1783).

Matthaei (1971) Rupprecht Matthaei, *Goethe's Colour Theory* (1971).

Meadows (1988) Peter Meadows, *Joseph Bonomi Architect 1739–1788* (1988).

Meikleham [*c.* 1835] Robert Meikleham (pseud. Robert Stuart), *A Dictionary of Architecture* [*c.* 1835].

Mercato (1717) Michele Mercato, *Metallotheca* (Rome, 1717).

Mérimée (1839) J.F.L. Mérimée, *The Art of Painting in Oil, and in Fresco* (1839).

Merret (1678) Christopher Merret, 'The Art of Refining', *Philosophical Transactions of the Royal Society*, vol. XII (1678), p. 1046ff.

Merret (1696) Christopher Merret, 'An Account of Several Observables in *Lincolnshire*', *Philosophical Transactions of the Royal Society*, vol. XIX (1695–7), pp. 343–53.

Merrifield (1849) Mary P. Merrifield, *Original Treatises . . . on the Art of Painting* (1849).

Middleton (1915) G.A.T. Middleton, *Building Materials* (2nd edn, 1915).

Mills & White 'Analyses' (1977) John Mills & Raymond White, 'Analyses of Paint Media', *National Gallery Technical Bulletin* (September 1977), pp. 57–9.

Mills & White 'Natural Resins' (1977) John Mills & Raymond White, 'Natural Resins of Art and Archaeology', *Studies in Conservation* (1952-date), vol. XXII (1977), pp. 12–31.

Monardes (1577/1925) Nicholas Monardes, *Joyfull Newes out of the Newe Founde Worlde* (tr. by John Frampton of *Primera y secunda y tercera partes de la historia medicinal* (Seville, 1574), originally printed in 1577, reprinted 1925).

Montfaucon (1724) Bernard de Montfaucon, *Supplement au livre de l'antiquité* (Paris, 1724).

Montfaucon (1725) Bernard de Montfaucon, *The Supplement to Antiquity Explained* (tr. David Humphries, 1725).

Morley (1984) John Morley, *The Making of the Royal Pavilion Brighton* (1984).

Morveau (1783) Guyton de Morveau, 'Recherches pour perfectionner la préparation des couleurs employées dans la peinture', *Nouveaux Mémoires de l'Académie de Dijon 1782* (Dijon, 1783), pp. 1–24.

Mount Vernon (1981) The Mount Vernon Ladies' Association of the Union, *Annual Report 1981* (Mount Vernon, 1982).

Moxon (1703) Joseph Moxon, *Mechanick Exercises* (3rd edn, 1703).

John Nash [1826] John Nash, *The Royal Pavilion at Brighton* [1826].

Joseph Nash (1839–49) Joseph Nash, *The Mansions of England in the Olden Time* (1839–49).

Neri (1662) Antonio Neri, *The Art of Glass* (tr. C[hristopher] M[erret], 1662).

Neve (1703) R. Neve (pseud. T.N. Philomath), *The City and Countrey Purchaser, and Builder's Dictionary* (1703).

New Decorators' Hand-Book *The New Decorators' Hand-book* (J. Tomlin, Barnsley, n.d.).

Newton (1672) Isaac Newton, letter dated 6 February 1672 published in *Philosophical Transactions of the Royal Society*, vol. 6 (1671), No. 80, pp. 3075–87.

Newton (1704) Isaac Newton, *Optics* (1704).

Nicholson (1819) Peter Nicholson, *An Architectural Dictionary* (1819).

Nicholson (1823–5) Peter Nicholson, *The New Practical Builder* (1823–5). Appended is 'The Practical Builder's Perpetual Price-book' with its own pagination.

Nicholson (1825) Peter Nicholson, *The Mechanic's Companion* (Oxford, 1825).

Nicholson (1834) Peter Nicholson, *The Builder's and Workman's New Director* (new edn, 1834). The first edition appeared in 1824, but did not contain any information on house-painting.

Nightingale (1813) — J. Nightingale, *The Beauties of England and Wales*, vol. XIII, part II, Staffordshire (1813).

Nostell Priory (1973); (1978) — *Nostell Priory* (National Trust guidebook, 1973, small format); ibid. (1978, larger format).

Osterley Park (1972) — *Osterley Park* (Victoria and Albert Museum guidebook, 1972).

Osterley Park (1985) — John Hardy & Maurice Tomlin, *Osterley Park House* (Victoria and Albert Museum guidebook, 1985).

Pain (1786) — William and James Pain, *Pain's British Palladio* (1786).

Pain (1794) — William Pain, *The Practical House Carpenter* (5th edn, 1794).

Painter's . . . Manual [*c.* 1830] — *The Painter's, Gilder's and Varnisher's Manual* (new edn, M. Taylor, [*c.* 1830]).

Painter's . . . Pocket Manual (1825) — *The Painter's and Varnisher's Pocket Manual* (Knight and Lacey, 1825).

Palladio (1738) — *The Four Books of Andrea Palladio's Architecture* (Isaac Ware, 1738). The first edition appeared as *I Quattro Libri dell'architettura* (Venice, 1570).

Palmer (1845) — C.F.R. Palmer, *The History of the Castle and Town of Tamworth* (1845).

Panelled Rooms (1914–1924) — Victoria and Albert Museum, Department of Woodwork, *The Panelled Rooms* (1914–1924).

Papworth (1857–8) — Wyatt Papworth, 'An Attempt to Determine the Periods in England, when Fir, Deal, and House Painting were first Introduced', *Transactions of the Royal Institute of British Architects*, 1st series, vol. VIII (1857–8), pp. 1–13.

Parsons (1950) — *A Tint Book of Historical Colours* (Thos. Parsons and Sons Ltd, 4th edn, 1950). (1st edn, 1934).

Payne (1798) — John Payne, *The Art of Painting in Miniature* (2nd edn, 1798).

Peacham (1606) — Henry Peacham, *The Art of Drawing with the Pen* (1606).

Peacock (1785) — James Peacock (pseud. Jose Mac Packe), *Οἰκίδια, or, Nutshells* (1785).

Pelletier (1792) — Bertrand Pelletier, 'Examens chimiques des cendres bleues', *Annales de chimie*, vol. XIII (Paris, 1792), p. 47ff.

Penny Magazine (August 1842) — 'A Day at a Floor-Cloth Factory', *Penny Magazine*, vol. XI (August, 1842), pp. 337–344.

Pepys (Murray, n.d.) — Samuel Pepys, *Diary 1659–1669* (abridged by Alex Murray, n.d.).

Petworth House — *Petworth House* (National Trust guidebook, 1978).

Philadelphia (1986) — *Philadelphia Museum of Art Bulletin* (vol. 82, Nos. 351–2, summer 1986) 'Drawing Room from Lansdowne House'. Includes chapter by Ian C. Bristow, 'The Room in the Context of Robert Adam's Work', pp. 12–19. (N.B. the colour illustrations of the interior are somewhat distorted in hue and misleading.)

Phillips (1804); (1812); (1821) — John Phillips, *Crosby's Builder's New Price-book* (1804); (19th edn, 1812); (31st edn, 1821).

Phillips (1971) — Morgan W. Phillips, 'Discoloration of Old House Paints: Restoration of Paint Colors at the Harrison Gray Otis House, Boston', *APT Bulletin*, vol. 3, No. 4 (Association for Preservation Technology, 1971), pp. 40–7.

Piccolpasso (1934) — Cipriano Piccolpasso, *The Three Books of the Potters Art* (tr. Bernard Rackham & Albert Van de Put, 1934).

Pincot [*c.* 1811] — John Pincot, *Pincot's Treatise on the Practical Part of Coach & House Painting* [*c.* 1811].

Piranesi (1769) — G.B. Piranesi, *Diverse maniere d'adornare i cammini* (Rome, 1769).

Piso (1658) — Guliemus Piso, *De Indiae Utriusque re naturali et medica* (Amsterdam, 1658).

Plesters (1956) — Joyce Plesters, 'Cross Sections and Chemical Analysis of Paint Samples', *Studies in Conservation* (1952-date), vol. II (1956), pp. 110–57.

Pliny (1938–62) — Caius Plinius secundus, *Natural History* (with an English translation by H. Rackham and others, 1938–62).

Plot (1677) — Robert Plot, *The Natural History of Oxford-Shire* (Oxford and London, 1677).

Plot (1686) — Robert Plot, *The Natural History of Stafford-Shire* (Oxford, 1686).

Pococke (1888–9) — *The Travels through England of Dr. Richard Pococke* (ed. James Joel Cartwright, Camden Society, 1888–9).

Powle (1678) — Henry Powle, 'An Account of the Iron-Works in the Forest of Dean', *Philosophical Transactions of the Royal Society*, vol. XII (1678), p. 931ff.

Powys (1899) — *Passages from the Diaries of Mrs. Lybbe Powys 1756–1808* (ed. E.J. Climenson, 1899).

Pozzo (1693–1700) — Andrea Pozzo, *Perspectiva pictorum et architectorum Andreae Putei* (Rome, 1693–1700).

Practical Treatise (1795) — *Practical Treatise on Painting in Oil-Colours* (1795).

Price (1796) — Sir Uvedale Price, *An Essay on the Picturesque* (new edn, 1796). (1st edn, 1794 – a further volume appeared in 1798.)

Primatt [1667] — Stephen Primatt, *The City & Country Purchaser & Builder* [1667].

Pückler-Muskau (1832) — Prince Pückler-Muskau, *Tour in England, Ireland, and France, in the years 1828 & 1829* (1832).

Pyne (1819) — W.H. Pyne, *History of the Royal Residences* (1819).

Raper (1924) — *The Receipt Book of Elizabeth Raper . . . written 1756–1770* (ed. Bartle Grant, 1924).

Raspe (1781) — R.E. Raspe, *A Critical Essay on Oil-Painting* (1781).

Ray (1673) — John Ray, *Observations Topographical, Moral, & Physiological* (1673).

Ray (1674) — John Ray, *A Collection of English Words* (1674).

Remington [1946] — John Stewart Remington, *Pigments their Manufacture and Properties* [1946].

Renwick (1909) — W.G. Renwick, *Marble and Marble Working* (1909).

Repertory of Arts — *The Repertory of Arts and Manufactures* (1794–1802).

Report from the Select Committee (1830) — *Report from the Select Committee on the Expense of Completing the Alterations and Improvements of Windsor Castle* (1830).

Repton (1816) — Humphry Repton, *Fragments on the Theory and Practice of Landscape Gardening* (1816).

Reynolds (1812) — Hezekiah Reynolds, *Directions for House and Ship Painting* (New Haven, 1812).

R.I.B.A. drawings, Cat. — *Catalogue of the Drawings Collection of the Royal Institute of British Architects* (1969–89).

Richardson (1776) — George Richardson, *A Book of Ceilings* (1776).

Richardson (1802–8) — George Richardson, *The New Vitruvius Britannicus* (1802–8).

Rigaud (1984) — Stephen Francis Dutilh Rigaud, 'Facts and Recollections of the XVIIIth Century in a Memoir of John Francis Rigaud Esq., R.A.' (abridged and edited by William L. Pressly, *Walpole Society*, vol. 50 (1984), pp. 1–164.

Rivington (1897–8) — *Rivington's Series of Notes on Building Construction* (new edn, 1897–8).

Roberts (1939) — Henry D. Roberts, *A History of the Royal Pavilion Brighton* (1939).

Rochefoucauld (1933) — François de la Rochefoucauld, *A Frenchman in England* (ed. Jean Marchand, 1933).

Rococo Exhibition (1984) — *Rococo Art and Design in Hogarth's England* (1984). (Catalogue of exhibition held at Victoria and Albert Museum, 16 May to 30 September 1984.)

Rondelet (1812–n.d.) — J. Rondelet, *Traité théoretique et pratique de l'art de bâtir* (Paris, 1812–n.d.).

Ruskin (1849) — John Ruskin, *The Seven Lamps of Architecture* (1849).

Rutter (1823) — John Rutter, *Delineations of Fonthill* (1823).

Sabin (1904) — A.H. Sabin, *The Industrial and Artistic Technology of Paint and Varnish* (New York & London, 1904).

Salmon (1672) — William Salmon, *Polygraphice* (1672).

Salmon (1734) — William Salmon, *Palladio Londinensis: or, the London Art of Building* (1734).

Salmon (1745); (1773) — William Salmon, *The London and Country Builder's Vade Mecum* (1745); (5th edn, 1773).

Saltram (1978) — *Saltram* (National Trust guidebook, 1978).

Sauval (1724) — Henri Sauval, *Histoire et recherches des antiquités de la ville de Paris* (Paris, 1724).

Scott (1857) — George Gilbert Scott, *Remarks on Secular & Domestic Architecture* (1857).

Seddon (1886) — H.C. Seddon, *Builder's Work and the Building Trades* (1886).

Serlio (1551) — Sebastiano Serlio, *Architettura* (Venice, 1551).

Serlio (1611) — Sebastiano Serlio, *The First [–fift] Booke[s] of Architecture translated out of Italian into Dutch, and out of Dutch into English* (London, Robert Peake, 1611).

Shellac (1965) — *Shellac* (Angelo Brothers Limited, Calcutta, 1965).

Shenstone (1939) — *The Letters of William Shenstone* (ed. Marjorie Williams, Oxford, 1939).

Sheraton (1793/1972) — Thomas Sheraton, *The Cabinet-Maker and Upholsterer's Drawing-Book . . . with a new introduction by Joseph Aronson* (New York, 1972).

Shoberl (1813) — Frederic Shoberl, *The Beauties of England and Wales*, vol. XVI, Suffolk (1813).

Skyring (1831) — W.H. Skyring, *Skyring's Builder's Prices* (21st edn, 1831). The first edition was: Z. Skyring, *Skyring's new and complete List of Builder's Prices* (1811).

Slive (1961) — Seymour Slive, 'Henry Henham's "Of Colours"', *Burlington Magazine*, vol. CIII (1961), pp. 378–80.

Smeaton (1760) — John Smeaton, *An Experimental Enquiry concerning the Natural Powers of Water and Wind* (1760).

Smirke (n.d.) — Robert Smirke (pseud. Roger Shanhagan), *The Exhibition* (n.d.).

George Smith (1808) — George Smith, *A Collection of Designs for Household Furniture* (1808).

George Smith (1812) — George Smith, *A Collection of Ornamental Designs after the Manner of the Antique, for the Use of Architects, Ornamental Painters, Statuaries, etc.* (1812).

George Smith (1826) — George Smith, *The Cabinet-Maker and Upholsterer's Guide* (1826).

James Smith (1815) — James Smith, *The Panorama of Science and Art* (Liverpool, 1815).

John Smith (1676); (1687); (1701); (1705); (1723) — *The Art of Painting* (1676); (2nd edn, 1687); (3rd edn, 1701); (4th edn, 1705); (5th edn, 1723). (Further editions appeared in 1738, 1753, and 1788.)

Soane (1802) — *Plans, Elevations, and Perspective Views, of Pitzhanger Manor-House* (1802).

Specification for Repainting (1939) — *Specification for Repainting Work* (Lead Industries Development Council, 1939).

Stalker & Parker (1688/1971) — John Stalker & George Parker, *A Treatise of Japanning and Varnishing 1688 . . . with an Introduction by H.D. Molesworth* (1971).

Stallybrass (1913) — B. Stallybrass, 'Bess of Hardwick's Building Accounts', *Archaeologia*, vol. LXIV (1913), pp. 347–98.

Stanhope (1932) — *The Letters of Philip Dormer Stanhope 4th Earl of Chesterfield* (ed. Bonamy Dobrée, 1932).

Stapleton & *al.* (1975) — H.E.C. Stapleton, G.G. Pace, & J.E. Day, *A Skilful Master-Builder* (York, 1975).

Stillman (1966) — Damie Stillman, *The Decorative Work of Robert Adam* (1966).

Stillman (1967) — Damie Stillman, 'Robert Adam and Piranesi', *Essays in the History of Architecture presented to Rudolph Wittkower* (ed. Douglas Fraser, Howard Hibbard, & Milton J. Lewine, 1967), pp. 197–206.

Stillman (1970) — Damie Stillman, 'The Gallery for Landsdowne House', *The Art Bulletin*, vol. 52 (1970), pp. 75–80.

Stitt (1819) — William Stitt, *The Practical Architect's Assistant* (Dublin, 1819).

Stratton [1920] — Arthur Stratton, *The English Interior* [1920].

Stroud (1961) — Dorothy Stroud, *The Architecture of Sir John Soane* (1961).

Stroud (1966) — Dorothy Stroud, *Henry Holland his Life and Architecture* (1966).

Stroud (1971) — Dorothy Stroud, *George Dance Architect 1741–1825* (1971).

Summerson (1969) — Sir John Summerson, *Architecture in Britain 1530 to 1830* (5th edn, 1969).

Survey of London — *The Survey of London* (1900–date).

Tessin/Cronström (1964) — *Les Relations artistiques entre France et Suède, 1693–1718. Extraits d'une correspondence entre l'architecte Nicodème Tessin le jeune et Daniel Cronström* (ed.

R.A. Weigert & C. Hernmarck, Stockholm, 1964).

Theophilus (1847) — *An Essay upon Various Arts in three books by Theophilus* (tr. Robert Hendrie, 1847).

Theophilus (1986) — Theophilus, *The Various Arts* (ed. & tr. C.R. Dodwell, Oxford, 1986).

Thomson (1943) — *Letters of a Grandmother* (ed. Gladys Scott Thomson, 1943).

Thornton (1978) — Peter Thornton, *Seventeenth-century Interior Decoration in England, France and Holland* (1978).

Thornton (1984) — Peter Thornton, *Authentic Decor* (1984).

Thornton & Tomlin (1980) — Peter Thornton & Maurice Tomlin, *The Furnishing and Decoration of Ham House* (1980).

Tingry (1803) — P.F. Tingry, *Traité théoretique et pratique sur l'art de faire et d'appliquer les vernis* (Geneva, 1803).

Tingry (1804); (1816) — P.F. Tingry, *The Painter and Varnisher's Guide* (1804); (2nd edn, 1816).

Tingry (1830) — P.F. Tingry, *The Painter's & Colourman's Complete Guide* (3rd, revised edn of the above, 1830).

Transactions of the Society . . . of Arts — *Transactions of the Society . . . of Arts* (1783–1823).

Turnbull (1740) — George Turnbull, *Treatise on Ancient Painting* (1740).

Turnbull (1741) — George Turnbull, *Curious Collection of Ancient Paintings* (1741).

Turner (1877) — T. Hudson Turner, *Some Account of Domestic Architecture in England* (2nd edn, vol. I, 1877).

Uppark (1976) — *Uppark* (National Trust guidebook, 1976).

Ure (1839) — Andrew Ure, *A Dictionary of Arts, Manufactures, and Mines* (1839).

Ure (1860) — *Ure's Dictionary of Arts, Manufactures, and Mines* (5th edn, ed. Robert Hunt, 1860).

Vanherman (1805) — T.H. Vanherman, 'On rendering Fish Oil and Linseed Oil drying; and on making Cheap Oil Paints', *Transactions of the Society for the Encouragement of Arts*, vol. XXIII (1805), pp. 193–210.

Vanherman (1828) — T.H. Vanherman, *The Painter's Cabinet, and Colourman's Repository* (1828).

Vanherman (1829) — T.H. Vanherman, *Every Man his own House-Painter and Colourman* (1829). Text and pagination identical with above.

Vasari (1927) — Georgio Vasari, *The Lives of the Painters, Sculptors, and Architects* (ed. William Gaunt, 1927).

Vauquelin (1797) — L.N. Vauquelin, 'Du plomb rouge de Sibérie', *Journal des mines*, vol. VI (Paris, 1797), pp. 737–60.

Vauquelin (1798) — L.N. Vauquelin, 'Mémoire sur une nouvelle substance métallique contenue dans le plomb rouge de Sibérie, et qu'on propose d'appeler *Chrôme*', *Annales de chimie*, vol. XXV (Paris, 1798), pp. 21–31.

Vauquelin (1809) — L.N. Vauquelin, 'Mémoire sur la meilleur méthode pour décomposer le chromâte de fer', *Annales de chimie*, vol. LXX (Paris, 1809), pp. 70–94.

Vernatti (1678) — Sir Philiberto Vernatti, 'A Relation of the Making of Ceruss', *Philosophical Transactions of the Royal Society*, vol. XII (1678), p. 935ff.

Very Proper Treatise (1573) — *A Very Proper Treatise, wherein is briefly sett forthe the Arte of Limming* (1573). See also facsimile (Michigan, 1932).

Vitruvius (1826) — *The Architecture of Marcus Vitruvius Pollio* (tr. Joseph Gwilt, 1826).

Waller (1686) — Richard Waller, 'A Catalogue of Simple and Mixt Colours', *Philosophical Transactions of the Royal Society*, vol. XVI (1686), pp. 24–8.

Wallington (1979) — *Wallington* (National Trust guidebook, 1979).

Walpole, 'Aedes', *Works* (1798) — Horace Walpole, 'Aedes Walpolianae', *The Works of Horatio Walpole Earl of Orford* (1798), vol. II, pp. [221]–278. (1st edn, 1747).

Walpole, 'Anecdotes', *Works* (1798) — Horace Walpole, 'Anecdotes of Painting', *The Works of Horatio Walpole Earl of Orford* (1798), vol. III.

Walpole, 'Description of . . . Strawberry Hill', *Works* (1798) — Horace Walpole, 'A Description of . . . Strawberry-Hill', *The Works of Horatio Walpole Earl of Orford* (1798), vol. II, pp. [393]–516. (1st edn was 1784).

Walpole, *Letters* (1903–25) — *The Letters of Horace Walpole* (ed. Mrs. Paget Toynbee, Oxford, 1903–25).

Ware [*c.* 1733] — Isaac Ware, *Designs of Inigo Jones* [*c.* 1733].

Ware (1756) — Isaac Ware, *A Complete Body of Architecture* (1756).

Watin (1785) — Jean Félix Watin, *L'Art du peintre, doreur, vernisseur* (4th edn, Paris, 1785). (1st edn, 1772).

Watkin (1968) — David Watkin, *Thomas Hope 1769–1831* (1968).

Watkin (1984) — David Watkin, *The Royal Interiors of Regency England* (1984).

Watson (1781–8) — Richard Watson, *Chemical Essays* (Cambridge, 1781–8).

Watson (1916) — John Watson, *British and Foreign Marbles and other Ornamental Stones* (Cambridge, 1916).

Welsh & Grandquist (1983) — F.S. Welsh & C.L. Grandquist, 'Restoration of the Exterior Sanded Paint at Monticello', *APT Bulletin*, vol. 15, No. 2 (Association for Preservation Technology, 1983), pp. 2–10.

Whitehead (1939) — A.D. Whitehead, 'The Micrography of Paint Films', *Journal of the Oil & Colour Chemists Association*, vol. XXII (1939), pp. 139–48.

Whittock (1827) — Nathaniel Whittock, *The Decorative Painters' and Glaziers' Guide* (1827).

Williams (1966) — J.D. Williams, *Audley End: The Restoration of 1762–1797* (Essex County Council, 1966).

Williams-Ellis (1919) — Clough Williams-Ellis, *Cottage Building in Cob, Pisé, Chalk & Clay* (1919).

Willis & Clarke (1886) — Robert Willis & John Willis Clark, *The Architectural History of the University of Cambridge* (Cambridge, 1886).

Wilsford (1659) — Thomas Wilsford, *Architectonice. The Art of Building* (1659).

Wilson (1960) — R.E. Wilson, *Two Hundred Precious Metal Years/A History of the Sheffield Smelting Company Limited 1760–1960* (1960).

John Wood (1749) — John Wood, *Essay Towards a Description of Bath* (2nd edn, 1749).

Margaret Wood (1965) — Margaret Wood, *The English Mediaeval House* (1965).

William Wood (1634) — William Wood, *New Englands Prospect* (1634).

Woodward (1724) — John Woodward, 'Praeparatio Caerulei Prussiaei', *Philosophical Transactions of the Royal Society*, vol. XXXIII (1724), pp. 15–17.

Wren Society — Volumes of the Wren Society (Oxford, 1924–42).

Zerr & Rübencamp — George Zerr & R. Rübencamp, *A Treatise on Colour Manufacture . . . English Edition by Dr. Charles Mayer* (1908).

2. MANUSCRIPTS AND OTHER UNPUBLISHED SOURCES

Abbott MS. — John Abbott's MS. design book in Exeter Record Office (404M/B1).

Armitage (n.d.) — F. Armitage, 'Lewis Berger & Sons Ltd. A New History' (n.d.). Copy at Hackney Archives Department, ref. D/B/BER, 2/7/51.

Arundel MS. — MS. at Arundel Castle, Sussex, MD 18 part II (bills of George Evans (painter) and John Cuenot (carver and gilder) for work at Norfolk House, London, 1753–6).

Berger MSS. — MSS. records of Lewis Berger and Sons, now at Hackney Archives Department, Rose Lipman Library, De Beauvoir Road, London, N1 5SQ, whose recent numbering (all preceded by D/B/BER) is given in brackets.

first experimental notebook: half-bound quarto volume labelled (on the back cover) 'Recipes & Experiments Various' (1/3/1);
second experimental notebook: similar volume bound in vellum containing formulae dating from between 1819 and 1831 with a final item dated 1840 (1/3/2);
third experimental notebook: similar volume containing formulae dated between 1830 and 1846 (1/3/3);
1831 formula book: tall vellum-bound volume containing costed production formulae dating from 1831 onwards (1/3/4);
'Lake & Carmine Book': similar volume thus labelled on front cover containing formulae and other entries from 1787 to 1829 (1/2/3);
letter book: quarto volume containing two series of copy letters covering the periods 1785 to 1788 and 1778 to 1788 (1/2/2);
'Sample Book': quarto volume identified by paper label as such, containing entries between 1778 and 1802 (1/2/1);
stock 1801–2: stock-list and accounts for 1801 showing stock held on 1st January 1802 (1/1/1);
stock 1805–6: corresponding volume for 1805–6 (1/1/5);
stock 1809–10: corresponding volume for 1809–10 (1/1/9).

B.L. MSS. — MSS. at Department of Manuscripts, British Library, British Museum, London:

MS. Sloane 2052 (notebook of Sir Theodore Turquet de Mayerne dating from *c.* 1620–40);
MS. Sloane 3292 (anonymous MS. in early seventeenth-century hand but containing material dated 1564);
MS. Sloane 6284 (MS. of *c.* 1603 containing list of colours by W. Rogers, engraver);
MS. Add. 36367 (drawings by the Bucklers);
MS. Add. 41133 (letter book of Sir William Chambers).

Boughton MS. — Accounts (in three volumes) of executors of 1st Duke of Montagu, in possession of the Duke of Buccleuch at Boughton House, Northamptonshire, to whom I am most grateful for access to this item.

Bowood MSS. — MSS., at Bowood House, Wiltshire:

Bowood bills, Spinnage's account: bill for painting work at Bowood by John Spinnage in 1764–5 (box 14/69);
diary: MS. diary of Lady Shelburne, 3 February 1765 to 21 September 1770;
Shelburne House bills, Adam's account: bill from Robert and James Adam covering designs supplied between 1764 and 1766, receipted 23 February 1771 (box AA5);
Shelburne House bills, Perfetti's account: bill from Joseph Perfetti for painting and gilding in 1775 and 1776, receipted 7 September 1776 (box AA5);
Shelburne House bills, Pitsala's account: bill covering painting work by Francis Pitsala in 1768 and 1769, receipted 16 May 1770 (box AA5).

I am grateful to Lord Shelburne for permission to quote from the above.

N.B. for part transcriptions of Shelburne House bills, see Philadelphia (1986), pp. 52–8; also Bolton (1922), vol. II, p. 12 (Perfetti's account), p. 340 (Adam's account).

Brighton/Crace MS. — Typed transcript of Crace ledgers at Royal Pavilion Archives, Brighton, Sussex (original believed destroyed, see Morley (1984), p. 78, and Roberts (1939), p. 43). I am most grateful to Jessica Rutherford for help in connection with this material.

Bristow MSS., notes — Paint samples and MS. notes filed by author under number quoted.

Bristow MSS., reports — Typescript reports:

British Museum (1983): Ian C. Bristow, 'Report on an Investigation of Paint Samples from the Front Railings of the British Museum' (2 September 1983);
British Museum (1984): Ian C. Bristow, 'British Museum, Main Entrance Hall, Report on an Investigation of Paint Samples' (3 July 1984);
Frogmore (1986): Ian C. Bristow, 'Frogmore House, Berkshire. Report on an Investigation of Paint Samples' (February 1986), quoted by gracious permission of Her Majesty the Queen;
Ham (1984): Ian C. Bristow, 'Ham House, Surrey, Report on an Investigation of Paint Samples from the North Drawing Room and North Front' (February 1984);
Ham (1989): Ian C. Bristow, 'Ham House, Surrey, Preliminary Report on the current state of Research into the Interior Colour Schemes of the Seventeenth Century' (March 1989);
Heveningham (1984a): Ian C. Bristow, 'The Print Room, Heveningham Hall, Suffolk. Report on an Investigation of Paint Samples' (30 September and 8 October 1984);
Heveningham (1984b): Ian C. Bristow, 'The Morning Room, Heveningham Hall, Suffolk, Report on an investigation of Paint Samples' (15 October 1984);
Heveningham (1984c): Ian C. Bristow, 'The State Staircase, Heveningham Hall, Suffolk.

Report on an Investigation of Paint Samples' (15 October 1984):
Marino Casino (1980): Ian C. Bristow, 'The Casino at Marino, Clontarf, Dublin. Report on an Investigation to determine the original Colour Schemes in the Vestibule, Saloon, and State Bedroom' (16 June 1980);
Osterley (1983): Ian C. Bristow, 'The Breakfast Room at Osterley Park, Middlesex, Report on an Investigation of Paint Samples' (19 August 1983);
Osterley (1989): Ian C. Bristow, 'Osterley Park, Middlesex, Report on an Investigation of Paint Samples from five rooms' (October 1989);
Pitzhanger (1986): Ian C. Bristow, 'Ealing, Pitzhanger Manor. Report on an Investigation of Paint Samples' (March 1986);
Queen's House (1986): Ian C. Bristow, 'Greenwich, the Queen's House, Report on an Investigation into the seventeenth-century painted finishes in the Hall and first-floor rooms' (December 1986);
Royal Academy (1988): Ian C. Bristow, 'The Royal Academy, London, Report on an Investigation of Paint Samples from the Saloon and Secretary's Office' (November 1988);
Soane Museum (1986a): Ian C. Bristow, 'Sir John Soane's House and Museum, Report on an Investigation of Paint Samples from the Exterior and North Drawing Room' (May 1986);
Soane Museum (1986b): Ian C. Bristow, 'Sir John Soane's House and Museum, Report on an Investigation of Paint Samples from the South Drawing Room and supplementary samples from the Monument Courtyard' (December 1986);
Soane Museum (1987–8): Ian C. Bristow, 'Sir John Soane's House and Museum, Report on an Investgation of paint samples from the Picture Room' (December 1987 and June 1988);
Soane Museum (1988): Ian C. Bristow, 'Report on an Investigation of Paint Samples from selected elements in the Study' (October 1988);
Soane Museum (1990a): Ian C. Bristow, 'The Soane Museum, London, Report on an investigation of paint samples from the Dressing Room' (September 1990);
Soane Museum (1990b): Ian C. Bristow, 'London, the Soane Museum, Report on a supplementary series of samples from the Study' (October 1990);
Soane Museum (1993a): Ian C. Bristow, 'London, the Soane Museum, Report on an Investigation of paint samples from the Hall and Staircase at No. 12 Lincoln's Inn Fields' (January 1993);
Soane Museum (1993b): Ian C. Bristow, 'London, the Soane Museum, Report on an Investigation of paint samples from the Dining Room at No. 12 Lincoln's Inn Fields' (January 1993);
Soane Museum (1993c): Ian C. Bristow, 'London, the Soane Museum, Report on an investigation of paint samples from the Breakfast Room at No. 12 Lincoln's Inn Fields' (January 1993);
Soane Museum (1993d): Ian C. Bristow, 'London, the Soane Museum, Supplementary report on additional paint samples from the Dome' (July 1993);
Soho House (1991): Ian C. Bristow, 'Birmingham, Handsworth, Soho House, Report on an Investigation of Paint Samples from the Hall and Dining Room' (July 1991);
Somerset House (1988): Ian C. Bristow, 'Report on an Investigation of Paint Samples from the First Floor' (November and December 1988);
Temple Newsam (1986): Ian C. Bristow, 'Temple Newsam, the Chinese Drawing Room. Report on an Investigation of Paint Samples' (October 1986);
Westminster (1985–6): Ian C. Bristow, 'Palace of Westminster, Lords Chamber, Throne Canopy, Report on an Investigation of Paint Samples' (23 May 1985, with supplement dated 1 January 1986);
York Assembly Rooms (1990): Ian C. Bristow, 'York Assembly Rooms. Report on an Investigation of Paint Samples from the Main Hall and North Room' (August 1990).

I am grateful to the Department of the Environment for permission to quote from reports commissioned by them.

Bristow, MSS., thesis (1983) — Ian C. Bristow, 'Interior House-painting from the Restoration to the Regency', DPhil thesis submitted to the University of York, December 1983.

Candee (1965) — Richard Candee, 'Materials towards a History of Housepaints' (1965), unpublished MA thesis submitted to the Faculty of State University of New York College at Oneonta.

Chester MS. — Cheshire Record Office, Chester. Chester Consistory Court Files, EDC.5 (1636), No. 65. Chorley (Lancs). Typed transcript of extracts kindly supplied by John Addy.

Claydon MS. — MS. book signed 'Mrs. Wynn, Plasnewydd' and dated 1766 at Claydon House, Buckinghamshire. I am most grateful to Christopher Wall of the National Trust for his kindness in supplying a typed transcript of two recipes for making green distemper.

C.M. & G. MS. — Volume of MS. bills relating to 15 St James's Square, London, in possession of Clerical, Medical & General Life Assurance Co. Ltd of that address (volume given by the Earl of Lichfield to Mr. Coles in April 1893).

Courtauld MS. — MS. notebook of George Field labelled 'Chromatography Specimens 1809' at Courtauld Institute, Somerset House, London.

Dickens House Museum MSS. — Tenancy agreements of Charles Dickens and his successor in respect of 48 Doughty Street, London, dated 1837 and 1840 respectively in ownership of Dickens House Museum at that address.

Dunham Massey MSS. — MSS. relating to Dunham Massey, Cheshire. (Although still at the house and uncatalogued in August 1980, it was then intended they should be transferred to the John Rylands Library, University of Manchester.)

Dyrham MSS. — MSS. relating to Dyrham Park, Gloucestershire (now Avon), deposited at Gloucester Record Office.

Farington's Diary — Typescript transcript of Joseph Farington's MS. diary in Print Room of British Museum, London.

G.L.R.O. MSS. — MSS. at Greater London Record Office:

Arlington Street: BRA/437/10 (inventory of 22 Arlington Street, London, taken after death of Henry Pelham in 1754);
Pepper: Q/STB/1–10 (notebooks of the surveyor, William Pepper). (Transcription of relevant parts kindly supplied by John Sambrooke.)

Gordon Castle MS. — MS. account for painting at Gordon Castle, Morayshire, now at Scottish Record Office, Edinburgh, MS. GD 44/51/387/2.

Haddon-Reece MS. (1985) — David Haddon-Reece. 'The tree-ring dating of Newington House, Oxfordshire', English Heritage A.M. Lab. report No. 4968 (1985).

Ham MSS. — Original MSS., typescript copies, and photocopies at Department of Furniture and Interior Design, Victoria and Albert Museum, London:

Carter's account: Thomas Carter's MS. bill for joinery work settled in September 1639;
Gooderick's account: Matthew Gooderick's MS. bill for painting in April 1638;
inventory (*c.* 1654): undated MS. inventory, probably made by Elizabeth Dysart in 1654 following death of first Earl of Dysart;
Kinsman's account: typescript copy of Joseph Kinsman's account for plastering work in 1637 and 1638;
Moore's account: account for work done at Ham by Nicholas Moore in 1673–4, certified 26 May 1674 (photocopy from original MS. at Buckminster Park, Leicestershire, bundle 443).

Harpur-Crewe MS. — MS. letter dated 25 May 1809 in Harpur-Crewe papers at Derbyshire Record Office (copy kindly furnished by Howard Colvin).

Hertford MS. — MS. at Hertford Record Office, QSB/12.

I.P.R.O. MSS. — MSS. at Public Record Office of Ireland, Four Courts, Dublin 7 (quoted by kind permission of the Deputy Keeper).

Kenwood MS. — Greater London Council photograph (serial No. 54/2894) of Antonio Zucchi's MS. account for painting the inset pictures in the Library at Kenwood House, Middlesex.

King's College, Cambridge MS. — MS. at King's College, Cambridge, Muniments, KCD 115 (transcript kindly furnished by Dr Terry Friedman, quoted by kind permission of the Librarian).

Lincoln Cathedral MSS. — MSS. in Lincoln Cathedral Library (reference D & C, Ciij.31.1.1): (i) contract for painting the Library dated 11 November 1676; (ii) list of rates for gilding and painting mentioned in the above and supplied by Christopher Wren. (Quoted by kind permission of the Dean and Chapter of Lincoln).

Lincoln Castle MS. — MS. in Lincoln Record Office, 'Minutes of Proceedings of the Commissioners for Erecting the County Hall, Lincoln' from 1822 (CO. C. 2/3).

Mansion House MSS. — Corporation of London Records Office, Mansion House Committee papers:

Downes (1748): Joseph Downes's proposal and agreement accepted 8 June 1748 for plasterer's work in the basement storey (box 2, 1748);
Fewkes (1749): George Fewkes's proposal dated 6 July 1749 for plastering work in the principal storey (box 2, 1749);
Fewkes (1755): George Fewkes's proposal dated 9 July 1755 for plastering work in the 'Great Hall' (box 3, 1755) – the wording is similar to that in the proposal of Humphrey Willmott (ibid.), who obtained the contract;
Rowe (1757): proposal for painting work in the 'Great Hall' dated 9 February 1757 (box 3, 1757) – the wording is similar to that in the proposal of Robert Ross (ibid.), who obtained the contract;
Rowe (1761): Joseph Rowe's bill for painting work in December 1761 (box 3, 1762);
Rowe (1768–71): Joseph Rowe's bill for painting work carried out between 1768 and 1771 (box 4, 1771);
Rowe (1774–5): Joseph Rowe's bill for painting work in 1774 and 1775 (box 4, 1776);
Stock (1751): John Stock's proposals for painting work dated 5 June 1751 (box 2, envelope marked '5 June, December 1751') – the wording is similar to that in the proposal of Thomas Wicks and Joseph Rowe (ibid.), and that of John Ventris (ibid.), who obtained the contract;
Willmot (1779–81): George Willmot's bill for plastering work executed in 1779–81 (box 5, 1781);
Willmot (1783–5): George Willmot's bill for plastering work executed in 1783–5 (box 5, 1785).

(I am grateful to Jeannie Chapel and Dr Sally Jeffery for transcriptions and photocopies of these documents.)

Newcastle MS. — MS. memorandum dated 17 July 1775 relating to improvements to be carried out to house in Arlington Street, London, among Newcastle MSS. at University of Nottingham (transcript kindly furnished by Gervase Jackson-Stops).

Northumberland MS. — Typescript in possession of Gervase Jackson-Stops of MS. notes by Duchess of Northumberland among various papers at Alnwick Castle, Northumberland, concerning the houses which she visited. Kedleston reference cited as 121/16.

Osterley MSS. — MSS. relating to Osterley Park at Department of Furniture and Design, Victoria and Albert Museum, London:

Adamson (1772–4): bill for work by David Adamson at Osterley in 1772–4;
Adamson (1787): bill for work by David Adamson at Osterley in 1787 (settled 26 June 1787);
Adamson (1788): bill for work by David Adamson at Osterley in 1788 (settled 6 January 1789);
Bacon (1779): bill for plastering work by George Bacon in 1779 (settled 18 March 1780);
Bacon (1780): bill for plastering work by George Bacon in 1780 (settled 6 March 1781);
Bacon (1781): bill for plastering work by George Bacon in 1781 (settled 19 February 1782);
Bacon (1783): bill for plastering work by George Bacon in 1783 (settled 28 January 1784);
Bacon (1784): bill for plastering work by George Bacon in 1784 (settled 10 January 1785);
Bacon (1785): bill for plastering work by George Bacon in 1785 (settled 3 January 1786);

Bacon (1788): bill for plastering work by George Bacon in 1788 (settled 3 January 1789);
Bacon (1789): bill for plastering work by George Bacon in 1789 (settled 2 January 1790);
Bacon (1791): bill for plastering work by George Bacon in 1791 (settled 3 January 1792);
Beauchamp-Proctor (1772): typescript transcription at Department of Furniture, Victoria and Albert Museum, of letter in private collection believed to be from Lady Beauchamp-Proctor;
Burchett (1775): bill from George Burchett for materials supplied between August and October 1775 (settled 22 January 1776);
Burchett (1779): bill from George Burchett for materials supplied between February and December 1779 (settled 12 January 1780);
Burchett (1780): bill from George Burchett for materials supplied between January and December 1780 (settled 11 January 1781);
Burchett (1781a): bill totalling £65 17*s.* 5*d* from George Burchett for materials supplied between January and December 1781 (settled 30 January 1782);
Burchett (1781b): bill totalling £33 2*s.* 6¼*d.* from George Burchett for materials supplied between January and December 1781 (settled 30 January 1782);
Inventory (1782): typescript transcription of now lost inventory of Osterley taken in August 1782;
Surveyor's notebook: Surveyor's notebook headed 'Rob.t Child Esq. 1763';
Thorogood (1774): bill from Richard Thorogood for materials supplied between April and December 1774 (settled 10 February 1775);
Wilkins (1784): bill from Joseph Wilkins for work at Osterley in 1784 (settled 12 February 1785);
Wilkins (1785): bill from Joseph Wilkins for work at Osterley in 1785 (settled 9 February 1786).

Painter-Stainers MS. — Court Minute books of the Painter-Stainers Company deposited at the Guildhall Library, London, MS. 5667.

Penn (1966) — Theodore Zuk Penn, 'Decorative and protective Finishes, 1750–1850: Materials, Process, and Craft' (1966), unpublished MA thesis submitted to the Faculty of the University of Delaware.

Petworth MSS. — MSS. at Petworth House, Sussex (available by arrangement at Chichester Record Office):
PHA 6614, No. 219 (George Evans's bill for painting work at Egremont House, London, 1759–64);
PHA 6615, No. 265 (bill for plastering work at house in Wood Street, 1763–4).

P.R.O. MSS. — MSS. at Public Record Office, Chancery Lane, London, or at Kew, Surrey.

R.I.B.A. MSS. — MSS. at Royal Institute of British Architects, London:
CHA 3/1, 3/2, 3/3 (accounts for Somerset House, London, 1776–95);
PEL/1 (the Pelham ledger, accounts for Henry Pelham's house in Arlington Street, London (now No. 22));
WiR/1/1/1 (contract between Robert Willson, carpenter, of the parish of St Mary Rotherhithe, and John Steinmetz for erection of a dwelling house, bakehouse, and lofts in the parish of St Anne, Middlesex, 5 April 1770);
WRE/2/19 (Royal Naval College, Greenwich, tender of William Thompson for paintwork, accepted on 14 August 1696);
WRE/2/20 (tender of Robert Abbott for the same [1696]);
WRE/2/21 (tender of John Dodson for the same [1696]).

R.I.A. MSS. — MSS. at Royal Irish Academy, Dublin, Charlemont letters.

St Bartholomew's MSS. — Manuscripts at St Bartholomew's Hospital, Smithfield, London, EC1A 7BE.

S.R.O. MSS. — MSS. at Scottish Record Office, Edinburgh:
4/62/3 (account for painting the dome at the General Register House, Edinburgh);
GD 150/3396 (recipe for green paint).

Soane MSS. — MSS. at Sir John Soane's House and Museum, London:
Berkeley Square: volume of MS. accounts relating to erection of No. 44 Berkeley Square for Lady Isabella Finch (AL. 39 B);
'Business': volume of MS. notes by Soane labelled 'Business to be done Sept 1795–1813';
Crace (1807): bill to Soane from John Crace dated 29 October 1807 (12 LIF);
'Ealing': volume of MS. notes by Soane labelled 'Ealing 1800–1803', bill pasted in at end;
Martin: MS. by John Martin (AL. 41 C).

S.A.L. MS. — MS. in Library of Society of Antiquaries, Burlington House, London, deed of transfer of completed rooms at Somerset House, London, to the Society, 15 February 1781.

Tredegar MSS. — Typed transcripts kindly furnished by the Curator of Tredegar House, Newport, Monmouthshire (now Gwent), of MS. bills in Tredegar papers at National Library of Wales for work done by Thomas Williams in 1688 (102/98) and by Rowland and Jacob Nicholas in 1792–3 (68/76).

V.A.M. MSS. — MSS. in Library at Victoria and Albert Museum, London:
L. 5203–1920 (volume of press cuttings containing at f. 19r a manuscript letter dated 18 February 1756 from William Farington to his sisters describing the opening reception at Norfolk House, London);
L. 1774–1935 (MS. attributed to Edmond Barton);
L. 1911–1939 (Robert Barnes, 'Papers in connection with early Floor Cloth Manufacture' (1857));
L. 4631C-1970 (MS. inventory of the contents of David Garrick's villa at Hampton, Middlesex, 1 March 1779).

Walton (1980) — Karin-Marina Walton, 'Eighteenth-century Upholstery in England, with particular emphasis on the Period 1754–1803: The Work and Status of the Upholsterer', unpublished M. Phil. thesis submitted to the University of Leeds (1980).

Woburn MSS. — MSS. relating to Woburn Abbey deposited at Bedford Record Office, box 394.

Y.A.S. MS. — MS. at Yorkshire Archaeological Society, Leeds Payne-Gallwey Collection, DD94, box 2 (copy furnished by Dr Derek Linstrum)

York City MSS.	MSS. in City Archives Department, York: Assembly Room minute books; M: 23.1; Mansion House painting account: Chamberlain's vouchers for 1729/30.

3. COLLECTIONS OF ARCHITECTURAL DRAWINGS

All Souls drawings	Drawings at All Souls College, Oxford.
Ashmolean drawings	Drawings in Print Room, Ashmolean Museum, Oxford.
Athenaeum drawings	Designs by Decimus Burton at the Athenaeum Club, London.
Audley End drawings	'Scrapbook' at Audley End, Essex.
B.M. drawings	Drawings in Print Room, British Museum, London.
Cooper-Hewitt drawings	Drawings at Cooper-Hewitt Museum, New York.
Eton College drawings	Topham Collection, Eton College Library, Berkshire.
Felbrigg drawings	Drawings at Felbrigg Hall, Norfolk.
G.L.R.O. drawings	Drawings in Greater London Record Office.
Heveningham drawings	Drawings formerly at Heveningham Hall, Suffolk, now at Heaton Hall, Manchester.
H.B.M.C. drawings	Drawings in Historic Plans Room, English Heritage.
Kedleston drawings	Drawings at Kedleston Hall, Derbyshire.
M.M.A. drawings	Drawings at Metropolitan Museum of Art, New York. N.B. The drawings in the Wyatt album (1958. 511) have two sets of numbering. Both are cited in the notes, the new before the old.
N.L.I. drawings	Drawings at National Library of Ireland, Dublin. The Wyatt collection is uncatalogued.
Nostell Priory drawings	Drawings relating to Nostell Priory, Yorkshire, in possession of Lord St Oswald.
Pierpont Morgan drawings	Drawings at Pierpont Morgan Library, New York.
R.A. drawings	Drawings in Library of Royal Academy, London.
R.I.B.A. drawings	Drawings at Royal Institute of British Architects Drawings Collection, British Architectural Library, 21 Portman Square, London. N.B. The published catalogue was incomplete when research commenced, and the then location reference is cited first, followed by the catalogue entry.
Royal Library drawings	Drawings in Royal Library, Windsor Castle, Berkshire.
Soane Museum drawings	Drawings at Sir John Soane's House and Museum, London: Pitzhanger album: volume labelled 'Pitzhanger, Ealing, Sundry views' in AL. Soane case, shelf C, left; 'Sketches & Drawings': volume labelled 'Sketches & Drawings of the House & Museum of J. Soane Esq.' in South Drawing Room cupboard; Soane perspective albums: volumes at AL. 22.
V.A.M. drawings	Drawings in Print Room, Victoria and Albert Museum, London.
Worcester College drawings	Drawings at Worcester College, Oxford.

4. PICTURES AND WATERCOLOURS

Arundel Castle, Sussex	Portrait of Alatheia Talbot, Countess of Arundel, *c.* 1618 by Daniel Mytens (National Portrait Gallery).
Attingham Hall, Shropshire	Watercolour at the house showing John Nash's design for the Gallery, 1806.
Blickling Hall, Norfolk	Watercolour by Buckler at the house showing the Hall and staircase in 1820.
British Library, London	Watercolour by Buckler in British Library MS. Add. 36370 (f. 38) showing the Drawing Room at 33 Upper Brook Street, London, in 1820.
Fairfax House, York	F.J. Nollekens, *Family in an Interior* (*c.* 1740).
Guildhall Library, London	Watercolour by Buckler in Guildhall Library, London, (Wakefield Collection, IV/BRO) showing Library-Drawing Room at Bromley Hill, Kent, in 1816.
Magdalene College, Cambridge	Drawing of Samuel Pepys's Library taken from his manuscript library catalogue and now hung in a reconstruction of this at the College.
Marble Hill House, Middlesex	Charles Philips. *George II* (*c.* 1740).
M.M.A.	Metropolitan Museum of Art, New York: Charles Philips. *The Strong Family* (1732).
National Gallery, London	William Hogarth, *Marriage à la Mode*: No. 114 'Shortly after the Marriage'; No. 116 'The Countess's Morning Levée'; No. 117 'The Killing of the Earl'; No. 118 'The Suicide of the Countess'.
National Gallery of Ireland, Dublin	No. 792 William Hogarth, *The Western Family*; No. 4304 Philip Hussey, *A Family Interior*.
National Portrait Gallery, London	No. 217 Francis Heyman, *Self Portrait with a Companion* (*c.* 1740–5); No. 2106 Francis Heyman, *John Hoadly and Maurice Green* (1747).
Petworth House, Sussex	Mid-nineteenth-century watercolour at the house, showing the Sculpture Gallery.
P.M.A.	Philadelphia Museum of Art: William Hogarth, *The Wanstead Assembly* (1729–31), McFadden, 28-1-13.
Private collections	Anonymous, *The Drawing Room at 45 Bedford Square, London* (*c.* 1830) (see *Interiors* (1981), No. 12); Mary Ellen Best, various watercolours exhibited at the Fine Art Society, 148 New Bond Street, London W1Y OJT, 3 to 28 February 1986 (see also Davidson (1985)); Arthur Devis, *The Reverend Streynsham Master and his Wife* (1742–4) (see Devis Exhibition (1983), No. 15, lent anonymously); Arthur Devis, *Sir Roger Newdigate in his Library at Arbury Hall* (*c.* 1756–8) (see Devis Exhibition (1983), No. 38, lent by Trustees of the Newdigate Settlement); Gawen Hamilton, *The Rawson Conversation Piece* (see Leger Galleries (1983), No. 1); Edward Haytley, *Portrait of Sarah Robinson* (?1744) (see Leger Galleries (1983), No. 11);

	William Hogarth, *The Wollaston Family* (1730) (see Rococo Exhibition (1984), No. B7, lent by Trustees of the late H.C. Wollaston);
	Barthélémy du Pan (attrib.), *The Shudi Family* (*c.* 1742) (see Rococo Exhibition (1984), No. B14, lent by the Broadwood Trust);
	John Zoffany, *The Dutton Family* (1771–2) (see Rococo Exhibition (1984), No. M31, lent by The Hon. P.M. Samuel).
Royal Borough of Kensington and Chelsea Central Library	Watercolours by Louisa Goldsmid (*c.* 1818) in Aubrey House album at Royal Borough of Kensington and Chelsea Central Library (accession No. 57/26302).
Soane Museum, London	James Thornhill, oil sketch in Picture Room for ceiling of Queen's State Bedchamber, Hampton Court, Middlesex;
	William Hogarth, *An Election* 'The Election Entertainment'.
Tate Gallery, London	No. 916 Antonio Verrio, oil sketch for painted ceiling at Moor Park, Hertfordshire, (*c.* 1670–85);
	No. 1153 William Hogarth, *The Strode Family* (*c.* 1738);
	No. 1943 Francis Cotes, *Paul Sandby* (*c.* 1760);
	No. 5359 William Hogarth, *The Staymaker* (*c.* 1744);
	No. 6200 James Thornhill, oil sketch for painted ceiling.
Temple Newsam House, Leeds, Yorkshire	William Hodges and John Zoffany, *Interior of the Pantheon, Oxford Street, London.*
V.A.M.	Victoria and Albert Museum, London:
	F.A. 116 C.R. Leslie, *Le Bourgeois Gentilhomme*;
	F.A. 145 William Mulready, *Choosing the Wedding Gown.*
	P. 31-1935 Arthur Devis, *The Duet* (1749).
Walker Art Gallery, Liverpool	Arthur Devis, *William Atherton and his Wife* (*c.* 1742–4).
Yale Center for British Art	Yale Center for British Art, New Haven, Connecticut, U.S.A:
	Arthur Devis, *The Bacon Family* (*c.* 1742–3), B1981.25.274;
	Arthur Devis, *Children in an Interior* (*c.* 1742–3), B1978.43.5.

5. OTHER OBJECTS, TRADE CARDS, &C.

B.M. trade cards	Heal and Banks Collections of Trade Cards in Print Room of British Museum, London.
Castle Museum, York	Trade cards in castle Museum, York.
I.G.S. samples	Mineralogical samples at Institute of Geological Sciences, now part of Natural History Museum, London.
N.M.R.	National Monuments Record, London, photographic library.
Patent Office	Printed series of patents at British Library, Science Reference, 25 Southampton Buildings, London (formerly part of the Patent Office).
V.A.M.	Victoria and Albert Museum, London:
	1736–1869 Boudoir de Madame de Sérilly;
	3-1891 Sizergh Castle Room;
	1029–1903 Cliffords Inn Room;
	W. 43–1936 Adelphi Room;
	W. 54-to-6-1953 Marble-topped table of *c.* 1820 formerly belonging to George Gwilt;
	W. 2-to-2V-1957 Painted arabesque panels from Ashburnham Place, Sussex;
	W. 36-to-40-1975 Painted panels by Agostino Brunias for Breakfast Room at Kedleston Hall, Derbyshire (1760);
	W. 76-1975 Bookcases from Library at Croome Court, Worcestershire;
	W. 41-1977 Pair of *bergères* from Drawing Room of David Garrick's house in the Adelphi;
	Graining and marbling samples by Thomas Kershaw of Bolton, on loan from Bolton Museum and Art Gallery , Lancashire.

GENERAL INDEX

GEOGRAPHICAL INDEX

to sources, manufacture, and trade in paint and painting materials